Major Problems in the History of World War II

MAJOR PROBLEMS IN AMERICAN HISTORY SERIES

GENERAL EDITOR
THOMAS G. PATERSON

Major Problems in the History of World War II

DOCUMENTS AND ESSAYS

EDITED BY
MARK A. STOLER
UNIVERSITY OF VERMONT

MELANIE S. GUSTAFSON
UNIVERSITY OF VERMONT

HOUGHTON MIFFLIN COMPANY
Boston   New York

Editor in Chief: Jean L. Woy
Senior Development Editor: Frances Gay
Senior Project Editor: Bob Greiner
Editorial Assistant: Wendy Thayer
Associate Production/Design Coordinator: Christine Gervais
Manufacturing Manager: Jane Spelman
Senior Marketing Coordinator: Sandra McGuire

Cover art:
Navajo Code Talkers by Colonel C. H. Waterhouse, courtesy U.S. Marine Corps Art Collection. Navajo "code talkers," who were U.S. Marines, were among the first assault forces to land on Pacific beaches. Dodging enemy fire, they set up radio equipment and transmitted vital information to headquarters, including enemy sightings and targets for American shelling. The Japanese never broke the special Navajo code.

Cover photos:
Mark Stoler: William Di Lillo. Media Photography Service. University of Vermont.
Melanie Gustafson: Diane Gabriel.

Printed in the U.S.A.

Library of Congress Control Number: 2001131557

ISBN: 0-618-061320

456789-MP-08 07 06

TO
Melvin E. and Mary Ann Gustafson
Nathan and Anne Stoler
Herbert and Jean Gabriel
And All the Other Members of the World War II Generation

Contents

Preface **xiv**

CHAPTER 1
U.S. Entry into World War II
Page 1

DOCUMENTS

1. The Neutrality Acts Seek to Avoid U.S. Participation in Another War, 1935–1939 **6**

2. President Franklin D. Roosevelt Proposes a "Quarantine" of Aggressors, 1937 **8**

3. President Franklin D. Roosevelt Proposes Lend-Lease Aid to Great Britain, December 17 and 29, 1940 **10**

4. Charles A. Lindbergh Opposes Lend-Lease, February 6, 1941 **14**

5. Americans Express Their Opinions on Aid to Britain and Entry into the War, 1940–1941 **16**

6. Secretary of State Cordell Hull Responds to Japan's Final Proposal, November 26, 1941 **17**

7. Japan Terminates Negotiations and Hull Replies Orally, December 7, 1941 **19**

8. President Roosevelt Asks Congress for a Declaration of War, December 8, 1941 **22**

ESSAYS

Bruce M. Russett • An Unnecessary and Avoidable War **23**

Gerhard Weinberg • A Necessary and Unavoidable War **33**

FURTHER READING **40**

CHAPTER 2
America Mobilizes for War
Page 42

DOCUMENTS

1. The Government Institutes and Revises the Draft, 1940 and 1943 **44**

2. Conscientious Objectors Explain Their Reasons for Refusing to Register for the Draft, 1941 **47**

3. Representative Edith Nourse Rogers Introduces the WAAC Bill, 1941 **48**

4. President Roosevelt Explains the Four Freedoms to the American People, 1941   **50**

5. The Office of Price Administration Reports on the Consequences of Defense Production, 1942   **51**

6. The War Affects Employment and Consumer Prices, 1940–1945   **53**

7. The Government Encourages Workers on the Home Front, 1943   **55**

8. Roosevelt Orders Japanese Relocation, 1942   **56**

E S S A Y S

Richard Overy • The Successes of American Mobilization   **58**

William L. O'Neill • The Problems of American Mobilization   **66**

F U R T H E R   R E A D I N G   **72**

C H A P T E R   3
Creating a Global Allied Strategy
Page 74

D O C U M E N T S

1. U.S. and British Military Officials Agree to a "Germany-First" Strategy: Admiral Stark's Memorandum and the ABC-1 Accord, November 1940/March 1941   **77**

2. Britain and the United States Reach Strategic Agreements at the ARCADIA Conference, Washington, D.C., December 1941–January 1942   **80**

3. Admiral Ernest J. King Calls for a Strategic Focus on Japan, March 1942   **83**

4. Roosevelt "Promises" the Soviets a Second Front, May–June 1942   **84**

5. Churchill Vetoes Crossing the Channel in 1942 and Proposes the North African Alternative, July 8, 1942   **86**

6. Admiral Ernest J. King and General George C. Marshall Respond with a "Pacific-First" Proposal, July 10, 1942   **87**

7. Roosevelt Rejects the "Pacific-First" Alternative, July 14, 1942   **88**

8. Britain and the United States Agree on a 1943 Mediterranean Strategy at the Casablanca Conference, January 1943   **88**

9. Stalin Angrily Responds to the Continued Delays in Establishing a Second Front, June 24, 1943   **89**

10. Roosevelt, Churchill, and Stalin Debate and Decide Future Allied Strategy at the Tehran Conference, November 29–30, 1943   **91**

E S S A Y S

Hanson W. Baldwin • The Political Shortsightedness of U.S. Strategy   **94**

Mark A. Stoler • The Political Wisdom of U.S. Strategy   **98**

Kent Roberts Greenfield • Roosevelt as Commander-in-Chief   **105**

F U R T H E R   R E A D I N G   **107**

CHAPTER 4
The War Against Germany: What Was Needed and What Was Done
Page 109

DOCUMENTS

1. Army Ground Versus Air Plans for the War Against Germany: The "Victory Program" (with AWPD-1) of September 1941   **111**

2. The Naval and Air Campaigns Against German U-Boats and Cities Receive High Priority at the Casablanca Conference, January, 1943   **113**

3. A Mother Questions and General Henry H. "Hap" Arnold's Staff Defends the Bombing of German Cities, 1943   **115**

4. The City of Dresden Before and After the Anglo-American Bombing of February, 1945   **117**

5. The Original OVERLORD Plan Proposes Landing on the Normandy Beaches and Explains the Problems to Be Overcome, July 27, 1943   **118**

6. General Dwight D. Eisenhower Addresses Allied Forces on D-Day, June 6, 1944   **121**

7. Generals Eisenhower and Montgomery Debate Broad- Versus Narrow-Front Strategies, September, 1944   **121**

8. General Marshall Explains the Key Military Events in German Defeat as Perceived by Captured Members of the German High Command, September, 1945   **125**

9. Tuskegee Airman Lieutenant Alexander Jefferson Recalls His Combat Missions and Imprisonment, 1944   **126**

10. Sergeant Bernard Bellush Recalls D-Day on Omaha Beach, November 14, 1944/March 16, 2000   **130**

ESSAYS

Richard Overy • The Naval and Air Campaigns as Critical to Allied Victory   **135**

Michael S. Sherry • Strategic Bombing as Technological Fanaticism   **149**

Michael D. Doubler • The Travails of the American Combat Soldier in Europe   **156**

FURTHER READING   **169**

CHAPTER 5
The War Against Japan: What Was Needed and What Was Done
Page 171

DOCUMENTS

1. Public Opinion Favors a Japan-First Strategy, 1942–1943   **174**

2. The Military Plans for the Defeat of Japan, May 21, 1943   **174**

3. Army Nurse Lieutenant Juanita Redmond Describes a Japanese Air Attack on Bataan in the Philippines, April 1942   **176**

4. Navy Pilot George Gay Survives the Battle of Midway, May 1942   **178**

5. Marine Private E. B. Sledge Remembers the Hellish Battle of Okinawa, 1945   **180**

6. Japanese Civilians Tomizawa Kimi and Kobayashi Hiroyasu Live Through the Firebombing of Tokyo, 1945   **183**

7. General Joseph Stilwell Bitterly Explains His Problems in China, 1944   **185**

8. President Roosevelt Attacks Colonialism in Asia, 1942–1943   **187**

9. Foreign Service Officers John Paton Davies and George R. Merrell Warn Against Support of British Colonialism in Asia, 1943   **189**

E S S A Y S

Ronald H. Spector • Strangers in Strange Lands   **190**

John W. Dower • The Pacific War as a Race War   **196**

Michael Schaller • The U.S. Failure in China   **202**

F U R T H E R   R E A D I N G   **209**

C H A P T E R   6
Cooperation and Conflict on the Home Front
Page 211

D O C U M E N T S

1. A Call to March on Washington, 1941   **213**

2. Rosie the Riveter Becomes a Symbol of Patriotic Womanhood   **215**

3. *Time* Magazine Contrasts Japanese Enemies and Chinese Allies, 1941   **216**

4. *Newsweek* Magazine Reports on Women's Stockings in Wartime, 1943   **216**

5. The Turmoil of Wartime Rapidly Changes Detroit, 1943   **217**

6. The Government Praises Spanish-Speaking Americans in the War Effort, 1943   **220**

7. The "Zoot Suit Riots" Reveal the Race Tensions on the West Coast, 1943   **222**

8. Labor Conflict and Questions of Patriotism Erupt in the Coal Fields, 1943   **224**

9. Japanese American Mikiso Hane Remembers His Wartime Internment, 1990   **227**

E S S A Y S

Karen Tucker Anderson • Conflicts Between White Women and Black Women, and Their Employers, in the Wartime Industrial World   **231**

Edward J. Escobar • Wartime Conflicts Between Sailors, Chicano Youths, and the Police in Los Angeles   **238**

F U R T H E R   R E A D I N G   **245**

CHAPTER 7
Challenges and Changes in Wartime American Culture
Page 247

D O C U M E N T S

1. Oveta Culp Hobby, Director of the Women's Army Auxiliary Corps, Talks to American Mothers, 1943   **249**

2. Robert P. Lane, Director of New York City's Welfare Council, Cites Home Front Concerns About "Victory Girls" and Venereal Disease, 1945   **251**

3. John Desmond, *New York Times* Writer, Praises Entertainers at the War Front, 1944   **252**

4. *Newsweek* Looks Back at Homosexuals in Uniform During Wartime, 1947   **254**

5. Wartime and Postwar Conditions Affect Marriage, Divorce, and Birth Rates, 1930–1950   **255**

6. Movie Star Ann Sothern Asks, "What Kind of Woman Will Your Man Come Home To?" 1944   **256**

7. Newspaper Columnist Ernie Pyle Depicts the Realities of War for Americans at Home, 1943   **258**

8. Editor and Publisher Henry Luce Proclaims the "American Century," 1941   **260**

9. Betty Grable Becomes a Favorite "Pin-up Girl" among Soldiers, 1943   **264**

10. Photographer Alfred Eisenstadt Captures the American Spirit of Victory, August 14, 1945   **266**

E S S A Y S

Robert B. Westbrook • The "Pin-up Girls" Taught Americans Less About Sex and More About Political Obligations   **267**

Leisa D. Meyer • Creating GI Jane   **275**

F U R T H E R   R E A D I N G   **280**

CHAPTER 8
The Impact of Science and Intelligence
Page 282

D O C U M E N T S

1. A Congressional Committee Assesses Blame for the Pearl Harbor Disaster, 1946   **284**

2. Bletchley Park Cryptologist Peter Calvocoressi Explains How ENIGMA Worked During the War   **286**

3. Americans Decode and Translate a Japanese Encrypted Message, 1944   **289**

4. The Navajo Language Becomes an Unbreakable American Code, 1945   **291**

5. Office of Strategic Services Official Allen Dulles Explains His Wartime Intelligence Activities, 1941–1945   **293**

6. Historian and OSS Official William Langer Describes the Contribution of Scholars to the Intelligence War, 1943–1946   **295**

7. Secretary of War Henry L. Stimson Raises Concerns to President Roosevelt about Communist Union Organizing in the Atomic Bomb Project, 1943   **297**

8. Office of Scientific Research and Development Director Dr. Vannevar Bush Reports to the President on the Importance of Science During and After the War, 1945   **298**

E S S A Y S

Roberta Wohlstetter • Pearl Harbor and the Limits of Signals Intelligence   **301**

Williamson Murray • Signals Intelligence As Critical to Allied Victory   **306**

Gordon Wright • Science Revolutionizes Warfare   **311**

F U R T H E R   R E A D I N G   **320**

CHAPTER 9
The United States and the Holocaust
Page 322

D O C U M E N T S

1. The National Origins Act Restricts Immigration, 1924   **324**

2. Henry Ford's *Dearborn Independent* Reveals American Anti-Semitism, 1921–1922   **324**

3. Public Opinion Polls Reveal American Attitudes About Jews in Europe, Refugees, and Immigration, 1938–1945   **327**

4. *The New York Times* Reports on the *St. Louis* Tragedy, 1939   **330**

5. Jan Karski of the Polish Underground Gives an Eyewitness Account of the "Final Solution," 1942–1944   **331**

6. The State Department Receives and Suppresses News of the "Final Solution," 1942   **335**

7. Secretary of the Treasury Henry Morgenthau, Jr., Denounces State Department Behavior to Roosevelt, 1944   **338**

8. U.S. Soldier Clinton C. Gardner Remembers the Liberation of the Buchenwald Concentration Camp, 1945   **339**

E S S A Y S

Henry L. Feingold • The American Failure to Rescue European Jews   **341**

William J. Vanden Heuvel • The Successes of American Rescue and The Limits of The Possible   **349**

F U R T H E R   R E A D I N G   **357**

CHAPTER 10
Franklin D. Roosevelt and Allied Diplomacy for War and Peace
Page 359

D O C U M E N T S

1. The Atlantic Charter States Allied War Aims, 1941   **361**

2. Josef Stalin Demands Territorial Settlements, 1941   **362**

3. The Allies Announce Formation of the Grand Alliance: The Declaration by the United Nations, 1942   **365**

4. Roosevelt Enunciates the Unconditional Surrender Policy, 1943   **366**

5. The Allies Agree on Postwar Policies: The Moscow Declaration on General Security, 1943   **366**

6. Roosevelt Informs His Allies of His Postwar Plans, 1942 and 1943   **367**

7. The Allies Agree to a Postwar International Organization: The Dumbarton Oaks Agreement, 1944   **370**

8. Churchill and Stalin Divide Eastern Europe, 1944   **372**

9. The Allies Reach Postwar Agreements at the Yalta Conference, 1945   **372**

10. Roosevelt Sends Letters to Stalin and Churchill, 1945   **377**

E S S A Y S

Frederick W. Marks III • The Ignorance and Naïveté of Roosevelt's Wartime Diplomacy   **379**

Robert Dallek • The Astuteness and Appropriateness of Roosevelt's Wartime Diplomacy   **387**

F U R T H E R   R E A D I N G   **393**

C H A P T E R   1 1
The Atomic Bomb and the End of World War II
Page 394

D O C U M E N T S

1. Albert Einstein Informs President Roosevelt of the Potential for an Atomic Bomb, 1939   **396**

2. Supreme Court Justice Felix Frankfurter Shares with FDR Physicist Niels Bohr's Suggestion that the Soviets Be Informed of the Atomic Bomb Project, 1944   **397**

3. Churchill and Roosevelt Reject Informing the Soviets, 1944   **398**

4. President Harry S Truman Recalls How He Learned About the Atomic Bomb Project, 1945   **398**

5. The Franck Committee Warns of a Nuclear Arms Race and Calls for a Noncombat Demonstration of the Bomb, 1945   **399**

6. The Scientific Panel of the Interim Committee Recommends Combat Use of the Bomb Against Japan, 1945   **402**

7. Undersecretary of the Navy Ralph Bard Objects to the Unannounced Use of the Bomb, 1945   **403**

8. Manhattan Project Commanding General Leslie Groves Reports the Results of the Alamagordo Test, 1945   **404**

9. A Photographer Captures Hiroshima Two Months After the Atomic Bomb of August 6, 1945   **405**

10. Public Opinion Polls Show Strong Support for the Atomic Bomb, August, September, and December 1945   **405**

11. Secretary of War Henry L. Stimson Has Second Thoughts on Atomic Secrecy, 1945   **406**

ESSAYS

Gar Alperovitz • Dropping the Atomic Bomb Was Neither Necessary Nor
Justifiable   **408**

Robert P. Newman • Dropping the Bomb Was Necessary and Justifiable   **412**

Barton J. Bernstein • Were There Viable Alternatives to Dropping the Atomic
Bomb?   **419**

FURTHER READING   **426**

CHAPTER 12
History and Memory: The Legacy of World War II
Page 427

ESSAYS

Michael C. C. Adams • Postwar Mythmaking About World War II   **428**

David M. Kennedy • The World the War Made   **437**

Alan Brinkley • The War Transformed American Liberalism   **441**

Roger Daniels • Americans Reevaluate Japanese American Incarceration   **448**

Richard H. Kohn • Culture War Erupts Over the 1994–1995 Smithsonian
Institution's *Enola Gay* Exhibition   **453**

Peter Novick • Why Did the Holocaust Become a Major Postwar Issue?   **461**

FURTHER READING   **470**

APPENDIX
General World War II Histories and Reference Works
Page 471

Preface

World War II was the largest and bloodiest conflict in human history. It was fought on virtually every continent and ocean, in the air, and against civilians as well as the armed forces of the major powers. These nations mobilized for total war, and it transformed every combatant as well as international relations in general.

The United States emerged as one of the major belligerents in this war. The nation suffered its greatest number of combat casualties since the Civil War, played a major role in the war's outcome, and was dramatically transformed in the process. Historians have long recognized the scope and impact of the war and have produced an enormous amount of literature on different aspects of U.S. participation. This volume introduces students to U.S. participation in this monumental conflict through both primary sources and scholarly interpretations.

The United States was just one of many nations to play a significant role in World War II. It officially entered the war later than any of the other great powers and suffered fewer deaths. This volume, then, published as part of Houghton Mifflin's *Major Problems in American History* series, deals only with part of the war— those aspects that actively engaged the American people. Although we have attempted to emphasize the global nature of the conflict, please be aware that the history presented here is but part of a much larger story.

During the first two to three decades after the war, American historians tended to focus on the diplomatic, military, and political aspects of U.S. participation. During the 1970s the declassification of major World War II official document collections in the United States and Great Britain, combined with the opening to scholars of numerous private manuscript collections, led to major interpretive reassessments that continue to this day. Simultaneously, the growth of social and cultural history within the historical profession spawned new explorations into previously ignored or understudied areas, such as race, class, gender, and popular culture, that also enrich our understanding of the war today. We have attempted in this volume to introduce students to all of these aspects of World War II history.

As with other volumes in this series, all but one of the chapters include primary sources, secondary and often-conflicting interpretive essays on controversial issues, headnotes for the documents and essays sections, chapter introductions that provide the context for the chapter topic, and suggestions for further reading. Chapter 1 deals with U.S. entry into the war, and its thorough introduction attempts to provide students with basic background on global as well as U.S. events before December 7, 1941. Chapter 2 focuses on the American mobilization effort. Chapter 3 explores the development of U.S. and Allied global strategy. Chapter 4 covers different aspects of the war against Germany, and Chapter 5, different aspects of the war against Japan—from controversies over air, naval, and ground operations to the experiences of the individuals who actually fought. Chapter 6 explores home-front issues such as the experiences of women and various ethnic groups during the war, and Chapter 7 examines the wartime culture that emerged within the United States. Chapter 8 studies the wartime revolution in science and intelligence. Chapters 9, 10, and 11 then approach three highly controversial politico-military issues: the U.S. response to the Holocaust, President Franklin D. Roosevelt's wartime diplomacy for the postwar world, and the decision to drop atomic bombs on Japan. We have provided a concluding Chapter 12 with essays that focus on the meaning and memory of World War II, a topic of great interest and controversy in recent years.

Many of the topics explored in this volume are relevant to more than one chapter. The attack on Pearl Harbor, for example, is an issue for Chapter 1 on U.S. entry and for Chapter 8 on science and intelligence. Wartime mobilization issues introduced in Chapter 2 are relevant to home front and wartime culture issues in Chapters 6 and 7. Strategic and diplomatic issues explored in Chapters 3, 4, 5, and 10 are related and interwoven. Three of the issues explored within Chapters 2, 9, and 11—the Japanese-American relocation, the U.S. response to the Holocaust, and the decision to use the atomic bomb—are all major issues also analyzed in Chapter 12 on controversies regarding the war's meaning and memory. We have pointed out these links in our introductions and "Further Reading" sections to refer the student to other relevant chapters.

Many of the documents reproduced in this volume were security classified during the war. In editing these documents for publication, we have deleted the actual security classification marks, such as "Top Secret." Students should realize, however, that these documents were available only to a few high-level officials during and for many years after the war. Indeed, most of these documents were not declassified and opened to scholars and the public until the 1960s and 1970s or later.

Numerous scholarly organizations deal extensively with World War II, and students interested in exploring specific wartime issues in greater depth should contact and consider joining one or more of them. Among the most notable are the Society for Historians of American Foreign Relations (SHAFR), which publishes the journal *Diplomatic History* and maintains a website at *www.ohio.edu/shafr/*; the Society for Military History (SMH), which publishes *The Journal of Military History* and has a website at *www.smh-hq.org*; the Peace History Society (PHS), which publishes *Peace & Change* and has a website at *www.theaha.org/affiliates/peace_his_soc.htm*; the World War II Studies Association (WWTSA), which has a website at *www.ksu.edu/history/institute/wwtsa*; and the MINERVA Center, which publishes *MINERVA: Quarterly Report on Women and the Military* and has a website at *www.minervacenter.com*. The websites of these organizations also provide information about membership, journals, newsletters, and other available resources. Numerous additional websites focus solely on World War II, but they vary enormously in quality and should be carefully selected with the assistance of a course instructor and/or a reference librarian.

We would like to thank the many individuals who helped us in this project. First and foremost is series editor Thomas G. Paterson, who first offered us the opportunity to prepare this volume and who has been a constant source of encouragement and sage advice. We profited from and are grateful for the detailed and constructive reviews of our original proposal provided by Benjamin L. Alpers,

University of Oklahoma; Susan A. Brewer, University of Wisconsin—Stevens Point; Kathleen A. Brown, St. Edward's University; Colonel Cole C. Kingseed, U.S. Military Academy; Elihu Rose, New York University; Steven E. Schoenherr, University of San Diego. We are also grateful for the gracious advice on specific documents and essays provided by the following colleagues at other universities: Harriet Alonso, Karen Anderson, Alexander Cochran, Conrad Crane, Justus Doenecke, Warren Kimball, Loyd Lee, Kurt Piehler, Steven Ross, Susan Ware, and Theodore Wilson. Editors and archivists Larry Bland at the George C. Marshall Library, Robert Parks at the Franklin D. Roosevelt Library, and Timothy Nenninger at the National Archives provided invaluable assistance in obtaining documents. Equally invaluable was the assistance provided by the faculty and staffs of the Documents, Reference, and Interlibrary Loan divisions of the Bailey-Howe Library of the University of Vermont. We are also deeply indebted to our University of Vermont departmental colleagues Jonathan Huener, Patrick Hutton, and Denise Youngblood for their advice and support, and to staff members Kathy Morris and Debbie Smail as well as graduate assistant James Heines for all their help. At Houghton Mifflin we would like to thank Editor in Chief for History and Political Science Jean Woy, Senior Development Editor Frances Gay, Senior Project Editor Bob Greiner, Editorial Assistant Wendy Thayer, and Permissions Editor Marie MacBryde. Special thanks at Houghton Mifflin go to Mary Stewart for exceptionally high quality copyediting. Special thanks also go to Alexander Jefferson and Bernard Bellush for sharing their unpublished works with us, and to Diane Gabriel and David Scrase for all the help and support they provided.

M.A.S.
M.S.G.

U.S. Entry into
World War II

World War II began long before the United States officially entered the conflict in December of 1941. Most historians cite September of 1939 as the starting date, for in the opening days of that month Germany invaded Poland, and France and Great Britain responded with formal declarations of war. Other scholars go back to 1937, when Japan began its undeclared war against China. Still others go back to 1933, when Nazi leader Adolf Hitler took power in Germany; or 1931, when the Japanese Kwantung Army conquered the northernmost Chinese province of Manchuria and established the puppet state of Manchukuo.

Whichever date one chooses, it is important to realize that the war had a history long before U.S. entry. And understanding that history is necessary to place U.S. entry and participation into their proper context.

Historians cite numerous "causes" for World War II. One of the most basic was the rise in Germany, Italy, and Japan of highly aggressive and militaristic regimes, commonly labeled fascist, which were determined to overthrow by force the international order established at the end of World War I. These fascist regimes emerged primarily because of domestic problems within the three nations and their dissatisfaction over the Versailles Treaties that had ended World War I (although Italy and Japan were victors in World War I, both felt cheated of their just rewards in the peace treaties) and because of the numerous economic problems that followed—most notably the Great Depression of the 1930s.

In Italy, Benito Mussolini and his Black Shirts had obtained power as early as 1922, quickly established a highly militarized dictatorship, and pursued an aggressive foreign policy designed to recapture the glory of ancient Rome; as part of that effort, Italian armies invaded and conquered the African nation of Ethiopia in 1935. In Japan, military officers took over Manchuria in 1931–1932 without government sanction, gradually wrested control of the government in Tokyo from civilians, pursued military conquest of China itself against Chiang Kai-shek's Nationalist forces, and sought to expand their colonial empire throughout East Asia and the western Pacific. In Germany, Hitler and his Nazi movement came to power in 1933 with the avowed aim of overthrowing the entire Versailles system and making Germany the dominant power of both Europe and the world. By 1936–1937, Hitler had quit the League of Nations, rearmed Germany and marched into the demilitarized Rhineland in violation of the Versailles Treaty, and formed an alliance with Italy and Japan—the Rome-Berlin-Tokyo Axis. Henceforth the three nations and their satellites would be known as the Axis powers.

Although the Axis posed a potentially mortal threat to the two major democratic nations of Europe, France and Great Britain, they were slow to challenge Axis aggression. World War I had proven a devastating experience for them, with each nation suffering the loss of virtually an entire generation in the bloody trenches. Anything, many people in these countries concluded, would be better than another war. A large number of these people had also concluded that Germany had been treated unjustly at Versailles and should be allowed to revise the punitive peace settlement. Nor did either power feel militarily prepared or sufficiently unified internally to risk war. Furthermore, successful opposition to the Axis powers would require alliance with the detested and feared Communist regime of Josef Stalin in the Soviet Union, a move neither power desired. Consequently Britain and France practiced a policy known as appeasement, whereby they acceded to Italian and Japanese military conquests, Italo-German military involvement in the Spanish Civil War, Hitler's violations of the Versailles Treaty, and his ensuing territorial demands. By the end of 1938, the German dictator had thus been able to annex Austria and the western portion of Czechoslovakia (the Sudetenland) without firing a shot.

Allied appeasement was reinforced by U.S. policies. Many Americans had also come to believe by the 1930s that Germany had been unfairly treated in the Versailles peace treaties. They had further concluded that their own entry into World War I in 1917 had been a mistake, and that a repetition was to be avoided at all costs. Although many historians no longer accept the simplistic definition of ensuing U.S. policies as "isolationist," they do concur that Americans sought to avoid political or military entanglements in Europe that could involve them in another world war. Congress also sought to avoid a repetition of 1917 by outlawing in the Neutrality Acts of 1935–1937 the arms trade, loans, and overseas travel that they believed had led them into World War I. By removing the United States from any potential coalition against the Axis, such behavior only reinforced the Anglo-French desire to appease rather than fight.

But Anglo-French appeasement did not satisfy Hitler's appetite for more territory, and in 1939 he occupied the rest of Czechoslovakia and began to make territorial demands on Poland. Britain and France now shifted policy and promised to support Poland, but Hitler countered with a surprising Non-Aggression Pact with the Soviet Union, his great racial and ideological enemy, on August 23, 1939. Within its secret sections were provisions for the two powers to divide Poland and the rest of Eastern Europe. With the threat of a two-front war thus removed, Hitler on September 1 invaded Poland; two days later Britain and France declared war.

Making use of new military technology and tactics known as blitzkrieg, or "lightning war," German armies quickly conquered Poland in the fall of 1939. More surprising and shocking to Americans, in the following spring those armies just as quickly conquered Denmark, Norway, Belgium, Luxembourg, the Netherlands, and France itself, with Italy entering the war on June 10 to obtain some of the spoils. Only Britain under its new prime minister, Winston S. Churchill, now stood between Hitler and total victory. During the summer and fall of 1940, the dramatic air campaign known as the Battle of Britain took place, with Hitler seeking to destroy Britain's Royal Air Force as the necessary prerequisite for an invasion of the island nation. Taking advantage of Anglo-French weakness during this time,

Japan simultaneously began to move military forces into French Indochina and to pressure Britain into closing the Burma Road, a major supply route to Chiang Kai-shek's forces in China.

The German conquests of 1940 precipitated a revolution in American thinking and a massive public debate over appropriate U.S. policies. Previously Americans had assumed that any European war would repeat the trench deadlock of 1914–1918. But German forces had avoided such a repeat of history and now stood triumphant on the shores of the English Channel and the Atlantic Ocean, poised to invade England and threaten the United States. The Atlantic no longer seemed to be the impenetrable barrier to invasion that Americans had long perceived it to be, and many of them joined President Franklin D. Roosevelt in arguing that the United States should provide Britain with military assistance so as to preclude a total German victory. Acting on this belief, Roosevelt in the so-called destroyer-bases deal during September of 1940 provided Britain with fifty overage U.S. warships in return for ninety-nine-year leases on British bases in the Western Hemisphere. But other Americans disagreed with the president and his supporters, arguing that Britain was doomed to defeat, that its defense was in no way vital to U.S. security, that the United States needed to build up its own defenses, and that a triumphant Germany need not be a threat to the United States. Americans also began to discuss whether military assistance should be given to Chiang Kai-shek in his struggle against the Japanese.

Seeking to preclude additional U.S. aid to either power, Germany, Italy, and Japan in September of 1940 signed the Tripartite Pact, a military alliance in which the three divided the world into spheres of influence and pledged military assistance to each other should any one of them be attacked by a presently neutral power. With the Soviet Union explicitly excluded, the threat was clearly aimed at the United States.

It did not work, however. Indeed, it boomeranged as Americans increased their support for both the Chinese and the British. In the Far East, the United States sought to curb further Japanese aggression by imposing limited economic sanctions against Tokyo and moving the fleet from California to Hawaii. Then in December Roosevelt proposed, and in March of 1941 Congress agreed to passage of, the Lend-Lease bill, which allowed the president to provide Britain, and any other country whose defense he deemed essential to U.S. security, with military assistance free of charge. But the split vote within each house illustrated continued strong divisions within the American populace.

In the spring of 1941, Hitler launched a new series of military offensives in the Balkans that resulted in the conquest of Yugoslavia and Greece as well as further military defeats for the British forces sent to aid the Greeks. Then on June 22 he launched Operation BARBAROSSA against the Soviet Union—the largest invasion in history. Churchill and Roosevelt quickly promised the Soviets aid on the grounds that Hitler was the immediate menace and that anyone fighting him, even a Communist regime led by a bloody dictator, should be assisted (if Hitler invaded hell, the prime minister commented, he [Churchill] would at least make a favorable reference to the devil in the House of Commons).

The promise of aid to the Soviet Union was but one of a series of executive actions that Roosevelt took in the summer and fall of 1941 to provide additional assistance to anti-Axis forces. Throughout this time period he extended eastward the self-proclaimed hemispheric security zone so as to allow for U.S. military occupation of first Greenland and then Iceland, as well as de facto naval assistance to the British in the western Atlantic. Then in August he and Churchill met off the coast of Newfoundland and promulgated the Atlantic Charter, a joint statement of idealistic dual war aims (see Chapter 10)—despite the fact that the United States was not an official belligerent in the war. In September, responding to a German submarine attack on the U.S. destroyer Greer in the Atlantic, Roosevelt ordered U.S. naval forces to "shoot on sight" when they encountered German U-boats and so informed the American people (though he did not mention that the Greer had been aiding British forces in their attack on that submarine). Roosevelt also asked Congress to end the "crippling provisions" of the Neutrality Acts so that U.S. merchant ships could be armed and carry Lend-Lease supplies to Britain. As the naval incidents mounted, Congress concurred. By November, the United States was in a full-scale if undeclared naval war with Germany in the Atlantic.

War officially came, however, as a result of events in the Pacific—not the Atlantic. Throughout 1941, Japanese-American tensions had continued to escalate. Special high-level negotiations in Washington failed to resolve the two nations' conflicting demands: the United States insisted that Japan withdraw its military forces from China as well as French Indochina, whereas Japan insisted on a free hand in Asia, no further U.S. aid to Chiang Kai-shek, and a full resumption of U.S. trade. In July, Washington responded to additional Japanese troops movements into French Indochina with a freeze on all Japanese assets in the United States, thereby creating a complete embargo on U.S.-Japanese trade. Consequently cut off from the raw materials they needed to continue their war in China, most notably oil, the Japanese decided to attack U.S., British, and Dutch possessions to obtain these resources and create a self-sufficient empire. Simultaneously, however, they continued to negotiate with the Americans in the hopes of achieving a diplomatic settlement on their terms that would make such an attack and war unnecessary.

American negotiators knew of Japanese plans and proposals because they had broken the Japanese diplomatic code (MAGIC). Unfortunately, however, MAGIC did not reveal where the Japanese would attack if negotiations failed. The ensuing December 7 assault on the Pearl Harbor naval base by Japanese naval aircraft thus came as a devastating surprise and decimated the U.S. fleet with the loss of over 2,400 American servicemen. One day later, the United States declared that war existed by act of Japan. On December 11, Hitler declared war on the United States, thereby joining the European and Asia/Pacific wars into one global conflict.

Soon after the war ended, historians such as Charles Beard and Charles Tansill charged that Roosevelt, desiring a full-scale declared war against Germany that neither Congress nor Hitler would give him, and knowing of Japanese plans, had allowed the Pearl Harbor attack to take place as a "back door to war." Although journalists and amateur historians have consistently revived this conspiracy theory over the last half-century, most if not all serious scholars now dismiss it. They do not dismiss the attacks on the wisdom of U.S. policies associated with the conspiracy theories, however. Indeed, many scholars argue, as did Roosevelt's early critics, that war with Japan could and should have been avoided, that U.S. diplomacy was too rigid, and that Roosevelt consistently abused his executive powers throughout 1940–1941. Ironically, however, other historians criticize the president for not moving faster and doing more to aid the anti-Axis nations.

The conflicting nature of these criticisms, and the ensuing defenses of Roosevelt's behavior by his supporters, raise a series of questions to consider as you read this chapter. Was Nazi Germany a threat to the United States? Should Roosevelt and the United States have acted earlier and more forcefully against Hitler and in support *of the nations he attacked, or less forcefully? Could and should war with Germany have been avoided? Could and should war with Japan have been avoided? Was U.S. diplomacy in Asia too rigid, or too timid? Did FDR lead or follow public opinion? Did he abuse his presidential powers? Did he manipulate a "back door to war" as critics charge? (For additional documents and questions concerning the Pearl Harbor attack itself, see Chapter 8).*

DOCUMENTS

Document 1 contains excerpts from the Neutrality Acts that outlawed the practices many Americans believed had led the United States into a needless war in 1917, most notably U.S. arms sales and shipments, loans to belligerents, and travel on belligerent ships. These acts illustrate the strength of antiwar sentiment, often labeled isolationist sentiment, in the United States during the 1930s. Document 2 contains excerpts from President Roosevelt's first public attempt to challenge such sentiment, his October 5, 1937, suggestion in Chicago that the United States join with other nations to "quarantine" aggressor states. The president quickly retreated from this proposal in the face of press criticism, but when war did break out in Europe in 1939, he made clear that the United States favored Britain and France and obtained from Congress an end to the arms embargo within the Neutrality Acts, thereby enabling the Allies to purchase arms as well as other items. All other provisions of the Neutrality Acts remained in effect, however, including the ban on U.S. loans and shipping. The Allies were thus limited to "cash and carry"—that is, purchases they could pay for and carry on their own ships.

Germany's stupendous military victories in the spring of 1940, culminating in French surrender, led many Americans to reconsider the wisdom of "cash and carry" and of the Neutrality Acts in general. Although British success in the Battle of Britain precluded German invasion, by year's end London no longer possessed the financial resources to continue purchasing arms from the United States. Document 3 is Roosevelt's resulting dramatic proposal that the United States henceforth lend such supplies to Britain via what would become known as Lend-Lease, thereby bypassing the ban on loans in the Neutrality Acts and making the United States in FDR's words, the "Arsenal of Democracy." It would also make the United States an unofficial belligerent in the war. FDR's proposal therefore led to a major debate in Congress and among the public over the wisdom of such extensive aid to Britain. In Document 4, aviator Charles Lindbergh, one of the most popular figures of the interwar era and a major spokesperson for the antiinterventionist cause, explains the reasons for opposing such aid. In March, Lend-Lease passed both houses of Congress by 2-1 majorities. Public opinion polls of the time, reproduced as Document 5, clearly reveal strong public support for the measure, but simultaneously strong opposition to an American declaration of war against Germany.

War came in the Pacific with the failure of Japanese-American negotiations and the ensuing Japanese attack on Pearl Harbor. Document 6, Secretary of State Cordell Hull's response to the final Japanese offer, presents the American perspective. Document 7 presents the Japanese perspective as revealed in Tokyo's final note, which was supposed to have been delivered simultaneously with the attack on Pearl Harbor but which was actually delivered hours later, and Secretary Hull's oral reply on December 7. Document 8, Roosevelt's war message to Congress, was delivered on the following day.

1. The Neutrality Acts Seek to Avoid U.S. Participation in Another War, 1935–1939

The 1935 Neutrality Act

Resolved by the Senate and House of Representatives of the United States of America in Congress assembled, That upon the outbreak or during the progress of war between, or among, two or more foreign states, the President shall proclaim such fact, and it shall thereafter be unlawful to export arms, ammunition, or implements of war from any place in the United States, or possessions of the United States, to any port of such belligerent states, or to any neutral port for transshipment to, or for the use of, a belligerent country. . . .

SEC. 3. Whenever the President shall issue the proclamation provided for in section 1 of this Act, thereafter it shall be unlawful for any American vessel to carry any arms, ammunition, or implements of war to any port of the belligerent countries named in such proclamation as being at war, or to any neutral port for transshipment to, or for the use of, a belligerent country. . . .

SEC. 6. Whenever, during any war in which the United States is neutral, the President shall find that the maintenance of peace between the United States and foreign nations, or the protection of the lives of citizens of the United States, or the protection of the commercial interests of the United States and its citizens, or the security of the United States requires that the American citizens should refrain from traveling as passengers on the vessels of any belligerent nation, he shall so proclaim, and thereafter no citizen of the United States shall travel on any vessel of any belligerent nation except at his own risk, unless in accordance with such rules and regulations as the President shall prescribe. . . .

The 1937 Neutrality Act

SECTION 1. (a) Whenever the President shall find that there exists a state of war between, or among, two or more foreign states, the President shall proclaim such fact, and it shall thereafter be unlawful to export, or attempt to export, or cause to be exported, arms, ammunition, or implements of war from any place in the United States to any belligerent state named in such proclamation, or to any neutral state for transshipment to, or for the use of, any such belligerent state.

(b) The President shall, from time to time, by proclamation, extend such embargo upon the export of arms, ammunition, or implements of war to other states as and when they may become involved in such war.

(c) Whenever the President shall find that a state of civil strife exists in a foreign state and that such civil strife is of a magnitude or is being conducted under such conditions that the export of arms, ammunition, or implements of war from the United States to such foreign state would threaten or endanger the peace of the

From *U.S. Statutes at Large,* 49 (1935–1936): 1081–1085; 50 (1937): 121–127; 54 (1939–1941): 4–12.

United States, the President shall proclaim such fact, and it shall thereafter be unlawful to export, or attempt to export, or cause to be exported arms, ammunition, or implements of war from any place in the United States to such foreign state, or to any neutral state for transshipment to, or for the use of, such foreign state. . . .

SEC. 2. (a) Whenever the President shall have issued a proclamation under the authority of section 1 of this Act and he shall thereafter find that the placing of restrictions on the shipment of certain articles or materials in addition to arms, ammunition, and implements of war from the United States to belligerent states, or to a state wherein civil strife exists, is necessary to promote the security or preserve the peace of the United States or to protect the lives of citizens of the United States, he shall so proclaim, and it shall thereafter be unlawful, except under such limitations and exceptions as the President may prescribe as to lakes, rivers, and inland waters bordering on the United States, and as to transportation on or over lands bordering on the United States, for any American vessel to carry such articles or materials to any belligerent state, or to any state wherein civil strife exists, named in such proclamation issued under the authority of section 1 of this Act, or to any neutral state for transshipment to, or for the use of, any such belligerent state or any such state wherein civil strife exists. The President shall by proclamation from time to time definitely enumerate the articles and materials which it shall be unlawful for American vessels to so transport. . . .

SEC. 3. (a) Whenever the President shall have issued a proclamation under the authority of section 1 of this Act, it shall thereafter be unlawful for any person with the United States to purchase, sell, or exchange bonds, securities, or other obligations of the government of any belligerent state or of any state wherein civil strife exists, named in such proclamation, or of any political subdivision of any such state, or of any person acting for or on behalf of the government of any such state, or of any faction or asserted government within any such state wherein civil strife exists, or of any person acting for or on behalf of any faction or asserted government within any such state wherein civil strife exists, issued after the date of such proclamation or to make any loan or extend any credit to any such government, political subdivision, faction, asserted government, or person, or to solicit or receive any contribution for any such government, political subdivision, faction, asserted government, or person. . . .

SEC. 6. (a) Whenever the President shall have issued a proclamation under the authority of section 1 of this Act, it shall thereafter be unlawful, until such proclamation is revoked, for any American vessel to carry any arms, ammunition, or implements of war to any belligerent state, or to any state wherein civil strife exists, named in such proclamation, or to any neutral state for transshipment to, or for the use of, any such belligerent state or any such state wherein civil strife exists. . . .

SEC. 10. Whenever the President shall have issued a proclamation under the authority of section 1, it shall thereafter be unlawful, until such proclamation is revoked, for any American vessel engaged in commerce with any belligerent state, or any state wherein civil strife exists, named in such proclamation, to be armed or to carry any armament, arms, ammunition, or implements of war, except small arms and ammunition therefor which the President may deem necessary and shall publicly designate for the preservation of discipline aboard such vessels.

The 1939 Neutrality Act

SEC. 2. (a) Whenever the President shall have issued a proclamation under the authority of section 1 (a) it shall thereafter be unlawful for any American vessel to carry any passengers or any articles or materials to any state named in such proclamation. . . .

(c) Whenever the President shall have issued a proclamation under the authority of section 1 (a) it shall thereafter be unlawful to export or transport, or attempt to export or transport, or cause to be exported or transported, from the United States to any state named in such proclamation, any articles or materials (except copyrighted articles or materials) until all right, title, and interest therein shall have been transferred to some foreign government, agency, institution, association, partnership, corporation, or national.

2. President Franklin D. Roosevelt Proposes a "Quarantine" of Aggressors, 1937

Some 15 years ago the hopes of mankind for a continuing era of international peace were raised to great heights when more than 60 nations solemnly pledged themselves not to resort to arms in furtherance of their national aims and policies. The high aspirations expressed in the Briand-Kellogg Peace Pact and the hopes for peace thus raised have of late given way to a haunting fear of calamity. The present reign of terror and international lawlessness began a few years ago.

It began through unjustified interference in the internal affairs of other nations or the invasion of alien territory in violation of treaties and has now reached a stage where the very foundations of civilization are seriously threatened. The landmarks and traditions which have marked the progress of civilization toward a condition of law, order, and justice are being wiped away.

Without a declaration of war and without warning or justification of any kind, civilians, including women and children, are being ruthlessly murdered with bombs from the air. In times of so-called peace ships are being attacked and sunk by submarines without cause or notice. Nations are fomenting and taking sides in civil warfare in nations that have never done them any harm. Nations claiming freedom for themselves deny it to others.

Innocent peoples and nations are being cruelly sacrificed to a greed for power and supremacy which is devoid of all sense of justice and humane consideration. . . .

[I]f we are to have a world in which we can breathe freely and live in amity without fear—the peace-loving nations must make a concerted effort to uphold laws and principles on which alone peace can rest secure.

The peace-loving nations must make a concerted effort in opposition to those violations of treaties and those ignorings of humane instincts which today are creating a state of international anarchy and instability from which there is no escape through mere isolation or neutrality.

From U.S. Department of State, *Papers Relating to the Foreign Relations of the United States: Japan, 1931–1941,* vol. 1 (Washington, D.C.: U.S. Government Printing Office, 1943), 379–383.

Those who cherish their freedom and recognize and respect the equal right of their neighbors to be free and live in peace, must work together for the triumph of law and moral principles in order that peace, justice, and confidence may prevail in the world. There must be a return to a belief in the pledged word, in the value of a signed treaty. There must be recognition of the fact that national morality is as vital as private morality. . . .

There is a solidarity and interdependence about the modern world, both technically and morally, which makes it impossible for any nation completely to isolate itself from economic and political upheavals in the rest of the world, especially when such upheavals appear to be spreading and not declining. There can be no stability or peace either within nations or between nations except under laws and moral standards adhered to by all. International anarchy destroys every foundation for peace. It jeopardizes either the immediate or the future security of every nation, large or small. It is therefore, a matter of vital interest and concern to the people of the United States that the sanctity of international treaties and the maintenance of international morality be restored.

The overwhelming majority of the peoples and nations of the world today want to live in peace. They seek the removal of barriers against trade. They want to exert themselves in industry, in agriculture, and in business, that they may increase their wealth through the production of wealth-producing goods rather than striving to produce military planes and bombs and machine guns and cannon for the destruction of human lives and useful property.

In those nations of the world which seem to be piling armament on armament for purposes of aggression, and those other nations which fear acts of aggression against them and their security, a very high proportion of their national income is being spent directly for armaments. It runs from 30 to as high as 50 percent.

The proportion that we in the United States spend is far less—11 or 12 percent.

How happy we are that the circumstances of the moment permit us to put our money into bridges and boulevards, dams and reforestation, the conservation of our soil, and many other kinds of useful works rather than into huge standing armies and vast supplies of implements of war.

I am compelled and you are compelled, nevertheless, to look ahead. The peace, the freedom, and the security of 90 percent of the population of the world is being jeopardized by the remaining 10 percent, who are threatening a breakdown of all international order and law. Surely the 90 percent who want to live in peace under law and in accordance with moral standards that have received almost universal acceptance through the centuries, can and must find some way to make their will prevail.

The situation is definitely of universal concern. The questions involved relate not merely to violations of specific provisions of particular treaties; they are questions of war and of peace, of international law, and especially of principles of humanity. It is true that they involve definite violations of agreements, and especially of the Covenant of the League of Nations, the Briand-Kellogg Pact, and the Nine Power Treaty. But they also involve problems of world economy, world security, and world humanity.

It is true that the moral consciousness of the world must recognize the importance of removing injustices and well-founded grievances; but at the same time it must be aroused to the cardinal necessity of honoring sanctity of treaties, of respecting the rights and liberties of others, and of putting an end to acts of international aggression.

It seems to be unfortunately true that the epidemic of world lawlessness is spreading.

When an epidemic of physical disease starts to spread, the community approves and joins in a quarantine of the patients in order to protect the health of the community against the spread of the disease.

It is my determination to pursue a policy of peace and to adopt every practicable measure to avoid involvement in war. It ought to be inconceivable that in this modern era, and in the face of experience, any nation could be so foolish and ruthless as to run the risk of plunging the whole world into war by invading and violating in contravention of solemn treaties the territory of other nations that have done them no real harm and which are too weak to protect themselves adequately. Yet the peace of the world and the welfare and security of every nation is today being threatened by that very thing. . . .

War is a contagion, whether it be declared or undeclared. It can engulf states and peoples remote from the original scene of hostilities. We are determined to keep out of war, yet we cannot insure ourselves against the disastrous effects of war and the dangers of involvement. We are adopting such measures as will minimize our risk of involvement, but we cannot have complete protection in a world of disorder in which confidence and security have broken down.

If civilization is to survive the principles of the Prince of Peace must be restored. Shattered trust between nations must be revived.

Most important of all, the will for peace on the part of peace-loving nations must express itself to the end that nations that may be tempted to violate their agreements and the rights of others will resist from such a cause. There must be positive endeavors to preserve peace.

America hates war. America hopes for peace. Therefore, America actively engages in the search for peace.

3. President Franklin D. Roosevelt Proposes Lend-Lease Aid to Great Britain, December 17 and 29, 1940

December 17, 1940, Press Conference

. . . Now, what I am trying to do is to eliminate the dollar sign, and that is something brand new in the thoughts of practically everybody in this room, I think—get rid of the silly, foolish old dollar sign. All right!

Well, let me give you an illustration: Suppose my neighbor's home catches fire, and I have got a length of garden hose four or five hundred feet away; but, my

---

Dec. 17 remarks in *Complete Presidential Press Conferences of Franklin D. Roosevelt,* vol. 15–16, 1940 (New York: DaCapo Press, 1972), 353–355. Dec. 29 radio address in State Department *Bulletin* 4 (1941): 3–8.

Heaven, if he can take my garden hose and connect it up with his hydrant, I may help him to put out his fire. Now what do I do? I don't say to him before that operation, "Neighbor, my garden hose cost me $15; you have got to pay me $15 for it." What is the transaction that goes on? I don't want $15—I want my garden hose back after the fire is over. All right. If it goes through the fire all right, intact, without any damage to it, he gives it back to me and thanks me very much for the use of it. But suppose it gets smashed up—holes in it—during the fire; we don't have to have too much formality about it, but I say to him, "I was glad to lend you that hose; I see I can't use it any more, it's all smashed up." He says, "How many feet of it were there?" I tell him, "there were 150 feet of it." He said, "All right, I will replace it." Now, if I get a nice garden hose back, I am in pretty good shape. In other words, if you lend certain munitions and get the munitions back at the end of the war, if they are intact—haven't been hurt—you are all right; if they have been damaged or deteriorated or lost completely, it seems to me you come out pretty well if you have them replaced by the fellow that you have lent them to. . . .

December 29, 1940, Radio Address

This is not a fireside chat on war. It is a talk on national security; because the nub of the whole purpose of your President is to keep you now, and your children later, and your grandchildren much later, out of a last-ditch war for the preservation of American independence and all of the things that American independence means to you and to me and to ours. . . .

Never before since Jamestown and Plymouth Rock has our American civilization been in such danger as now.

For, on September 27, 1940, by an agreement signed in Berlin, three powerful nations, two in Europe and one in Asia, joined themselves together in the threat that if the United States interfered with or blocked the expansion program of these three nations—a program aimed at world control—they would unite in ultimate action against the United States.

The Nazi masters of Germany have made it clear that they intend not only to dominate all life and thought in their own country, but also to enslave the whole of Europe, and then to use the resources of Europe to dominate the rest of the world. . . .

Some of our people like to believe that wars in Europe and in Asia are of no concern to us. But it is a matter of most vital concern to us that European and Asiatic war-makers should not gain control of the oceans which lead to this hemisphere. . . .

Does anyone seriously believe that we need to fear attack while a free Britain remains our most powerful naval neighbor in the Atlantic? Does anyone seriously believe, on the other hand, that we could rest easy if the Axis powers were our neighbor there?

If Great Britain goes down, the Axis powers will control the continents of Europe, Asia, Africa, Australasia, and the high seas—and they will be in a position to bring enormous military and naval resources against this hemisphere. It is no exaggeration to say that all of us in the Americas would be living at the point of a gun—a gun loaded with explosive bullets, economic as well as military.

We should enter upon a new and terrible era in which the whole world, our hemisphere included, would be run by threats of brute force. To survive in such a world, we would have to convert ourselves permanently into a militaristic power on the basis of war economy.

Some of us like to believe that even if Great Britain falls, we are still safe, because of the broad expanse of the Atlantic and of the Pacific.

But the width of these oceans is not what it was in the days of clipper ships. At one point between Africa and Brazil the distance is less than from Washington to Denver—five hours for the latest type of bomber. And at the north of the Pacific Ocean, America and Asia almost touch each other. . . .

There are those who say that the Axis powers would never have any desire to attack the Western Hemisphere. This is the same dangerous form of wishful thinking which has destroyed the powers of resistance of so many conquered peoples. The plain facts are that the Nazis have proclaimed, time and again, that all other races are their inferiors and therefore subject to their orders. And most important of all, the vast resources and wealth of this hemisphere constitute the most tempting loot in all the world. . . .

The experience of the past two years has proven beyond doubt that no nation can appease the Nazis. No man can tame a tiger into a kitten by stroking it. There can be no appeasement with ruthlessness. There can be no reasoning with an incendiary bomb. We know now that a nation can have peace with the Nazis only at the price of total surrender. . . .

The American appeasers ignore the warning to be found in the fate of Austria, Czechoslovakia, Poland, Norway, Belgium, the Netherlands, Denmark, and France. They tell you that the Axis powers are going to win anyway; that all this bloodshed in the world could be saved; and that the United States might just as well throw its influence into the scale of a dictated peace, and get the best out of it that we can.

They call it a "negotiated peace." Nonsense! Is it a negotiated peace if a gang of outlaws surrounds your community and on threat of extermination makes you pay tribute to save your own skins?

Such a dictated peace would be no peace at all. It would be only another armistice, leading to the most gigantic armament race and the most devastating trade wars in history. And in these contests the Americas would offer the only real resistance to the Axis powers.

With all their vaunted efficiency and parade of pious purpose in this war, there are still in their background the concentration camp and the servants of God in chains.

The history of recent years proves that shootings and chains and concentration camps are not simply the transient tools but the very altars of modern dictatorships. They may talk of a "new order" in the world, but what they have in mind is but a revival of the oldest and the worst tyranny. In that there is no liberty, no religion, no hope.

The proposed "new order" is the very opposite of a United States of Europe or a United States of Asia. It is not a government based upon the consent of the governed. It is not a union of ordinary, self-respecting men and women to protect themselves and their freedom and their dignity from oppression. It is an unholy alliance of power and pelf to dominate and enslave the human race.

The British people are conducting an active war against this unholy alliance. Our own future security is greatly dependent on the outcome of that fight. Our ability to "keep out of war" is going to be affected by that outcome.

Thinking in terms of today and tomorrow, I make the direct statement to the American people that there is far less chance of the United States getting into war if we do all we can now to support the nations defending themselves against attack by the Axis than if we acquiesce in their defeat, submit tamely to an Axis victory, and wait our turn to be the object of attack in another war later on.

If we are to be completely honest with ourselves, we must admit there is risk in *any* course we may take. But I deeply believe that the great majority of our people agree that the course that I advocate involves the least risk now and the greatest hope for world peace in the future.

The people of Europe who are defending themselves do not ask us to do their fighting. They ask us for the implements of war, the planes, the tanks, the guns, the freighters, which will enable them to fight for their liberty and our security. Emphatically we must get these weapons to them in sufficient volume and quickly enough, so that we and our children will be saved the agony and suffering of war which others have had to endure.

Let not defeatists tell us that it is too late. It will never be earlier. Tomorrow will be later than today.

Certain facts are self-evident.

In a military sense Great Britain and the British Empire are today the spearhead of resistance to world conquest. They are putting up a fight which will live forever in the story of human gallantry.

There is no demand for sending an American Expeditionary Force outside our own borders. There is no intention by any member of your Government to send such a force. You can, therefore, nail any talk about sending armies to Europe as deliberate untruth.

Our national policy is not directed toward war. Its sole purpose is to keep war away from our country and our people.

Democracy's fight against world conquest is being greatly aided, and must be more greatly aided, by the rearmament of the United States and by sending every ounce and every ton of munitions and supplies that we can possibly spare to help the defenders who are in the front lines. It is no more unneutral for us to do that than it is for Sweden, Russia, and other nations near Germany to send steel and ore and oil and other war materials into Germany every day.

We are planning our own defense with the utmost urgency; and in its vast scale we must integrate the war needs of Britain and the other free nations resisting aggression. . . .

As planes and ships and guns and shells are produced, your Government, with its defense experts, can then determine how best to use them to defend this hemisphere. The decision as to how much shall be sent abroad and how much shall remain at home must be made on the basis of our over-all military necessities.

We must be the great arsenal of democracy. For us this is an emergency as serious as war itself. We must apply ourselves to our task with the same resolution, the same sense of urgency, the same spirit of patriotism and sacrifice, as we would show were we at war. . . .

4. Charles A. Lindbergh Opposes
Lend-Lease, February 6, 1941

Mr. Chairman and gentlemen, in the hope that it will save time and add to clarity, I have attempted to outline briefly my reasons for opposition to this bill. In general, I have two. I oppose it, first, because I believe it is a step away from the system of government in which most of us in this country believe. Secondly, I oppose it because I think it represents a policy which will weaken rather than strengthen our Nation. . . .

. . . I would like to say that I have never taken the stand that it makes no difference to us who wins this war in Europe. It does make a difference to us, a great difference. But I do not believe that it is either possible or desirable for us in America to control the outcome of European wars. When I am asked which side I would like to have win, it would be very easy for me to say "the English." But, gentlemen, an English victory, if it were possible at all, would necessitate years of war and an invasion of the Continent of Europe. I believe this would create prostration, famine, and disease in Europe—and probably in America—such as the world has never experienced before. This is why I say that I prefer a negotiated peace to a complete victory by either side.

This bill is obviously the most recent step in a policy which attempts to obtain security for America by controlling internal conditions in Europe. The policy of depleting our own forces to aid England is based upon the assumption that England will win this war. Personally, I do not believe that England is in a position to win the war. If she does not win, or unless our aid is used in negotiating a better peace than could otherwise be obtained, we will be responsible for futilely prolonging the war and adding to the bloodshed and devastation in Europe, particularly among the democracies. In that case, the only advantage we can gain by our action lies in whatever additional time we obtain to prepare ourselves for defense. But instead of consolidating our own defensive position in America, we are sending a large portion of our armament production abroad. In the case of aviation, for instance, we have sent most of it, yet our own air forces are in deplorable condition for lack of modern equipment. The majority of the planes we now have are obsolescent on the standards of modern warfare.

This bill even authorizes the transfer of the equipment that our air forces now possess. From the standpoint of aviation, at least, I believe this policy weakens our security in America rather than strengthens it. . . .

. . . I believe it is obvious that England cannot obtain an air strength equal to Germany's without great assistance from the United States; and my personal opinion is that, regardless of how much assistance we send, it will not be possible for American and British aviation concentrated in the small area of the British Isles, to equal the strength of German aviation, with unlimited bases throughout the Continent of Europe. We would have a disadvantageous geographical position from

From Senate Foreign Relations Committee Hearings, *To Promote the Defense of the United States,* 77th Cong., 1st sess. (January 3, 1941, through January 2, 1942) (Washington, D.C.: U.S. Government Printing Office, 1941), 490–492.

which to fight, and an ocean to cross with aircraft, men, fuel, and supplies, while our ships would be constantly subjected to the bombs and torpedoes of our enemy.

With this picture of Europe in mind, I now return to my statement that, from the standpoint of aviation, the attempt to gain supremacy of the air in Europe weakens our security in America. If we follow the policy represented by this bill, we will find ourselves with England as a bridgehead in Europe; and, one might say, with the American neck stretched clear across the Atlantic Ocean. . . .

It is also essential to take into consideration the fact that we have another island bridgehead in the Philippines; so that if we follow out the policy represented by this bill, we will have to maintain and protect supply lines which stretch two-thirds of the way around the earth, and which end in positions exposed to attack by the most powerful nations of both Europe and Asia.

This would be an audacious undertaking even if our nation were fully prepared for war. But we are not prepared for war, and the attempt to hold control of island positions off the coasts of Europe and Asia, at the same time, would necessitate depleting even the small defense forces that we now have, as the terms of this bill clearly show.

What we are doing in following our present policy, is giving up an ideal defensive position in America for a very precarious offensive position in Europe. I would be opposed to our entering the internal wars of Europe under any circumstances. But it is an established fact today, that our army and our air force are but poorly equipped on modern standards, and even our Navy is in urgent need of new equipment. If we deplete our forces still further, as this bill indicates we may, and if England should lose this war, then, gentlemen, I think we may be in danger of invasion, although I do not believe we are today. If we ever are invaded in America, the responsibility will lie upon those who send our arms abroad.

I advocate building strength in America because I believe we can be successful in this hemisphere. I oppose placing our security in an English victory because I believe that such a victory is extremely doubtful.

I am opposed to this bill because I believe it endorses a policy that will lead to failure in war, and to conditions in our own country as bad as or worse than those we now desire to overthrow in Nazi Germany.

I do not believe that the danger to America lies in an invasion from abroad. I believe it lies here at home in our own midst, and that it is exemplified by the terms of this bill—the placing of our security in the success of foreign armies, and the removal of power from the Representatives of the people in our own land.

5. Americans Express Their Opinions on Aid to Britain and Entry into the War, 1940–1941

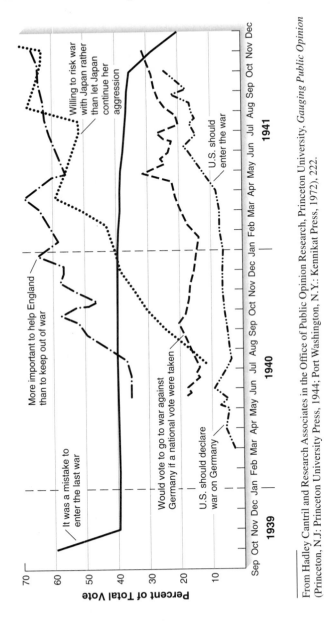

From Hadley Cantril and Research Associates in the Office of Public Opinion Research, Princeton University, *Gauging Public Opinion* (Princeton, N.J.: Princeton University Press, 1944; Port Washington, N.Y.: Kennikat Press, 1972), 222.

6. Secretary of State Cordell Hull Responds to Japan's Final Proposal, November 26, 1941

[T]he Government of the United States offers for the consideration of the Japanese Government a plan of a broad but simple settlement covering the entire Pacific area as one practical exemplification of a program which this Government envisages as something to be worked out during our further conversations.

The plan therein suggested represents an effort to bridge the gap between our draft of June 21, 1941 and the Japanese draft of September 25 by making a new approach to the essential problems underlying a comprehensive Pacific settlement. This plan contains provisions dealing with the practical application of the fundamental principles which we have agreed in our conversations constitute the only sound basis for worthwhile international relations. We hope that in this way progress toward reaching a meeting of minds between our two Governments may be expedited.

OUTLINE OF PROPOSED BASIS FOR AGREEMENT
BETWEEN THE UNITED STATES AND JAPAN

SECTION I
Draft Mutual Declaration of Policy

The Government of the United States and the Government of Japan both being solicitous for the peace of the Pacific affirm that their national policies are directed toward lasting and extensive peace throughout the Pacific area, that they have no territorial designs in that area, that they have no intention of threatening other countries or of using military force aggressively against any neighboring nation, and that, accordingly, in their national policies they will actively support and give practical application to the following fundamental principles upon which their relations with each other and with all other governments are based:

(1) The principle of inviolability of territorial integrity and sovereignty of each and all nations.
(2) The principle of non-interference in the internal affairs of other countries.
(3) The principle of equality, including equality of commercial opportunity and treatment.
(4) The principle of reliance upon international cooperation and conciliation for the prevention and pacific settlement of controversies and for improvement of international conditions by peaceful methods and processes.

The Government of Japan and the Government of the United States have agreed that toward eliminating chronic political instability, preventing recurrent economic collapse, and providing a basis for peace, they will actively support and practically apply the following principles in their economic relations with each other and with other nations and peoples:

(1) The principle of non-discrimination in international commercial relations.
(2) The principle of international economic cooperation and abolition of extreme nationalism as expressed in excessive trade restrictions.

From U.S. Department of State, *Papers Relating to the Foreign Relations of the United States: Japan, 1931–1941*, vol. 2 (Washington, D.C.: U.S. Government Printing Office, 1943), 767–769.

(3) The principle of non-discriminatory access by all nations to raw material supplies.

(4) The principle of full protection of the interests of consuming countries and populations as regards the operation of international commodity agreements.

(5) The principle of establishment of such institutions and arrangements of international finance as may lend aid to the essential enterprises and the continuous development of all countries and may permit payments through processes of trade consonant with the welfare of all countries.

SECTION II
*Steps to Be Taken by the Government of the United States and by the
    Government of Japan*

The Government of the United States and the Government of Japan propose to take steps as follows:

1. The Government of the United States and the Government of Japan will endeavor to conclude a multilateral non-aggression pact among the British Empire, China, Japan, the Netherlands, the Soviet Union, Thailand and the United States.

2. Both Governments will endeavor to conclude among the American, British, Chinese, Japanese, the Netherland and Thai Governments an agreement whereunder each of the Governments would pledge itself to respect the territorial integrity of French Indochina and, in the event that there should develop a threat to the territorial integrity of Indochina, to enter into immediate consultation with a view to taking such measures as may be deemed necessary and advisable to meet the threat in question. Such agreement would provide also that each of the Governments party to the agreement would not seek or accept preferential treatment in its trade or economic relations with Indochina and would use its influence to obtain for each of the signatories equality of treatment in trade and commerce with French Indochina.

3. The Government of Japan will withdraw all military, naval, air and police forces from China and from Indochina.

4. The Government of the United States and the Government of Japan will not support—militarily, politically, economically—any government or regime in China other than the National Government of the Republic of China with capital temporarily at Chungking.

5. Both Governments will give up all extraterritorial rights in China, including rights and interests in and with regard to international settlements and concessions, and rights under the Boxer Protocol of 1901.

Both Governments will endeavor to obtain the agreement of the British and other governments to give up extraterritorial rights in China, including rights in international settlements and in concessions and under the Boxer Protocol of 1901.

6. The Government of the United States and the Government of Japan will enter into negotiations for the conclusion between the United States and Japan of a trade agreement, based upon reciprocal most-favored-nation treatment and reduction of trade barriers by both countries, including an undertaking by the United States to bind raw silk on the free list.

7. The Government of the United States and the Government of Japan will, respectively, remove the freezing restrictions on Japanese funds in the United States and on American funds in Japan.

8. Both Governments will agree upon a plan for the stabilization of the dollar-yen rate, with the allocation of funds adequate for this purpose, half to be supplied by Japan and half by the United States.

9. Both Governments will agree that no agreement which either has concluded with any third power or powers shall be interpreted by it in such a way as to conflict with the fundamental purpose of this agreement, the establishment and preservation of peace throughout the Pacific area.

10. Both Governments will use their influence to cause other governments to adhere to and to give practical application to the basic political and economic principles set forth in this agreement.

7. Japan Terminates Negotiations and Hull Replies Orally, December 7, 1941

Memorandum Handed by the Japanese Ambassador (Nomura) to the Secretary of State at 2:20 P.M. on December 7, 1941

. . .

2. It is the immutable policy of the Japanese Government to insure the stability of East Asia and to promote world peace and thereby to enable all nations to find each its proper place in the world.

Ever since [the] China Affair broke out owing to the failure on the part of China to comprehend Japan's true intentions, the Japanese Government has striven for the restoration of peace and it has consistently exerted its best efforts to prevent the extension of war-like disturbance. It was also to that end that in September last year Japan concluded the Tripartite Pact with Germany and Italy.

However, both the United States and Great Britain have resorted to every possible measure to assist the Chungking régime so as to obstruct the establishment of a general peace between Japan and China, interfering with Japan's constructive endeavours toward the stabilization of East Asia. Exerting pressure on the Netherlands East Indies, or menacing French Indo-China, they have attempted to frustrate Japan's aspiration to the ideal of common prosperity in cooperation with these regions. Furthermore, when Japan in accordance with its protocol with France took measures of joint defence of French Indo-China, both American and British Governments, wilfully misinterpreting it as a threat to their own possessions, and inducing the Netherlands Government to follow suit, they enforced the assets freezing order, thus severing economic relations with Japan. While manifesting thus an obviously hostile attitude, these countries have strengthened their military preparations perfecting an encirclement of Japan, and have brought about a situation which endangers the very existence of the Empire. . . .

4. From the beginning of the present negotiation the Japanese Government has always maintained an attitude of fairness and moderation, and did its best to reach a settlement, for which it made all possible concessions often in spite of great difficulties. As for the China question which constituted an important subject of the

From U.S. Department of State, *Papers Relating to the Foreign Relations of the United States: Japan, 1931–1941*, vol. 2 (Washington, D.C.: U.S. Government Printing Office, 1943), 787–792.

negotiation, the Japanese Government showed a most conciliatory attitude. As for the principle of non-discrimination in international commerce, advocated by the American Government, the Japanese Government expressed its desire to see the said principle applied throughout the world, and declared that along with the actual practice of this principle in the world, the Japanese Government would endeavour to apply the same in the Pacific Area including China, and made it clear that Japan had no intention of excluding from China economic activities of third powers pursued on an equitable basis. Furthermore, as regards the question of withdrawing troops from French Indo-China, the Japanese Government even volunteered, as mentioned above, to carry out an immediate evacuation of troops from Southern French Indo-China as a measure of easing the situation. . . .

On the other hand, the American Government, always holding fast to theories in disregard of realities, and refusing to yield an inch on its impractical principles, caused undue delay in the negotiation. It is difficult to understand this attitude of the American Government and the Japanese Government desires to call the attention of the American Government especially to the following points:

1. The American Government advocates in the name of world peace those principles favorable to it and urges upon the Japanese Government the acceptance thereof. The peace of the world may be brought about only by discovering a mutually acceptable formula through recognition of the reality of the situation and mutual appreciation of one another's position. An attitude such as ignores realities and imposes one's selfish views upon others will scarcely serve the purpose of facilitating the consummation of negotiations.

Of the various principles put forward by the American Government as a basis of the Japanese-American Agreement, there are some which the Japanese Government is ready to accept in principle, but in view of the world's actual conditions, it seems only a utopian ideal on the part of the American Government to attempt to force their immediate adoption. . . .

2. The American proposal contained a stipulation which states—"Both Governments will agree that no agreement, which either has concluded with any third power or powers, shall be interpreted by it in such a way as to conflict with the fundamental purpose of this agreement, the establishment and preservation of peace throughout the Pacific area." It is presumed that the above provision has been proposed with a view to restrain Japan from fulfilling its obligations under the Tripartite Pact when the United States participates in the War in Europe, and, as such, it cannot be accepted by the Japanese Government.

The American Government, obsessed with its own views and opinions, may be said to be scheming for the extension of the war. While it seeks, on the one hand, to secure its rear by stabilizing the Pacific Area, it is engaged, on the other hand, in aiding Great Britain and preparing to attack, in the name of self-defense, Germany and Italy, two Powers that are striving to establish a new order in Europe. Such a policy is totally at variance with the many principles upon which the American Government proposes to found the stability of the Pacific Area through peaceful means.

3. Whereas the American Government, under the principles it rigidly upholds, objects to settle international issues through military pressure, it is exercising in conjunction with Great Britain and other nations pressure by economic power. Recourse to such pressure as a means of dealing with international relations should be condemned as it is at times more inhumane than military pressure.

4. It is impossible not to reach the conclusion that the American Government desires to maintain and strengthen, in coalition with Great Britain and other Powers, its dominant position it has hitherto occupied not only in China but in other areas of East Asia. It is a fact of history that the countries of East Asia for the past hundred years or more

have been compelled to observe the *status quo* under the Anglo-American policy of imperialistic exploitation and to sacrifice themselves to the prosperity of the two nations. The Japanese Government cannot tolerate the perpetuation of such a situation since it directly runs counter to Japan's fundamental policy to enable all nations to enjoy each its proper place in the world.

The stipulation proposed by the American Government relative to French Indo-China is a good exemplification of the above-mentioned American policy. . . .

5. All the items demanded of Japan by the American Government regarding China such as wholesale evacuation of troops or unconditional application of the principle of non-discrimination in international commerce ignored the actual conditions of China, and are calculated to destroy Japan's position as the stabilizing factor of East Asia. The attitude of the American Government in demanding Japan not to support militarily, politically or economically any régime other than the régime at Chungking, disregarding thereby the existence of the Nanking Government, shatters the very basis of the present negotiation. This demand of the American Government falling, as it does, in line with its above-mentioned refusal to cease from aiding the Chungking régime, demonstrates clearly the intention of the American Government to obstruct the restoration of normal relations between Japan and China and the return of peace to East Asia.

5. In brief, the American proposal contains certain acceptable items such as those concerning commerce, including the conclusion of a trade agreement, mutual removal of the freezing restrictions, and stabilization of yen and dollar exchange, or the abolition of extra-territorial rights in China. On the other hand, however, the proposal in question ignores Japan's sacrifices in the four years of the China Affair, menaces the Empire's existence itself and disparages its honour and prestige. Therefore, viewed in its entirety, the Japanese Government regrets that it cannot accept the proposal as a basis of negotiation. . . .

7. Obviously it is the intention of the American Government to conspire with Great Britain and other countries to obstruct Japan's efforts toward the establishment of peace through the creation of a new order in East Asia, and especially to preserve Anglo-American rights and interests by keeping Japan and China at war. This intention has been revealed clearly during the course of the present negotiation. Thus, the earnest hope of the Japanese Government to adjust Japanese-American relations and to preserve and promote the peace of the Pacific through cooperation with the American Government has finally been lost.

The Japanese Government regrets to have to notify hereby the American Government that in view of the attitude of the American Government it cannot but consider that it is impossible to reach an agreement through further negotiations. . . .

After the Secretary had read two or three pages he asked the Ambassador whether this document was presented under instructions of the Japanese government. The Ambassador replied that it was. The Secretary as soon as he had finished reading the document turned to the Japanese Ambassador and said,

> I must say that in all my conversations with you [the Japanese Ambassador] during the last nine months I have never uttered one word of untruth. This is borne out absolutely by the record. In all my fifty years of public service I have never seen a document that was more crowded with infamous falsehoods and distortions—infamous falsehoods and distortions on a scale so huge that I never imagined until today that any Government on this planet was capable of uttering them.

8. President Roosevelt Asks Congress for a Declaration of War, December 8, 1941

Yesterday, December 7, 1941—a date which will live in infamy—the United States of America was suddenly and deliberately attacked by naval and air forces of the Empire of Japan.

The United States was at peace with that Nation and, at the solicitation of Japan, was still in conversation with its Government and its Emperor looking toward the maintenance of peace in the Pacific. Indeed, one hour after Japanese air squadrons had commenced bombing in Oahu, the Japanese Ambassador to the United States and his colleague delivered to the Secretary of State a formal reply to a recent American message. While this reply stated that it seemed useless to continue the existing diplomatic negotiations, it contained no threat or hint of war or armed attack.

It will be recorded that the distance of Hawaii from Japan makes it obvious that the attack was deliberately planned many days or even weeks ago. During the intervening time the Japanese Government has deliberately sought to deceive the United States by false statements and expressions of hope for continued peace.

The attack yesterday on the Hawaiian Islands has caused severe damage to American naval and military forces. Very many American lives have been lost. In addition American ships have been reported torpedoed on the high seas between San Francisco and Honolulu.

Yesterday the Japanese Government also launched an attack against Malaya.

Last night Japanese forces attacked Hong Kong.

Last night Japanese forces attacked Guam.

Last night Japanese forces attacked the Philippine Islands.

Last night the Japanese attacked Wake Island.

This morning the Japanese attacked Midway Island.

Japan has, therefore, undertaken a surprise offensive extending throughout the Pacific area. The facts of yesterday speak for themselves. The people of the United States have already formed their opinions and well understand the implications to the very life and safety of our Nation.

As Commander-in-Chief of the Army and Navy I have directed that all measures be taken for our defense.

Always will we remember the character of the onslaught against us.

No matter how long it may take us to overcome this premeditated invasion, the American people in their righteous might will win through to absolute victory.

I believe I interpret the will of the Congress and of the people when I assert that we will not only defend ourselves to the uttermost but will make very certain that this form of treachery shall never endanger us again.

Hostilities exist. There is no blinking at the fact that our people, our territory, and our interests are in grave danger.

With confidence in our armed forces—with the unbounded determination of our people—we will gain the inevitable triumph—so help us God.

From U.S. Department of State, *Papers Relating to the Foreign Relations of the United States: Japan, 1931–1941*, vol. 2 (Washington, D.C.: U.S. Government Printing Office, 1943), 793–794.

I ask that the Congress declare that since the unprovoked and dastardly attack by Japan on Sunday, December seventh, a state of war has existed between the United States and the Japanese Empire.

E S S A Y S

Pearl Harbor ended the massive public debate between those in favor of and those opposed to U.S involvement in overseas conflicts not simply for the duration of the World War II, but actually for the next thirty years. "Isolationism" was said to have died on December 7, 1941, thoroughly discredited by the Japanese attack. Henceforth the United States would in its own interests have to play a major role in halting any aggression in the international arena. During the 1950s and 1960s, however, such beliefs played a major role in leading the United States into war in Vietnam. This conflict sharply divided the American people and ended the national foreign policy consensus long before it resulted in a humiliating defeat. Consequently it led many Americans to a new look at what by this time appeared to be the prophetic warnings of Roosevelt's prewar critics regarding the long-term negative consequences of the president's internationalist policies, and therefore to a reconsideration of the wisdom of those policies. The first essay, by Bruce M. Russett of Yale University, belongs to this school of thought. In it the author maintains that the United States could and should have avoided not only war with Japan, but also war with Nazi Germany.

Most scholars disagreed sharply with Russett's provocative conclusions. Among the most notable of these was Gerhard Weinberg of the University of North Carolina, a World War II scholar who had previously unearthed a second book Hitler had written after his *Mein Kampf.* In that second book, the Nazi dictator made clear his plans for global, not simply European, war and conquest, with the United States as one of his principal enemies. In the second essay, Weinberg shows Hitler acting on these plans in 1940–1941, and the global nature and interrelationships of German, Japanese and U.S. policies in 1940–1941. Combining his reassessment of Hitler's goals with recent and harsh reassessments of Japanese policies, Weinberg argues that Nazi Germany and militaristic Japan posed a mortal threat to the United States—one that required (and left the United States with no alternative to) full-scale participation in the war, despite Roosevelt's contrary desire to keep that participation limited, and the ensuing total destruction of Axis power.

An Unnecessary and Avoidable War

BRUCE M. RUSSETT

American participation in World War II brought the country few gains; the United States was no more secure at the end than it could have been had it stayed out. First, let us look at the "might have beens" in Europe. The standard justification of American entry into the war is that otherwise Germany would have reigned supreme on the continent, victor over Russia and Britain. With all the resources of Europe at the disposal of his totalitarian government, plus perhaps parts of the British fleet, Hitler would have posed an intolerable threat to the security of the United States. He could have consolidated his winnings, built his war machine, established bridgeheads in South America, and ultimately could and likely would have moved against North America to achieve world domination.

Several links in this argument might deserve scrutiny, but by far the critical one is the first, that Hitler would have won World War II. Such a view confuses the ability of Germany's enemies to *win* with their ability to achieve a *stalemate*. Also, it tends to look more at the military-political situation of June 1940 than at that of December 1941, and to confuse President Roosevelt's decision to aid Britain (and later Russia) by "all measure short of war" with an actual American declaration of war. Let me say clearly: I basically accept the proposition that German domination of all Europe, with Britain and Russia prostrate, would have been intolerable to the United States. By any of the classical conceptions of "power-balancing" and "national interest," the United States should indeed have intervened if necessary to prevent that outcome. . . .

But . . . [b]y the end of 1941 Hitler had already lost his gamble to control Europe. In large part this was due to British skill, courage, and good luck in the summer of 1940. Given German naval inferiority, Hitler had to destroy the British air force for an invasion to be possible. But the RAF won the Battle of Britain and Hitler decided against undertaking Operation Sea Lion; it was too risky. From that point onward German relative capabilities for a cross-channel attack declined rather than improved. The ebb of the tide against Hitler was very greatly assisted, as an absolutely essential condition, by American military and economic assistance to the British.

Recall American initiatives during the first two years of war in Europe. In the fall of 1939 the Neutrality Act was amended to repeal the arms embargo and make any goods available to all belligerents on a cash-and-carry basis. Thanks to the British fleet, only the Allies could take advantage of this measure. The destroyers-for-bases exchange with Britain was agreed upon in September 1940. Many of the old American warships were of doubtful military value, but the trade's symbolism was extremely significant. The Lend-Lease Act, which was to pour billions of dollars of supplies into Britain and, beginning later, to Russia, was signed in March 1941. In July 1941 United States forces occupied Iceland and President Roosevelt had agreed that American ships would escort convoys—including British ships—as far as Iceland. Convoying meant that if German U-boats approached the American escorts were to "shoot on sight" to insure that the goods got through. These steps played central roles in British survival. By August Roosevelt and Churchill could meet in a cruiser off Argentia, Newfoundland to discuss military collaboration and, with the Atlantic Charter, to begin planning for the postwar world.

I do not, therefore, argue that American nonbelligerent assistance to Britain was a mistake, quite the contrary. Yet that is just the point—by the end of 1941 Britain's survival was essentially assured. . . .

If British survival into 1941 raised the specter of deadlock or war of attrition to Hitler, the failure of his attack on Russia brought the specter to life. . . . With the onset of the Russian winter and Hitler's inability to take Moscow—Napoleon had at least managed that—the prospect of German failure was sharp. Looking back, we now can see that *this* was in fact the hinge of fate; the more visible turning a year later was more nearly the outward sign of a predetermined shift. . . .

The essential point is that the Russian success, like the British, occurred quite independently of American military action. . . .

Had America remained in the status of twilight belligerence Germany probably would not have been defeated, though as I have argued above, neither could it have won. Probably World War II would have ended in some sort of draw and negotiated settlement, or would have continued on for a decade or two with occasional truces for breathing spells—not unlike the Napoleonic Wars. Or perhaps most likely is some combination of the two, in which the negotiated peace was uneasy and soon broken. What I imagine, then, is a very long and bloody war, longer and even more bloody than the one that really was fought, with protracted savage fighting in east and central Europe. . . .

Some contemporaries of course took a more alarmist view, especially immediately after the fall of France. A *Fortune* magazine survey of Americans in July 1940 found that 63 percent expected that an Axis triumph would bring an immediate German attempt to seize territory in the Western Hemisphere; 43 percent expected an imminent attack on the United States. American army generals feared a Nazi invasion of South America, and to forestall it wanted a major base in Trinidad. The continued resistance of Britain calmed such alarm for a while, though it was to be revived in somewhat similar form in 1942 with the anticipation of German aerial attacks on American cities and towns. Seacoast areas were allotted major antiaircraft units. Blackout regulations were widely enforced. School children were taught how to crouch against basement walls clenching corks between their teeth in the event of bombardment. Fiorello LaGuardia, then head of the Office of Civilian Defense, wanted 50 million gas masks.

All of this of course seems more than a little absurd in light of known—then as well as now—German capabilities. Not a single German bomb ever did fall in North or South America. Any kind of troop landing required naval and logistic support utterly beyond Hitler's reach. After all, it was not until two and a half years of war, with vast shipping and naval superiority, and a base in Britain, that the Allies felt able to cross even the English Channel in an invasion the other way. The bogeyman of Nazi troops in America had no more substance than that, several years later, of Russian landings.

This is not to say that ultimately a German victory might not have posed some such dangers, nor to imply any certainty about limitations to Hitler's intentions. A. J. P. Taylor paints Hitler as essentially a classical German statesman without real ambition to dominate Europe; Alan Bullock sees ambition, but directed largely toward Eastern Europe and certainly not toward the new world. We need not accept either of these views. Other writers grant that the documents have turned up no German plan before December 1941 for a military attack on the United States, but contend that such plans might well have developed ultimately. One does show some Hitlerian ravings and notions of ultimate war with America, beginning in October 1940. This same author emphasizes that the mere absence of plans is no proof that Hitler did not have, or could not have developed, the intent. At this point the argument of those who posit the possibility of a later threat becomes impossible to refute. One must ask realistic questions about German capability, not intention.

Very possibly a stalemate would not have marked the end of Hitler's ambitions, but that is not really the point. For some time at least, Germany would not have been

supreme as an immediate menace to the United States. One further step in still another war would first be required—the ultimate victory over Britain and/or Russia,
and if that should in fact be threatened, the United States could still have intervened
then, and done so while allies existed. By the end of 1941 the pressure for such intervention had really passed for *that* war. Even those who most heavily stress the
dangers of Nazi subversion in North and South America grant that "There still
would be ominous eddies, but by the summer of 1940 the Nazi cause was in retreat
in the new world." . . .

Finally, we ought to confront the argument that sheer morality demanded American intervention against Hitler. I have deliberately left this issue aside, defining our
concern to be only with the structure of the international system, the relative weight
of power facing the United States and its potential allies. My argument has accepted
the "realist" one that fears the concentration of great power in other hands regardless
of the apparent goals, ideology, or morality of those wielding that power. Concern
with the morality of others' domestic politics is an expensive luxury, and evaluations all too subject to rapid change. . . .

Yet some would maintain that Hitler was just too evil to tolerate, that the United
States had a moral duty to exterminate him and free those under his rule. . . .

Still, in this context Hitler must be compared with Stalin, who was hardly a
saint, and who as a result of the complete German collapse in 1945 emerged from
the war with an immensely greater empire. We must remember the terror and paranoid purges of his rule, and such examples of Stalinist humanity as the starvation
of millions of kulaks. The worst Nazi crimes emerged only in 1943 and later at
Nuremberg. German "medical experiments" and extermination camps were unknown to the world in 1941. Though the Hitler regime had anything but a savory
reputation then, the moral argument too is essentially one made in hindsight, not a
primary motivation at the time war was declared. . . .

If one rejects the purely moral justification of American entry into the war against
Hitler, no very effective moral brief can then be made for the war in the Pacific.
True, the Japanese were often unkind conquerors, though this can easily be exaggerated by American memories of the Bataan death march and other horrors in the
treatment of prisoners. Japanese occupation was often welcomed in the former European colonies of Southeast Asia, and Japan retains some reservoir of good will for
its assistance, late in the war, of indigenous liberation movements. In any case it is
Hitler, not Tojo, who is customarily presented as the personification of evil. Possibly
Americans did have some vague obligation to defend Chinese independence, but
more clearly than in Europe the basis for American participation has to be *realpolitik.*
The case has to be founded on a conviction that Japan was too powerful, too dangerously expansionist without any apparent restraint, to have been left alone. An
extreme but widely accepted version is given by an early chronicler of the war:

> Japan in the spring and summer of 1941 would accept no diplomatic arrangement
> which did not give it everything that it might win in the Far East by aggression, without
> the trouble and expense of military campaigns.

The evidence, however, shows quite a different picture both of intent and capability. Nor is it enough simply to assert that, because Japan attacked the United States

at Pearl Harbor, America took no action to begin hostilities. This is formally true, but very deceptive. The Japanese attack would not have come but for the American, British, and Dutch embargo on shipment of strategic raw materials to Japan. Japan's strike against the American naval base merely climaxed a long series of mutually antagonistic acts. In initiating economic sanctions against Japan the United States undertook actions that were widely recognized in Washington as carrying grave risk of war. To understand this requires a retracing of the events of the preceding years....

... [The Japanese] apparently believed that their Empire's status as an independent world power depended on military equality with Russia and the United States in the Far East; that in turn depended on a hegemonical position, preferably economic but achieved by force if necessary, in the area of China. Though this seems strange now, an adequate view of Japanese policy in its contemporary context has to remember Tokyo's position as a latecomer to colonialism, in a world where France, Britain, and the United States all had their own spheres of influence.

Japanese forces made important initial gains by occupying most of the Chinese coast and most of China's industrial capacity, but with a trickle of American aid the nationalist armies hung on in the interior. By 1941 the Japanese armies were bogged down, and their progress greatly impeded by raw material shortages. In 1940 Congress placed fuel oil and scrap iron under the new National Defense Act as goods which could not be shipped out of the Western Hemisphere without an export license. Although commerce in these products was not actually cut off for another year, the threat to Japan of a raw material scarcity was obvious, and deliberately invoked by an American government seeking to apply pressure against the Japanese campaign in China. This strategy was exercised in a series of dozens of gradually tightening economic measures—an escalation that was to drive Japan not to capitulation, as it was intended to do, but to war with the United States.

Following the July 1941 freeze on Japanese assets in America, and the consequent cessation of shipment of oil, scrap iron, and other goods from the United States, Japan's economy was in most severe straits and her power to wage war directly threatened. Her military leaders estimated that her reserves of oil, painfully accumulated in the late 1930s when the risk of just such a squeeze became evident, would last at most two years. She was also short of rice, tin, bauxite, nickel, rubber and other raw materials normally imported from the Dutch East Indies and Malaya. Negotiations with the Dutch authorities to supply these goods, plus extraordinary amounts of oil from the wells of Sumatra, had failed, ostensibly on the grounds that the Dutch feared the material would be reexported to the Axis in Europe. The United States, and the British and Dutch, made it quite clear that the embargo would be relaxed only in exchange for Japanese withdrawal from air and naval bases in Indochina (seized in order to prosecute better the war against China) and an agreement which would have meant the end of the Japanese involvement in China and the *abandonment* of any right to station troops in that country, not just a halt to the fighting. The purpose of the Western economic blockade was to force a favorable solution to the "China incident."

Under these conditions, the High Command of the Japanese navy demanded a "settlement" of one sort or other that would restore Japan's access to essential raw materials, most particularly oil. Without restored imports of fuel the fleet could not very long remain an effective fighting force. While the navy might have been willing to abandon the China campaign, it was utterly opposed to indefinite continuation of the status quo. Either raw material supplies had to be restored by a peaceful settlement with the Western powers, or access to the resources in Thailand, Malaya, and the Indies would have to be secured by force while Japan still retained the capabilities to do so.

If the navy demanded either settlement or war, most members of the Japanese elite were opposed to any settlement which would in effect have meant withdrawal from China. No serious thought was given to the possibility of peace with Chiang's government, for it would have meant the end of all hopes of empire in East Asia and even, it was thought, of influence on the continent of Asia. Moderate Foreign Minister Shigenori Togo reacted to the most forceful statement of American demands, on November 27, 1941, "Japan was asked not only to abandon all the gains of her years of sacrifice, but to surrender her international position as a power in the Far East." In his view that surrender would have been equivalent to national suicide. . . .

Thus, for the various elements in the Japanese government, and for somewhat different reasons, a peaceful settlement ultimately became unacceptable. They could not accede to the American demands, and they could not even continue to drag out the negotiations because of the increasingly precarious nature of the war economy and especially the Navy's fuel supplies. On rejecting this unpalatable alternative they were again thrown back on the other; the necessary raw material could be obtained only by seizing Thailand, where there was rice; Malaya, with its sources of tin, nickel, and rubber; and the Dutch East Indies, with their oil. But, according to the Japanese calculations, the United States was certain to fight if British or Dutch territory in the Far East were attacked. Japanese analysts reached the latter conclusions despite the absence of any American threat or promise. . . .

Having decided against withdrawal from China, failed to negotiate a settlement with America, and decided on the necessity of seizing supplies from Southeast Asia, they were faced with the need to blunt what they regarded as the inevitable American response. Thus they launched a surprise attack on Pearl Harbor to destroy any American capability for immediate naval offensive. For all the audacity of the strike at Hawaii, its aims were limited: to destroy existing United States offensive capabilities in the Pacific by tactical surprise. The Japanese High Command hoped only to give its forces time to occupy the islands of the Southwest Pacific, to extract those islands' raw materials, and to turn the whole area into a virtually impregnable line of defense which could long delay an American counteroffensive and mete out heavy casualties when the counterattack did come. As a result of their early success the Japanese naval and military chiefs extended this line a little farther than they had first meant to do, but their original intentions were not grandiose.

In deciding to attack Pearl Harbor the Japanese took what they fully recognized to be a great risk. There is no doubt but that the Imperial government realized it could not win a long war with the United States if the Americans chose to fight such a war. Japanese strategists calculated that America's war potential was seven to eight times greater than their own; they knew that Japan could not hope to carry the war to the continental United States. General Suzuki, chairman of the Planning Board, had reported that Japan's stockpile of resources was not adequate to support a long war. Admiral Yamamoto, the brilliant inventor of the Pearl Harbor attack plan, warned: "In the first six months to a year of war against the U.S. and England

I will run wild, and I will show you an uninterrupted succession of victories; I must also tell you that, should the war be prolonged for two or three years, I have no confidence in our ultimate victory."

Because the proposed attack seemed an escape from the dilemma it was grasped with more enthusiasm than it deserved. The Japanese never seriously considered exactly what would cause the United States to forego crushing Japan, or how Japan might best create the proper conditions for a negotiated peace. Certain key elements, such as the probable effect of the Pearl Harbor attack on the American will to win, were left completely unanalyzed. Japan's sole strategy involved dealing maximum losses to the United States at the outset, making the prospects of a prolonged war as grim as possible, and counting, in an extremely vague and ill-defined way, on the American people's "softness" to end the war. . . .

. . . [T]he Japanese attack on Pearl Harbor, and for that matter on Southeast Asia, [was] not evidence of any unlimited expansionist policy or capability by the Japanese government. It was the consequence only of a much less ambitious goal, centering on an unwillingness to surrender the position that the Japanese had fought for years to establish in China. When that refusal met an equal American determination that Japan should give up many of her gains in China, the result was war. Japanese expansion into Southeast Asia originated less in strength than in weakness; it was predominantly instrumental to the China campaign, not a reach for another slice of global salami. Of course there were Japanese political and military leaders with wider ambitions, but they were not predominant in policy-making.

Throughout the 1930s the United States government had done little to resist the Japanese advance on the Asian continent. There were verbal protests, but little more. Even in early 1941 Washington apparently would have settled for a *halt* in China, and saw little danger of a much wider move into Southeast Asia. But the application of economic sanctions against Tokyo was very successful; it was obviously hurting, and the moderate Premier Prince Konoye proposed a direct meeting with Roosevelt to try to reach an understanding. At about that point the American Government seems to have been so impressed with its success that it rebuffed Konoye's approach, demanding that he agree in advance on terms of a settlement. Konoye's cabinet fell, and American observers concluded—on the basis of untestable evidence that sounded a bit like sour grapes—that he could not have enforced a "reasonable" settlement in Japanese politics anyway. Washington then raised the ante, calling for a Japanese *withdrawal* from all occupied territory in China. Several officials in the State Department proposed settling for a halt, giving China a breathing spell that would have served it better for several more years of war while America made its main effort in the Atlantic. Hull considered and then rejected their plan for such a *modus vivendi,* which rather closely resembled the second of two Japanese proposals ("Plan B") that represented Tokyo's last efforts. Economic sanctions continued to provide a warm moral glow for those who disapproved of trading with an aggressor, but they then served to make inevitable an otherwise avoidable war which was peripheral to American vital interests and for which the country was ill-prepared. . . .

Why then did President Roosevelt and his advisers embark on a series of incremental pressures that had the effect of pushing the Japanese into war? In large part, of course, they decided that Japanese ambitions in China posed a long-term threat to American interests, and so they forced a confrontation. A sentimental American attitude toward China as a "ward" also must not be forgotten. From missionary days they had been a people "we had always helped," to whom there was a sense of obligation. Roosevelt had a long-time emotional attachment to China, and from his days as Assistant Secretary of the Navy had allegedly "become imbued with the Navy's conviction that Japan was America's Number One enemy."

Nor should economic, as opposed to strategic, motives be ignored as they have been in most conventional histories of the period. . . . But as for the Far East, by embargoing Japan in 1941 the United States was giving up an export trade at least four times that with China. While one must not equate dollar volume perfectly with relative political influence, the impact of China traders can easily be exaggerated. . . .

On purely strategic grounds some observers might argue that the danger was not from Germany, Italy, or Japan alone, but rather from their combination in an aggressive alliance encircling the Western Hemisphere. The rhetoric of the time could suggest such a threat, but in fact the Tripartite Pact of Germany and Italy with Japan had become quite fragile. As explained [previously] . . . it was designed to deter United States entry into either of the then still-separate conflicts. The Japanese foreign minister in early 1941, Yosuke Matsuoka, had negotiated the Pact and was by far its strongest supporter in the cabinet. He tried to persuade his colleagues to follow the German attack on Russia with a similar act by Japan, but failed and was deposed. Thereafter the Pact faded in importance to the Tokyo government. In considering their subsequent negotiations with the United States the Japanese leaders were fully willing to sacrifice the Pact in return for the necessary economic concessions. Had Hitler managed to get himself into war with America in the Atlantic he could not successfully have invoked the Pact unless the Japanese clearly had seen war to be in their own interests.

Moreover, this drift away from Germany was, it has been well argued, adequately known to American and British officials—Ambassadors Grew and Craigie, Cordell Hull, Roosevelt and Churchill—thanks in part to American ability to crack the codes used in all Japanese secret cables. "After Matsuoka's fall . . . no Axis leader was able even to keep up the pretense of expecting Japanese intervention in behalf of Germany and Italy." In the context of late 1941, therefore, the prospects of close cooperation among Germany, Italy and Japan were not very menacing. Given their very diverse long-run interests, and Hitler's racial notions, a "permanent" alliance surely does not seem very plausible. A special irony of the situation is that Roosevelt was particularly anxious to see Hitler beaten first, and that British and Dutch colonial possessions in Southeast Asia, which seemed essential to the European war, be unmolested. His belated insistence on Japanese evacuation from China then pushed the Axis back together and endangered his other goals. . . .

In retrospect, the fear that America would be left alone in the world against two great victorious empires in Europe and Asia seems terribly exaggerated. Clear-cut victory was not in prospect for either, nor does the assumption that they could long have maintained a close alliance seem especially plausible. The critical American mistake may well have been in backing the Japanese into a corner, for without war in the Pacific the American conflict with Germany very possibly could have been held to limited naval engagements, but no clash of ground troops. In short, we might at most have fought a limited war.

These conclusions are highly speculative; the situation of the time cannot be reproduced for another run, searching for an alternate future. Perhaps I underestimate the risks that an American determination to avoid war would have entailed. On the other hand, the proposition that the war was unnecessary—in a real sense premature, fought before the need was sufficiently clearly established, though the need might well have become apparent later—is worth considering. Just possibly the isolationists were right in their essential perspective.

This last may be unpalatable, especially because the intellectual company of some of the most famous isolationists—William Borah, Hiram Johnson, and Burton Wheeler—is not very distinguished. Others like Father Coughlin were home-grown fascists, or, like Charles Lindbergh, are remembered as naive admirers of Germany. But once more, I do not imagine that the United States should have carried on blithely in 1941 as though nothing were happening elsewhere in the world. Complete isolation would have been much worse than intervention. All Americans would agree that American strategic interests required substantial assistance to the belligerents against Germany. Both Britain and Russia had to be preserved as independent and powerful states. With a little less certainty I would also grant the need to keep a significant portion of China viable.

It seems, however, that those goals could have been achieved by the belligerents themselves, with great American economic and noncombatant military aid. As insurance, American rearmament had to go on. A sustained defense effort not less than what was later accepted during the cold war would have been required. That would imply 10 percent of the American GNP devoted to military purposes, as compared with about that amount actually expended in 1941 and a mere one and one-half percent in 1939. That much, incidentally, would with Lend-Lease have been quite enough to revive the economy from the depression and assuredly does not imply idle resources.

With this prescription I find myself at odds with the extreme critics of Roosevelt's policy, men who spoke at that time and again, briefly, after the war. Most of the President's military and economic acts seem appropriate and, in deed, necessary. I have no quarrel with the decisions for rearmament or to institute Selective Service, with revision of the Neutrality Act to permit "cash-and-carry" by belligerents (effectively by the Allies only), with the destroyers-for-bases exchange, with Lend-Lease, or with the decision to convoy American vessels as far as Iceland. Even the famous "shoot-on-sight" order, even as interpreted to allow American destroyers to seek out the sight of U-boats, seems necessary if the convoys were to be protected on the first stage of the critical lifeline to Britain. I do have some serious reservations about the way in which those decisions were publicly justified, a matter for discussion below. But the content of those decisions seems fully defensible. And irritating as they surely were, Hitler would probably have continued to tolerate them in preference to more active American involvement.

Only two major exceptions to the content of American policy in 1941 appear worth registering. One is the vote by Congress in mid-November 1941, at the President's behest, removing nearly all the remaining restrictions of the Neutrality Act. It permitted American ships to carry supplies all the way across the Atlantic, instead of merely as far as Iceland. This almost certainly would have been too much for Hitler to bear. . . .

The other and still more serious exception I take is with President Roosevelt's policy toward Japan as described [previously]. . . . It was neither necessary nor desirable for him to have insisted on a Japanese withdrawal from China. An agreement for a standstill would have been enough, and he did not make an honest diplomatic attempt to achieve it. He refused to meet Prince Konoye in the Pacific to work out a compromise, and after Konye's fall he rejected, on Hull's advice, a draft proposal that could have served as a basis for compromise with the Japanese. We have no guarantee that agreement could have been reached, but here was at least some chance and the effort was not made. . . .

It would of course be unfair and inaccurate to trace all the developments cited in this chapter, and especially the adoption of interventionist policies, only back to 1940, just as it is wrong to think they emerged full-blown at the beginning of the cold war. One can find roots in our earlier Caribbean policy, in Woodrow Wilson's acts, in the war of 1898, and even earlier. But World War II, rather like monosodium glutamate, made pungent a host of unsavory flavors that had until then been relatively subdued. We cannot really extirpate contemporary "global policeman" conceptions from American thinking unless we understand how, in World War II, they developed and became ingrained.

Preface to the Twenty-fifth Anniversary Edition

. . . [W]here did the book come from in my personal history? As I stated clearly in the original preface, it stemmed from my experience, as a scholar of American foreign policy, of the Vietnam War. Published at the height of the war, it originated from my disgust and represented my effort to understand why the war had happened and persisted. I believed then, and still do, that such standard interpretations as bureaucratic inertia on Pennsylvania Avenue, economic interest on Wall Street, or anti-communist ideology on Main Street, constitute at best partial explanations that missed a broader kind of ideological underpinning. I would characterize that ideological underpinning as a particular kind of "realist" view of international power politics that exaggerated both the necessity and the possibility of effectively exerting American military power all over the globe. A shorthand label for such a view now comes under the expression "imperial overstretch." And I believe that view was, for many Americans, born out of the experience of World War II. . . .

The fundamental problem with the World War II experience—rightly judged in some degree to be a success—was, in my view, that it led to an exaggerated sense of American power and wisdom; *hubris,* in effect. It seemed such a success that the limits and the particular circumstances of that success were ignored in subsequent policy. And that hubris led to the intervention in Vietnam, a military expedition for which the motivation and the need were far less clear than in World War II. Consequently, the national will for a total commitment in Vietnam was, properly, lacking, and thus the prospects for that intervention were poor. In other words, the construction put upon the World War II experience was an invitation to subsequent failure; to understand that failure, and to avoid repeating it, required some deconstruction of World War II's lessons. It required speculating about whether active American participation in the war could have been avoided, and if so, what the costs and benefits of such an alternative might have been. It was a task for historical evaluation as well as a practically oriented form of theoretical discussion. . . .

A Necessary and Unavoidable War

GERHARD WEINBERG

Hitler's view of the United States was based on an assessment that this was a weak country, incapable because of its racial mixture and feeble democratic government of organizing and maintaining strong military forces. The antagonism of Americans, both in government and among the public, toward Germany was therefore no cause for worry. Certain that Allied victory in World War I was the result of Germany's having been stabbed in the back by the home front, he was never interested in the American military effort in that conflict or any possible renewal of it. He had long assumed that Germany would have to fight the United States after conquering Eurasia, and he had begun preparations toward that end both in airplane and naval construction. The outbreak of war in Europe in 1939, however, forced a temporary postponement in the program to construct a big navy of huge battleships and numerous other surface ships. Although it is not clear when Hitler learned the facts, the project for building planes which could reach the American east coast was also not going well.

Under these circumstances, Hitler preferred to defer war with the United States, not because he was greatly worried about that prospect, but because he saw no reason to rush into premature hostilities when he had not completed his blue-water navy, and the navy actually at his disposal did not yet have the number of submarines which might really seal off the British Isles. Nothing that had happened in 1939 changed his basic views of the United States. . . .

[In mid-1940 t]he great problem for the future was the fact that the Germans had been obliged by the outbreak of war in 1939 to postpone construction of the navy needed for the war which Hitler expected to wage against the United States. The first of the battleships designed with the British navy in mind, the *Bismarck* and the *Tirpitz,* were being completed; but work on the super-battleships which were expected to outclass anything the United States might build had been halted in September 1939. Knowing that the completion of these enormous ships took years, Hitler was eager to have work on them resumed as soon as possible. On July 11, 1940, the orders to do so were agreed upon between him and the Commander-in-Chief of the navy. At a time when Hitler still had some hope that Britain might pull out of the war, he was looking forward to the contest ahead when a great blue-water navy would enable him to defeat the United States with England either conquered or allied with *either* of the two major contestants. Nothing more clearly illuminates the world-wide ambitions of the Third Reich than the decision to press forward with a vast program for constructing battleships, aircraft carriers, and other warships at a time when the war that began in September 1939 was believed to be over. Unlike some post-war German apologists and many non-German historians, Hitler recognized, and acted on the recognition, that a pre-condition for any successful war with the United States was not the selection of American beaches on which to land but the building of a navy that could project German power across the Atlantic. . . .

From Gerhard Weinberg, *A World at Arms: A Global History of World War II* (New York: Cambridge University Press, 1994), 86–87, 175–178, 182, 238–245, 248, 250–252, 254–259, 261–263. Reprinted by permission of Cambridge University Press.

The navy proposed and Hitler very much made his own a series of projects for bases on and off the coast of Northwest Africa. Included in these plans were bases to be constructed and owned by Germany not only in formerly French colonial possessions, especially the French protectorate of Morocco, but also on Portuguese and Spanish territory, in particular the Spanish Canary Islands. This project, to which the German government clung rigidly in the summer and fall of 1940, is especially illuminating for our understanding of the priorities of Berlin, since the Germans sacrificed the possibility of Spanish participation in the war to it. . . .

. . . The fact that the Germans were willing to forgo Spain's participation in the war rather than abandon their plans for naval bases on and off the coast of Northwest Africa surely demonstrates the centrality of this latter issue to Hitler as he looked forward to naval war with the United States.

For years Hitler had been calling for an airplane capable of bombing the United States, and work on such a plane had been under way since 1937. The realization of this project, however, was still not imminent in 1940, and the Germans could only push forward with it in the hope that by the time the planes were ready, refueling in the Portuguese Azores would be possible and would increase the possible bomb load. The prerequisites for war with the United States were being worked on, but it was obvious that they would take time to complete. While the preparations went forward, a project which was thought to be much simpler and capable of completion long before the huge blue-water navy and swarms of four-engined bombers had been built was to be carried out by Germany's victorious army: the invasion of the Soviet Union and the defeat of that country so that huge portions of it could be annexed and settled by German farmers, and the area's metal and oil resources harnessed to the subsequent campaign against the United States.

The whole project of crushing France and England had, after all, been undertaken only as a necessary preliminary, in Hitler's eye, to the attack in the East which would enable Germany to take the living space, the *Lebensraum,* he believed she needed. . . .

The limited industrial resources of Germany at their relatively low level of mobilization were not, however, capable of coping simultaneously with the preparations for the new land campaign in the East and the construction of the great battleship navy. Once again—as in September 1939—these projects had to be postponed. Victory over the Soviet Union would release the necessary resources for a resumption of construction on the big ships; in the interim, Germany would concentrate at sea on the blockade of Great Britain by submarines and airplanes.

The postponement of fleet building, in turn, had immediate implications for Germany's direct and indirect relations with the United States. In the direct sense, it meant that the German submarines were instructed to be careful of incidents with the United States, and Hitler ordered restraint on a navy ever eager to strike at American shipping. Simultaneously, in the indirect sense the position and role of Japan with its great navy became more important in German eyes. As already mentioned, Hitler anticipated that an attack on the Soviet Union would help propel Japan forward in Asia, thus tying up the United States in the Pacific in the years that Germany was still building her own surface navy. Between the decision to attack Russia and the implementation of that decision, however, there were now the intervening months to consider.

It was in this context that lining up Japan with the Axis came to be seen as increasingly important, a process which met the interests of the new leadership which had come to power in Tokyo in the days of decision in Berlin. The Tripartite Pact of Germany, Italy and Japan was not signed until September 27, but the new impetus from Berlin, in spite of earlier German unhappiness with Japan, needs to be seen in the context of the decisions of late July. Furthermore, the slow dawning on Germany's leaders of the realization that England was not going to give in operated to reinforce the policy choice previously made. A Japanese attack on Britain's possessions in Southeast Asia, particularly on Singapore, could not help but assist Germany's own fight against the United Kingdom. . . .

. . . Since by this time [Hitler] had already decided to attack the Soviet Union, he assumed and repeatedly assured his associates that this step would free Japan to move south, thereby drawing American power into the Pacific. This aspect of German policy will be reviewed in the context of the analysis of Japan's policy leading to the Pacific War, but it must always be kept in mind in assessing Hitler's orders to the German navy in the second half of 1940 and the first half of 1941. Since he planned to attack the Soviet Union and to defeat that country quickly, he would first get America diverted to the Pacific and subsequently be enabled to shift resources to naval construction to deal with the United States directly. In the interim, it made no sense to him to provoke the United States into open hostilities by incidents attendant upon what he believed would be a relatively small increment in U-Boat and surface raider sinkings. He learned from a study he ordered the navy to undertake that a surprise attack by submarines on the American fleet in American harbors was not practically feasible; if that sort of blow was not possible, it made more sense to wait. If an under-water "Pearl Harbor attack" could not be mounted, it would be better to postpone hostilities with the United States until either Germany acquired an ally with a large navy or had time to build one of its own.

The converse of this policy of restraints imposed on the existing German navy was a double one. In the diplomatic field, it meant, as we shall see, urging Japan forward in the Pacific, if necessary with the promise to go to war against the United States alongside Japan if that was what the Japanese believed they needed to do. In the military field, it meant returning from emphasis on the army to emphasis on naval construction and on the air force just as soon as the war in the East seemed to be going as well as Hitler confidently anticipated. It is in this context that one must understand why the moment he (quite incorrectly) believed that the campaign in Russia was going well, Hitler ordered the big program of battleship, aircraft carrier, and cruiser construction resumed. That program had to be set aside in the fall of 1941, as had been necessary in the fall of 1940, when the fighting went very differently from the way Hitler had expected. The failure of the German navy to cancel one of the contracts led to the delivery in *June 1944* of four completed battleship engines. Promptly scrapped, these relics of earlier dreams show how seriously the Germans had held at one time their plans for fighting the American navy.

The American President hoped to avoid open warfare with Germany altogether. He urged his people to aid Great Britain, and he devised and proposed, as we shall see, a whole variety of ways to do just that and to make sure that the aid actually reached its destination; but he hoped until literally the last minute that the United States could stay out of the war. . . .

The general assumption of many that countries are either at war or at peace with each other was not shared by Roosevelt, who knew that the American navy had originated in the quasi-war with France at the turn of the eighteenth to the nineteenth century and that more recently Japan and the Soviet Union had engaged in bloody encounters at specific points in East Asia while continuing to have diplomatic relations and without entering into general hostilities with each other. Some of Roosevelt's advisors did think the United States should or would have to enter the war to assure the defeat of Hitler, but there is no evidence that the President himself abandoned his hope that the United States could stay out. He had been proved right in his belief that Britain could hold on in 1940—against the view of many; he would be proved right in his expectation that the Soviet Union could hold on in 1941—again against the view of many. In a way he would be proved right on the question of formal American entrance into the war. We now have his comments on October 8, 1940; "the time may be coming when the Germans and the Japs [sic] will do some fool thing that would put us in. That's the only real danger of our getting in. . . ."

[In June 1941 t]he President quickly determined to send the Soviet Union whatever help could be provided; the fact that he placed his closest confidante, Harry Hopkins, in charge of this endeavor testifies to the importance he attached to it. Hopkins was sent to Moscow to get the whole project moving and took along Colonel Philip Faymonville, a strong believer in the ability of the Red Army to hold out, to handle aid at the Russian end. Knowing of popular opposition to aid to the Soviet Union, Roosevelt worked hard to try to have people see that this dictatorship was less threatening than the immediate menace of the German dictatorship, and he was especially concerned about calming the widespread concern over the lack of religious freedom in the Soviet Union. There were great worries and enormous difficulties, some growing out of the fact that there had been such vast differences between United States and Soviet policies in the preceding years. The Moscow conferences of early August 1941 produced an agreement on major shipments of military supplies in the face of the preference of United States and British military leaders who preferred to keep what weapons were coming off the assembly lines for their own forces. In the face of the German advances in the East, which if victorious would then free them for a renewed push in the Atlantic, Roosevelt pressed his associates to get the materials moving. In a way, he understood better than many contemporaries and most subsequent observers the anti-American component in Hitler's planning and hoped to preclude its success by making the German search for victory in the East as hard as possible. Difficulties in the production process and the problem of reconciling United States and British needs with those of the Soviet Union kept down actual shipments in 1941, but the fall of that year saw the beginnings of a vast flow. . . .

The American government's greatest concern was that the advance of Japan in Asia would threaten both itself and the British and thereby simultaneously aid Germany and possibly precipitate the United States into war. In the fall of 1940 and the winter of 1940–41 the United States government, under the prodding of Chiang Kai-shek and with Henry Morgenthau as the main advocate of assistance, took new steps to provide credits to China. The hope was that such support would restrain Chiang from making a settlement with the Japanese, because such a settlement would release Japanese forces for adventures elsewhere. It was not a coincidence that on November 30, 1940, the same day that the Japanese recognized the puppet government of Wang Ching-wei, Roosevelt announced plans for a one hundred million dollar credit for Chiang, and Hull explained that the United States recognized only his government. . . .

All through 1940 and 1941 the Roosevelt administration tried to find ways to hold off Japan while the United States rearmed itself, aided Britain, and, after the German invasion of the Soviet Union, aided the latter. Concentrating primary attention on the Atlantic and the dangers there, the administration hoped to restrain Japan, possibly pry her loose from the Tripartite Pact, and figure out ways to keep her from expanding the war she had already started in China. The assistance provided to the Chinese Nationalists was one element in this policy. The end of the US-Japan trade agreement, which left the Japanese guessing as to the next American step, was another. Roosevelt did not want to take steps which might drive Japan to take radical action, but he was being pushed by a public opinion which objected to the United States selling Japan the materials it needed for the war against China; on this subject the same people who objected to aid for Britain for fear of war were among the most vociferous advocates of a forward policy in East Asia. . . .

The hope of the administration that some accommodation could be reached with Japan which would restrain the latter by a combination of patient negotiations, continued American rearmament, and a passive stance in the Pacific, was dashed by the insistence of the Japanese government on a sweeping offensive in Southeast Asia; but for months there at least appeared to be a prospect of success. That prospect turned out to be a deliberately manufactured illusion created by a few private individuals, who pretended to the Americans that a project they had concocted had the approval of some elements in Japan, at the same time pretending to the Japanese that it had American approval—when in reality neither assertion was true. . . .

In September 1940 the [Japanese] government decided to ally itself with Germany. Now was the time to move in an alignment with Germany to seize all of Southeast Asia, quite possibly adding Burma and India and the islands of the South Pacific. If that meant war with the United States, so be it. Even the navy, at one time reluctant, was now prepared to go along; because of the American naval building program, "now is the most advantageous time for Japan to start a war." . . .

From time to time, the Japanese would point out to the Germans that Japan would be ready to move in 1946, the year when the last United States forces were scheduled to leave the Philippines, to which the Germans responded by pointing out that by that time the war in Europe would be over and the American fleet doubled. Perhaps more important was the German assurance that if Japan could move against Singapore only if she struck the United States at the same time, then she could count on Germany to join her.

This was a point von Ribbentrop had already made in 1939. A detailed examination of the issue by the German naval attaché in Tokyo seemed to show that this would be a good bargain for Germany; Japan as an open ally would more than offset the disadvantages of converting the United States from a tacit to an open enemy of Germany. Here is a key point which most analysts of the situation have overlooked and which has led them to puzzle endlessly and needlessly over Germany's declaration of war on the United States in December 1941. Hitler had long intended to fight the United States. He had tried to begin air and naval preparations for this in the late

1930s. These had been aborted by the outbreak of war in 1939, but on each occasion thereafter, when it looked as if the campaign immediately at hand was over, he had returned to the big blue-water navy program. It was always his belief that Germany needed a big navy to tackle the United States that made him want to postpone war and avoid incidents with the United States; when the right time came he was confident that he would find a good excuse—he always had with other countries.

But if the Japanese, who had hung back so long, took the plunge, then the naval deficit would automatically disappear. He had thought of removing that discrepancy by a German sneak under-water attack on the United States navy in port. Told by his navy that this was impossible, there was the obvious alternative of Japan providing a navy for his side of the war; that the Japanese would do from above the water what he had hoped to do from underneath was not known to him beforehand, but that made no difference. The key point was that Japan's joining openly on the Axis side would provide a big navy right away, not after years of building, and hence remove the main objection to going to war with the United States now rather than later. It was therefore entirely in accord with his perception of the issues that he promised Matsuoka on April 4 that if Japan believed that the only way for her to do what the Germans thought they should do, namely attack the British, was also to go to war at the same time with the United States, they could move in the knowledge that Germany would immediately join them. This policy was fully understood in German headquarters and would be voiced repeatedly thereafter. . . .

The definitive Japanese decision to shift from concentrating on war with China to war against the Western Powers came in early June 1941. The hinge of decision was the shift from occupying *northern* French Indo-China, which was part of the war against China because that country could then be blockaded more effectively, to occupying *southern* Indo-China, which pointed in the opposite direction, that is, to war against the British and Dutch to the south and against the Americans in the Philippines and on the Pacific flank of the southern advance. . . .

Reviewing the situation in a series of meetings between August 16 and September 6, 1941, the Japanese decided to go forward with war. They would seize Southeast Asia, talking with the United States but going to war with her if she did not give in on all points. The sooner war came once the Japanese and navy were ready, the better. Germany and Italy were likely to come in on Japan's side while the Soviet Union could not move against her when engaged in bitter fighting with Germany. The expectation was that in the early stages of war Japan would win great victories and that there would then be a stalemate and a new peace acknowledging her gains. All the key figures, including the Prime Minister, the army and the navy, were in agreement. Only Emperor Hirohito had doubts, but in the face of unanimous advice, he could only assent.

Because of the insistence of the United States government on continuing negotiations and the desire of the Japanese ambassador in the United States (who was not informed about his government's intention) to do so also, the authorities in Tokyo had to reexamine the issues several times in October and November, always coming back to the same conclusion: now was the time to fight. In the process, Konoe became tired of the discussion of a policy he had himself launched and was replaced by War Minister Tojo Hideki, but there was no inclination within the government to reverse the course for war. The new Foreign Minister, Togo Shigenori, and Finance

Minister Kaya Okinori had doubts but were overridden by the others. The Japanese would demand control of Southeast Asia, the end of American aid to Chiang Kai-shek and guarantee of American oil deliveries with more demands to come if these were accepted. War would come in early December, and once the Western Powers had been defeated, Japan would attack the Soviet Union. Germany and Italy would be asked to join in. With all at the end of the discussions again in agreement, the Emperor's plaintive asking of questions (probably inspired by Kido), such as how could Japan justify invading Thailand and how would Japan cope with airplane and submarine attacks on oil transports, were brushed aside. The course was set for war. . . .

The Japanese had decided to provide a public explanation by making extensive demands on the United States which they expected to be refused and which could be increased if accepted. A lengthy memorandum was therefore sent to Washington following on earlier such demands. In between, they received and disregarded a restatement of the American position (which they afterwards for propaganda purposes called an ultimatum). All this was shadow-boxing. The Japanese government had decided on war; had kept this fact from their own diplomats in Washington so that these could appear to be negotiating in good faith; and instructed them to present a lengthy note in time for Japan to initiate hostilities. . . .

In reality, the Pearl Harbor attack proved a strategic and tactical disaster for Japan, though the Japanese did not recognize this. The ships were for the most part raised; by the end of December, two of the battleships [Admiral] Yamamoto [Isoroku] had imagined sunk were on their way to the West Coast for repairs. All but the *Arizona* returned to service, and several played a key role . . . in a great American naval victory in October 1944. Most of the crew members survived to man the rebuilding American navy. These tactical factors were outgrowths of the basic strategic miscalculation. As anyone familiar with American reactions to the explosion on the *Maine* or the sinking of the *Lusitania* could have predicted, an unprovoked attack in peacetime was guaranteed to unite the American people for war until Japan surrendered, thus destroying in the first minutes of war Japan's basic strategy. The hope that the American people would never expend the blood and treasure needed to reconquer from Japan all sorts of islands—most of which they had never heard of—so that these could be returned to others or made independent, became completely unrealistic with the attack on Pearl Harbor. The attainment of surprise guaranteed defeat, not victory, for Japan.

Others were eager to join Japan in war with the United States. The Germans and Italians had been asked by Japan to join in and enthusiastically agreed. Mussolini had already promised to join in on December 3 and now did so, an extraordinary situation given Italy's string of defeats. Hitler had repeatedly urged the Japanese to move against Britain and was positively ecstatic that they had acted at last. The idea of a Sunday morning air attack in peacetime was especially attractive to him. He had started his campaign against Yugoslavia that way a few months earlier; here was an ally after his own heart. Now there would be a navy of battleships and aircraft carriers to deal with the Americans. His own navy had been straining at the leash for years and could now sink ships in the North Atlantic to its heart's content. Since the Japanese had not told Hitler precisely when they planned to move, he had just returned to East Prussia from the southern end of the Eastern Front, where he had dealt with a crisis caused by a Soviet counter-offensive, when the news of Pearl

Harbor reached him. It would take a few days to organize the proper ceremonies in Berlin on December 11, but that did not have to hold up the open hostilities he was eager to begin. In the night of December 8–9, at the earliest possible moment, orders were given to sink the ships of the United States and a string of countries in the Western Hemisphere. Two days later Hitler told an enthusiastic Reichstag the good news of war with America. Those who really believed that Germany had lost World War I because of a stab-in-the-back, not defeat at the front, were certain that it was American military power which was the legend. For once the unanimity in the Reichstag mirrored near unanimity in the government of the Third Reich. The German government's only worry was that the Americans might get their formal declaration of war in before they could deliver one themselves; they would get their way.

President Roosevelt asked and obtained declarations of war against Germany and Italy from Congress in response to the German and Italian declarations, steps which those countries had followed up by a treaty with Japan promising never to sign a separate peace. When Romania, Hungary, and Bulgaria also declared war on the United States, the President tried to get these declarations withdrawn. Perhaps the peoples of those countries could live quite happily without having a war with the United States. But the effort to persuade them of this truth failed, and in June the Congress reciprocated. The whole world was indeed aflame.

FURTHER READING

Barnhart, Michael. *Japan Prepares for Total War* (1987).
———. "The Origins of the Second World War in Asia and the Pacific: Synthesis Impossible?" *Diplomatic History* 20 (1996): 241–260.
Beard, Charles A. *President Roosevelt and the Coming of the War, 1941* (1948).
Borg, Dorothy. *The United States and the Far Eastern Crisis of 1933–1938* (1964).
Borg, Dorothy, and Shumpei Okamoto, eds. *Pearl Harbor as History* (1973).
Burns, James M. *Roosevelt*, 2 vols. (1956, 1970).
Butow, Robert J. C. *The John Doe Associates* (1974).
———. *Tojo and the Coming of the War* (1961).
Chadwin, Mark. *The Hawks of World War II* (1968).
Clifford, J. Garry, and Samuel R. Spencer Jr. *The First Peacetime Draft* (1986).
Cole, Wayne S. *America First: The Battle Against Intervention, 1940–1941* (1953).
———. *Charles A. Lindbergh and the Battle Against American Intervention in World War II* (1974).
———. *Roosevelt and the Isolationists* (1983).
Cull, Nicholas J. *Selling War* (1995).
Dallek, Robert D. *Franklin D. Roosevelt and American Foreign Policy, 1932–1945* (1979).
Davis, Kenneth S. *FDR* (1993, 2000).
Divine, Robert A. *The Reluctant Belligerent* (1979).
Doenecke, Justus D. *Storm on the Horizon: The Challenge to Intervention, 1939–1941* (2000).
———. "U.S. Policies and the European War, 1939–1941," *Diplomatic History* 19 (Fall 1995): 669–698.
———, ed. *In Danger Undaunted: The Anti-Interventionist Movement of 1940–1941 as Revealed in the Papers of The America First Committee* (1990).
Doenecke, Justus D., and John E. Wilz. *From Isolation to War, 1931–1941* (1991).
Feis, Herbert. *The Road to Pearl Harbor* (1950).
Freidel, Frank. *Franklin D. Roosevelt: A Rendezvous with Destiny* (1990).
Gardner, Lloyd C. *Economic Aspects of New Deal Diplomacy* (1964).

————. *Spheres of Influence* (1993).

Hearden, Patrick. *Roosevelt Confronts Hitler* (1987).

Heinrichs, Waldo. *Threshold of War: Franklin D. Roosevelt and American Entry into World War II* (1988).

Herzstein, Robert E. *Roosevelt & Hitler* (1989).

Iriye, Akira. *The Origins of the Second World War in Asia and the Pacific* (1987).

Iriye, Akira, and Warren I. Cohen, eds. *American, Chinese and Japanese Perspectives on Wartime Asia, 1931–1949* (1990).

Jonas, Manfred. *Isolationism in America* (1966).

Kennedy, David M. *Freedom from Fear: The American People in Depression and War, 1929–1945* (1999).

Kimball, Warren F. *The Most Unsordid Act: Lend-Lease, 1939–1941* (1969).

Langer, William L., and S. Everett Gleason. *The Challenge to Isolationism* (1952).

————. *The Undeclared War, 1940–1941* (1953).

Marks, Frederick W. III. *Wind Over Sand: The Diplomacy of Franklin Roosevelt* (1988).

Offner, Arnold A. *American Appeasement* (1969).

————. *The Origins of the Second World War* (1975).

Reynolds, David. *The Creation of the Anglo-American Alliance, 1937–1941* (1982).

————. *From Munich to Pearl Harbor* (2001).

Russett, Bruce M. *No Clear and Present Danger* (1997).

Schroeder, Paul W. *The Axis Alliance and Japanese-American Relations, 1941* (1958).

Tansill, Charles C. *Back Door to War* (1952).

Utley, Jonathan G. *Going to War with Japan, 1937–1941* (1985).

Weinberg, Gerhard. *A World at Arms* (1994).

Wilson, Theodore A. *The First Summit: Roosevelt and Churchill at Placentia Bay, 1941* (1991).

For Pearl Harbor, see Chapter 8.

For Roosevelt, see also Chapters 3 and 10.

CHAPTER
2

America Mobilizes
for War

Sweeping changes in the United States were first set in motion by growing American concerns about defense and by American aid to Britain through Lend-Lease. As the blitzkrieg and the Battle of Britain raged, government and business leaders began transforming American industry for the production of war materials. The Japanese attack on Pearl Harbor and the American declaration of war that followed brought on even more dramatic changes.

Overall, the American mobilization for war centered on four major areas: the mobilization of armed forces; the conversion of civilian industrial production to military purposes; a government propaganda campaign aimed at all Americans; and the creation of a West Coast "safety zone" as a way to deal with fears raised by the very visible presence of Japanese Americans, who were viewed as potential enemy aliens.

The War Manpower Commission oversaw the mobilization of forces for the military effort. By the end of the war in 1945, over 16 million Americans had served in the armed forces. Mobilizing Americans into the military through the use of a draft, or conscription, had first been established during the Civil War and was again introduced in World War I. The United States adopted the first peace-time draft with the Selective Training and Service Act of 1940. All male citizens between the ages of twenty-one and thirty-six were required to register for the draft. After the war declaration of December 1941, the draft was extended to all men between the ages of eighteen and forty-five. About 12,000 conscientious objectors did civilian public service. Those who refused, whether for religious or political reasons, faced fines and imprisonment.

Women were also militarily mobilized. In 1942, the U.S. Army created the Women's Army Auxiliary Corps (WAAC), which became the Women's Army Corps (WAC) the next year. Ovetta Culp Hobby directed the almost 100,000 women who joined. About 10,000 served in Europe and 6,000 in the Pacific. World War II also saw the establishment of the Navy's WAVES, Women Accepted for Voluntary Emergency Service; the Air Force WAFS, the Women's Auxiliary Ferrying Squadron, which became the WASPs, Women Airforce Service Pilots; and the U.S. Coast Guard Women's Reserve, also known as the SPARs—the name an acronym for the Coast

Guard's motto, "*Semper Paratus—Always Ready.*" Women also served in gender-segregated units in the Marine Corps. Black women were accepted into the WAACs in the same proportion as black men in the army. In 1948, the Women's Armed Services Integration Act gave women full regular status in the military, but not full equality, as the act limited women to 2 percent of regulars, capped ranks, and forbade them from serving aboard ships or aircraft involved in combat.

In the arena of economic mobilization, a centrally planned economy was put under the management of new government agencies, including the Office of Price Administration (OPA), established in April 1941, and the War Production Board (WPB), established in January 1942. The leaders of these agencies were often corporate executives serving as "dollar-a-year men" who volunteered their time and expertise to the war effort. They worked with military leaders to set the conditions for the production and distribution of goods and services, and to determine how resources would be allocated for military and civilian needs. The two successive directors of the WPB—Donald M. Nelson (1942–1944) and Julius A. Krug (1944–1945)—had vast powers to coordinate the creation and procurement of materials to maximize defense production, and in its three years of existence the WPB supervised the production of $185 billion worth of weapons and supplies. The WPB mobilized industries for the war effort with such measures as financing the conversion of existing factories and the construction of new defense plants. During the war, the government also suspended antitrust laws, intervened in labor-management disputes, and regulated wages. The OPA controlled rents in defense areas, restricted the sale of consumer goods, and issued ration books.

As defense mobilization transformed the nation's economic life, the government also went full steam ahead with a propaganda campaign to teach Americans how they could best help the war effort individually and collectively. An Office of War Information created and disseminated posters, movies, and radio commentaries that, unlike the antiimmigrant campaigns of World War I, emphasized the need for all Americans to pull together for the sake of the "good war." Unity and freedom dominated the government's propaganda. Specific propaganda campaigns were aimed at those on the home front. Women were encouraged to join the industrial work force to release a man to fight, and more than 6 million did so. Consumers were reminded that, like the men at the front, they too had to make sacrifices by accepting rationing, planting victory gardens, and buying war bonds. Workers were prompted to accept the no-strike pledge, adapt to new assembly-line techniques, and keep quiet about the production of war equipment.

Before Pearl Harbor, about 90 percent of the 125,000 Japanese Americans lived in California, Oregon, and Washington. Two-thirds were Nisei, native-born American citizens, while the other third were Issei, born in Japan and ineligible for citizenship because of the 1882 and 1924 immigration laws. After Pearl Harbor, fear of a Japanese invasion led President Roosevelt to issue Executive Order 9066 in February 1942. This order authorized the military, under the leadership of General John L. DeWitt, to "proscribe military areas" and exclude "any or all persons" from the areas for security reasons. The army interpreted the order to mean the entire West Coast and all Japanese Americans. The result was the removal of Japanese Americans from their homes to internment camps set up in the interior of the country. Even the Supreme Court agreed that the relocation of Japanese Americans was a wartime necessity with a 5-3 decision in the case of Korematsu v. the United States (1944). Japanese Americans were required to register with local police and turn over all items in their possession that might foster sabotage, including weapons, chemicals, shortwave radios, and cameras. Overall, about 120,000 Japanese Americans were interned, including 77,000 who were Nisei. In 1988 Congress awarded the 60,000 surviving Japanese American internees $20,000 and a public apology.

The huge and multifaceted American wartime mobilization played a major role in Allied victory. It also had enormous wartime as well as postwar consequences for the United States. But exactly how and why was the nation able to mobilize for a total war effort? Just what role did mobilization play in Allied victory? Furthermore, what were the specific wartime and postwar consequences, both positive and negative, of this mobilization?

D O C U M E N T S

The Selective Training and Service Act of 1940 narrowly passed Congress to become the nation's first peacetime military draft. Document 1, the beginning of the Selective Service Act, and a 1943 *Time* magazine article, together show the "selective" nature of the draft process, which was amended to meet the ongoing need for soldiers. Document 2 is a 1941 statement of a group of students from New York City who refused to register for the draft. Document 3 also deals with military mobilization. It is the May 28, 1941, speech given by Representative Edith Nourse Rogers of Massachusetts introducing a bill in Congress to establish a women's army auxiliary corps. The mix of facing both the practical and ideological needs of the hour are also evident in Document 4, President Roosevelt's annual message to Congress of January 6, 1941, often referred to as the "Four Freedoms" speech. Document 5 is an excerpt from the April 1942 report of the Office of Price Administration, which demonstrates how the transition to defense production began before December 1941 as well as the enormous economic changes brought on by wartime production. The report also indicates how these changes influenced every citizen on a daily basis. One of the most dramatic changes felt by consumers was the rise in price for food, clothing and other items, as shown in Document 6. Document 7 is a reproduction of a popular, and optimistic, propaganda poster issued by the War Manpower Commission in 1943. It was designed to remind workers of their obligations to those at the front. Document 8, Roosevelt's Executive Order 9066, deals with Japanese relocation. Also reprinted as part of Document 8 is a map of relocation centers and internment camps.

1. The Government Institutes and Revises the Draft, 1940 and 1943

An Act

To provide for the common defense by increasing the personnel of the armed forces of the United States and providing for its training.

Be it enacted by the Senate and House of Representatives of the United States of America in Congress assembled, That (a) the Congress hereby declares that it is imperative to increase and train the personnel of the armed forces of the United States.

From Selective Training and Service Act of 1940, *U.S. Statutes at Large,* 1939–1941 54, pt. 1: 885–897; "The Draft: Navy Spanking," *Time,* May 24, 1943, p. 69.

(b) The Congress further declares that in a free society the obligations and privileges of military training and service should be shared generally in accordance with a fair and just system of selective compulsory military training and service.

(c) The Congress further declares, in accordance with our traditional military policy as expressed in the National Defense Act of 1916, as amended, that it is essential that the strength and organization of the National Guard, as an integral part of the first-line defenses of this Nation, be at all times maintained and assured. To this end, it is the intent of the Congress that whenever the Congress shall determine that troops are needed for the national security in excess of those of the Regular Army and those in active training and service under section 3 (b), the National Guard of the United States, or such part thereof as may be necessary, shall be ordered to active Federal service and continued therein so long as such necessity exists.

Sec. 2. Except as otherwise provided in this Act, it shall be the duty of every male citizen of the United States, and of every male alien residing in the United States, who, on the day or days fixed for the first or any subsequent registration, is between the ages of twenty-one and thirty-six, to present himself for and submit to registration at such time or times and place or places, and in such manner and in such age group or groups, as shall be determined by rules and regulations prescribed hereunder.

Sec. 3. (a) . . . The President is authorized from time to time, whether or not a state of war exists, to select and induct into the land and naval forces of the United States for training and service, in the manner provided in this Act, such number of men as in his judgment is required for such forces in the national interest: . . . *Provided* . . . That except in time of war there shall not be in active training or service in the land forces of the United States at any one time under subsection (b) more than nine hundred thousand men inducted under the provisions of this Act. The men inducted into the land or naval forces for training and service under this Act shall be assigned to camps or units of such forces.

(b) Each man inducted under the provisions of subsection (a) shall serve for a training and service period of twelve consecutive months, unless sooner discharged, except that whenever the Congress has declared that the national interest is imperiled, such twelve-month period may be extended by the President to such time as may be necessary in the interests of national defense. . . .

Sec. 4. (a) The selection of men for training and service under section 3 (other than those who are voluntarily inducted pursuant to this Act) shall be made in an impartial manner, under such rules and regulations as the President may prescribe, from the men who are liable for such training and service and who at the time of selection are registered and classified but not deferred or exempted: *Provided,* That in the selection and training of men under this Act, and in the interpretation and execution of the provisions of this Act, there shall be no discrimination against any person on account of race or color. . . .

Sec. 5. (e) The President is authorized, under such rules and regulations as he may prescribe, to provide for the deferment from training and service under this Act in the land and naval forces of the United States of those men whose employment in industry, agriculture, or other occupations or employment, or whose activity in other endeavors, is found in accordance with section 10 (a) (2) to be necessary to the maintenance of the national health, safety, or interest. The President is also authorized, under such rules and regulations as he may prescribe, to provide for the deferment from training and service under this Act in the land and naval forces of the United States (1) of those men in a status with respect to persons dependent upon them for support which renders their deferment advisable, and (2) of those men found to be physically, mentally, or morally deficient or defective. No deferment from such training and service shall be made in the case of any individual except upon the basis of the status of such individual, and no such deferment shall be made of individuals by occupational groups or of groups of individuals in any plant or institution. . . .

(g) Nothing contained in this Act shall be construed to require any person to be subject to combatant training and service in the land or naval forces of the United States who, by reason of religious training and belief, is conscientiously opposed to participation in war in any form. Any such person claiming such exemption from combatant training and service because of such conscientious objections whose claim is sustained by the local board shall, if he is inducted into the land or naval forces under this Act, be assigned to noncombatant service as defined by the President, or shall, if he is found to be conscientiously opposed to participation in such noncombatant service, in lieu of such induction, be assigned to work of national importance under civilian direction. . . .

Time Magazine on 1943 Draft Revisions

Still straining to feed the armed services' hunger for manpower, Selective Service took another step last week toward the draft of fathers by August.

It ordered the one-week furlough now granted to new recruits restored to the old period of two weeks. Family men will need more time to wind up their affairs before going off to camp; by Sept. 1 the furlough is to be three weeks.

Heart specialists, meanwhile, were winnowing lists of 4-Fs in a nationwide experiment to determine how many men rejected for cardiac ailments might be salvaged for limited service. First reports were encouraging: of 2,000 men examined in New York and Philadelphia, 400 were found fit. If that percentage held up, Selective Service would have tapped a useful pool of manpower in its own backyard.

Another agency for military procurement, FBI, put on a special weekend roundup that located 638 draft-dodgers in 20 cities. G-men are handling about 15,000 draft complaints a month, have "located and made available" 86,543 men—enough for six infantry divisions.

But the week's spiciest draft news came from the House Committee on Naval Affairs, which soundly and publicly birched the Navy Department for: 1) deferring too many of its civilian employees; 2) maintaining a landlubber corps of young, healthy sailors in Washington.

An investigating subcommittee headed by New Dealer Lyndon B. Johnson, of Texas, a naval lieutenant commander on inactive status, discovered that the Navy had belatedly revised its policy after investigators turned up records of 893 deferments, at least 207 of them open to criticism. It also found that the Navy had 6,556 enlisted men (more than three battleship crews) working in Washington alone, sternly recommended that they be replaced by WAVES, draft-proof civilians or limited-service recruits now barred by the Navy's strict physical standards.

2. Conscientious Objectors Explain Their Reasons for Refusing to Register for the Draft, 1941

It is impossible for us to think of the conscription law without at the same time think-ing of the whole war system, because it is clear to us that conscription is definitely a part of the institution of war.

To us, the war system is an evil part of our social order, and we declare that we cannot cooperate with it in any way. War is an evil because it is in violation of the Way of Love as seen in God through Christ. It is a concentration and accentuation of all the evils of our society. War consists of mass murder, deliberate starvation, vandalism, and similar evils. Physical destruction and moral disintegration are the inevitable result. The war method perpetuates and compounds the evils it purports to overcome. It is impossible, as history reveals, to overcome evil with evil. The last World War is a notorious case of the failure of the war system, and there is no evidence to believe that this war will be any different. It is our positive proclama-tion as followers of Jesus Christ that we must overcome evil with good. We seek in our daily living to reconcile that separation of man from man and man from God which produces war.

We have also been led to our conclusion on the conscription law in the light of its totalitarian nature. It is a totalitarian move when our government insists that the manpower of the nation take a year of military training. It is a totalitarian move for the President of the nation to be able to conscript industry to produce certain materials which are deemed necessary for national defense without considering the actual physical needs of the people. We believe, therefore, that by opposing the Selective Service law, we will be striking at the heart of totalitarianism as well as war. . . .

We feel a deep bond of unity with those who decide to register as conscien-tious objectors, but our own decision must be different for the following reasons:

If we register under the act, even as conscientious objectors, we are becom-ing part of the act. The fact that we as conscientious objectors may gain personal exemption from the most crassly un-Christian requirements of the act does not compensate for the fact that we are complying with it and accepting its protec-tion. If a policeman (or a group of vigilantes) stops us on the street, our posses-sion of the government's card shows that we are "all right"—we have complied

From "Excerpts from the Joint Statement of Donald Benedict, Joseph J. Bevilacqua, Meredith Dallas, David Dellinger, George M. Houser, William H. Lovell, Howard E. Spragg, and Richard J. Wichlei," in *Why We Refused to Register* (New York: Fellowship of Reconciliation, Keep America Out of War Con-gress, National Council for Prevention of War, Youth Committee Against War, Young Peoples Socialist League, and War Resisters League, 1941); reprinted in *Nonviolence in America: A Documentary History,* ed. Staughton Lynd (Indianapolis: Bobbs-Merrill, 1966), 269–299.

with the act for the militarization of America. If that does not hurt our Christian consciences, what will? If we try to rationalize on the theory that we must go along with the act in order to fight the fascism and militarism of which it is a part, it seems to us that we are doing that very thing which all pacifist Christians abhor: we are consciously employing bad means on the theory that to do so will contribute to a good end. . . .

In similar vein, it is urged that great concessions have been won for religious pacifists and that we endanger these by our refusal to accept them. Fascism, as it gradually supplanted democracy in Germany, was aided by the decision of Christians and leftists to accept a partial fascism rather than to endanger those democratic concessions which still remained. It is not alone for our own exemption from fighting that we work—it is for freedom of the American people from fascism and militarism.

Partial exemption of conscientious objectors has come about partly through the work of influential pacifists and partly through the open-mindedness of certain nonpacifists. But it has also been granted because of the fear of the government that, without such a provision, public opposition to war would be too great to handle. In particular, it seems to us that one of the reasons the government has granted exemption to ministers and theological students is to gain a religious sanction for its diabolical war. Where actual support could not be gained, it hoped to soothe their consciences so that they could provide no real opposition.

We do not contend that the American people maliciously choose the vicious instrument of war. In a very perplexing situation, they lack the imagination, the religious faith, and the precedents to respond in a different manner. This makes it all the more urgent to build in this country and throughout the world a group trained in the techniques of nonviolent opposition to the encroachments of militarism and fascism. Until we build such a movement, it will be impossible to stall the war machine at home. When we do build such a movement, we will have forged the only weapon which can ever give effective answer to foreign invasion. Thus, in learning to fight American Hitlerism, we will show an increasing group of war-disillusioned Americans how to resist foreign Hitlers as well.

For these reasons we hereby register our refusal to comply in any way with the Selective Training and Service Act. We do not expect to stem the war forces today; but we are helping to build the movement that will conquer in the future.

3. Representative Edith Nourse Rogers Introduces the WAAC Bill, 1941

Mr. Speaker, I introduced this bill with a view to having women enlist, not to be drafted, in the Women's Army Auxiliary Corps, for noncombatant service in the Army of the United States, for the purpose of making available to the national defense the knowledge, skill, and special training of the women of this Nation. I understand the War Department favors this bill. I am told that the Budget favors the bill with certain minor modifications. I know that the gentlemen of the Congress

From *Congressional Record,* 77th Cong., 1st sess., 89, pt. 9: 9747–9749.

who have returned from England can testify as to the very splendid work done by the women in England. In the World War I saw the work of women with the British forces; some of them did work with our Army. Many men can be released for other duty. Women can take the place of cooks, waiters, telephone operators, and chauffeurs. They can take places as hostesses, librarians, in technical positions, in radio, in the Signal Corps, as dietitians, and physiotherapists. They can join the corps and thereby release men to go back to do vital defense work in industry. This bill will release men for work of vast importance in our national defense. There are many positions that women can fill, the Army believes, that will be of great benefit to the Army as the need arises. Many women have expressed eagerness to enlist in an auxiliary corps of this kind. The women of America are anxious to serve their country. They are intensely patriotic. . . .

This does not in any way interfere with volunteer work without pay, but it does allow a great group of women to enlist who could not afford to do patriotic national-defense work for nothing. Mr. Speaker, the women of America want to make every sacrifice; they want in every way to aid, in this war, the march to victory.

Be it enacted, etc., That the President is hereby authorized to establish a Women's Army Auxiliary Corps for noncombatant service with the Army of the United States for the purpose of making available to the national defense the knowledge, skill, and special training of the women of this Nation.

SEC. 2. . . . The Director shall receive a salary of $3,000 per annum, together with such other allowances as may be provided for hereinafter. . . .

SEC. 3. The Secretary is authorized to establish and maintain such number of schools as he may consider necessary for the purpose of training candidates for officers of the corps. . . . Candidates for such schools may be selected from women volunteers who are citizens of the United States and during their attendance at such schools shall be furnished living quarters, uniforms as hereinafter provided, medical and dental service, medicines, medical and hospital supplies, hospitalization, subsistence, texts, necessary school supplies, and pay at the rate of $50 per month. . . . *Provided,* That the whole number of officers so appointed initially shall not exceed 750, together with the Director and Assistant Directors; but the Secretary is authorized to increase this number when he deems such action necessary. The pay of officers so appointed shall be $2,000 per annum for each first officer, $1,575 per annum for each second officer, and $1,500 per annum for each third officer, together with such allowances as may be hereinafter provided. . . .

SEC. 5. The Secretary is authorized to have enrolled initially in the corps, in addition to the Director, Assistant Directors, and officers hereinabove provided for, by voluntary enrollment, not to exceed 25,000 women of excellent character in good physical health, between the ages of 21 and 45 years and citizens of the United States: *Provided,* That . . . [t]he pay of first leaders shall be $864 per annum, of leaders $720 per annum, of junior leaders $648 per annum, and for auxiliaries not otherwise classified $21 per month for the first 4 months of service and $30 per month thereafter. Specialists of the first class shall be paid, in addition to their base pay, the sum of $15 per month, specialists of the second class shall similarly be paid $10 per month, and specialists of the third class shall similarly be paid $5 per month.

4. President Roosevelt Explains the Four Freedoms to the American People, 1941

The Nation takes great satisfaction and much strength from the things which have been done to make its people conscious of their individual stake in the preservation of democratic life in America. Those things have toughened the fibre of our people, have renewed their faith and strengthened their devotion to the institutions we make ready to protect.

Certainly this is no time for any of us to stop thinking about the social and economic problems which are the root cause of the social revolution which is today a supreme factor in the world.

For there is nothing mysterious about the foundations of a healthy and strong democracy. The basic things expected by our people of their political and economic systems are simple. They are:

Equality of opportunity for youth and for others.

Jobs for those who can work.

Security for those who need it.

The ending of special privilege for the few.

The preservation of civil liberties for all.

The enjoyment of the fruits of scientific progress in a wider and constantly rising standard of living.

These are the simple, basic things that must never be lost sight of in the turmoil and unbelievable complexity of our modern world. The inner and abiding strength of our economic and political systems is dependent upon the degree to which they fulfill these expectations.

Many subjects connected with our social economy call for immediate improvement.

As examples:

We should bring more citizens under the coverage of old-age pensions and unemployment insurance.

We should widen the opportunities for adequate medical care.

We should plan a better system by which persons deserving or needing gainful employment may obtain it.

I have called for personal sacrifice. I am assured of the willingness of almost all Americans to respond to that call. . . .

If the Congress maintains these principles, the voters, putting patriotism ahead of pocketbooks, will give you their applause.

In the future days, which we seek to make secure, we look forward to a world founded upon four essential human freedoms.

The first is freedom of speech and expression—everywhere in the world.

The second is freedom of every person to worship God in his own way—everywhere in the world.

The third is freedom from want—which, translated into world terms, means economic understandings which will secure to every nation a healthy peacetime life for its inhabitants—everywhere in the world.

From Franklin D. Roosevelt, Annual Message to Congress, January 6, 1941, in *Public Papers and Addresses of Franklin D. Roosevelt,* vol. 9, *1940* (New York: Macmillan, 1941), 663–678.

The fourth is freedom from fear—which, translated into world terms, means a world-wide reduction of armaments to such a point and in such a thorough fashion that no nation will be in a position to commit an act of physical aggression against any neighbor—anywhere in the world.

That is no vision of a distant millennium. It is a definite basis for a kind of world attainable in our own time and generation. That kind of world is the very antithesis of the so-called new order of tyranny which the dictators seek to create with the crash of a bomb.

To that new order we oppose the greater conception—the moral order. A good society is able to face schemes of world domination and foreign revolutions alike without fear.

5. The Office of Price Administration Reports on the Consequences of Defense Production, 1942

From an orderly, though accelerating, transition to a wartime economy as "the arsenal of democracy"—a transition in which selective price controls were proving effective—the country was catapulted overnight into a full-fledged fighting war by the attack on Pearl Harbor on December 7. Although complete details of the physical damage of that attack to our naval strength were not available, its major military implications were apparent at once. No less apparent were the economic implications.

Of immediate concern was the threat to our supplies of a long list of vitally important Asiatic imports: rubber, tin, Australian wool, copra, kapok, tea, pepper, and other spices, various essential and vegetable oils, and numerous minerals and chemicals originating in the Far East.

Even more pressing to the Office than the supply situation—i.e., how much we had and how much more we were going to be able to bring through in the face of war in the Pacific—was the prospect that, in the absence of swift and bold action, the domestic prices of many of these commodities would skyrocket with the opening of business on the following day. Such a development, sympathetically communicated to the more volatile of our domestic commodities, would touch off a speculative upsurge. . . .

The crisis precipitated by the attack on Pearl Harbor marked a change of basic significance in operations of the Office. As a result of the serious rubber situation, the War Production Board "froze" all sale of automobile tires and directed their rationing by OPA. This brought the Office back directly into the field of civilian supply from which it had been separated the previous August, and gave it responsibility for a major wartime job, the job of rationing. . . .

It is appropriate to note here that tire rationing marked the Office's first direct contact with a large segment of the consuming public and that the establishment of local rationing boards in every county of the United States supplied a basic framework, not only for other rationing, but for the effective administration of general price control which events soon were to force upon a nation at war.

From *First Quarterly Report for the Period Ending April 30, 1942* (Washington, D.C.: U.S. Government Printing Office, 1942), 15–16, 18–19.

Such was the immediate impact of Pearl Harbor upon the operations of the Office. . . . The war had become global in character and our involvement no less universal.

This meant the prompt equipping of American armies to move to the battle fronts in all parts of the world. It meant the stepping up of production schedules to supply planes and munitions for the new Pacific war. It meant the diversion of shipping to carry men and material across the vast Pacific. And it meant the further expansion of shipbuilding to overcome the toll taken by submarines. Beyond all this, it meant the realization that war production must henceforth be not merely the dominant factor but the one great single objective of the entire economy.

The Blueprint for Victory

The change was made crystal clear on January 6, 1942, when the President sent to the Congress his message on the state of the Union, outlining a "blueprint for victory" that called for 60,000 planes, 45,000 tanks, 20,000 antiaircraft guns, and 8,000,000 tons of shipping for 1942, with the sights raised even higher for 1943. The budget message "of a nation at war in a world at war" followed the next day and forecast expenditures for the coming fiscal year of 53 billion dollars for war, as compared with 24 billion dollars in the fiscal year 1942.

"These huge expenditures for ships, planes, and other war equipment will require prompt conversion of a large portion of our industrial establishment to war production," the President said. "These estimates reflect our determination to devote *at least one-half of our national production to the war effort.*"

The full meaning of this statement in terms of its impact on the entire economy forecast the end of selective price control.

The reasons were three:

1. To devote one-half of our national production to the war effort meant that whatever slack remained in the economy would be taken up, and that capacity would be strained to the utmost.

2. Supplies of civilian goods, already shrinking, would be curtailed much more acutely, and scarcity, hitherto confined largely to consumer durable goods, would spread to virtually every type of product.

3. The increase in expenditures for war meant an enormous expansion of money incomes paid out in the form of wages, salaries, rents, profits, and cash farm income and a constantly accelerating demand for a declining amount of civilian goods.

At the time the President sent his budget message to Congress, about one-fifth of our national production was devoted to the war program, and monthly expenditures on this account approximated 2 billion dollars. As the message indicated, attainment of the 50-percent-for-war goal would raise these monthly outlays to more than 5 billion dollars before the close of the 1943 fiscal year.

This vast expansion of war output could not be obtained by bringing into production additional idle plant facilities and manpower, as in 1940 and 1941, since industry was rapidly approaching the limits of existing capacity. The disappearance of the slack in our industrial machine was reflected in the slowing down of the increase in industrial production from the rapid pace of 1940 and the first half of 1941.

Total production would continue to climb, of course, but the increase would reflect further extension of multiple shift operations, more overtime, and the coming into production of newly completed plants.

6. The War Affects Employment and Consumer Prices, 1940–1945

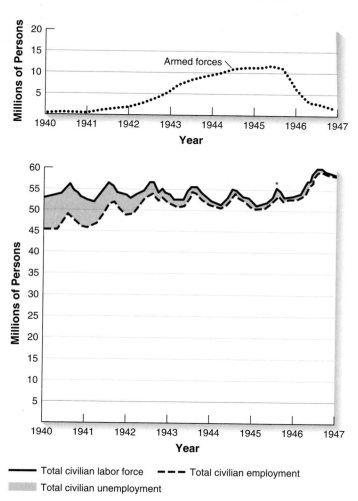

Not surprisingly, the number of men and women in the armed forces increased dramatically during the war and unemployment rates for the civilian labor force decreased as employment increased.

From *Economic Report of the President Transmitted to Congress,* January 8, 1947 (Washington, D.C.: U.S. Government Printing Office, 1947), 3 and 23.

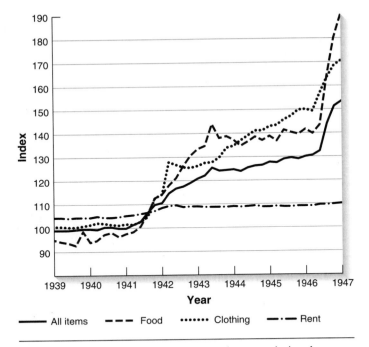

Despite government controls, consumer prices rose during the war, especially for food. However, rents held steady.

7. The Government Encourages Workers on the Home Front, 1943

"United We Win," photograph by Alexander Liberman, 1943. Printed by the Government Printing Office for the War Manpower Commission, NARA Still Picture Branch (NWDNS-44-PA-370). Library of Congress, Prints & Photographs Division, FAS/OWI collection.

8. Roosevelt Orders Japanese Relocation, 1942

**Authorizing the Secretary of War to Prescribe Military Areas,
Executive Order No. 9066**

WHEREAS the successful prosecution of the war requires every possible protection against espionage and against sabotage to national-defense material, national-defense premises, and national-defense utilities as defined in section 4, Act of April 20, 1918, 40 Stat. 533, as amended by the act of November 30, 1940, 54 Stat. 1220, and the Act of August 21, 1941, 55 Stat. 655 (U. S. C., Title 50, Sec. 104):

NOW, THEREFORE, by virtue of the authority vested in me as President of the United States, and Commander in Chief of the Army and Navy, I hereby authorize and direct the Secretary of War, and the Military Commanders whom he may from time to time designate, whenever he or any designated Commander deems such actions necessary or desirable, to prescribe military areas in such places and of such extent as he or the appropriate Military Commanders may determine, from which any or all persons may be excluded, and with such respect to which, the right of any person to enter, remain in, or leave shall be subject to whatever restrictions the Secretary of War or the appropriate Military Commander may impose in his discretion. The Secretary of War is hereby authorized to provide for residents of any such area who are excluded therefrom, such transportation, food, shelter, and other accommodations as may be necessary, in the judgement of the Secretary of War or the said Military Commander, and until other arrangements are made, to accomplish the purpose of this order. The designation of military areas in any region or locality shall supersede designations of prohibited and restricted areas by the Attorney General under the Proclamations of December 7 and 8, 1941, and shall supersede the responsibility and authority of the Attorney General under the said Proclamations in respect of such prohibited and restricted areas.

I hereby further authorize and direct the Secretary of War and the said Military Commanders to take such other steps as he or the appropriate Military Commander may deem advisable to enforce compliance with the restrictions applicable to each Military area hereinabove authorized to be designated, including the use of Federal troops and other Federal Agencies, with authority to accept assistance of state and local agencies.

I hereby further authorize and direct all Executive Departments, independent establishments and other Federal Agencies, to assist the Secretary of War or the said Military Commanders in carrying out this Executive Order, including the furnishing of medical aid, hospitalization, food, clothing, transportation, use of land, shelter, and other supplies, equipment, utilities, facilities and services.

This order shall not be construed as modifying or limiting in any way the authority heretofore granted under Executive Order No. 8972, dated December 12, 1941, nor shall it be construed as limiting or modifying the duty and responsibility of the Federal Bureau of Investigation, with respect to the investigation of alleged acts of

From President, "Executive Order 9066 (February 19, 1942)," *Federal Register* 7, no. 38 (February 25, 1942): 1407.

sabotage or the duty and responsibility of the Attorney General and the Department of Justice under the Proclamations of December 7 and 8, 1941, prescribing
regulations for the conduct and control of alien enemies, except as such duty and
responsibility is superseded by the designation of military areas hereunder.

FRANKLIN D. ROOSEVELT
February 19, 1942

Relocation Centers and Internment Camps

- ○ Assembly centers
- ■ Relocation centers
- ● Justice department internment camps
- △ Citizen isolation camps

From Michi Weglyn, *Year of Infamy: The Untold Story of America's Concentration Camps* (New York:
Morrow, 1976). *Who Built America?* by Nelson Lichtenstein, Susan Strasser, and Roy Rosenzweig. Copyright © 2000 by American Social History Productions, Inc. Used with the permission of Worth Publishers.

ESSAYS

In the first essay, British historian Richard Overy of King's College, Cambridge
University, analyzes the U.S. mobilization effort and the reasons why that effort and
its Soviet counterpart were so successful when compared with the German effort.
While not disputing the eventual importance of the U.S. effort to Allied victory, in the
second essay, American historian William O'Neill of Rutgers University focuses on
the numerous failures of that mobilization—before as well as after Pearl Harbor—
and the reasons for those failures.

The Successes of American Mobilization

RICHARD OVERY

There was no doubt that America had the resources for a prodigious war effort. British leaders had longed before Pearl Harbor to have that abundance at their disposal. "There is one way, and one way only," the British economist Sir William Layton told an audience of American industrialists in October 1940, "in which the three to one ratio of Germany's steel output can be overwhelmed and that is by the 50 to 60 million ingot tons of the United States." In 1941 America produced more steel, aluminum, oil and motor vehicles than all the other major states together.

The problem was how to turn this abundance from the purposes of peace to those of war. The United States had no tradition of military industry. Intervention in the First World War came too late to build up war production of any real size. The "military-industrial" complex was the product of a later age. By the 1930s twenty years of disarmament and detachment left the world's richest economy with an army ranked eighteenth in size in the world, and an air force of 1,700 largely obsolescent aircraft and a mere twenty thousand men. In 1940 military expenditure made up just 2 per cent of America's national product. Military weakness was a consequence of an isolation both geographical and political. The American public displayed a deep-felt hostility to war and militarism. In 1937 comprehensive neutrality legislation passed through Congress, intended to keep the United States out of other people's wars, and to limit the trade and production of armaments. Many Americans regretted the intervention of 1917 and were determined not to make the same mistake twice.

This was not the only political issue. America's was a free market economy, emerging in the late 1930s from a decade of economic hardship into the full glare of a consumer boom. The American government could not simply suppress its people's expectations and turn butter into guns. Both business and labour distrusted state power, no more so than when the state was planning to spend their money on arms. The effort to increase federal responsibilities under Roosevelt's "New Deal" for economic recovery in the 1930s brought bitter disputes. Unlike Germany or the Soviet Union, the growth of the military economy depended on reaching a broad consensus across the whole political spectrum, from hard-nosed Republican bosses to tough-minded Democrat unions. This remained the case even after Pearl Harbor gave Roosevelt the perfect opportunity to cut across all the objections to economic mobilisation at a stroke. The American people reacted with a fiery indignation to the Japanese attack in the early months of 1942, but the United States itself was not threatened with invasion; no bombs fell on American cities. The conflicts were an ocean away, and sustaining a popular commitment to production and economic sacrifice was an altogether different issue than it appeared in Britain or the Soviet Union.

For all these reasons, American rearmament was slow to materialise before 1942. Roosevelt was able to win additional budget funds for the navy only on the grounds that the navy was a genuine instrument of defence rather than offence. The tiny American military aircraft industry was stimulated from 1939 onwards by the demand for aviation equipment from Britain and France. Only in 1941, with a third Presidential election successfully behind him, did Roosevelt feel confident enough of popular support to begin to rearm more earnestly. On 9 July 1941 he asked the army and navy to draw up a comprehensive plan of all the resources they would need to defeat America's potential enemies. The programme became known informally as the "Victory Programme." The results were presented to the President in September, but a final estimate could not be prepared until British and Soviet requests for military aid were drawn up and approved. As a result a final programme for war production was barely ready before the United States found themselves at war with Japan and Germany in December. Until a clear general picture of the scale of America's planned rearmament was available, the President could do little more than authorise temporary and uncoordinated contracts, many of them to feed the needs of the other warring states for whom he had promised in December 1940 to make the United States the "arsenal of democracy." In the whole of 1941 military expenditure was just 4 per cent of the amount America spent between 1941 and 1945.

When war broke out the United States was still a predominantly civilian economy, with a small apparatus of state, low taxes, and a military establishment that had only reached the foothills of re-equipment. America faced states which had been arming heavily for eight or nine years and now had more than half their national product devoted to the waging of war. American leaders were conscious of how much there was to catch up. The giant plans approved by Roosevelt and Congress in the first weeks of war did not just result from America's great wealth of resources, but reflected a genuine fear of military inferiority. In four years these plans turned America from military weakling to military super-power. American industry provided almost two-thirds of all the Allied military equipment produced during the war: 297,000 aircraft, 193,000 artillery pieces, 86,000 tanks, 2 million army trucks. In four years American industrial production, already the world's largest, doubled in size. The output of the machine-tools to make weapons trebled in three years. The balance between the United States and her enemies changed almost overnight. Where every other major state took four or five years to develop a sizeable military economy, it took America a year. In 1942, long before her enemies had believed it possible, America already outproduced the Axis states together, 47,000 aircraft to 27,000, 24,000 tanks to 11,000, six times as many heavy guns. In the naval war the figures were more remarkable still: 8,800 naval vessels and 87,000 landing craft in four years. For every one major naval vessel constructed in Japanese shipyards, America produced sixteen.

Production on this scale made Allied victory a possibility, though it did not make victory in any sense automatic. For all the obvious advantages of resources and remoteness from the field of battle, the arming of America on this scale and with such speed could not be taken for granted. In the first weeks of war the administration struggled to produce a coherent picture of where and when military goods could be supplied. On 5 January 1942 the automobile industrialist, William Knudsen, appointed by Roosevelt to run the pre-war rearmament agency, the Office of Production Management, resorted to the extreme of calling together a room full of businessmen where he read out a long list of military products and simply asked for volunteers to produce them. For all its curious informality this was an approach more calculated to work with an industrial community that disliked taking orders and thrived on technical challenges. The urgency of mobilisation left the government with little choice but to rely on the initiative and technical flair of American business. The strengths of the American industrial tradition—the widespread experience with mass-production the great depth of technical and organisational skill, the willingness to "think big," the ethos of hustling competition—were just the characteristics needed to transform American production in a hurry.

Even before the outbreak of war Roosevelt had begun to mend the bridges between his Democrat administration and the largely Republican business elite. The liberal, pro-labour stance of Roosevelt's government was played down. He needed the political cooperation of business, for he knew that he could not just impose a state-run war economy. When war broke out he sought their support by building a structure for wartime planning and supervision largely run by business recruits. This made practical sense. Corporate bosses had as much, if not more, experience of the kind of planning and coordination needed in a wartime economy than did government officials, whose only real experience was the ill-starred New Deal. They preferred a strategy where business was given a good deal of responsibility to get on with the job. The new agencies—the War Production Board under the Sears-Roebuck director, Donald Nelson, the Controlled Materials plan, the Manpower Commission—dealt only with those issues that the marketplace could imperfectly direct in wartime.

There was a scramble of volunteers for war contracts, in which the largest corporations were in a strong position, not least because co-opted directors sat side by side with the officials placing the orders. By the time the first rush was over four-fifths of all war orders had been given to the country's hundred largest businesses. American industrial plants eclipsed in size even the gigantic factories of the Urals. Some of them were so large that they were able to undertake war tasks on a scale no other economy could match. The General Motors Corporation alone supplied one-tenth of all American war production, and hired three-quarters of a million new workers during the war to produce it. The great scale of American prewar output, made possible by the size and wealth of its domestic market, allowed the widespread use of the most modern techniques of mass-production. Though there existed some skepticism in military circles about the feasibility of manufacturing technically complex weapons with the methods used for Cadillacs, even the largest equipment, heavy-bombers and shipping, ultimately proved amenable. No story better exhibits that "genius for mass-production" summoned up by Roosevelt than the story of the Liberty Ship.

In 1940 the British government ordered sixty cargo vessels from American dockyards to make good losses from submarine warfare. Working from the original British designs, American shipbuilders came up with a standard vessel, 420 feet in length, capable of carrying 10,000 tons of cargo at a plodding 10 knots. It was a plain, workmanlike vessel. Roosevelt thought it a "dreadful-looking object"; *Time* magazine christened it the "Ugly Duckling," and the name stuck until the US Maritime Commission, which was in charge of the building programme, insisted that what they were making amounted to nothing less than a Liberty Fleet. When the first ship was launched in September 1941 from the brand-new Bethlehem-Fairfield shipyard in Baltimore, the President himself lent dignity to the occasion. It was a gala celebration; the ugly duckling became overnight the Liberty Ship.

Over the next three years the initial order for sixty ships swelled into a programme for 2,700. Each new demand placed an ever greater burden on the over-stretched shipbuilding industry, short of skilled labour and berths. At first sight the ships did not lend themselves easily to mass-production, but at the west coast shipyards of Henry J. Kaiser the old principles of shipbuilding were overturned in 1942. Kaiser was new to shipwork. He began life running a photographer's shop in New York, moved into the gravel business, and ended up in California running a multi-million dollar construction company that built the Hoover Dam and the Bay Bridge. He had a reputation for tackling the impossible. When the shipbuilding programme started his initial involvement was the construction of four of the new yards on the west coast, but he then began to produce the ships as well. At his Permanente Metals Yards No. 1 and No. 2 at Richmond, on the northern edge of San Francisco Bay, the young Kaiser manager, Clay Bedford, set out literally to mass-produce ships.

The secret of the new method was to build much of the ship in large prefabricated sections. Instead of setting down a keel on the slipway, and slowly building the ship from the hull upwards, riveting one piece of steel to the next, the Liberty Ships were built in parts, away from the slipway, and then assembled there by modern welding methods. The shipyards were designed like a long production line, stretching back vertically from the coast. A mile from the shore vast assembly sheds and storehouses were built, where the superstructure of three ships at a time was built up along a moving line. At points along the line, components and sub-assemblies were fed in from the storehouses by conveyors and overhead pulleys. Each job was broken down into a series of simple tasks which could be mastered by even the most briefly trained worker. Outside the sheds, in the open air, were 80-foot conveyors on which the completed superstructure and bulkheads, complete with plumbing and wiring, were moved to the berths, to be lifted by four great cranes on to the welded hull. The whole complex of conveyors, rail lines, cranes, the piles of preassembled, standardised parts, the army of hurriedly-trained workers distributed by time-and-motion experts along the line, the factory banners exhorting workers to build "ships for victory," became an unexpected monument to that American obsession, rationalisation. At the start of the programme ships took 1.4 million man-hours and 355 days to build. By 1943 the figure was under 500,000 man-hours and an average of 41 days. At Richmond No. 2 the Liberty Ship *Robert E. Peary* was launched in just eight days. The methods gradually filtered out to other shipyards. Over the war years productivity in the shipbuilding industry increased by 25 per cent a year. "We are more nearly approximating the automobile industry than anything else," the head of the Maritime Commission told a Congressional hearing in 1942.

To any American audience the motor industry was an obvious benchmark. It had pioneered modern methods of production; its commercial history was one of the distinctive success stories of American enterprise. If the rationalisation of shipbuilding was a surprising bonus, the motor industry, because of its core of mass-production giants—Ford, General Motors, Chrysler—was expected to play a major role in the efficient production of war equipment from the start. American vehicle manufacture grew up in the mid-western states, on the edge of the Great Lakes. Here, in the American equivalent of the Urals-Volga heartland, was concentrated the largest manufacturing complex in the world. In 1941 over three and a half million passenger cars were produced there. During the war production dropped to the extraordinary figure of just 139 cars. This decline freed enormous industrial capacity for the war effort. By 1945 the industry supplied one-fifth of all the country's military equipment, including almost all the vehicles and tanks, one-third of the machine guns and almost two-fifths of aviation supplies. The Ford company alone produced more army equipment during the war than Italy.

The conversion of an industry of this size presented all kinds of problems. Until the very eve of war the powerful car-makers resisted efforts to reduce civilian output; 1941 was a record year for the motor industry. When war came they were quite unprepared for the changeover. The last day for civilian output was fixed for 10 February 1942. Small ceremonies were held in the car plants as the last chassis came down the line. Then, under the energetic supervision of a former Ford manager, Ernest Kanzler, the machinery was ripped out and new tools were installed to begin the mass-production of weapons. This was a daunting task. Although the authorities assumed that the car plants could be turned off and on again like a tap, the manufacture of armaments on a large scale was very different from assembling cars. Weapons exhibited a greater degree of complexity and required higher precision; they needed periodic updating and improvement, which made long production runs hard to sustain. That the motor industry did adapt so successfully owed a good deal to the character of the industry. Annual model changes accustomed managers and workers to regular large-scale adjustments on the factory floor; the large companies were used to a wide product range; the workforce was compelled by the nature of the manufacturing process to be flexible and adaptive. Car manufacture was in most cases a job of assembling parts and equipment provided by outside firms, and the practice of employing specialist sub-contractors—General Motors used nineteen thousand of them during the war—was carried over to the production of tanks, aircraft and engines. Once the conversion was completed the industry began to overfulfil its orders. As early as the autumn of 1942 the motor industry could provide enough vehicles, ordnance and equipment to provision America's new armies throughout 1943, and to do so with weapons of high quality and standard construction.

The ultimate challenge was to produce an aircraft by the same method used to mass-produce a car. The consensus was that it could not be done. This was a technical challenge too great to resist for that apostle of progress, Henry Ford. He was the archetype of the unschooled heroic entrepreneur of American legend, a man whose faith in the possibilities of the machine age was boundless and uncritical. Early in 1941 the Ford company was invited to produce parts for the new B-24 Liberator bomber being built by the Consolidated aircraft plant in San Diego. When Ford's general manager, Charles Sorensen, visited Consolidated he was appalled at the modesty of their plans and the primitive methods of construction. That evening, 8 January, Sorensen sketched out the plan of a plant to mass-produce bombers. It was the start of one of the most famous projects of the American war effort. The army was lukewarm about the idea when Sorensen and Ford suggested it a few days later, but Ford persisted: he would either produce the whole aircraft in a purpose-built plant, or nothing at all. The army reluctantly concurred and by March 1941 work began on the factory foundations.

The site chosen was dictated by the sheer dimensions of the plan and the need to have an adjacent airfield for aircraft testing. In the open country south of Detroit Ford had bought some flat, tree-covered farmland. A small creek meandered across it till it hit the river Huron. It was known as Willow Run. The name was adopted for the project itself. Within months the quiet rural vista was transformed into a sprawl-ing, noisy building site over 900 acres in extent. The centerpiece was the main assembly hall, "the most enormous room in the history of man," a vast L-shaped construction that eventually housed an assembly line 5,450 feet long, and covered an area of 67 acres. Ford's aim was to break down the construction of the aircraft in such a way that the components could be fed into a continuous moving assembly line. With a car this could be done relatively easily, for it averaged fifteen thousand parts; but the B-24 had thirty thousand different parts, and a total of 1,550,000 parts in all. To mass-produce something so complex was to push mechanised production to its very limits.

The project was so difficult that it almost collapsed. Constant delays in the sup-ply of tools and labour, pressure from the army to stick to building the components, the erratic intervention of Ford himself who insisted on re-siting the whole plant when he discovered that the boundary of a Democrat county ran through the com-plex, all conspired to hold up the promised supply of one bomber an hour. While Ford struggled with Willow Run, the "enormous room" was even eclipsed by a room yet bigger, a vast plant for Oerlikon anti-aircraft guns built by the Chrysler Corporation in Chicago. But Ford's technical persistence paid off. By 1943 over ten bombers a day were delivered; during 1944 over five thousand were produced, reaching a rate of one bomber every 63 minutes. Willow Run, for all its problems, came to symbolise all the self-confidence and drive of American industry. Looking across the giant assembly hall was like gazing at a scene from Fritz Lang's futuristic movie, *Metropolis*. The glare of the machinery and polished aluminum and the clouds of dust made it impossible to see its whole length. At one end four moving lines carried the core of the aircraft; the four merged to two as the aircraft took shape; 1 mile from the start there was just one line of completed bombers, fed out through a cavernous opening on to the airfield beyond. It was, observed the aviation hero, Charles Lindbergh, "the Grand Canyon of the mechanised world."

Long before Willow Run redeemed its author's ambitions the rest of American industry turned to modern methods. Productivity in the aircraft industry doubled between 1941 and 1944. By 1944 each American aircraft worker produced more than twice his German counterpart, four times the output of a Japanese worker. The war revived America's flagging enterprise culture. After a decade of depres-sion and high unemployment, both business and labour profited from war. The contrast not only with the Soviet Union but with every other warring population was striking. In America there was enough left over from the booming war effort to provide civilians with supplies of consumer goods and food in generous quanti-ties. Rationing was limited and loosely applied, except for petrol. Wages boomed, with an average increase, even allowing for price rises, of 70 per cent across the war years. As the nine million unemployed were absorbed into the workforce, and women—fourteen million in all—took up paid work, family earnings rose even faster. For millions of Americans who had lived on state relief and handouts in the 1930s the wartime economy was a windfall. The lure of high wages drew almost four million workers from the poorer south to the boom cities of the west coast, Michigan and the north-east. That haunting photographic image of the 1930s, the Madonna of the Depression, gave way to the propaganda ideal of war-working womanhood, Rosie the Riveter (though given the changes in work practices Wanda the Welder might have been more appropriate). In reality the high demand for labour and the unwillingness of the government to regiment the workforce led to high labour turnover, and a strike movement that produced almost five thousand strikes in 1944. The migration of labour exacerbated racial tension, and strained the housing market. But compared with the hugely deprived Soviet workforce and the bombed and bullied workforces in Germany and Japan, American labour was able to work without danger, well-fed and well-shod. This may have made it harder to exact a higher level of effort or self-sacrifice, but it certainly fostered a productive workforce.

Without the wartime opportunities the American population would presumably have done its patriotic duty with more or less enthusiasm. But can we doubt that economic opportunism spurred on the war effort as much as raw desperation fired the Soviet population? Over the war more than half a million new businesses were started up in America. Like the Soviet over-achievers, the new entrepreneurs were hailed as examples of economic individualism at work. But in wartime American workers really could become bosses overnight. The son of a Syrian immigrant, Tom Saffody, worked as a machinist at the start of the war for a Detroit company. During the course of his work he invented a machine for metal measurement in his home garage. He left his job, built a factory using secondhand piping welded together, and by 1943 ran a business with an annual turnover of 4.5 million dollars. The entrepreneurial ideal did not explain America's wartime economic performance any more than socialist emulation explained that of the Soviet Union, but it would be wrong to ignore its motivating power entirely. Much of America's economic effort was voluntary; it was therefore all the more important that it should be prosperous. "If you are going to try to go to war or prepare for war in a capitalist country," wrote Henry Stimson, Roosevelt's Secretary for War, with unusual frankness in his diary, "you have got to let business make money out of the process, or business won't work." . . .

Hitler had little respect for American economic power. "What is America," he asked, "but millionaires, beauty queens, stupid records and Hollywood?" He had even less for the Soviet Union. On the eve of Barbarossa he told [Nazi Propaganda Minister Josef] Goebbels that between German and Soviet strength there was no comparison; "Bolshevism will collapse like a pack of cards." These turned out to be profound misjudgements, though who, in the summer of 1941, could have clearly foreseen how rapidly and on what a scale America and the Soviet Union would arm themselves? Two years of production turned both states into the superpowers Hitler's Germany hankered to become.

What Hitler failed to see was how central industry was to the Allied view of warfare. "Modern war is waged with steel," Churchill told Hopkins when he weighed up the imbalance between American and Japanese economic strength. Stalin's view of the war was entirely conditioned by economics, as befitted any disciple of Marx: "The war will be won by industrial production," he told an American delegation in October 1941. Roosevelt's opinion of American power was every bit as determinist. In planning the Victory Programme in 1941 he told War Secretary Stimson to work on the assumption "that the reservoir of munitions power available to the United States and her friends is sufficiently superior to that available to the Axis powers to insure defeat of the latter." Though Hitler was the inspiration behind the German adoption of mass-production in 1941, he did not consider economics as central to the war effort. Rather, he stuck to the view that racial character—willpower, resolve, endurance—was the prime mover; weapons mattered only to the extent that they could be married to the moral qualities of the fighting man.

There was much in common between the Soviet and American experience. One of the correspondents that made the trip to Magnitogorsk observed that the Russian people were "in many ways like Americans . . . they have a fresh and unspoiled outlook which is close to our own." These were sentiments that pre-dated the Cold War, but they contained a grain of truth. In both countries mobilisation was a hustling, improvised affair; technical tasks were tackled head-on and quickly; production was big in scale and easily standardised; engineers and managers were given wide scope to solve problems themselves. Both economies had a good deal of central planning, but here the similarity ends, for the one enjoyed a supervised abundance, the other a regimented scarcity. Both countries shared the sudden shock of unprovoked aggression, which gave a genuine urgency to economic planning, and forced their economies to give priority to finding a cluster of advanced weapons on which to concentrate production energies.

The situation facing Germany was very different. There was no direct threat to the homeland until the onset of serious bombing. German planners and designers had almost two years at war before conflict with the Soviet Union and America. During that time there was little pressure to mass-produce, even if the military had approved it, or to concentrate on a narrow band of designs. The military slowly built up their version of a heavily bureaucratic command economy, which displayed a ponderous inflexibility beside the enemy. A few hours before the attempt to assassinate Hitler on 20 July 1944, [German Armaments Minister Albert] Speer wrote to him that the great strength of the American and Soviet systems was their ability to use "organisationally simple methods." He drew a contrast between Germany's "overbred organisation" and the "art of improvisation" on the other side. Speer was a man constantly banging his head against officialdom. Posterity, he warned Hitler, would judge that Germany lost the struggle by clinging on to an "arthritic organisational system." Posterity might find this view a little harsh, for Speer himself had given the system a good shaking. But the contrast between American and Soviet productionism and Germany's bureaucratised economy was more than superficial. No war was more industrialised than the Second World War. Factory for factory, the Allies made better use of their industry than their enemy.

The Problems of American Mobilization

WILLIAM L. O'NEILL

Bad as America's diplomacy was, its defenses were even worse. Had it been strongly armed Germany and Japan would not have declared war. Or, if they had done so despite the odds, retribution would have been swift and lethal. Instead, peacetime mobilization lagged, ensuring that when war came disaster would follow disaster. Yet, for years before Pearl Harbor polls had shown that a majority of Americans favored rearmament—on its merits to be sure, but also because defense orders would create more jobs at a time of high unemployment: 15 percent of the work force remaining idle as late as 1940.

Why necessity and a popular mandate did not inspire vigorous preparations goes back to the democratic process. For one, it seems to have been a fixed rule that politicians did not believe that people were willing to sacrifice, no matter what the polls said. A strong defense effort would have created many jobs, but also higher taxes and fewer consumer goods. Congress and the President alike shrank from testing voter resolution on these sensitive topics.

Moreover, a strong defense meant strengthening the executive branch, which alone could oversee it. Congress had reservations about this, and so did the President, because expansion raised knotty questions about delegating power, recruiting personnel, and managing the aims of contending interest groups. In retrospect it all seems perfectly obvious. A collapsing world order made military strength the number one national priority. America had the means to build a great armed force and should have done so at once. However, to contemporaries balancing long-term need against short-term pain, it was not that easy.

At first few voices were raised on behalf of preparedness. Chief among them was Bernard M. Baruch, who, as chairman of the War Industries Board [WIB] in 1918, had directed American mobilization. . . . Throughout the interwar years Baruch repeatedly stressed how important it was to build upon America's World War I experience. . . . He wanted the WIB revived as an advisory commission that would, in an emergency, be given complete control of mobilization. In addition, price control was essential to maintain a stable economy. . . .

Baruch's failure as an advocate was very nearly total. Isolationists were quick to reject his stand. . . . New Dealers never supported full mobilization if that required, as it did, putting all power over it in the hands of a businessman—or someone acceptable to business. Whenever the need for a mobilization "czar" was addressed, New Dealers balked, certain that Baruch, or a man like him, would be appointed. Accordingly, for Roosevelt a weak mobilization in the prewar era was politically expedient, appealing as it did to both liberal and conservative isolationists. On July 1, 1939, the day he received his first preparedness budget, Roosevelt ordered the Chiefs of Staff and the Army-Navy Munitions Board, plus a handful of planning and management agencies, directly into the Executive Office of the President. In war, as in peace, all

From William O'Neill, *A Democracy at War: America's Fight at Home and Abroad in World War II* (New York: Free Press, 1993), 75–76, 78–80, 82–84, 90, 98–101, 214–215, 218, 222. Copyright © 1993 by William L. O'Neill. Reprinted with permission of The Free Press, an imprint of Simon & Schuster Adult Publishing Group.

roads would lead to the White House. This centralization was portrayed as an aid to efficiency. In fact it would set civilians against the military, cut the service secretaries out of the power loop, and leave Roosevelt as the only one fully informed.

On May 25, 1940, while France was falling, Roosevelt took additional steps. By executive order he formed an Office of Emergency Management in the White House, through which he proposed to direct mobilization. He invoked the Defense Act of 1916 to create a new Advisory Commission. . . . that would report directly to him. . . . The President's reorganization ensured once again that there would be no super agency to bleed away his power. . . . The President genuinely wanted a stronger national defense, but first he wanted to be reelected in 1940. If this necessitated appointing the wrong men to key mobilization jobs, setting them at cross purposes, and creating a maze of overlapping and poorly defined authorities to give the impression of doing much while actually doing little, so be it. . . .

On March 11, 1941 Roosevelt signed the Lend-Lease Act, which would in time greatly expand the shipment of munitions to Great Britain. As the threat of inflation could no longer be ignored Roosevelt, instead of giving control of prices to OPM [the Office of Production Management], created the Office of Price Administration and Civilian Supply, under his budget chief Leon Henderson. This further complicated an already bewildering power structure. . . .

Shortages, and the government's failure to provide leadership, forced manufacturers to bend the rules. Henry J. Kaiser could not have become the most famous industrialist of the war had he lacked that ability. A heavy-construction man who had built many roads and dams, he found his true calling in the war as an industrialist. Though in peacetime he had never laid a keel, he became the world's biggest shipbuilder. . . . In 1941 it took a year to build a Liberty Ship. Kaiser's dozen yards, which ultimately built a third of the 2,708 Liberty Ships made during the war, would cut that to a matter of days, assembling the *Robert E. Peary* in fewer than five. . . .

For auto makers, on the other hand, it remained business as usual. In 1941, as in 1917, they went on producing civilian vehicles while attempting to gear up for war. The companies hoarded materials, and enlarged passenger-car inventories, at the expense of their own defense contracts. At the same time, they were laying men off by closing down assembly lines so as to install the new equipment required for war production. As late as the summer of 1941 the all-important machine-tools industry was still working only one shift a day. With Japanese-American relations worsening fast, it was time to end the anarchy that characterized what passed for mobilization.

Roosevelt's answer to bureaucratic confusion and production delays was yet another monstrosity, the Supplies Priorities and Allocations Board [SPAB]. He created it on August 28, 1941, when Russia's survival, and therefore the only real hope of defeating Germany, hung in the balance. . . .

After Pearl Harbor it was obvious that SPAB and OPM must go: There had to be a wholehearted mobilization directed by someone with authority. Roosevelt could no longer avoid having a powerful assistant to coordinate production. What he could avoid was a "ministry of supply" comparable to Britain's. On January 15, 1942, Roosevelt told Henry Wallace and Donald Nelson that a new instrument, the War Production Board, would take charge of mobilization, with Nelson as Chairman, whose decisions, the President announced, "will be final." On paper WPB looked like the answer to Baruch's prayers. The powers given it were those outlined in the suppressed report submitted by the War Resources Board in 1939, so WPB bore at least some resemblance to the super agency that Baruch had been asking for all along. But its authority was not complete, and even if it had been, WPB required aggressive leadership, which Nelson could not provide. Hopkins would have been a good choice, but, considering his frail health, he was already overextended.

To those like Baruch who favored complete centralization, Nelson was bound to be a disappointment, and not just because of his failings as an administrator. WPB was a big improvement over its predecessors, but it had not been given control over the entire war procurement and production effort. Nelson was obliged to compete with the military services, which retained their authority to place orders, thus undermining WPB in ways that Nelson should not have permitted. He had to contend with international raw materials and allocations boards, and with various little czars who had considerable autonomy. A more forceful individual might have created order out of this madness, but most likely not even Baruch could have done the job without broader powers. As it was, everyone raided, or tried to raid, each other's programs in order to obtain the crucial materials they needed to meet inflated production quotas. . . .

. . . Everywhere in Washington there existed duplication and confusion, overlapping grants of authority, and divided tasks. A host of agencies fought each other to gain power, funds, and breathing space. Decisions were made on the basis of immediate or local needs, rather than according to an overall design, or anything resembling one. What planning did take place was short-term and specific.

Roosevelt's working habits contributed to this disorder. Access to him was limited and capricious. Important men cooled their heels outside his office while nobodies who had caught his eye engaged the President's attention. Letters were answered or not as fancy dictated. Often the President made conflicting pronouncements on the same subject, leaving frustrated officials to find out for themselves what his intentions were. He ignored all complaints, and they were incessant, or else airily dismissed them. Not even discovering that enemy news agencies were using the "mess in Washington" to support Japanese morale made any difference to the man who was apparently responsible for it.

In some respects the American war effort resembled that of Nazi Germany. This would have come as a surprise to Americans at the time, who believed that Germany was a model of Teutonic precision and police-state efficiency. In fact, the Nazi state was remarkable for its overlapping authorities and plagued by bureaucratic chaos. As in America, personalities were vitally important, favored administrators expanding their reach at the expense of those outside the magic circle of power. As also in America the supreme leader, for political reasons, did not wish mobilization to inconvenience civilians. Though Hitler increased armament production before the war, he resisted stockpiling essential materials and cutting back on inessentials. As in America again, German munitions were produced over and above consumer goods more than might be expected. America got away with doing so because of its immense industrial base and because it still produced most of its raw materials. Germany made up for domestic shortages by plundering captive nations. . . .

By this standard the American war effort looks more impressive than when studied by itself. On the other hand, if compared with Great Britain's, the shortcomings become apparent. Churchill, who was both Prime Minister and Minister of Defence, conducted national affairs with the aid of a five-man War Cabinet—a highly efficient mechanism that had no counterpart in America. There was no mobilization czar in Britain either, for, like Roosevelt, Churchill did not wish to share power. To a large extent the War Cabinet made one unnecessary. While he created some new ministries, notably the Ministry of Production in 1942, much of the war effort was administered through existing agencies by professional civil servants. Though some business executives were brought into government, Britain got along without the horde of dollar-a-year men (the WPB alone had 800) who in America did, along with much good, much to promote big business.

Once [James F.] Byrnes became Director of War Mobilization, the war effort was at least adequately managed, yet American mobilization never was what it could have been. Paul Koistinen, the leading authority on this subject, estimates that the United States could easily have increased its supply of munitions by 10 to 20 percent. Production during the war was only about what could have been achieved in peacetime, given full employment. The results were striking just the same.

Much criticism of Roosevelt's wartime leadership missed the point, which was that even if Roosevelt had made efficiency his god, the American system of government would still have obstructed him. Here again the comparison with Great Britain is useful. In America individualism, pluralism, and mistrust of government made extemporizing not just desirable but absolutely necessary. Americans put a premium on leadership as well, the success or failure of any war agency depending to a large extent on whoever happened to run it. As the existing bureaucracy was relatively small and inelastic, it seemed easier, and was culturally more acceptable, to solve each new problem by creating a new organization and inviting businessmen to staff it. The tradition of public service being weak, and civil service a synonym for time wasting incompetence, business was the primary source of executive talent.

Business was also the interest group that worried Roosevelt most. A *Fortune* magazine survey published in November 1941 revealed that three-quarters of all businessmen feared that Roosevelt would use the war crisis to promote what they saw as undesirable reforms. Because some businessmen were still resisting mobilization, it was all the more important for Roosevelt to appease corporate America. Since expanding the federal service would only have further upset it, Roosevelt followed the easier course of creating temporary new bodies for business leaders to run. Despite his mistrust of dollar-a-year men, expediency won out. . . .

. . . Ultimately the nation would stand or fall according to how well the job was done on thousands of shop floors. FDR recognized this even before Pearl Harbor. In a fireside chat on December 29, 1940, President Roosevelt said "We must be the great arsenal of democracy." Still, after Pearl Harbor, far from equipping its allies, an ill-prepared United States could not even arm itself, and soon cut Lend-Lease aid to Russia and Great Britain. But within two years the production curve grew so rapidly that shipments were later resumed, and then hugely expanded. A few figures indicate the magnitude of this feat. In 1944 the United States produced over 96,000 aircraft, many with four engines, compared to just under 68,000 planes manufactured by the Axis states, which did not make heavy bombers. During the Battle of the Atlantic the Allies lost 8.3 million tons of shipping, yet the United States by itself produced 9 million tons of merchant shipping to more than wipe out the shortfall.

The amounts manufactured for Lend-Lease alone were staggering. At war's end the Soviet Union possessed 665,000 motor vehicles, 400,000 of them made in America. The United States also supplied 2,000 locomotives, 11,000 freight cars, and 540,000 tons of rail, with which the Soviets laid more track than during the 11 years of ruthlessly enforced industrialization that began in 1928. At the same time, America was providing Great Britain with much of its armament, rising to a peak of 28.7 percent of all British military equipment in 1944.

Many new inventions and discoveries came out of the war. However, though Americans viewed them proprietorially, most came from overseas. The British invented sonar, radar, penicillin, and the proximity fuse, while sulfa and DDT were German products. The theoretical work behind the atomic bomb was done mostly by European scientists. America's genius was for engineering and putting inventions into mass production.

At its peak the United States was building a ship a day and an airplane every five minutes. Between 1941 and 1943 America realized more than an 80 percent increase in military production, the GNP rising in constant dollars from $88.6 billion in 1939 to $135 billion in 1945. By then more than half of all world manufacturing was taking place inside the United States. Much of this output was achieved simply by putting what had been excess plant capacity to use. Many who worked in the wartime factories also had been surplus during the Depression. Although 12.5 million Americans were in uniform in 1945, the work force that year amounted to 65,290,000, up from 56,180,000 five years earlier, even though the birth rate had declined for years before the war.

This miracle of industrial growth, an extraordinary achievement that reflected the American "can do" spirit and its willingness to attempt the impossible, was not without its problems. The explosive growth of war industries affected every part of the country, areas with few or no government contracts losing population to luckier regions. . . .

The most famous wartime industrial site was Henry Ford's huge bomber plant at Willow Run, Michigan, 27 miles west of Detroit. The scale of the place made it a favorite of journalists, who liked to dwell on such impressive statistics as that the main building occupied 67 acres, the final-assembly line was over a mile in length, the airfield covered 1,434 acres and had six runways, one of which was 7,366 feet long. Enough concrete had been poured to build 115 miles of highway. The "Run" would produce 8,564 B-24 Liberators. At top plant speed, one would roll off the assembly line every 63 minutes.

Seemingly a monument to America's industrial greatness, Willow Run was actually one of the most badly planned and managed of all new industrial plants, a result of the haste and competing pressures of democratic America at war. One federal housing official described conditions there as "the worst mess in the whole United States." The first error was the choice of location. When construction began in April 1941, planners assumed that the workers would commute from Detroit on a state expressway built for that purpose. After Southeast Asia fell to the Japanese, the resulting rubber shortage and gasoline rationing made commuting from Detroit impractical. Before long there was not a vacant room within 15 miles of the plant. Because of the failure to build housing on a large enough scale, Willow Run would never realize its potential.

Thanks to federal inefficiency and local opposition, the first dormitory for single workers did not open until February 1943, the first family units in Willow Village, known also as Bomber City, were not available until July, and there were no shopping services for residents until February 1944. Native Michiganders, who resented and looked down on the out-of-state "hillbillies" (those from Kentucky, Tennessee, and West Virginia in particular, who constituted about half of the work force), blocked or delayed every effort to provide housing and support services. Ultimately the government built housing for only 10 percent of the workers and their dependents, a major reason why the bomber plant at its busiest employed only 42,331 workers instead of the projected 100,000. . . .

Living conditions for new workers in Washtenaw County remained harsh. Most workers and their families lived in cramped and often squalid quarters, half of them in shacks, tents, and trailers, often miles from the nearest shops, without laundry facilities or even running water. School construction lagged as well, so most of their children were in badly overcrowded classrooms or else on half-day schedules. Two years went by before the first family case worker was assigned to Willow Run. Local churches made few efforts to reach newcomers. Little was done to provide organized entertainment. These deficiencies caused a high level of absenteeism in the plant and an enormous turnover. The daily number of absentees ranged from 8 percent to 17 percent, while 10 percent of the work force quit every month. Over the three and a half years during which Willow Run was operational, Ford hired a total of 114,000 workers to maintain an average strength of 27,400. No one calculated what this churning meant in terms of lost production, but it must have amounted to hundreds, if not thousands, of aircraft.

Sociologists Lowell Carr and James Stermer, from the nearby University of Michigan, made a study of Willow Run. In one of the angriest monographs ever written, they spread the blame for its failures very widely. Except for the United Autoworkers, nobody seemed to care about the plight of Ford's employees. The federal government "dawdled and bungled." War production was subordinated to selfish local interests. Ford resisted every effort to provide public housing—and so did local businessmen and the county supervisors who wanted to protect real estate values and "keep Washtenaw county safe for the Republicans."

One Ford executive told a protest committee that "Ford Motor Company's business is to build the best bombers in the world, and how our workers live off the job is a community problem, not ours." This callousness infuriated the authors, and, though they neglected to mention it, was particularly offensive in light of Henry Ford's previous record of meddling into the private lives of his workers. Ford's security department, which during the war was still run by a notorious thug named Harry Bennet, who, despite his uncouthness, was a Henry Ford favorite, used to spy on workers constantly, not only to weed out union organizers but to enforce the owner's spartan code of personal morality.

Ultimately, the authors maintained, it all came down to politics. How to adequately care for the needs of workers and their families involved merely technical questions to which there were technical answers. But, for lack of any other system or procedure, each difficulty was treated as a political issue and resolved according to clout. Because few bomber-plant workers were eligible to vote in local elections, politicians could ignore them—and did. . . .

Willow Run embodied just about everything that could go wrong with war plants. In addition to callous management, hostile locals, and terrible planning, it was just too big to be absorbed by a small community. Even well-developed cities had trouble when they doubled in size—as did San Diego, California and Hampton Roads, Virginia—or even increased by a seemingly far less significant amount ("only" 40 percent), like the San Francisco Bay Area. Because war workers and their families might disappear when the emergency was over, few private or public bodies wanted to make capital investments for needs that were considered temporary. Thus, it was rare to have bonds issued to pay for schools, water, and sewers, and businessmen too were reluctant to expand if growth had to be financed with their own money.

FURTHER READING

Barber, William J. *Designs Within Disorder: Franklin D. Roosevelt, the Economists, and the Shaping of American Economic Policy, 1933–1945* (1996).
Brinkley, Alan. *The End of Reform: New Deal Liberalism in Recession and War* (1995).
Campbell, D'Ann. *Women at War with America: Private Lives in a Patriotic Era* (1984).
Chatfield, Charles. *The American Peace Movement: Ideals and Activism* (1992).
Daniels, Roger. *Concentration Camps U.S.A.: Japanese Americans and World War II* (1971).
———. *The Decision to Relocate the Japanese Americans* (1973).
———. *Prisoners Without Trial: Japanese Americans in World War II* (1993).
———, ed. *American Concentration Camps: A Documentary History of the Relocation and Incarceration of Japanese Americans, 1941–1945,* 9 vols. (1989).
DeBenedetti, Charles. *Origins of the Modern American Peace Movement* (1978).
Dreisziger, N. F., ed. *Mobilization for Total War: The Canadian, American and British Experience, 1914–1918, 1939–1945* (1981).
Earley, Charity Adams. *One Woman's Army: A Black Officer Remembers the WAC* (1989).
Fletcher, Marvin E. *America's First Black General: Benjamin O. Davis Sr., 1880–1970* (1989).
Flynn, George Q. *The Draft, 1940–1973* (1993).
———. *The Mess in Washington: Manpower Mobilization in World War II* (1979).
Gesensway, Deborah. *Beyond Words: Images from America's Concentration Camps* (1987).
Gropman, Alan. *Mobilizing U.S. Industry in World War II* (1996).
Gruhzit-Hoyt, Olga. *They Also Served: American Women in World War II* (1995).
Hooks, Gregory M. *Forging the Military-Industrial Complex* (1991).
Irons, Peter. *Justice at War: The Story of the Japanese American Internment Cases* (1983).
Janeway, Eliot. *The Struggle for Survival: A Chronicle of Economic Mobilization in World War II* (1951).
Kennett, Lee. *For the Duration: The United States Goes to War: Pearl Harbor, 1942* (1985).
Koistinen, Paul A. C. *The Military-Industrial Complex* (1996).
Matsumoto, Valerie. *Farming the Home Place: A Japanese American Community in California, 1919–1982* (1993).
Miller, Sally M., and Daniel A. Cornford, eds. *American Labor in the Era of World War II* (1995).
Moore, Brenda L. *To Serve My Country, To Serve My Race: The Story of the Only African American WACs Stationed Overseas During World War II* (1996).
Okihiro, Gary Y. *Whispered Silences: Japanese Americans and World War II* (1996).
Poulos, Paula Nassen, ed. *A Women's War Too: U.S. Women in the Military in World War II* (1996).
Schwartz, Jordan A. *The Speculator: Bernard M. Baruch in Washington, 1917–1965* (1981).

Smith, Page. *Democracy on Trial: The Japanese-American Evacuation and Relocation in World War II* (1995).

Sparrow, Bartholomew H. *From the Outside In: World War II and the American State* (1996).

Sutton, Antony C. *Wall Street and FDR* (1975).

Tateishi, John, ed. *And Justice for All: An Oral History of the Japanese American Detention Camps* (1984).

Treadwell, Mattie E. *The Women's Army Corps,* in *United States Army in World War II* (1954).

Vatter, Harold G. *The U.S. Economy in World War II* (1985).

Winkler, Allan. *Home Front U.S.A.* (2000).

———. *The Politics of Propaganda: The Office of War Information, 1942–1945* (1978).

See also Chapters 6 and 7.

CHAPTER
3

Creating a
Global Allied Strategy

The industrial and human mobilization described in Chapter 2 could not by itself win the war. That would require the creation, acceptance, and implementation of a global military strategy for the effective use of U.S. and Allied resources. These would prove to be extremely difficult and time-consuming tasks, for each member of the Allied coalition favored a different strategic approach reflecting its own unique situation and interests in the war. Furthermore, American strategists and policymakers were split as to the best approach for the nation to follow. The result was a series of major disagreements within the United States and between the Allies that dominated coalition relations from 1941 through late 1943, when agreement was finally reached. This chapter examines those disagreements, both within the United States and between the Allies. In the process it also explores the relationship between President Franklin D. Roosevelt, the U.S. commander in chief, and his key military advisers.

The three most militarily powerful members of the Allied coalition were the United States, Great Britain, and the Soviet Union. All three agreed that they had to concentrate first on the more dangerous German enemy, halting Hitler's numerous offensives and totally defeating him before refocusing on the Japanese. They also agreed that victory would require coordinated military operations. But they could not agree as to what those operations should be, or where they should be launched.

Great Britain favored an indirect "peripheral" approach, for its own and U.S. forces, centering on four types of military operations: a naval blockade of German-occupied Europe; the bombing of Germany's cities to destroy its industry and the morale of its people; encouragement and support of indigenous guerrilla forces in Axis-occupied Europe to stretch and weaken Axis military forces; and relatively small ground campaigns in North Africa and the Mediterranean— primarily against Vichy France and Germany's weak Italian ally—to "close the ring," in Churchill's famous words. All of these in combination would, London argued, force an Axis collapse at a relatively low cost in Allied casualties. That was particularly important to the British because of their relatively small population and the memories of the horrible losses they had suffered in the World War I trenches. It was also the only strategy possible for them after their disastrous 1940 defeats and the French surrender.

In 1941–1942, however, Britain's new Soviet ally objected vehemently to continuation of this strategy and called instead for a more direct approach designed to confront and defeat the German armies in western Europe as quickly and decisively as possible. For the Soviets, the British strategy was unacceptable because it would not establish a "second front" in western Europe capable of diverting German forces from Russia and thus would provide no relief to the hard-pressed Red armies. Indeed, it would minimize British and American casualties only by maximizing those of the Soviet Union, something the Soviets suspected to be a secret British goal: for if the Germans and Russians were left to bleed each other to death, Britain's postwar position would be enhanced. That position would also be enhanced by the presence of British forces throughout the Mediterranean and Middle East, areas of great imperial interest.

The United States maintained an unprecedented level of military cooperation with the British during World War II. Nevertheless it joined the Soviets in objecting to London's peripheral strategy and in calling instead for the establishment of an Anglo-American second front in western Europe, to be created by crossing the English Channel into northern France as quickly as possible. American planners believed that the peripheral approach would be militarily indecisive, and that the only way to guarantee victory was to confront and defeat the German armies in western Europe while the Soviets did the same in the east, thereby forcing Hitler into a two-front war. They also feared that without the military assistance a second front would provide, the Soviet Union would be defeated or would sign a separate peace with the Germans, either of which would preclude the possibility of an Allied military victory in Europe. It would also preclude a much-desired Soviet entry into the war against Japan. Even if such worst-case scenarios did not develop, an indecisive and time-consuming peripheral strategy in the Mediterranean would delay victory over Germany, thereby delaying offensive operations against Japan that large segments of the public as well as the navy, Southwest Pacific commander General Douglas MacArthur, and the Allied governments of China, Australia, and New Zealand all demanded in the aftermath of Pearl Harbor and the Japanese onslaught.

The ensuing strategic debate dominated and seriously weakened Allied relations from 1941 to late 1943. It also had a major negative impact on U.S. civil-military relations, as Roosevelt in 1942 supported the British position and overruled his own Joint Chiefs of Staff. The debate was finally settled in late 1943, however, thereby setting the stage for the highly successful and decisive Allied military victories of 1944–1945.

This chapter traces the development of U.S. strategic proposals and the ensuing disagreements within both the United States and the Grand Alliance as a whole. In examining those disagreements, keep in mind the numerous, complex, and interrelated issues and questions that were involved. Why, for example, did American planners conclude even before official U.S. entry into the war that they would need to defeat Germany before Japan? Why did they believe in close military coordination with the British but oppose British strategy? Did Roosevelt "promise" the Russians a second front in 1942? Why? Why did the president wind up supporting the British approach over that advocated by his military advisers in 1942? What impact did this dispute have on Allied relations and the conduct of the war? How was it finally resolved in late 1943?

DOCUMENTS

Document 1 consists of excerpts from the first formal call for an Anglo-American "Germany-first" strategy, by Chief of Naval Operations Admiral Harold E. Stark in November 1940, and the ensuing ABC-1 military accord negotiated by U.S. and British military planners between January and March of 1941. Immediately after Pearl Harbor, Prime Minister Winston Churchill and his military advisers traveled to Washington to reaffirm the Germany-first decision, set additional strategic priorities, and establish the bases for future military collaboration. Document 2 summarizes the most important of the agreements reached at this conference, code-named ARCADIA.

A major reason Churchill came to Washington was his fear that Pearl Harbor might lead the United States to abandon the Germany-first strategy and instead seek immediate revenge against Japan. Although Washington continued to adhere to Germany-first, numerous Americans wanted to abandon it in favor of the "Pacific-first" strategy that Churchill feared. Included in the latter group was Admiral Ernest J. King, the new Chief of Naval Operations. In Document 3, King explains his Pacific-first reasoning to Roosevelt.

Army Chief of Staff General George C. Marshall countered with a proposal for an immediate buildup of forces in the United Kingdom (Operation BOLERO) to launch a cross-channel attack and establish a second front in western Europe, either on a large scale in 1943 (Operation ROUNDUP) or on a smaller scale during 1942 (Operation SLEDGEHAMMER). Roosevelt concurred. After British acquiescence, the president discussed the proposal with visiting Soviet foreign minister Vyacheslav Molotov in May and June of 1942. Document 4 summarizes these conversations. But any 1942 operation would have to consist largely of British troops, and, as shown in Document 5, in July 1942 Churchill vetoed such an operation and proposed as an alternative the invasion of French North Africa, code-named GYMNAST. Incensed by what they considered British duplicity, King and Marshall responded with a formal proposal for a Pacific-first strategy, excerpted in Document 6. Document 7 presents excerpts from Roosevelt's memos to Marshall rejecting the Pacific-first strategy. Instead, Roosevelt insisted that his military advisers immediately go to Britain and agree to the North African invasion, which was renamed Operation TORCH and launched in November of 1942.

TORCH succeeded, and in January 1943 Churchill and Roosevelt met with their military advisers in the captured Moroccan city of Casablanca to consider additional operations. With major forces now committed in North Africa, the Americans were forced to agree to continuation in the Mediterranean despite their continued desire to cross the English Channel. Document 8 reproduces that agreement. The resulting postponement of cross-channel operations in turn enraged Soviet leader Josef Stalin, who in June 1943 responded to Churchill with a list of Anglo-American broken promises regarding the establishment of a second front in western Europe. Document 9 reproduces Stalin's message to Churchill. The ensuing crisis in Allied relations was resolved in November 1943 during the "Big Three" summit conference in Tehran. Document 10 consists of excerpts from the minutes of that conference, illustrating how Roosevelt and Stalin pressured Churchill into agreeing to limit future Mediterranean operations in order to cross the channel in Operation OVERLORD during the spring of 1944.

1. U.S. and British Military Officials Agree to a "Germany-First" Strategy: Admiral Stark's Memorandum and the ABC-1 Accord, November 1940/March 1941

The Stark Memorandum, November 1940

The strong wish of the American government and people at present seems to be to remain at peace. In spite of this, we must face the possibility that we may at any moment become involved in war. With war in prospect, I believe our every effort should be directed toward the prosecution of a national policy with mutually supporting diplomatic and military aspects, and having as its guiding feature a determination that any intervention we may undertake shall be such as will ultimately best promote our own national interests. We should see the best answer to the question: "Where should we fight the war, and for what objective?" . . .

. . . As I see affairs today, answers to the following broad questions will be most useful to the Navy:

(A) Shall our principal military effort be directed toward hemisphere defense, and include chiefly those activities within the Western Hemisphere which contribute directly to security against attack in either or both oceans? An affirmative answer would indicate that the United States, as seems now to be the hope of this country, would remain out of war unless pushed into it. If and when forced into war, the greater portion of our Fleet could remain for the time being in its threatening position in the Pacific, but no major effort would be exerted overseas either to the east or the west; the most that would be done for allies, besides providing material help, would be to send detachments to assist in their defense. It should be noted here that, were minor help to be given in one direction, public opinion might soon push us into giving it major support, as was the case in the World War.

Under this plan, our influence upon the outcome of the European War would be small.

(B) Shall we prepare for a full offensive against Japan, premised on assistance from the British and Dutch forces in the Far East, and remain on the strict defensive in the Atlantic? If this course is selected, we would be placing full trust in the British to hold their own indefinitely in the Atlantic, or, at least, until after we should have defeated Japan decisively, and thus had fully curbed her offensive power for the time being. Plans for augmenting the scale of our present material assistance to Great Britain would be adversely affected until Japan had been decisively defeated. The length of time required to defeat Japan would be very considerable.

If we enter the war against Japan and then if Great Britain loses, we probably would in any case have to reorient towards the Atlantic. There is no dissenting view on this point.

Stark Memorandum from Franklin D. Roosevelt Presidential Library; ABC-1 Accord from National Archives, Washington, D.C. Both are reproduced in *America War Plans, 1919–1941*, ed. Steven T. Ross (New York: Garland, 1992), vol. 3, pp. 225–250; vol. 4, pp. 5–13.

(C) Shall we plan for sending the strongest possible military assistance both to the British in Europe, and to the British, Dutch and Chinese in the Far East? The naval and air detachments we would send to the British Isles would possibly ensure their continued resistance, but would not increase British power to conduct a land offensive. The strength we could send to the Far East might be enough to check the southward spread of Japanese rule for the duration of the war. The strength of naval forces remaining in Hawaii for the defense of the Eastern Pacific, and the strength of the forces in the Western Atlantic for the defense of that area, would be reduced to that barely sufficient for executing their tasks. Should Great Britain finally lose, or should Malaysia fall to Japan, our naval strength might then be found to have been seriously reduced, relative to that of the Axis powers. It should be understood that, under this plan, we would be operating under handicap of fighting major wars on two fronts.

Should we adopt Plan (C), we must face the consequences that would ensue were we to start a war with one plan, and then, after becoming heavily engaged, be forced greatly to modify it or discard it altogether, as, for example, in case of a British fold up. On neither of these distant fronts would it be possible to execute a really major offensive. Strategically, the situation might become disastrous should our effort on either front fail.

(D) Shall we direct our efforts toward an eventual strong offensive in the Atlantic as an ally of the British, and a defensive in the Pacific? Any strength that we might send to the Far East would, by just so much, reduce the force of our blows against Germany and Italy. About the least that we would do for our ally would be to send strong naval light forces and aircraft to Great Britain and the Mediterranean. Probably we could not stop with a purely naval effort. The plan might ultimately require capture of the Portuguese and Spanish Islands and military and naval bases in Africa and possibly Europe; and thereafter even involve undertaking a full scale land offensive. In consideration of a course that would require landing large numbers of troops abroad, account must be taken of the possible unwillingness of the people of the United States to support land operations of this character, and to incur the risk of heavy loss should Great Britain collapse. Under Plan (D) we would be unable to exert strong pressure against Japan, and would necessarily gradually reorient our policy in the Far East. The full national offensive strength would be exerted in a single direction, rather than be expended in areas far distant from each other. At the conclusion of the war, even if Britain should finally collapse, we might still find ourselves possessed of bases in Africa suitable for assisting in the defense of South America.

. . . I believe that the continued existence of the British Empire, combined with building up a strong protection in our home areas, will do most to ensure the status quo in the Western Hemisphere, and to promote our principal national interests. As I have previously stated, I also believe that Great Britain requires from us very great help in the Atlantic, and possibly even on the continents of Europe or Africa, if she is to be enabled to survive. In my opinion Alternatives (A), (B), and (C) will most probably not provide the necessary degree of assistance, and, therefore, if we undertake war, that Alternative (D) is likely to be the most fruitful for the United States, particularly if we enter the war at an early date. . . . [S]hould we be forced into a war with Japan, we should, because of the prospect of war in the Atlantic also, definitely plan to avoid operations in the Far East or the Mid-Pacific that will prevent the Navy from promptly moving to the Atlantic forces fully adequate to safeguard our interests and policies in the event of a British collapse. We ought not now willingly engage in any war against Japan unless we are certain of aid from Great Britain and the Netherlands East Indies.

No important allied military decision should be reached without clear understanding between the nations involved as to the strength and extent of the participation which may be expected in any particular theater, and as to a proposed skeleton plan of operations.

Accordingly, I make the recommendation that, as a preliminary to possible entry of the United States into the conflict, the United States Army and Navy at once undertake secret staff talks on technical matters with the British military and naval authorities in London, with Canadian military authorities in Washington, and with British and Dutch authorities in Singapore and Batavia. The purpose would be to reach agreements and lay down plans for promoting unity of allied effort should the United States find it necessary to enter the war under any of the alternative eventualities considered in this memorandum.

United States–British Staff Conversations Report [ABC-1 Accord]

3. The purposes of the Staff Conference, as set out in the instructions to the two representative bodies, were as follows:

(a) To determine the best methods by which the armed forces of the United States and British Commonwealth, with its present Allies, could defeat Germany and the Powers allied with her, should the United States be compelled to resort to war.

(b) To coordinate, on broad lines, plans for the employment of the forces of the Associated Powers.

(c) To reach agreements concerning the methods and nature of Military Cooperation between the two nations, including the allocation of the principal areas of responsibility, the major lines of the Military strategy to be pursued by both nations, the strength of the forces which each may be able to commit, and the determination of satisfactory command arrangements, both as to supreme Military control, and as to unity of field command in cases of strategic or tactical joint operations. . . .

6. The High Command of the United States and United Kingdom will collaborate continuously in the formulation and execution of strategical policies and plans which shall govern the conduct of the war. They and their respective commanders in the field, as may be appropriate, will similarly collaborate in the planning and execution of such operations as may be undertaken jointly by United States and British forces. This arrangement will apply also to such plans and operations as may be undertaken separately, the extent of collaboration required in each particular plan or operation being agreed mutually when the general policy has been decided. . . .

13. . . .

(a) Since Germany is the predominant member of the Axis Powers, the Atlantic and European area is considered to be the decisive theatre. The principal United States Military effort will be exerted in that theatre, and operations of United States forces in other theatres will be conducted in such a manner as to facilitate that effort. . . .

15. To effect the collaboration outlined in paragraph 6, and to ensure the coordination of administrative action and command between the United States and British Military Services, the United States and United Kingdom will exchange Military Missions. These Missions will comprise one senior officer of each of the Military Services, with their appropriate staffs.

2. Britain and the United States Reach Strategic Agreements at the ARCADIA Conference, Washington, D.C., December 1941–January 1942

Memorandum by the United States and British Chiefs of Staff [December 31, 1941.]

AMERICAN–BRITISH GRAND STRATEGY

I. GRAND STRATEGY

1. At the A–B Staff conversations in February, 1941, it was agreed that Germany was the predominant member of the Axis Powers, and consequently the Atlantic and European area was considered to be the decisive theatre.

2. Much has happened since February last, but notwithstanding the entry of Japan into the War, our view remains that Germany is still the prime enemy and her defeat is the key to victory. Once Germany is defeated, the collapse of Italy and the defeat of Japan must follow.

3. In our considered opinion, therefore, it should be a cardinal principle of A–B strategy that only the minimum of force necessary for the safeguarding of vital interests in other theatres should be diverted from operations against Germany.

II. ESSENTIAL FEATURES OF OUR STRATEGY

The essential features of the above grand strategy are as follows. Each will be examined in greater detail later in this paper.

a. The realization of the victory programme of armaments, which first and foremost requires the security of the main areas of war industry.

b. The maintenance of essential communications.

c. Closing and tightening the ring around Germany.

d. Wearing down and undermining German resistance by air bombardment, blockade, subversive activities and propaganda.

e. The continuous development of offensive action against Germany.

f. Maintaining only such positions in the Eastern theatre as will safeguard vital interests (see paragraph 18) and denying to Japan access to raw materials vital to her continuous war effort while we are concentrating on the defeat of Germany.

From U.S. Department of State, *Foreign Relations of the United States: The Conferences at Washington, 1941–1942, and Casablanca, 1943* (Washington, D.C.: U.S. Government Printing Office, 1968), 214–217, 232–234.

III. STEPS TO BE TAKEN IN 1942 TO PUT INTO EFFECT
THE ABOVE GENERAL POLICY

The Security of Areas of War Production . . .
Maintenance of Communications . . .
Closing and Tightening the Ring Around Germany

13. This ring may be defined as a line running roughly as follows:

> Archangel—Black Sea—Anatolia—The Northern Seaboard of the Mediterranean—
> The Western Seaboard of Europe.

The main object will be to strengthen this ring, and close the gaps in it, by sustaining the Russian front, by arming and supporting Turkey, by increasing our strength in the Middle East, and by gaining possession of the whole North African coast.

14. If this ring can be closed, the blockade of Germany and Italy will be complete, and German eruptions, e.g. towards the Persian Gulf, or to the Atlantic seaboard of Africa, will be prevented. Furthermore, the seizing of the North African coast may open the Mediterranean to convoys, thus enormously shortening the route to the Middle East and saving considerable tonnage now employed in the long haul around the Cape.

The Undermining and Wearing Down of the German Resistance

15. In 1942 the main methods of wearing down Germany's resistance will be:
   a. Ever-increasing air bombardment by British and American Forces.
   b. Assistance to Russia's offensive by all available means.
   c. The blockade.
   d. The maintenance of the spirit of revolt in the occupied countries, and the organization of subversive movements.

Development of Land Offensives on the Continent

16. It does not seem likely that in 1942 any large scale land offensive against Germany except on the Russian front will be possible. We must, however, be ready to take advantage of any opening that may result from the wearing down process referred to in paragraph 15 to conduct limited land offensives.

17. In 1943 the way may be clear for a return to the Continent, across the Mediterranean, from Turkey into the Balkans, or by landings in Western Europe. Such operations will be the prelude to the final assault on Germany itself, and the scope of the victory program should be such as to provide means by which they can be carried out.

The Safeguarding of Vital Interests in the Eastern Theatre

18. The security of Australia, New Zealand, and India must be maintained, and the Chinese war effort supported. Secondly, points of vantage from which an offensive against Japan can eventually be developed must be secured. Our immediate object must therefore be to hold:—
   a. Hawaii and Alaska.
   b. Singapore, the East Indies Barrier, and the Philippines.
   c. Rangoon and the route to China.
   d. The Maritime Provinces of Siberia.

The minimum forces required to hold the above will have to be a matter of mutual discussion.

POST-ARCADIA COLLABORATION [January 14, 1942]

1. In order to provide for the continuance of the necessary machinery to effect collaboration between the United Nations after the departure from Washington of the British Chiefs of Staff, the Combined Chief of Staffs . . . propose the broad principles and basic organization herein outlined.

2. To avoid confusion we suggest that hereafter the word "Joint" be applied to Inter-Service collaboration of one nation, and the word "Combined" to collaboration between two or more of the United Nations.

3. Definitions.—

    a. The term "Combined Chiefs of Staff" is defined as the British Chiefs of Staff (or in their absence from Washington, their duly accredited representatives), and the United States opposite numbers of the British Chiefs of Staff.

    b. The term "Combined Staff Planners" is defined as the body of officers duly appointed by the Combined Chiefs of Staff to make such studies, draft such plans, and perform such other work as may from time to time be placed on the "Combined Chiefs of Staff Agenda" by that Body, and duly delegated by them to the Combined Staff Planners.

    c. The "Combined Secretariat" is defined as the body of officers duly appointed by the Combined Chiefs of Staff to maintain necessary records, prepare and distribute essential papers, and perform such other work as is delegated to them by the Combined Chiefs of Staff. . . .

5. The Combined Chiefs of Staff shall develop and submit recommendations as follows:

    a. For the ABDA [American-British-Dutch-Australian Command] Area, specifically as set forth in the Directive, Annex 2 to U.S. ABC–4/5, British WW–6, dated January 5, 1942.

    b. For other areas in which the United Nations may decide to act in concert, along the same general lines as in *a* above, modified as necessary to meet the particular circumstances.

6. The Combined Chiefs of Staff shall accordingly:

    a. Recommend the broad program of requirements based on strategic considerations.

    b. Submit general directives as to the policy governing the distribution of available weapons of war. (It is agreed that finished war equipment shall be allocated in accordance with strategical needs; to effectuate this principle, we recommend the utilization of appropriate bodies in London and Washington, under the authority of the Combined Chiefs of Staff).

    c. Settle the broad issues of priority of overseas military movements.

7. The question of the production and dissemination of complete Military Intelligence to serve the Combined Chiefs of Staff and Combined Staff Planners has been referred to the latter body for a report. Here also, it is contemplated that existing machinery will be largely continued.

8. It is planned that the Combined Chiefs of Staff will meet weekly, or more often if necessary; an agenda will be circulated before each meeting.

3. Admiral Ernest J. King Calls for a Strategic Focus on Japan, March 1942

March 5, 1942

Memorandum for the President:

1. The delineation of general areas of responsibility for operations in the Pacific is now taking place, in which it appears that we—the U.S.—will take full charge of all operations conducted eastward of the Malay Peninsula and Sumatra.

2. You have expressed the view—concurred in by all of your chief military advisers—that we should determine on a *very few* lines of military endeavor and concentrate our efforts on these lines. It is to be recognized that the *very few* lines of U.S. military effort may require to be shifted in accordance with developments but the total number should be kept at a *very few*.

3. Consideration of what war activities we (U.S.) should undertake in the Pacific requires to be premised on some examination of our (U.S.) relationship with respect to world-wide war activities—the Pacific being one part of the larger whole.

4. Other than in the Pacific our principal allies—Great Britain and Russia—are already committed to certain lines of military effort, to which our (U.S.) chief contribution in the case of Russia will continue to be munitions in general.

5. As to Britain's lines of military effort:

(a) It is apparent that we (U.S.) must enable the British to hold the citadel and arsenal of Britain itself by means of the supply of munitions, raw materials and food—and to some extent by troops, when they will release British troops to other British military areas.

(b) The Middle East is a line of British military effort which they—and we—cannot afford to let go. This effort should continue to receive our (U.S.) munitions.

(c) The India-Burma-China line of British military effort is now demanding immediate attention on their part—and will absorb its proportion of our (U.S.) munitions—in addition to the munitions which we are committed to furnish to China.

6. The chief sources of munitions for the United Nations are Britain, the U.S. and, to some degree, Russia. The chief sources of manpower for the United Nations are China, Russia, the U.S., and to less degree, the British Commonwealth. The only mobile factors are those available to Britain and to the U.S., because of their use of sea power—navies and shipping.

7. Australia—and New Zealand—are "white man's countries" which it is essential that we shall not allow to be overrun by Japanese because of the repercussions among the non-white races of the world.

8. Reverting to the premise of paragraph 2—a *very few* lines of military endeavor —the general area that needs immediate attention—and is in our (U.S.) sphere of responsibility—is Australasia, which term is intended to include the Australian

From Ernest J. King Papers, Navy Historical Center, and Franklin D. Roosevelt Presidential Library: reproduced in Thomas B. Buell, *Master of Seapower: A Biography of Fleet Admiral Ernest J. King* (Boston: Little, Brown, 1980), 531–533.

continent, its approaches from the northwest—modified ABDA [American-British-Dutch-Australian Command] area—and its approaches from the northeast and east—ANZAC [Australia-New Zealand Sea Command] area. These approaches require to be actively used—continuously—to hamper the enemy advance and/or consolidation of his advance bases.

9. Our primary concern in the Pacific is to hold Hawaii and its approaches (via Midway) from the westward and to maintain its communications with the West Coast. Our next care in the Pacific is to preserve Australasia (par. 8 above) which requires that its communications be maintained—via eastward of Samoa, Fiji and southward of New Caledonia.

10. We have now—or will soon have—"strong points" at Samoa, Suva (Fiji) and New Caledonia (also a defended fueling base at Bora Bora, Society Islands). A naval operating base is shortly to be set up in Tongatabu (Tonga Islands) to service our naval forces operating in the South Pacific. Efate (New Hebrides) and Funafuti (Ellice Islands) are projected additional "strong points."

11. When the foregoing 6 "strong points" are made reasonably secure, we shall not only be able to cover the line of communications—to Australia (and New Zealand) but—given the naval forces, air units, and amphibious troops—we can drive northwest from the New Hebrides into the Solomons and the Birmarck Archipelago after the same fashion of step-by-step advances that the Japanese used in the South China Sea. Such a line of operations will be offensive rather than passive—and will draw Japanese forces there to oppose it, thus relieving pressure elsewhere, whether in Hawaii, ABDA area, Alaska, or even India.

12. The foregoing outline (of U.S. participation in the war) points the way to useful lines in U.S. military endeavor in the Pacific, which may be summarized in an integrated, general plan of operations, namely:

Hold Hawaii

Support Australasia

Drive northwestward from New Hebrides.

4. Roosevelt "Promises" the Soviets a Second Front, May–June 1942

May 30, 1942

Mr. Molotov thereupon remarked that, though the problem of the second front was both military and political, it was predominantly political. There was an essential difference between the situation in 1942 and what it might be in 1943. In 1942 Hitler was the master of all Europe save a few minor countries. He was the chief enemy of everyone. To be sure, as was devoutly to be hoped, the Russians might hold and fight on all through 1942. But it was only right to look at the darker side of the picture. On the basis of his continental dominance, Hitler might throw in

From U.S. Department of State, *Foreign Relations of the United States, 1942*, vol. 3 (Washington, D.C.: U.S. Government Printing Office, 1961), 576–577, 582–583, 593–594.

such reinforcements in manpower and material that the Red Army might *not* be able to hold out against the Nazis. Such a development would produce a serious situation which we must face. The Soviet front would become secondary, the Red Army would be weakened, and Hitler's strength would be correspondingly greater, since he would have at his disposal not only more troops, but also the foodstuffs and raw materials of the Ukraine and the oil-wells of the Caucasus. In such circumstances the outlook would be much less favorable for all hands, and he would not pretend that such developments were all outside the range of possibility. . . .

Mr. Molotov therefore put this question frankly: could we undertake such offensive action as would draw off 40 German divisions which would be, to tell the truth, distinctly second-rate outfits? If the answer should be in the affirmative, the war would be decided in 1942. If negative, the Soviets would fight on alone, doing their best, and no man would expect more from them than that. He had not, Mr. Molotov added, received any positive answer in London. Mr. Churchill had proposed that he should return through London on his homeward journey from Washington, and had promised Mr. Molotov a more concrete answer on his second visit. Mr. Molotov admitted he realized that the British would have to bear the brunt of the action if a second front were created, but he also was cognizant of the role the United States plays and what influence this country exerts in questions of major strategy. Without in any way minimizing the risks entailed by a second front action this summer, Mr. Molotov declared his government wanted to know in frank terms what position we take on the question of a second front, and whether we were prepared to establish one. He requested a straight answer.

The difficulties, Mr. Molotov urged, would not be any less in 1943. The chances of success were actually better at present while the Russians still have a solid front. "If you postpone your decision," he said, "you will have eventually to bear the brunt of the war, and if Hitler becomes the undisputed master of the continent, next year will unquestionably be tougher than this one."

The President then put to General Marshall the query whether developments were clear enough so that we could say to Mr. Stalin that we are preparing a second front. "Yes," replied the General. The President then authorized Mr. Molotov to inform Mr. Stalin that we expect the formation of a second front this year. . . .

June 1, 1942

The President . . . went on to say that on the previous day he had discussed questions of tonnage and shipping with the Chiefs of Staff. Every week we were building up troop and plane concentrations in England with a view to getting at the Germans from there as quickly as possible. . . .

. . . The President . . . proposed that the Soviet Government consider reducing its lease-lend requirements from 4,100,000 tons to 2,000,000 tons. This reduction would release a large number of ships that we could divert to shipping to England munitions and equipment for the second front, and thus speed up the establishment of that front. . . .

The President repeated that we expected to set up a second front in 1942, but that every ship we could shift to the English run meant that the second front was so much the closer to being realized. After all, ships could not be in two places at once, and hence every ton we could save out of the total of 4,100,000 tons would be so much to the good. The Soviets could not eat their cake and have it too.

To this statement Mr. Molotov retorted with some emphasis that the second front would be stronger if the first front still stood fast, and inquired with what seemed deliberate sarcasm what would happen if the Soviets cut down their requirements and then no second front eventuated. Then, becoming still more insistent, he emphasized that he had brought the new treaty out of England. "What answer," he asked, "shall I take back to London and Moscow on the general question that has been raised? What is the President's answer with respect to the second front?"

To this direct question the President answered that Mr. Molotov could say in London that, after all, the British were even now in personal consultation with our staff-officers on questions of landing craft, food, etc. We expected to establish a second front. . . .

Press Release Issued by the White House, June 11, 1942

The People's Commissar of Foreign Affairs of the Union of Soviet Socialist Republics, Mr. V. M. Molotov, following the invitation of the President of the United States of America, arrived in Washington on May 29 and was for some time the President's guest. This visit to Washington afforded an opportunity for a friendly exchange of views between the President and his advisers on the one hand and Mr. Molotov and his party on the other. . . .

In the course of the conversations full understanding was reached with regard to the urgent tasks of creating a second front in Europe in 1942. In addition, the measures for increasing and speeding up the supplies of planes, tanks, and other kinds of war materials from the United States to the Soviet Union were discussed. Also discussed were the fundamental problems of cooperation of the Soviet Union and the United States in safeguarding peace and security to the freedom-loving peoples after the war. Both sides state with satisfaction the unity of their views on all these questions.

5. Churchill Vetoes Crossing the Channel in 1942 and Proposes the North African Alternative, July 8, 1942

July 8, 1942, 1:45 A.M.

From Former Naval Person to President Personal and Secret.

1. No responsible British General, Admiral or Air Marshal is prepared to recommend SLEDGEHAMMER as a practicable operation in 1942. The Chiefs of the Staff have reported "The conditions which would make SLEDGEHAMMER a sound sensible enterprise are very unlikely to occur." They are now sending their paper to your Chiefs of Staff. . . .

From Franklin D. Roosevelt Presidential Library; reproduced in *Churchill & Roosevelt: The Complete Correspondence*, vol. 1, ed. Warren F. Kimball (Princeton: Princeton University Press, 1984), 520.

3. In the event of a lodgement being effected and maintained it would have to be nourished and the bomber effort on Germany would have to be greatly curtailed. All our energies would be involved in defending the Bridgehead. The possibility of mounting a large scale operation in 1943 would be marred if not ruined. All our resources would be absorbed piecemeal on the very narrow front which alone is open. It may therefore be said that premature action in 1942 while probably ending in disaster would decisively injure the prospect of well organized large scale action in 1943.

4. I am sure myself that GYMNAST is by far the best chance for effective relief to the Russian front in 1942. This has all along been in harmony with your ideas. In fact it is your commanding idea. Here is the true second front in 1942. I have consulted cabinet and defence committee and we all agree. Here is the safest and most fruitful stroke that can be delivered this autumn.

6. Admiral Ernest J. King and General George C. Marshall Respond with a "Pacific-First" Proposal, July 10, 1942

July 10, 1942.

MEMORANDUM FOR THE PRESIDENT:

. . . Our view is that the execution of Gymnast, even if found practicable, means definitely no Bolero-Sledgehammer in 1942 and that it will definitely curtail if not make impossible the execution of Bolero-Roundup in the Spring of 1943. We are strongly of the opinion that Gymnast would be both indecisive and a heavy drain on our resources, and that if we undertake it, we would nowhere be acting decisively against the enemy and would definitely jeopardize our naval position in the Pacific. . . .

Neither Sledgehammer nor Roundup can be carried out without full and whole-hearted British support. They must of necessity furnish a large part of the forces. Giving up all possibility of Sledgehammer in 1942 not only voids our commitments to Russia, but either of the proposed diversions, namely Jupiter [invasion of Norway] and Gymnast, will definitely operate to delay and weaken readiness for Roundup in 1943. If the United States is to engage in any other operation than forceful, unswerving adherence to full Bolero plans, we are definitely of the opinion that we should turn to the Pacific and strike decisively against Japan; in other words assume a defensive attitude against Germany, except for air operations; and use all available means in the Pacific. Such action would not only be definite and decisive against one of our principal enemies, but would bring concrete aid to the Russians in case Japan attacks them.

It is most important that the final decision in this matter be made at the earliest possible moment.

From National Archives and the Franklin D. Roosevelt Presidential Library.

7. Roosevelt Rejects the "Pacific-First" Alternative, July 14, 1942

Gen. Marshall

. . . I have carefully read your estimate of Sunday. My first impression is that it is exactly what Germany hoped the United States would do following Pearl Harbor. Secondly it does not in fact provide use of American troops in fighting except in a lot of islands whose occupation will not affect the world situation this year or next. Third it does not help Russia or the Near East.

Therefore it is disapproved as of the present.

Roosevelt CinC
[Commander-in-Chief]

General Marshall:

I have definitely decided to send you, King and Harry [Hopkins] to London immediately. . . .

I want you to know now that I do not approve the Pacific proposal. Will see you in the morning. . . .

Roosevelt

8. Britain and the United States Agree on a 1943 Mediterranean Strategy at the Casablanca Conference, January 1943

Memorandum by the Combined Chiefs of Staff

[Casablanca], January 19, 1943.

CONDUCT OF THE WAR IN 1943

The Combined Chiefs of Staff have agreed to submit the following recommendations for the conduct of the war in 1943.

1. *Security:*
   The defeat of the U-boat must remain a first charge on the resources of the United Nations.
2. *Assistance to Russia:*
   The Soviet forces must be sustained by the greatest volume of supplies that can be transported to Russia without prohibitive cost in shipping.
3. *Operations in the European Theater:*
   Operations in the European Theater will be conducted with the object of defeating Germany in 1943 with the maximum forces that can be brought to bear upon her by the United Nations.

(Document 7) From Franklin D. Roosevelt Presidential Library.

(Document 8) From U.S. Department of State, *Foreign Relations of the United States: The Conference at Washington, 1941–1942, and Casablanca, 1943* (Washington, D.C.: U.S. Government Printing Office, 1968), 774–775.

4. The main lines of offensive action will be:

In the Mediterranean:

(*a*) The occupation of Sicily with the object of:

(1) Making the Mediterranean line of communications more secure.

(2) Diverting German pressure from the Russian front.

(3) Intensifying the pressure on Italy.

(*b*) To create a situation in which Turkey can be enlisted as an active ally.

In the U.K.:

(*c*) The heaviest possible bomber offensive against the German war effort.

(*d*) Such limited offensive operations as may be practicable with the amphibious forces available.

(*e*) The assembly of the strongest possible force (subject to (*a*) and (*b*) above and paragraph 6 below) in constant readiness to reenter the Continent as soon as German resistance is weakened to the required extent.

5. In order to insure that these operations and preparations are not prejudiced by the necessity to divert forces to retrieve an adverse situation elsewhere, adequate forces shall be allocated to the Pacific and Far Eastern Theaters.

6. *Operations in the Pacific and Far East:*

(*a*) Operations in these theaters shall continue with the forces allocated, with the object of maintaining pressure on Japan, retaining the initiative and attaining a position of readiness for the full scale offensive against Japan by the United Nations as soon as Germany is defeated.

(*b*) These operations must be kept within such limits as will not, in the opinion of the Combined Chiefs of Staff, jeopardize the capacity of the United Nations to take advantage of any favorable opportunity that may present itself for the decisive defeat of Germany in 1943.

(*c*) Subject to the above reservation, plans and preparations shall be made for:

(1) The recapture of Burma (ANAKIM) beginning in 1943.

(2) Operations, after the capture of Rabaul, against the Marshalls and Carolines if time and resources allow without prejudice to ANAKIM.

9. Stalin Angrily Responds to the Continued Delays in Establishing a Second Front, June 24, 1943

From your [Winston Churchill's] messages of last year and this I gained the conviction that you and the President were fully aware of the difficulties of organising such an operation and were preparing the invasion accordingly, with due regard to the difficulties and the necessary exertion of forces and means. Even last year you told me that a large-scale invasion of Europe by Anglo-American troops would

From Ministry of Foreign Affairs of the U.S.S.R., *Correspondence Between the Chairman of the Council of Ministers of the U.S.S.R. and the Presidents of the U.S.A. and the Prime Ministers of Great Britain During the Great Patriotic War of 1941–1945*, vol. 2, (Moscow: Foreign Languages Publishing House, 1957), 73–76.

be effected in 1943. In the Aide-Mémoire handed to V. M. Molotov on June 10, 1942, you wrote:

> Finally, and most important of all, we are concentrating our maximum effort on the organisation and preparation of a large-scale invasion of the Continent of Europe by British and American forces in 1943. We are setting no limit to the scope and objectives of this campaign, which will be carried out in the first instance by over a million men, British and American, with air forces of appropriate strength.

Early this year you twice informed me, on your own behalf and on behalf of the President, of decisions concerning an Anglo-American invasion of Western Europe intended to "divert strong German land and air forces from the Russian front." You had set yourself the task of bringing Germany to her knees as early as 1943, and named September as the latest date for the invasion.

In your message of January 26 you wrote:

> We have been in conference with our military advisers and have decided on the operations which are to be undertaken by the American and British forces in the first nine months of 1943. We wish to inform you of our intentions at once. We believe that these operations together with your powerful offensive, may well bring Germany to her knees in 1943.

In your next message, which I received on February 12, you wrote, specifying the date of the invasion of Western Europe, decided on by you and the President:

> We are also pushing preparations to the limit of our resources for a cross-Channel operation in August, in which British and United States units would participate. Here again, shipping and assault-landing craft will be the limiting factors. If the operation is delayed by the weather or other reasons, it will be prepared with stronger forces for September.

Last February, when you wrote to me about those plans and the date of invading Western Europe, the difficulties of that operation were greater than they are now. Since then the Germans have suffered more than one defeat: they were pushed back by our troops in the South, where they suffered appreciable loss; they were beaten in North Africa and expelled by the Anglo-American troops; in submarine warfare, too, the Germans found themselves in a bigger predicament than ever, while Anglo-American superiority increased substantially; it is also known that the Americans and British have won air superiority in Europe and that their navies and mercantile marines have grown in power.

It follows that the conditions for opening a second front in Western Europe during 1943, far from deteriorating, have, indeed, greatly improved.

That being so, the Soviet Government could not have imagined that the British and U.S. Governments would revise the decision to invade Western Europe, which they had adopted early this year. In fact, the Soviet Government was fully entitled to expect that the Anglo-American decision would be carried out, that appropriate preparations were under way and that the second front in Western Europe would at last be opened in 1943.

That is why, when you now write that "it would be no help to Russia if we threw away a hundred thousand men in a disastrous cross-Channel attack," all I can do is remind you of the following:

First, your own Aide-Mémoire of June 1942 in which you declared that preparations were under way for an invasion, not by a hundred thousand, but by an Anglo-American force exceeding one million men at the very start of the operation.

Second, your February message, which mentioned extensive measures preparatory to the invasion of Western Europe in August or September 1943, which, apparently, envisaged an operation, not by a hundred thousand men, but by an adequate force.

So when you now declare: "I cannot see how a great British defeat and slaughter would aid the Soviet armies," is it not clear that a statement of this kind in relation to the Soviet Union is utterly groundless and directly contradicts your previous and responsible decisions, listed above, about extensive and vigorous measures by the British and Americans to organise the invasion this year, measures on which the complete success of the operation should hinge.

I shall not enlarge on the fact that this responsible decision, revoking your previous decisions on the invasion of Western Europe, was reached by you and the President without Soviet participation and without inviting its representatives to the Washington conference, although you cannot but be aware that the Soviet Union's role in the war against Germany and its interest in the problems of the second front are great enough.

There is no need to say that the Soviet Government cannot become reconciled to this disregard of vital Soviet interests in the war against the common enemy.

You say that you "quite understand" my disappointment. I must tell you that the point here is not just the disappointment of the Soviet Government, but the preservation of its confidence in its Allies, a confidence which is being subjected to severe stress. One should not forget that it is a question of saving millions of lives in the occupied areas of Western Europe and Russia and of reducing the enormous sacrifices of the Soviet armies, compared with which the sacrifices of the Anglo-American armies are insignificant.

10. Roosevelt, Churchill, and Stalin Debate and Decide Future Allied Strategy at the Tehran Conference, November 29–30, 1943

November 29 Meeting

[Prime Minister Churchill] went on to say that personally all he wanted was landing craft for two divisions in the Mediterranean and that with such a force many operations would be feasible, for example, it could be used to facilitate the operations in Italy or to take the islands of Rhodes if Turkey will enter the war, and could be used for these purposes for at least six months and then employed in support of OVERLORD. He pointed out that this force of landing craft could not be supplied for the forces in the Mediterranean without either delaying OVERLORD six to eight weeks or without withdrawing forces from the Indian theater. This is the dilemma. . . . THE PRIME MINISTER concluded that if Turkey declared war on Germany it would be a terrible blow to German morale, would neutralize Bulgaria and would directly affect Rumania which even now was seeking someone to surrender unconditionally to. Hungary likewise would be immediately affected. He said that

From U.S. Department of State, *Foreign Relations of the United States: The Conferences at Cairo and Tehran, 1943* (Washington, D.C.: U.S. Government Printing Office, 1961), 536–539, 576–577.

now is the time to reap the crop if we will pay the small price of the reaping. He summed up the task before the conference as: (1) to survey the whole field of the Mediterranean, and (2), how to relieve Russia, and (3), how to help OVERLORD.

MARSHAL STALIN said that Mr. Churchill need have no worry about the Soviet attitude toward Bulgaria; that if Turkey entered the war the Soviet Union would go to war with Bulgaria, but even so he did not think Turkey would come in. He continued that there was no difference of opinion as to the importance of helping the Partisans, but that he must say that from the Russian point of view the question of Turkey, the Partisans and even the occupation of Rome were not really important operations. He said that OVERLORD was the most important and nothing should be done to distract attention from that operation. He felt that a directive should be given to the military staffs, and proposed the following one:

> (1). In order that Russian help might be given from the east to the execution of OVER-LORD, a date should be set and the operation should not be postponed. (2). If possible the attack in southern France should precede OVERLORD by two months, but if that is impossible, then simultaneously or even a little after OVERLORD. An operation in southern France would be a supporting operation as contrasted with diversionary operations in Rome or in the Balkans, and would assure the success of OVERLORD. (3). The appointment of a Commander-in-Chief for OVERLORD as soon as possible. Until that is done the OVERLORD operation cannot be considered as really in progress. MARSHAL STALIN added that the appointment of the Commander-in-Chief was the business of the President and Mr. Churchill but that it would be advantageous to have the appointment made here.

THE PRESIDENT then said he had been most interested in hearing the various angles discussed from OVERLORD to Turkey. He attached great importance to the question of logistics and timing. He said it is clear that we are all agreed as to the importance of OVERLORD and the only question was one of when. He said the question was whether to carry out OVERLORD at the appointed time or possibly postpone it for the sake of other operations in the Mediterranean. He felt that the danger of an expedition in the eastern Mediterranean might be that if not immediately successful it might draw away effectives which would delay OVERLORD. He said that in regard to the Balkans, the Partisans and other questions are pinning down some 40 Axis Divisions and it was therefore his thought that supplies and commando raids be increased to that area to insure these Divisions remaining there. THE PRESIDENT then said he was in favor of adhering to the original date for OVERLORD set at Quebec, namely, the first part of May.

MARSHAL STALIN said he would like to see OVERLORD undertaken during the month of May; that he did not care whether it was the 1st, 15th or 20th, but that a definite date was important.

THE PRIME MINISTER said it did not appear that the points of view were as far apart as it seemed. The British Government was anxious to begin OVERLORD as soon as possible but did not desire to neglect the great possibilities in the Mediterranean merely for the sake of avoiding a delay of a month or two.

MARSHAL STALIN said that the operations in the Mediterranean have a value but they are really only diversions.

THE PRIME MINISTER said in the British view the large British forces in the Mediterranean should not stand idle but should be pressing the enemy with vigor.

He added that to break off the campaign in Italy where the allied forces were holding a German army would be impossible.

MARSHAL STALIN said it looked as though Mr. Churchill thought that the Russians were suggesting that the British armies do nothing.

THE PRIME MINISTER said that if landing craft [are] taken from the Mediterranean theater there will be no action. He added that at Moscow the conditions under which the British Government considered OVERLORD could be launched had been fully explained, and these were that there should not be more than 12 mobile German divisions behind the coastal troops and that German reinforcements for sixty days should not exceed 15 Divisions. He added that to fulfill these conditions it was necessary in the intervening period to press the enemy from all directions. He said that the Divisions now facing the allies in Italy had come . . . [for the most part from France], and to break off the action in Italy would only mean that they would return to France to oppose OVERLORD. Turning again to the question of Turkey, THE PRIME MINISTER said that all were agreed on the question of Turkey's entrance into the war. If she refused, then that was the end of it. If she does enter, the military needs will be slight, and it will give us the use of Turkish bases in Anatolia, and the taking of the island of Rhodes which he felt could be done with one assault Division. Once Rhodes was taken the other Aegean islands could be starved out and the way opened to the Dardanelles. MR. CHURCHILL pointed out that the operation against Rhodes was a limited operation and would not absorb more effectives, and that in any case the troops for this purpose would come from those now used for the defense of Egypt. Once Rhodes was taken these forces from Egypt could proceed forward against the enemy. All he wanted was a small quantity of landing craft. . . .

. . . MARSHAL STALIN then said he wished to ask Mr. Churchill an indiscreet question, namely, do the British really believe in OVERLORD or are they only saying so to reassure the Russians.

THE PRIME MINISTER replied that if the conditions set forth at Moscow were present it was the duty of the British Government to hurl every scrap of strength across the channel. He then suggested that the British and American Staffs meet tomorrow morning in an endeavor to work out a joint point of view to be submitted to the conference. It was further agreed that the President, Marshal Stalin and the Prime Minister would lunch together at 1:30. . . .

November 30 Meeting

GENERAL BROOKE said that sitting in combined session the United States and British Staffs had reached the following agreement, which had been submitted for the approval of the President and the Prime Minister. It was agreed:

(1). That OVERLORD will be launched during the month of May, 1944.
(2). That there will be a supporting operation in southern France on as large a scale as possible, depending on the number of landing craft available for this operation. . . .

MARSHAL STALIN said he fully understood the importance of the decision reached and the difficulties which would be encountered in the execution of OVERLORD. He added that the danger in the beginning of the operation was that the Germans might attempt to transfer troops from the eastern front to oppose OVERLORD. In order to deny to the Germans the possibility of maneuvering he pledged that the Red Army would launch simultaneously with OVERLORD large scale offensives in a number of places for the purpose of pinning down German forces and preventing the transfer of German troops to the west. He said that he had already made the foregoing statement to the President, and Mr. Churchill but he thought it necessary to repeat it to the conference.

☯ E S S A Y S

The acrimonious debate over Allied wartime strategy sparked an equally acrimonious debate among historians in all three countries. In general, scholars in each country tended to defend the positions taken by their wartime political and military leaders. Simultaneously, however, the breakup of the Grand Alliance immediately after Axis surrender led many American writers to attack U.S. strategy in general, with particular emphasis on Roosevelt's supposed naiveté regarding the Soviet Union, his wartime leadership and relations with his military chiefs of staff, and the apolitical "pure military" nature of the advice those chiefs offered him as well as of the decisions he reached.

   The first essay, by American journalist Hanson W. Baldwin, summarizes these criticisms. Although it was written only a few years after the war ended and before the release of key archival documents, this essay remains illustrative of a still-powerful strand of thought in the United States highly critical of Roosevelt and U.S. wartime strategy for its political naiveté. In the second essay, Mark A. Stoler, professor of history at the University of Vermont, disagrees with such criticisms by emphasizing the political aspects of the strategies pursued by the United States as well as its allies. In the third essay, U.S. Army Chief Historian Kent Roberts Greenfield emphasizes the extent to which Roosevelt controlled his military advisers, rather than vice versa, while noting the political nature of his military decisions.

The Political Shortsightedness of U.S. Strategy

HANSON W. BALDWIN

The United States has fought wars differently from other peoples. We have fought for the immediate victory, not for the ultimate peace. Unlike the British or the Russians, we have had no grand design, no over-all concept. This lack of a well-defined political objective to chart our military action has distinguished, to greater or lesser degree, much of our past history. During World War II our political mistakes cost us the peace. The British and the Russians thought and fought in terms of the big picture, the world after the war; we thought and fought in terms of what we could do to lick Germany and Japan *now*. . . .

   The major American wartime errors were all part and parcel of our political immaturity. We fought to win—period. We did not remember that wars are merely

From Hanson W. Baldwin, *Great Mistakes of the War* (New York: Harper & Brothers, 1950), 1–3, 8, 14–15, 24–27, 29, 33–37, 41–42, 45, 107–108. Copyright © 1950 by Hanson W. Baldwin. Reprinted by permission of Curtis Brown, Ltd.

an extension of politics by other means; that wars have objectives; that wars without objectives represent particularly senseless slaughters; that unless a nation is to engage in an unlimited holocaust those objectives must be attainable by the available strength, limited by the victor's capacity to enforce them and the willingness of the vanquished state to accept them; and that the general objective of war is a more stable peace. We forgot that the "unity of outlook between allies in war never extends to the subsequent discussion of peace terms." We forgot that "while the attainment of military objectives brings victory in war, it is the attainment of political objectives which wins the subsequent peace." The United States, in other words, had no peace aims; we had only the vaguest kind of idea, expressed in the vaguest kind of general principles (the Atlantic Charter, the United Nations) of the kind of postwar world we wanted.

Our judgments were emotionally clouded by the perennial American hope for the millenium, the Russian military accomplishments, the warm sense of comradeship with our Allies which the common purpose of victory induced, and by the very single-mindedness of our military-industrial effort. Wartime propaganda added to illusion; all our enemies were knaves, all our Allies friends and comrades—military victory our only purpose. We were, in other words, idealists but not pragmatists. We embarked upon Total War with all the zeal and energy and courage for which Americans are famous, but we fought to win; in the broader sense of an objective, we did not know what we were fighting for. . . .

One of our greatest weaknesses in the policy field during the war was the failure to equate, evaluate, and integrate military and political policy; there was then no adequate government mechanism, save in the person of the President himself, for such integration. . . .

Unconditional Surrender

This was perhaps the biggest political mistake of the war. In the First World War Wilson took care to distinguish between the Kaiser and the militaristic Junkers class and the German people; in the Second, Stalin drew a clear line between Hitler and the Nazis, and the German people, and even the German Army. The opportunity of driving a wedge between rulers and ruled, so clearly seized by Wilson and by Stalin, was muffed by Roosevelt and Churchill. Unconditional surrender was an open invitation to unconditional resistance; it discouraged opposition to Hitler, probably lengthened the war, cost us lives, and helped to lead to the present abortive peace.

This policy grew in part out of the need for a psychological war cry; in part it was intended, as Langer puts it, as a reassurance to "the Bolshevik leaders that there would be no compromise with Hitler and that the Allies would fight on to total victory." The haunting fear that motivated so many of our actions during the war—the fear of a separate Russian peace with Germany—and Russia's growing suspicions of her Western Allies because of their inability until that time (January, 1943) to open a "second front" on land in Western Europe, dictated the famous declaration of Casablanca. . . .

Unconditional surrender was a policy of political bankruptcy, which delayed our military objective—victory—and confirmed our lack of a reasoned program for peace. It cost us dearly in lives and time, and its essentially negative concept has handicapped the development of a positive peace program.

By endorsing the policy, we abandoned any pragmatic political aims; victory, as defined in these terms, could not possibly mean a more stable peace, for "unconditional surrender" meant, as Liddell Hart has noted, the "complete disappearance of any European balance.

"War to the bitter end was bound to make Russia 'top dog' on the Continent, to leave the countries of Western Europe gravely weakened and to destroy any buffer."

Unconditional surrender could only mean unlimited war, and unlimited war has never meant—save in the days when Rome sowed the fields of Carthage with salt and destroyed her rival with fire and sword—a more stable peace.

This political policy, coupled with a military policy of promiscuous destruction by strategic bombing, could not help but sow the dragon's teeth of future trouble.

Loss of Eastern Europe

The long wartime history of strategic differences between Britain and the United States started soon after Pearl Harbor. From then until just before the invasion of southern France in August, 1944, when the British finally failed in their last effort to persuade us to undertake a Balkan invasion, we steadily championed an invasion of Western Europe and the British consistently proposed an alternative or complementary invasion of the "underbelly."

The two differing strategic concepts were separated, not only by geography and terrain, but by centuries of experience. We sought only military victory—the quickest possible victory. The British looked toward the peace; victory to them had little meaning if it resulted in political losses. We saw in the British insistence upon Southern European "adventures" all sorts of malevolent motives. . . .

. . . [F]undamentally the British evaluation was politico-military; we ignored the first part of that compound word. The British wanted to invade Southern Europe because its lands abut on the Mediterranean and are contiguous to the Near East, important to Britain's power position in the world. For centuries Britain had had major politico-economic interests in Greece, other Balkan states, and Turkey; for centuries her traditional policy had been to check the expansionism of Russia, to support Turkish control of the Dardanelles, to participate in Danubian riparian rights. In 1942 and 1943, with the Russians in deep retreat and the Germans almost at the Caspian, the British may not have foreseen 1944 and 1945, with the Russians entering the Balkans, but they perceived clearly the political importance of this area, and they saw that an invasion there would preserve it—in the best possible manner, by soldiers on the ground—against either Russian or German interests, and in so doing, would safeguard the British "lifeline" through the Mediterranean. Thus the British believed Germany could be beaten and the peace won "by a series of attritions in northern Italy; in the eastern Mediterranean, in Greece, in the Balkans, in Rumania and other satellite countries." . . .

. . . [I]n retrospect it is now obvious that our concept of invading Western Europe in 1942 was fantastic; our deficiencies in North Africa, which was a much needed training school for our troops, proved that. The British objection to a 1943 cross-Channel operation was also soundly taken militarily; we would have had in that year neither the trained divisions, the equipment, the planes, the experience, nor (particularly) the landing craft to have invaded the most strongly held part of the continent against an enemy whose strength was far greater than it was a year later.

Sicily inevitably led to an invasion of Italy, an operation envisaged first as a limited one against the boot of the Italian peninsula, then later for the seizure of air bases at Foggia, the quick capture of Rome, and the consequent political-psychological advantage. Churchill saw Italy and Sicily as bases for a jump eastward into the Balkans, and he continued, with the aid of his military leaders, to push this project. . . .

At Teheran the British again advocated the Balkan invasion, but Roosevelt, stressing the geographical advantages of the cross-Channel assault and the terrain difficulties of the Balkans, said that only an invasion of western France could be considered, from the Russian point of view a "second front." Stalin naturally sided with Roosevelt; indeed, the two "got along" not only at Teheran but at Yalta. . . .

. . . And so it was that on November 30, 1943, the invasion of Normandy was finally decided at Teheran, and *Stalin strongly supported the southern France invasion,* rather than a trans-Adriatic operation into the Balkans which was mentioned by Roosevelt and backed strongly by Churchill.

This Teheran decision, in which Stalin's unequivocal insistence upon an invasion of western France and the unanimity of the American military were the decisive factors, really settled the postwar political fate of Eastern Europe.

Major General John R. Deane in his book says of Teheran: "Stalin appeared to know exactly what he wanted at the Conference. This was also true of Churchill, but not so of Roosevelt. This is not said as a reflection on our President, but his apparent indecision was probably the *direct result of our obscure foreign policy.* President Roosevelt was thinking of *winning the war;* the others were thinking of their *relative positions when the war was won.* Stalin wanted the Anglo-American forces in Western not Southern Europe; Churchill thought our postwar position would be improved and British interests best served if the Anglo-Americans as well as the Russians participated in the occupation of the Balkans." (italics mine) . . .

Despite these arguments it was not to be; the British, despite the great eloquence of Churchill and the reasoned logic of his staff, had failed; the American strategy— heartily endorsed by the Russians—was the pattern of conquest.

It was, of course, a successful pattern, for it was a very sound plan militarily, probably sounder in a military sense than a Balkan invasion, and it led to unconditional surrender. But it also led to the domination of Eastern and Central Europe by Russia and the postwar upset in the European balance of power which has been so obvious since the war. . . . For we forgot that all wars have objectives and all victories conditions; we forgot that winning the peace is equally as important as winning the war; we forgot that politico-military is a compound word.

Such mistakes as those outlined in these pages—the attempt to find total victory, to inflict absolute destruction, to use unlimited means, and to mistake military victory for political victory—have been heretofore in history the peculiar characteristics of totalitarian or dictator-led states. The long view, the greatest good of the greatest number, a desire for world tranquilization and peace, have never characterized absolute rulers.

One reflection from a prison cell by the German General Kleist ought to be emblazoned above every doorway in the Pentagon and in the State Department:

> The German mistake was to think that a military success would solve political problems. Indeed, under the Nazis we tended to reverse Clausewitz's dictum, and to regard peace as a continuation of war.

The Political Wisdom of U.S. Strategy

MARK A. STOLER

War, as Carl von Clausewitz perceived, is an instrument of policy, and military strategy should be geared to the accomplishment of national political goals. According to popular belief, Americans have traditionally rejected such a concept, naively insisting that their wartime strategy be geared solely to achieving quick and decisive victory while politics awaited the peace conference. Following this unrealistic duality during World War II, the United States supposedly gave no thought to the importance of placing troops in key areas for bargaining purposes once the war ended, and vehemently opposed British attempts to follow such a "politically inspired" strategy. The State Department, which should have pointed out the necessity of controlling key areas, refused to meddle in what it considered "purely military" matters. Thus, it excluded itself from the decision-making process during the war and left the president with only military advice from the joint chiefs of staff.

According to this interpretation, the American military chiefs thus wound up determining foreign as well as military policy without ever realizing it—and with disastrous results. Their victory in the long and bitter strategic debate with Britain, signified by the Normandy invasion in June 1944, ensured decisive victory over Germany. But the political cost of such blindness to reality was a dangerous extension of Soviet power, thereby denying the United States the fruits of victory and adding another chapter to the supposed American tradition of winning the wars but losing the peace.

While such an explanation of events appears correct on the surface, it actually raises more questions than it answers. Why, for example, were the president and the joint chiefs so intent upon defeating Germany as quickly as possible? Was "military efficiency" the sole reason for the Army's almost fanatical adherence to the cross-Channel concept and opposition to British Mediterranean plans? Did the State Department totally ignore what had become by 1942 the biggest political as well as military issue of the war? How could a president known for his incredible political acumen, and military leaders trained in Clausewitzian and Mahanite principles of warfare, totally ignore the political aspects of strategy?

Careful examination of American military and political records for the war years casts doubt upon the validity of traditional assumptions regarding American naiveté during the war. From its very inception, the second-front issue was highly political and was so recognized by the leadership in Washington. The United States developed and backed this concept not simply as a way to win the war as quickly and decisively as possible, but as a way to win it on American, rather than British or Soviet, terms. Furthermore, the military did not develop its concept in a political vacuum. It asked for and received advice from political agencies, increased its contact with the president, and politicized itself to an unprecedented degree during the war. If the "military mind" did triumph with the Normandy invasion, it was a

From Mark A. Stoler, *The Politics of the Second Front: American Military Planning and Diplomacy in Coalition Warfare, 1941–1943* (Westport, Conn.: Greenwood Press, 1977), xi–xii, 6–7, 160–168. Reprinted by permission of Greenwood Publishing Group, Inc. http://www.greenwood.com.

military mind very concerned with and knowledgeable of the political aspects of strategy-making. . . .

Accustomed to working with an abundance of manpower and material on a continent with no other major land power, the American military was firmly convinced of the validity of the "direct" approach of strategy; the quickest and the most efficient way to win a war was to meet the enemy in a massive confrontation. Continuing British insistence on a wasteful Mediterranean alternative, the planners felt, could be explained and justified historically and in the present only by reference to its political implications; London's strategy always had been and was once again being orientated not to winning a war as quickly as possible, but to preserving the British Empire. American acquiescence in such a strategy, the Joint Army-Navy Planning Committee (JPC) warned in January 1941, could hurt American interests and should therefore be avoided. "We cannot afford," it bluntly stated, "nor do we need to entrust our national future to British direction." London's proposals at the coming conference "will probably have been drawn up with chief regard for support of the British Commonwealth. Never absent from British minds are their postwar interests, commercial and military. We should likewise safeguard our own eventual interests."

American military planners thus did not naively believe in following a strategy based solely on ideas of military efficiency. They were well aware of the fact that war is an instrument of policy and should be conducted so as to facilitate the accomplishment of national political goals. The definition of such goals, they further realized, was not their job but that of the civilian leadership of the country. . . .

The second-front issue was basically a political controversy within the Grand Alliance based on differing national conceptions of the proper way to defeat the Axis. These conceptions were in turn products of the histories, interests, and immediate positions of each member of the Alliance. London, Moscow, and Washington all perceived the war from their own vantage points and generalized their particular positions into concepts of the only "proper" way to win. Each viewpoint was thus as incorrect for an ally as it was correct for the nation propounding it. The result was a politico-military conflict that became the basic theme of Allied diplomacy through 1943.

Army planners in Washington developed the second-front concept as a way of winning the war on American, rather than British, terms. They defined those terms through a host of politico-military factors that represented a generalization of Army into national as well as national into Allied interests. While their position seemed to rest on the military need to achieve concentration and aid Russia in order to gain a quick and decisive victory, these needs were highly political.

Britain's peripheral approach through the Mediterranean, designed to minimize casualties and place troops in areas of imperial interest, would take longer to defeat Germany than a massive cross-Channel assault. The American Navy and public, insistent upon revenge against Japan, would not countenance such a dilatory approach and would demand further action in the Pacific, perhaps to the extent of overthrowing the Germany-first strategy. Such a move would not only imperil final victory, but would also replace Army influence in the White House with that of the Navy. From the War Department's viewpoint, the Mediterranean approach had already succeeded in replacing its influence with that of Churchill, thus creating this series of problems in the first place. Furthermore, continued dispersion of forces in either the Mediterranean or Pacific would destroy both Army power in Washington and American power within the Grand Alliance.

The necessity to aid Russia through a second front was based not only on the military situation, but also on the fact that Moscow had made the operation a political prerequisite for continued participation in the war. That participation was in turn mandatory in order to successfully launch the cross-Channel attack and maintain the Germany-first approach. Moreover, Russia's aid would be needed in the Pacific, and Stalin would eventually supply such aid only if he were given equivalent help against Germany.

While agreeing to the Army plan, Roosevelt perceived it as providing an immediate as well as a decisive front in Europe. Besides keeping Russia in the war, such immediate action would enable him to counter the Pacific thrust in American thought and mollify the offensive demands of the American public, thus silencing his critics and protecting his own political position. It would also allow him to take the lead in Allied diplomacy and define the alliance on American terms by offering Stalin a second front in return for an end to Russian demands for recognition of the 1939–1940 conquests in Eastern Europe.

Such an approach to foreign and domestic problems suffered from numerous deficiencies. The Army had developed the 1942 assault as an emergency operation in case disaster threatened on the Eastern front and as a method of forcing concentration for the massive 1943 assault. The 1942 operation was thus too small to fulfill Russian needs and too risky to guarantee the victory Roosevelt needed for domestic purposes. Furthermore, it depended upon British troops, and London was totally unwilling to risk another Dunkirk.

Most of these facts were known to all three partners. Yet, each ignored them in hopes of achieving specific aims. London agreed to the 1942 plan in order to prevent an American shift to the Pacific, but from the beginning had absolutely no intention of launching the operation. Despite strong hints of the true British position, Roosevelt promised the Russians a 1942 second front on a scale that was logistically impossible in return for a nonterritorial treaty. The Soviets demanded such a promise from him, although they knew London would have to supply the forces and would not agree to such a sacrifice. Churchill then played on Roosevelt's need for a 1942 victory in Europe so that the British could replace the cross-Channel attack with an invasion of North Africa. This switch in turn virtually destroyed the possibility of any second front until 1944.

In the short run, this series of deceptions produced benefits for all three countries. Roosevelt gained his nonterritorial treaty and 1942 action in Europe for domestic political purposes; London kept American forces in Europe and operations centered in the Mediterranean; and the Soviets received a "promise" they could show their war-weary people and perhaps use as a bargaining point in later Allied negotiations. In the long run, the deceptions proved disastrous, however. The political necessity for 1942 action, coupled with the British refusal to cross the Channel that year, led to a two-year delay in the second front and a slowing down of Western aid to Russia. Together with the nonterritorial treaty, this meant that Stalin had been denied everything he had demanded from his allies at the most critical juncture of the war. His suspicions of the West were increased by this "second-front diplomacy," rather than decreased as the Americans had hoped, and his reaction precipitated a diplomatic crisis within the Grand Alliance. The wounds engendered by this conflict never fully disappeared.

The episode also split the American military services, hardened the planners' beliefs regarding British motives and their inherent danger to American interests, and forced the military to further recognize the inseparability of political and strategic issues. As a result, in late 1942 and 1943 the planners began to delve deeply into the political aspects of strategy-making in order to convince the president of the validity of their views and to defeat the British in combined staff discussions. Those discussions increasingly resembled battles rather than conferences between allies.

The planners had long recognized the inseparability of political and military issues, but they had always felt that the political leadership of the country should play the key role in defining the relationship between the two. Roosevelt refused to give such a definition beyond unconditional surrender, and he appeared to be under British influence to a dangerous extent. As a result, the planners insisted on a greater role for themselves in defining the political and military aspects of national goals. By mid-1943, they had evolved a statement of these goals as well as those of Britain and Russia, the relationship of strategy to national aims, and the necessity of a second front to accomplish American desires. In the process, they called upon the State Department and the OSS [Office of Strategic Services] for political advice and achieved a degree of unofficial liaison with these two services. At the same time, the military improved its own coordination through the JCS [Joint Chiefs of Staff] and joint committees, planned combined staff conversations on a political basis, and increased its influence with the White House.

The planners' basic conclusion was that London's Mediterranean strategy was a reflection of British political interests and ran counter to American interests as defined during the 1942 debate. In 1943, however, new political interests were added to these old ones. Most important was the fear now expressed, often in terms quite similar to [George F.] Kennan's 1947 "Containment" theory, over the combination of Russian victories and diplomatic truculence resulting from the postponement of the second front. This combination seemed to threaten either a separate peace or Soviet domination of the peace conference and postwar Europe.

According to the planners, the only way to avoid this menace without negating either unconditional surrender or the goals expressed in 1942 was to establish a second front. The Soviets had demanded such an operation in return for continued cooperation both during and after the war. Furthermore, only a second front could enable the West to land enough troops in Europe to give it an effective bargaining position at the peace conference and block any Soviet attempts to dominate Europe without alienating Moscow before the war ended. An approach via the Balkans would immediately alienate the Russians and was logistically incapable of defeating either them or the Germans. In short, the planners perceived the second front as an "umbrella" policy, capable of fulfilling all American goals and handling any future possibility with the Soviets. British Mediterranean strategy was rejected not because it was political, but because it was logistically unfeasible and attempted to fulfill British goals at the expense of those of the United States.

Roosevelt's military advisers stressed these points in their conversations with him, and by mid-1943 the president was in complete accord with them. During that entire year, his degree of support for the cross-Channel assault increased as the Red armies moved westward and Soviet-American relations deteriorated. Stalin had already told him that any future cooperation hinged on this operation. His advisers reinforced this point as well as the fact that only a second front could block Soviet domination of the peace conference and Europe.

The results of this united American front were the TRIDENT* and QUAD-RANT† decisions on Operations OVERLORD and RANKIN, the successors to the original ROUNDUP and SLEDGEHAMMER projects in 1942. RANKIN, however, was a good deal more political than its predecessor. It had little military value, and it was basically designed to get Western forces onto the continent rapidly if Germany collapsed before OVERLORD could be launched. Not the least of the reasons for such a plan was the desire to prevent Russian domination of the peace conference and Europe.

RANKIN was, of course, never communicated to the Soviets. OVERLORD was, and it led to a great improvement in relations between the USSR and the West, culminating in the Moscow Foreign Ministers' Conference and the promise of a future Big Three meeting. The Soviets again made clear, however, that future cooperation depended upon a successful OVERLORD.

London now attempted to postpone the cross-Channel assault once more so that further operations could be launched in the Mediterranean. In an ironic twist, the Soviets backed this proposal. The worried Americans decided to explain their position to Moscow. They realized, however, that cooperation was the key goal and, if the Soviets insisted, OVERLORD would have to be delayed or canceled.

The final decision on the second front at Tehran was thus arranged not as a military decision, but as political one to be made totally within the context of Allied diplomatic relations. Ironically, Stalin would determine future Anglo-American strategy. But before the conference opened Roosevelt moved to protect American interests, in case the Soviets sided with the British, by insisting on Far Eastern action to aid China and on a RANKIN plan to get American forces into Berlin. Stalin, however, backed the American position fully at Tehran, and the British were overruled. Roosevelt, still thinking in terms of 1942, saw this agreement as the foundation for all future cooperation. He never did realize the changes in the situation caused by the two-year delay, nor did he understand that a 1944 second front could not be the all-encompassing politico-military operation he had hoped the 1942 assault would be. Hard political compromises were now necessary. Unfortunately, they were not forthcoming.

The findings developed in this study contradict many popular assumptions regarding the second front and American advocacy of that operation. From its very inception, the cross-Channel controversy was heavily involved in political issues and was a basic factor in the origins of the Cold War. Furthermore, both President Roosevelt and his military planners were well aware of the political factors involved

---

*TRIDENT was the May 1943 Anglo-American Conference in Washington, D.C.

†QUADRANT was the August 1943 Anglo-American Conference in Quebec.

and acted accordingly. In retrospect, the American plan appears more realistic on both military and political levels than Britain's approach.

While historians have recognized the crucial importance of the second-front controversy in the coming of the Cold War, most of them still maintain that the planners, and perhaps the president, were naive regarding the political aspects of this operation. Such conclusions appear to stem from two basic facts: the nature of the documents involved and the questions historians have asked relating to politics and strategy.

World War II records are so enormous that no individual historian can read all of them. Consequently, each historian writing on this period has concentrated on a specific set of documents. Studies based on such examinations have been extremely valuable, and this work has relied heavily upon many of them. Such concentration, however, can easily lead to a distorted view of the entire picture. Certain Army records, for example, show that logistical problems were the basic factors in delaying and modifying the cross-Channel assault. But such a conclusion ignores the fact that many of these logistical problems were caused by earlier political decisions. TORCH is a prime example.

Furthermore, the documents themselves do not tell the entire story. Roosevelt's statements (or lack thereof), if taken literally, would lead one to the conclusion that the president was a political and strategic moron. Yet, his political wisdom is famous, and as an ex-Navy man, he was well aware of Mahanite principles regarding the link between strategy and politics. One of the problems here stems from the fact that Roosevelt's goals, by his very position as the chief of state, were broader than and often different from those of his advisers. Although these advisers theoretically realized this fact, they as well as later historians reached the erroneous conclusion that Roosevelt was either ignorant of strategic and political realities or naively under the influence of Churchill.

Neither judgment is correct. Roosevelt was usually very consistent, and his few inconsistencies were the result more of the contradictory nature of his many goals than of any ignorance of the realities of the situation. Roosevelt may have been indulging in wishful thinking, for example, in his belief that the Soviets would accept TORCH as an effective second front. But since a true second front was impossible for 1942 and his political goals demanded some offensive action, he was forced to hope that the North African assault could accomplish everything the defunct cross-Channel attack would have achieved.

Another key problem regarding Roosevelt and the documentation available is his notorious insistence upon secrecy. Throughout his White House career, Roosevelt refused to divulge his innermost thoughts to the men around him. By his standards, only the president should weigh all the factors involved in a decision, and no one, future historians included, should know how he reached such a decision. Nor was Roosevelt above the temptation of distorting the record for the sake of his future reputation, as is clearly shown by his desire to expunge the 1942 record of all references to the Pacific alternative. Even more revealing of his secretiveness was his 1943 comment to Cordell Hull that the notes of conversations between Wilson, Lloyd George, and Clemenceau should never have been written. Had the president been able to have his way, there probably would have been no official record of the Tehran Conference.

Such secretiveness is in no way ignorance. Roosevelt's refusal to inform his advisers of his political goals beyond unconditional surrender may have been a grave error which led the military into political discussions, but that is not equivalent to a total ignorance of or refusal to deal with political goals. His actions and statements during the war clearly show that those goals were constantly on his mind.

The situation is similar in regard to the planners on both sides of the Atlantic. Because of their beliefs and training, these men seldom set down their political thoughts in official documents. Historians reading these documents have thus concluded that the American planners ignored political factors. Furthermore, since British strategic papers show no strong political desire either to enter the eastern Mediterranean or to cancel OVERLORD, Washington's stated beliefs in this regard appear to be figments of paranoid imaginations rather than reflections of the facts. Again, one must realize that the official documents do not tell the entire story. In their memoirs and unofficial correspondence, the planners expressed their concern with political factors, and this concern sometimes did spill onto official papers. Some unguarded British comments even suggest that the American suspicions were correct.

Furthermore, even the political leadership often discussed political matters on purely military grounds because of the standards of the times. According to Eisenhower, Churchill once argued for a change in strategy on military grounds for seven straight hours, although both men knew the rationale for such a change was political. Since military men were not supposed to consider these issues, and since the Americans had carefully kept such issues out of their official statements, Churchill apparently concluded that he would be on safer ground if he stuck to military arguments with Eisenhower. The American commander quickly realized this, informed Churchill of his knowledge as to the real situation, and suggested he discuss the issue with Roosevelt on political grounds if he desired a change in strategic plans.

The second key problem centers on the questions historians have asked regarding the relationship between strategy and politics. Most have searched for a "right" versus a "wrong" approach to strategy and have often based their conclusions on statements of "military" versus "political" factors. Both dichotomies are artificial. The key question here is not right or wrong, but right or wrong for *whom;* the missing factor is the *merging* of the political and military aspects of an issue into a truly grand strategic design. Churchill's primary motive for pushing Aegean operations in the fall of 1943 was not his fear of communism in the area. However, this was definitely *one* of the factors in his mind, and he merged it with his other desires—the indirect approach to victory, low casualties, a purely British victory, proving his World War I ideas correct, and placing British troops in areas of great imperial interest—into a grand strategic design. As he himself stated later, "It is not possible in a major war to divide military from political affairs. At the summit they are one." The American planners wholeheartedly agreed with such a judgment and planned accordingly. Ironically, future historians, and not the characters themselves, created this artificial split.

In later years, American planners spoke out sharply against the growing belief in their political naiveté during the war. General Marshall in particular pointed out that, with the exception of the landing craft shortage, nothing "came to our minds more frequently than the political factors." Dean Acheson, who worked under Marshall in the State Department during the postwar era, often discussed this point with the general and later concluded that when Marshall thought about military problems, "non-military factors played a controlling part." In fact, Marshall's explanation and knowledge of the complex political and military factors involved in the second-front controversy convinced Acheson of the brilliance of the man considered by many to have been America's greatest soldier. One might also add that such knowledge enabled Marshall to become secretary of state. He, along with his advisers and JCS colleagues, learned a valuable lesson during the war in the inseparability of political and military factors. Hence, within the second-front controversy may lie one of the origins of military influence in the formulation of post–World War II foreign policy.

If one disagrees with that foreign policy, then one may conclude that Roosevelt's greatest failing as a war leader was his unwillingness to share his political thoughts with his advisers. Yet from a larger vantage point, his very ability to perceive the link between strategy and politics, and to act accordingly, proved his greatest failing. This ability, shared by the other two heads of state and the different advisers, meant that no one within the Grand Alliance was capable of viewing the war, politically or militarily, from an *Allied* rather than a national perspective. Such a broad outlook was beyond the power of men trained in terms of national interest and facing the supreme threat to the very existence of their countries. While this situation may appear natural, or even inevitable, it set definite limits to the cooperation possible within the alliance both during and after the war. Common danger may bring nations together, but the desire to survive as a national entity means that the cooperation stops far short of its desired goals.

In World War II, those goals included future international cooperation. Men hoped that the second front and the alliance as a whole would bring the anti-Axis nations together and further the idea of internationalism in the process of defeating the enemy. The merging of strategy and politics did the exact opposite by reinforcing national desires and suspicions, and thus future rivalries. No one during the war wanted this to happen, but no one proved capable of breaking through established national thought patterns to prevent it. No national leader has to this very day.

Roosevelt as Commander-in-Chief

KENT ROBERTS GREENFIELD

Without going beyond the published histories one can count more than twenty cases in which Mr. Roosevelt overruled the considered judgment of his responsible military chiefs and substituted for theirs his own estimate of the military situation, or his own concept of the strategy that the situation required. To these can be added twelve other instances in which the initiative for taking an important military measure came, as far as one can see, from him. . . .

From the date of the Military Order of 1939 until Pearl Harbor, F.D.R. made all of his important decisions regarding the use of American military power either

From Kent Roberts Greenfield, *American Strategy in World War II: A Reconsideration* (Baltimore: Johns Hopkins Press, 1963), 51–53, 55–56, 69, 77–80. © 1973 by copyright holder. Reprinted with permission of Johns Hopkins University Press.

independently of his military chiefs, or against their advice and over their protests; and this was the period in which the kind of war the United States was going to fight, as well as the weapons with which we were to fight it, was determined. . . .

In striking contrast with Mr. Churchill, Mr. Roosevelt seemed to be content, once the United States had entered the war, to leave his military chiefs free to work out their own strategic ideas, subject to his general direction and approval; and to intervene only very rarely and then as a mediator between conflicting views. Mr. Churchill, on the other hand, was notoriously articulate and active in arguing for his concepts not only of strategy, but of tactics, weapons, equipment, and every other aspect of the British military effort by land, by sea, and in the air; and pressing these on his associates in the Government and on commanders in the field, at all hours of the day and night.

It is easy to overdo this contrast, which cannot be reconciled with facts that are of record. Of the cases noted in which F.D.R. overruled his military chiefs, more than half of the twenty-odd . . . can be cited as having occurred in 1942, 1943, and 1944. And this reckoning does not include the cases in which the Joint Chiefs of Staff probably refrained from proposing a plan which represented their best military judgment, because they knew that they could not get Mr. Roosevelt to support it.

But if Mr. Roosevelt exercised a more positive control over the military conduct of the war than is immediately apparent, it was mainly in 1942 and 1943 that this was true. In 1944–45, with one important exception—the relief of General [Joseph] Stilwell in October, 1944—he backed his Joint Chiefs one hundred percent. Regarding 1944–45, but only regarding this period, one can agree with Professor Ehrman that "American strategy emerged from the White House much as it had emerged from the Pentagon." . . .

The strategy of the Allies, then, in 1943, the year in which it became fixed by the deployment of their military resources, was not what it would have been if the American Joint Chiefs had had their way, or if the British had had their way. It crystallized out of compromises between the American Joint Chiefs and the British, and within the Joint Chiefs of Staff between the Army, the Air Forces, and the Navy, in a sequence of realistic adjustments to changing conditions. But the timing and balance of the compromises was determined by Mr. Roosevelt. . . .

Given Mr. Roosevelt's ways of getting things done, and with no such memoirs as Mr. Churchill's to assist them, historians have had almost as much difficulty in tracing the course of Mr. Roosevelt's influence on the military direction of America's war effort as the Joint Chiefs had in anticipating his decisions. But one certainly cannot say, given the record, that he had any compunctions about overriding—or ignoring—the counsels of his military experts, or agree with Mr. Churchill that he was "oppressed by the prejudices of his military advisers."

The principles that guided him as war leader of the American nation, and his determination to follow them, he made clear at an early date, and if the military chiefs had difficulties in foreseeing what practical application he would give them, they could have no doubt that he would overrule any proposal or measure of theirs that in his judgment conflicted with these principles. They can be summarized as follows:

1. The solidarity of the Anglo-American coalition must be maintained for military reasons, and also because the interest of the United States required the survival of Great Britain and its postwar freedom of action as a great power.

2. Nazi Germany is the Number One enemy and must be defeated and crushed at the earliest possible date.

3. Soviet Russia must be given unstinted aid and kept fighting to the end.

4. Germany and Japan must be forced to unconditional surrender.

5. China must be kept in the war, with the object of having it enter the postwar world as a great power.

6. The interest of the United States in the postwar world requires an international organization of "United Nations," and this, to establish itself, must at first be directed by a firm union of the victorious allies: the United States, Great Britain and its Commonwealth, the U.S.S.R., and China.

These were political as well as military objectives. What is important in a study of Mr. Roosevelt as Commander-in-Chief is that the decisions he made to achieve these objectives—with the glaring exception of China—made military sense. . . .

. . . In short, thanks largely to Mr. Roosevelt's exercise of his military authority, the United States had developed a strategy appropriate to a two-front war on a global scale, which brought Japan to terms within a few months after the unconditional surrender of Germany, and without the redeployment of our forces.

FURTHER READING

Beitzell, Robert. *The Uneasy Alliance: America, Britain, and Russia, 1941–1943* (1972).

Buell, Thomas. *Master of Seapower: A Biography of Fleet Admiral Ernest J. King* (1980).

Butler, J. R. M., ed. *History of the Second World War: Grand Strategy*, 6 vols. (1957–1972).

Cline, Ray S. *Washington Command Post: The Operations Division*, in *United States Army in World War II* (1951).

Danchev, Alex. *Very Special Relationship: Field-Marshal Sir John Dill and the Anglo-American Alliance, 1941–1944* (1986).

Dunn, Walter S., Jr. *Second Front Now, 1943* (1980).

Edmonds, Robin. *The Big Three* (1991).

Ellis, John. *Brute Force: Allied Strategy and Tactics in the Second World War* (1990).

Greenfield, Kent Roberts. *American Strategy in World War II* (1963).

———, ed. *Command Decisions* (1960).

Hayes, Grace Person. *The History of the Joint Chiefs of Staff in World War II: The War Against Japan* (1982).

Herring, George C. *Aid to Russia, 1941–1946* (1973).

Higgins, Trumbull. *Soft Underbelly: The Anglo-American Controversy over the Italian Campaign, 1939–1945* (1968).

Howard, Michael. *The Mediterranean Strategy in the Second World War* (1968).

James, D. Clayton. *A Time for Giants: The Politics of the American High Command in World War II* (1987).

Kimball, Warren F. *Forged in War: Roosevelt, Churchill and the Second World War* (1998).

———. *The Juggler: Franklin Roosevelt as Wartime Statesman* (1991).

Laqueur, Walter, ed. *The Second World War* (1982).

Larrabee, Eric. *Commander in Chief: Franklin D. Roosevelt, His Lieutenants, and Their War* (1987).

Leighton, Richard M., and Robert W. Coakley. *Global Logistics and Strategy*, 2 vols., in *United States Army in World War II* (1955, 1968).

Matloff, Maurice, and Edwin Snell. *Strategic Planning for Coalition Warfare*, 2 vols., in *United States Army in World War II* (1953, 1959).

O'Connor, Raymond. *Diplomacy for Victory: FDR and Unconditional Surrender* (1971).

Paret, Peter, ed. *Makers of Modern Strategy* (1986).

Pogue, Forrest C. *George C. Marshall,* 4 vols. (1963–1987).

Reynolds, David, Warren F. Kimball, and A. O. Chubarian, eds. *Allies at War* (1994).

Sainsbury, Keith. *Churchill and Roosevelt at War* (1994).

———. *The Turning Point: Roosevelt, Stalin, Churchill, and Chiang-Hai-Shek, 1943— The Moscow, Cairo, and Teheran Conferences* (1985).

Sherwood, Robert. *Roosevelt and Hopkins* (1950).

Steele, Richard. *The First Offensive, 1942* (1973).

Stoler, Mark A. *Allies and Adversaries: The Joint Chiefs of Staff, the Grand Alliance, and U.S. Strategy in World War II* (2000).

———. *George C. Marshall* (1987).

———. *The Politics of the Second Front* (1977).

Thorne, Christopher. *Allies of a Kind: The United States, Britain, and the War Against Japan, 1941–1945* (1978).

See also Chapter 10.

The War Against Germany:
What Was Needed
and What Was Done

The war against Germany took place on the high seas and in the air as well as on land, with numerous debates occurring within the U.S. armed forces as well as the Grand Alliance over correct strategy and priorities. In general, each of the major services—army, navy, and air—argued that its role was the most important and should receive priority on available resources and personnel.

One of the most important of such arguments focused on the proper use of a relatively new weapon—aircraft. Although airplanes had been used during World War I, it was only during the interwar years that military theorists began to explore their full potential and debate the best way to use them. This debate continued throughout World War II. Advocates of so-called strategic bombing within the U.S. and British air forces (the World War II U.S. air force was an autonomous branch of the army known as the Army Air Forces [AAF] and did not become a totally separate service until 1947) argued that massed bombers attacking German cities could destroy both the industrial capacity of Germany and the will of its people to resist, thereby guaranteeing victory. Army and navy critics disagreed. They maintained that strategic bombing could not achieve these goals and that ground and naval success remained the keys to victory. Consequently the United States should focus on "tactical" use of airpower in support of both ground forces fighting the German army in Europe and naval forces fighting the crucial campaign against German submarines in the Atlantic. Without success in that latter campaign, naval personnel argued, the critical Atlantic supply line would be cut and the war would be lost. Army planners similarly noted and argued that ultimate victory depended on Allied ability to defeat the German army on the ground.

Inter-Allied as well as interservice disagreements over appropriate theater strategy and priorities also took place. The British Air Force favored nighttime area bombing of German cities to destroy German morale, for example, whereas their American counterparts believed in daylight "precision" bombing to cripple German industry. Once OVERLORD was launched in 1944, British and American ground *commanders disagreed incessantly over which forces should receive priority in supplies and mission, and whether attacks on the German army should be launched along a "broad front" from the English Channel to the Swiss border as Supreme Allied Commander Dwight D. Eisenhower proposed, or along a much narrower front as his ground commanders, most notably Generals Bernard Montgomery, Omar Bradley, and George Patton, preferred.*

Behind these disagreements stood the fate of all the soldiers, sailors, and airmen who fought in the Atlantic/European theater. Their personal experiences in the air, naval, and ground campaigns are as much a part of the war against Germany as the disagreements within the U.S. and Allied high commands.

The strategic arguments discussed in this chapter continued after the war ended. To this day, scholars disagree over the high priority and effectiveness (as well as the morality) of the strategic bombing campaign, whether Eisenhower should have followed a broad- or narrow-front strategy, and if the latter, whether priority should have been given to British or U.S. forces. How effective was strategic bombing? Was the campaign worth its enormous human and material costs (bomber crews had one of the highest casualty rates in the war) as well as the moral opprobrium it added to the Allied cause because of the killing of civilians? Should it have received an even higher priority, or a lower one so that more critical air support could have been given to naval forces in the Atlantic and ground forces in Europe? Why did Eisenhower favor a broad-front approach while his ground commanders preferred a narrow-front approach? In retrospect, which approach appears preferable, and what were the most important factors in the Allied victory over Germany?

🌎 D O C U M E N T S

The different strategic approaches of the U.S. services were muted but still apparent in the prewar plans of the Army Ground and Air Forces contained within the so-called Victory Program of September 1941, excerpted in Document 1 (the AAF section was entitled AWPD-1). Document 2, from the Combined Chiefs of Staff minutes and conclusions of the Casablanca Conference of January 1943, shows the very high priority given to the naval campaign against German U-boats and the use of heavy bombers for both this purpose and the high-priority strategic bombing campaign against German cities. Document 3 is a defense and explanation of that controversial campaign, written by one or more AAF staff members in reply to the expressed and enclosed concerns of a bomber pilot's mother and friend of AAF chief General Henry H. "Hap" Arnold. Document 4 shows the German city of Dresden before and after it was destroyed by Anglo-American bombers in February of 1945.

U.S. and British ground forces first invaded Europe via Sicily and Italy in 1943, and then via Normandy in northern France on June 6, 1944, in Operation OVERLORD, the largest amphibious operation in military history. Document 5, taken from the original OVERLORD plan of July 1943, explains why the Normandy beaches were selected and lists the numerous obstacles that would have to be overcome if the operation were to succeed. Document 6 is General Eisenhower's inspiring Order of the Day to his forces on June 6, 1944, part of which also appears on the base of his statue at West Point. In Document 7, Eisenhower and Montgomery explain and debate the merits of a broad- versus narrow-front strategy in an argument that would continue until the fall of Berlin in April of 1945; in the process they also reveal their sharply different personalities. In Document 8, Army Chief of Staff General George C. Marshall explains at war's end what the captured German generals considered to have been the most important factors in their defeat. Note their emphasis on Soviet and British as well as U.S. actions.

The men who had to complete all these military missions in Europe came from diverse backgrounds and often faced racial discrimination. Blacks, for example, were racially segregated within the services as well as within civilian society and frequently were given only menial tasks by the armed forces. One of the most notable exceptions in this regard were the Tuskegee airmen, African American fighter pilots who amassed an enviable record during the war. Document 9 comes from the unpublished memoirs of one of those airmen, Lieutenant Alexander Jefferson, who was shot down in 1944 and became a German prisoner of war (POW). Document 10 comes from an unpublished wartime company history by Sergeant Bernard Bellush, a Jewish American from New York City who landed on bloody Omaha Beach on June 6, 1944, and from his postwar recollections of that experience. Jefferson later rose to the rank of lieutenant colonel and became a public school science teacher and assistant principal in Detroit; Bellush became a professor of history at the City College of New York.

1. Army Ground Versus Air Plans for the War Against Germany: The "Victory Program" (with AWPD-1) of September 1941

Ultimate Requirements Study Estimate of Army Ground Forces

1. The specific operations necessary to accomplish the defeat of the Axis Powers cannot be predicted at this time. Irrespective of the nature and scope of these operations, we must prepare to fight Germany by actually coming to grips with and defeating her ground forces and definitely breaking her will to combat. Such requirement establishes the necessity for powerful ground elements, flexibly organized into task forces which are equipped and trained to do their respective jobs. The Germans and their associates with between 11 and 12 million men under arms, now have approximately 300 divisions fully equipped and splendidly trained. It is estimated that they can have by 1943, a total of 400 divisions available in the European Theater.

2. The important influence of the air arm in modern combat has been irrefutably established. The degree of success attained by sea and ground forces will be determined by the effective and timely employment of air supporting units and the successful conduct of strategical missions. No major military operation in any theater will succeed without air superiority, or at least air superiority disputed. The necessity for a strong sea force, consisting principally of fast cruisers, destroyers, aircraft carriers, torpedo boats and submarines, continues in spite of the increased fighting potential of the air arm. Employment of enemy air units has not yet deprived naval vessels of their vital role on the high seas, but has greatly accelerated methods and changed the technique in their employment. It appears that the success of naval operations, assuming air support, will still be determined by sound strategic concepts

From "Over-all Production Requirements Required to Defeat United States Potential Enemies," RG 225, National Archives; reproduced in *American War Plans,* vol. 5, ed. Steven T. Ross (New York: Garland, 1992), 190–191, 199–201, 210–217.

and adroit leadership. A sea blockade will not accomplish an economic strangulation or military defeat of Germany. Nor will air operations alone bring victory. Air and sea forces will make important contributions but effective and adequate ground forces must be available to close with and destroy the enemy within his citadel. . . .

4. . . . Accepting the promise, that we must come to grips with the enemy ground forces, our principal theater of war is Central Europe. . . .

5. . . . Task Forces consisting principally of armored and motorized divisions, must be created for possible operations in North Africa, the Middle East, France and the Low Countries. . . . The realization of our present national policies may require operations in distant theaters by military forces of unprecedented strength. It would be folly to create strong fighting forces without providing the transportation to move and maintain them in the contemplated theaters of operations. The maximum possible shipbuilding capacity of our country, coordinated of course with other essential demands upon industry and raw materials, must be exploited and continued in operation for the next several years.

6. The foregoing considerations clearly indicate the importance of creating a productive capacity in this country, that will provide the most modern equipment designed to give mobility and destructive power to our striking forces. The forces that we now estimate as necessary to realize our national objectives and for which production capacity must be provided, may not be adequate or appropriate. No one can predict the situation that will confront the United States in July, 1943. We may require much larger forces than those indicated below, and correspondingly greatly increased quantities of equipment. Emphasis has been placed on destructive power and mobility, with a view to offensive maneuvers in our principal theater of operations (Europe). The forces deemed necessary to accomplish the role of ground units in the supreme effort to defeat our potential enemies, total 5 Field Armies consisting of approximately 215 divisions (infantry, armored, motorized, airborne, mountain and cavalry) with appropriate supporting and service elements.

Air Intelligence—Estimate of the Situation [AWPD-1]

3. *b.* The German offensive against Russia and the other German war operations have placed a considerable strain upon the economic structure of the Reich, and the Russian Campaign engaged a major portion of the German army and most of the German Air Force in Eastern Europe.

c. The declaration of war by Germany against Russia improved the conditions for enforcing the sea blockade and the means of applying pressure through economic warfare. Even in the event of Russian collapse, the German economic structure will continue to operate under heavy strain, and there will be a period of at least a year before Russian economy could be resuscitated and incorporated into the German system.

d. The extent of the economic strain on Germany is indicated by the following: at present there are 6½ million men under arms in the German army, 100,000 in the German Navy, and 1½ million in the German Air Force. Behind this armed front, there are 8½ million men engaged in armaments works alone, about half of whom are working in steel industries. Nearly 17 million men are directly engaged in this war, to the exclusion of all normal civil pursuits and production. Hence, there is a very heavy drain on the social and economic structure of the state. Destruction of that structure will virtually break down the capacity of the German nation to wage war. The basic conception on which this plan is based lies in the application of air power for the breakdown of the industrial and economic structure of Germany. This conception involves the selection of a system of objectives vital to continued German war effort, and to the means of livelihood of the German people, and tena-ciously *concentrating all bombing* toward destruction of those objectives. The most effective manner of conducting such a decisive offensive is by destruction of precise objectives, at least initially. As German morale begins to crack, area bomb-ing of civil concentrations may be effective.

e. It is improbable that a land invasion can be carried out against Germany proper within the next three years. If the air offensive is successful, a land offen-sive may not be necessary.

2. The Naval and Air Campaigns Against German U-Boats and Cities Receive High Priority at the Casablanca Conference, January, 1943

Combined Chiefs of Staff Minutes, January 14, 1943

[General Marshall] repeated that our first concern must be the defeat of Germany's submarine warfare.

[British Air Chief] SIR CHARLES PORTAL then said that the British Chiefs of Staff also felt that the defeat of the submarine menace must be given first priority in the use of air power, particularly in the protection of our line of communications. . . .

SIR CHARLES PORTAL said that the air had proved the most effective weapon against the U-boat. The estimated German output of U-boats was twenty a month. He gave the following figures for attacks on U-boats during the last two months:

		November	*December*
U-Boats sunk / U-Boats damaged	by aircraft	8 / 24	2 / 9
U-Boats sunk / U-Boats damaged	by other means	8 / 7	6 / 6

Air patrols over the U-boat routes to the hunting grounds were very costly in aircraft since it was calculated that there was only one sighting for 250 hours flying time. Nevertheless, even if a large number of U-boats were not actually destroyed by this means, aircraft patrols had a good effect in compelling U-boats to remain submerged and thereby reducing their time on the hunting grounds. A further method of attack on U-boats was the laying of mines from the air at the exits of the U-boat bases and construction yards.

From U.S. Department of State, *Foreign Relations of the United States: The Conferences at Washing-ton, 1941–1942, and Casablanca, 1943* (Washington, D.C.: U.S. Government Printing Office, 1968), 545, 565, 774, 781–782.

GENERAL ARNOLD inquired whether it was not possible to use flying boats for anti-submarine work, both over the hunting grounds and on the routes to them. This would avoid the use of valuable long-range bombers.

SIR CHARLES PORTAL said that the long-range bomber was essential for work over the convoys, since flying boats, owing to their slow speed, took too long to reach them after a call for assistance. Moreover, the load of the flying boat in bombs and depth charges was less than that of the Liberator. . . . A considerable number of Catalinas were being used in spite of these disadvantages. It was estimated that the minimum requirements for the whole of the Atlantic and British Home Waters was between 120 and 135 long-range bombers. . . .

Memorandum by the Combined Chiefs of Staff, January 19, 1943

CONDUCT OF THE WAR IN 1943

The Combined Chiefs of Staff have agreed to submit the following recommendations for the conduct of the war in 1943.

1. *Security:*
    The defeat of the U-boat must remain a first charge on the resources of the United Nations.
2. *Assistance to Russia:*
    The Soviet forces must be sustained by the greatest volume of supplies that can be transported to Russia without prohibitive cost in shipping.
3. *Operations in the European Theater:*
    Operations in the European Theater will be conducted with the object of defeating Germany in 1943 with the maximum forces that can be brought to bear upon her by the United Nations.
4. The main lines of offensive action will be:
    In the Mediterranean:
    (*a*) The occupation of Sicily with the object of:

    (1) Making the Mediterranean line of communications more secure.
    (2) Diverting German pressure from the Russian front.
    (3) Intensifying the pressure on Italy.

    (*b*) To create a situation in which Turkey can be enlisted as an active ally.
    In the U.K.:
    (*c*) The heaviest possible bomber offensive against the German war effort.
    (*d*) Such limited offensive operations as may be practicable with the amphibious forces available. . . .

Memorandum by the Combined Chiefs of Staff, January 21, 1943

THE BOMBER OFFENSIVE FROM THE UNITED KINGDOM

Directive to the appropriate British and U.S. Air Force Commanders, to govern the operation of the British and U.S. Bomber Commands in the United Kingdom (Approved by the Combined Chiefs of Staff at their 65th Meeting on January 21, 1943)

1. Your primary object will be the progressive destruction and dislocation of the German military, industrial and economic system, and the undermining of the

morale of the German people to a point where their capacity for armed resistance is fatally weakened.

2. Within that general concept, your primary objectives, subject to the exigencies of weather and of tactical feasibility, will for the present be in the following order of priority:

(*a*) German submarine construction yards.
(*b*) The German aircraft industry.
(*c*) Transportation.
(*d*) Oil plants.
(*e*) Other targets in enemy war industry.

The above order of priority may be varied from time to time according to developments in the strategical situation. Moreover, other objectives of great importance either from the political or military point of view must be attacked. Examples of these are:

(1) Submarine operating bases on the Biscay coast. If these can be put out of action, a great step forward will have been taken in the U-boat war which the C.C.S. [Combined Chiefs of Staff] have agreed to be a first charge on our resources. . . .

(2) Berlin, which should be attacked when conditions are suitable for the attainment of specially valuable results unfavorable to the morale of the enemy or favorable to that of Russia. . . .

5. You should take every opportunity to attack Germany by day, to destroy objectives that are unsuitable for night attack, to sustain continuous pressure on German morale, to impose heavy losses on the German day fighter force, and to contain German fighter strength away from the Russian and Mediterranean theaters of war.

3. A Mother Questions and General Henry H. "Hap" Arnold's Staff Defends the Bombing of German Cities, 1943

May 3, 1943

Dear Hap:

Last month my son Ted won his wings at Randolph Field. He is now going through a bombardment school, and in a short time expects to go to the front.

Will you tell me—has he become what our enemies call him, "A Hooligan of the Air?" Is he expected to scatter death on men, women, children—to wreck churches and shrines—to be a slaughterer, not a fighting man? . . .

Very sincerely,

/s/ Katherine A. Hooper
(Mrs. James E. Hooper)

From the Frederick L. Anderson Collection, Hoover Institution, Stanford University, Stanford, California; "Suggested Reply" reproduced in Conrad C. Crane, *Bombs, Cities, and Civilians* (Lawrence: University Press of Kansas, 1993), 163–164. Reprinted with permission from the Hoover Institution Archives.

Suggested Reply to Letters Questioning
Humanitarian Aspects of Air Force

The most fundamental difference between beast and man is in the fact that the beast is a realist, taking life at its face value, while man attempts by his emotions to camouflage, and thereby to make more bearable, unpleasant prospects which he faces.

War, no matter how glorious the cause, is horrible by every civilized standard. Clothing it in shining armor does not hide the blood and suffering except from him who would be blind; neither does changing the vehicle of destruction alter the fact that death and destruction form the inevitable body and face of war.

By drawing aside the curtain, we see air warfare as being different only in the range of its potential destruction. The air gives uncurbed bestial instincts a wider field of expression, leaving only humanity and common sense to dictate limitations. Law cannot limit what physics makes possible. We can depend for moderation only upon reason and humane instincts when we exercise such a power.

We believe that we are using those curbs to the proper extent in our application of Air Power, but I can well understand your confusion in the light of propaganda and misguided reports of air operations. The fact that no adequate explanation has ever been offered has likewise confused others in a much better position to understand.

All of us have seen the result of air power as used by the beast. To one such as he, any horror is justified so long as his end is accomplished. [B]ut he fails to realize that even his purpose could be better accomplished if he used methods which are more efficient and which happen, at the same time, to be most humane.

This can best be illustrated by our own concept of the proper role of air power in war. It works on the principle of the old adage to the effect that for the lack of a nail the house fell down. We take away the nail.

It has always been recognized that armies can be defeated through the killing of men; but are not modern armies as futile without weapons and equipment? The armored force is nothing without a tank, and we can take the tank by killing its occupants and, at the same time, suffering casualties on our part. But we can also take the tank away, in effect, "before it is born," thereby saving the casualties on both sides. We can hit the factory where it is built, the steel plant where the armor is made, or the refinery from which it gets its fuel. We do not mean the cities containing the factories, but by exercising the precision which is the keynote of America, we mean that we carefully select and, to the best of our ability, hit the precise spot which is most vital to the enemy. We hold no brief for terror bombing. True that will cause casualties on both sides, and there will still be ground fighting, but the final score in blood will be much less.

Those are the factors of reason and humanity which we allow to curb the awful weapon at our disposal. Those are the factors which the brute mind of the beast cannot conceive. With the understanding cooperation of you and thousands of others like you, we will prove to the beast that humanity pays and that Air Power is the most powerful urge for peace.

4. The City of Dresden Before and After the Anglo-American Bombings of February, 1945

View of the Frauenkirche in Dresden, Germany, 1945.

From Saxon State Library, Dresden, Germany; reproduced in Library of Congress, "Treasures of Saxon State Library," http://lcweb.loc.gov/exhibits/dres/dresphot.html.

View of the Frauenkirche in Dresden, Germany, summer, 1947, after Anglo-American bombing.

5. The Original OVERLORD Plan Proposes Landing on the Normandy Beaches and Explains the Problems to Be Overcome, July 27, 1943

The object of Operation "Overlord" is to mount and carry out an operation with forces and equipment established in the United Kingdom, and with target date the 1st of May, 1944, to secure a lodgement on the Continent from which further offensive operations can be developed. The lodgement area must contain sufficient port facilities to maintain a force of some twenty-six to thirty divisions, and enable that force to be augmented by follow-up shipments from the United States or elsewhere of additional divisions and supporting units of the rate of three to five divisions per month.

Selection of a Lodgement Area

. . . 4. [T]aking beach capacity and air and naval considerations together, it appears that either the Pas de Calais area or the Caen-Cotentin [Normandy] area is the most suitable for the initial main landing.

From U.S. Department of State, *Foreign Relations of the United States: The Conferences at Washington and Quebec,* 1943 (Washington, D.C.: U.S. Government Printing Office, 1970), 488–496.

5. As the area for the initial landing, the Pas de Calais has many obvious advantages such that good air support and quick turn round for our shipping can be achieved. On the other hand, it is a focal point of the enemy fighters disposed for defence, and maximum enemy air activity can be brought to bear over this area with the minimum movement of his air forces. Moreover, the Pas de Calais is the most strongly defended area on the whole French coast. The defences would require very heavy and sustained bombardment from sea and air: penetration would be slow, and the result of the bombardment of beach exits would severely limit the rate of build-up. Further, this area does not offer good opportunities for expansion. It would be necessary to develop the bridgehead to include either the Belgian ports as far as Antwerp or the Channel ports Westwards to include Havre and Rouen. But both an advance to Antwerp across the numerous water obstacles, and a long flank march of some 120 miles to the Seine ports must be considered unsound operations of war unless the German forces are in a state not far short of final collapse. . . .

8. . . . The Caen Sector is weakly held; the defences are relatively light and the beaches are of high capacity and sheltered from the prevailing winds. Inland the terrain is suitable for airfield development and for the consolidation of the initial bridgehead; and much of it is unfavorable for counterattacks by Panzer divisions. Maximum enemy air opposition can only be brought to bear at the expense of the enemy air defence screen covering the approaches to Germany; and the limited number of enemy airfields within range of the Caen area facilitates local neutralisation of the German fighter force. The sector suffers from the disadvantage that considerable effort will be required to provide adequate air support to our assault forces and some time must elapse before the capture of a major port.

After a landing in the Caen sector it would be necessary to seize either the Seine group of ports or the Brittany group of ports. To seize the Seine ports would entail forcing a crossing of the Seine, which is likely to require greater forces than we can build up through the Caen beaches and the port of Cherbourg. It should, however, be possible to seize the Brittany ports between Cherbourg and Nantes and on them build up sufficient forces for our final advance Eastwards.

Provided that the necessary air situation can first be achieved, the chances of a successful attack and of rapid subsequent development are so much greater in this sector than in any other that it is considered that the advantages far outweigh the disadvantages.

The Lodgement Area Selected

9. In the light of these factors, it is considered that our initial landing on the Continent should be effected in Caen area, with a view to the eventual seizure of a lodgement area comprising the Cherbourg-Brittany group of ports (from Cherbourg to Nantes).

Opening Phase up to the Capture of Cherbourg

. . . 11. The main limiting factors affecting such an operation are the possibility of attaining the necessary air situation; the number of offensive divisions which the enemy can make available for counter attack in the Caen area; the availability of landing ships and craft and of transport aircraft; and the capacity of the beaches and ports in the sector. . . .

Major Conditions Affecting Success of the Operation

32. It will be seen that the plan for the initial landing is based on two main principles—concentration of forces and tactical surprise. Concentration of the assault forces is considered essential if we are to ensure adequate air support and if our limited assault forces are to avoid defeat in detail. An attempt has been made to obtain tactical surprise by landing in a lightly defended area—presumably lightly defended as, due to its distance from a major port, the Germans consider a landing there unlikely to be successful. This action, of course, presupposes that we can offset the absence of a port in the initial stages by the provision of improvised sheltered waters. It is believed that this can be accomplished.

33. The operation calls for a much higher standard of performance on the part of the naval assault forces than any previous operation. This will depend upon their being formed in sufficient time to permit of adequate training.

34. Above all, it is essential that there should be an over-all reduction in the German fighter force between now and the time of the surface assault. From now onwards every practical method of achieving this end must be employed. This condition, above all others, will dictate the date by which the amphibious assault can be launched.

35. The next condition is that the number of German offensive divisions in reserve must not exceed a certain figure on the target date if the operation is to have a reasonable chance of success. The German reserves in France and the Low Countries as a whole, excluding divisions holding the coast, G. A. F. [German Air Force] divisions and training divisions, should not exceed on the day of the assault twelve full-strength first-quality divisions. In addition, the Germans should not be able to transfer more than fifteen first-quality divisions from Russia during the first two months. Moreover, on the target date the divisions in reserve should be so located that the number of first-quality divisions which the Germans could deploy in the Caen area to support the divisions holding the coast should not exceed three divisions on D day, five divisions by D plus 2, or nine divisions by D plus 8.

During the preliminary period, therefore, every effort must be made to dissipate and divert German formations, lower their fighting efficiency and disrupt communications.

36. Finally, there is the question of maintenance. Maintenance will have to be carried out over beaches for a period of some three months for a number of formations, varying from a maximum of eighteen divisions in the first month to twelve divisions in the second month, rapidly diminishing to nil in the third month. Unless adequate measures are taken to provide sheltered waters by artificial means, the operation will be at the mercy of the weather. Moreover, special facilities and equipment will be required to prevent undue damage to craft during this extended period. Immediate action for the provision of the necessary requirements is essential.

37. Given these conditions—a reduced G. A. F., a limitation in the number or effectiveness of German offensive formations in France, and adequate arrangements to provide improvised sheltered waters—it is considered that Operation "Overlord" has

a reasonable prospect of success. To ensure these conditions being attained by the 1st May, 1944, action must start *now* and every possible effort made by all means in our power to soften German resistance and to speed up our own preparations.

6. General Dwight D. Eisenhower Addresses Allied Forces on D-Day, June 6, 1944

Soldiers, Sailors and Airmen of the Allied Expeditionary Force:

You are about to embark upon the Great Crusade, toward which we have striven these many months. The eyes of the world are upon you. The hopes and prayers of liberty-loving people everywhere march with you. In company with our brave Allies and brothers-in-arms on other Fronts you will bring about the destruction of the German war machine, the elimination of Nazi tyranny over oppressed peoples of Europe, and security for ourselves in a free world.

Your task will not be an easy one. Your enemy is well trained, well equipped and battle-hardened. He will fight savagely.

But this is the year 1944! Much has happened since the Nazi triumphs of 1940–41. The United Nations have inflicted upon the Germans great defeats, in open battle, man-to-man. Our air offensive has seriously reduced their strength in the air and their capacity to wage war on the ground. Our Home Fronts have given us an overwhelming superiority in weapons and munitions of war, and placed at our disposal great reserves of trained fighting men. The tide has turned! The free men of the world are marching together to Victory!

I have full confidence in your courage, devotion to duty and skill in battle. We will accept nothing less than full victory!

Good luck! And let us all beseech the blessing of Almighty God upon this great and noble undertaking.

Dwight D. Eisenhower

7. Generals Eisenhower and Montgomery Debate Broad- Versus Narrow-Front Strategies, September, 1944

September 15, 1944

Dear Montgomery:

. . . I have been considering our next move.

As I see it, the Germans will have stood in defense of the Ruhr and Frankfurt and will have had a sharp defeat inflicted on them. Their dwindling forces, reinforced

---

(Document 6) From Forrest C. Pogue, *The Supreme Command,* a volume in *United States Army in World War II* (Washington, D.C.: U.S. Government Printing Office, 1945), 545.

(Document 7) From Eisenhower Papers, Eisenhower Presidential Library, Abilene, Kans.; reproduced in *The Papers of Dwight David Eisenhower: The War Years,* vol. 4, ed. Alfred D. Chandler, Jr. (Baltimore: Johns Hopkins Press, 1970), 2148–2149, 2164–2165; and in *The Memoirs of Field-Marshal Montgomery* (Cleveland: World Publishing Co., 1958), 248–253.

perhaps by material hastily scratched together or dragged from other theaters, will probably try to check our advance on the remaining important objectives in Germany. By attacking such objectives we shall create opportunities of dealing effectively with the last remnants of the German forces in the West. Moreover, we shall be occupying further key centers and increasing our stranglehold on the German peoples.

Clearly, Berlin is the main prize, and the prize in defense of which the enemy is likely to concentrate the bulk of his forces. There is no doubt whatsoever, in my mind, that we should concentrate all our energies and resources on a rapid thrust to Berlin.

Our strategy, however, will have to be coordinated with that of the Russians, so we must also consider alternative objectives.

There is the area of the northern ports, Kiel-Lubeck-Hamburg-Bremen. Its occupation would not only give us control of the German Navy and North Sea bases, of the Kiel Canal and of a large industrial area, but would enable us to form a barrier against the withdrawal of German forces from Norway and Denmark. Further, this area, or a part of it, might have to be occupied as flank protection to our thrust on Berlin.

There are the areas Hanover–Brunswick and Leipzig–Dresden. They are important industrial and administrative areas and centers of communications, on the direct routes from the Ruhr and Frankfurt to Berlin, so the Germans will probably hold them as intermediate positions covering Berlin.

There are the Nurnberg-Regensburg and the Augsburg-Munich areas. Apart from their economical and administrative importance, there is the transcending political importance of Munich. Moreover, there may be an impelling demand to occupy these areas and cut off enemy forces withdrawing from Italy and the Balkans.

Clearly, therefore, our objectives cannot be precisely determined until nearer the time, so we must be prepared for one or more of the following:

    a. To direct forces of both Army Groups on Berlin astride the axes Ruhr-Hanover-Berlin *or* Frankfurt-Leipzig-Berlin, *or* both.
    b. Should the Russians beat us to Berlin, the Northern Group of Armies would seize the Hanover area and the Hamburg group of ports. The Central Group of Armies would seize part, or the whole, of Leipzig-Dresden, depending upon the progress of the Russian advance.
    c. In any event, the Southern Group of Armies would seize Augsburg-Munich. The area Nurnberg-Regensburg would be seized by Central or Southern Group of Armies, depending on the situation at the time.

Simply stated, it is my desire to move on Berlin by the most direct and expeditious route, with combined U.S.-British forces supported by other available forces moving through key centers and occupying strategic areas on the flanks, all in one coordinated, concerted operation.

It is not possible at this stage to indicate the timing of these thrusts or their strengths, but I shall be glad to have your views on the general questions raised in this letter.

Sincerely,

[Dwight D. Eisenhower]

18th September

My dear Ike,

I have received your letter dated 15-9-44, and I give below my general views on the questions you raise—as asked for by you.

1. I suggest that the whole matter as to what is possible, and what is NOT possible, is very closely linked up with the administrative situation. The vital factor is time; what we have to do, we must do quickly.
2. In view of para. 1, it is my opinion that a concerted operation in which all the available land armies move forward into Germany is not possible; the maintenance resources, and the general administrative situation, will not allow of this being done QUICKLY.
3. But forces adequate in strength for the job in hand could be supplied and maintained, provided the general axis of advance was suitable, and provided these forces had complete priority in all respects as regards maintenance.
4. It is my own personal opinion that we shall not achieve what we want by going for objectives such as Nurnberg, Augsburg, Munich, etc., and by establishing our forces in central Germany.
5. I consider that the best objective is the Ruhr, and thence on to Berlin by the northern route. . . .
6. If you agree with para. 5, then I consider that 21 Army Group, plus First U.S. Army of nine divisions, would be adequate. Such a force must have *everything it needed in the maintenance line*; other Armies would do the best they could with what was left over.
7. If you consider that para. 5 is not right, and that the proper axis of advance is by Frankfurt and central Germany, then I suggest that 12 Army Group of three Armies would be used and would have all the maintenance. 21 Army Group would do the best it could with what was left over; or possibly the Second British Army would be wanted in a secondary role on the left flank of the movement.
8. In brief, I consider that as time is so very important, we have got to decide what is necessary to go to Berlin and finish the war; the remainder must play a secondary role. It is my opinion that three Armies are enough, if you select the northern route, and I consider that, from a maintenance point of view, it could be done. I have not studied the southern route.
9. I consider that our plan, and objectives, should be decided NOW, and everything arranged accordingly. I would not myself agree that we can wait until nearer the time, as suggested in your letter.
10. Finally to sum up.
    I recommend the northern route of advance via the Ruhr, vide para. 5.
    Para. 6 would then apply. . . .

Yours ever

(Sgd) B. L. Montgomery

20th September

Dear Monty,

Generally speaking I find myself so completely in agreement with your letter of 18 September (M-526) that I cannot believe there is any great difference in our concepts.

Never at any time have I implied that I was considering an advance into Germany with all armies moving abreast.

Specifically I agree with you in the following: My choice of routes for making the all-out offensive into Germany is from the Ruhr to Berlin. A prerequisite from the maintenance viewpoint is the early capture of the approaches to Antwerp so that that flank may be adequately supplied.

Incidentally I do not yet have your calculations in the tonnage that will be necessary to support the 21 Army Group on this move. There is one point, however, on which we do not agree, if I interpret your ideas correctly. As I read your letter you imply that all the divisions that we have, except those of the 21st Army Group and approximately nine of the 12th Army Group, can stop in place *where they are* and that we can strip all these additional divisions from their transport and everything else to support one single knife-like drive towards Berlin. This may not be exactly what you mean but it is certainly not possible.

What I do believe is that we must marshal our strength up along the Western borders of Germany, to the Rhine if possible, insure adequate maintenance by getting Antwerp working at full blast at the earliest possible moment and then carry out the drive you suggest. All of Bradley's Army Group, except his left Army, which makes his main effort, will move forward sufficiently so as always to be in supporting position for the main drive and to prevent concentration of German forces against its front and flanks. . . .

As you know I have been giving preference to my left all the way through this campaign including attaching the First Airborne Force to you and adopting every possible expedient to assure your maintenance. All other forces have been fighting with a halter around their necks in the way of supplies. You may not know that for four days straight Patton has been receiving serious counterattacks and during the last seven days, without attempting any real advance himself, has captured about 9000 prisoners and knocked out 270 tanks. . . .

Sincerely,

(Sgd) Dwight D. Eisenhower

21st September

Dear Ike, thank you very much for your letter of 20 Sep sent via Gale. I cannot agree that our concepts are the same and I am sure you would wish me to be quite frank and open in the matter. I have always said stop the right and go with left, but the right has been allowed to go on so far that it has outstripped its maintenance and we have lost flexibility. In your letter you still want to go on further with your right and you state in your para. 6 that all of Bradley's Army Group will move forward sufficiently etc. I would say that the right flank of 12 Army Group should be given a very direct order to halt and if this order is not obeyed we shall get into greater difficulties. The net result of the matter in my opinion is that if you want to get the Ruhr you will have to put every single thing into the left hook and stop everything else. It is my opinion that if this is not done then you will not get the Ruhr. Your very great friend Monty.

8. General Marshall Explains the Key Military Events in German Defeat as Perceived by Captured Members of the German High Command, September, 1945

The steps in the German defeat, as described by captured members of the High Command, were:

1. *Failure to invade England.* Hitler's first military setback occurred when, after the collapse of France, England did not capitulate. According to Colonel General Jodl, Chief of the Operations Staff of the German High Command, the campaign in France had been undertaken because it was estimated that with the fall of France, England would not continue to fight. The unexpectedly swift victory over France and Great Britain's continuation of the war found the General Staff unprepared for an invasion of England. . . .

2. *The Campaign of 1941 in the Soviet Union.* In the autumn of 1941 after the battle of Vysma, the Germans stood exhausted but apparently victorious before Moscow. According to Jodl, the General Staff of the armed forces considered that one last energetic push would be sufficient to finish the Soviets. The German High Command had neither envisioned nor planned for a winter campaign. A sudden change in the weather brought disaster. The Red Army defense, a terrific snowstorm, and extremely unseasonable cold in the Christmas week of 1941 precipitated the strategic defeat of the German armed forces. Impatient of all restraint, Hitler publicly announced that he had more faith in his own intuition than in the judgment of his military advisers. He relieved the Commander in Chief of the Army, General Von Brauschitsch. It was the turning point of the war.

3. *Stalingrad.* Even after the reverse before Moscow in 1941, Germany might have avoided defeat had it not been for the campaign in 1942 which culminated in the disaster at Stalingrad. Disregarding the military lessons of history, Hitler, instead of attacking the Soviet armies massed in the north, personally planned and directed a campaign of which the immediate objectives were to deprive the Soviet Union of her vital industries and raw materials by cutting the Volga at Stalingrad and seizing the Caucasian oil fields. Beyond these concrete objectives was evidently the Napoleonic dream of a conquest of the Middle East and India by a gigantic double envelopment with one pincer descending from the Caucasus through Tiflis and the other from North Africa across Egypt, Palestine, and the Arabian

From *Biennial Report of the Chief of Staff of the United States Army, July 1, 1943 to June 30, 1945, to the Secretary of War;* reprinted in *World War II Policy and Strategy: Selected Documents with Commentary,* ed. Hans-Adolf Jacobsen and Arthur L. Smith (Santa Barbara, Calif.: ABC-Clio, 1979), 331–333.

desert. The campaign collapsed before Stalingrad with the magnificent Russian defense of that city and in the northern foothills of the Caucasus. . . .

4. *Invasion of North Africa.* Allied landings in North Africa came as a surprise to the German High Command. . . . Allied security and deception measures for the landing operations were found to have been highly effective. . . .

5. *The Invasion of France.* All German headquarters expected the Allied invasion of France. According to Colonel General Jodl, both the general direction and the strength of the initial assault in Normandy were correctly estimated; but Field Marshal Keitel states that the Germans were not sure exactly where the Allies would strike and considered Brittany as more probable because of the three major U-boat bases located in that region. Both agree that the belief of the German High Command that a second assault would be launched, probably by an army under General Patton, held large German forces in the Pas-de-Calais area. Both Keitel and Jodl believed that the invasion could be repulsed or at worst contained, and both named the Allied air arm as the decisive factor in the German failure. . . .

6. *The Ardennes Counterattack.* The German offensive in December 1944 was Hitler's personal conception. According to Jodl, the objective of the attack was Antwerp. It was hoped that overcast weather would neutralize Allied air superiority, and that an exceptionally rapid initial break-through could be achieved. Other German officers believe that this operation was reckless in the extreme, in that it irreparably damaged the comparatively fresh armored divisions of the Sixth Panzer Army, the principal element of Germany's strategic reserve, at a moment when every available reserve was needed to repulse the expected Soviet attack in the east.

7. *The Crossing of the Rhine.* Even after the failure of the German counter-offensive in the Ardennes, the Germans believed that the Rhine line could be held. The loss of the Remagen bridge, however, exploded this hope. The entire Rhine defensive line had to be weakened in the attempt to contain the bridgehead, and the disorderly German retreat in the Saar and Palatinate rendered easy the subsequent drive eastward of the Allied armies toward Hamburg, Leipzig, and Munich.

9. Tuskeegee Airman Lieutenant Alexander Jefferson Recalls His Combat Missions and Imprisonment, 1944

I wish that I had a detailed record of the missions that I flew. I flew as a wing man on the 18 missions in just over one month, tail end Charlie most of the time or near it. I made every mission that was scheduled from the first P-51 flights until I was shot down on August 12, 1944. All of the missions were long range escort missions, escorting B-24s and B-17s to targets in Greece, Bulgaria, Hungary, Poland, Germany and France. I did not have my own plane, I always flew the extra until just before my last mission. I named her "Margo." Planes were arriving and new engines were being installed. Older pilots began to claim the first available planes as their own. As a replacement, I had to wait my turn.

From Alexander Jefferson, "Memoirs of a Luft Gan[g]ster" (unpublished).

A Typical Mission

Weather was warm. Three men in the tent now that Dickson was gone, Elsberry, Faulkner and me. . . . We would mark course, altitude, position, bomber ID and other fighter ID on a pad that strapped on the knee. Maps would be marked and folded. Intelligence would then come forth and give the latest flack report, which areas to avoid because of heavy flak concentration. And it invariably turned out to be wrong. We would encounter the most devastating flak over some areas that intelligence had said was perfectly safe. We still laughed at intelligence. The weather officer would then give us the weather condition to the target and back. They would then give us the latest information on partisan activity in the area in case you are forced down. Davis would then indicate which squadron would lead the group that day and end with instruction about radio silence, tight formation and protect the bombers, and who is in second command. We would hack watches on time, take off time given . . . the order of squadron take off given. Planes, meanwhile, had been preflighted. The mechanics had been up maybe all night. We would then pile out of the briefing shack, get in jeeps and trucks and ride to our planes. We would walk around the plane, talk with the crew chief, find out what to expect the ship to do etc., strap in, start engines on certain time, watching dials, feet on brakes trying to keep 2500 pounds of plane from moving, 92 gallons of gas in each wing, 100 gallons hanging under each wing, 85 gallons in a tank behind you, three 50 caliber guns in each wing with 300 rounds for each gun, with that big eleven foot prop spinning and the 1500 HP pulling, your pulse starts to race when you look down the line and see fifteen other planes of your squadron slowly ease forward and turn 30 degrees and start to taxi down the ramp. The canopy is still open, the noise is deafening but exhilarating. You just hope that the bastard behind you doesn't let up on his brakes and chew your tail off, or that so and so on your left has his gun switch off and keeps his finger off the trigger so that he doesn't blow you to smithereens. You sit there, the plane vibrating, throbbing, shaking, threatening to move, [y]our legs are tied in knots with heels on brakes, the air is filled with fumes and dust. Funny how it gets into the oxygen mask. You just sit there locked in, can't move, a big prop chewing on your left and your prop threatening the guy on your right. And then you look to your left and watch the 99th start taking off down the strip toward you and the first few guys pass about 50 feet out in front of you. Then as number five and six start to hit the turbulence of the previous guys, they start to waiver left and right. And then you look up and a P-51 with two wing tanks full and that big eleven foot prop sails over your head with about 10 to 15 feet to spare! The rest straggle and fight turbulence. When the 18 get off . . . 16 plus 2 spares, it becomes 301st turn to take off. . . . Four squadrons, 64 planes, off to pick up the B-17s that left Foggia about three hours ago. We might pick them up about 200 miles inside Hungary on the way to Ploesti. We would relieve another fighter group who would have to return to base because of low fuel. . . .

Many escort missions were monotonous 5 and 6 hour rides. My fourth or fifth mission was a wild ride. The group got eight or nine kills and I didn't see a single one. I was too busy flying my element's wing and watching our rear end. . . .

My first mission to Ploesti will stay with [me] until I die. It was an uneventful escort from the border of Hungary and Romania where we picked up the bomber string. . . . relieving another P-51 group that had carried them that far. They encountered sporadic anti-aircraft fire on the way to the target.

And then I saw, far ahead, 15 or 20 miles, a huge black cloud, shaped like a hockey puck, from 20,000 feet to about 26,000 feet. There was a series of fires and smoke rising from the ground underneath it, which appeared to be an oil refinery complex. The B-17s flew out on a 60 degree angle and then aimed directly for that black cloud. We pulled off to the left and orbited while they disappeared into the black cloud. Then we saw four or five 17's falling out of the bottom of the cloud, spinning down lazily, trailing smoke and flame, we unconsciously yelled, "Bail out damned it. . . . get out!" Then we counted, one . . . two . . . three chutes coming out and opening up, and then with a big whoosh . . . a B-17 would explode in a huge red ball of flame, and realism would hit you . . . three chutes . . . that meant seven men died, right there in front of your eyes . . . seven men gone. I got sick at 31,000 feet inside of my oxygen mask. It is burned into the back of my mind . . . I'll never forget. My crew-chief refused to clean out my oxygen mask. . . .

I was shot down by ground fire, 20 mm fire, Friday, August 12, 1944, while strafing radar stations on the coast of Southern France, Toulon Harbor at 1047 hours. The radar stations at that time were possibly second in secrecy only to the atomic bomb. The 332nd was assigned the task of knocking them out previous to the proposed invasion on the 15th. Each squadron was assigned a target, the 301st was assigned Toulon. Those radar stations must be destroyed to prevent them detecting American troop ship[s] and directing gun fire. There had been a stand down for three days prior to that mission, but we did not know what the mission was going to be until we walked into the briefing room that morning. The day was a beautiful clear day, unlimited visibility and warm. Sixteen planes went over at 15,000 feet and then split-s down to hit the target at low level and high speed, and then out to sea on the deck. My tanks were hung up and I was slow in getting them off when the squadron leader called for them to be dropped. By the time we were down to 300 feet and indicating more than 400 mph, I was in position. . . . Tail-End-Charlie, the last man in the formation. Looking up ahead I could see the first flight of four getting hits on the towers and veering out to sea. Then the second flight of four right behind them getting hits on target and veering out to sea, followed by the third flight and then we came into position. Air speed was above 400 mph, ship was bucking and shaking, a couple of the needles were in the red, the oil pressure and coolant temp . . . everything else was in the top of the green, about to go red. Targets came into range and we started firing, and as we did so, out of the corner of my eye I saw Robert Daniels get hit, a black explosion was seen on the bottom of his fuselage. He started to veer out to sea. The whole side of the sea wall appeared to be covered with little red lights, blinking on and off. Tremendous anti aircraft fire was coming up against us. I fired on a tower and got good hits. As I passed over the target at about 50 feet, there was a loud thump, that shook the plane. I glanced at the instrument panel, everything was in the red. I was startled and looked up and suddenly there was a hole in the top of the canopy just in front of my head, and I said to myself, "What the hell." Then when I looked down, fire was coming up through a hole in the floor in front of the stick between my feet scorching my gloves and boots. So . . . pull up into a loop. While going up, reach forward, pull the red knob and pop the canopy, rack in forward trim tab on the elevator with the left hand. . . . When on the top of the loop, punch the safety belt release, coordinated with letting the stick go, and the forward trim tab would pitch the nose down, but in this case since the plane is upside down, the nose would go up and I was thrown out.

As the tail went by, I can still see it, even noticing the rivets, I pulled the "D" ring, the rip cord, and remember looking at the "D" ring in my hand and saying to myself, "Those ^%$##@&*'s sold the silk." (The chute had not yet opened and the rumor back at the base that there had been someone who was stealing the silk out of the parachutes and selling it to the Italians.) Just then the chute popped, and all I could see was green, I was going down through the trees and I hit squarely on my feet. Good thing that I was wearing paratrooper jump boots, giving extra support to my ankles. I figured that I got out at about 800 feet.

Intelligence had instructed us that, if you parachute into French territory, dig a hole, hide your chute, lay low and contact the Free French who were in the area. Well, I hit the ground, rolled over, looked up into the muzzle of a mauser, and the German soldier said, "Yah, Auch Zo . . . Yah. Leointnant . . . Yah Neger . . . Vor you, der var ist ovar." They were the very gun crew that shot me down, I landed right in the midst of them.

I was Tail-End-Charlie. No one saw me get out. When the flights looked back, all they saw was the plane go in and explode and they thought that I had bought the farm. A "KIA" (Killed In Action) telegram was sent to my parents. They found out of my being a POW a month later through the Red Cross. . . .

Then [I was] taken to a villa, on the sea, ushered onto the veranda, at which a German officer sat at a glass topped table. I saluted, and he replied in perfect English, "Have a seat Lieutenant, thanks for the Lucky Strikes!" After having been bombarded by German soldiers, this floored me. He then asked how were things in the States. I replied "fine." He then asked if I had ever been in Michigan, of course I said, "No Sir," name, rank serial number. He then asked if I had ever been in Atlanta, of course I said, "No Sir," although I had spent four years in the attending Clark College. He then asked if I had ever been in Washington, D.C., which I said, "No Sir," although I attended Howard University. He then reminisced about his days at the University of Michigan, naming streets, fraternity houses, eating places, and his fond inspection on the plane that I had flown; my crew chief's entire school record. I simply sat there and smoked his cigarettes, they had taken mine away. He had my entire collegiate record of Clark College and Howard University. . . .

Our arrival in camp was met with a certain aloofness. Many of the men avoided us, almost acting that we did not exist. A few were curious, as to our rank, position and how did we get in uniform and what were we flying. There was never a hint of outward racism. And then, five days later, men came in from a bomber group in the 15th, and when they saw me, they yelled, ran over hugged me and exclaimed in loud accolades, "If the Red Tails had been our top cover, we wouldn't have been shot down. Those Sons-o-Bitches always brought us back home!!!!" The word spread throughout the camp, the Red Tails of the 15th never lost a bomber that they escorted to German fighters. Morgan and Hathcock had been flying P-40s, performing ground support, which was not as sensitive and far reaching. Immediately, the word spread that Black men were flying P-51s, long range escort, and hadn't lost a bomber. We made a lot of friends, many who are close friends today.

10. Sergeant Bernard Bellush Recalls D-Day on Omaha Beach, November 14, 1944/March 16, 2000

During the evening of June 3rd, our LST [landing ship, tank] 376 pulled up anchor and headed out for the open channel waters, only to be called back to port at about 0700 the following morning. The channel was too stormy for an amphibious assault. This respite was shortlived for the evening of the 4th found us off again, this time to be halted only when 10 miles off the French coastline. We slept fairly well that night. During the morning of the 5th, after hearing the announcement over the loud-speaker that, "France is now dead ahead," we cleaned our carbines, had our final briefing and made last minute preparations. As far as the eye could see were LST's, and their rhinos [pontoon barges] in tow, LCT's [landing craft, tank], LCC's [land-ing craft, control] with their tremendous antennae, and American destroyers flitting between their protected breed. Navy men aboard our LST were continuously at battle stations, with look-outs identifying the endless squadrons of friendly planes flying overhead towards France. All was in readiness for any eventuality, yet tragedy, in the form of a torpedo, was to strike her a few days later. In the early after-noon the First team assembled forward on the top deck for mixed services. Sgt. Bernard Bellush of The Bronx, N.Y., read the convocation and offered the sermon, while Sgt. Sam Godino of Jersey City, N.J., led us in The Lord's Prayer. With this completed we returned to our "cubby holes" to while away the time playing cards, reading or just talking. Darkness finally descended and we tried to snatch a few hours of sleep. About 0300 on June 6th the motors went dead—we were 10 miles from France. The Navy "Huskies" aboard rocket firing speedboats were lowered away to the rough waters and then slid off into the darkness. Within an hour, the 105 Howitzer-laden dukws [army amphibious truck] backed out of the tank deck into the water and then moved off. All was in readiness for our transfer to the rhino ferry which was to carry us to shore. Off in the distance could be seen flashes of explod-ing shells and rockets. Finally, when darkness gave way to light, we found ourselves surrounded by LST's, troop transports and smaller type vessels. Overhead P-38's flew by in an unending line, ranging over the entire sky. We anxiously waited for the rhino-ferry to swing around and back up to the bow of the ship. Twice the rough waters squelched the plans of the Seabees, but the third attempt was successful. We shook hands all around as we said farewell to our navy friends, many who now lie interred with the 376 in Davey Jones' locker. May their stay there be peaceful. . . .

The water was choppy, and though we rocked slightly—and continued to do so for days after hitting the beach—men of the first team became sick. We were eleven miles out to sea when we started for shore and so did not come close to land until 1300 hours. There was little movement on shore. Shells could be seen burst-ing on all sides, with many vehicles aflame. An LCI [landing craft, infantry] ordered us back and we heaved a deep sigh of relief, especially after seeing the rhino dead ahead of us receive direct hits and burst into flames. Things looked bad. As we moved aimlessly, paralleling the beach, mention was heard of this invasion

From Bernard Bellush, "The Making of an Ammunition Company" (616th Ord. Amm. Co.), November 14, 1944, National Archives, and author's March 16, 2000, afterword.

being a failure, and our returning to England for another year of training and preparation. This pessimist was quickly corrected by the expressed thoughts of another who maintained that we couldn't fail. We had unlimited, and overpowering, supplies of men and material. And we had complete mastery of the skies. No! Success was inevitable. They couldn't stop us. In the midst of these thoughts we were ordered onto the beach once more by a passing LCC which told us to "Get going." On went our packs and pistol belts, as we silently prayed for our safety, while verbally cursing the cumbersome loads on our shoulders. Later, we were to be grateful that we had kept most of our stuff, especially the blankets.

As we approached the shrapnel-strewn shore a second time, an LCI with a loudspeaker attached, told us to "get the hell away from the beach." And once more we felt deeply relieved. The boys on the beach were going through hell. . . .

And what of the third team of the company? They had left their transport on two LCVP's [landing craft, vehicle and personnel], led by Lt. Bertram I. Sherman, of Cleveland Heights, Ohio, and Lt. Richard D. Cameron, of Battle Creek, Michigan. After circling for over an hour with eight other LCVP's, they headed for shore, but only four of these vessels beached at about 1330 hours. The other six had found things too hot because of 88 shells, and machine gun fire which had ricocheted off the front ramps. Meanwhile some 80 per cent of the men became sick—and were they sick. With the lowering of the front ramps the men jumped into water up to their necks, and shuffled shorewards for the psychological protection of the beach. [There they found] the rock-laden sands already strewn with wounded and dead. The time table had been upset. We were lying side by side with the infantrymen of the 26th Regt. of the First Division. We had been warned time and again, but had never believed, that we might someday be fighting alongside infantrymen. Shrapnel was hitting all about us, cutting through the trousers of our evil-smelling impregnated clothes (chemically treated against possible gas attacks), lifting helmets from heads and bodies from the ground. We crawled behind a wrecked LCI and LCT for protection, then edged farther up the beach behind stalled half-tracks. A few minutes after leaving the "protection" of those vehicles they were blown to smithereens by direct mortar hits. And before we could finally edge our way through the mine field to safe shelter at the base of the cliff, we left James S. Isbell, of Falkville, Alabama, a fervently religious lad, fatally wounded, and two shrapnel-hit men, James Devine, of Philadelphia, Pennsylvania, and Carl Umhelts, of Sunbury, Pennsylvania. We had had our first taste of actual combat, and we didn't like it. . . .

And so we all dug in for the night, hoping that falling ack-ack and enemy bombs—would not strike us. It was a cold, damp night of fitful snatches of sleep— a night to forget. Before dawn of D plus 1, we were told by messenger to prepare ourselves to advance to the front lines as replacements for the infantry. But the final orders never came through. Our footsloggers were suffering terrific casualties. . . .

On the morning of D plus 1 the third team sent two men in search of the separated group of twelve men. They eventually returned with them late in the afternoon. At the same time a group of men . . . were detailed . . . to remove German ammunition from a concrete emplacement on the beach. Despite possible booby traps attached to the German ammunition, American wounded lying within the emplacement, and mortar shells falling without, the dangerous task was completed by early afternoon. Outside the emplacement Father Schultz, our Catholic Chaplain from Washington, D.C., calmly gave last rites to our dying, as mortars and shrapnel continued to fall nearby.

Some other men were directed to unload the only munition-laden LCT to land safely on our beach. And they continued to do so despite mortar fire and exploding mines which shook you so that you soon felt that you had just been through a clothes wringer. They were shortly joined in this task by men from the separated group of the first team. Continued mortar firing, and increased temperature readings, made it uncomfortably hot as we struggled to empty the craft of its valuable cargo—the only reserve ammunition for our valiant fighting men up front. Have you ever lifted, and then carried, a 155mm shell across, and up a large pebble-strewn beach, with the sand giving way under every step, and then stacked them amongst our tarp-covered dead? It's a heartbreaking and wearying task. We finally left the work when ordered back to our outfit, which we rejoined late that afternoon. But before we left the beach we had been told by a Colonel from our Brigade that our ammunition company was the most important outfit on the beach that day. It is true that he exaggerated the situation, but we later learned that up to D plus 6, ours was the only ammunition dump on this beach supplying practically any ammunition to the boys up front.

By early evening of D plus 1, we were still unable to open either of the predetermined ASP [Ammunition Supply Point] sites, because the areas had not yet been demined. Thus, we set up shop about an eighth of a mile from the beach and ammunition started trickling and then flowing, in. We didn't have to go far to supply the artillery for our 105's were shooting from fields next to us. . . .

. . . We received and issued ammunition during the night of D plus 1, although the dump was often lit up as pre-war Times Square by the anti-aircraft fire which greeted Jerry flying overhead. Those of us who did have opportunity to rest fell asleep from sheer exhaustion and were not awakened by the AA [anti-aircraft] fire, falling ack-ack, nor even sniper or machine gun fire. We slept in the inevitable hedgerow of Normandy, which offered excellent natural protection. Most of us froze that night because the duffel bags containing our blankets had not yet arrived. . . .

. . . The S.O.P. (Standard Operating Procedure), set during maneuvers in Tennessee, S. Wales, and S. England, provided for a bivouac site some distance away from the ammunition. But this is war in all its reality, and cruelty. Thus, we camped in the hedgerows, surrounded on all sides by TNT, 155mm shells, charges, and ground force ammunition of all types. One lucky hit from Jerry's nightly visits and ——: well, lets forget about it. Our work was cut out for us and we did it, and we're darn proud of our achievements. . . .

Respectfully submitted by,
Sgt. Bernard Bellush, 32629761
November 14, 1944

Fifty-six years after the completion of this manuscript, I was able to secure a copy of it from the National Archives and read it once more. . . .

During a quick reading of the manuscript . . . , I realized that there were a number of instances where the narrative could have been more fully developed. One of

them was a very brief reference to a sermon I gave on LST 376 while we were crossing the English Channel, on our way to Omaha Beach. The other was too brief references to my feelings and actions as our rhino ferry approached the beach. So, let me
try to expand on at least these two events.

On that bitterly cold and blustery day of June 5th, as the Allied armada was
slowly making its way across the English Channel towards Omaha Beach, my
shortish commanding officer suddenly approached me. He remarked that there was
no Chaplain aboard our LST to conduct religious services and then said that he was
appointing me Acting Chaplain, but only for that day. My assignment was to
shortly conduct religious services for the men of our company. I called upon the
help of a Catholic as well as a Protestant member of our Army unit, and asked one
to read the Lord's Prayer and the other another relevant section from the Army
Prayer book. They did their chores after we gathered our unit together on the heav-
ing deck of this lumbering ship.

In the short space of time accorded me, I decided to offer a sermon based upon
the tragic but memorable experiences of the Jewish fighters of the Warsaw Ghetto.
Apparently, from reading the weekly *New Republic* magazine, which reached me
regularly overseas, I had learned about this comparatively recent revolt long before
the general public was alerted to it. Surrounded by ships as far as the eye could see,
and looking into the eyes of fearful men who knew not what to expect the next day
on the beaches of Normandy, I sought to reassure them as best I could.

I reminded them that the Warsaw Ghetto Jews had revolted against the mighty
German Nazi Army with a miniscule number of rifles and grenades. And despite the
overwhelming German cannon, machine guns, howitzers and lumbering, huge tanks
which mowed them down street by street, the Jews of Warsaw fought on coura-
geously to the last man and woman. At the least, they were models for us to emulate.
We, on the other hand, I reminded my companions, would land on Omaha Beach
supported by the greatest array of armament, ships and planes ever assembled by
any one group of nations in the history of man and womankind. Did I calm or
strengthen any of these soldiers? I don't know to this day.

But I do know that it took over half a century before someone confirmed the
fact that I had given a sermon on the Warsaw Ghetto uprising, aboard LST 376,
the day before we landed on Omaha Beach. In my manuscript on the history of the
616th Ordinance Ammunition Company, I had apparently avoided devoting too
much space to myself by detailing the contents of the sermon. Thus, there was no
written or oral record of its contents, except from my own recollections. This situation was finally altered in the Fall of 1998.

After a luncheon in New York's Marriot Hotel, in late September of 1998,
where I had just debated a conservative economist on the merits of our nation's tax
system before some 500 retired unionists, I was approached by a shortish man in his
late sixties, He asked me, "What does the 616th Ordinance Ammunition Company
mean to you." I immediately replied that it was my army unit during World War II.
He then excitedly threw his hands around me and blurted out: "I am Tony Bisogno
and I was in the same outfit with you. And I remember you giving the sermon on the
Warsaw Ghetto Jews on LST 376 as we were crossing the English Channel."

Fifty-four years after D-Day, I lived to hear Tony Bisogno, from Long Island,
confirm my memories and the Warsaw Ghetto sermon I had given on LST 376.

Why didn't I originally describe, in much greater detail, the reactions of the men of the 616th Ordinance Ammunition Company, as we left LST 376? I don't know. But I knew we were heading for Omaha Beach, directly in line with the Church spire at Colleville-sur-Mer. But, let me now, 56 years later, try to remedy that situation. . . .

. . . While heading towards the beach, we passed an endless array of battleships, cruisers and then destroyers, all of which were firing away at German defenses and embankments on and beyond the beach.

Finally, we spotted the beach and, to our utter amazement, gradually discerned immense, overhanging cliffs. The indoctrination lectures given us in England, just before we shoved off across the Channel, never adequately described these mountainous heights. They reminded those of us who came from the New York area of the towering Palisades which line the west side of the Hudson River, north of the George Washington Bridge. Unlike Utah Beach, which was level into the surrounding countryside, those GIs who landed on Omaha Beach in the early morning hours of D-Day were decimated by the bristling German armor on the beach and above it in the awesome Palisades.

A rhino ferry, which is almost a basketball court wide, has no side walls. Thus, we were afforded no psychological protection, especially when we observed German artillery shells hitting a rhino ferry to our right, and then another to our left, setting them ablaze. Fearing that we would be the next ones hit, and expecting then to have to jump into the water and swim to shore to save our lives, I started shedding clothes from my overweight knapsack. The most valuable items I threw overboard, which really made no sense or logic, because of their infinitesimal weight, were my size 14 socks—an extremely rare item in Uncle Sam's army. But who, at this critical moment, was sensible or logical. We were never more frightened in our entire lives. Fortunately, our rhino-ferry was not hit, that day, and we survived to hit hellish Omaha Beach long after we were scheduled to do so. But we had survived.

Bernie Bellush
March 16, 2000

ESSAYS

While the strategic bombing campaign remains one of the most controversial aspects of the Anglo-American war effort, the naval campaign against German U-boats in the Atlantic remains one of its least known aspects. In the first essay, British historian Richard Overy of King's College, Cambridge University, explains the critical importance of both and, in the process, defends the air campaign against its numerous critics. In the second essay, U.S. historian Michael S. Sherry of Northwestern University focuses on the reasons Americans were so enamored with strategic bombing and offers a damning critique of the campaign. In the third essay, Michael D. Doubler, a Ph.D. historian and retired U.S. Army colonel, describes some of the experiences of combat soldiers in Europe.

The Naval and Air Campaigns
as Critical to Allied Victory

RICHARD OVERY

For both Britain and the United States naval power was a geographical necessity, though for different reasons. British naval strategy was chiefly concerned with protecting overseas trade and safeguarding a far-flung colonial empire. Britain purchased half her food and two-thirds of her raw materials from abroad. Without this flow of supplies homewards, and the flood of manufactured exports sent in return, Britain might have remained what she was until the eighteenth century, an impoverished, underdeveloped island off the European mainland. Without a powerful navy Britain would not have been able to protect her trade, or build the network of imperial possessions that nourished and guarded it. Without the navy Britain would not for centuries have been blessed with the means to defend the home islands from assault and the luxury of being able to fight on other people's soil at times and places of her own choosing. There were drawbacks. British strategy was global rather than local. The seamless cloth of ocean made for a vast, unmasterable field of conflict. Britain was manifestly vulnerable to the interruption of her sea traffic by states with pretensions to regional maritime power, and even, in the worst case, to the blockade of the home islands. In the fifty years before the Second World War these dangers had become first apparent, then real. The rise of American sea power challenged British maritime primacy, though not dangerously so. The growth of German naval power, though blunted by defeat in the Great War, was regarded as much more dangerous, particularly when it revived again in the 1930s, and even more so when Germany began to drift closer to Italy and Japan, both of whom had large modern navies in menacing proximity to Britain's chief imperial interests. By 1939 Britain simply could not afford a navy of a size sufficient to ensure global security. Yet she entered the war in September 1939 reliant for her very survival on the ability of her navy to defend the arteries of trade and to shepherd troops and supplies worldwide.

America was much less vulnerable than Britain. Geographically remote from potential enemies, the United States possessed abundant food supplies and extravagant natural sources. Foreign trade made her richer, but it was not a lifeline. Neither did America have a far-flung empire on which she relied for men and supplies. Her few overseas possessions, in the Pacific and the Caribbean, were sentry posts to the western hemisphere and not stepping stones to world empire. The American navy was not a means to other ends but was mustered purely for the armed defence of the New World. Ever since 1822, when President James Monroe announced his famous Doctrine for the Americas, the United States assumed unsolicited responsibility for the defence of the New World against outside military interference. Its vital strategic function brought it the lion's share of Congressional appropriations for defence.

In the crisis-ridden international order of the 1930s it was the navy's task to insulate America from the dangers of war, east and west. If it ever became necessary to commit American forces to battle, as Roosevelt realised might be the case sooner than most, the existence of a powerful navy ensured that the fighting would be overseas in distant theatres, provisioned and protected by American ships. Without naval power American intervention in World War II could not have been contemplated, even less attempted. . . .

. . . No Allied strategy was possible across the Atlantic Ocean without the defeat of the submarine. The supply of goods and oil to Britain and the Soviet Union was threatened on every route, from the Arctic convoys to Murmansk and Archangel, to the long hauls from Trinidad or around the Cape of Good Hope. Any operation, whether in the Libyan desert, in north-west Africa, or across the Channel, relied on securing the sea-lanes first. Almost immediately on American entry into the war the advantage in the Battle of the Atlantic swung towards the submarines, and Allied naval power faced its most severe test. . . .

In an area as vast as the Atlantic the submarine was an inherently difficult enemy to defeat. Cruising on the surface it could outrun most ships; submerged it was invisible without the right scientific equipment. The initiative lay with the submarines who could choose where and when to engage enemy traffic. The Allies by 1942 were faced with a daunting but not insoluble mission. They adopted two very distinct approaches. The first was to find ways of avoiding the submarine altogether. Indeed the chief priority was not to sail pell-mell into a submarine trap in the hope that a handful of small escort vessels could sink the attacker in time, but to get across the Atlantic entirely unmolested. If this was galling to naval commanders who relished combat, it was none the less the best way of getting supplies (and relieved sailors!) across the ocean. The second was to find a way of accurately locating submarines so that effective anti-submarine forces, naval and air, could be brought to bear without wasting endless time on long sweeping searches. It was never enough simply to avoid the submarines: at some point they had to be fought. . . .

Direct attack on the submarines required information of a different kind. There was little chance of a kill without some way of locating to within feet the position of the enemy. At night-time, against submarines operating on the surface, this knowledge could not be acquired with conventional technology and naval tactics, and chance played a part in any densely packed convoy battle. During 1941 and for much of 1942 the number of submarines destroyed in all theatres remained small, only 35 in 1941, and only 21 in the first six months of the following year. This was a rate of attrition that could comfortably be supported by the U-boat arm. The only way to increase that rate was to apply to the naval conflict the new weapons of war—long-range aircraft, radio and radar.

The importance of aircraft was plain to see. Wherever air patrols were in operation submarine activity was much reduced. Aircraft were the "the great menace for the submarines." [U-boat Chief Admiral Karl] Dönitz told Hitler in September 1942. But until well into 1942 the aircraft was a limited weapon in the actual destruction of U-boats. The number of aircraft allocated to over-sea duty was small in relation to the task, and it proved difficult to persuade the RAF to divert larger bombing aircraft from the attack on Europe to the war at sea. The original anti-submarine bomb proved to have almost no destructive power, and was replaced by an aerial depth-charge, though only in the course of 1942 were weapons of enhanced destructive power, charged with a new explosive (Torpex), finally intro-duced. The central problem for the anti-submarine aircraft was to find the subma-rine and, having found it, to sustain an attack before it submerged to the safety of waters beyond the range of depth-charges. The answer lay with Radio-Direction Finding, later known by its familiar name of radar. . . .

The war in the Mediterranean did nothing to solve the U-boat war. At the end of 1942 the Battle of the Atlantic was delicately poised. Allied shipping was still dangerously vulnerable; the morale of the merchant mariners was low and casual-ties high. But U-boat losses were rising too, and German submariners were faced with the stark reality that they would now survive no more than two or three sorties at most. Between January and May the Battle of the Atlantic reached its final climax. . . .

. . . In London the U-boat war was placed under the direction of a remarkable British submariner, Admiral Sir Max Horton. In November 1942 he was appointed Commander-in-Chief of the Western Approaches. His brief was to find some way to reverse the downward slide in the anti-submarine war. . . .

With the arrival of Horton to duel with Dönitz came the changes that would eventually tilt the Battle of the Atlantic the Allies' way. He campaigned immediately for more aircraft, particularly long-range aircraft to fill the Atlantic Gap. He insisted that all aircraft hunting submarines at night should be fitted with Leigh Lights and centimetric radar. He set about reorganising the whole escort system, insisting on employing more up-to-date ships and escort carriers, and on the establishment of "support groups" of submarine hunter-killers which could be moved quickly about the Atlantic battlefield to the point of greatest danger. He insisted on higher standards of training and preparation. . . . Rather than avoid the submarines, Horton drove his convoys into their midst. . . . By the end of the month only half the mer-chant losses of March were recorded, for the loss of nineteen more U-boats. . . .

Horton's offensive did all that he had hoped and more. During May sinkings in the North Atlantic fell to 160,000 tons, the lowest figure since the end of 1941. The new tactics and technology blunted the U-boat threat in a matter of weeks. During May the U-boat arm lost 41 vessels. This was a catastrophic rate of loss. By the end of the month U-boats were being sunk faster than cargo ships. With great reluc-tance Dönitz bowed to reality and on 24 May he ordered all submarines to retreat from the Atlantic until his forces could be reformed and rearmed. On 31 May he reported to Hitler that the Atlantic Battle was lost for the moment. His retreating forces were harried home to their bases across the Bay of Biscay where they were forced to fight it out with enemy aircraft armed with rockets, depth charges and pin-point radar. In June and July his force lost 54 more boats. For submarine crews each mission was more and more likely to be their last. . . .

So sudden was the end of the campaign that had hung dangerously in the bal-ance only weeks before that it is tempting to assume that some special factor, lately introduced into the battle, explained its abrupt conclusion. The explanation is more routine that this: victory was the product of all those elements of organisation and invention mobilised in months of patient, painstaking labour. Under Horton's in-spirational command these elements reached a critical mass by the late spring of 1943. German directives could again be read by British cryptanalysts at almost exactly the time that new Allied codes blinded their opposite number for the rest of the war. Radar and anti-submarine weaponry had evolved at last the necessary level of reliability and sophistication. Better training and tactics turned the escort vessel into a genuine help-mate for the convoys and a true deterrent to its hunters. Finally, air power worked its transforming art in the Atlantic as it had done in the Pacific and the Mediterranean. This was the most important change of all. Not until April did Horton get the escort carriers long promised, but from then on the number of carriers increased more rapidly, and air cover could be provided throughout the seaborne theatres. The number and quality of aircraft plying backwards and forwards over the Bay of Biscay or far out into the Atlantic, in lengthy, often unrewarding, cold reconnaissance, increased sharply by the spring of 1943. In January 1942 there had been only 127 of which just ten were converted long-range bombers; a year later there were 371 aircraft, including almost one hundred long-range aircraft. But the VLR [very long range] aircraft, the Liberators with their extra fuel tanks, which could fly for eighteen hours or more, came in numbers only in April and May 1943, although only a fraction of what had been requested was supplied. Why the RAF [Royal Air Force] remained resistant for so long to the idea of releasing bombers for work over the ocean defies explanation. A mere 37 aircraft succeeded in closing the Atlantic Gap, whose existence had almost brought the Allies' war plans to stalemate.

The Battle of the Atlantic was not won like other naval conflicts, fleet face to face with fleet in decisive engagement. Its start and its finale were ragged and ill-defined, though real enough. The outcome of the struggle owed a great deal to organisations and staff far distant from the seamen and ships whose job it was to fight for the convoys' passage: the submarine Tracking Rooms in London and Washington, the Trade Plot Room that masterminded the global movement of merchant shipping, and the offices for radio interception and decipherment. It was a victory neither easy nor inevitable. Allied navies were stretched to the limit to achieve it. But victory in the Atlantic sea-lanes, like the victory at Midway, represented a decisive shift in the fortunes of war.

The war at sea was won not by the traditional instruments of maritime strategy, but by modern weapons—aircraft, radar and radio intelligence. Where ships sailed unprotected by aircraft, without benefit of modern means to detect other vessels and blind to the intentions of the enemy, they were all but defenceless. If either the British or American navies had been unwilling to recognise that maritime strategy had to undergo a fundamental revolution in the early years of the war, the sea-lanes might well have remained blocked. The Japanese navy was compromised for too long by the search for the big battleship confrontation, while the German navy was handicapped throughout the war by the reluctance of the German air force to develop a serious maritime strategy.

Under the impact of modern weaponry and tactics the sea war became a war of costly attrition conducted in the main by aircraft, submarines and small escort vessels. These spent the bulk of their time in monotonous routine, sweeping the skies and oceans for sight of the enemy, adding a tiny piece to the intelligence puzzle or supplying another statistic in the trade war. This kind of sea war, Churchill later observed, had none of the flavour of the past, no "flaming battles and glittering achievements." Instead its end product was "statistics, diagrams, and curves unknown to the nation, incomprehensible to the public." Attrition warfare had none of the spectacular bloodletting of great land battles; there was no Somme, no Stalingrad. Yet the war at sea was exceptionally costly in men, who had to fight one small engagement after another, with all the skills of old-fashioned seamanship, against both the enemy and the harsh marine environment. Out of 39,000 German submariners, 28,000 were killed, or almost three-quarters of the force. From the 55,800 crewmen who went down with Britain's merchant ships, over 25,000 were drowned. Chances of rescue on the high sea were slight. Life and death at sea were peculiarly harsh. "There is no margin for mistakes in submarines." Horton once told British submariners stationed at Malta, "You are either alive or dead."

The victory of the Allied navies was the foundation for final victory in the west and in the Pacific. It permitted Britain and the United States to prepare seriously for the largest amphibious assault yet attempted, the re-entry to Hitler's Europe. It allowed the Allies to impose crippling sea blockades on Italy and Japan that destroyed 64 percent of all Italy's shipping tonnage, and reduced the Japanese merchant fleet from over 5 million tons in 1942 to 670,000 tons in 1945. The stranglehold on Italian and Japanese supply lines sapped fatally the industrial strength of these nations and made their reinforcement of distant fronts sporadic and costly. Finally, victory gave a growing immunity to Allied shipping so that the disparity in naval strengths and merchant tonnage between the two sides became unbridgeable. From the beginning of 1943 onward the Royal Navy lost no more battleships or aircraft carriers; only six more cruisers were lost compared with 26 between 1939 and 1942; and only 36 destroyers against 112. In the Atlantic the Allied merchant marine lost only 31 ships in 1944 against a figure of 1,006 in 1942, despite the fact that the U-boat arm actually had almost four hundred submarines in 1944, bottled up in their home ports or kept at arm's length by an almost impenetrable curtain of anti-submarine defences.

The source of this enhanced naval presence was the vast production of American shipyards. The United States navy ended the war with 1,672 major naval vessels, the Royal Navy with 1,065 major warships, and 2,907 minor ones. The American merchant shipbuilding programme was a production miracle: 794,000 tons of shipping were built in 1941, 21 million tons in the next three years. It is tempting to argue that sheer material strength won the sea war. Yet this is to ignore the question of timing. Midway was won against overwhelming Japanese superiority in warships. The convoy battles were won by a tiny number of maritime aircraft and limited numbers of escort vessels. The great imbalance in resources only began to tell later in the war, when it helped to prevent any re-entry by the Japanese navy or the U-boats as a serious peril in the sea war. In the critical year between Midway and the defeat of the submarine Allied resources were stretched to the limit. Tactical and technical innovation won the war at sea before sheer numbers came to matter. . . .

[Except for the United States and Great Britain], none of the other warring states saw much merit in long-range "strategic" bombing. . . . Why, then, did Britain and the United States fly in the face of conventional military wisdom and persist with bombing? At best the answer is a patchwork. Public opinion in both states was unusually susceptible to the science-fiction view of air power, first popularised by writers such as H.G. Wells, whose *War in the Air*, published in London as long ago as 1908, painted a lurid picture of "German air fleets" destroying "the whole fabric of civilisation." . . . This was hardly a basis for military strategy. Yet British airmen and politicians stuck by the view in the inter-war years that indiscriminate bombing, to achieve a rapid "knock-out blow," was likely to be the central feature of the next war. To counter the threat of bombing you needed bombers of your own. The roots of post-war deterrence reach back to the British decision in the 1930s to build a powerful striking force of bombers to frighten potential enemies into restraint.

There were, to be sure, more solid reasons for pursuing bombing than fear of being its victim. No one wanted to repeat the awful bloodletting of the Great War. A bombing war, for all its manifold horrors, promised a quicker, cleaner conflict. . . . Here was war on the cheap, saving not only lives, but money: an economical strategy to appeal to the democratic taxpayer and the parsimonious treasury alike.

All of this begged a very large question: what should the bombers bomb? In Germany and France, with politically powerful armies, the issue was easily resolved: aircraft attacked enemy aircraft, and when they had finished doing that they bombed enemy armies. This met the Clausewitzian test of war, the concentration of effort against the military forces of the enemy. But British and American airmen, much freer from the smothering constraints of old-established armies, wanted a strategy that gave them real independence, one that complemented the novelty and modernity of the weapon itself. They chose what became known as "strategic" bombing, to distinguish it from mere "tactical" bombing in support of armies and navies. The target of the strategic bomber was the very heart of the enemy state, its home population and economy. The Great War had opened the way to a new kind of conflict, total war, in which the distinction between civilian and soldier was eliminated. The bomber was the instrument of total war *par excellence,* capable of pulverising the industries of the enemy and terrorising the enemy population into surrender. Air strategists were fond of using the analogy of the human body. Bombing did not just weaken the military limbs of the victim, but destroyed the nerve centres, the heart, the brain, the arteries (lungs remained a curiously neglected metaphor)—the very ability of a nation to make war at all.

Much of this was fantasy. In the 1920s the RAF, and in particular its overbearing, truculent commander, Sir Hugh Trenchard, clung to the quite unproved assertion that the moral effect of bombing was twenty times greater than the effect of material damage. It was an assumption that lingered on past Trenchard's retirement in 1930. Though air leaders in Britain, and later in the United States, hesitated to urge attacks on civilian populations for the sake of terror, the whole logic of independent, strategic bombing was to crush popular willingness and capacity to wage war. If there was not quite a straight line between Trenchard's dogmatic views on morale and the ghastly apotheosis of bombing at Hiroshima, the curve was barely noticeable. For those airmen with qualms about attacking civilians, there developed in the 1930s a second assumption, that bombers could precisely attack selected economic targets, whose destruction would dry up the supply of arms and drain away the material life-blood of the enemy's armed forces. Whatever the justification, the object of attack was the home front and not the military shield in front of it. For all of the 1930s, and even in the early years of war, this strategy was technically unfeasible and operationally amateur. Nevertheless in December 1937

British Bomber Command was ordered to plan for the destruction of the German economy through bombing, and from that date the groundwork was laid for what became the Combined Bomber Offensive launched in 1943. . . .

The early bombing of Germany demonstrated all the limitations of Bomber Command. Daylight raids were soon abandoned once it was found that some attacks suffered the loss of almost the entire force. Bombing by night, on the other hand, though safer for the crews, could only be attempted when it was clear and moonlit. Without the moon it was difficult to locate the area of the target, let alone the target itself, and without the clear night sky navigation by the stars was impossible. There were no radio navigation aids, no radar, not even effective bomb-sights. So inaccurate was British bombing that German intelligence had considerable difficulty in grasping exactly what strategy the British were pursuing. The offensive was continued only because, following the defeat of French and British forces in June 1940, there was no other way left for Britain to demonstrate to the world her willingness to continue fighting: "We are hitting that man hard," Churchill wired Roosevelt at the end of July.

In fact Bomber Command was doing anything but. Moreover the pinprick attacks did exactly what Chamberlain had always feared: they provoked fierce German retaliation. . . .

With the coming of the Blitz the British got the war they had expected all along. The German attacks were costly and terrifying, but the Blitz was not the Super-Armageddon. When Gallup polled Londoners early in 1941 about what made them most depressed that winter, the weather came out ahead of bombing. Bombing did little to dent British production, and if anything morale was stiffened rather than reduced. Hitler, who had started the Blitz in a rage at British "terrorism," soon became disillusioned with city bombing. What the Blitz *did* achieve was the firm commitment of both British and American leaders to the idea that strategic bombing as a way of conducting war was here to stay. The bombing of London shocked world opinion in ways that the bombing of Berlin evidently could not. In thousands of American cinemas the newsreels showed the famous image of St Paul's cathedral, majestically, incredibly rising above the tide of flame that licked all round it. The American newsman Ed Murrow's poignant reports of ordinary British courage and tenacity kept alive western optimism at a dark moment of the war. The public perception of the Blitz in the United States perhaps did more than anything to switch American opinion to the view that bombing mattered, and that the United States should do it too.

During the course of 1941 Roosevelt and his military advisers began seriously to make ready for war. Roosevelt himself was the inspiration behind the planning of a bombing offensive as a central part of American preparation for war. . . .

Without the support of Roosevelt and other senior American politicians for a policy of bombing it is unlikely that it would ever have materialised as one of the key elements in the western war effort. Without Churchill's championship of "a ceaseless and ever growing air bombardment," whose strategic necessity he regularly endorsed in his correspondence with the American President, Bomber Command would almost certainly have remained auxiliary to the activities of the army and navy. Even with such powerful allies, the bombing offensive found the senior services snapping at its heels throughout the period of trial and error. Admirals and generals pleaded with Roosevelt and Churchill to release the bombers to help them overcome the armed power of the Axis at the battlefront. Without the urgent pressure of Soviet demands for a Second Front in 1942, which bombing was used to placate, even Churchill and Roosevelt might have given way. Strategic bombing emerged as a major commitment not from proven operational success but from political necessity. It was chosen by civilians to be used against civilians, in the teeth of strong military opposition. Now bombing had to prove that the politicians' confidence was not misplaced. . . .

The 8th air force, for all the painful delays in its establishment, was a blood transfusion for the bombing campaign. It was not just that American airmen, brash, confident, eager for combat, brought a breath of fresh air to a stale campaign. It was also that they brought with them the enthusiastic conviction that bombing, whatever its limitations hitherto, was the answer to destroying German power. Unlike the British, American airmen believed that the destruction of Germany's vital industries, her transport system and her fuel supply could be precisely calculated in terms of aircraft despatched and bomb tonnages dropped. The source of that conviction was the technology available. American bombing forces were composed largely of the Boeing B-17 "Flying Fortress" which had been developed as early as 1935. It was robust, had a high ceiling and long range and was so heavily armed that it was assumed that it could fly in daylight and defend itself effectively on the wing. Flying by day meant a better view of the target; the use of the Norden bombsight, which the American air force refused to pass on to the RAF, increased accuracy even more. Bombing tests in the United States demonstrated not quite the ability to hit a "pickle-barrel" that some American airmen claimed, but were more than satisfactory. Armed with equipment for accurate, daylight bombardment, the 8th air force deliberately distinguished their practice of "precision bombing" of individual targets from the more random efforts of the Royal Air Force. The choice of daylight tactics would prevent the two forces from treading on each other's toes: the RAF bombed industrial areas by night, the 8th air force would pick off factories and railway stations and oil depots by day.

In practice it was a long time before the American air forces could do anything of the sort. . . .

By the end of 1942 both bomber forces were poised to mount a much more dangerous and effective campaign than anything they had carried out hitherto. Yet even at this late stage, with large resources mortgaged to the endeavour, it was far from clear what strategy bombing was supposed to support. For much of the autumn and winter of 1942–3 the bombers were directed to attack targets to help in the Battle of the Atlantic, which was reaching its desperate finale. Wave after wave of heavy-bombers all but obliterated the French ports of Lorient and Brest where the German submarine pens were based, without once inflicting serious damage on the reinforced concrete structures that protected the U-boats. And while the arguments continued about opening a Second Front in Europe, bombing was generally regarded by the military chiefs on both sides of the Atlantic as a mere adjunct to that greater enterprise, a means of weakening the enemy before invasion. The decision to embark on Torch rather than invade mainland Europe in the foreseeable future, left the bombing offensive in limbo once again, with no clearly defined objective.

The turning-point for the bombing effort came in January 1943 when Roosevelt and Churchill at last agreed to give priority to the bombing campaign. . . .

At Casablanca the two leaders agreed to postpone the Second Front, almost certainly until 1944, and to continue with the Mediterranean strategy of attacking what Churchill called the "soft underbelly" of the Axis "crocodile." To bridge the now widening time-lag between Torch and the invasion of northern Europe the two leaders agreed to intensify the air campaign with the "heaviest possible bomber offensive against the German war effort." Though neither leader expected bombing to bring Germany to defeat on its own, the task it was allocated at Casablanca went well beyond anything yet asked of it. On 21 January the Combined Chiefs-of-Staff issued a directive to the air forces to bring about "the progressive destruction and dislocation of the German military, industrial and economic system, and the undermining of the morale of the German people to a point where their capacity for armed resistance is fatally weakened." The go-ahead was given to see what bombing could do; a high priority was given to the production of the tools for the job. . . .

In post-war arguments about the morality of bombing a great deal has always been made of the unequal nature of the contest between bombers and defenceless civilians, and there is no disguising the fact that the collapse of German civilian morale was one of the objectives agreed when the Combined Bomber Offensive was launched at Casablanca. But the actual combat was not between bombers and ordinary people, but between bombers and the defensive forces of the enemy, the fighters and anti-aircraft fire. When the bombers streamed into Europe, their crews knew that they had to fight their way to the target and fight their way back. They sat in uncomfortable, surprisingly noisy, vulnerable aircraft, cold and cramped. They had to avoid heavy anti-aircraft fire from the massive concentration of fifty thousand anti-aircraft guns in the German defences; with the constant refinement of the Kammhuber Line and German fighter tactics they faced periods of brief but fierce engagement with an enemy who held all the advantages of timing and manoeuvrability. On the return flight poor weather, fuel shortages, or damage from anti-aircraft fire added to what hazards the enemy could still supply. If it now seems disingenuous of surviving crewmen to claim, as they often do, that they were too absorbed with battle against the elements and the enemy to think of those they were bombing, we should be reminded that each bombing mission *was* a military confrontation with a statistically increased risk of death the more missions each crewman flew. . . .

In the winter of 1943–4 the two bomber forces were compelled to rethink the campaign. Schweinfurt for the Americans, Berlin and Nuremberg for the British, showed the limitations of bombing, even though the defence had been stretched to the limit. It gradually dawned on the western forces that one thing, and one thing only, would secure the skies over Germany: the defeat of the German air force. They had ignored Clausewitz at their peril. Concentration of force against the armed forces of the enemy was not mere dogma; it was proved again and again in the harsh crucible of combat.

To be fair, American service chiefs saw this sooner than the British. When bombing plans were first drawn up in August 1941, American planners pointed to the Luftwaffe as an intermediate priority, whose destruction would permit uninterrupted assault on the economy. But British airmen had always dismissed attacks against an enemy air force as a waste of time. The targets were regarded as too dispersed and too small, and, as they had ably demonstrated in the Battle of Britain, recuperation from attack was relatively easy. When the 8th air force began operations in the summer of 1943, the Combined Bomber Offensive directive (codenamed "Pointblank") placed the undermining of German air power as a top priority. American attacks that year did have some success in limiting the expansion of German fighter production; the attack on Schweinfurt on 14 October reduced ball-bearing output by 67 per cent. But the defeats suffered in these attacks were a reflection of the complete failure to confront the direct sources of German air power, the fighters, pilots and airfields of the Luftwaffe.

The defeat of the German air force became a matter of urgency. Without that defeat the projected invasion of Europe in the late spring of 1944, Operation "Overlord," would be placed in jeopardy. Without the bombing offensive, which was supposed to weaken German resistance to invasion and re-conquest, the western Allies faced a long and bloody contest. There was no alternative but to defeat the Luftwaffe if western strategy was not to be thrown into disarray. On New Year's Day 1944 the Commander-in-Chief of the American air forces, General "Hap" Arnold, sent the following to his commanders in Europe: "My personal message to you—this is a MUST—is to, *'Destroy the Enemy Air Force wherever you find them in the air, on the ground and in the factories.'* "

Here, crudely expressed, was the central issue of this zone of conflict. It was resolved not by some revolution in air warfare, but through a tactic of remarkable simplicity: the introduction of additional, disposable, fuel tanks on Allied fighters. It might well be asked with hindsight why it took the Allies so long to recognise that they needed fighters to fight German aircraft, and that their range could only be increased by giving them more fuel. The straight answer is that no one thought it was possible without sacrificing speed and manoeuvrability. It was a technical possibility quite early in the war, but neither the Allies nor the Germans saw any real gains in pursuing it. For too long it was assumed that heavily armed bombers could defend themselves. In fact the bombers were like unescorted merchant ships: to deliver their bomb cargoes they needed to be convoyed.

By good fortune more than by sound planning the convoy vessels were to hand. The standard American fighter aircraft, the P-38 Lightning and the P-47 Thunderbolt, had been fitted with extra fuel tanks under the wings when they were ferried long distances. By repeating this simple expedient the escort range of both fighters was increased from 500 miles to 2,000 miles. But the attention of the bombing commanders became focused on a hitherto neglected fighter, the P-51 Mustang. Built originally for the RAF in American factories, the marriage of an American airframe and the British Rolls-Royce "Merlin" engine produced a fighter of exceptional endurance and capability, even when loaded with heavy supplies of extra petrol. The first group of adapted Mustangs joined the 8th air force in November 1943, and flew a mission to Kiel and back in December, the farthest any fighter had yet flown and fought in Europe. A crash production programme in American factories turned out enormous quantities in a matter of months. By March 1944 the P-51, with a maximum armed range of 1,800 miles, flew with the bombers all the way to Berlin and back.

The long-range escort fighter transformed the air war overnight. . . .

During the last year of the war the bombing campaign came of age. With the thin veil of German air defence in tatters, the economy was at last exposed to the full fury of the bombers. Most of the bomb tonnage dropped by the two bomber forces was disbursed in the last year of the war—1.18 million tons out of a total for the whole war of 1.42 million. These attacks did not go entirely unresisted. There were over fifty thousand heavy and light anti-aircraft guns at the peak, organised into heavy batteries, concentrated around the most important industrial targets. There remained an exiguous fighter force by day and night (including a few of the new jet fighters), whose pilots continued with almost reckless bravery to pit their tiny strength against the air armadas. The force now available to the Allies was one of overwhelming power. . . .

Did bombing help the Allies to win the war? The arguments began even before the war was over, when American and British technical intelligence teams scoured the bomb sites trying to decide what effect bombing had had on the enemy war effort. The air force commanders wanted the civilian investigators to confirm that if bombing had not quite won the war, it had at least made a major contribution to victory. The civilians, drawn in the main from academic or business backgrounds, were at best sceptical of air power claims, at worst hostile to bombing. Their concluding reports damned with faint praise: bombing had certainly contributed to undermining resistance in Germany in the last months of war, but until then it had done nothing to reverse the sharp upward trajectory of German production, and it had clearly not dented morale sufficiently to reduce production or produce revolution. It was estimated that Germany lost only 10 per cent of its production in 1944, which could hardly be regarded as critical. The view has persisted ever since that bombing was a strategic liability, a wasteful diversion of resources that might more fruitfully have been used building tanks or laying down ships.

Bombing has also occasioned a chorus of moral disapproval. Yet to understand what bombing achieved it is necessary, though agonisingly difficult, to lay aside the moral issue. Its strategic merits or limitations are distinct from its ethical implications, however closely entwined they have become in the contemporary debate. Even on the strategic questions there is a great deal of confusion. There persists the myth that bombing was supposed to win the war on its own, and was thus a failure in its own terms. This was never the expectation of Allied leaders. Bombers were asked to contribute in a great many ways to what was always a combined endeavour of aircraft, ships and armies. The popular view of bombing has concentrated far too much on the narrow question of how much German production was affected by bomb destruction, at the expense of looking at bombing's other functions, and the other theatres of combat in which it was used. To give a more balanced answer to the question of how much bombing contributed to victory we must be clear about the nature of its achievement.

Let us examine Allied strategy first. Bombing met some significant objectives of western engagement in war. Though the costs were far from negligible—over six years the death of 140,000 American and British airmen, and the loss of 21,000 bombers—bombing did reduce the overall level of western casualties in Europe and in the Far East, by weakening German resistance and by knocking Japan out of the war before invasion. Western losses were far lower than those of the other fighting powers. Bombing also permitted Britain and the United States to bring their considerable economic and scientific power to bear on the contest. The campaign was capital intensive, where the great struggle on the eastern front was based on military labour. This suited the preferences of the west, which did not want to place a much higher physical strain on their populations. For all the criticism directed at the waste of resources on bombing, the whole campaign absorbed, according to a post-war British survey, only 7 per cent of Britain's war effort. . . .

The bombing offensive was for most of its course a fighting contest between the two western bomber forces and the German defences. From the middle of 1943 the defeat of the German air force became a central objective. Until that date German air power, deployed in the main as a tactical offensive arm, was a critical factor in German success on land and sea. The bombing offensive caused German military leaders to drain much needed air strength away from the main fighting fronts to protect the Reich, weakening German resistance in the Soviet Union and the Mediterranean. Though Stalin remained sceptical of Churchill's claim that bombing somehow constituted a Second Front, the facts show that German air power declined steadily on the eastern front during 1943 and 1944, when over two-thirds of German fighters were sucked into the contest with the bombers. By the end of 1943 there were 55,000 anti-aircraft guns to combat the air offensive—including 75 per cent of the famous 88-millimetre gun, which had doubled with such success as an anti-tank weapon on the eastern front. As the bombing war developed, the whole structure of the Luftwaffe was distorted. On the eastern front it was the bombers that had caused the damage to Soviet forces in 1941 and 1942. The shift to producing fighters reduced the German bombing threat over the battlefield. In 1942 over half the German combat aircraft produced were bombers; in 1944 the proportion was only 18 per cent. The German air threat at the battle of Kursk and in the long retreat that followed visibly melted. By compelling Germany to divide its air forces there were reductions in effectiveness on all fronts, which could not be reversed even by the most strenuous production effort.

Once the Allies had the long-range fighter pouring out in numbers from America's industrial cornucopia, German air power could be blunted once and for all. The result was not a single, spectacular victory, but a slow and lethal erosion of fighting capability. For the Allies this was an essential outcome, if their re-entry to the Continent was not to face hazardous risk. For all Stalin's impatience, the western Allies knew the stunning effect on their war effort that a German victory on the invasion beaches would generate. Without the defeat or neutralisation of the German air force the Allies might well have hesitated to take the risk. Without the successful diversion of the heavy-bomber force to the job of pulverising roads, railways and bridges, in order to stifle German efforts to reinforce the anti-invasion front, D-Day might have failed at the first attempt. That story remains to be told below, but it weighs heavily in the scales of any judgement on bombing. All of these factors, the defeat of the German air force, the diversion of effort from the eastern front at a critical point in that struggle, the successful preliminaries to D-Day, belie the view that bombing was a strategy of squandered effort. It is difficult to think of anything else the Allies might have done with their manpower and resources that could have achieved this much at such comparatively low cost.

Beyond these military gains lay the German economy and German morale. No one would argue with the view that for much of the war the bombing forces exaggerated the degree of direct physical destruction they were inflicting on German industry. Neither can it be denied that between 1941 and 1944, in step with the escalating bombardment, German military output trebled. The effect of bombing on the German economy was not to prevent a sustained increase in output, but to place a strict ceiling on that expansion. By the middle of the war, with the whole of continental Europe at her disposal, Germany was fast becoming an economic superpower. The harvest of destruction and disruption reaped by bomb attack, random and poorly planned as it often was, was sufficient to blunt German economic ambitions.

The effects of bombing on the economy were both direct and indirect. The direct physically reduced the quantity of weapons and equipment flowing from German factories; the indirect forced the diversion of resources to cope with bombing, resources which German industry could have turned into tanks, planes and guns. Direct effects were felt from both area bombing and precision bombing, as the city attacks hit water, gas and electricity supplies, cut railway lines, blocked roads, or destroyed smaller factories producing components. Much of this, it is true, could be made good within weeks, sometimes within days. But for the German manager in the last two years of war there were two battles to fight: a battle to increase production, and a battle against the endless inconveniences produced by bombing, the interruptions to work, the loss of supplies and raw materials, the fears of the workforce. Where the businessman in America or Britain could work away at the task of maximising output, German managers were forced to enter an uncomfortable battlefield in which they and their workers were unwitting targets. The stifling of industrial potential caused by bombing is inherently difficult to quantify, but it was well beyond the 10 per cent suggested by the post-war bombing survey, particularly in the cluster of war industries specifically under attack. At the end of January 1945 Albert Speer and his ministerial colleagues met in Berlin to sum up what bombing had done to production schedules for 1944. They found that Germany had produced 35 per cent fewer tanks than planned, 31 per cent fewer aircraft and 42 per cent fewer lorries as a result of bombing. The denial of these huge resources to German forces in 1944 fatally weakened their response to bombing and invasion, and eased the path of Allied armies.

The indirect effects were more important still, for the bombing offensive forced the German economy to switch very large resources away from equipment for the fighting fronts, using them instead to combat the bombing threat. By 1944 one-third of all German artillery production consisted of anti-aircraft guns; the anti-aircraft effort absorbed 20 per cent of all ammunition produced, one-third of the output of the optical industry, and between half and two-thirds of the production of radar and signals equipment. As a result of this diversion, the German army and navy were desperately short of essential radar and communications equipment for other tasks. The bombing also ate into Germany's scarce manpower: by 1944 an estimated two million Germans were engaged in anti-aircraft defence, in repairing shattered factories and in generally cleaning up the destruction. From the spring of that year frantic efforts were made to burrow underground, away from the bombing. Fantastic schemes were promoted which absorbed almost half of all industrial construction and close to half a million workers. Of course, if German efforts to combat the bombing had succeeded the effort would not have been wasted. As it was the defences and repair teams did enough to keep production going until the autumn of 1944, but not enough to prevent the rapid erosion of German economic power thereafter, and not enough to prevent the massive redirection of economic effort from 1943. Bombing forced Germany to divide the economy between too many competing claims, none of which could, in the end, be satisfied. In the air over Germany, or on the fronts in Russia and France, German forces lacked the weapons to finish the job. The combined effects of direct destruction and the diversion of resources denied German forces approximately half their battle-front weapons and equipment in 1944. It is difficult not to regard this margin as decisive.

The impact of bombing on morale is a different question altogether. The naive expectation that bombing would somehow produce a tidal wave of panic and disillusionment which would wash away popular support for war and topple governments built on sand, was exposed as wishful thinking. Neither in Germany nor Japan did bombing provoke any serious backlash against the regime from those who suffered. But there can surely be little doubt that bombing was a uniquely demoralising experience. No one enjoyed being bombed. The recollections of its victims are unanimous in expressing feelings of panic, of fear, of dumb resignation. The chief ambition of ordinary Germans in the last years of war was survival, *das Überleben,* the desperate struggle to secure food and shelter, to cope with regular and prolonged cuts in gas and light, to keep awake by day after nights of huddling in cramped shelters. The last thing on the minds of those living under the hail of bombs was political resistance. Not even the prospect of vengeance against the bombers could sustain morale. Bombed populations developed an outlook both apathetic and self-centred; each night they hoped that if there had to be bombing, it would be on someone else. . . .

The impact of bombing was profound. People became tired, highly strung and disinclined to take risks. Industrial efficiency was undermined by bombing workers and their housing. In Japan absenteeism from work rose to 50 per cent in the summer of 1945; in the Ford plant in Cologne, in the Ruhr, absenteeism rose to 25 per cent of the workforce for the whole of 1944. At the more distant BMW works in Munich the rate rose to one-fifth of the workforce by the summer of 1944. A loss of work-hours on this scale played havoc with production schedules. Even those who turned up for work were listless and anxious. "One can't get used to the raids," complained one respondent. "I wished for an end. We all got nerves. We did not get enough sleep and were very tense. People fainted when they heard the first bomb drop." For the bombed cities the end of the war spelt relief from a routine of debilitating terror and arbitrary loss. No one could doubt who walked through the ghost towns of Germany and Japan, past the piles of rubble and twisted concrete, the rusting machines and torn up rails, miles and miles of burned-out houses, their few frightened inhabitants eking out a half-life in the cellars and ruined corners, no one could doubt but that bombing shattered civilian lives.

There has always seemed something fundamentally implausible about the contention of bombing's critics that dropping almost 2.5 million tons of bombs on tautly-stretched industrial systems and war-weary urban populations would not seriously weaken them. Germany and Japan had no special immunity. Japan's military economy was devoured in the flames; her population desperately longed for escape from bombing. German forces lost half of the weapons needed at the front, millions of workers absented themselves from work, and the economy gradually creaked almost to a halt. Bombing turned the whole of Germany, in Speer's words, into a "gigantic front." It was a front the Allies were determined to win; it absorbed huge resources on both sides. It was a battlefield in which only the infantry were missing. The final victory of the bombers in 1944 was, Speer concluded, "the greatest lost battle on the German side. . . ." For all the arguments over the morality or operational effectiveness of the bombing campaigns, the air offensive was one of the decisive elements in Allied victory.

Strategic Bombing as Technological Fanaticism

MICHAEL S. SHERRY

The leaders and technicians of the American air force were driven by technological fanaticism—a pursuit of destructive ends expressed, sanctioned, and disguised by the organization and application of technological means. Destruction was rarely the acknowledged final purpose for the men who made air war possible. Rather, they declared that it served the purpose of securing victory and that its forms were dictated by technological, organizational, and strategic imperatives. In practice, they often waged destruction as a functional end in itself, without a clear comprehension of its relationship to stated purposes.

To label these men fanatics or their mentality and behavior as fanatical may defy the usual understanding of the terms, which sees in fanaticism the workings of a single-minded, frenzied emotional devotion to a cause. Intensity of emotion hardly seemed to characterize men whose virtue was their capacity for rational examination of problems. "The fanatic cannot tolerate scientific thought," it has been said. Moreover, "fanaticism is a megalomaniacal condition," one notable for "a jealous, vindictive and monomaniacal faith," usually in a party, an organization, or a leader in which is invested a "unique saving function." The air force certainly inspired among its professional officers an intense loyalty but rarely a monomaniacal allegiance. While some wartime scientists maintained an unquestioning faith in their methodology and its beneficence, by no means did all. Nor was faith in the American or the Allied cause always intense or evenly shared. What characterized the experts in air war was their flexibility and control, the ease with which they worked among a variety of organizations serving many purposes, and the skills with which they balanced personal, professional, bureaucratic, and ideological goals. Indeed, the practice of air war grew out of a convergence of diverse appeals, needs, and opportunities, diversity imparting to the bombing much of its momentum.

Fanaticism in the context of World War II usually refers to America's enemies—the Nazis, genocidal in ideology and practice, and the Japanese, whose cult of spiritual strength sent thousands of men to their deaths in kamikaze attacks. In more recent expressions of fanaticism—the acts of terrorism carried out by shadowy religious organizations from the Middle East, for example—self-destructiveness seems the salient characteristic, indeed the hidden desire of the fanatic. In contrast, if anything seemed to bind Americans together during World War II, it was self-preservation, the lowest common denominator of support for the war effort.

Why, then, call the practitioners of air war fanatics, and what shared mentality constituted their fanaticism? For one thing, fanatical acts are not always the product of frenzied or hateful individuals, as Hannah Arendt has shown in capturing the banality of Adolph Eichmann. For another, there was a suggestion of the megalomaniacal among the practitioners of air war in their aspirations for technological omnipotence over the natural universe for some of the scientists, over the geographic and political world for the airmen striving to achieve a "global" air force, with men like John von Neumann embracing both aspirations. For sure, these aspirations did not often appear suicidal or self-destructive to the men who held them. Yet the technology they created or promoted—finally the atomic bomb but to some degree the apparatus of "conventional" air war as well—carried that self-destructive potential for the nation and the world, and not simply in retrospect inasmuch as the world-ending potential of aerial warfare had been recognized before the war by writers like H. G. Wells and during the war by some atomic scientists and policymakers.

The shared mentality of the fanatics of air war was their dedication to assembling and perfecting their methods of destruction, and the way that doing so overshadowed the original purposes justifying destruction. Their coolness, their faith in rational problem-solving, did not easily appear fanatical because its language was the language of rationality and technique. It apparently expressed the triumph of a new set of values, ones often called modern or bureaucratic, which displaced more traditional ones by which people were defined according to racial, ethnic, religious, and national differences. Yet it is by no means clear that such values had entirely displaced more traditional ones. For one thing, whatever their individual value system, those who waged air war served as the instrument of national passions that were often decidedly racist in character. For another, their rhetoric, as in the use of the term "dehousing," allowed them to express aggressive and destructive impulses in other terms, impulses that did not necessarily disappear from motivation, simply from view.

It was easier to regard the decisions that took lives as the products of technological, strategic, and bureaucratic imperatives. In the face of these imperatives, men felt a helplessness that allowed them to escape responsibility or fulfilled a wish to do so. Actions ceased to be recognized as the product of aggressive wills and became foreordained, irresistible. Certainly, the complexities of modern technology, bureaucracy, and war-making were real enough. The American political system had built-in impediments to accountability because of its diffuse nature, aggravated by the division of responsibilities among the three services. The functional distribution of power along the chain of command and the compartmentalization that accompanied it had much the same effect. Efforts to centralize power, as with Arnold's command of the Twentieth Air Force, did not necessarily enhance accountability at the top because leaders were so remote from war's realities. Rarely were these arrangements designed deliberately to negate accountability—as usual, they were a response to perceived necessities. Yet, for a nation with a benign image of its role in the world, eager to mete out punishments to its enemies but reluctant to proclaim its intent to do so, these arrangements were also attractive, desirable.

The lack of a proclaimed intent to destroy, the sense of being driven by the twin demands of bureaucracy and technology, distinguished America's technological fanaticism from its enemies' ideological fanaticism. That both were fanatical was not easily recognizable at the time because the forms were so different. The enemy, particularly the Japanese, had little choice but to be profligate in the expenditure of manpower and therefore in the fervid exhortation of men to hatred and sacrifice—they were not, and knew they were not, a match in economic and technological terms for the Allies. The United States had different resources with which to be fanatical: resources allowing it to take the lives of others more than its own, ones whose accompanying rhetoric of technique disguised the will to destroy. As lavish with machines as the enemy was with men, Americans appeared to themselves to practice restraint, to be immune from the passion to destroy that characterized their enemies and from the urge to self-destruction as well.

The distinction between technological and ideological fanaticism was not absolute. It could not be, given how war often elicits similar behavior from disparate combatants. On occasion, particularly when their backs were to the wall early in the war, Americans celebrated the suicidal defense of hopeless positions, and if the rhetoric of technique dominated official expression, a rhetoric of racial and martial passion often dominated the larger culture. Allies like the Soviet Union, although zealous in pursuing technological advantage when possible, also could be profligate indeed in the expenditure of manpower. When conditions were favorable, the Japanese relied on technical superiority; it was not suicidal tactics that destroyed the American fleet at Pearl Harbor. Even when frankly suicidal tactics were employed, they had a military rationale, for the intent was to take the enemy along.

Likewise, the fact that both the United States and its enemies were fanatical did not mean that the differences between them in the forms of fanaticism were inconsequential. Destruction disguised as technique carried the gravest implications for the fact of enemy civilians. At the same time, it had inherent limits because it had little sanction apart from the prosecution of war. Since destruction was felt, but rarely proclaimed officially, as a good in itself, its sanction continued only as long as the war and the mobilization of technique that went with it continued. It made all the difference in the world to the Japanese—if we are to contrast their fate to that of the Jews—that however much vengeance may have motivated Americans, it did not become official policy and remained fulfilled by policies undertaken for other stated reasons.

Technological fanaticism had many sources: in the nature of strategic air power, whose benefits promised to be so large yet whose consequences were so hard to observe; in its demands for technique that distanced men from its consequences; in war's powerful emotions, difficult to recognize given America's strategic position and its own self-image. At bottom, technological fanaticism was the product of two distinct but related phenomena; one—the will to destroy—ancient and recurrent; the other—the technical means of destruction—modern. Their convergence resulted in the evil of American bombing. But it was sin of a peculiarly modern kind because it seemed so inadvertent, seemed to involve so little choice. Illusions about modern technology had made aerial holocaust seem unthinkable before it occurred and simply imperative once it began. It was the product of a slow accretion of large fears, thoughtless assumptions, and at best discrete decisions.

In one sense, the disjunction between means and ends that characterized the bombing seems at odds with the tenor of wartime political culture in the United States. The very vagueness of American purposes and the difficulty of achieving consensus about them in a diverse nation immune to immediate destruction led American leaders to define purposes by the lowest common denominators of survival and victory. If victory was a dominant, rationalizing value, was not a premium placed on how destruction would contribute to it? In practice, the focus on victory tended to validate any form of destruction that vaguely promised to secure it. Since political authority defined the path to victory as lying so substantially through production and technological effort, the focus tended to remain on means rather than ends. And progress by the preferred method of victory, war by air, could be measured most easily in terms of the destruction it wrought; the connection of that destruction to the end of victory was as easily presumed as it was hard to prove.

In their long journey from Pearl Harbor to the enemy's surrender on the decks of the *Missouri,* Americans might be likened to a man forced to set out on a cross-country car trip. As he drives along, the trip gathers its own interest, momentum, and challenge. He finds himself diverting to places he had not imagined; he tinkers with his car and enjoys feeling it run faster and smoother and discovers a power and mastery in manipulating it. Perhaps he did not choose this mode of travel conscious of the pleasures it would bring; he thought it necessary because of the baggage he wanted to bring along and because it was cheaper to travel this way, and after all, he already knew how to drive. Nor does he forget what his destination is, but as he travels he does not dwell on its importance; it will take care of itself if he makes the trip properly. Once the trip is done, it rapidly fades from memory, its pleasures and challenges now comfortably tucked away in his mind as necessities imposed on him in order to enable him to reach his destination, not as choices he had the freedom to make.

By December 1944, Americans were close to their destination, closer than most of them realized. Proximity was not evident, not with one more range of mountains to cross, not with the trip itself generating such excitement and anxiety, not with the machine built to make the trip yet to be fully tested. There was perhaps even a hope that the mountains would stand tall, to provide full measure for the test. "To test the [atomic] bomb's real destructiveness," Arnold later wrote about his concerns near the end of the war, "three or four cities must be saved intact from the B-29's regular operations as unspoiled targets for the new weapon. Which cities should be spared was a problem," he added. To Arnold, it seems, the test was as important as the destination. It lay ahead, with not only the atomic bomb but the "regular" forms of fire his bombers could hurl at Japanese cities. Technological fanaticism, long developing, could now be fully expressed. . . .

Impatience to finish off Germany quickly and by a decisive contribution from the air, along with the collapse of German capacity to defend and retaliate, culminated in the bombing that took place over the war's last winter. The climax came at Dresden, struck on the night of February 13–14 in two ferocious assaults brilliantly executed by British bombers, followed the next day by American bombers (except for forty that mistakenly hit Prague). The resulting firestorm, visible to bomber crews two hundred miles away, struck a city clotted with refugees fleeing other crumbling towns and advancing Soviet armies. Residents of Dresden were also unusually ill-prepared, believing their city exempted from Allied bombing perhaps to save it as the capital of a new Germany. The Dresden death toll, even as later revised downward to thirty-five thousand, was catastrophic and became the focal point of postwar debate about the moral distinctions between the Allies and the Axis. Dresden added to a tally of German civilian fatalities from Anglo-American bombing that reached somewhere between three hundred thousand and six hundred thousand; untold thousands more were killed in other Allied operations, the Red Army in particular razing cities by shelling and tactical air strikes.

The Dresden raids were less the product of conscious callousness than of casual destructiveness. Indeed, so many had a hand in the decision and so many reasons were available to run it that no clear rationale had to be furnished. One source was plans advanced from the previous summer for terror attacks to force the final breakdown of German morale. Supported by some AAF leaders, momentarily resisted by others and by Eisenhower, indirectly encouraged by Roosevelt, those plans—"baby killing schemes," as one AAF officer complained—generated intense debate over whether terror attacks would complement the precision campaign or dilute it, enhance the AAF's reputation or tarnish it, teach Germans a lasting lesson or only embitter them, and inflict righteous revenge or cause American shame. Slow to gain explicit approval, such plans were informally implemented anyway over the winter, particularly in Spaatz's February 3 raid on Berlin, claimed to have taken twenty-five thousand lives.

For the RAF's Harris, the obliteration of cities was routine practice, and Dresden was one city on his list as yet relatively unscathed. Yet the impetus within British circles to attack Dresden itself came more from Churchill, who knew well how "increasing the terror" could take place "under other pretexts." Dresden's marginal war industries, though sometimes cited as justification for the attacks, were not even targeted. With Marshall's support, Eisenhower's headquarters probably cut the explicit orders for Dresden, having in mind German morale, plus assisting the Soviet advance westward by disrupting German rail transport and fouling it with refugees. For their part, the Russians encouraged the assistance, though they did not specifically request an attack on Dresden. At least a few British and Americans also sought to impress and perhaps intimidate the Soviets with Anglo-American air power. Certainly Arnold was chagrined that "Stalin hasn't the faintest conception of the damage done to Germany and Japan by strategic bombing," and his representatives came to the Yalta conference in February with Hollywood pictures and combat footage to make an impression on the assembled Big Three leaders.

But to the bomber commanders involved, the Dresden raids did not appear unusual before they were run except for the circuitous channels and prodding by superiors that produced them. Indeed, had the hands of Churchill, Eisenhower, and Marshall not been evident and had not fortuitous factors produced a firestorm, Dresden would probably have escaped critical scrutiny. Harris's Bomber Command had, on its own authority, already demolished other German cities with a ferocity exceeding that displayed in Dresden. Darmstadt, for example, had been incinerated in a September firestorm because it was destroyable, not because it had even the strategic importance Dresden momentarily possessed. But the world had not noticed, any more than it noticed Hankow or the fate of other German, Italian, and Asian cities.

Dresden also stirred controversy because of its status as the cultural capital of Germany and because of an Associated Press story based on a SHAEF [Supreme Headquarters, Allied Expeditionary Force] officer's briefing and unaccountably cleared by censors. The AP reported that "the Allied air commanders have made the long-awaited decision to adopt deliberate terror bombing of the great German population centers as a ruthless expedient to hasten Hitler's doom." Both the British and American high commands were shocked by the appearance of such a claim and fearful of the controversy it seemed destined to arouse. An assistant to the ailing Arnold warned Spaatz of the "nation-wide serious effect on the Air Forces as we have steadily preached the gospel of precision bombing against military and industrial targets."

Spaatz's headquarters labored to assure Washington that there had been "no change in the American policy of precision bombing directed at military objectives." In a sense the claim was technically correct, and these men really believed that because American planes still flew under directives assigning precise targets, nothing in American targeting practices had changed. But by the end of 1944, American bombers relied on radar or "blind bombing" techniques so often, for roughly three-fourths of their missions, that terror became their inevitable consequence even when defined targets were the avowed objectives. Because that consequence seemed inadvertent and because it came about through a slow erosion of the distinction between precision and area bombing, any confrontation with moral scruples was forestalled for American commanders, just as it had been earlier for the British until civilians were finally acknowledged as the target. "Radar bombing was better than no bombing," air force historians aptly paraphrased the bomber commanders' thinking. On paper there was a policy against "indiscriminate bombing," Schaffer has pointed out: "Sometimes it was adhered to; often it was not, or it was so broadly reinterpreted as to become meaningless." In those circumstances, it was hard to recognize, or at least easy to deny, when the line to a different kind of bombing had been crossed.

Strangely, a drift in the reverse direction had received equally little recognition from the British. "By a curious development of the war's circumstances," it was explained to Arnold, "the AAF now bombs blind by day, while the RAF bombs visually (through the use of visual markers) by night. RAF bombing is now in fact frequently more accurate than our own." However, although unavoidable inaccuracy had originally justified the RAF's switch to area bombing, Harris refused to redirect his bombers. In general, greater accuracy was employed simply to perfect the wholesale destruction of cities.

In assessing responsibility for this destruction, Marshall's biographer has not exempted the chief of staff. Like other responsible commanders, he "did not so much direct the specific bombing as leave the choice of targets in the hands of subordinates who found it difficult to stop the momentum of attacks on a hated enemy." In fact, Marshall, Arnold, and Eisenhower did more than "leave the choice" to subordinates, for they had often talked of terror bombing and tacitly approved it by offering objections rooted only in timing and tactics. In connection with Operation CLARION, a plan to hit smaller German towns, Marshall had already spoken of bombing Munich "because it would show the people that are being evacuated to Munich that there is no hope." Even after Dresden, CLARION was formally ordered by Eisenhower's headquarters.

Earlier, Eaker had objected that CLARION would show the Germans "that we are the barbarians they say we are, for it would be perfectly obvious to them that this is primarily a large scale attack on civilians, as, in fact, it of course will be." But in a climate of degraded sensibilities and informal encouragement, Dresden, like other cities, was razed as the casually accepted by-product of attacks still designated as precise and limited. Spaatz's deputy revealed as much when he parried Washington's queries about what happened at Dresden. "These attacks [on cities he listed] have not been hailed as terror attacks against populations. . . . There has been no change of policy . . . only a change of emphasis in locale." The wording simultaneously implied that "terror attacks" were taking place, and yet that they were not because they had not been "hailed" as such.

Whatever concern Dresden evoked among American leaders was limited. The matter apparently never came to Roosevelt's attention. Stimson was upset over a German account that made "the destruction seem on its face terrible and probably unnecessary," but his stated reasons for concern were political: since Dresden was in the "least Prussianized part of Germany," he explained to Marshall in an eerie echo of the dashed hopes of its residents, it needed to be saved as the "center of a new Germany." There may have been more than this to Stimson's anxiety. Stimson knew the language of realpolitik, but he was also a moralist. But for the moment Dresden was a passing concern for him. For his part, Arnold's response to Stimson's concern was characteristically brutal: "We must not get soft—war must be destructive and to a certain extent inhuman and ruthless."

The "careful investigation" Stimson requested was pursued with little urgency and came too late to affect the subsequent course of bombing. Dresden itself was struck not only on February 14 by the Americans, but again on February 15, March 2, and April 17. Perhaps the additional raids seemed necessary because for all that the city's marshaling yards had justified the initial firestorm, in fact they had escaped major damage, and railway lines had quickly resumed operations. Only the exhaustion of targets and the desire not to complicate further the task of occupying Germany brought the campaign against its cities to a halt in mid-April. . . .

In general . . . American military leaders had feared an outcry that never arose. Yet their nervousness had significance, indicating their perceptions of limits to what the nation might accept in the way of destruction against the Germans. Although uncritical, press coverage of Germany's destruction was notably free of the spirit of revenge, implying that bombing was acceptable only as a military necessity. And as the Joint Chiefs were advised by Elmer Davis, long-standing distinctions made by Americans between their two major enemies were still evident in the muted reactions offered to the winter's bombing campaign: "There did not appear to be a great deal of opposition from the humanitarian point of view to the bombing of Japan," the head of the Office of War Information reported on February 27, "but some opposition is being expressed to the continual bombing of Berlin."

The Travails of the American
Combat Soldier in Europe

MICHAEL D. DOUBLER

Another departure from prewar doctrine was the need to fight without adequate reserves. Doctrine advised commanders to commit two-thirds of their strength into the fight and to hold the remainder in reserve. But constant attrition whittled away at combat units, and the demands of attacking prepared German defenses prompted generals to throw every man they had into the fight. Fighting with every unit committed became standard practice, and generals learned to live with the calculated risks of fighting without a reserve. . . .

Lack of reserves also meant that units had to stay on the fighting line for long periods without relief or rest. By May of 1945 American forces in the ETO [European Theater of Operations] included forty-six infantry and fifteen armored divisions. Between D-Day and V-E Day stretched 337 days, during which many divisions endured near continuous commitment in battle. Half of the infantry divisions spent over 150 days in combat, and 40 percent spent 200 days or more. Two divisions saw more than 300 days of action. The 2nd Division marched across Omaha Beach on 8 June and went on to spend an incredible 303 days in battle. The 90th Division saw its first fight in Normandy and in a stormy combat career managed to accumulate 308 days of combat, the highest of any division in the ETO. The armored divisions also had to endure long periods under fire. Of the fifteen armored divisions in the ETO, four saw more than 200 days of battle. . . .

A survey of casualties in the ETO shows why officers may have been so worried over their losses. Overall, U.S. army air and ground forces suffered 936,259 battle casualties in all theaters during World War II. The European theater alone accounted for the loss of 586,628 soldiers and airmen. Over 78 percent of the losses, or a total of 456,779 casualties, came from fighting divisions. The resulting picture is sobering: of the total American air and ground casualties in World War II, 49 percent occurred in the ETO's ground units between 6 June 1944 and 8 May 1945. The final body count of the ETO's casualties included 80,211 killed, 325,969 wounded, 40,271 prisoners of war, and 10,328 missing in action. Leaders in the ETO's ground units could take little consolation in the fact that they were participating in the greatest American bloodletting since Grant's 1864 drive on Richmond.

A review of divisional casualties conveys the intensity of the fighting. Of the sixty-one divisions in the theater, twenty had a personnel turnover rate of 100 percent or higher due to battle and nonbattle casualties. The infantry divisions suffered horribly; eighteen out of forty-six lost the equivalent of an entire division's worth of troops. Five divisions—the 1st, 3d, 4th, 9th, and 29th—had the dubious distinction of suffering more than 200 percent casualties during their careers in the ETO. The 4th Division had the unenviable distinction of being the most blooded division in Europe, suffering a ghastly casualty rate of 252.3 percent. In early

1945, forty-seven infantry regiments serving throughout nineteen divisions had sustained casualty rates between 100 and 200 percent. The armored divisions lost fewer in total numbers, but the proportion of the suffering was also grim. The 3d and 6th Armored Divisions had a turnover rate exceeding 100 percent. Three others followed close behind with casualty rates above 95 percent, so that one-third of the armored divisions had a turnover rate of 95 percent or higher.

To study the wounded and the dead is, to a great extent, to study the infantryman's burden; they represented 14 percent of the army's overseas strength but suffered 70 percent of the total battle casualties. Before D-Day army planners estimated the casualty rate for riflemen at around 70 percent. In reality the rate was much higher, about 83 percent, and the typical rate of loss in infantry platoons exceeded 90 percent. Riflemen accounted for 68 percent of an infantry division's authorized strength, but suffered almost 95 percent of its casualties. An AGF study on casualties concluded that in a typical battle, 90 percent of a division's casualties took place in the forward sectors assigned to the rifle battalions.

The other combat arms suffered much less than the infantry. Artillery men were 16 percent of an infantry division's authorized strength but only absorbed 3 percent of its casualties. The lion's share of artillery casualties took place among FO teams operating on the front lines rather than among gun crews. Engineers composed 4 percent of the division and lost only 2 percent of the casualties. Definite patterns emerged during tank-infantry operations. Armored infantry equaled 29 percent of an armored division's authorized strength but suffered an average of 62 percent of all casualties. Likewise, tankers filled 20 percent of authorized spaces but accounted for only 23 percent of the casualties. Losses between tankers and infantrymen varied in direct proportion to the tactical situation, but whoever led the attack absorbed the brunt of the losses. In one attack in Europe, tank battalions pushed ahead and suffered 50 percent of an armored division's losses, while the infantry absorbed 40 percent of the casualties. When armored infantry led attacks they suffered as much as 66 percent of the division's losses, the tankers just over 16 percent. The pattern of tanker to infantry losses holds true for the entire ETO. For all of the infantry and armored divisions that fought in Europe, the average rate of battle casualties per thousand men per day of combat were 3.2 and 2.7, respectively.

Two types of casualties caught the army off guard and caused serious problems throughout the European campaigns. The first was an epidemic of cold weather casualties that occurred in the form of trench foot and frostbite. Cold weather injuries usually took place in combat units forced to live in cold and wetness during static periods in which soldiers could not warm themselves, change socks and footgear, or receive warm food and hot drinks. Long periods of inactivity manning defenses and the restriction of blood flow to the extremities caused by poor clothing and footgear made troops vulnerable to cold weather injuries.

Cold weather injuries ravaged the American ranks like a medieval plague. In all of World War II, air and ground forces suffered a total of 91,000 cold weather casualties, and the lion's share of these occurred in the fighting units in the ETO. Between November 1944 and April 1945 hospitals in Europe admitted 45,283 cold weather casualties, just under 50 percent of all air and ground cold weather injuries for the war and about 9 percent of the total ground battle casualties suffered during the same period. In general, for every 1,000 soldiers in the ETO, 76 suffered a cold weather casualty. During November and December 1944, the American armies lost 23,000 soldiers to cold weather causes. In raw numbers the losses equaled the strength of one-and-a-half infantry divisions. However, most of the injuries took place among the 4,000 riflemen in a division, so cold weather injuries in reality incapacitated the equivalent fighting power of five-and-a-half divisions. Between November 1944 and March 1945, First and Third armies suffered 115,516 battle casualties and another 32,163 losses to cold injuries, a ratio of roughly 4 to 1. General Patton captured the flavor of the trench foot crisis in a memorandum of 21 November 1944 sent to all Third Army corps and division commanders: "The most serious menace confronting us today is not the German Army, which we have practically destroyed, but the weather which, if we do not exert ourselves, may well destroy us through the incidence of trench foot. . . . To win the war we must conquer trench foot." The explosion of cold weather injuries eroded the army's combat power and put unbearable demands on the replacement and medical evacuation systems.

A number of factors precipitated the cold weather injury epidemic. The winter of 1944 was the coldest, wettest period Europe had experienced in thirty years. Heavy rains in October and November and winter months with long periods of record-breaking cold caused frostbite and trench foot cases to mount. The American army was slow to gather and disseminate lessons learned on cold weather injuries in other theaters. Stateside and overseas training programs paid little attention to cold weather injury prevention, and soldiers did not know enough about the care and treatment of their own feet. General Bradley took a calculated risk in the early fall of 1944 and deliberately gave priority of shipment to ammunition and gasoline to sustain the drive into Germany rather than moving forward stocks of winter clothing and supplies. When the German army stopped the Allied advance and bad weather set in, American troops were ill equipped for it. . . .

The army also suffered heavy losses to a much more serious and complicated disease—combat exhaustion. American forces in World War I learned to cope with the effects of "shell shock," but 1941 found the army unprepared to deal with large numbers of soldiers suffering from combat-related mental disorders. At the time of Pearl Harbor the army lacked a treatment system, a definition, or even a name for a vexing problem that by 1945 would drain combat power from fighting units at an alarming rate. Large numbers of cases developed during the Tunisian campaign when the army first coined the term "combat exhaustion." The army's chief neuropsychiatrist graphically described the distinctive symptoms of a combat exhaustion casualty: "Typically he appeared as a dejected, dirty, weary man. His facial expression was one of depression, sometimes of tearfulness. Frequently his hands were trembling or jerky. Occasionally he would display varying degrees of confusion, perhaps to the extent of being mute or staring into space. Very occasionally he might present classically hysterical symptoms." Medical channels believed the "social and psychological background of the individual" helped determine the incidence and severity of combat exhaustion cases. Other determining factors were a soldier's military training and experience as well as the cumulative effects of fatigue, hunger, and fear. Perhaps the most telling indication that the army was not prepared to deal with the problem is that throughout the war it never considered combat exhaustion as a category of disease for reporting purposes.

Psychiatric casualties winnowed the ranks at an alarming rate. The armies in Europe evacuated 151,920 cases of neuropsychiatric disorders to hospitals in 1944 and 1945, and combat units discovered that on average, for every three men killed or wounded, one other soldier became a psychiatric casualty. High incidences of combat exhaustion paralleled peak fighting periods and was most prevalent in units in action for the first time. . . .

Combat exhaustion casualties usually fell into two broad categories. The first type occurred among new soldiers just before entry into combat or during their first five days on the front lines. Infantry replacements without adequate training or proper integration into their new units experienced unusually high combat exhaustion rates. Acute, traumatic incidents of fear or carnage induced combat exhaustion in many new soldiers. In the Huertgen Forest a new replacement in the elite 2d Ranger Battalion saw the head of a fellow ranger less than three feet away blown completely off. The new soldier became speechless, did not know his name, and could not recognize anyone around him. The unit evacuated the replacement, who finally ended up in a stateside psychiatric ward.

A second type of combat exhaustion occurred among experienced veterans who had endured continuous, severe fighting for four months or more. In the spring of 1945, First Army determined that the longest any man could remain in combat and retain his wits was about 200 days. The first indications of developing combat exhaustion among veterans were increased irritability, apathy, inefficiency, and carelessness about their own safety. Soldiers easily identified the phenomenon among veterans and began to call it the "old sergeant syndrome." Although this second kind of combat exhaustion developed over time, a specific occurrence usually brought on the final breakdown. A platoon leader in a rifle company of the 1st Division observed a classic, graphic example of the syndrome. In late March 1945 his company was fighting within the Remagen bridgehead. One of the squad leaders had landed on Omaha Beach on 6 June, was never wounded, and had not missed a day of action in all of the 1st Division's battles across Europe. But on 22 March the sergeant finally succumbed to combat exhaustion. The platoon leader wrote, "Now more than 270 combat days after first engagement, he suddenly reached the limit . . . the woods were silent except for his sobbing. Clutching his rifle he sat at the foot of a tree completely hysterical. He refused to release the rifle, apparently heard no commands, was unaffected by solicitude, and was incapable of further action." Fearing that the sergeant's collapse would demoralize the other men, the platoon leader evacuated him to the rear. After a few days of rest the squad leader rejoined the company but was never again "an effective fighting man."

Attitudes toward men suffering from combat exhaustion varied widely. Even the army's senior leaders held mixed opinions. Bradley believed that every soldier had his breaking point. The infamous Patton slapping incident during the Sicilian campaign personified the attitudes of many others who contended that combat exhaustion casualties really suffered from cowardice, poor motivation, or weakness of character. Soldiers in fighting units were much more understanding. Most officers in leadership positions believed that combat exhaustion and extreme reactions to fear were medical, not disciplinary, problems and required treatment rather than punishment. In 1944 as many as 77 percent of the officers assigned to two infantry divisions in the ETO indicated that combat exhaustion casualties should be treated as sick men, and a clear majority of the enlisted men held the same view. But there was little tolerance toward those trying to use combat exhaustion or extreme fear reactions to avoid combat. Troops expected everyone to make an effort to overcome fear and exhaustion. Soldiers visibly shaken by danger, who trembled and cried openly, were not considered cowards if they made an effort to regain their composure and to go back to their duties. If a man showed exhaustion symptoms and simply declared that he could not go any further and required evacuation, other soldiers branded him a coward and expressed their contempt and scorn.

Treatment methods and systems emerged slowly early in the war because many senior leaders tended to ignore or minimize the depth of the problem. But by 1944 the need for an organized medical response was clear to everyone. Commanders and medical channels had to improvise and experiment to develop effective treatment programs. Three principles guided treatment regimes: immediacy, proximity, and expectancy. Commanders learned to evacuate combat exhaustion casualties as quickly as possible for immediate treatment. Early in the war the army evacuated these soldiers far to the rear, where patients lost touch with their comrades, began to question their own worth and esteem, and tended to exaggerate the seriousness of their problem. In the ETO the army learned that by treating soldiers at the lowest adequate level of care and keeping them close to the front, most patients maintained a desire to return to their old units. Medical channels also conveyed to soldiers that their condition was temporary and treatable, and that after proper care they would return to the fighting. Many of the psychiatric care channels required to treat combat exhaustion were not included in the army's prewar force structure, and surgeons and commanders had to reorganize personnel and equipment to form treatment channels from scratch.

Battalion aid stations within 400 yards of the front lines were the army's most forward treatment centers. Battalion surgeons knew most of the troops in the unit and took a personal approach to their care. Common treatments included a few hours' rest, hot coffee, warm food, and a chance to wash. For more serious cases, surgeons administered sedatives from whiskey to morphine. Drug-induced sleep and food seemed the best remedies for mild cases and brought most soldiers back to full duty status. Battalion surgeons also separated malingerers and soldiers suffering temporary effects of extreme fear reactions from those with combat exhaustion symptoms. It was not unusual for troops to undergo immediate treatment and to return quickly to their unit. When soldiers did not respond to treatment, battalion surgeons evacuated them further to the rear. Regimental aid stations served as triage points for a more careful investigation of cases suspected of malingering and as rest areas for soldiers with persistent symptoms. The next level of evacuation was division clearing stations, where doctors tended to focus on battle casualties and the sick and hesitated to divert their time and resources to neuropsychiatric cases. Most divisions began to segregate physical casualties from mental cases and created separate combat exhaustion triage and treatment centers operated by the division's neuropsychiatrist. Most soldiers responded to treatment and moved on to division retraining centers that prepared them for return to the front lines. The most severe mental patients went on to newly formed hospitals controlled by the field armies or the COMZ. Patients responding to rehabilitation went back to their divisions for reassignment. Those who did not improve went to the ETO's central neuropsychiatric hospital at Ciney, Belgium, for more extensive treatment or rehabilitation. . . .

One of the army's greatest challenges was to keep battle-torn divisions up to strength with a constant flow of individual replacements. Fresh troops usually came from two sources: stateside replacements who entered the ETO through the Replacement System, which was a separate command within the COMZ, or soldiers from a variety of overstrength specialties retrained within the ETO to fight in critically short combat positions. The theater attempted to support a replacement pool of 70,000 troops. The key challenge was to maintain a manpower pool containing the right number of soldiers in the correct military specialties. Before D-Day the ETO determined that 64 percent of the replacement pool should consist of infantrymen, but after the heavy fighting in Normandy, the number went up to almost 80 percent. Casualty rates and the tempo of operations were variables that caused fluctuations in manpower demands. Matching the military specialties of incoming troops against the numbers and types of soldiers out of action was a balancing act commanders and personnel officers had a hard time mastering. Not until April 1945, when the stockage of replacements reached 86,000 men, was the Replacement System entirely capable of meeting the theater's demands.

Responsibility for administering the ETO's replacement infrastructure fell to the Replacement System, which was composed of a series of depots. By January 1945 twelve depots assisted in the movement of troops. The key nodes were four forward depots that supported the major field armies. Behind the army depots a varying number of intermediate depots assisted in the flow of replacements. Two depots acted as receiving stations for hospital returnees, commonly known as "casuals." The typical replacement set foot in the ETO through one of the entry depots at Le Havre or Marseilles. There he had a stop of several hours or an overnight rest while awaiting transportation to another depot further inland. At intermediate depots troops received individual weapons and equipment, clerks updated personnel records, and instructors gave lectures and classes. Replacements finally reached army depots where they underwent administrative processing before loading on trucks for the final leg of their trip to the front. Replacements ended their odyssey through the human pipeline under a variety of conditions. The lucky ones joined divisions in rest areas where they had a chance to become part of their unit before going into combat, while others went directly onto the firing line with little knowledge of their location, unit, or mission.

Replacements voiced acute dissatisfaction with the depot system. The army seemed incapable of providing quality amenities, and soldiers began to refer derisively to depots as "repple depots." The spartan facilities provided little more than the most basic shelter, sanitation, and dining comforts. Replacements moved from depot to depot in open trucks or in unheated and crowded train cars normally used to haul cargo or livestock. With little to do, soldiers became bored or frustrated and worried about what lay ahead. Lengthy delays in transit gnawed at replacements' physical conditioning, mental keenness, and discipline. Morale suffered tremendously, and casuals returning to units were quick to fuel replacements' anxieties with horror stories of what it was like at the front. A new officer replacement remembered talking to veterans in one repple depot:

> I met several individuals who had come back from the line. Invariably they recounted their hair-raising experiences—their outfits had been "wiped out," or "pinned down for days"; "officers didn't have a dogs' chance of survival," etc. One platoon sergeant . . . said his platoon had lost sixteen officers in one two-week period. I expected confidently that I would be blown to bits within fifteen minutes after my arrival at the front.

For the average soldier, life in the Replacement System was a hardship that seemed meaningless and unnecessary.

By the late fall of 1944 there were enough complaints about the poor physical and mental quality of replacements to cause concern. The COMZ made a concerted effort to provide better billets, recreational facilities, mess halls, and transportation. Improvised training programs attempted to reduce boredom, and the army began to segregate replacements from the dour casuals. A consensus developed that the term replacement had an adverse impact on morale because it suggested a soldier's expendability. In late December fresh troops became known as reinforcements, an effort to emphasize the replacement's function as a combat reserve rather than as a human repair part. The most fundamental reform did not come until March 1945. Recognizing the replacement system's adverse effects on the morale, discipline, and training of individual soldiers, the ETO began to move troops through depots in organized groups. Reinforcements became members of ad hoc squads, platoons, or companies organized for movement to the front. When possible, soldiers remained in these units until they reached their final destination. Keeping soldiers grouped together successfully warded off the impersonal nature of the depot system, but reform came too late to indicate any other real benefits.

The army transferred soldiers from a variety of military specialties to the combat arms to provide additional replacements. The ETO drew from three sources in an effort to fill critical shortages: noninfantry replacements, men taken from overstrength units, and troops reassigned from COMZ and AAF units. As combat casualties grew, the theater vigorously retrained these soldiers as infantrymen and sent them to the front lines. Commanders everywhere seemed displeased with the retraining program. Most division commanders preferred to receive infantry replacements from stateside than from the ETO's retraining centers, complaining that soldiers released by the COMZ and AAF were of poorer quality than those coming from the United States. Undoubtedly, both the COMZ and AAF used the retraining program to clean house. Many troops transferred to the infantry were undesirables. In April 1945 First Army complained that of 514 retrained soldiers received from AAF, 231 had court-martial convictions. Later that month an investigation revealed that 22 percent of all AAF airmen transferred to the infantry had records of court-martial conviction. . . .

Although the army had trained many of its divisions for as long as two years with the full realization that they were headed for a combat zone, the best efforts could not completely close the gap between training and battle. Officers felt they had received adequate tactical training but needed more instruction on leadership methods and how to train their own soldiers. A majority of rifle company officers in three divisions preparing to deploy overseas felt they did not know enough about developing pride and motivation in soldiers or how to cope with troops' personal problems. They also wanted more instruction on how to train troops on specific soldier skills. They believed physical training and conditioning, close order drill, and military courtesy and discipline were the strengths of American training programs. The enlisted ranks were more thorough and critical in evaluating training. A slim majority of combat veterans believed their overall training had been "about right," while 30 percent thought it had not been demanding enough. Most soldiers felt that field exercises with tough, realistic battle conditions, regular and rigorous physical fitness training, running obstacle courses, and long field marches of 25 miles with full field equipment best prepared them for battle. These activities reflected the broad consensus that the single best way to prepare a soldier for combat was to improve his stamina and physical strength.

Veterans were quick to point out training shortcomings. Inadequate knowledge of the enemy was one of the army's greatest training deficiencies. Approximately 80 percent of soldiers said that they did not know enough about German weapons or how to defend against them. Knowledge of German tactics was deficient, and soldiers lacked training on how to attack various types of enemy defenses. Almost two-thirds of American soldiers felt they were weak on aircraft identification. Many veterans criticized their precombat training for not giving them enough exposure to live fire ammunition. Almost 90 percent of American soldiers indicated that they were unprepared for mine warfare. The detection and removal of mines and booby traps challenged units in the ETO and resulted in heavy losses in men and equipment. Veterans felt they did not know enough about how to deal with trench foot. Considering the army's heavy trench foot losses, it is no surprise that training on the prevention and treatment of the malady was one of the military's greatest training oversights.

A broad consensus existed among enlisted men on the best and worst aspects of training. Soldiers felt that weapons training, instruction in seeking cover and concealment, how to stay dispersed and not bunch up, and skills in digging foxholes and defensive positions helped them the most. Soldiers held the view that close order drill, military courtesy, inspections, bayonet and hand-to-hand combat drills, and chemical warfare training had little relevance to their work on the battlefield. A paradox in soldiers' evaluations of training programs is that those areas in which officers felt training programs excelled—close order drill and military courtesy and discipline—were perceived by the troops as not very important in preparing them for combat. The opposing views probably reflected the officer corps' attitude that instilling discipline was a vital function of training programs, while the enlisted ranks tended to believe that the exclusive purpose of training was to teach them the specific skills required for combat.

Actual combat revealed a number of defects in American battlefield performance. New units experiencing their baptism of fire in the ETO failed to follow close behind supporting artillery fire, tended to slow down upon initial enemy contact, and allowed German indirect fire to pin them down in the open. Tank-infantry cooperation was poor across the board but improved over time. Commanders put excessive emphasis on protecting their flanks and maintaining contact with adjacent outfits. Units put too much faith in artillery firepower and often failed to generate enough fire with their own organic weapons. The performance of individual soldiers indicated other training weaknesses. The tendency of soldiers to bunch together under fire was a universal complaint. American troops displayed carelessness in close proximity to the enemy and tended to expose their locations because of poor noise and light discipline.

Commanders believed that their soldiers did not fire enough and that units needed better fire discipline and training in distributing fire throughout objective areas. Soldiers trained on known-distance rifle ranges found many reasons for not shooting in combat. Instead of placing fire in the general area of the objective, many wanted to identify specific targets before firing, while others preferred to remain under cover rather than exposing themselves while trying to get off a few shots. Some soldiers believed that firing at anything other than a good target was a waste of ammunition. Lt. Col. John A. Hentges, commander of the 3d Division's 7th Infantry, summed up the views of many as to why soldiers did not shoot enough:

> Our greatest need in training is to get riflemen to fire their weapons. New men will not fire. This is caused primarily by not wanting to disclose their position and inability to see the enemy or something to aim at. I believe our policy of putting so much of our basic weapon training on known distance ranges where men are cautioned so often on holding, squeezing and marking the target causes this.

A training memorandum of the 78th Division told commanders that "new men must be told and re-indoctrinated" that aggressive fire kept the Germans pinned down and allowed their own units to advance. It reminded soldiers that "the M-1 and the BAR throw a lot of lead" and that "the unit that keeps firing intelligently" could always move on the battlefield. Col. S. L. A. Marshall, one of the leading combat historians in the ETO, interviewed many units after engagements and came up with a surprising and controversial finding on infantry firepower. Marshall believed that in an "average experienced infantry company" only 15 percent of soldiers fired their weapons, while the best units under extreme, heavy combat managed to produce fire from 25 percent of all soldiers.

The army adopted a technique known as "marching fire" to increase infantry firepower and aggressiveness. In attacks across open ground, infantry platoons deployed into skirmish lines with their BARs and light machine guns scattered along the line. The idea was for soldiers to keeping pressing forward while throwing a wall of lead before them. . . .

While the army as an institution changed its ways of employing combat power, individual soldiers tried to adjust to life in the combat zone. Soldiers instinctively knew that increasing their own survivability and effectiveness would make the combined arms team more powerful and help hasten the war's end. A number of tremendous stresses faced soldiers on the battlefield: getting used to the notion of killing or being killed; the incessant presence of danger, noise, and confusion; living in a world of frustration and uncertainty; and having to always depend on others for personal safety and welfare. Veterans came to realize that the combat zone was a forbidding, tiring place, and constant threats to life and limb drained their mental stamina and will to fight. Lack of shelter, wetness, extreme hot or cold, filth, and sleep deprivation caused misery and mindnumbing fatigue. The loss of friends and the sights and sounds of the dead and wounded unnerved even the strongest. Isolation from loved ones, normal social activities, and female companionship bothered many soldiers. Conflicts between fundamental values—the paradox between morality and the horrors of war and loyalty between duty and friends—confused and distressed many soldiers. Soldiers had to learn to deal with all of these problems while pushing ahead against the enemy.

Without a doubt coping with fear was the greatest human challenge soldiers faced on the battlefield. During stateside training the army tried to reduce adverse reactions from fear in three ways. Trainees underwent systematic psychological screening to weed out those mentally unfit for combat, and about 10 percent of all draftees were rejected on psychiatric grounds. The army also encouraged soldiers to take a permissive attitude toward their own symptoms of fear. Soldiers were taught that feeling afraid in dangerous situations was not shameful and that fear was normal and felt by everyone. Training stressed that even though a man felt fear he could overcome it and that eventually the symptoms of fear would abate. A handbook issued to all trainees conveyed these notions in easy-to-understand language:

> YOU'LL BE SCARED. Sure you'll be scared. Before you go into battle, you'll be frightened at the uncertainty, at the thought of being killed. . . . If you say you're not scared, you'll be a cocky fool. Don't let anyone tell you you're a coward if you admit being scared. Fear before you're actually in the battle is a normal emotional reaction. . . . After you've become used to the picture and the sensations of the battlefield, you will change. All the things you were taught in training will come back to you. . . . That first fight—that fight with yourself—will have gone. Then you will be ready to fight the enemy.

Last, the army tried to reduce the disruptive effects of fear by ingraining soldiers with automatic responses to certain kinds of dangers and exposing them to simulated battle conditions. Instructors drilled trainees time and time again on how to clear weapons malfunctions, don gas masks, "hit the dirt" when taken under fire, move with "your head down," and dozens of other reflex responses to danger. Trainees had to crawl over rough ground for about 80 yards with live machine-gun bullets clipping over their heads. Sometimes the army exposed infantry trainees to close artillery shelling to give them a feel for the noise and concussion of exploding rounds. The efficacy of such steps is hard to measure, but veterans believed that more exposure to fear in training would have better prepared them for combat.

On the front lines, commanders saw that fear and anxiety before battle were just as great as when bullets began to fly, and officers and NCOs learned specific leadership techniques to reduce fear before it overwhelmed their troops. Before combat, soldiers tended to multiply and exaggerate the unknown dangers that lay ahead. Almost 70 percent of veterans admitted to worrying about becoming a casualty in the next fight. Commanders counteracted prebattle fear by giving soldiers as much information as they could about the tactical situation while explaining their battle plans in detail. Leaders appealed to teamwork and cooperation, the sense of responsibility for the welfare of others, unit pride, the hope of winning and going home, and hatred for the enemy. However, commanders discovered that troops did not respond well to patriotic appeals, and though humor worked to dispel fear, those in charge learned to never joke about death or wounds. Leaders making promises they could not keep—telling soldiers the fight would be over in a few days or promising a rest period after the battle—created morale problems. Officers learned that they could not threaten or browbeat soldiers into overcoming fear and that it was impossible to talk rationally to men panicked or hysterical with fear. Soldiers preparing for battle did not have time to dwell on their anxieties, so leaders kept them busy with weapons and equipment maintenance and inspections. Commanders talked informally with troops and found that humor, encouragement, prayer, and talking about any variety of subjects diverted attention from the dangers ahead.

Training could not introduce soldiers to stark fear, so they felt the physical symptoms of fear for the first time in battle. The most common physiological sign of fear experienced by roughly 80 percent of troops was violent pounding of the heart. A majority of soldiers also felt a "sinking feeling" in the stomach, shaking or trembling of the hands and body, cold sweat, and nausea. Fewer than 20 percent of soldiers admitted to losing control of their bowels, another 10 percent said that they urinated in their pants, and runaway bodily functions may have been even more common. A new replacement was next to a veteran when a German 88 fired on them. The older sergeant swore, and the new troop asked him if he was hit:

> He sort of smiled and said no, he had just pissed his pants. He always pissed them, he said, when things started and then he was okay . . . and then I realized something wasn't quite right with me. . . . There was something warm down there and it seemed to be running down my leg . . . I told the sarge. I said, "Sarge, I've pissed too," or something like that and he grinned and said, "Welcome to the war."

A survey of 277 wounded in the ETO revealed that some symptom of fear at one time or another kept 65 percent of them from performing adequately, and almost half admitted recurring incidents of disruptive fear reactions.

Training did not prepare soldiers for coping with the fear of enemy weapons. Enemy machine guns and mines inflicted heavy casualties, but Americans' familiarity with the weapons made them less fearful. GIs identified the 88-mm gun, German aircraft, and mortars as the most fearful weapons they faced. Soldiers seemed to respect most the weapons they could not hear coming or take protection against, and they linked fear with a weapon's noise. Enemy machine guns had a high cyclic rate of fire that Americans said sounded like a sheet being torn in two, while their own machine guns had a slower, thumping rhythm. A weapon that struck widespread fear was the German Nebelwerfer, a mobile, multibarreled rocket launcher that induced fear not from its accuracy or ordnance, but because its shells made a terrifying, moaning noise in flight. Soldiers learned to detect the accuracy of incoming artillery from the noise of the shells in flight. Veterans came to fear German mortars more because their shells exploded without warning. Over time, fear of weapons often changed to healthy respect as soldiers got used to enemy weapons, listened for approaching danger, and learned to take cover.

Despite the army's best efforts to provide realistic training, soldiers still had to learn fundamental survival lessons and were quick to discover ways to stay alive in combat. Veterans stated emphatically that staying put under fire was one of the best ways to get killed. Soldiers had to overcome the tendency to freeze upon initial enemy contact, and units learned to minimize casualties by moving quickly through preplanned mortar and artillery fire and by maneuvering aggressively against enemy defenses. The Germans tended to return fire when fired upon, so troops learned to use reconnaissance by fire to detect enemy positions at long range. Soldiers stressed the importance of proper cover and concealment and taught replacements to avoid open fields, roads, and paths. The easiest route forward was often the quickest way to get killed or wounded. Soldiers learned to dig deep foxholes—two feet or more to provide adequate protection—and to get some type of overhead cover against shell fragments. Despite warnings that they had to stay dispersed under fire, soldiers sought mutual protection by crowding together during engagements. A wounded rifleman warned, "The minute you bunch up they let you have it. Men bunch up for company. When you get into battle you just naturally want to get close—but we learned the hard way—don't bunch." Soldiers learned better light and noise discipline to avoid giving away their positions. Riflemen tried to remain calm when wounded because panicked shouting and thrashing about endangered themselves and the lives of others nearby. New troops learned that the Germans often booby-trapped abandoned weapons and tempting souvenirs. Moving forward to take custody of surrendering Germans could be hazardous, and Americans learned always to make prisoners come to them. Soldiers also developed a wariness for overly friendly civilians.

The maintenance of troop morale in fighting units was one of the army's greatest concerns. Soldiers with high morale had a zeal to accomplish tasks, a discipline that allowed them to subordinate individual interests to those of the group, a confidence in themselves and their equipment, and an absence of discontent and worry regarding their duty position and role in combat. Soldiers with low morale were lethargic and ineffective, had discipline problems, and contributed little on the combined arms battlefield. Mental anxiety was perhaps the greatest cause of low morale. The army learned that war fostered worries that could drain a soldier's working and fighting efficiency. Troops thousands of miles from home, living and fighting under heartbreaking and nerve-wracking conditions, worried about immediate problems and the welfare of loved ones at home. Common concerns among officers and enlisted men included being gone from the United States for long periods, family matters at home, and the overall progress of the war. Footsoldiers seemed to worry about very practical matters: their overall mental and physical health, fear of wounds or death, the uncertainties that came with each day on the front lines, and a concern that America might not achieve its war aims. Officers tended to worry more about the future than the present and about how they would resume normal lives and careers after the war.

Commanders on the front lines learned that they could do much to maintain esprit. Soldiers responded readily to measures that promoted teamwork, unit pride, and improved officer-enlisted relations. Soldiers respected and followed leaders who looked after their needs, and boasts from troops that they had "a damn good company commander and a fine first sergeant" were one of the best indicators of high morale. Teamwork existed in units where officers led by example, enlisted men cooperated with one another, and everyone pulled together to get through tough times. Leaders who remained calm under fire and maintained a sense of humor fostered high morale. Efforts to give soldiers adequate meals, shelter, rest, and recreation whenever possible also paid great dividends, while the absence of any or all of these conditions made morale suffer. A thoroughly trained, physically fit soldier with high morale responded to training, maintained discipline during periods of quiet and boredom, and performed well in battle.

The army's greatest cause of low morale was far beyond the power of frontline commanders to repair: extended periods overseas and the lack of a rotation policy for ground soldiers. As units moved across France combat troops came to realize that only peace, wounds, or death would bring release from the war's burdens. Veteran infantrymen believed they had done their part and that others should come forward to assume their share of the burden. Soldiers began to talk about the "million dollar wound," one serious enough to require evacuation to rear areas or even stateside but inflicting no permanent disfigurement or injury.

Officers detected a distinct lack of animosity for the enemy among their troops, and postwar surveys revealed that Americans had fairly moderate attitudes toward enemy troops and the German people. A substantial minority of soldiers admitted that some hatred for the Germans motivated them in combat, but most soldiers were not vindictive. More than half the riflemen in one division in Europe admitted that viewing enemy prisoners close up made them realize that Germans were "men just like us" and that it was "too bad we have to be fighting them." The War Department seemed appalled by American soldiers' tepid feelings of hatred and cautioned commanders, "Many soldiers who lack vindictiveness are probably standing on the shaky ground of too much identification with the enemy as a human being. . . . These men need to be convinced that America's very survival depends upon killing the enemy with cold, impersonal determination, that the enemy must be destroyed if America is to live." Despite the army's desire to perpetuate hatred for the enemy, about two-thirds of American soldiers believed that after the war the Allies should punish Nazi leaders but not the German people.

Outside the parameters of combat, behavior between Americans and Germans ranged from savagery to compassion. Only 13 percent of a sample of riflemen from Europe observed atrocities, but sometimes Americans found it difficult not to kill their enemies in the heat of passion. At Brest a German sniper shot a medic square in the center of the red cross on his helmet, so infantrymen avenged his death by refusing to take prisoners for the next several hours. North of Aachen a surrendering German officer killed a soldier of the 30th Division with a concealed pistol. The other members of the platoon threw the officer against a pillbox, killed him with a volley from almost every one of their weapons, and then continued the attack. Not all captured Germans made it into PW handling channels, and some rifle companies developed reputations for taking few prisoners. At the other end of the spectrum, opposing forces often held short truces to evacuate the dead and the wounded. In the midst of the gruesome fighting in the Huertgen Forest, German troops blocking the 28th Division's supply line along the Kall Trail let medical vehicles and stretcher teams pass unharmed.

The high number of incidents in which small numbers of isolated Germans and Americans encountered one another without firing a shot was one of the more peculiar aspects of soldiers' behavior. When small groups unexpectedly ran into one another at close quarters, both sides tended to back off quickly without firing a shot and to go about their business somewhere else. During the Battle of the Bulge, two American riflemen moving through the woods came upon a line of skirmishers moving in the opposite direction. One of the soldiers remembers:

> I say to Carl, "Hey, look at the long overcoats." Carl turns, takes one quick look, and says, "Oh, my God, those are Germans!" . . . I whisper "What do we do now?" And Carl, he was an old-timer, says to me, "Don, we don't do nothing, we just keep going." They passed us, we passed them. I think both [Carl] Bauer and I were scared stiff. I know I was. We kept this to ourselves, we never told anyone.

Soldiers on both sides seemed to believe that killing one another as a result of a meaningless, unexpected encounter was folly. They tended to save their hostilities for days when they could fight as a unit and when their killing might have some bearing on the war's outcome.

If American soldiers were unemotional about the enemy, they also held sober attitudes toward their own work. Soldiers viewed the war in pragmatic terms and rarely discussed the broader values and principles for which they were fighting. All across Europe, Americans manned guns, drove vehicles, and marched against the enemy with a matter-of-fact attitude toward the fighting. They faced combat with grim determination. During the bloody fighting in the Huertgen Forest, a group of squad leaders in the 4th Division received another order from their platoon leader. When the lieutenant finished, an awkward silence fell over the men. One sergeant stood up with his rifle, said "Well, we can't do a damn thing sitting here," and walked away to get his men ready for the attack. . . .

In retrospect, the army's philosophy of getting the war over with as quickly as possible while inflicting maximum damage on the Germans and minimizing its own casualties motivated much of what went on in the ETO. Soldiers knew the only way to get the war over and go home was through hard fighting. When Creighton Abrams stood on the west bank of the Moselle River at Dieulouard and told his superiors that the shortest way to end the war and go home was to attack and capture the hills on the far bank, his words personified the attitudes of most soldiers. Americans stayed on the offensive as much as logistical constraints and the enemy situation would allow. GIs closed with the enemy with a sense of grim determination but without developing a consuming hatred for their opponents. . . .

⊕ FURTHER READING

Ambrose, Stephen E. *Band of Brothers: E Company, 506th Regiment, 101st Airborne* (1992).
———. *Citizen Soldiers* (1997).
———. *D-Day, June 6, 1944* (1994).
———. *Eisenhower,* 2 vols. (1983–1984).
Crane, Conrad C. *Bombs, Cities, and Civilians: American Airpower Strategy in World War II* (1993).
Craven, Wesley Frank, and James Lea Cate, eds. *The Army Air Forces in World War II,* 7 vols. (1948–1958).
D'Este, Carlo. *Patton: A Genius for War* (1995).
———. *World War II in the Mediterranean, 1942–1945* (1990).
Doubler, Michael D. *Closing with the Enemy: How GI's Fought the War in Europe* (1994).
Eisenhower, John. *Allies: Pearl Harbor to D-Day* (1982).
Gray, J. Glenn. *The Warriors: Reflections on Men in Battle* (1959).
Hastings, Max. *Overlord* (1984).
Keegan, John. *Six Armies in Normandy* (1984).
Kennett, Lee. *GI: The American Soldier in World War II* (1987).
Linderman, Gerald F. *The World Within War: America's Combat Experience in World War II* (1997).
Millett, Allan R. and Murray Williamson, eds. *Military Effectiveness,* vol. 3, *The Second World War* (1988).
Morison, Samuel E. *History of United States Naval Operations in World War II,* 15 vols. (1947–1962).
Overy, Richard J. *The Air War* (1980).
———. *Why the Allies Won* (1995).
Perret, Geoffrey. *Winged Victory: The Army Air Forces in World War II* (1993).
Roskill, Stephen W. *The War at Sea, 1939–1945,* 3 vols. (1954–1961).
Sandler, Stanley. *Segregated Skies: All-Black Combat Squadrons in World War II* (1992).

Schaffer, Ronald. *Wings of Judgment: American Bombing in World War II* (1985).
Schoenfeld, Max. *Stalking the U-Boat: USAF Offensive Antisubmarine Operations in World War II* (1994).
Sherry, Michael S. *The Rise of American Air Power* (1987).
U.S. Department of the Army, Center for Military History. *United States Army in World War II: European Theater of Operations* series and *Mediterranean Theater of Operations* series (multivolume).
Van Creveld, Martin. *Fighting Power: German and U.S. Army Performance, 1939–1945* (1982).
Weigley, Russell F. *Eisenhower's Lieutenants* (1981).
Wells, Mark K. *Courage and Air Warfare: The Allied Aircrew Experience in the Second World War* (1995).

See also Chapters 2, 3, 5, and 11.

CHAPTER
5

The War Against Japan:
What Was Needed
and What Was Done

The war against Japan differed in many ways from the war against Germany. Although interservice disagreements about the relative importance of ground, naval, and air operations took place, they were quite dissimilar from the debates in Europe. So were the political disagreements between the Allied powers and the nature of the actual fighting.

Although the United States officially maintained a Germany-first strategy as per prewar plans (see Chapter 3), Washington sent major forces to the Pacific in 1942 in an effort to halt the Japanese offensives that followed the Pearl Harbor attack. This effort was demanded by America's Chinese, Australian, and New Zealand allies; by the U.S. Navy; by Philippine commander General Douglas MacArthur; and by a public insistent on revenge for Pearl Harbor. As a result, more U.S. forces were deployed against Japan than against Germany throughout 1942, and even into 1943 (not until 1944 would the bulk be deployed against Germany). These forces failed to prevent Japanese conquest of the Philippines, Burma, the Dutch East Indies, and all the other European colonies in Southeast Asia, but they did halt the Japanese tide at the 1942 naval battles of Coral Sea and Midway as well as the six-month campaign for the island of Guadalcanal in the South Pacific Solomons chain. Nevertheless Japan still possessed in 1943 one of the largest empires in history, and how to defeat the Japanese became a matter of intense interservice and inter-Allied disputes.

In the air war, those disputes did not focus on daylight precision versus night area bombing as they did in Europe. Reversing the air strategy they championed in the European theater, American military planners came to favor the eventual area bombing of Japanese cities. But how to get within bombing range of the Japanese home islands, and whether bombing itself would be sufficient to obtain Japanese surrender, led to major debates as to the relative importance of different geographic theaters.

The enormous Pacific theater, which was totally under the control of the U.S. Joint Chiefs of Staff, had been divided in 1942 into the Pacific Ocean Areas under Admiral Chester W. Nimitz in Hawaii and the Southwest Pacific under General Douglas MacArthur in Australia. The latter pressed for major offensives in New Guinea and New Britain to destroy the major Japanese base at Rabaul and advance northwestward to liberate the Philippines, while Nimitz and the navy pressed instead for a naval drive due westward across the central Pacific, through the Gilbert, Marshall, and Marianas island groups, to the island of Formosa off the China coast. Either approach would require major amphibious assaults, and land as well as naval battles against Japanese forces.

Most of the Japanese Army was already deployed in China, however, and U.S. military planners hoped to keep it that way. So did President Roosevelt, who wanted China to play a major role in the war and to become one of the "Four Policemen" in the postwar world (see Chapter 10). Consequently China constituted a third important geographic theater in the war against Japan. To maintain and support Nationalist Chinese leader Chiang Kai-shek's forces, General Joseph Stilwell was appointed Chiang's chief of staff as well as Lend-Lease administrator and commanding general of all U.S. forces in the China-Burma-India [CBI] theater. His major tasks were to train the Chinese armies and, in conjunction with British and U.S. forces, reconquer Burma so that supplies could flow to Chiang's armies.

Numerous political as well as military disagreements plagued Stilwell's mission. General Claire Chennault, head of U.S. Army Air Forces in the China theater, discounted the need for ground operations and pressed instead for the establishment of air bases from which to bomb the Japanese. Chiang Kai-shek supported this strategy, at least partially because he did not wish to risk his armies in battles against the Japanese. Rather, as Stilwell discovered, he was most interested in obtaining training and military aid for his forces to prepare for continuation of the civil war against Mao Tse-tung's Communists that had begun before the Japanese invasion. Nor were the British anxious for Burma operations or a major role for China in the war—or in the postwar era. Churchill did not believe China could or should be considered a major power, and he clashed with Roosevelt over the entire question of the future of colonialism in Asia.

By 1944 these factors had led to consistent military failure in China and Burma. Simultaneously General MacArthur and Admiral Nimitz obtained great success in the Pacific, where each was allowed to pursue his own approach. By late 1944 their forces had met in the Philippines and thereby cut the Japanese off from the resources of Southeast Asia.

This dual advance in the Pacific involved warfare quite different from what was taking place in the war against Germany. Once again control of the seas was critical, but in the Pacific U.S. rather than German submarine forces took the offensive and succeeded in destroying much of the Japanese merchant marine. Furthermore, naval warfare in the Pacific focused to a much greater extent than in the Atlantic on battles between surface ships—most importantly the aircraft carriers that replaced battleships as the key capital vessels of both navies. (So extensive was the reach of these ships and their planes that in many naval battles the opposing fleets did not even see each other.) In such critical battles as Coral Sea, Midway, Philippine Sea, and Leyte Gulf, U.S. forces virtually destroyed Japan's carrier fleet and naval air forces as well as its other surface ships. Along *with these naval battles went amphibious landings and major land campaigns on the invaded islands by marine and army units. These battles were particularly brutal, with little if any quarter asked or given by either side.*

With its navy and merchant marine decimated and the U.S. forces within air range, Japan by early 1945 was under a strangling blockade and intense air bombardment. The situation was hopeless. Nevertheless Japanese forces fought fiercely, using suicide tactics in the Philippines and on the islands of Iwo Jima and Okinawa to inflict on the Americans the heaviest casualties they had yet received in the Pacific theater.

Numerous questions have arisen regarding the nature of the war against Japan. Did the United States devote too much attention to this war at the expense of the more critical conflict against Germany, not enough attention, or just the right amount? Why? Why did the Joint Chiefs of Staff violate their principle of unity of command by allowing two competing theaters to exist in the Pacific? Was this "dual offensive" effective or counterproductive? Why were the Pacific island battles so bloody, and why were so few prisoners taken? What were the reasons for the failures of the U.S. military and diplomatic efforts in China, and what were the consequences of these failures? What impact did all of the above have on the 1945 decision to use the atomic bomb against Japan in 1945? (See Chapter 11.)

DOCUMENTS

The public opinion polls in Document 1 reveal the Japan-first mentality of many Americans in 1942–1943, despite Washington's continued official adherence to a Germany-first strategy. Document 2 is taken from a Joint and Combined Chiefs of Staff 1943 plan for Japanese defeat and illustrates the numerous theaters and approaches involved in Allied planning.

The next four documents illustrate different aspects of the actual fighting in Asia and the Pacific. Document 3 is from the memoir of a U.S. Army nurse on the Bataan Peninsula in the Philippines, where U.S. forces made their unsuccessful stand against the Japanese in 1942, followed by the notorious Bataan Death March. Document 4, written by a U.S. pilot at the pivotal battle of Midway (the sole survivor of a U.S. torpedo squadron), describes naval air warfare in the Pacific. Document 5 is from a memoir by a U.S. marine, E. B. Sledge, and illustrates the horrors of ground warfare in the Battle of Okinawa. Document 6, the recollections of two Japanese civilians, illustrates the equal if not greater horrors of the air campaign.

The final three documents deal with the political aspects of the war against Japan. Document 7, excerpted from General Stilwell's acerbic diary, illustrates the political as well as the military problems and frustrations he faced in the China theater, with particular reference to the 1944 crisis that led to his recall; it also illustrates why he was nicknamed "Vinegar Joe." In Document 8, President Roosevelt makes clear his desire to do away with European colonialism in Asia. In Document 9, U.S. Foreign Service officers John Paton Davies and George R. Merrell pointedly note the conflict between this U.S. postwar goal and the contradictory desire to maintain Great Britain as a major power, as well as the negative consequences that would flow from adherence to the latter goal.

1. Public Opinion Favors a Japan-First Strategy, 1942–1943

Japan First or Germany First, 1942

40. . . . . Granting that it's important for us to fight the Axis every place we can, which do you think is more important for the United States to do right now?

	Mar 28 '42	June 17 '42
Put most of our effort into fighting Japan	62%	37%
Put most of our effort into fighting Germany	21	46
Don't know	17	14
Both		1
No answer		2

Nation's Chief Enemy, 1943

Interviewing Date 2/5–10/43
Survey #289-K   Question #1

*In this war, which do you think is our chief
enemy—Japan or Germany?*

Japan 53%
Germany 34
No opinion 13

2. The Military Plans for the Defeat of Japan, May 21, 1943

4. Burma-China Theater

The Combined Chiefs of Staff have agreed on:

a. The concentration of available resources as first priority within the Assam-Burma Theater on the building up and increasing of the air route to China to a capacity of 10,000 tons a month by early Fall, and the development of air facilities in Assam with a view to—

(1) Intensifying air operations against the Japanese in Burma;
(2) Maintaining increased American air forces in China;
(3) Maintaining the flow of airborne supplies to China.

b. Vigorous and aggressive land and air operations from Assam into Burma via Ledo and Imphal, in step with an advance by Chinese forces from Yunnan, with the

---

(Document 1) From *The Gallup Poll, 1935–1971* by George Gallup, vol. 1, 370. Copyright © 1972 by American Institute of Public Opinion. Used by permission of Random House, Inc.

(Document 2) From U.S. Department of State, *Foreign Relations of the United States: The Conferences at Washington and Quebec, 1943* (Washington, D.C.: U.S. Government Printing Office, 1970), 349–350.

object of containing as many Japanese forces as possible, covering the air route to China, and as an essential step towards the opening of the Burma Road.

  c. The capture of Akyab and of Ramree Island by amphibious operations.

  d. The interruption of Japanese sea communications into Burma.

5. Operations in the Pacific—1943–44

The courses of action examined by the Combined Chiefs of Staff and the conclusions reached by them are as follows:

  a. Far Eastern Theater.

  (1) *Operations in Burma to Augment Supplies to China.*
    Vital to implementing the strategic plan for the defeat of Japan and to keeping China in the war.
  (2) *Air Operations in and from China.*
    Close coordination with other elements of plan are essential.

  b. Pacific Theater.

  (1) *Operations in the Solomons and Bismarck Archipelago.*
    Provides for retaining the initiative, maintaining pressure on Japan, and the defense of Australia.
  (2) *Operations in New Guinea.*
    The capture of New Guinea will facilitate the opening of a line of communications to the Celebes Sea and contribute to the defense of Australia.
  (3) *Operations in Eastern Netherlands East Indies.*
    Due to limitation of forces, operations other than air warfare should be restricted to the seizure of those islands necessary to the capture of New Guinea.
  (4) *Operations in the Marshall Islands.*
    Shortens line of communications to Southwest Pacific and Celebes Sea.
  (5) *Operations in the Caroline Islands.*
    Necessary to gain control of central Pacific, thereby facilitating establishment of line of communications to Celebes Sea. Will enable United Nations forces to directly threaten the Japanese Archipelago.
  (6) *Intensification of Operations Against Enemy Lines of Communication.*
    All the foregoing operations are essential to the attainment of positions which enable the intensification and expansion of attacks on the enemy lines of communication in the Pacific.

Conclusions

  a. Offensive operations in the Pacific and Far East in 1943–1944 should have the following objectives:

  (1) Conduct of air operations in and from China.
  (2) Operations in Burma to augment supplies in China.
  (3) Ejection of the Japanese from the Aleutians.
  (4) Seizure of the Marshall and Caroline Islands.

(5) Seizure of the Solomons, the Bismarck Archipelago, and Japanese held New Guinea.

(6) Intensification of operations against enemy lines of communication.

b. Operations to gain these objectives will be restricted by the availability of trained amphibious divisions and amphibious craft.

3. Army Nurse Lieutenant Juanita Redmond Describes a Japanese Air Attack on Bataan in the Philippines, April 1942

At ten o'clock on Easter Monday the first wave of bombers struck us.

Someone yelled, "Planes overhead!" But those had become such familiar words that most of us paid them little attention. I went on pouring medications, and then the drone of the planes was lost in the shrill crescendo and roar of a crashing bomb.

It landed at the hospital entrance and blew up an ammunition truck that was passing. The concussion threw me to the floor. There was a spattering of shrapnel and pebbles and earth on the tin roof. Then silence for a few minutes.

I heard the corpsmen rushing out with litters, and I pulled myself to my feet. Precious medicines were dripping to the ground from the shattered dressing carts, and I tried to salvage as much as possible.

The first casualties came in. The boys in the ammunition truck had been killed, but the two guards at the hospital gate had jumped into their fox holes. By the time they were extricated from the débris that filled up the holes they were both shell-shock cases.

There were plenty of others.

Outside the shed a guard yelled, "They're coming back!"

They were after us, all right.

In the Orthopedic ward nurses and corpsmen began to cut the traction ropes so that the patients could roll out of bed if necessary, broken bones and all. In my ward several of the men became hysterical; I would have joined them if I could. It was all I could do to go on being calm and acting as if everything were all right and I had everything under control.

"They're very near us!" came the warning from outside.

Father Cummins had come in, and standing in the middle of the shed where all the boys could see him, he asked us to repeat the Lord's Prayer with him.

Then the second wave of bombs fell.

That one hit the mess and the Doctors' and Nurses' Quarters. When the ripping and tearing sound of crashing wood and the roar of minor explosions diminished, I could hear shrieks of pain outside, the helpless sobbing of the men in the wards, and Father Cummins' quiet voice praying.

Through the open sides of the sheds came flying débris, clouds of dust, wrenched boards with protruding nails, limbs of trees.

From Juanita Redmond, *I Served on Bataan.* (Philadelphia: J. B. Lippincott, 1943), 106–111, 117–118. Reprinted by permission of HarperCollins Publishers, Inc.

It wasn't over.

Even in the first few moments of quiet, we heard the planes coming back.

We couldn't do anything but wait. That was the awful part; we couldn't do anything.

This time they scored a direct hit on the wards. A thousand-pound bomb pulverized the bamboo sheds, smashed the tin roofs into flying pieces; the iron beds doubled and broke jaggedly like paper matches. Sergeant May had pulled me under a desk, but the desk was blown into the air, he and I with it.

I heard myself gasping. My eyes were being gouged out of their sockets, my whole body was swollen and torn apart by the violent pressure. This is the end, I thought.

Then I fell back to the floor, the desk landing on top of me and bouncing around drunkenly. Sergeant May knocked it away from me, and gasping for breath, bruised and aching, sick from swallowing the smoke of the explosive, I dragged myself to my feet. I heard Freeman, our boy with no legs, calling out:

"Where's Miss Redmond? Is Miss Redmond alive?"

He was being carried out; fortunately, he had rolled out of bed and, though he had been covered with débris, except for a few scratches he was unhurt.

Father Cummins said calmly: "Somebody take over. I'm wounded." He had shrapnel in his shoulder.

Only one small section of my ward remained standing. Part of the roof had been blown into the jungle. There were mangled bodies under the ruins; a bloodstained hand stuck up through a pile of scrap; arms and legs had been ripped off and flung among the rubbish. Some of the mangled torsos were almost impossible to identify. One of the few corpsmen who had survived unhurt climbed a tree to bring down a body blown into the top branches. Blankets, mattresses, pajama tops hung in the shattered trees.

We worked wildly to get to the men who might be buried, still alive, under the mass of wreckage, tearing apart the smashed beds to reach the wounded and the dead. These men were our patients, our responsibility; I think we were all tortured by an instinctive, irrational feeling that we had failed them.

The bombing had stopped, but the air was rent by the awful screams of the new-wounded and the dying, trees were still crashing in the jungle and when one near by fell on the remaining segment of tin roof it sounded like shellfire. We were shaking and sick at our stomachs, but none of us who was able to go on dared to stop even for a moment. . . . .

That night we stayed in our fox holes. I didn't sleep. We hadn't eaten since breakfast, but I wasn't hungry. We were like hunted animals, waiting for the kill, almost hoping it would happen quickly so that the torment of waiting would end. But stronger than that was anger; anger and hate and a hot desire to fight back, to avenge our dead.

What kind of human beings would deliberately bomb a hospital, defenseless, openly marked for what it was, filled with the wounded and the sick?

I don't know. The only answer I had found when I crawled out of my hole in the morning, my head aching, a crick in my back, my legs cramped, was not an answer but a conviction. This isn't a war in which anybody—*anybody*—is let off. Each single individual of us is in it and each must give everything he has to give. An enemy that will bomb hospitals and undefended cities—sick and injured men, or women and children and helpless old people—isn't an enemy you can ever come to terms with; not in the usual meaning of the phrase. The war must end without compromise.

It wasn't particularly original thinking, I know, but somehow it comforted me to have it clear and simple in my own mind. I could put the long thoughts of the people I would never see again into the background and go on about my work.

4. Navy Pilot George Gay Survives the Battle of Midway, May 1942

We were now in a position, those of us still left, to turn west again to intercept the ship we had chosen to attack, but the Zeros were still intent on not letting us through, and our planes kept falling all around me. We were on the ship's starboard side, or to the right and ahead of our target, and as we closed range, the big carrier began to turn toward us. I knew immediately from what the skipper had said so often in his lectures that if she got into a good turn she could not straighten out right away, and I was glad that she had committed herself. At that moment there were only two planes left of our squadron besides our own. One was almost directly ahead of me, and I could hardly see him over the nose of my plane. The other was also ahead of me, but off just a bit to my left. I skidded to the left and avoided more 20 MM slugs just in time to pull my nose up and fire another Zero as he got in front of me. I only had one .30 caliber gun, and although I knew I hit this Zero also, it did little damage. I had a number of such chances, but I didn't get anywhere near the satisfaction that I wanted out of spitting at those Zeros with that one pea-shooter. When I turned back to the right, the plane that had been directly ahead of me was gone, and the other was out of control. . . .

My target, which I think was the *Kaga,* was now in a hard turn to starboard and I was going toward her forward port quarter. I figured that by the time a torpedo could travel the distance it should be in the water, the ship should be broadside. I aimed about one quarter of the ship's length ahead of her bow, and reached out with my left hand to pull back the throttle. It had been calculated that we should be at about 80 knots when we dropped these things, so I had to slow down.

I had just got hold of the throttle, when something hit the back of my hand and it hurt like hell. My hand didn't seem to be working right, so I had to pull the throttle back mostly with my thumb. You can well imagine that I was not being exactly neat about all this, I was simply trying to do what I had come out to do. When I figured that I had things about as good as I was going to get them, I punched the torpedo release button.

Nothing happened. "Damn those tracers," I thought. "They've goofed up my electrical release and I'm getting inside my range." I had been told that the ideal drop was 1,000 yards range, 80 knots speed, and 80 feet or so of altitude. But by the time I got the control stick between my knees and put my left hand on top of it to fly the plane, and reached across to pull the cable release with my good right hand, I was into about 850 yards. The cable, or mechanical release, came out of the

From George Gay, *Sole Survivor: A Personal Story About the Battle of Midway* (Florida: Midway Publishers, 1979; rev. ed., 1986), 121–126.

instrument panel on the left side, designed to be pulled with the left hand. But those damn Zeros had messed up my program. My left hand did not work. Anyhow, it was awkward, and I almost lost control of the plane trying to pull out that cable by the roots. I can't honestly say I got rid of that torpedo. It felt like it. I had never done it before so I couldn't be sure, and with the plane pitching like a bronco, I had to be content with trying my best.

"Okay, so I've gotten rid of the G.D. torpedo. Now what do I do?" Slamming that throttle forward was no problem. Now it was "balls to the wall" as we would say. We had talked about this and decided that this was no place to turn around. If you threw your belly up to all those guns on that ship, you would increase your size by about 300 per cent. The only thing to do was fly right at them and present the smallest target possible.

God, but that ship looked big! I remember thinking, "Why in the hell doesn't the *Hornet* look that big when I'm trying to land on her?" There was a Jap on a Pom-Pom gun shooting at me, and I just bore-sighted right back at him and flew him eye to eye. He must have thought I was fool enough to be one of his kamikaze types, because he jumped off his gun and I flew right over him.

I looked up on the bridge, and I could see a guy there waving his arms. I could even see a pair of binoculars in one hand and a Samurai sword in the other. He was pointing at me like they couldn't see me. I think he was the captain.

Here again, you just keep thinking. I remember that I did not want to fly out over the starboard side and let all those gunners have a chance at me, so I headed out over the stern.

Maybe that guy back there on that Pom-Pom hadn't been so wrong after all. I looked down on the flight deck and there were not only planes and men there, but bombs, torpedoes, gas hoses, and all kinds of gear.

I thought, "I could crash into all this and make one great big mess, maybe even get myself a whole carrier, but I'm feeling passably good, and my plane is still flying, so the hell with that—I'll keep going. Maybe I'll get another crack at them and do more damage in the long run." . . .

Flying as low as I could, I went between a couple of cruisers, and out past the destroyers. If you have ever seen movies of this sort of thing, you may wonder how anything could get through all that gunfire. I am alive to tell you that it *can* be done. I think my plane was hit a few times, but here again, I really wasn't going to the trouble to keep track of these small details.

The Zeros had broken off me when I got into ack-ack, but they had no trouble going around to meet me on the other side. A 20 MM cannon slug hit my left rudder pedal just outside my little toe, blew the pedal apart and knocked a hole in the firewall. This set the engine on fire, and it was burning my left leg through that hole.

When the rudder pedal went, the control wire to the ailerons and the rudder went with it. Don't ask me how or why, but the thing that was left for me was the only thing I had to have. I had the elevators so I could pull the nose up. Reaching over with my right hand, I cut the switch. That was also on the left side. Anyhow, I was able to hold the nose up and slow down to almost a decent ditching speed.

Most airplanes will level out if you turn them loose, especially if they are properly trimmed. Mine was almost making it, but I was crosswind, so the right wing hit first. This slammed me into the water in a cartwheel fashion and banged the hood shut over me before it twisted the frame and jammed the hood tight.

As I unbuckled, water was rising to my waist. The nose of the plane was down, so I turned around and sat on the instrument panel while trying to get that hood open. It wouldn't budge. When that water got up to my armpits and started lapping at my chin, I got scared—and I mean really scared. I knew the plane would dive as soon as it lost buoyancy and I didn't want to drown in there. I panicked, stood up and busted my way out.

The Zeros were diving and shooting at me, but my first thought now was of Bob Huntington. I was almost positive he was dead. I think he took at least one of those cannon slugs right in the chest, but I thought that the water might revive him and I had to try and help him. I got back to him just as the plane took that dive, and I went down with it trying to unbuckle his straps and get him out.

The beautiful water exploded into a deep red, and I lost sight of everything. What I had seen confirmed my opinion of his condition and I had to let Bob go. The tail took a gentle swipe at me as if to say goodbye and I came up choking. . . . Zeros were still strafing me and I ducked under a couple of times as those twacking slugs came close. As I came up for air once, I bumped my head on my life raft out of the plane. . . .

I noticed that the Zeros had stopped strafing me and I wondered why. Looking around, I saw the whole Jap Navy steaming right down on me. They were landing planes again, and though I thought they were going to run right over me, I was fascinated by their landing procedure. Their planes did not come by the ship downwind as we did, then turn for a base leg and come off the final turn at the cut. They were coming straight in from astern and I thought, "How awkward. How do they get the proper interval? That doesn't give them much of a chance to judge relative speed."

Then I saw why the Zeros had left me. Our dive bombers were coming down. There is no way I can describe what a beautiful sight that was! I could see that the Zeros that had come down after us were not up there bothering them and I knew that some of those fellows were not only pushing over in their first dive, but it was also their first time they had ever flown that type of plane. They were magnificent and I did not see a single splash indicating a miss! They laid those bombs right where they belonged and caused the most devastating damage possible. Some pilots would see their target explode, and pull off to pick another one and then come on down. It was almost unbelievable, but I was seeing it. Almost simultaneously, three Jap carriers were wiped out. I knew what that meant. By golly, we did it! We caught them just as we had hoped to while they were retrieving aircraft that were low on fuel and out of bombs and ammunition.

5. Marine Private E. B. Sledge Remembers the Hellish Battle of Okinawa, 1945

After digging in the gun, registering in on the aiming stakes, and preparing ammo for future use, I had my first opportunity to look around our position. It was the most ghastly corner of hell I had ever witnessed. As far as I could see, an area that previously had been a low grassy valley with a picturesque stream meandering

From E. B. Sledge, *With the Old Breed at Peleliu and Okinawa* (Novato, Calif.: Presidio Press, 1981), 252–253, 267, 276–278.

through it was a muddy, repulsive, open sore on the land. The place was choked with the putrefaction of death, decay, and destruction. In a shallow defilade to our right, between my gun pit and the railroad, lay about twenty dead Marines, each on a stretcher and covered to his ankles with a poncho—a commonplace, albeit tragic, scene to every veteran. Those bodies had been placed there to await transport to the rear for burial. At least those dead were covered from the torrents of rain that had made them miserable in life and from the swarms of flies that sought to hasten their decay. But as I looked about, I saw that other Marine dead couldn't be tended properly. The whole area was pocked with shell craters and churned up by explosions. Every crater was half full of water, and many of them held a Marine corpse. The bodies lay pathetically just as they had been killed, half submerged in muck and water, rusting weapons still in hand. Swarms of big flies hovered about them.

"Why ain't them poor guys been covered with ponchos?" mumbled my foxhole buddy as he glanced grimly about with a distraught expression on his grizzled face. His answer came the moment he spoke. Japanese 75mm shells came whining and whistling into the area. We cowered in our hole as they crashed and thundered around us. The enemy gunners on the commanding Shuri Heights were registering their artillery and mortars on our positions. We realized quickly that anytime any of us moved out of our holes, the shelling began immediately. We had a terrible time getting our wounded evacuated through the shell fire and mud without the casualty- and stretcher-bearers getting hit. Thus it was perfectly clear why the Marine dead were left where they had fallen.

Everywhere lay Japanese corpses killed in the heavy fighting. Infantry equipment of every type, U.S. and Japanese, was scattered about. Helmets, rifles, BARs [Browning automatic rifles], packs, cartridge belts, canteens, shoes, ammo boxes, shell cases, machine-gun ammo belts, all were strewn around us up to and all over Half Moon.

The mud was knee deep in some places, probably deeper in others if one dared venture there. For several feet around every corpse, maggots crawled about in the muck and then were washed away by the runoff of the rain. There wasn't a tree or bush left. All was open country. Shells had torn up the turf so completely that ground cover was nonexistent. The rain poured down on us as evening approached. The scene was nothing but mud; shell fire; flooded craters with their silent, pathetic, rotting occupants; knocked-out tanks and amtracs; and discarded equipment—utter desolation.

The stench of death was overpowering. The only way I could bear the monstrous horror of it all was to look upward away from the earthly reality surrounding us, watch the leaden gray clouds go skudding over, and repeat over and over to myself that the situation was unreal—just a nightmare—that I would soon awake and find myself somewhere else. But the ever-present smell of death saturated my nostrils. It was there with every breath I took.

I existed from moment to moment, sometimes thinking death would have been preferable. We were in the depths of the abyss, the ultimate horror of war. During the fighting around the Umurbrogol Pocket on Peleliu, I had been depressed by the wastage of human lives. But in the mud and driving rain before Shuri, we were surrounded by maggots and decay. Men struggled and fought and bled in an environment so degrading I believed we had been flung into hell's own cesspool. . . .

Our buddies who had gone back had been greeted enthusiastically—as those of us who survived were received later on. But the folks back home didn't, and in retrospect couldn't have been expected to, understand what we had experienced, what in our minds seemed to set us apart forever from anyone who hadn't been in combat. We didn't want to indulge in self-pity. We just wished that people back home could understand how lucky they were and stop complaining about trivial inconveniences. . . .

At dusk on one of those last few days of May, we moved onto a muddy, slippery ridge and were told to dig in along the crest. One of the three 60mm mortar squads was to set up its gun down behind the ridge, but my squad and the remaining squad were ordered to dig in along the ridge crest and to function as riflemen during the night. The weather turned bad again, and it started to rain.

Mac, our mortar section leader, was nowhere to be seen. But Duke, who had been our section leader on Peleliu and who was by then leading the battalion's 81mm mortar platoon, came up to take charge. He ordered an NCO to have us dig two-man foxholes five yards apart along the crest of the ridge. My buddy went off down the ridge to draw ammo and chow while I prepared to dig.

The ridge was about a hundred feet high, quite steep, and we were on a narrow crest. Several discarded Japanese packs, helmets, and other gear lay scattered along the crest. From the looks of the muddy soil, the place had been shelled heavily for a long time. The ridge was a putrid place. Our artillery must have killed Japanese there earlier, because the air was foul with the odor of rotting flesh. It was just like being back at Half Moon Hill. Off toward our front, to the south, I had only a dim view through the gathering gloom and curtain of rain of the muddy valley below.

The men digging in on both sides of me cursed the stench and the mud. I began moving the heavy, sticky clay mud with my entrenching shovel to shape out the extent of the foxhole before digging deeper. Each shovelful had to be knocked off the spade, because it stuck like glue. I was thoroughly exhausted and thought my strength wouldn't last from one sticky shovelful to the next.

Kneeling on the mud, I had dug the hole no more than six or eight inches deep when the odor of rotting flesh got worse. There was nothing to do but continue to dig, so I closed my mouth and inhaled with short shallow breaths. Another spadeful of soil out of the hole released a mass of wriggling maggots that came welling up as though those beneath were pushing them out. I cursed, and told the NCO as he came by what a mess I was digging into.

"You heard him, he said put the holes five yards apart."

In disgust, I drove the spade into the soil, scooped out the insects, and threw them down the front of the ridge. The next stroke of the spade unearthed buttons and scraps of cloth from a Japanese army jacket buried in the mud—and another mass of maggots. I kept on doggedly. With the next thrust, metal hit the breastbone of a rotting Japanese corpse. I gazed down in horror and disbelief as the metal scraped a clean track through the mud along the dirty whitish bone and cartilage with ribs attached. The shovel skidded into the rotting abdomen with a squishing sound. The odor nearly overwhelmed me as I rocked back on my heels.

I began choking and gagging as I yelled in desperation, "I can't dig in here! There's a dead Nip here!"

The NCO came over, looked down at my problem and at me, and growled, "You heard him; he said put the holes five yards apart."

"How the hell can I dig a foxhole through a dead Nip?' I protested.

Just then Duke came along the ridge and said, "What's the matter, Sledge-hammer?"

I pointed to the partially exhumed corpse. Duke immediately told the NCO to have me dig in a little to the side away from the rotting remains. I thanked Duke and glared at the NCO. How I managed not to vomit during the vile experience I don't know. Perhaps my senses and nerves had been so dulled by constant foulness for so long that nothing could evoke any other response but to cry out and move back.

6. Japanese Civilians Tomizawa Kimi and Kobayashi Hiroyasu Live Through the Firebombing of Tokyo, 1945

Kobayashi: March 9, 1945. I was there. Air-raid warnings came every day, so we weren't particularly shaken when we saw red spots far away, but soon the airplanes were flying above us. Places near us were turning red. Over there, it's red. Here, it's red! Some were still at the switchboards. The others were trying to extinguish the flames after the building caught fire. Outside, huge telephone poles, set against the building and meant to protect the windows and withstand any bomb blast, became like kindling under the incendiary bombs. When the poles started burning, there were still some working the phone lines.

Tomizawa: Our place had communication lines to the antiaircraft batteries and the fire-fighting units for the whole Shitamachi area. There weren't any wireless communications in use then, so crucial government lines passed through our switchboard. Until the last second, many operators were still working, plugging lines into the jacks.

Kobayashi: Parts of the building were still made of wood. The windowframes, for instance, and the rest areas. Wood, covered with stucco. Up on the roof, there was a water tank. Through pipes, it was supposed to lay down a curtain of water over the whole building. But the water in the tank, when it was released, was soon exhausted. We opened up fire plugs, and though water poured out fast at first, everyone was using them, too, so it soon trickled to a stop. We had a small pond, maybe two meters long. It had goldfish we kept for fun. We drained that water, throwing it onto the windows to cool them down. The glass shattered, *"Ping!"* because of the heat. I remember those kids carrying buckets. Helter-skelter. Even the water in the teakettle was used up.

Outside, the world was ablaze. We had no more water. It was all gone. That was it. The operators and the night supervisor, Matsumoto Shūji, were there. Mr. Matsumoto was found dead in the shelter. Burned to death. He was a marathon runner, but he was responsible for them. According to a survivor, Miss Tanaka, they finally did try to leave the building. "Get out, get out!" they were told, but the flames were too strong. They couldn't flee.

Tomizawa: Only four of them survived. Fortunate to escape that dangerous situation. The remaining thirty-one all perished.

Kobayashi: When we left, we men thought we were the last ones. We couldn't really get the gate open, so we climbed over the side wall. The bridge over the Arakawa was jammed. People coming this way from the far side, and trying to go there from this side. They packed together in the middle and couldn't move. People are greedy. Even at times like that, people are carrying things. Our phone cable was next to the bridge, partially submerged in the water. We took a chance. There was no other way. We hung on to it and moved across hand over hand, our bodies in the water. All the way across the river to escape the burning air. It was like a circus act.

If there'd still been water, water coming from the hydrants, we probably wouldn't have made it. But there was no water. No way to fight the fire. Besides, our line of command was separate from that of the girls. We were later questioned. "Why did only the men flee?" They wanted to know why we didn't take more girls with us. But when they investigated, they found that even the coin boxes on the public phones had melted completely. Then they understood.

Not even a single line was still operational. When I returned the next day, where the thick cables went in, they had melted down. There were no windowframes. All the metallic things had melted in the heat and were bowing down, all bent over. The switchboards, anything made of wood, all burned. Gone.

Tomizawa: The interior cables were still hanging in the empty concrete box. A chill went through me.

Kobayashi: Some people could be identified. By their stomach wraps. Where it had been tight against their skin a name could be found written on it. It wasn't burned. To tell you the truth, I couldn't tell if they were men or women. They weren't even full skeletons. Piled on top of each other. The bottom of the pile, all stuck together. A few bits of clothing could be found on them. The underpants of Mr. Matsumoto were left. Touching the wall of the shelter. When Matsumoto-san's wife came, nobody could bear to tell her that her husband was not there anymore. "You have to tell her," everyone told me. "You were on night duty together." There's nothing more painful than that. His wife confirmed that they were her husband's underwear.

Even after all the bones were buried, when it rained, a blue flame burned. From the phosphorus. Soldiers stationed there used to say, "Maybe they'll come out tonight," thinking of the ghosts and the blue flames.

I wonder what war is. I wonder why we did it. I'm not talking about victory or loss. I merely feel heartbroken for those who died. It's not an issue of whether I hate the enemy or not. However much you're glorified, if you're dead, that's it. Young kids worked so hard. Without complaint. It makes me seethe. Burning flames, huge planes flying over, dropping bombs. My feeling of hatred—"You bastards! Bastards!" you shout. But there was no sense that you're capable of doing anything about it. If you win, you're the victors. You can justify anything. It's all right if the ones who have rifles are killed. That's OK. But these kids didn't have weapons, they had only their breasts. Those are the one whose end was tragic.

I wonder, does war bring happiness to anyone? The ones who perished here on duty were merely promoted two ranks. They got a medal from the Emperor. A long time afterwards. Their parents didn't even get their pensions. Only the men with stars are enshrined in Yasukuni. But where are those who perished here? Girls of fifteen and sixteen. Who did their best. [*His voice breaks.*] People even ask, "Why didn't they escape earlier? They should have fled earlier."

Tomizawa: They are the ones who should be enshrined.

Kobayashi: No! Not that! Their parents want them back!

7. General Joseph Stilwell Bitterly Explains His Problems in China, 1944

SEPTEMBER 17, THE MANURE PILE: LETTER TO MRS. STILWELL   We are in the midst of a battle with the Peanut [Chiang Kai-shek], and it is wearing us out. Crises are rising in quick succession here and there; there is disaster in Hunan and Kwangsi: Dorn [in command on the Salween] is screaming for help: and hell to pay generally. Hell has been to pay before so I guess we can take it again. You may be interested to know that everything is turning out exactly as I told them it would in May 1943, when I was the Voice of One Howling in the Wilderness and when I was voted the Horse's-Neck-Most-Likely-to-Succeed-in-that-Role. I don't know if the Knowitalls have learned their lesson or not, but even if they have it has been an expensive experiment for me. A year and a half lost. In the so-called campaign for Changsha, Hengyang and Kweilin, the Peanut insisted on conducting operations by remote control and by intuition as usual, with catastrophic results. The enormity of his stupidity is shown by the fact that he thinks it was a pretty good show, considering. Considering what? I don't know. They throw away 300,000 men in Hunan [East China] without batting an eye and I break my back trying to get 10,000 to replace battle casualties [in the Burma campaign]. Co-operation in capital letters. Why can't sudden death for once strike in the proper place. It would really be funny if it weren't so tragic. The picture of this little rattlesnake being backed up by a great democracy, and showing his backside in everything he says and does, would convulse you if you could get rid of your gall bladder. But to have to sit there and be dignified, instead of bursting into guffaws, is too much to ask for the pay I get. What will the American people say when they finally learn the truth?

I see that the Limeys [British] are going to rush to our rescue in the Pacific. Like hell. They are going to continue this fight with their mouths. Four or five old battleships will appear and about ten RAF planes will go to Australia but in twenty years the schoolbooks will be talking about "shoulder to shoulder" and "the Empire struck with all its might against the common enemy" and all that crap. The idea, of course, is to horn in at Hongkong again, and our Booby is sucked in. . . .

SEPTEMBER 19   Mark this day in red on the calender of life. At long, at very long last, F.D.R. has finally spoken plain words, and plenty of them, with a firecracker in every sentence. "Get busy or else." A hot firecracker. I handed this bundle of paprika to the Peanut and then sank back with a sigh. The harpoon hit the little

From Theodore H. White, ed. *The Stilwell Papers* (New York: William Sloan Associates, 1948: reprint, New York: Shocken Books, 1972), 331–333, 339–341.

bugger right in the solar plexus, and went right through him. It was a clean hit, but beyond turning green and losing the power of speech, he did not bat an eye. He just said to me, "I understand." And sat in silence, jiggling one foot. We are now a long way from the "tribal chieftain" bawling out. *Two long years lost,* but at least F.D.R.'s eyes have been opened and he has thrown a good hefty punch.

I came home. Pretty sight crossing the river: lights all on in Chungking.

SEPTEMBER 21, LETTER TO MRS. STILWELL   A lot of mail in but nothing but junk. I throw it at Carl. The only mail I want to see has the Carmel postmark. It has taken two and a half years for the Big Boys to see the light, but it dawned finally and I played the avenging angel.

> I've waited long for vengeance—
> At last I've had my chance.
> I've looked the Peanut in the eye
> And kicked him in the pants.
>
> The old harpoon was ready
> With aim and timing true,
> I sank it to the handle,
> And stung him through and through.
>
> The little bastard shivered,
> And lost the power of speech.
> His face turned green and quivered
> As he struggled not to screech.
>
> For all my weary battles,
> For all my hours of woe,
> At last I've had my innings
> And laid the Peanut low.
>
> I know I've still to suffer,
> And run a weary race,
> But oh! the blessed pleasure
> I've wrecked the Peanut's face.

* * *

[OCTOBER 1], LETTER TO MRS. STILWELL   It looks very much as though they had gotten me at last. The Peanut has gone off his rocker and Roosevelt has apparently let me down completely. If old softy gives in on this, as he apparently has, the Peanut will be out of control from now on. A proper fizzle. My conscience is clear. I have carried out my orders. I have no regrets. Except to see the U.S.A. sold down the river. So be ready, in case the news isn't out sooner, to have me thrown out on the garbage pile. At least, I'll probably get home and tell you all about it. God help the next man.

It hasn't happened yet, but it is a thousand to one that it will soon.

8. President Roosevelt Attacks Colonialism in Asia, 1942–1943

June 1, 1942 (Minutes of the Meeting between Roosevelt and Molotov)

The President then recalled that he had already developed his ideas about disarming Germany and Japan, about control and inspection of their munitions industries to preclude surreptitious rearmament, about the future police activities of the four major nations, and about their role as guarantors of eventual peace. He had omitted one other point: viz., that there were, all over the world, many islands and colonial possessions which ought, for our own safety, to be taken away from weak nations. He suggested that Mr. Stalin might profitably consider the establishment of some form of international trusteeship over these islands and possessions.

In reply Mr. Molotov declared that he had considered and reported to Moscow the President's earlier proposals as to post-war organization. He had received an answer from Mr. Stalin, who was in full accord with the President's ideas on disarmament, inspection, and policing with the participation of at least Great Britain, the United States, and the Soviet Union, and possibly China. This idea had the full approval of the Soviet Government, which would support it fully. He had no doubt that the President's trusteeship principle would be equally well received in Moscow.

The President then pointed out that the acceptance of this principle would mean the abandonment of the mandate system. For example, after the last war the Japanese had received a mandate over the previously German islands in the Pacific, which they had fortified. These islands were small, but they ought not to be given to any one nation. The Japanese should, of course, be removed, but we did not want these islands, and neither the British nor the French ought to have them either. Perhaps the same procedure should be applied to the islands now held by the British. The islands obviously ought not to belong to any one nation, and their economy was substantially the same everywhere. The easiest and most practical way to handle the problem of these islands over a long period would be to put them under an international committee of 3–5 members. . . .

Turning to the question of colonial possessions, the President took as examples Indo-China, Siam, and the Malay States, or even the Dutch East Indies. The last-mentioned would some day be ready for self-government, and the Dutch know it. Each of these areas would require a different lapse of time before achieving readiness for self-government, but a palpable surge toward independence was there just the same, and the white nations thus could not hope to hold these areas as colonies in the long run. Generalissimo Chiang Kai-shek therefore had the idea that some form of interim international trusteeship would be the best mode of administering these territories until they were ready for self-government. They

From U.S. Department of State, *Foreign Relations of the United States, 1942,* vol. 3 (Washington D.C.: U.S. Government Printing Office, 1961), 580–581; ibid., *Foreign Relations of the United States: The Conferences at Cairo and Tehran* (Washington, D.C.: U.S. Government Printing Office, 1961), 485–486 and 872–873.

might, the President added, be ready for self-government in 20 years, during which the trustees might endeavor to accomplish what we accomplished in the Philippines in 42 years. . . .

November 28, 1943 (Minutes of the Tehran Conference)

THE PRESIDENT . . . remarked that after 100 years of French rule in Indochina, the inhabitants were worse off than they had been before. He said that Chiang Kai-shek had told him China had no designs on Indochina but the people of Indochina were not ready yet for independence, to which he had replied that when the United States acquired the Philippines, the inhabitants were not ready for independence which would be granted without qualification upon the end of the war against Japan. He added that he had discussed with Chiang Kai-shek the possibility of a system of trusteeship for Indochina which would have the task of preparing the people for independence within a definite period of time, perhaps 20 to 30 years.

MARSHAL STALIN completely agreed with this view.

THE PRESIDENT went on to say that Mr. Hull had taken to the Moscow Conference a document which he (the President) had drawn up for the purpose of a National [*International?*] Committee to visit, every year, the colonies of all nations and through use of instrumentalities of public opinion to correct any abuse that they find.

MARSHAL STALIN said he saw merit in this idea.

THE PRESIDENT continued on the subject of colonial possessions, but he felt it would be better not to discuss the question of India with Mr. Churchill, since the latter had no solution of that question, and merely proposed to defer the entire question to the end of the war.

MARSHAL STALIN agreed that this was a sore spot with the British.

THE PRESIDENT said that at some future date, he would like to talk with Marshal Stalin on the question of India; that he felt that the best solution would be reform from the bottom, somewhat on the Soviet line.

MARSHAL STALIN replied that the India question was a complicated one, with different levels of culture and the absence of relationship in the castes. He added that reform from the bottom would mean revolution. . . .

The President to the Secretary of State

WASHINGTON, January 24, 1944.

MEMORANDUM FOR THE SECRETARY OF STATE

I saw Halifax [British Ambassador to the United States] last week and told him quite frankly that it was perfectly true that I had, for over a year, expressed the opinion that Indo-China should not go back to France but that it should be administered by an international trusteeship. France has had the country—thirty million inhabitants for nearly one hundred years, and the people are worse off than they were at the beginning.

As a matter of interest, I am wholeheartedly supported in this view by Generalissimo Chiang Kai-shek and by Marshal Stalin. I see no reason to play in with the

British Foreign Office in this matter. The only reason they seem to oppose it is that they fear the effect it would have on their own possessions and those of the Dutch. They have never liked the idea of trusteeship because it is, in some instances, aimed at future independence. This is true in the case of Indo-China.

F[RANKLIN] D R[OOSEVELT]

9. Foreign Service Officers John Paton Davies and George R. Merrell Warn Against Support of British Colonialism in Asia, 1943

The Chargé in India (Merrell) to the Secretary of State

No. 249

NEW DELHI, October 26, 1943.
[Received November 5.]

SIR: I have the honor to enclose a copy of a most interesting memorandum prepared by Mr. John Davies, Second Secretary of the American Embassy in Chungking attached to the staff of Lieutenant General Joseph W. Stilwell, on the subject of "British Intimations for the Future." The memorandum was prepared as a result of a conversation between Mr. Davies, two British propaganda officials, and representatives of the United States Office of War Information in New Delhi and Chungking. . . .

There is almost complete unanimity among British officials in New Delhi that post-war Anglo-American collaboration is essential but one has a definite feeling that they view British fighting in Asia as having the primary purpose of re-establishing and extending British imperialist interests. Distrust of the Chinese and fear of a strong and united post-war China are characteristic of British officialdom here.

The chief points made in the conversation by Mr. Davies are:

1. In the minds of most Americans a better world is identified with the abolition of imperialism, and there is a very real danger that the United States may again become isolationist after the war as a result of a feeling by the American people that they have been made dupes of British imperialism.

2. Our policy is apparently based on the conviction that we need Britain as a first-class power; Britain cannot be a first-class power without its empire; we are accordingly committed to the support the British empire.

3. If Britain does not want the United States to go isolationist it must be careful to leave us some freedom to state our own case in Asia.

The Mission considers Mr. Davies' appraisement of the consequences which may be expected to flow from our apparent policy of supporting British aims in Asia to be sound. It matters little whether this is our actual policy or whether by our

From U.S. Department of State, *Foreign Relations of the United States, 1943, China* (Washington, D.C.: U.S. Government Printing Office, 1957), 878–880.

silence we allow that conclusion to be drawn by Asiatics. The result is the same, namely, a growing conviction among the people of this part of the world that American policy is at one with the British in desiring the restoration and extension of "whitetocracy" in Asia. The long-range consequence of such a conviction will, it would seem, be an alignment of the colored races against the whites as their only hope of freedom and progress.

Respectfully yours,

GEORGE R. MERRELL

E S S A Y S

The three essays that follow focus on three of the major aspects of the war against Japan. In the first essay, Ronald H. Spector of George Washington University surveys the experiences of different groups of American service personnel amidst the unfamiliar environments and cultures of Asia and the Pacific. In the second essay, John W. Dower of the University of California at San Diego analyzes the nature and impact of Japanese and American racist beliefs. In the third essay, Michael Schaller of the University of Arizona explains the reasons for the failure of U.S. policies in China and the 1944 crisis that resulted in the recall of General Stilwell.

Strangers in Strange Lands

RONALD H. SPECTOR

Approximately a million and a quarter American men and women served in the Pacific and other Asian theaters between 1941 and 1945; from India to Hawaii, from Alaska to New Zealand, the zones of operations embraced one third of the globe. Men worked, fought, and died in terrain as diverse as the icy, fog-bound Aleutians and the beautiful islands of Polynesia, but the war against Japan was conducted mainly in the tropics, that jungle-covered zone of the earth where rain is plentiful, heat and sweat constant, mud, insects, and decay universal. . . .

In this inhospitable environment the American serviceman—and woman— spent one, two, or often three years. . . .

. . . Combat in the Pacific was usually, but not always, characterized by short periods of intense fighting followed by long intervals of waiting. One army division which spent nineteen months in the Pacific had thirty-one days in combat. Another, which had been there for twenty-seven months, saw fifty-five days in combat. By contrast, American troops in the European theater often spent months on the battle line.

In most other respects the combat soldier and marine in the Pacific had a tougher time than his counterpart in Europe. He was likely to have spent a longer time overseas and his rear base was often in an area as hot, primitive, and unhealthy as the battlefield itself. In two divisions studied by army psychologists in the spring of 1944, 66 percent and 41 percent of the infantrymen had been sent to a malaria treatment center at least once.

As in all modern wars, the infantryman bore a disporportionate share of the risks. In U.S. Army divisions, infantry units constituted less than 70 percent of unit strength but suffered over 90 percent of the casualties. If a division remained in combat more than three months, the laws of probability suggested that every one of its 132 second lieutenants would be killed or wounded.

If he were wounded, the World War II soldier, marine, or airman had a better chance of survival than ever before, thanks to the availability of new sulfa drugs, penicillin, blood plasma, and such innovations as air evacuation. . . .

Wounds and death in battle were hazards faced by a minority of servicemen who saw combat. Less dramatic but far more common were the hardships of boredom, isolation, and loneliness. These were enemies faced by almost every soldier, sailor, or marine: at times they could seem more terrible than combat. . . .

One group of servicemen had more than the usual problems of boredom, isolation, loneliness, and danger. These were the Black GIs serving in army, navy, and Marine Corps units throughout the Pacific and Asia. Blacks had a long and honorable record of service in the American wars. But by the eve of World War II, there were fewer than 4,000 American Negroes in the armed services—less than there had been in 1900. Even the famous old outfits like the army's Ninth and Tenth Cavalry had been reduced to service as truck drivers, orderlies, cooks, and grooms. The Marine Corps had no Black personnel at all; the navy had none outside the stewards branch. This was the result of a tradition of racism and discrimination stretching back to the turn of the century. According to widespread opinion in the military, Blacks made only mediocre soldiers, took longer to train, and could perform at all well only if led by white officers.

Over a million Black men and women ultimately served in the armed forces. Branches and specialties like the WACs, the Coast Guard, the Seabees, Officer Candidate Schools and the Red Cross were opened to Blacks. There were Black officers, Black combat pilots, even a Black general. Yet much of this was window dressing. Wartime magazines and newspapers featured pictures of Black fighter aces and Black radar technicians, but the vast majority of Negro servicemen spent their tours in so-called service units, performing hard manual labor such as road building, stevedoring, and laundering. Despite promising experiments, rigid segregation remained the rule—from the induction station to the combat zone. Most Black units had at least some white officers but few, if any, white units included Black officers. . . .

The army's only Black combat units to see action in the Pacific were elements of the 93d Division, which fought on Bougainville and later served on Morotai, in the Moluccas and on Saipan. The 24th Infantry of that division did such an outstanding job in mopping-up operations on Saipan that the War Department's inspector general singled them out for special praise: these men were collectively awarded the Combat Infantryman's Badge and an additional battle star for their theater service ribbon. Yet it was a Black sister unit, the 25th Regimental Combat Team, which received most attention.

On Bougainville in April 1944, Company K of the 25th was on its first patrol when a platoon encountered a Japanese machine-gun position. The inexperienced troopers became confused; platoons began firing on each other. One of the platoon sergeants panicked and fled, and the entire company withdrew in disorder, ignoring pleas from the company commander to hold their position and cease fire. Ten men were killed and twenty wounded in this fiasco; the dead were left behind—along with a radio, a mortar, and several small arms.

Although an inglorious episode, the Company K incident was no worse—and in some respects not so bad—as many other experiences of green troops in the South Pacific. Yet such was the climate of opinion at the time, so deep were the prejudices and doubts about Negro combat troops, that the incident became a cause célèbre. Stories circulated that the entire 25th Regimental Combat Team had broken and run or that its men "wouldn't fight—couldn't get them out of the caves to fight." Many Blacks believed that the company had been deliberately thrown into combat without adequate training and that the company commander, who was white, deserted his men under fire and fled to the rear. Later in the war the 25th conducted many successful patrols, including one which resulted in the capture of one of the highest-ranking Japanese officers on the island of Morotai. Nevertheless, it was the story of Company K that was repeated, often in distorted form, and remembered.

While the 25th's record in action continued to be debated, other Black combat units saw no action at all. After arduous and lengthy training in the United States, many Blacks found themselves performing manual labor or guard duties once they arrived in the Pacific. In part this was due to the chronic shortage of service troops in all overseas theaters—but Black leaders also suspected, with good reason, that the large number of Negro units converted to labor service was due to white stereotyping of the Negro as timid, untrainable, and useful only for manual labor.

In the Marine Corps, the policy of assigning a large proportion of Blacks to service units had an especially ironic result. The Marine Corps had initially organized its Black recruits into defense battalions, like the unit which had fought so valiantly at Wake Island in 1941. The defense battalion appeared to be an organization well suited to the needs of a segregated Marine Corps: it was a small, almost self-contained, unit employing a wide variety of weapons and utilizing a large number of different specialties, from radar technicians to machine gunners. But by the time these Black defense battalions were trained, organized, and ready for action, the war in the Pacific had progressed to the point where purely defensive outfits were no longer needed. So the Black defense battalions, trained for combat, spent their time in garrison duties.

In contrast, Black marine ammunition- and depot companies, that is, labor troops, were in the thick of the fighting in the central Pacific, from Saipan to Iwo Jima. The reason was that such companies served in assault landings as part of the shore parties. Earlier experience with amphibious landings had shown that specially trained, experienced troops were needed to perform the difficult task of moving supplies and ammunition quickly from the landing craft to the troops in action further inland. As a result, specialized beach- and shore units were organized for the assault on the Marinas and for subsequent invasions. . . .

"The Negro Marines are no longer on trial," announced Marine Corps Commandant A. A. Vandegrift after the assault on Saipan. "They are Marines, period." Yet despite such ringing affirmations, it was not until the 1950s that Blacks would be accepted on anything like an equal basis in the Marine Corps and the other services.

Overseas, Blacks often encountered much the same type of discrimination they had known in "the good old U.S.A." British officials worried about the possibility that the appearance of Black soldiers—well-fed, well-educated, and well-paid—in their colonial possessions might give dangerous ideas to their own subject populations. Australia, with its "white Australia" policy, protested against receiving Negro troops, which eventually constituted over 8 percent of MacArthur's forces there and in New Guinea. . . .

However difficult their position, Black soldiers were hardly a novelty in the army. Women were another matter. They had been involved in American wars since the Revolution; some had even received awards for bravery. But until World War I, women had been rigorously excluded from serving in uniform as part of the regular armed forces.

During the First World War, the navy had enlisted women to serve as clerks (yeomen) in the navy and marines, but this experiment was hastily discontinued at the conclusion of the war. At the beginning of 1941 the only military organizations in the United States which accepted women were the army and navy Nurse corps. The nurses wore uniforms and were under military control, but they lacked military rank, equal pay, retirement privileges, and veterans rights. In short, they were considered simply as a kind of auxiliary.

With the outbreak of World War II and the passage of the Selective Service Act in the United States, there were demands from women's groups and other citizens that women be permitted to serve in the armed forces. Both Eleanor Roosevelt and Congresswoman Edith Nourse Rogers called for the establishment of some type of military organization for women. During the summer of 1941 the War Department began planning for a women's force "so that when it is forced upon us, as it undoubtedly will, we shall be able to run it our way."

The War Department's "way" was to establish a "Women's Army Auxiliary Corps." The key word was "Auxiliary," for the women's corps was to be *in* the army but not *of* it. "Auxiliary" status meant that the women GIs would have pay and benefits inferior to those of their male counterparts. It was not until late in 1943 that the "WAACs" became "WACs" with full army status, equivalent ranks, and equal pay.

Legislation to create an army and navy women's force finally passed Congress in the spring of 1942, despite the misgivings of congressmen who wondered who would now be left to "do the cooking, the washing, the mending, the humble homey tasks to which every woman has devoted herself?" Mrs. Oveta Culp Hobby, a prominent businesswoman and civic leader from Texas, was appointed director of the new corps. The first 440 officer candidates were chosen from more than 30,000 applicants with something of the same care which was later devoted to the selection of the first astronauts. They reported to Fort Des Moines, Iowa, an abandoned cavalry post, in July 1942.

During the next year the corps expanded rapidly. By November 1942 the first WAACs were en route overseas in answer to an urgent call from General Eisenhower for skilled typists and telephone operators to serve in North Africa. By this time, the Women's Army Auxiliary Corps had expanded to three training centers, nine service companies, and twenty-seven Aircraft Warning Units. The War Department was beginning to talk about recruiting a million WAACs.

The navy's turn came a few weeks later with the creation of the WAVES (Women Accepted for Volunteer Emergency Service) under Wellesley College's former president Mildred McAfee. Over 80,000 women eventually served in the navy, marines and Coast Guard, but federal law prohibited them from serving outside the continental United States or aboard combatant ships or aircraft. In late 1944 that restriction was eased somewhat to allow WAVES to serve in Alaska, Hawaii, and the Caribbean. All the same, Admiral Nimitz refused to allow women at his headquarters: it was not until CINCPAC [Commander in Chief, Pacific Area Command] headquarters moved to Guam at the beginning of 1945 that WAVES were finally assigned to Pearl Harbor.

The unprecedented spectacle of large numbers of women in uniform, many of them serving in or near the combat zones, gave rise to amazement and disapproval among the more conservative male soldiers and civilians. An Arkansas radio evangelist told his listeners that WAAC recruits were paraded naked before their male officers. At Daytona Beach, Florida, where there was a WAAC training center, local citizens reported that these women "were touring in groups, seizing and raping sailors and coastguardsmen." Large numbers of WAAC's were reported as being returned home from overseas pregnant: it was widely believed that "WAAC's were really taken into service to take care of the sex problems of soldiers."

War Department authorities pointed out in vain that illicit pregnancy among WAAC's was almost unknown, and that their venereal disease rate was lower than in any known civilian community. The colorful stories continued to circulate throughout the war years. One war correspondent drily noted that if even some of the devoutly believed stories of WAAC promiscuity were true, each of the 200-odd women serving in North Africa in 1943 must have been shipped home pregnant several times.

In the war against Japan the largest number of women—about 5,500—served in the southwest Pacific theater. Here McArthur's forces, which had become dependent for administrative support on locally recruited Australian civilians, suddenly found themselves shorthanded when American units moved west and north into New Guinea and the Philippines, where civilians could not go. An urgent call went out for all the WAACs that could be spared. In May 1944 the first shipment of 640 WAACs arrived in Sydney, soon to move north to New Guinea.

Employment of WAACs in MacArthur's theater got off to a shaky start because of MacArthur's chief of staff's maneuvers to have his Australian girl friend, who doubled as his secretary, commissioned in the WAACs. Sutherland, by insisting that MacArthur himself desired the commissioning of the lady and two other Australian secretaries, was able to push the case through. He did so over the heated objections of Colonel Hobby, who pointed out that all WAAC officers had been selected from the ranks.

When General MacArthur eventually learned of Sutherland's machinations, and was further informed that the woman in question might be sued for divorce, "the lady was sent back to Australia with all the suddenness of the circus man shot from the cannon." Yet the damage had been done. Army officers, both male and female, were infuriated. All the old stories that WAACs were simply officers' concubines were dusted off and took on a new lease on life. Examination of soldiers' mail from the southwest Pacific in the month before the first WAACs arrived "showed that 90 percent of the comments about all WAACS were unfavorable, many obscene."

Undaunted, WAAC technicians, secretaries, radio operators, postal workers, supply clerks, and mechanics took up their duties in remote New Guinea and the Philippines. At most bases the WAACs lived in guarded, barbed-wire compounds which they could leave only in groups escorted by armed guards. Such precautions were thought necessary to protect them from the thousands of sex-starved GIs nearby. Off-duty activities were limited to unit parties and other group entertainment. Even attendance at movies required a formation and a guard, and all women were required to be back in quarters by midnight.

At Hollandia, army and air force WAACs lived in wooden-floored tents pitched in ankle-deep mud, an elysian field for mosquitoes. At Leyte the first WAACs landed at Tacloban—on an airfield which was then being strafed by Japanese planes. The women spent their first three months working long night hours in lantern-lit tents, frequently interrupted by air raids. In Manila, they lived on K rations, dodged Japanese snipers, and took turns washing up out of their helmets.

"We began to see a steady influx of WAC's, female nurses and Red Cross workers," recalled Rear Admiral Daniel E. Barbey. "All tried to be helpful but, on the whole, they were a nuisance. . . . If we had been given the chance, we would have shipped them home." Most of Barbey's colleagues disagreed. Favorable comment on women's services, as measured by remarks in mail from soldiers in the Southwest Pacific Area, rose from less than 15 percent in August 1944 to over 50 percent by March of 1945; by the end of the war over 70 percent spoke highly of them.

For one group of Americans the war was an unrelieved nightmare. They were the 20,000-odd soldiers, sailors, airmen, and marines captured by the Japanese at the surrender of the Philippines. Of these unlucky men, less than 60 percent survived Japanese imprisonment to return home in 1945. Some perished at the outset of their captivity on the notorious Bataan Death March—a ghastly, forced-march evacuation of troops who had surrendered in southern Bataan, to clear the way for the final Japanese drive on Corregidor. Over 600 Americans and 5–10,000 Filipinos perished on this trek from the town of Balanga, halfway up the peninsula, to their final internment at the former Philippine Army post of Camp O'Donnell, sixty-five miles north. Sixteen thousand more Americans and Filipinos died in the first few weeks at the camp. . . .

Survivors of the Death March, as well as other Allied prisoners in Japanese camps and prisons scattered from Singapore to Manchuria had a long ordeal before them. The Japanese military code forbade surrender under any circumstances, so the Japanese tended to regard prisoners of war as disgraced, cowardly criminals, scarcely human. Guarding these prisoners was almost as dishonorable as being one. Consequently, the Japanese tended to assign misfits, troublemakers, alcoholics, and even the insane to prison-camp duty. The Japanese claimed to abide by the Geneva Convention rules for the treatment of prisoners of war. But few, if any, of these rules were ever followed in practice. The International Red Cross was never permitted to visit camps in the Philippines; rarely were visits allowed elsewhere. Red Cross parcels were seldom distributed. Even POW mail was frequently delayed—or never delivered.

Conditions differed considerably from one prison camp to another. But in most camps the prisoners faced a daily struggle for survival. The death rate in the camps was lower than on the Death March but dysentery, diet deficiencies, malaria, heat, and overwork still took a heavy toll. Camp diet usually consisted of a cup of cooked rice served three times daily, along with a bowl of watery soup. The prisoners' main source of protein was the Japanese *miso* or soybean paste, which occasionally accompanied these dishes. . . .

As the war progressed, more and more prisoners were moved north from the Philippines to northern China, Taiwan, or Japan. Under the best of circumstances, these journey through waters patrolled by American planes and submarines were highly uncomfortable and dangerous. At worst, the voyages exceeded the horrors of the Death March. . . .

For those American prisoners still in the Philippines, liberation came early in 1945 as MacArthur's forces reoccupied the islands. Other prisoners—in remote camps in Japan or Manchuria—were not released until late September. Nine years later a survey found that of the men who had fought in the Bataan campaign, only one out of seven was still alive in 1954.

Whether in the South Pacific, the mountains of south China, or the parched, brown plains of India, thousands of servicemen encountered societies and countries they had heard of before only in the pages of their grammar-school geography books. Everywhere in Asia and the Pacific, Americans found unfamiliar cultures and strange peoples, and everywhere—in small ways and in large—the GIs left their mark. In remote parts of New Guinea and the New Hebrides, they inspired bizarre "cargo cults" among the local inhabitants, some of which have continued into the present day. In Australia, at least 15,000 women married American servicemen. Several thousand emigrated to America, inspiring fears that the island continent, with only 7 million inhabitants, was being depopulated. In India GIs introduced the dill pickle to Calcutta restaurants and taught their Indian bearers to act as fielders and shortstops in scratch games of baseball. In China their presence fueled the already roaring black market and inflation and, for good or ill, gave millions of Chinese a chance to observe large groups of Americans at close hand. What they saw aroused both their admiration and their contempt. In all places where American GIs worked, fought, and died, societies and economies were mightily affected—and sometimes changed.

The Pacific War as a Race War

JOHN W. DOWER

World War Two changed the face of the globe. It witnessed the rise and fall and rise again of empires—the swiftly shifting fortunes of the European powers and the Axis allies, the emergence of the American and Soviet superpowers—and no policymaker was unaware of the stakes involved. Control of territory, markets, natural resources, and other peoples always lay close to the heart of prewar and wartime planning. This was certainly true of the war in Asia, where nationalist aspirations for genuine liberation and independence met resistance from Europeans, Americans, and Japanese alike. In Asia, the global war became entangled with the legacies

From *War Without Mercy: Race and Power in the Pacific War* by John W. Dower, 3–14. Copyright © 1986 by John W. Dower. Used by permission of Pantheon Books, a division of Random House, Inc.

of Western imperialism and colonialism in a manner that proved explosive, not only at the time but for decades thereafter.

To scores of millions of participants, the war was also a race war. It exposed raw prejudices and was fueled by racial pride, arrogance, and rage on many sides. Ultimately, it brought about a revolution in racial consciousness throughout the world that continues to the present day. Because World War Two was many wars, occurring at different levels and in widely separated places, it is impossible to describe it with a single phrase; and to speak of the global conflict as a race war is to speak of only one of its many aspects. Nonetheless, it is a critical aspect which has rarely been examined systematically.

Apart for the genocide of the Jews, racism remains one of the great neglected subjects of World War Two. . . .

The blatant racism of the Nazis had a twofold impact in the anti-Axis camp. On the one hand, it provoked the sustained critique of "master-race" arguments in general, with a wide range of Western scientists and intellectuals lending the weight of their reputations to the repudiation of pseudoscientific theories concerning the inherently superior or inferior capabilities of different races. At the same time, this critique of Nazi racism had a double edge, for it exposed the hypocrisy of the Western Allies. Anti-Semitism was but one manifestation of the racism that existed at all levels in the United States and the United Kingdom. Even while denouncing Nazi theories of "Aryan" supremacy, the U.S. government presided over a society where blacks were subjected to demeaning Jim Crow laws, segregation was imposed even in the military establishment, racial discrimination extended to the defense industries, and immigration policy was severely biased against all nonwhites. In the wake of Pearl Harbor, these anti-"colored" biases were dramatically displayed in yet another way: the summary incarceration of over 110,000 Japanese-Americans. . . .

. . . World War Two contributed immeasurably not only to sharpened awareness of racism within the United States, but also to more radical demands and militant tactics on the part of the victims of discrimination.

This was equally true abroad, especially in Asia, where the Allied struggle against Japan exposed the racist underpinnings of the European and American colonial structure. Japan did not invade independent countries in southern Asia. It invaded colonial outposts which the Westerners had dominated for generations, taking absolutely for granted their racial and cultural superiority over their Asian subjects. Japan's belated emergence as a dominant power in Asia, culminating in the devastating "advance south" of 1941–42, challenged not just the Western presence but the entire mystique of white supremacism on which centuries of European and American expansion had rested. This was clear to all from an early date: to the Japanese; to the imperiled European and American colonials; and, not least, to the politically, economically, and culturally subjugated peoples of Asia.

Japan's Pan-Asiatic slogans played upon these sentiments, and the favorable response of many Asians to the initial Japanese victories against the Americans, British, and Dutch intensified Western presentiments of an all-out race war in Asia. In China, the Japanese had persuaded Wang Ching-wei, formerly a respected nationalist leader, to head their puppet government. After Pearl Harbor, Indian and Burmese patriots both formed independent nationalist armies in collaboration with the Japanese, while in Indonesia pro-Japanese sentiments were expressed by the rousing triple slogan of the so-called AAA movement: Japan the Leader of Asia, Japan the Protector of Asia, Japan the Light of Asia. In the highly publicized Assembly of the Greater East Asiatic Nations convened in Tokyo in November 1943, a succession of Asian leaders voiced support for Japan and placed the war in an East-versus-West, Oriental-versus-Occidental, and ultimately blood-versus-blood context. Thus, Burma's passionately outspoken leader Ba Maw told delegates to the conference, "My Asiatic blood has always called to other Asiatics," and declared that his dreams of Asiatic solidarity had at long last become reality. "This is not the time to think with our minds," Ba Maw exclaimed; "this is the time to think with our blood, and it is this thinking with the blood that has brought me all the way from Burma to Japan." The Burmese prime minister spoke repeatedly of the solidarity of "a thousand million Asiatics," a vision also evoked by other Asian leaders.

Burma and the Philippines, long colonies of Britain and the United States respectively, were granted nominal independence by Japan in 1943. Occupied Indonesia was later also given independence, although the quick end of the war made the transfer of authority untidy. The Tokyo conference of November 1943 was designed to be an inspiring symbol of Pan-Asian idealism and the demise of white colonial rule in Asia; and although it was ultimately a hollow exercise, it fueled both Asian racial dreams and Western racial fears. Officials in the West took the rhetoric of Asian solidarity painfully to heart. During the first year of the war, for example, Admiral Ernest King worried about the repercussions of Japanese victories "among the non-white world" while Roosevelt's chief of staff Admiral William Leahy wrote in his diary about the fear that Japan might "succeed in combining most of the Asiatic peoples against the whites." William Phillips, Roosevelt's personal emissary to India in 1943, sent back deeply pessimistic reports about a rising "color consciousness" that seemed to be creating an insurmountable barrier between Oriental and Occidental peoples. In March 1945, a month before he died, President Roosevelt evoked in a negative way much the same image of Pan-Asian solidarity that the Asian leaders had emphasized in Tokyo in 1943. "1,100,000,000 potential enemies," the president told a confidant, "are dangerous."

The media in the West were frequently even more apocalyptic in their expression of such fears. Thus, the Hearst newspapers declared the war in Asia totally different from that in Europe, for Japan was a "racial menace" as well as a cultural and religious one, and if it proved victorious in the Pacific there would be "perpetual war between Oriental ideals and Occidental." Popular writers described the war against Japan as "a holy war, a racial war of greater significance than any the world has heretofore seen." Spokesmen for the cause of China and a free Asia like Pearl Buck and Lin Yutang were so appalled and alarmed by the way Westerners instinctively saw the fight against Japan in sweeping racial terms that they warned of a Third World War between whites and nonwhites within a generation.

In fact, Pan-Asian unity was a myth, albeit a myth that died hard for all sides. In the end, their own oppressive behavior toward other Asians earned the Japanese more hatred than support. Ba Maw, dreamer of Asian blood calling to Asian blood, eventually became a bitter, scathing critic of Japanese "brutality, arrogance, and racial pretensions"; in his disillusion, as in his dreams, he was typical. As a symbol of Asian audacity, defiance, and—fleetingly—strength vis-à-vis the West, the Japanese commanded admiration throughout Asia. As the self-designated leaders of the

Greater East Asia Co-Prosperity Sphere, however, they proved to be as overweening as the Westerners had been before them, and in many instances even more harsh: dominating the political scene, taking over local economies, imposing broad programs of "Japanization," slapping non-Japanese in public, torturing and executing dissidents, exploiting native labor so severely that between 1942 and 1945 the death toll among such workers numbered in the hundreds of thousands. Untold millions of Asian civilians died during the brief existence of the Co-Prosperity Sphere—from fighting, atrocities, disastrous labor and economic policies, and the starvation and disease that followed the war destruction. To some critics, this oppression reflected the fascist nature of the Japanese state. To some, it was better understood as the desperate reflex of an overly ambitious imperialist power that had arrived late on the scene. Still other critics argued that Japanese behavior betrayed a racial supremacism as virulent in its own way as the master-race theories of the Nazis.

That there was a decidedly racist component to the very conception of the Co-Prosperity Sphere is indisputable. Although the Japanese government frequently admonished its officials and citizens to avoid all manifestations of racial discrimination, the operative language of the new sphere was in fact premised on the belief that the Japanese were destined to preside over a fixed hierarchy of peoples and races. An Imperial Army document from the summer of 1942, for example, divided the nationalities of Asia into "master races," "friendly races," and "guest races," reserving the position of undisputed leadership for the "Yamato race." A massive secret study prepared in the civilian bureaucracy in 1942–43 was entitled "Global Policy with the Yamato Race as Nucleus," and expatiated upon the destiny of the Japanese as the "leading race" in Asia and implicitly the world. The Co-Prosperity Sphere, it was argued there, would contribute in both material and psychological ways to maintaining that superiority "eternally." For the Japanese, Pan-Asianism was thus a hydra-headed ideology, involving not merely a frontal attack on the Western colonial powers and their values but also discrimination vis-à-vis the other races, nationalities, and cultures of Asia.

When the struggle in Asia is taken into consideration, it becomes apparent that neither anti-Semitism nor white supremacism in its wider manifestations suffices to illuminate the full impact of racism during World War Two. In the United States and Britain, the Japanese were more hated than the Germans before as well as after Pearl Harbor. On this, there was no dispute among contemporary observers. They were perceived as a race apart, even a species apart—and an overpoweringly monolithic one at that. There was no Japanese counterpart to the "good German" in the popular consciousness of the Western allies. At the same time, the Japanese themselves dwelled at inordinate length on their own racial and cultural superiority, and like their adversaries, who practiced discrimination while proclaiming they were "fighting for democracy," they too became entangled in a web of contradictions: creating new colonial hierarchies while preaching liberation; singing the glories of their unique Imperial Way while professing to support a broad and all-embracing Pan-Asianism.

The racist code words and imagery that accompanied the war in Asia were often exceedingly graphic and contemptuous. The Western Allies, for example, persisted in their notion of the "subhuman" nature of the Japanese, routinely turning to images of apes and vermin to convey this. With more tempered disdain, they portrayed the Japanese as inherently inferior men and women who had to be understood in terms of primitivism, childishness, and collective mental and emotional deficiency. Cartoonists, songwriters, filmmakers, war correspondents, and the mass media in general all seized on these images—and so did the social scientists and Asia experts who ventured to analyze the Japanese "national character" during the war. At a very early stage in the conflict, when the purportedly inferior Japanese swept through colonial Asia like a whirlwind and took several hundred thousand Allied prisoners, another stereotype took hold: the Japanese superman, possessed of uncanny discipline and fighting skills. Subhuman, inhuman, lesser human, superhuman—all that was lacking in the perception of the Japanese enemy was a human like oneself. An endless stream of evidence ranging from atrocities to suicidal tactics could be cited, moreover, to substantiate the belief that the Japanese were a uniquely contemptible and formidable foe who deserved no mercy and virtually demanded extermination.

The formulaic expressions and graphic visual images which the Japanese relied on to distinguish themselves from others were, on the surface, quite different. Their leaders and ideologues constantly affirmed their unique "purity" as a race and culture, and turned the war itself—and eventually mass death—into an act of individual and collective purification. Americans and Europeans existed in the wartime Japanese imagination as vivid monsters, devils, and demons; and one had only to point to the bombing of Japanese cities (or the lynching of blacks in America) to demonstrate the aptness of this metaphor. In explaining their destiny as the "leading race," the Japanese also fell back upon theories of "proper place" which had long been used to legitimize inequitable relationships within Japan itself.

These dominant perceptions of the enemy on both the Allied and Japanese sides, intriguing in themselves, become even more interesting when it is recognized that they all existed independently of the conflict in Asia. Indeed, both the stereotypes and the explanations used to justify them really had little to do with Americans, Englishmen, Australians, Japanese, or other Asian nationalities per se. They were archetypical images associated with inequitable human relations in general, and their roots traced back centuries on both sides. . . .

These neglected aspects of the war in Asia do more than illuminate general patterns of racial and martial thinking. They also are a reminder of how merciless the conflict was. It was a common observation among Western war correspondents that the fighting in the Pacific was more savage than in the European theater. Kill or be killed. No quarter, no surrender. Take no prisoners. Fight to the bitter end. These were everyday words in the combat areas, and in the final year of the war such attitudes contributed to an orgy of bloodletting that neither side could conceive of avoiding, even though by mid-1944 Japan's defeat was inevitable and plain to see. As World War Two recedes in time and scholars dig at the formal documents, it is easy to forget the visceral emotions and sheer race hate that gripped virtually all participants in the war, at home and overseas, and influenced many actions and decisions at the time. Prejudice and racial stereotypes frequently distorted both Japanese and Allied evaluations of the enemy's intentions and capabilities. Race hate fed atrocities, and atrocities in turn fanned the fires of race hate. The dehumanization of the Other contributed immeasurably to the psychological distancing that facilitates killing, not only on the battlefield but also in the plans adopted by strategists far removed from the actual scene of combat. Such dehuman-ization, for example, surely facilitated the decisions to make civilian populations the targets of concentrated attack, whether by conventional or nuclear weapons. In countless ways, war words and race words came together in a manner which did not just reflect the savagery of the war, but contributed to it by reinforcing the impres-sion of a truly Manichaean struggle between completely incompatible antagonists. The natural response to such a vision was an obsession with extermination on both sides—a war without mercy.

And yet, despite this, the two sides did have things in common, including not only race hate and martial fury but also battlefield courage and dreams of peace. "Proper-place" theorizing was hardly alien to Western ways of thinking, which also viewed the world in terms of status, inequality, and a hierarchical division of labor and reward. Purity and purification through battle, so conspicuous a part of the carefully cultivated mystique of the Yamato race, were ideals frequently espoused in the West and elsewhere in Asia, where ideologues of the political left and right launched campaigns against spiritual pollution, patriots burned with ardor at the prospects of a holy war, and militarists extolled the purifying nature of life-and-death struggle. No side had a monopoly on attributing "beastliness" to the other, although the Westerners possessed a more intricate web of metaphors with which to convey this.

Even the most basic attitudes toward life and death, which many participants in the war claimed were fundamentally different among Japanese and Westerners, prove on closer scrutiny not to have been so drastically unalike. Many Japanese fighting men died instead of surrendering because they had little choice in the matter, owing not only to pressure from their own side but also to the disinterest of the Allies in taking prisoners. After the initial wave of humiliating Allied defeats and mass surrenders, Allied fighting men also almost never surrendered voluntar-ily. Indeed, the kill-or-be-killed nature of combat in the Pacific soon made personal decisions about living or dying almost irrelevant for combatants on either side. . . . Even as Americans were belittling Japanese who fought to the last man, treating them as virtually another species of being, they were cherishing their own epics of defeat such as the Alamo and the Little Bighorn. On the eve of Pearl Harbor one of Hollywood's most popular offerings was *They Died with Their Boots On,* an Errol Flynn movie commemorating Custer's last stand.

In the heat of war, such points of common ground were lost sight of and the be-havior of the enemy was seen as unique and peculiarly odious, with the issue of atrocities playing an exceptionally large role in each side's perception of the other. Savage Japanese behavior in China and throughout Southeast Asia, as well as in the treatment of Allied prisoners, was offered as proof of the inherent barbarity of the enemy. In a similar way, the Japanese stimulated hatred of the Allies by publicizing grisly battlefield practices such as the collection of Japanese skulls and bones, and responded with profound self-righteousness to the terror bombing of Japanese civil-ians. It is conventional wisdom that in times of life-and-death struggle, ill-grounded rumors of enemy atrocities invariably flourish and arouse a feverish hatred against the foe. This is misleading, however, for in fact atrocities follow war as the jackal follows a wounded beast. The propagandistic deception often lies, not in the false claims of enemy atrocities, but in the pious depiction of such behavior as peculiar to the other side. There is room for debate over the details of alleged incidents of atrocity in the war in Asia; room for discussion about the changing definition of legitimate targets of war; room for argument concerning how new technologies of firepower and air power may have altered the meaning of atrocity in the modern world. However, just as no one can return to Custer and the Little Bighorn any more without observing how vicious the fighting was on both sides, so it is also necessary to acknowledge that atrocious behavior occurred on all sides in the Pacific War. Such acts, and the propagandizing of them, became part of the vicious circle of war hates and race hates and contributed to the deaths of hundreds of thousands of individuals—millions, if the civilian deaths of the Japanese as well as other Asians are counted—long after Japan's defeat was a foregone conclusion. . . .

To a conspicuous degree, the racial and racist ways of thinking which had contributed so much to the ferociousness of the war were sublimated and transformed after August 1945. The merciless struggle for control of Asia and the Pacific gave way, in a remarkably short time, to an occupation in which mercy was indeed displayed by the conquerors, and generosity and goodwill characterized many of the actions of victor and vanquished alike. That vicious racial stereotypes were transformed, however, does not mean that they were dispelled. They remain latent, capable of being revived by both sides in times of crisis and tension. At the same time, these patterns of thinking also were transferred laterally and attached to the new enemies of the cold-war era: the Soviets and Chinese Communists, the Korean foe of the early 1950s, the Vietnamese enemy of the 1960 and 1970s, and hostile third-world movements in general. The patterns persist, even as specific circumstances change. They are only part of the picture, but still a telling and potentially tragic part.

The U.S. Failure in China

MICHAEL SCHALLER

Allies in a New War

The allies [the United States and China] had joined together, but had begun two different wars. While American planners expected to use Chinese manpower as a vast force against Japan, the Nationalist regime hoped to utilize its alliance to accumulate reserves of money, weapons, and influence which would help achieve domestic supremacy. Americans who supposed that aid could be used as a lever to encourage reform confronted a Chinese leadership convinced that foreign assistance obviated the need for reform. These contradictions cast the first of many long shadows over the imaginary "key to the strategy of the Pacific."

Even as Japan overran the scattered American outposts of the Pacific, military and diplomatic officials in China sought to warn Washington against the danger of attributing too much importance to the Chinese alliance. . . .

From Michael Schaller, *The U.S. Crusade in China, 1938–1945* (New York: Columbia University Press, 1979), 87–92, 99–100, 102–104, 106–108, 110–111, 115, 122–123, 147, 158–160, 164–165, 169–170, 174–175.

These reports from Chungking, though quite dissimilar in political content, attested to the dubious military value of China in the current war effort. The judgment they rendered upon Chinese politics showed scant trace of the romantic or heroic propaganda which had dominated popular discussions about China. To understand why these and most later recommendations from "experts" in China were ignored, we must look again at Franklin D. Roosevelt, the individual most responsible for charting the course of American diplomacy. Early in the war, Roosevelt adopted an Asian strategy centered upon elevating Nationalist China to "great power" status, something Lauchlin Currie had previously urged him to do. This decision had major implications for both the conduct of the war and postwar diplomacy.

Not surprisingly, Roosevelt assumed that following Japan's eventual defeat Asia would enter a new stage of political evolution. Japan would be gone as a dominant military power, but so would the mighty British, Dutch, and French empires—soon if not immediately. Two major forces would probably rush in to fill this power vacuum: Soviet power extending from northeast Asia and nationalist political movements emerging within the former colonial and neocolonial societies. Wartime decisions made by the United States could influence the pace of decolonization, the dimensions of the Soviet sphere, and, perhaps most importantly, the nature of Asian nationalism. Neither Roosevelt nor his advisors were deadset against any of these developments, since they hoped that a carefully reordered Asia would contribute to world stability and prosperity. But they were determined that the United States should play a major role in outlining the contours of postwar Asia.

Constraining this concern, however, was the demand imposed upon American resources by the global war. The massive battlefronts of Europe and the Pacific, deemed strategically more vital than mainland Asia, meant that the American war effort in China stood in third place. Neither the best minds in Washington, sufficient material, nor many troops would be spared for the China front. Yet for a variety of reasons, both pragmatic and romantic, Roosevelt sought to include China among the ranks of the Grand Alliance. Encouraged by the advice of such men as Lauchlin Currie, Harry Hopkins, James McHugh, Claire Chennault, Joseph Alsop, and Chiang Kai-shek, the President believed he could join American power to the KMT [Kuomintang, the Nationalist Party] and thereby create an effective wartime and postwar ally. This policy, he believed, might encourage the development of a liberal, pro-American China to replace the influence of the imperialist powers in Asia and counter the appeal of revolutionary doctrines among the masses of the East. A thought expressed by Roosevelt and Hopkins at several points during the war clinched the argument: "in any serious conflict of policy with Russia," Nationalist China "would line up on our side."

Roosevelt's concern, however, was not fixated upon a Soviet or revolutionary threat. During the war American planners were equally concerned with easing the European imperialists out of Asia. The British in particular feared that American policy had determined to pull down the foundations of the empire even before a final verdict was rendered. Throughout the war the British growled about extending aid to Chiang Kai-shek, largely because they saw Chinese nationalism as a direct threat to colonialism. Churchill believed Roosevelt's game was to make China strong enough to "police" Asia while remaining essentially dependent upon the United States. The prime minister complained to subordinates that the Americans expected to use China as a "faggot vote on the side of the United States in an attempt to liquidate the British overseas Empire."

Before fulfilling either Roosevelt's hope or Churchill's fear, the United States had first to succeed in prodding the Nationalist regime to begin the military and political reforms which might transform China into a powerful and unified state. Without change, little could be expected of China. Yet Roosevelt never really understood that in his effort to forge a new order in Asia he had linked the United States to a crumbling regime, a situation reminiscent of the Austrian "corpse" to which Germany found itself allied in World War I. From 1941 on, despite a brave façade, the KMT's claim to popular support and power grew only weaker. The party and government apparatus devolved from an instrument of class and military rule to a jumble of family-oriented cliques and semi-independent military commanders. As this occurred, the forces of social revolution grew consistently stronger, accelerating the internal crisis and unraveling the web of American policy. The demise of the United Front and Nationalist power removed the buffer between the Chinese Communists and the United States, placing these two powerful forces on a collision course. . . .

From the beginning of the war, Roosevelt groped for a China policy which would do several, sometimes contradictory, things at once. At a minimum, he wished to sustain China as an active ally, tying down several million Japanese troops on the Asian mainland. A policy of generous aid, combined with elevating China's importance in world political councils, could contribute to the acceptance of China as a great power. Meanwhile, a reformed, unified China could cooperate with the United States in insuring a stable postwar Asia. Also, the President remained largely convinced that within China the agency of transformation must be Chiang Kai-shek and his regime. Thus Chiang must be supported and indulged, with a view toward future cooperation. Until late in the war, the President ignored or misunderstood signs indicating that the U.S.-KMT alliance yielded results fundamentally opposed to the objectives of U.S. policy. . . .

The most significant contradictions and strains in China policy developed between the President and his aides, who in Washington took a broad, long-term view of events, and the military and diplomatic officers stationed in China, who faced the realities of the political and military battlefield. While Roosevelt could project a future "great China," General Stilwell had to deal with a crumbling army. The staff of the American embassy, witnessing the grave political deterioration of the KMT, had little faith in predictions that a liberal China was about to assume the mantle of Asian leadership. While all acknowledged that the political future of China held tremendous importance for the United States, few Americans agreed upon exactly why this was so or which China really represented America's—or China's—best interests. Since the United States had resolved to begin a massive program of aid to a Chinese government engaged in both a foreign and civil war, the unresolved questions of basic policy could only contribute to eventual disaster. . . .

American Military Strategy and the Chinese Nationalists

. . . During his first official meeting with Chiang, Stilwell requested the power to command the Chinese Fifth and Sixth armies, which had moved into Burma at British request. Chiang nominally acceded to this request, but privately complained of Stilwell's arrogance and failure to show the generalissimo sufficient deference. The American had not behaved at all like a "chief of staff," an advisor, but like an independent commander.

When he left for the Burmese front on March 11, Stilwell was unprepared for the situation which he found there. Neither Chinese nor British commanders wished to sacrifice men and material for an area they considered marginal. British forces desired to withdraw to protect India, while Chinese commanders balked at serving under an American. Chiang, of course, had never given Stilwell more than nominal authority. Stilwell scurried around Burma and revisited Chungking in a vain effort to have Chiang order Chinese field commanders that Stilwell be obeyed. The verbal assurances given to Stilwell dissolved upon his return to the battlefield.

Given these circumstances, the battle in Burma during March 1942 proved disastrous in almost every way. The disorganized and defeatist Anglo-Chinese troops were no match for the well-supplied, disciplined, and highly motivated Japanese army. Stilwell found it impossible to rally his troops and soon discovered he had no real power to command the Chinese armies assigned to him. The Japanese assumed command of the air, making both resupply and movement of his forces nearly impossible. By mid-April the battle was clearly lost, and early in May the British, Indian, and Chinese units in Burma had become isolated and disorganized. Stilwell himself led one column through the jungles and mountain passes in a desperate effort to reach safety in India. When the weary and embittered survivors reached India on May 29, the general admitted publicly that the Allies had taken "a hell of a beating" in Burma. . . .

Characteristically, almost as soon as he had reached the safety of India, Stilwell began to evaluate the causes of the military disaster which had overtaken him in Burma. Working furiously, he prepared a fifty-page report on the Burma campaign which graphically recounted the bungling of British and Chinese commanders. The British, he concluded, only cared about defending strategic colonies, and then only when it suited a larger imperial strategy. They balked at cooperating with China, since that nation represented a long-term nationalistic threat to colonialism. But Stilwell came down hardest on Chiang Kai-shek, especially for interfering with the American's effort to command Chinese troops. While "the wasteful and inefficient system of political juggling" of Chinese armies might be necessary to maintain Chiang's political power, it "emasculated the effectiveness of Chinese troops." The existing political and military organization of China was virtually hopeless, Stilwell wrote. Only by relying on the individual Chinese soldier, retrained, rearmed, and commanded by officers in a "New Army," could military victory be achieved. Stilwell's dream of a New Army, conceived in the Burma debacle, took determined root in his mind as he prepared to return to Chungking. There he would present Chiang with "notes" calling for the complete reorganization of the armed forces which the generalissimo had spent his life building. . . .

The military reform proposals centered on the creation of two new Chinese army groups. One would be organized in India, built up from the remnants of the Chinese units which retreated from Burma. They would be supplemented by new conscripts. At the same time a second, larger group of thirty Chinese divisions would be assembled in China's western Yunnan province. Retrained, rearmed, and commanded by Chinese officers who themselves were under American guidance, the two groups would move into Burma, where, assisted by British military action, they would reopen the land route to China. This "simple" reform would create an active military front in China as well as paving the way for increased aid to flow across Burma. It also meant that a new Chinese army, not under Chiang's control or patronage, would probably emerge as the most powerful force in China. Such a scheme had already been angrily rejected by Soong at the time of the negotiations for the $500 million loan.

From the summer of 1942 on through his recall late in 1944 Stilwell's plans centered on the dual reform and Burma campaign projects. . . .

Chiang balked at the essence of Stilwell's proposals, assuaging the American only by agreeing to permit the creation of a small Chinese force in India. Since they would be outside the country, the troops posed no immediate threat. But Chiang adamantly refused to consider reorganizing thirty divisions in Yunnan. Only when and if the Americans delivered substantial military aid would such a force be possible. The generalissimo spoke indignantly of how he was asked to create new armies while the United States had failed to send promised aid. Here he had a good debating point, since the military crisis in the Middle East, marked by the fall of Tobruk on June 21, caused planners to divert aircraft and weapons from China. Without additional transport aircraft, the 10th Air Force could not carry sufficient cargo from India over the Hump of the Himalayas. The diversion of supplies also starved the small air task force which Chennault had begun to operate within China. To make matters still worse, the MAB [Munitions Assignment Board] cut China's monthly Lend-Lease allotment to thirty-five hundred tons in view of the undeliverable stockpiles accumulating in India.

Stilwell provided an easy and obvious target for Chiang's wrath. He had already proposed to meddle in the Chinese power structure, while T. V. Soong in Washington reported that Stilwell was "deliberately and disloyally" responsible for delaying aid. Soong and Chiang found Stilwell to be anything but putty in their hands. They sought to salvage the situation by boosting the reputation of their favorite American officer—and Stilwell's archrival-to-be—Claire Chennault. . . .

. . . Marshall informed Soong that Stilwell would not be recalled and that any possible successor would occupy the same role and exercise similar control of Lend-Lease. . . .

Following this episode, the relationship between Stilwell and Chiang Kai-shek took on a bitterness unrelieved until their final confrontation late in 1944. In Stilwell's diary and headquarters Chiang was referred to as the "Peanut," his wife as "Snow White"—terms originally used for code transmissions but now as epithets. Privately, Stilwell began to think of alternatives to KMT rule. . . .

Chiang's most powerful ally in this successful extortion of American aid remained the myth of his genius and invincibility. The American public knew only the Chiang Kai-shek of *Time* and *Life* cover stories, the China of the Big Four fighting on the side of democracy. In public Roosevelt continually boosted Chiang's status as the leader of a "great power." Although later in the war a handful of dissenting journalists sought to shatter this myth, neither the public nor the American government were seriously challenged to examine their preconceptions. . . .

In a letter to Marshall early in March, the President explained his reluctance to adopt a stern approach toward Chiang. The United States and China were allies, both great powers. It would be counterproductive to attempt to command Chiang, a man who had struggled to become the "undisputed leader of 400,000,000 people" and who had created in China "what it took us a couple of centuries to attain." The President would not "speak sternly to a man like that or exact commitments from him as we might do from the Sultan of Morocco." In place of threats, Roosevelt preferred to indulge the generalissimo and win his support. Since this meant endorsing an air strategy in China, the President went on to order the creation of an independent 14th Air Force of five hundred planes under Chennault, and the increase of Hump deliveries toward ten thousand tons per month. Although a Burma campaign still remained possible, Roosevelt's insistence that Chennault receive a guaranteed monthly minimum of supplies reduced the likelihood of Stilwell accumulating necessary supplies.

What at first appeared to be a technical, nonpolitical, and unextraordinary debate over military strategy actually masked a political chasm. Chennault and Stilwell fully understood, as did their Chinese hosts, that in China it was next to impossible to separate military and political strategies. For example, the impact of a few hundred planes and pilots on China, as compared to Stilwell's massive reorganization program, would be miniscule. Yet the debate in Washington, and Roosevelt's awareness, barely reflected this fact. For the Chinese and a growing number of Americans in China, however, this issue had become linked to overall policymaking and the smoldering civil war.

The General or the Generalissimo?

The converging forces of revolution, foreign invasion, and a contradictory American aid program placed an almost unbearable strain on China during 1944. Fighting reached its highest pitch since 1938, as allied forces finally entered Burma and the Japanese launched an offensive in southeast China. Chiang's continuing refusal to commit his forces against the Japanese and the growing signs of internal warfare prompted not only Stilwell but Roosevelt as well to consider a radical shift in policy. For a few months it appeared the President saw a new reality and even considered the partial abandonment of Chiang's regime. The failure to pursue this course marked a true turning point in America's Asian policy. . . .

As the fighting in Burma escalated in the spring and summer of 1944, there arose yet another impasse in Sino-American relations. Both Stilwell and Roosevelt resumed efforts to establish contacts with Yenan, presumably to incorporate Communist forces into the Chinese government and American military aid program. This issue lay at the core of China's internal crisis and bore directly on U.S. relations with the Soviet Union. To prevent civil war—thus reducing the twin dangers of either a Communist victory or Soviet intervention—Americans looked for a way to control both Yenan and Chungking. If the United States appeared willing to balance its assistance between the Communists and Nationalists, both parties might be restrained from attacking the other. In any event, such an American stance would give Washington far greater flexibility than it had previously enjoyed. The Foreign Service officers serving in the embassy and with Stilwell had long advocated this strategy, arguing that the United States must send a mission to Yenan. This, they understood, was the ultimate test of whether the United States would sever itself from an unrealistic dependence on the KMT. It also represented a trial run for Washington's ability to come to terms with and possibly influence revolutionary nationalism in Asia.

When, in February 1944, Chiang refused Roosevelt's initial request that he permit an American team to visit Yenan, few observers were surprised. The generalissimo had no reason to accept the proposal, given the success he had previously enjoyed in rejecting all political demands. But by March 1944 both Roosevelt's attitude and the situation within China were reversed. With unexpected fury the Japanese army launched yet another major offensive (Operation Ichigo) in southeastern China. Japanese forces struck hammer blows against provinces supposedly under firm KMT control. The provincial armies, which Chiang had long insisted needed none of Stilwell's reorganization, were no match for the Japanese and began disorderly retreats on all fronts. For a time, it even seemed that Chungking might be threatened. To make matters even worse, the Japanese overran the provinces in which Chennault's forward air bases were located. As Stilwell had long predicted, air bases left unprotected were easy prey to the Japanese. Now the precious aid which had built up Chennault's air force and bases was lost because there was no adequate Chinese army to defend them.

The debacle of Ichigo (which lasted through the early autumn) made its mark on the President. It seemed that Stilwell's tactics had been right, after all. If this was the case, perhaps it was also true that sending a group of Americans to Yenan was worth pressing for. At the least, it might frighten Chiang into cooperating more fully with Stilwell. By early March Roosevelt believed the time had come to press Chiang directly on the matter of a mission to Yenan. . . .

Chiang's reaction to the Japanese Operation Ichigo offensive made American action imperative. The generalissimo suddenly began to demand that Chinese troops be brought back from the thick of the battle in Burma to meet the Japanese in China. Since it was highly unlikely that Chiang would really commit these troops against the Japanese, Stilwell suggested to Marshall that Chiang be stripped of command powers. In his place Stilwell would assume complete freedom to direct China's war effort, command troops, remove recalcitrant officers, and even incorporate Communist units into his military plans. After convincing the Joint Chiefs they should back this proposal, Marshall presented the idea to the President on July 4, 1944.

The Army Chief of Staff asked Roosevelt to endorse a message which accused Chiang and Chennault of responsibility for a long chain of blunders. The President affixed his signature on July 6 to a cable warning Chiang that a "critical situation" now existed. Because of this it was imperative for Stilwell to assume "command of all Chinese and American forces . . . including the Communist forces.". . .

Reacting to Stilwell's warnings, Marshall's staff in Quebec drafted a message, which Roosevelt approved, rebuking Chiang. The time for stalling, it declared, had passed and unless Stilwell was given complete power to command troops, United States aid would be terminated. Blaming Chiang for courting "catastrophic consequences," the reprimand intoned that it was "evident to all of us here . . . that all your and our efforts to save China are to be lost by further delays."

Stilwell delivered this ultimatum in person to Chiang on September 19, interrupting a private meeting between the generalissimo and Hurley. The consummate joy of revenge felt by Stilwell was expressed in the poem he wrote to commemorate the occasion [see Document No. 7]. . . . Believing he now had the President's full support, Stilwell could at last "play the avenging angel."

While Stilwell may have felt secure in this new role, he had won a Pyrrhic victory. During the following weeks it became clear that Patrick Hurley had secretly taken it upon himself to work with Chiang in ridding the generalissimo of the tiresome American general. Hurley's motives and methods are shrouded in mystery. His own records reveal his collusion with Chiang but fail to adequately explain his reasons for this. Hurley's behavior over the next year does show that he believed it imperative to sustain Chiang in power. He feared that any American decision either to work directly with the Communists or to topple Chiang would open up China to the several dangers of a Communist victory, European meddling, or Soviet expansion. Thus a man almost totally ignorant of the actual situation in China took it upon himself to once again steer American policy firmly in the direction of sustaining Chiang's unchallenged supremacy in China. It is a dubious testament to Hurley's skills that he managed to accomplish this task. . . .

On October 18, [1944], Roosevelt made the expedient decision to recall Stilwell. Hurley was asked to suggest the names of a possible successor and FDR soon selected General Albert Wedemeyer from among the nominees. In appointing the new commander, Roosevelt announced the division of the CBI Theater into a separate China Theater and Burma-India Theater. Wedemeyer would serve as commander of American forces and as the generalissimo's chief of staff but would not be expected to command any Chinese forces.

On October 21, after composing a sheaf of farewell letters to his friends and adversaries in China, Stilwell left his command. He would never again return to China. Gauss, now more superfluous than ever, soon resigned, with Hurley shortly assuming the title of ambassador. Chiang had accomplished one of the most crucial victories in his remarkable career.

Upon his arrival in Washington only George Marshall met Stilwell. Their discussion convinced Stilwell that he was to be kept "out of the way and muzzled until after the elections." Henry Stimson admitted to his diary that he, among others, was treating Stilwell terribly shabbily. Nevertheless the administration's priority was "to keep him out of reach of all newsmen and not give them an opportunity to catch and distort any unwary word just before [the] election."

FURTHER READING

Bergerud, Eric. *Touched with Fire: The Land War in the South Pacific* (1996).

Blair, Clay, Jr. *Silent Victory: The U.S. Submarine War Against Japan* (1975).

Cameron, Craig M. *American Samurai: Myth, Imagination, and the Conduct of Battle in the First Marine Division, 1941–1951* (1994).

Cook, Haruko Taya, and Theodore F. Cook. *Japan at War: An Oral History* (1992).

Costello, John. *The Pacific War* (1982).

Craven, Wesley Frank, and James Lea Cate, eds. *The Army Air Forces in World War II,* 7 vols. (1948–1958).

Crowl, Philip A., and Jeter A. Isely. *The U.S. Marines and Amphibious War* (1951).

Dower, John W. *War Without Mercy: Race and Power in the Pacific War* (1986).

Hayes, Grace P. *The Joint Chiefs of Staff and the War Against Japan* (1982).

Iriye, Akira. *Power and Culture: The Japanese-American War, 1941–1945* (1981).

James, D. Clayton. *The Years of MacArthur,* 3 vols. (1964–1973).

Linderman, Gerald F. *The World Within War: America's Combat Experience in World War II* (1997).

Lindstrom, Lamont, and Geoffrey M. White. *Island Encounters: Black and White Memories of the Pacific War* (1990).

Miller, John, Jr. *Guadalcanal: The First Offensive* (1949).

Morison, Samuel E. *History of United States Naval Operations in World War II,* 15 vols. (1947–1962).

Potter, E. B. *Nimitz* (1976).

Sledge, E. B. *With the Old Breed at Peleliu and Okinawa* (1981).

Spector, Ronald H. *Eagle Against the Sun: The American War with Japan* (1985).

Thorne, Christopher. *Allies of a Kind: The United States, Britain, and the War Against Japan* (1978).

Tuchman, Barbara. *Stilwell and the American Experience in China* (1970).

U.S. Department of the Army, Center for Military History. *United States Army in World War II: The China-Burma-India Theater* series and *The War in the Pacific* series (multivolume).

U.S. Marine Corps, Historical Division. *History of U.S. Marine Corps Operations in World War II* (1958–1968).

Willmott, H. P. *Empires in the Balance: Japanese and Allied Pacific Strategies to April 1942* (1982).

———. *The Barrier and the Javelin: Japanese and Allied Pacific Strategies, February to June 1942* (1983).

See also Chapters 2, 3, 4, and 11.

CHAPTER 6

Cooperation and Conflict

on the Home Front

World War II brought enormous economic and social changes to the American home front, and with these changes came both conflict and cooperation. The wartime employment boom and the opening of new occupational opportunities for many Americans led to declining unemployment, increasing wages, and a flourishing business climate. At the same time, the conversion of the economy to military purposes meant a shortage of consumer goods and rationing. People may have had more cash but in most cases they could not buy new cars or gasoline to run them with, radios, or foods like butter and sugar. In an era when silk stockings were replaced by nylons, women even found these new fashion items in short supply.

The war also changed the demographic contours of the United States when over 30 million Americans migrated from one region to another. The population of western states increased dramatically; the populations of California and Arizona increased 53 percent and 50 percent respectively. Just as dramatic was the migration of African Americans from rural areas to cities, including about 1.5 million blacks who moved out of the South to northern and western cities. This mobility was, in part, about jobs. The numbers of African Americans who worked in defense industries increased. So too did the numbers of women of all races. The Office of War Information helped recruit and keep women on the job with a propaganda campaign centered on the idea that the war could not be won without women's cooperation and women's work. As a result, the number of employed women rose from 11 million to almost 20 million during the war. In 1940, one out of every twenty production workers in the auto industry was a woman; by 1944, as the factories turned out tanks instead of personal automobiles, the number was one in five.

Conflict on the home front existed alongside cooperation. Many blacks were turned away from defense jobs, or were the last hired when no more whites were available. They also faced discriminatory practices once on the shop floor. Workplace discrimination was nothing new, but the government's defense programs created a new political and economic context for black political leaders who demanded changes. One of the most important results was President Roosevelt's executive order outlawing racial discrimination in the hiring of defense industry workers.

The dramatic growth in established communities with the influx of new factory workers and military personnel, the disruptions to established patterns, and the everyday adjustments required during wartime, coupled with race and ethnic tensions, resulted in riots in Detroit and Los Angeles in June 1943. The group that might have been the most direct target of these attacks on the West Coast, Japanese Americans, had already been removed to relocation camps in the interior of the country. There, tensions between the relocated Japanese Americans and the surrounding communities were minimized by government supervision.

Despite the agreement of the "no-strike-pledge" between government and labor unions, "wildcat" (unauthorized) strikes broke out across the country with disputes over wages and working conditions. Considering that workers involved in the strikes were denounced as unpatriotic and even guilty of sabotage, these strikes provide an illustration of the ongoing tensions between labor and management and the new tensions brought on by government and industry's all-out production efforts. The longest wartime strike occurred in the coal industry as miners sought higher wages and to challenge the unprecedented power government wielded over labor. The United Mine Workers called over 400,000 workers out on strike four separate times in 1943, but the miners and their leader, John L. Lewis, faced an enormous negative response. Roosevelt seized the mines, and Congress passed the Smith-Connally War Labor Disputes Act, which increased government power over workplaces where laborers were striking.

How deeply did wartime conditions change American society? One way to assess this question is to focus on different social groups. Was World War II a watershed for American women in the area of work and family? How profoundly did wartime disruption influence the lives of people of color? Did internment have a long-term impact on not only Japanese American lives but also American ideas of civil liberties? Related to these questions is whether or not different groups had the right to make demands for better working conditions or greater civil rights, or if self-interest was inappropriate during wartime. Was such behavior selfish and even disloyal? Or was it a reasoned response to conditions on the home front?

DOCUMENTS

Document 1 is a call for black Americans to march on Washington to bring pressure on the president and Congress to eliminate discrimination in the workplace and segregation in the armed forces. This effort was led by civil rights leader A. Philip Randolph. Document 2 is an example of the government's creative campaign to enlist women for the war effort and shows the positive image of Rosie the Riveter, a fictional industrial woman worker. Also depicted in a positive light were American allies, as shown in Document 3, which contrasts America's Chinese allies with its Japanese enemies and reveals the inherent racism of the era. Document 4, a magazine article on women's stockings, highlights how the war changed consumer patterns, and the levity with which some changes were dealt with. On a more serious level, Document 5, excerpts from two *Life* magazine articles, explores the changes brought on by the expansion of industry, the ongoing race and labor tensions in urban areas, and the responses of business and government. Document 6, a government pamphlet highlighting the contributions of Mexican Americans in the war, provides evidence of the cooperation on the home front and the battlefield. It is also an example of how wartime labor concerns reached every segment of the American population. Documents 7 and 8 look at the wartime conflicts of the zoot suit riots and the coal strike respectively. Finally,

Document 9 is a reflection on the changes this era brought to one young Japanese American. It is the recollection of Mikiso Hane, now a professor of history at Knox College, who as a young man was relocated from his family farm in California to an internment camp in Arizona.

1. A Call to March on Washington, 1941

We call upon you to fight for jobs in National Defense.

We call upon you to struggle for the integration of Negroes in the armed forces, such as the Air Corps, Navy, Army and Marine Corps of the Nation.

We call upon you to demonstrate for the abolition of Jim-Crowism in all Government departments and defense employment.

This is an hour of crisis. It is a crisis of democracy. It is a crisis of minority groups. It is a crisis of Negro Americans.

What is this crisis?

To American Negroes, it is the denial of jobs in Government defense projects. It is racial discrimination in Government departments. It is widespread Jim-Crowism in the armed forces of the Nation.

While billions of the taxpayers' money are being spent for war weapons, Negro workers are being turned away from the gates of factories, mines and mills—being flatly told, "NOTHING DOING." Some employers refuse to give Negroes jobs when they are without "union cards," and some unions refuse Negro workers union cards when they are "without jobs."

What shall we do?

What a dilemma!

What a runaround!

What a disgrace!

What a blow below the belt!

'Though dark, doubtful and discouraging, all is not lost, all is not hopeless. 'Though battered and bruised, we are not beaten, broken or bewildered.

Verily, the Negroes' deepest disappointments and direst defeats, their tragic trials and outrageous oppressions in these dreadful days of destruction and disaster to democracy and freedom, and the rights of minority peoples, and the dignity and independence of the human spirit, is the Negroes' greatest opportunity to rise to the highest heights of struggle for freedom and justice in Government, in industry, in labor unions, education, social service, religion and culture.

With faith and confidence of the Negro people in their own power for self-liberation, Negroes can break down the barriers of discrimination against employment in National Defense. Negroes can kill the deadly serpent of race hatred in the Army, Navy, Air and Marine Corps, and smash through and blast the government, business and labor-union red tape to win the right to equal opportunity in vocational training and re-training in defense employment.

Most important and vital to all, Negroes, by the mobilization and coordination of their mass power, can cause PRESIDENT ROOSEVELT TO ISSUE AN EXECUTIVE ORDER

ABOLISHING DISCRIMINATIONS IN ALL GOVERNMENT DEPARTMENTS, ARMY, NAVY, AIR CORPS AND NATIONAL DEFENSE JOBS.

Of course, the task is not easy. In very truth, it is big, tremendous and difficult.

It will cost money.

It will require sacrifice.

It will tax the Negroes' courage, determination and will to struggle. But we can, must and will triumph.

The Negroes' stake in national defense is big. It consists of jobs, thousands of jobs. It may represent millions, yes, hundreds of millions of dollars in wages. It consists of new industrial opportunities and hope. This is worth fighting for.

But to win our stakes, it will require an "all-out," bold and total effort and demonstration of colossal proportions.

Negroes can build a mammoth machine of mass action with a terrific and tremendous driving and striking power that can shatter and crush the evil fortress of race prejudice and hate, if they will only resolve to do so and never stop, until victory comes.

Dear fellow Negro Americans, be not dismayed in these terrible times. You possess power, great power. Our problem is to harness and hitch it up for action on the broadest, daring and most gigantic scale.

In this period of power politics, nothing counts but pressure, more pressure, and still more pressure, through the tactic and strategy of broad, organized, aggressive mass action behind the vital and important issues of the Negro. To this end, we propose that ten thousand Negroes MARCH ON WASHINGTON FOR JOBS IN NATIONAL DEFENSE AND EQUAL INTEGRATION IN THE FIGHTING FORCES OF THE UNITED STATES.

An "all-out" thundering march on Washington, ending in a monster and huge demonstration at Lincoln's Monument will shake up white America.

It will shake up official Washington.

It will give encouragement to our white friends to fight all the harder by our side, with us, for our righteous cause.

It will gain respect for the Negro people.

It will create a new sense of self-respect among Negroes.

But what of national unity?

We believe in national unity which recognizes equal opportunity of black and white citizens to jobs in national defense and the armed forces, and in all other institutions and endeavors in America. We condemn all dictatorships, Fascist, Nazi and Communist. We are loyal, patriotic Americans, all.

But, if American democracy will not defend its defenders; if American democracy will not protect its protectors; if American democracy will not give jobs to its toilers because of race or color; if American democracy will not insure equality of opportunity, freedom and justice to its citizens, black and white, it is a hollow mockery and belies the principles for which it is supposed to stand.

To the hard, difficult and trying problem of securing equal participation in national defense, we summon all Negro Americans to march on Washington. We summon Negro Americans to form committees in various cities to recruit and register marchers and raise funds through the sale of buttons and other legitimate means for the expenses of marchers to Washington by buses, train, private automobiles, trucks, and on foot.

We summon Negro Americans to stage marches on their City Halls and Councils in their respective cities and urge them to memorialize the President to issue an executive order to abolish discrimination in the Government and national defense.

However, we sternly counsel against violence and ill-considered and intemperate action and the abuse of power. Mass power, like physical power, when misdirected is more harmful than helpful.

We summon you to mass action that is orderly and lawful, but aggressive and militant, for justice, equality and freedom. . . .

2. Rosie the Riveter Becomes a Symbol of Patriotic Womanhood

Of all the images of working women during World War II, the image of women in factories predominates. Rosie the Riveter—the strong, competent women dressed in overalls and bandanna—was introduced as a symbol of patriotic womanhood. The accoutrements of war work—uniforms, tools, and lunch pails—were incorporated into the revised image of the feminine ideal.

From J. Howard Miller, "We Can Do It!" National Archives and Records Administration.

3. *Time* Magazine Contrasts Japanese Enemies and Chinese Allies, 1941

HOW TO TELL YOUR FRIENDS FROM THE JAPS

There is no infallible way of telling [Chinese and Japanese] apart, because the same racial strains are mixed in both. Even an anthropologist, with calipers and plenty of time to measure heads, noses, shoulders, hips, is sometimes stumped. A few rules of thumb—not always reliable:

• Some Chinese are tall (average: 5 ft. 5 in.). Virtually all Japanese are short (average: 5 ft. 2½ in.).

• Japanese are likely to be stockier and broader-hipped than short Chinese.

• Japanese—except for wrestlers—are seldom fat; they often dry up and grow lean as they age. The Chinese often put on weight, particularly if they are prosperous (in China, with its frequent famines, being fat is esteemed as a sign of being a solid citizen).

• Chinese, not as hairy as Japanese, seldom grow an impressive mustache.

• Most Chinese avoid horn-rimmed spectacles.

• Although both have the typical epicanthic fold of the upper eyelid (which makes them look almond-eyed), Japanese eyes are usually set closer together.

• Those who know them best often rely on facial expression to tell them apart: the Chinese expression is likely to be more placid, kindly, open; the Japanese more positive, dogmatic, arrogant.

• In Washington, last week, Correspondent Joseph Chiang made things much easier by pinning on his lapel a large badge reading "Chinese Reporter—NOT *Japanese*—Please."

• Some aristocratic Japanese have thin, aquiline noses, narrow faces and, except for their eyes, look like Caucasians.

• Japanese are hesitant, nervous in conversation, laugh loudly at the wrong time.

• Japanese walk stiffly erect, hard-heeled. Chinese, more relaxed, have an easy gait, sometimes shuffle.

4. *Newsweek* Magazine Reports on Women's Stockings in Wartime, 1943

The Office of War Information last week concerned itself to the extent of eight pages on "Women's Hosiery," and the report's only bright note was a half promise of no plans to ration them.

Most of the rest of the information was what women already knew or suspected—almost all (85 per cent) of next year's hose will be rayon, and even these won't be too plentiful since a good deal of rayon has gone to war in tire cords, and other equipment. Only five shades will be permitted, but there will be the usual range of lengths. These, however, will average an inch shorter than silk or nylon hose, because of rayon's "stretching properties."

The biggest blow was a warning that sheer stockings are a war casualty—they don't wear well. So, the War Production Board has banned production of 50-denier (sheer) hose of standard yarn and discourages production of those of special yarn, not much of which is available for hosiery anyway. As one WPB representative put it: "A 50-denier stocking that doesn't wear is a waste."

5. The Turmoil of Wartime Rapidly Changes Detroit, 1943

Detroit Is Dynamite

The news from Detroit is bad this summer. Few people across the country realize how bad it is. Wildcat strikes and sitdowns, material shortages and poor planning at the top have cut into Detroit's production of war weapons. Detroit's workers, led by the lusty U.A.W. [United Auto Workers], seem to hate and suspect their bosses more than ever. Detroit's manufacturers, who are the world's best producers, have made a failure of their labor relations. And the Government, which is asking Detroit to produce more and more, is divided within itself on how to get the most production.

The result is a morale situation which is perhaps the worst in the U.S. When workers in a great new tank arsenal strike because they can't smoke during work hours; when workers in an anti-aircraft gun plant quit making guns to help win a grocery-store strike; when a worker in a bomber plant tells a reporter: "I'm going to stay home tonight and go fishing: we're not getting anything done over there"; and another worker in the same plant punches 18 holes in a bomber's gas line because he has been called in the draft—when scores of incidents like these happen every week, as they do in Detroit—then it is time for the rest of the country to sit up and take notice. For Detroit can either blow up Hitler or it can blow up the U.S.

What the nation pictures when it thinks of Detroit today is a great stream of tanks, guns, engines and bombers flowing off the assembly lines in invincible profusion. But that picture has been achieved to date in only a few plants and a few specific categories. On tanks and guns, Detroit is ahead of schedule. On planes it has scarcely begun. Ford's Willow Run plant, advertised the world over as a symbol of U.S. industrial might, has not completed one plane on its assembly lines and is working now at a fraction of capacity, making sub-assemblies for other factories.

Detroit, which gave the nation its first miracles of production, has worked no miracles in this war like Henry Kaiser's shipbuilding miracle on the Pacific Coast. Detroit's unsung heroes—technicians and engineers and production bosses who work in shirtsleeves—have worked long and hard but they are caught in the middle of a fierce war between labor and management. Now they are facing other serious troubles—shortages of steel and other materials which have closed some war plants for as long as seven weeks.

In the first six months after Pearl Harbor, Detroit made $1,400,000,000 in war goods, less than it would have made in autos in a good half year in peacetime. The rate is now rising fast. In 1943, says Production Boss Donald Nelson, Detroit will have to shoulder a load of $12,000,000,000 or about one-sixth of U.S. war production.

Few people doubt that Detroit *can* do this colossal job. It has the machines, the factories, the know-how as no other city in the world has them. The weary months of conversion and retooling are over. If machines could win the war, Detroit would have nothing to worry about. But it takes people to run machines and too many of the people of Detroit are confused, embittered and distracted by factional groups that are fighting each other harder than they are willing to fight Hitler.

Detroit is a city of violent extremes. In the 1920's it made so many automobiles that it got rich and expanded beyond its wildest dreams. But in the 1930's it sank lower into the great depression than any big U.S. city. Its large banks were the first to close and its labor wars were the most vicious in the nation. The greatest battle of all, between Henry Ford and the auto-workers union, was hardly over when the U.S. was plunged into World War II.

Now Detroit is flushed with feverish prosperity again but it still seethes with racial, religious, political and economic unrest. More than half its population of nearly two million came to Detroit in the last 20 years. They have no great love for their city and they give their loyalty to their own group, creed or union. Largest single bloc is the 260,000 Polish Catholics, who also dominate the city of Hamtramck (pop. 50,000) which forms a kind of Polish island inside Detroit. After them come the 200,000 Southern whites who have migrated to Detroit with their barbecue stands and tent shouting evangelists, and 150,000 Negroes. The remainder are old-line Detroiters, Canadians, Ukrainians, Germans, Bulgars, Yugoslavs, Maltese, Italians and Syrians.

In this melting pot flourish demagogues of every persuasion—Communists, Fascists, Ku-Kluxers, Coughlinites, pro-Nazi leaders of the National Workers League and such recent arrivals as Gerald L. K. Smith. Even the auto-workers union, which fights as a unit against employers, has a constant civil war going on inside its ranks among the Catholics (who form more than 50% of its members), the Communists, the Negroes and a small, fierce Ku-Klux element which has helped foment one race riot in Detroit this year and is attempting to stir up more.

One day in June, employees of Henry Ford walked into a Ford-owned field near Willow Run, yanked out stakes planted by Federal surveyors and ordered the surveyors off the land. In Dearborn, Ford announced through his handyman, Harry Bennett, that he would "resist by every legal method" the Government's attempt to build a new "Bomber City" to house about 33,000 Willow Run workers. This ended the most ambitious effort towards solving Detroit's incredible housing mess. As early as April 98.7% of all dwelling units in Detroit were occupied (85% is considered the danger mark). It is now impossible to rent a decent house within 50 miles of the city. Around Willow Run hundreds of tents, trailers and shacks have sprung up in woods, fields, barnyards. Ford objects to a big Federal project on the grounds that: (1) it is a waste of money and materials, and (2) it would concentrate people where they might be bombed.

The foes of Ford say what he really fears are: (1) a change in political control of Republican Washtenaw County, where the Willow Run plant is located, and (2) higher taxes. But aside from Willow Run there are other thousands of war workers in Detroit who can afford good homes but simply cannot get them. Only two small Federal projects have been completed this year—and one of these was the cause of a race riot in February. A determined, housing program backed by Federal, State and city governments, as well as by industry and labor, would go far toward solving Detroit's morale worries.

Detroit Six Months After

In its issue for Aug. 7, 1942, *Life* published a report on Detroit entitled "Detroit Is Dynamite." It disclosed that wildcat strikes, bad morale, material shortages, poor planning at the top and Government indecision were cutting seriously into Detroit's 1942 war production. It warned the rest of the country to take notice, for "Detroit can either blow up Hitler or it can blow up the U.S."

Just six months after that article was printed, *Life* asked its Detroit correspondent to report again on the Detroit situation. . . . Detroit's worries over labor disputes, slowed production, food shortages, and the thousands of obstacles encountered in transforming the great auto industry to war production have largely disappeared. (But Detroit, like the rest of the country, still has not solved the absentee problem.) Labor-management friction has declined: Detroit has not had a real strike in the last six months. And Detroit's production of munitions has soared and soared until it is greater than any city in the world. Everyone agrees that Detroit is now doing a real job of blowing up Hitler.

Another piece of good news from Detroit is that the Government is giving Detroit a freer hand in working out some of its problems. The Army, for instance, has moved its whole Tank Automotive Center out of Washington and set it down in the 34-story Union Guardian Building in Detroit. Under Brigadier General A. R. Glaney, a former General Motors vice president, the "T-A" Center supervises "everything that rolls" for the Army. It is responsible for the design, production, delivery and servicing all over the world of tanks, trucks, jeeps, tank destroyers and a whole flock of secret weapons on wheels. This move makes good sense; it is saving untold thousands of man-hours that used to be lost shuttling between Detroit and Washington.

Last month Detroit also got a regional War Labor Board with real powers to act on the spot. Until then all Detroit labor contracts and disputes were referred to a board in Cleveland and then on to Washington. Even when an agreement was reached it sometimes took months to put it in effect, causing grumbling and bad feeling. Detroiters believe that their new board will make any future work stoppage in the Detroit area unnecessary.

Detroit is no longer so worried about wartime race relations. Negroes are working in more places and making better money than they did six months ago, and there has been no instance of serious friction. Detroit's No. 1 loud-mouth and demagog[ue], Gerald L. K. Smith, was roundly squelched last fall by the voters of Michigan when he tried to talk his way into the Republican Senatorial nomination.

But Detroit still has grave problems. The worst now is manpower. Detroit will need 100,000 new migrant workers by the end of 1943, over and above the 700,000 now employed in its war plants, and the additions that will come from housewives and non-essential industries. Detroit's housing situation, which was bad last August, is still bad. There is no room for the new workers Detroit must have. And local transportation is close to the breaking point. Before gas rationing came to Detroit last December, 80% of its workers drove to work in their own cars. Now most of them ride buses—and stand in long lines to wait for them. "The face of Detroit has changed tremendously in six months," concludes *Life*'s correspondent. "But with most of the old problems solved, new problems are springing up to take their place."

6. The Government Praises Spanish-Speaking Americans in the War Effort, 1943

War came, and all America changed—small town, big city, North and West. One change above all—young men went off to fight. The sons of the races and nations of the world, who came here to make this America, went off to fight for freedom the globe around.

The southwestern states gave their full complement, among them thousands of their Spanish speaking sons. One of them is a boy named Ricardo Noyola. He was born 26 years ago on a ranch "Los Potreros," in Texas near the Rio Grande. Like his father, Ricardo could speak no English. He had had no schooling, working as a farm hand growing cotton and wheat since he was 13. It took war, and the new world America entered, to bring about a change for Noyola and his people, to give him his chance.

At Camp Robinson, Arkansas, where Noyola found himself, without English, awkward, confused, unhappy, the U.S. Army stepped in and did an unusual, an important thing. It took Noyola and 54 other Spanish speaking boys—the majority from Texas, some from New Mexico, a few from California—and formed a special platoon. It gave them a leader who could teach them in their own language, share their troubles, advise and encourage. It sent them to Fort Benning, Georgia, and put them through 13 weeks of intensive training in weapons, drills, tactics. The result—a body of men who, in final battalion maneuvers, received high commendation for stamina, enthusiasm, and ingenuity. Specially cited for leading a night reconnaissance patrol was Ricardo Noyola: "at all times very alert . . . use of arm and hand signals . . . taking advantage of the terrain and natural cover . . . all during the patrol Pvt. Noyola showed excellent quality of leadership over his men."

But the Army did more—it gave "the platoon" extra weeks to learn to read and write English. And today, their special training over, Noyola and his comrades are scattered throughout the 300th Infantry, 3 and 4 to a company. Reports the Army: "They have fallen in on an equal plane with the English speaking men and more

From *Spanish Speaking Americans in the War: The Southwest* (Washington, D.C.: Office of the Coordinator of Inter-American Affairs, 1943).

than hold their own." Reports their commander: "The experiment has proved that
... Spanish speaking Americans from the Southwest make topnotch soldiers 'en el
ejercito del Tio Samuel' [in Uncle Sam's army]."

This is but one story, one proof. There are others, in the camps, on the battlefields.

Before Benning, it was proved in blood at Bataan.

Bataan was a National Guard tragedy. The first soldiers ready, they were the first
to go. Unlike the regular army, the Guards were home town units, local soldiers, local
leaders. The threat of war was too great to allow time to regroup them. They went to
the Philippines as they were. The 200th and 515th Coast Artillery of New Mexico
were sent because they could talk Spanish and above all because they were the crack
anti-aircraft units the Filipino people needed.

On April 9th, it was over. The glory of Bataan is the nation's but the grief is in
the homes of the small towns of America—from Harrodsburg, Kentucky, to Salinas,
California, on the faces of this New Mexican mother, these Kentucky parents. New
Mexico gave the fullest measure of devotion—one quarter of the 9,000 men from
the mainland lost.

Action was America's answer to Bataan.

America demanded fighters, workers, farmers. All these the Spanish speaking
Americans gave to their country.

Along the U.S. side of the Rio Grande 1 out of every 2 Spanish speaking males
between the ages of 15 and 65 is either in the armed forces or has left his home to
farm, to mine, to build ships and planes.

Some have been cited, some have died, all fight for their country.

Pvt. Raymondo Lara of Berg's Mill, Texas, with his father, mother, sister, brother
and niece, and Col. Stanton T. Smith at Brooks Field, Texas, during the presentation of the soldier's medal for valor to Pvt. Lara for acting above and beyond the
line of duty in rescuing two flyers from a burning plane after a crash.

First Lieut. Roger Vargas, Army Air Corps, home Morenci, Arizona, decorated
five times, awarded the Silver Star for gallantry, the Purple Heart for wounds in
action, the Air Medal for ability and courage in bombing Rabaul and the Oak
Leaf Cluster for his part in the battle of the Bismarck Sea.

Paratroopers Frank Romero, Taos, New Mexico, who spent a month sabotaging
communications far behind enemy lines in North Africa. He and four other American soldiers led by Lieut. Dan Deleo of Chicago, successfully escaped by driving
through German held territory in an Italian truck.

Food—in this global war we have learned the old lesson that the man who
works the earth is basic to us all, soldiers, civilians and allies.

As President Roosevelt said to the United Nations Food Conference: "Never
before have nations representing over 80 per cent of the world's two billion inhabitants set out to bend their united efforts to the development of the world's resources
so that all men might seek to attain the food they need.

The Spanish speaking Americans, heirs to the oldest agricultural tradition in
America, are working with their hands and their machines to add the citrus fruits
of California and Texas, the beet sugar of California and Colorado, the wheat of New
Mexico and the cattle and sheep of the Rio Grande to the stores of the United Nations.

Where fascism adds hunger to slavery, the democracies fight both to free men and to feed them. From the United States food goes to England and to Russia, to Europe and Africa. With so many of our men in the armed forces and in war production plants, we needed help to grow and harvest the food we send our armies and our allies.

This our Mexican neighbours provided when they came into the Southwest to help us harvest our crops—and they came with full faith in the common cause.

Here, across our border, is an example of the collaboration on which final victory must rest.

Machines and the skilled hands they require have changed life in the Southwest. To her copper mines war has added the airplane plants, and shipyards the length of the Pacific Coast. Through training courses many thousands of Spanish speaking Americans have found a place in these front line industries of modern war.

These fighters, this worker are one.

The very meaning of democracy lies in the bond between fighter and worker in a common cause.

Todos—all of us are in this war.

Spanish speaking women are nurses and Red Cross aids, Spanish speaking girls are in the Waacs, the Marines, the Waves.

And Spanish speaking women have gone to work beside their men in the plants of the Southwest. One of many examples of the special contribution they make—at the Consolidated assembly plant at Tucson, Arizona the needle craft of the Spanish speaking women has proved the very skill necessary to complete the intricate cloth and leather fittings of the planes.

A young Spanish speaking boy put it this way: "I am the last of my family—my mother and my father are dead. My brother—I am very glad now—they thought he got killed out there some place; but now the War Department has sent me a telegram, saying that's not so—he's alive. I think I'm going out there, too, just where my brother is, then we can fight together. We got to fight—got to win this war—maybe we die for liberty—maybe not—but we got to fight—we got to win. It was for such as these that Presidents Roosevelt and Camacho met and spoke at Monterrey."

"We know that the day of exploitation of the resources and the people of one country for the benefit of any group in another country is definitely over." —President Roosevelt.

7. The "Zoot Suit Riots" Reveal the Race Tensions on the West Coast, 1943

"Kill the pachuco bastard!"

That was the battle cry. The zoot war began on the West Coast—in Los Angeles —with servicemen doing battle against young civilians of Mexican descent, called pachucos for the Pachuca district in Mexico where natives affect gaudy clothes. It flared up also in Toronto, in Detroit and Philadelphia, and its reverberations reached the State Department in Washington. Though its deeper causes were mixed—including

From "Zoot Suits and Service Stripes: Race Tension Behind the Riots," *Newsweek,* June 21, 1943, pp. 35–40. © 1943 *Newsweek,* Inc. All rights reserved. Reprinted by permission.

some race prejudice and much resentment of hooliganism—the servicemen's hated target everywhere was the zoot suit.

Gangs.   Between 1914 and 1929 Mexicans by the thousands crossed the border into Southern California to work on section gangs, desert mines, and farms. The depression settled many of them in Los Angeles, where they encountered much of the social ostracism accorded Negroes—in schools, movie houses, playgrounds, community swimming pools. Their American-born children grew up in a jangled environment: at home they were Americans, speaking a language different from their parents; outside they were Mexicans.

Outside, too, they banded into gangs, at first just for sociability, later for plainly vicious purposes. The advent of the zoot suit gave them a distinctive badge of defiance. In bizarre details of drape, pleat, and cuff they outdazzled their Harlem counterparts. They went the limit in pork-pie hats, ballooning trousers, and spectacularly long coats. They called themselves the Mateo Bombers, the Main Street Zooters, the Califa, the Sleepy Lagoon, and the Black Legion. And for months they engaged in cruel, bludgeoning internecine warfare or came to grips with the law on charges varying from violation of the juvenile curfew to murder, rape, and robbery.

Finally, the gangs had their "cholitas" or "slick chicks," female partners who affected black blouses and slacks or short black skirts and mesh stockings. Sometimes the girls fought side by side with the zooters; sometimes they merely carried their weapons.

Los Angeles authorities noted an ominous connection between the zoot suit and mounting hooliganism, but the delinquency mounted. Meanwhile servicemen by the thousand were being funneled into the city and its naval and military areas. Everything was set for the explosion.

The War.   A sailor with a pocketful of money has always been fair game for loose women, and the girls of the Los Angeles Mexican quarter were no exception. Soon stories of assaults by zoot suiters on servicemen were getting back to the barracks. Three weeks ago pachucos badly mauled two sailors who tried to steal their girls at a Venice dance hall. The yard was itching for a fight.

On the night of June 4 bands of sailor vigilantes invaded the squalid Mexican quarter on the east side, harrying all zoot suiters they met, thrashing those who refused to discard their fancy clothes, ripping to shreds baggy pants and long coats. By the next night the "sharpies" had forgotten their own back-alley strife to join forces. They waded in with tire irons, chains, knives, broken bottles, clubs, steel bars, wrenches, and rope lengths weighted with wire and lead.

And by last Monday night the soldiers and sailors were pouring into Los Angeles by the hundreds seeking a showdown. Downtown a pachuco of 17 tried to sneak through the crowd of civilians following a band of soldiers. Men pushed him back; fists smashed into his frightened brown face. The boy went down; hands ripped off his coat and pants and tossed him into a garbage truck while the crowd roared approval. Dozens of pachucos were stripped and left naked on street corners. The police either could or would do little except make belated arrests.

Finally, naval and military authorities declared Los Angeles and certain suburbs out of bounds. But the fighting continued sporadically, with cholitas taking up the battle. Three attacked and slashed a waitress; one said the battle would go on till one side or the other was wiped out. At the end of six nights of fighting an unofficial tabulation showed 94 civilians and eighteen servicemen had been treated for serious injuries, and 94 civilians and twenty servicemen had been arrested.

As a leader of the pachucos, police named Miguel Minijares Guerrero, 26, unmarried, and Texas-born, now serving a 50-day sentence in the county jail. Guerrero has a long record of arrests, chiefly for assaults. Like most of the other zooters, Guerrero's draft classification is 4-F—morally unfit because of his police record.

Alarmed by the outbreaks, the Los Angeles city council passed an ordinance making the wearing of a zoot suit a misdemeanor. Gov. Earl Warren appointed a five-man citizens committee to investigate the violence; it demanded that those responsible be punished: "No group has the right to take the law into its own hands." County and city authorities began an inquiry, and narcotics agents stepped in when reports reached them some of the zooters were marihuana addicts. Field representatives of Nelson Rockefeller, Coordinator of Inter-American Affairs, also began an inquiry. There was talk of an official Mexican protest, but this collapsed when it was pointed out that most of the zooters were American-born. Secretary of State Cordell Hull said there had been only informal exchanges between officials.

8. Labor Conflict and Questions of Patriotism Erupt in the Coal Fields, 1943

The nation's coal mines were open this week, but again it was a temporary reopening, and the strike threat still hung over the land.

The nation's 530,00 miners agreed to go to work on Monday after a strike begun June 1 and lasting six days during which the steel production rate faltered, because at least eleven blast furnaces were obliged to shut down, during which also the men had ignored President Roosevelt's order to cease their strike.

But John L. Lewis kept a string on his United Mine Workers of America. No sooner had he recommended to the union's policy committee, 24 hours after the President issued his order, that the men were to go back, than Lewis set a new "deadline." There is to be another strike on June 20 unless agreement is reached with the Appalachian bituminous and anthracite operators.

Shock.   This deadline came as a shock to the Interior Department, whose chief, Secretary Ickes, is operating the mines for the government, although earlier there were hints that Lewis and Ickes had worked together in planning to reopen the mines. Officials had thought the miners would keep on digging indefinitely while some form of agreement was worked out. But the union needed some club to keep behind the chair, ready for use, at that conference, and the strike threat was the biggest club Lewis could find.

On the other hand the War Labor Board also produced a club. On May 25 it had directed the operators and union officials to submit to it within fifteen days any differences that still remained. Once the miners agreed to return to work, the WLB reiterated that June 9 deadline and broadly hinted that, in the event of no contract by then, it would write one itself.

Almost the sole remaining difference between miners and operators was the amount of portal-to-portal pay. During the negotiations in Washington preceding the strike, the conferees had agreed that this "travel time" would apply to all mine workers—clerks and checkers in the offices above ground, as well as those who actually had to travel the underground labyrinths to their diggings. They had likewise agreed that the payment would be a flat rate—regardless of the distance traveled or the time involved. But they had not agreed on whether it should be the $2 a day Lewis demanded or the 80 cents the operators had counterproposed. (After the strike began, Lewis dropped to $1.50 while the operators came up to $1.) Since there was no agreement when the Lewis truce expired May 31, there was no contract. And in accordance with a policy almost as old as the 53-year-old union, "no contract, no work."

Order.   This time there had been no way out for the White House, and President Roosevelt, cornered, acted. His order was issued after the miners had been out for 48 hours, tending to their Victory gardens and playing cards for the newspaper photographers.

When a strike threatened in April, Mr. Roosevelt had "appealed" to the miners not to cease production. This time he was curt: "As President and Commander-in-Chief, I order and direct the miners . . . to return to their work on Monday, June 7, 1943." Then he went on to remind the men that they were working for the government on essential war work and said it was their duty "no less than that of their sons and brothers in the armed forces to fulfill their war duties." The President's order was made over Lewis's head, and it upheld the authority and jurisdiction of the WLB, which Lewis has repeatedly ignored.

This action resulted in a bit of comedy. Secretary Ickes followed up Mr. Roosevelt's order with a letter to Lewis saying he expected the UMW [United Mine Workers] chief to direct his men to return to the pits. Lewis replied with a letter saying he had no power to direct but would, however, recommend to the UMW policy committee (which always rubberstamps his decisions) that it do the directing.

The public sighed with relief. The policy committee met and did what Lewis ordered. And then, when it had sent its identical telegrams to all local unions, Lewis sprang his surprise:

It was one of those steamy hot days in Washington, with a half dozen reporters lolling in the green overstuffed reception couches in the office of K. C. Adams, Lewis's press man. Adams walked into his inner office without saying a word. He sat down at his littered desk as the news writers ambled after him to make small talk. Adams inquired lazily if all wire services were represented. They were. Would they like a press release? They would. Without saying a word Adams started peeling off typed copies of the order that work be resumed—but only "up to and including June 20." Adams cackled gleefully as wire reporters scrambled for telephones to dictate the 50-word wire as a flash. Then he nonchalantly set about something else; he has seen similar shows many times.

Thus the strike was begun, stopped, and replaced by a threat of a new stop-page. In the six days the miners had been out this is what happened:

¶   The War Labor Board's power and prestige diminished. When the miners went out it soon halted the negotiations, issued a stinging statement attacking Lewis, and left the mess up to the White House.

¶   Gaps began to appear in the ranks of the miners; some went back to the pits.

¶   Donald M. Nelson warned that virtual paralysis of war production would fol-low any serious curtailment of coal to plants making steel, synthetic rubber, aviation gasoline, and other items.

¶   Soldiers in North Africa, questioned by *The Stars and Stripes,* their news-paper, were 90 per cent in favor of drastic action against the strikers. Some offered to trade places with the miners. Others suggested that the recalcitrants be taken into the Army and ordered to work in the mines.

¶   The public temper rose. Some speakers used the word "treason" in attacking Lewis. It was clear that the citizens would not stand for much more.

¶   Selective Service officials in Tennessee and Alabama were ordered by their governors to reclassify all striking miners. And the President himself at his Friday press conference pointed out that a striking miner was no different from a man in a nonessential industry—he could be drafted if he failed to do essential work.

¶   The House, getting angry, passed by the wide margin of 231 to 141 the Smith-Connally anti-strike and labor control bill already approved in slightly different form by the Senate and War Mobilization Director Byrnes was reported to have asked the two chambers quickly to compose their differences so that the measure might soon be put on the statute books.

Significance

The miners prepared to return to work because Lewis said so, not because of the President's order. In that situation lies future trouble, as shown in Lewis's new "deadline" for an agreement, for the fundamental issue is still unsolved.

That issue is twofold. On the labor side, it is whether Lewis is to be sub-jected to the wartime rules obeyed by other unions or whether he is to be allowed to dictate his own terms, to obey orders if they suit him, to defy the public and the government if such defiance suits his purpose. On the Administration side, it is whether the government is going to end its vacillating policies on labor, on price and wage freezing, and on the steady rush of the nation toward the perils of inflation.

Out of all the confusion have come ominous results. Already the country has lost not only a week's production of coal, at the estimated rate of 2,000,000 tons a day, but the rate of production of the machines of war has been slowed all along the line. Morale at home and abroad has suffered. And the Axis radio has made hay.

While the Administration may be able to claim a technical victory at least for two weeks, what with the resumption of mining, the actual winner is more likely to be Lewis, since his miners are going to get more money one way or another—a victory that will spur other workers to pressure their own leaders for increases puncturing the "hold the line" orders. Nevertheless, there is one big loser: the American war effort.

9. Japanese American Mikiso Hane Remembers His Wartime Internment, 1990

I suppose the place to start is "Where was I on December 7, 1941?" I was helping on the family farm. I had just learned to maneuver the Farmall tractor and was spreading fertilizer on the field all day that Sunday. It wasn't until after five that I went home. That was when I first heard about the Japanese attack on Pearl Harbor. My reaction was one of shock . . . and then fear about what public reaction toward us would be like.

For Japanese-American citizens growing up in California, racial bias and discrimination were facts of life that we had been conditioned to live with since childhood. Discrimination against Asian immigrants started with measures taken against the Chinese immigrants, culminating in the Chinese Exclusion Act of 1882 and the Geary Act of 1892. The next wave of Asian immigrants who became the target of the exclusionists was made up of Japanese. The door to Japanese immigrants was closed by the Immigration Act of 1924.

After 1924 anti-Japanese sentiments abated somewhat, but in the 1930s when Japan began to commit acts of aggression against China, the antagonism felt toward Japan resurfaced and was once again directed against people of Japanese descent on the West Coast. So our situation was fraught with a double-edged threat: the traditional anti-immigrant, racist sentiment and the anger at Japanese imperialism.

I was especially sensitive about this in 1941 because I had just returned from Japan in 1940. I was one of four sons and my parents, hoping to strike it rich in America and to retire in Japan, wanted one of us there. So in 1932 when I was ten I was sent back to a village near the outskirts of Hiroshima to live with my uncle's family and attend school. When relationships between the United States and Japan began to worsen and there was talk of the possibility of war breaking out between Japan and the United States, I asked my parents if I could return to the States. To my surprise they agreed to let me come back. The eight years in Japan made me feel that the American perception that all Japanese were different and not acceptable as Americans would apply more directly to me than to other Nisei (second-generation Japanese). I would be classified as a Kibei—a returnee to America, less of an American than Nisei, who were also not regarded as "real" Americans by the white population.

Because I had returned to the U.S. after eight years I was still in high school as an overaged nineteen-year-old student in 1941. I think all Nisei went to school on December 8 with an acute sense of anxiety and trepidation. The most uncomfortable experience that day was congregating in the assembly hall to listen to President Franklin D. Roosevelt deliver his "day of infamy" speech.

Our schoolmates and teachers did not show any overt hostility toward us, so we continued going to school without suffering any untoward incidents. . . .

But the atmosphere in the society at large was a different matter. Almost immediately there was a hue and cry about spies in the Japanese community. All "Japs" were seen as sneaky, treacherous, disloyal, untrustworthy elements. A curfew was

From Mikiso Hane, "Wartime Internment," *Journal of American History* 77, no. 2 (September 1990): 569–575.

established to keep us from traveling beyond a certain limit, and during the hours from 8 P.M. to 6 A.M., we were confined to our homes. Japanese community leaders were immediately arrested by the Federal Bureau of Investigation (FBI). (On the first day, 736 Japanese immigrant leaders were detained; 2,192 people had been picked up by the FBI by February). It was said that anyone who possessed books, magazines, or letters in the Japanese language could be apprehended. I had such materials, so I immediately disposed of all my books, magazines, photographs, letters, and diaries. I either burned them or dumped them in the outhouse.

Soon rumors began to spread about lynch mobs and about people being attacked in other communities. We had no way of verifying these rumors, but the hysteria being whipped up by the press led us to believe that some of the stories must be true. In fact two Nisei sisters in the neighboring town were abducted and raped. All things considered, the actual number of acts of violence was not as horrendous as we had feared it would be: seven killings and thirty-six other acts of violence. When the evacuation and internment order came, there was talk that all of us were going to be herded into camps and machine-gunned to death. . . . Gen. John L. De Witt, who was in charge of evacuating us, asserted that there was no distinction between Japanese in Japan and Japanese Americans in the United States. "A Jap's a Jap," he asserted. In testifying before a congressional committee in early 1943, he said, "We will have to worry about the Japs until they are wiped off the face of the map." In other words, what he had in mind was akin to Adolph Hitler's "final solution." In this respect we were fortunate that the administration of the camps was turned over to a civilian agency and not kept under the control of the army. . . .

. . . President Roosevelt signed Executive Order No. 9066 on February 19, 1942, authorizing the evacuation and internment of all West Coast Japanese including Japanese-American citizens. . . .

Ultimately, 119,803 of us ended up behind barbed wire fences. Sixty-five percent of those were American citizens. . . .

Well, in May 1942 those of us living in Hollister were rounded up and bused to Salinas to a temporary camp set up in the old rodeo grounds. Then in August we were put on the train with armed guards and sent to the internment camp in Poston, Arizona, a barren desert where the temperature in the summer hit about 120 degrees. Eventually twenty thousand of us were interned in Poston.

We arrived late at night but it was still oppressively hot. We trudged through the ankle-deep sand, headed to the empty barracks with our mattresses (straw-filled cloth sacks), and tried to sleep, wondering what was in store for us. For the next several months we struggled with the heat, the sandstorms, the scorpions, the rattlesnakes, the confusion, the overcrowded barracks, and the lack of privacy. But eventually a semblance of order and normality set in. We were all asked to serve in some capacity to make the camp a livable place. I took a job as a kitchen helper in the community mess hall. Water was drawn into the camp; grass and trees were planted; vegetables were grown.

In retrospect it is clear that the decision to evacuate and intern all people of Japanese blood from the West Coast was based not on military but on racial and political grounds. . . . Of course this was not clear to us then, and we succumbed to the mass hysteria that was overwhelming us and meekly accepted our plight. Virtually no one, except three persons, had the courage to challenge the authorities.

Why didn't the Nisei leadership lodge even a pro forma protest rather than urging us to cooperate fully with the authorities? . . . To explain the lack of strong leadership, we could note that most Nisei were very young, had very little political experience, and were conditioned by their parents to be submissive and obedient to authority.

If our inability to resist the evacuation and internment is understandable, how can we justify our meek behavior in camp when we were asked to prove our loyalty after we had been judged as potentially dangerous enemy aliens and had been interned? On this occasion we might have shown some gumption and defied the authorities by refusing to say yes to the loyalty questions. (They were questions 27: "Are you willing to serve in the armed forces of the United States on combat duty, wherever ordered?" and 28: "Will you swear unqualified allegiance to the United States of America and faithfully defend the United States from any or all attack by foreign or domestic forces, and forswear any form of allegiance or obedience to the Japanese emperor, to any other foreign government, power or organization?")

Not only did the Japanese-American leadership urge us to answer yes to these questions, but we were also encouraged to volunteer for the Japanese-American combat team. . . . I recall reading in an article in a Hearst paper that we were digging cellars under our barracks to hoard food for the Japanese force whose invasion we were anticipating. In fact, we were digging cellars under the barracks to try to stay cool. We would sit around in the hole and play cards to while our time away. That is where I learned to play pinochle.

Well, most of us, 65,000 out of 75,000 citizens, complied and said yes to questions 27 and 28. There were some, however, who had the courage to say no. But instead of praising them for their courage, the Japanese-American loyalists condemned them. Those who answered no to the loyalty questions were segregated and sent to the camp in Tule Lake, California, which came to resemble a high-pressure concentration camp.

After answering yes to questions 27 and 28, I even volunteered for combat—not out of patriotism or courage or desire to join the army, but essentially because of faintheartedness. After I said yes to questions 27 and 28, the sergeant who had processed my answer then asked me if I was willing to volunteer for the Japanese-American combat unit. I was nonplussed by this question because I had just said I was loyal to the United States and was willing to serve in the army. If I said no to his question then logically he could conclude that I was lying when I said yes to questions 27 and 28. I was already afraid that I was more vulnerable than other Nisei because I was a Kibei. If I did not volunteer, it was possible, I thought, that I would be included among those who answered no to questions 27 and 28 and be sent off to a camp set up for disloyal Nisei and eventually be sent back to Japan. At any rate the situation seemed ominous. So I said yes and signed on the dotted line.

Eventually I was turned down by the army who classified me as 4-C, an enemy alien. So my concern that I would automatically be judged disloyal because I had just returned from Japan may not have been far off the mark.

By mid-1943 the War Relocation Authority began to allow internees to leave the camps if they received FBI clearances and could find employment away from the West Coast. Soon after I received a letter from Adj. Gen. J. A. Ulio declining my services as a soldier, I got an opportunity to leave the camp to become a tutor in

Japanese in the army specialized training program at Yale University. The camp authorities gave me a temporary pass, so I left camp for New Haven in October 1943.

I cannot say that I had suffered much living in camp. So far as life in camp was concerned, for me it was merely a matter of inconvenience, time lost, and discomfort, and of course the humiliation and indignity that we experienced. But my reaction to life in camp would not be typical because I had lived in somewhat straitened circumstances as a peasant boy in Japan.

Those who underwent greater hardships were people who had more to lose than I did, especially professional people. I was paid sixteen dollars a month as kitchen help in the community kitchen. Doctors, who labored day and night with only primitive facilities at their disposal to take care of many of us who got sick, were paid nineteen dollars a month. When I entered the barracks hospital, after collapsing from spontaneous pneumothorax, the young doctor who took care of patients in the crowded ward worked tirelessly day and night. The doctors and the nurses are the unsung heroes of Poston and all the other internment camps. . . .

. . . When my oldest brother returned to Hollister to see if it would be possible to resume farming there, he saw nothing but signs that said, "No Japs allowed." He had to find a place to eat, so he finally entered a small diner, hoping that, it being a simple place, he would be allowed to have a hot dog. The owner pulled out a shotgun and threatened to shoot him if he didn't get the hell out of there. That was the end of his attempt to return to Hollister.

As for the impact that the internment and evacuation had on my life, it turned out to have positive results. It got me out to the East Coast, gave me an opportunity to work in an army language program in a university setting, and eventually provided me with the chance to go on to college and graduate school and enter the teaching profession. I shudder to think what my life would have been like if I had not been allowed to return to the States in 1940. Recently I was asked to review a book about the experiences of Japanese widows who lost their husbands in the atomic holocaust. Their vivid accounts made me reflect upon what might have happened to me if I had stayed in Hiroshima working in the post office where I had started to work just before I returned to the States. I too could well have been food for the maggots and worms because the boardinghouse where I lived was in the epicenter of the blast. If I, like other Japanese Americans, was destined to pay for the military actions of Japan because of our race, I am grateful that I paid for them in Poston rather than in Hiroshima.

E S S A Y S

The following two essays look at how race and sex were determining factors in how people interacted during the era of World War II. Both essays focus on conflict, but they do so in very different ways. The first essay, by Karen Tucker Anderson, a pioneering women's historian who teaches at the University of Arizona, focuses on the arena of the workplace and looks at the impact of the war on working patterns of black women. In the second essay, Edward J. Escobar, who teaches at Arizona State University, shifts the focus to the community of Los Angeles and examines what became known as the zoot suit riots.

Conflicts Between White Women and Black Women, and Their Employers, in the Wartime Industrial World

KAREN TUCKER ANDERSON

As a result of the increasing demand for workers in all categories of employment, and especially in the high-paying manufacturing sector, the full employment economy of World War II posed the most serious challenge in American history to the traditional management preference for white male labor in primary-sector jobs. The war years were especially important for blacks, who benefited from an expanding labor force, changing racial values, a revitalized migration out of the rural South, and the attempted enforcement of equal employment opportunity under a presidential executive order. Although scholars have given some attention to the labor-force fortunes of blacks in the war economy, few have considered the impact of the wartime expansion on black women, who constituted 600,000 of the 1,000,000 blacks who entered paid employment during the war years. Those who have focused on black women have stressed the degree to which the war opened new job categories and fostered mobility. William Chafe, for example, contends that the opportunities generated by the wartime economy and the long-term changes they fostered constituted a "second emancipation" for black women. According to Dale L. Hiestand, occupational shifts by black women workers during the 1940s promoted substantial income improvement.

A careful examination of the labor-force status of black women during the 1940s brings into question such sanguine pronouncements. Focusing on the wartime experiences of black women provides insight into the nature of prejudice as manifested and experienced by women and into the sources and mechanisms of labor-force discrimination in a particular historical context. It also facilitates an examination of the relative importance of managerial intransigence and coworker prejudice in perpetuating discriminatory employment practices. In addition, it gives an indication of the importance of tight labor markets in fostering economic mobility for minority group women.

Labor force statistics support the contention that the war marked an important break with the historic allocation of work by race and sex. Between 1940 and 1944 the proportion of employed black women engaged in domestic service declined from 59.9 percent to 44.6 percent, although their share of jobs in this field increased because white women exited from private household work in even greater proportions. In addition, the percentage of the black female labor force in farm work was cut in half, as many from the rural South migrated to urban areas in response to the demand for war workers. The shift of large numbers of black women from work in farms and homes to work in factories resulted in the proportion of black females employed in industrial occupations rising from 6.5 percent to 18 percent during the war. A comparable expansion also occurred in personal service

From Karen Tucker Anderson, "Last Hired, First Fired: Black Women Workers During World War II," *Journal of American History* 69 (June 1982): 82–97.

work outside of the private household, which claimed 17.9 percent of black women workers in 1944.

To stress only the improvement wrought during the war, however, is to understate the extent to which discrimination persisted and to ignore the fact that the assumptions of a historically balkanized labor force continued to determine the distribution of the benefits of a full employment economy. When faced with a shortage of white male workers, employers had various options. They could seek workers from other areas of the country, hoping that this would enable them to minimize the changes produced by the wartime expansion, or they could rely on underutilized elements of the local labor supply—workers in nonessential employment, women, blacks, and older and younger workers. If unable to secure large numbers of white male in-migrants and unwilling to modify hiring patterns too dramatically, they could limit production, sacrificing output to prejudice.

Those who decided to employ substantially increased numbers of women and/or minorities established a complex hierarchy of hiring preferences based on the composition of the local labor force and the nature of the work to be done. In light industries, women workers became the first recourse of employers unable to recruit large numbers of white males. In the airframe industry, for example, women constituted 40.6 percent of the employees by November 1943, while blacks claimed only 3.5 percent of airframe jobs. Employers in heavy industries, by contrast, sought minority males as a preferred source of labor, with the result that the level of utilization of women depended on the minority population of an area. In Baltimore, for example, blacks comprised up to 20 percent of the shipbuilding workers while women represented only 4 percent. Seattle, which had only a small black population, relied on women for 16 percent of its shipyard employees.

Whatever the hierarchy of preference, however, black women could always be found at the bottom. The dramatic expansion of jobs for women did not necessarily mean the opening up of new categories of employment for minority group women. A survey conducted by the United Auto Workers (UAW) in April 1943 found that only 74 out of 280 establishments that employed women in production work were willing to hire black women. Similarly, a 1943 study by the National Metal Trades Association revealed that only twenty-nine out of sixty-two plants that used women workers had black women in their employ. Moreover, most of them used black women only in janitorial positions. Even some employers willing to hire white women and black men in large numbers balked at including black women in their work forces. At the Wagner Electric Corporation in Saint Louis, for example, 64 percent of the employees were white women, 24 percent were black males, and 12 percent were white males. The company refused to hire black women throughout the war, even in the face of a January 1945 order from the President's Committee on Fair Employment Practice (FEPC) to cease all discrimination.

Because of the mobilization of large numbers of young men by the military, the availability of white women for aircraft and munitions work, the nature of the jobs being created during the war, and the depth of the prejudice against black women, the male labor force proved to be more racially flexible than the female labor force. While the number of all blacks employed in manufacturing increased 135 percent between April 1940 and January 1946, the number of black women in such work rose only 59 percent. Blacks made their greatest wartime gains in heavily male-employing industrial fields; by January 1945 they constituted 25 percent of the labor force in foundries, 11.7 percent in shipbuilding, and 11.8 percent in blast furnaces and steel mills. By contrast, nonwhites accounted for only 5.8 percent of employees in aircraft and 2.7 percent of those in electrical equipment production. In the traditional female fields of clerical and sales, the gains of black women were negligible—their share of female clerical jobs rose from 0.7 percent to 1.6 percent while their proportion in the female sales force declined from 1.2 percent to 1.1 percent.

One of the most important and obdurate of the industries that fought the employment of black women during the war was the auto industry. Led by the negative example of the Ford Motor Company, which refused to hire nonwhite women in any but token numbers, the auto companies persisted in rejecting trained black female applicants or in limiting their employment to a few work categories until very late in the war. When referred to the automakers by the United States Employment Service (USES) in response to calls for women workers, black women found that the white women accompanying them would be hired immediately while they would be told to await a later call, a call that would never come. When Samella Banks, along with five white women, applied to Cadillac Motor Company in November 1942, she was told that there might be a janitress opening in a day or two while they were hired as welder trainees. As a result, much of the expansion of the female labor force in industrial work occurred before economic or political pressures necessitated the hiring of black women. By February 1943 nonwhite women had claimed only 1,000 of the 96,000 jobs held by women in major war industries in Detroit. Consequently, most nonwhite females were confined to work in low-paying service and other unskilled categories, and those who landed industrial jobs had so little seniority that their postwar fate was guaranteed.

As was generally the case with wartime racial discrimination in employment, the most frequent employer rationale for excluding nonwhite women was the fear that white opposition to the change might cause work slowdowns or strikes. An examination of the nature and goals of coworker prejudice during the war years provides some possible answers to the question of whether such prejudice is rooted in an aversion to social contact in a context of equality or is primarily a calculated attempt on the part of whites to maintain an exploitative economic advantage. When the former issue is the basic concern, it is manifested in a desire to exclude blacks altogether or to segregate them on the job. When the latter is the wellspring of white workplace prejudice, it is evidenced, not in a wish to segregate black workers, but in an attempt to prevent the hiring of blacks or to limit them to particular low-paying job categories.

During the war years, white male hostility to expanded job opportunities for black men focused primarily on the issue of promotion rather than on hiring or segregation. Although some strikes occurred when black men were admitted to entry-level jobs or over the issue of integrating the workplace, most white-male hate strikes took place when black male workers were promoted into jobs at higher skill and pay levels. This was a product of the fact that black men had been employed as janitors and unskilled laborers in many defense industries prior to the war and sought promotions as opportunities expanded. White males thus seemed to be concerned primarily with maintaining their advantaged economic position. Moreover, their resistance to the elimination of discrimination was more tenacious and more effective than was the opposition of white women to the opening of opportunities for black women. Control over labor unions, whose opposition to black entry into previously white jobs proved an effective barrier to change in many cases, gave white males more power to translate prejudice into employer discrimination.

For women workers, on the other hand, the desire to maintain social distance, rather than a wish to safeguard economic prerogatives, seemed to be the dominant motivation in many cases. White female workers frequently objected to working closely with black women or sharing facilities with them because they feared that blacks were dirty or diseased. Work stoppages occurred in several places after the introduction of black women into the female work force. More than 2,000 white women employed at the U.S. Rubber plant in Detroit walked off the job in March 1943, demanding separate bathroom facilities. A similar walkout occurred at the Western Electric plant in Baltimore in summer 1943. In both cases management refused to segregate the facilities and appealed to patriotic and egalitarian values to persuade the striking workers to return to their jobs. Significantly, the one hate strike by white women workers that focused on upgrading as well as integration, the Dan River strike in 1944, was in a traditional female-employing industry. . . .

As a result of the idiosyncratic nature of employer practices during the war, some areas and some employers offered greater employment opportunities for black women than others. Aircraft plants in the Los Angeles area, for example, began hiring black women for production work relatively early by comparison with similar operations in other areas of the country. As a result, by 1945 black women could be found doing industrial work in all Los Angeles aircraft plants; 2,000 were employed by North American Aviation alone. Among the automakers, the Briggs plant in Detroit deviated from industry patterns and hired substantial numbers of black women. In Saint Louis, where defense industry discrimination against black women was the general rule, the Curtiss-Wright Company and the U.S. Cartridge Company eased the situation somewhat by providing industrial jobs for hundreds of nonwhite women. These examples, however, were not typical of employer response; restrictive hiring and segregation remained the rule, even in industries faced with severe labor shortages. Nowhere was this truer than in the South, where traditional practices remained virtually unchanged.

Even when defense employers broke with tradition and hired nonwhite women, they generally segregated them from other women workers and employed them only for certain kinds of work, usually that which was arduous, dirty, hot, or otherwise disagreeable. A cursory study of black women workers done by the Women's Bureau of the United States Department of Labor in 1945 revealed that in many cases nonwhite women were disproportionately represented among women employed in outside labor gangs, in foundries, and in industrial service work. On the ore docks of the Great Lakes, for example, the survey found women, predominantly black, shoveling the leavings of ore from the bottoms of ships onto hoists. According to the USES, the meat-packing industry in Detroit resorted to black women in large numbers during the war years to take jobs others had spurned. On the railroads minority group women found employment in substantial numbers as laborers, loaders, car cleaners, and waitresses. The city of Baltimore first broke with its policy of hiring only whites for street-cleaning work in the immediate prewar period when it began hiring black males; by 1943, when the black male labor force was completely exhausted, the city turned to the only labor reserve left—the large numbers of unemployed and underemployed black females.

The insistence by some employers on segregated work arrangements and facilities served as a rationale for excluding black women altogether or limiting their numbers to conform to physical plant requirements. The Glenn Martin Aircraft Company, for example, hired the same proportion of nonwhite women for its integrated plant in Omaha, where the black population was quite small, as it did for its Baltimore operations, where black women constituted a substantial proportion of the local labor supply. In Baltimore, however, their numbers were limited because they had to be assigned only to a small separate subassembly plant. A small aircraft parts firm in Los Angeles asserted that it could not hire black women because it separated workers by sex as well as by race and could not further complicate its managerial and supervisory difficulties. At the Norfolk Navy Yard, management excluded black women from most production jobs on the grounds that women workers had to be segregated by race, although the racial integration of male workers was an accomplished fact. As a result, black men worked in a wide variety of jobs at all skill levels in the yard while the jobs assigned to women were virtually monopolized by whites. . . .

The major agency charged with enforcing equal opportunity in employment regardless of race, religion, or national origin was the FEPC, an agency created in 1941 by executive order of President Franklin D. Roosevelt in response to a threatened march on Washington by civil rights groups protesting discriminatory policies by war contractors. Although the FEPC could theoretically recommend the removal of war contracts from those who continued to discriminate and the WMC [War Manpower Commission] could restrict work permits to enforce federal hiring policies, the federal government was not inclined to hamper the production of essential war materials in order to foster racial equity. As a result, the agency had to rely on behind-the-scenes negotiations and the possibility of adverse publicity generated by public hearings. Although effective in some cases, such tools proved ineffectual against recalcitrant violators, whose ranks included some major war industries. The large volume of complaints and the bureaucratic delays inherent in the situation facilitated evasion, even on the part of blatant violators officially ordered to cease restrictive hiring practices. Moreover, the reliance on individual, documented complaints rather than on employer hiring patterns as the basis for action hampered effective enforcement.

The decision by Roosevelt to place the FEPC under the jurisdiction of the WMC in July 1942 also handicapped the agency in its efforts to end employment discrimination. WMC head Paul McNutt, never enthusiastic regarding the FEPC's goals and afraid that they were incompatible with his agency's responsibility for allocating scarce manpower within war industries, canceled scheduled FEPC hearings on discrimination by the railroads and generally made racial equity a low priority within WMC. Even after the FEPC was removed from the WMC in May 1943, it was hampered in its efforts to enforce the law by the unwillingness of southern representatives of the WMC and the USES to cooperate in reporting and seeking to change discriminatory practices. Although the USES had agreed in September 1943 to refuse to fill employer requests for workers when they included racial restrictions, its agents in the South frequently disregarded this directive.

Thus, when blacks with defense training applied for appropriate work, they were often referred to jobs outside the area. The persistence of discrimination, despite a federal commitment to eliminate it, hampered the ability of all blacks, male and female, to find industrial employment in the region that still claimed a majority of the black population.

In its official policies the FEPC treated discrimination against black women as seriously as discrimination against black males, although its rate of success in enforcing compliance in women's cases lagged somewhat behind the rate for men. After its 1944 hearings in Saint Louis, the FEPC ruled that a company that hired black males while discriminating against black women was still in violation of the executive order, noting that "partial compliance is partial violation." Despite pressure from civil rights groups on behalf of black women workers and occasional threats of strikes by black male workers, the equal opportunity machinery of the government proved unable to aid minority women in any substantial way. By the time the agency had investigated, negotiated, or held hearings, much valuable time had been lost. For women, this could be especially damaging because it meant that anything beyond token conformity could be jeopardized by employer unwillingness to expand the female work force late in the war.

The Carter Carburetor Company in Saint Louis, for example, managed a minimal compliance with an FEPC order to cease discriminating when it came to black men, but refused in April 1944 to hire any black women on the grounds that it had no intention of hiring any more women. Although the government continued to pressure the company, it stood by its policies. The Allied Tent Manufacturing Company in New Orleans claimed to have instituted a nondiscriminatory policy regarding women workers when it announced its intention in June 1945 to replace all its women machine operators with men (white and black), having decided that women workers had proved themselves "unsatisfactory." Federal enforcement officials thus found that labor-market forces late in the war provided a rationale and a means for continued resistance by those employers intent on circumventing federal hiring policies regarding black women.

The organization that was most cognizant of persisting discrimination against black women and most active in fighting against it was the National Association for the Advancement of Colored People (NAACP). As early as August 1942, Detroit NAACP officer Gloster Current wrote to McNutt of the WMC, complaining that the Ford Motor Company was discriminating against black females as it hired thousands of whites for work at the Willow Run Bomber Plant. In March 1943 the Detroit NAACP cooperated with the United Auto Workers Inter-Racial Committee in staging a large rally to protest continued discrimination against black women in hiring and black men in promotion on the part of Detroit's war industries. Thereafter both groups continued to pressure employers and government officials at all levels on the issue. In a statement prepared for presentation to the House manpower committee, the NAACP evinced its awareness that the situation was not unique to Detroit but was a national problem resulting in the serious underutilization of black womanpower. . . .

Job retention was a serious issue for those women who landed industrial work during the war. The persistence of discrimination and the late entry of black women into production work, rather than their on-the-job conduct, meant that nonwhite females were more likely than others to experience layoffs resulting from contract completions or seasonal cutbacks. Once fired, they faced great difficulties in finding comparable work. According to an official of the Baltimore Urban League, white women there with industrial experience were easily reabsorbed by war industries while black women were being referred by the USES to work as maids, counter girls, and laundry pressers. As would be the case for all unemployed women after the war, those who turned down such jobs faced the possibility of losing their unemployment benefits for refusing suitable work. Black women thus experienced a much greater degree of job discontinuity than others during the war, hampering their ability to accumulate seniority.

Once the war was over and American industry began its postwar contraction, those black women who had held industrial jobs during the war found that their concentration in contracting industries, their low seniority, and their sex contributed to employment difficulties in the postwar period. American women, black and white, were overrepresented among those experiencing layoffs in durable good industries. When management began rehiring workers in the reconversion period, it reinstituted most prewar discriminatory policies regarding working women, even to the point of disregarding their seniority rights, a practice facilitated by union acquiescence. USES officials reinforced employer policies by denying unemployment benefits to those women who refused referrals to jobs in traditional female-employing fields. To a greater extent than white women, black women were victimized by the postwar eviction of women from jobs in durable goods industries. . . .

In other work categories black women fared somewhat better in the postwar years. Although some apparently lost employment in service, sales, and clerical work as a result of competition from displaced white women, most managed to maintain their hold on lower-level jobs in the female work force. Despite attempts by USES officials in some local offices to force black women to return to domestic service work by threatening to withhold unemployment compensation benefits, enough job opportunities in other categories remained available to prevent a massive return to household work. Even so, domestic service remained the primary occupation of black women, providing employment to 782,520 in 1950, 40 percent of the black female work force.

As a result of the wartime experience, black women made substantial progress in the operatives occupational category, although their position in this area deteriorated somewhat in the late 1940s. One of the most important areas of expansion for nonwhite women was the apparel industry, which witnessed a 350 percent increase in black female employment during the 1940s. By 1950, it offered employment to 56,910 black women and ranked second in the operatives category behind laundry and dry cleaning establishments, where 105,000 black females were employed. Other major sources of industrial work for women, including textiles, remained virtually closed to blacks during the 1940s. In the durable goods industries, which had experienced the greatest wartime expansion, black women were a rarity in the postwar period. In 1950, only 60 black women held jobs as operatives in aircraft plants, while 2,730 claimed similar positions in the auto industry.

In the long run, the greatest benefit of the wartime experience for black women workers derived from their movement in large numbers out of the poverty of the rural South to the possibilities provided by an urban, industrialized economy. The extent to which those possibilities were realized in the decade of the 1940s can be overstated, however. Both during and after the war, black women entered the urban female labor force in large numbers only to occupy its lowest rungs. Largely excluded from clerical and sales work, the growth sectors of the female work force, black women found work primarily in service jobs outside the household and in unskilled blue-collar categories. Although many experienced some upward mobility during the war, their relative position within the American economy remained the same.

Wartime circumstances illustrate the extent to which an economic system that had historically allocated work according to race and sex could tolerate a high level of unemployment and underemployment even in a time of labor shortage in order to minimize the amount of change generated by temporary and aberrant conditions. By stressing the modification of traditional patterns fostered by rapid economic growth, scholars ignore the degree to which prejudices inhibited change and constrained the rate of economic expansion even in the face of strong patriotic, political, and economic incentives favoring expanded output at all cost. For black women, especially, what is significant about the war experience is the extent to which barriers remained intact.

Wartime Conflicts Between Sailors, Chicano Youths, and the Police in Los Angeles

EDWARD J. ESCOBAR

Between 3 and 10 June 1943 the city of Los Angeles was rocked by the worst rioting it had seen to that point in the twentieth century. For eight days scores of American servicemen, sometimes joined by civilians and even police officers, roamed the streets of the city in search of Mexican American youths wearing a distinctive style of dress called a zoot suit. When they found the zoot-suiters, the servicemen attacked and beat them, tearing off their clothes and leaving them naked and bleeding in gutters. As the riots progressed, the level of violence escalated, with servicemen entering bars, theaters, dance halls, restaurants, and even private homes in search of victims. Toward the end of the rioting, the servicemen expanded their attacks to include all Mexican Americans, whether they wore zoot suits or not, as well as African Americans. The rioting did not subside until the War Department made Los Angeles out of bounds to military personnel.

An illuminating aspect of the riots was the role of the Los Angeles Police Department (LAPD). Rather than enforcing the law impartially, police officers handled the rioting in a biased manner. They allowed the servicemen to beat and strip the zoot-suiters, and after the servicemen had left the scene, they moved in and arrested the Mexican American youths for disturbing the peace. Police, in fact, detained

From Edward J. Escobar, "Zoot-Suiters and Cops: Chicano Youth and the Los Angeles Police Department During World War II," in *The War in American Culture: Society and Consciousness* by Lewis A. Erenberg and Susan E. Hirsch, eds., 284–291, 293–300, 302–303. Copyright © 1996 by copyright holder. Reprinted with permission of the University of Chicago Press.

only a handful of servicemen but arrested over six hundred Mexican Americans during the riots.

. . . Police, along with local civic leaders, believed that Mexican American youths, especially young males, were inclined toward violent crime and constituted a severe social problem. . . .

. . . [B]efore World War II the LAPD, like other big city police departments, had not yet linked race and crime in any systematic manner. . . . The zoot suit riots and the anti-Mexican hysteria that preceded them changed all that, convincing the LAPD that Mexican Americans constituted a serious crime problem and that the department needed to develop training, deployment, and general policing strategies for dealing with Mexican American crime. . . . [T]he assumptions reached and the strategies developed by the LAPD regarding the inherent criminality of racial minorities would have profound consequences for policing during the second half of the twentieth century.

A variety of factors during the war years contributed to the conclusion that Mexican American youths were criminally inclined and that stern measures had to be taken to control them. These included the misinterpretation of arrest statistics; the LAPD's adoption of the police professionalism model; general wartime anxieties; and the sensational press coverage of Mexican American crime that led to public hysteria over an alleged Mexican-American crime wave. More important, however, were the rise of the zoot suit fad among Mexican American youth and a corresponding belief among local civic leaders that the zoot suit represented a severe social problem and even reflected criminality within the Mexican American community.

. . . Since the mid-1920s the LAPD had kept detailed statistics on arrests, cross-referenced by charge and race. These statistics show that the LAPD consistently arrested Mexican Americans at a rate higher than the best estimates of their representation within the general population. During the war years, however, the LAPD began arresting significantly higher numbers of Mexican Americans, especially youths, and the department claimed that these increased arrests demonstrated that Mexican American crime was getting out of control and that Mexican Americans were criminally inclined.

By equating arrests with the actual rate of crime, however, police officials misinterpreted their own statistics. Reported crime, which is a more accurate measure of the crime rate, actually fell during 1942 and 1943, the years of the alleged crime wave. The increases in arrests resulted more from changes in the law and in police practices than from changes in Mexican Americans' behavior. Specifically, the enactment and enforcement of new statutes, such as immigration and draft laws for adults and curfew ordinances for juveniles, created new classes of laws that Mexican Americans violated, thus swelling the arrest statistics. . . . Although arrests of Mexican Americans rose, only a fraction of them resulted in criminal prosecutions.

To a great extent the LAPD's excessive arrests of Mexican American youths resulted from the "war on crime" orientation that was part of the professional reform model the LAPD began adopting in 1938. An unforeseen but significant outcome of professionalism was a different relationship between the police and the community, as police changed from a responsive to a preventive force. . . .

Probably the most important factor in the growing popular fear of Mexican Americans was the development of a decidedly rebellious and potentially hostile Mexican American youth culture. The symbols of this youthful rebellion were the zoot suits worn by many Mexican American youths, the distinctive argot they spoke, and a general attitude of both hostility and scorn toward white society. Whites, however, interpreted this rebelliousness not merely as a sign of youthful rambunctiousness but as evidence of the inherently pathological, antisocial, and even criminal nature of Mexican Americans.

The zoot suit phenomenon resulted primarily from the racism, discrimination, and extreme poverty that people of Mexican descent faced in the United States. Economic and social indicators confirmed that Mexican Americans constituted the most destitute racial group in the Los Angeles area during the early 1940s. Because of discrimination by employers and unions, they found employment only in the lowest-paying, most menial jobs. Thus in 1941 Mexican Americans had a yearly median family income of only $790, or more than 29 percent below "the minimum required for decent food and housing for the average family of five persons." . . .

Mexican American youth suffered from blatant educational discrimination. Los Angeles city school officials placed Mexican American children into segregated "Mexican schools." In addition, whether in the Mexican schools or in mainstream schools, these children had to endure the racist attitudes and actions of school officials, from superintendents to classroom teachers. One school official, for example, stated that Mexican Americans were "lazy, have no ambition and won't take advantage of opportunities offered them." . . .

Such attitudes led directly to the undereducating of Mexican American children. . . . The head of a high-school business department, for example, stated: "I have no problems with the Mexicans. I take care that the first few days' work is so difficult and involved that they become discouraged and quit."

These practices proved disastrous for Mexican American children. . . . Many others, frustrated and angry, simply dropped out before finishing their education.

Mexican American youths also suffered from other forms of discrimination, especially in public places. Local officials, for example, prohibited them from using particular parks and public pools except for certain days of the week or month. . . . Some theaters seated Mexican Americans only in certain sections, and some restaurants, dance halls, and other amusements refused them admittance.

Even social service agencies designed to help citizens and promote the war effort discriminated against Mexican Americans. According to War Manpower Commission representative Guy Nunn, the activities of the Civilian Defense, the Red Cross, the War Bonds program, the Office of Price Administration Consumer Division, and the Office of Defense Health and Welfare Service "have persistently been characterized by discrimination and neglect in Spanish-speaking districts." . . .

Although these forms of public humiliation served to remind Mexican American youths of their inferior position in American society and to embitter many, perhaps no other form of discrimination created more anger in the community than the mistreatment they received from police. Probably the most common type of police misconduct was verbal abuse, in particular racial slurs. Former congressman Edward R. Roybal, who grew up in East Los Angeles, states that police officers regularly referred to Mexican Americans as "dirty Mexicans" or "cholos."

Sexual harassment occurred as male officers hand-searched women's bodies, allegedly looking for weapons or drugs. The LAPD had such a bad reputation regarding treatment of young women that Mexican American parents told their daughters that if stranded or in trouble they should walk home rather than seek assistance from a police officer.

The practice of arbitrary "field interrogations" of Mexican Americans also angered the community. In a typical field interrogation officers would stop a car with Mexican American passengers, order everyone out, then search the car and the people for contraband. Anyone of Mexican descent was subject to these searches, but the police seem to have focused on youths. . . .

The police practice that most angered the Mexican American community was the excessive use of force or police brutality. Typically, if police officers felt young men failed to show proper deference and respect for authority, they could expect a violent reaction; but just about any response, from a look to a question, could be interpreted as lack of respect and result in a beating. . . .

The extreme poverty, the pervasive discrimination, and the constant police abuse and brutality led to rebellion and to alienation from American society by a significant segment of Mexican American youths. This rebellion generally did not manifest itself through direct challenges to constituted authority, however. Rather, Mexican American youth engaged in what sociologist Joan Moore calls a "symbolic challenge to the world" through the zoot-suiter.

The zoot suit or "drapes" represented an exercise in excess. It consisted of very baggy pants that fit high on the waist (in extreme cases all the way to the armpits), deep "reet" pleats, and narrow pegged cuffs. The coat had wide lapels and shoulder pads that resembled epaulets; it was sometimes so long that it extended to the knees. Accessories included a broad-brimmed "pancake" hat, long watch chain, and thick-soled shoes. The female equivalent of the zoot-suiter, the "cholita," also wore distinctive clothes, if not as outlandish. Her outfit, which many found sexually provocative, consisted of either a flared or a tight short skirt, tight sweater, and distinctive earrings and makeup. Boys wore long hair combed in a ducktail, while girls stacked their hair high on their heads in a pompadour. In addition to the way they dressed, some Mexican American youths spoke a special argot called Caló. The use of Caló, a derivative of a fifteenth-century Iberian Gypsy dialect, made them incomprehensible to Spanish-speaking elders and to white English-speaking authority figures, and it intensified their sense of uniqueness and generational solidarity. The youths who most completely adopted the zoot suit lifestyle were called pachucos.

With the zoot suit, Mexican American youths reciprocated the rejection they experienced from white society. . . .

Zoot-suiters flaunted their outlandish clothes, and both boys and girls gained a measure of satisfaction and a sense of unity from the looks of ridicule and disgust they received from "squares" when they walked down the street. United Farm Workers leader César Chávez remembers that as a teenager he wore a zoot suit and that he and others "needed a lot of guts to wear those pants, and we had to be rebellious to do it, because the police and a few of the older people would harass us." While only a handful were hard-core pachucos, as many as two-thirds of all Mexican American youths in Los Angeles judged wearing some version of the zoot suit worth the harassment, for it gave them a sense of belonging to at least one group in a society from which they generally felt alienated. . . .

. . . In fact these youths took special pride in their Mexican heritage and rejected any thought of assimilation into American culture. . . .

The extreme alienation of some zoot-suiters went beyond symbolic rebellion and led them into much more aggressive and often even violent behavior. These youths, however, directed much of their hostility inward within the Mexican American community. Almost all the violence the press reported with such great alarm during the war years consisted of Mexican American youths fighting and often killing other Mexican American youths. . . .

Finally, although zoot-suiters never developed a political movement, at least some pachucos had a political consciousness. On at least two occasions during the war years Mexican American youths burned the American flag and tore down posters promoting the war effort. The vice principal of Garfield high school accused Mexican American students who formed their own organization of having "pro-Nazi designs," and police officials became extremely alarmed when a convicted German spy waiting to be transferred to a federal penitentiary began telling his Mexican American jail mates that they were victims of racial discrimination. In fact, during the war years Los Angeles community leaders, both white and Mexican American, believed the pachuco fad was a scheme of an extreme right-wing and possibly pro-Axis Mexican movement known as the Sinarquistas that allegedly hoped to disrupt the war effort by sowing disunity between Mexican Americans and Anglo-Americans.

We should remember, however, that although most Mexican American youths wore some part of the zoot suit costume, the overwhelming majority did not engage in illegal acts, politically motivated or otherwise. . . .

. . . [I]t seems that above all the zoot-suiters wanted respect. Despite their outlandish clothes and sometimes outlandish behavior, what the pachucos really wanted—indeed what they demanded—was to be treated like all other members of their age group. They wanted to get the same kinds of jobs, to be treated fairly in school, to frequent the same entertainment spots, to be treated fairly by the police, and above all, they wanted in all these interactions to be treated with respect.

White society, however, was unwilling to respect Mexican Americans, especially zoot-suiters. Whites were repelled by the zoot suit precisely because of what it represented: rebellion against traditional forms of discrimination and subordination. Mexicans were not supposed to have as good jobs as whites, they were not supposed to get an equal education, they were not supposed to go to the same dances or sit in the same section of theaters—and the role of the police was to keep them in their place. Moreover, Mexicans were supposed to be humble and meek and generally invisible, and youths were supposed to obey authority figures. That Mexican American youth chose to attack these norms of behavior not directly through political action, but symbolically through actions that showed their defiance and hostility toward white society made it easier for whites to dismiss their protests and label them as deviant, criminal, and even pathological. . . .

To a certain extent, a popular belief that Mexican American juvenile delinquency was sweeping Los Angeles was an outgrowth of wartime. Los Angeles became the West Coast center for war-related production, which resulted in rapid population increases and concomitant social dislocations. In addition, public offi-cials across the nation expected a significant rise in juvenile delinquency once the United States entered the war. Such an increase had occurred in the United States during World War I and in Great Britain earlier in the current war.

The United States' actual entry into the war raised fears of internal enemy con-spiracies and demands for total conformity. Even before the United States entered the war, the Los Angeles Police Commission recommended that the City Council pass an ordinance ordering all noncitizens to register with the chief of police. Once the war started, the expulsion of Japanese nationals and Japanese Americans from the West Coast and their "internment" in concentration camps was the most ob-vious consequence of this paranoia and demand for conformity. After the removal of the Japanese, municipal officials, the press, and much of the public transferred their anxiety to the city's largest minority group, Mexican Americans. That fear eventually led to public hysteria over an alleged Mexican American crime wave.

Los Angeles newspapers helped create the hysteria with a campaign of sen-sational headlines and lurid news stories depicting the latest depredations of so-called Mexican American youth gangs. Beginning in the spring of 1942, six months after Pearl Harbor and only weeks after the internment of the Japanese and Japanese Americans, newspapers featured stories on Mexican American juvenile delinquency. These stories continued through the summer, growing in intensity and reaching a peak in August 1942. Because of protests from the federal government that the stories hurt the war effort, newspapers cut back on their sensational cover-age for a time. They resumed in early 1943, however, and continued throughout the spring until they peaked again in May. The coverage of Mexican American crime and the frenzy it created culminated with the zoot suit riots of 3–10 June 1943. . . .

From mid-1942 onward, the theme that dominated the Los Angeles press's treatment of Mexican American youth was that of the gang, and local newspapers consistently assumed that any Mexican who committed a crime must belong to a gang. . . .

The incident that fixed the public's attention on Mexican American crime was the infamous Sleepy Lagoon case. . . . On the morning of Sunday, 2 August 1942, José Díaz was found severely injured next to a dirt road close to a gravel pit called Sleepy Lagoon. He was taken to a local hospital, where he died of head injuries later that day. The next day Los Angeles newspapers attributed his death to "Mexican Boy Gangs," and over the next several weeks and months the local press repeatedly charged that a "Boy Gang Terror Wave" was sweeping the city. . . .

. . . There was no proof that anyone actually killed Díaz. Nevertheless, prosecu-tors filed first-degree murder charges against twenty-two Mexican American boys from the Thirty-eighth Street neighborhood on the grounds that they had been in a fight at a party that Díaz also attended.

The trial was a mockery of justice and demonstrated the prevailing attitudes of government officials and the press toward Mexican American youths. . . . [T]he jury found the defendants guilty of charges ranging from assault to first-degree murder. Thanks to the efforts of a citizens' group called the Sleepy Lagoon Defense Com-mittee, however, the verdicts were overturned on appeal.

The LAPD used the death of José Díaz and the fears it raised as an excuse to repress the growing rebelliousness of Mexican American youth. On the weekend following Díaz's death, police conducted a massive three-day sweep of the barrios, apprehending over six hundred youths. . . . [P]olice arrested anyone who looked as if he or she could have committed a crime sometime in the past. Police charged the youths with "suspicion," usually of robbery or assault with a deadly weapon. . . .

In the midst of this crisis atmosphere, the Los Angeles County Grand Jury initiated hearings into the extent, nature, and causes of Mexican American juvenile delinquency. The hearings and the debate they sparked among government officials and community leaders were the clearest articulation ever of law enforcement's attitude toward the Mexican American community. . . . [T]hey agreed that the zoot-suiters and the pachuco lifestyle represented a grave social ill that must be repressed. . . .

The testimony that caused the most controversy and most closely reflected the thinking of the Los Angeles law enforcement community came from the Sheriff Department's Captain Ayres. Although he acknowledged that discrimination was a factor, Ayres believed the main cause for Mexican American criminality was biological. He attributed this "biological basis" to the Los Angeles Mexican Americans' descent from the inherently violent Indians of Mexico. After all, the Aztecs were known for sacrificing 30,000 Indians in one day, he maintained, and "this total disregard for human life has always been universal throughout the Americas among the Indian population, which of course is well known to everyone." . . . To dramatize the difference between whites and Mexican Americans, Ayres used the analogy of a house cat and a wild cat. A house cat could be domesticated and treated leniently; a wild cat, Ayres argued, would always be wild and must therefore be caged. . . .

Ayres and the other officers who testified before the grand jury thus developed a broad strategy for dealing with Mexican American youth. They recommended prosecuting all juveniles suspected of lawbreaking or simply belonging to a gang and called for filing charges of contributing to the delinquency of a minor against any adult gang members. Another part of the law enforcement plan called for an increase in arrests and "field investigations" of Mexican American youth and the creation of a central juvenile delinquency file of information on all potential juvenile delinquents—that is, anyone who was arrested and put on probation as well as students who got into trouble in school.

Police officials thus saw Mexican American youths as a criminal and dangerous element within society that must be suppressed even at the cost of violating their civil liberties. . . .

. . . Since the function of the police was to fight crime and since Mexican Americans were either biologically or environmentally inclined toward criminality, the police had to do everything in their power to suppress this evident social danger. Anything else would have been an unprofessional dereliction of duty.

In the short term, however, despite the consensus regarding the seriousness of "the Mexican problem," law enforcement could not implement the most repressive aspects of its proposed campaign against Mexican American youth. After the initial police actions in the wake of Sleepy Lagoon, the need for the United States to maintain good relations with its Latin American allies and the effectiveness of German propaganda in that part of the world precluded any more mass arrests or other wholesale repression. For the duration of the war, at least, the LAPD would have to satisfy itself with piecemeal responses to pachuco rebelliousness and to passing along to the newspapers information about the latest instance of Mexican American juvenile delinquency. Officers' complicity during the zoot suit riots shows the frustration they must have felt over their inability to take more vigorous action.

In the long term, the consensus regarding Mexican American criminality changed the way the LAPD policed the Mexican American community. It . . . began training officers, both formally and informally, to expect more crime from Mexican Americans than from the white population. In addition, since theories of scientific management and other aspects of police professionalism directed that police be aggressively deployed in high-crime areas, the concentration of officers became much greater in the Mexican American community than in other areas of the city. The combination of these two factors and the department's more aggressive posture toward fighting crime resulted in chronic overarresting of Mexicans in Los Angeles. Since the police used arrest statistics to determine the crime rate within a given population, the idea that Mexican Americans were criminally inclined became a self-fulfilling prophecy. . . .

The war years thus saw the LAPD adopt a theory of criminality that linked crime with race. After the war that theory was increasingly institutionalized in police policies and practices. Moreover, the LAPD transferred both the theory and the policies and practices regarding Mexican American criminality to African Americans when that community began to grow in Los Angeles after the war. Aggressive police tactics against the black and Chicano communities continued and intensified, and so did allegations of police abuse from minorities.

F U R T H E R   R E A D I N G

Abrahamson, James. *The American Home Front* (1983).
Anderson, Karen. *Wartime Women: Sex Roles, Family Relations, and the Status of Women During World War II* (1981).
Bentley, Amy. *Eating for Victory: Food Rationing and the Politics of Domesticity* (1998).
Bernstein, Alison R. *American Indians in World War II: Toward a New Era in Indian Affairs* (1991).
Campbell, D'Ann. *Women at War with America: Private Lives in a Patriotic Era* (1984).
Capeci, Dominic J., Jr. *The Harlem Riot of 1943* (1977).
———. *Race Relations in Wartime Detroit: The Sojourner Truth Housing Controversy of 1942* (1984).
Chafe, William. *The American Woman* (1972).
Dalfiume, Richard M. *Desegregation of the U.S. Armed Forces: Fighting on Two Fronts, 1939–1953* (1969).
Erenberg, Lewis A., and Susan E. Hirsch, eds. *The War in American Culture* (1996).
Gamboa, Erasmo. *Mexican Labor and World War II* (1990).
Glaberman, Martin. *Wartime Strikes: The Struggle Against the No-Strike Pledge in the UAW During World War II* (1980).
Gluck, Sherna Berger. *Rosie the Riveter Revisited: Women, the War, and Social Change* (1987).
Goodwin, Doris Kearns. *No Ordinary Time: Franklin and Eleanor Roosevelt: The Home Front in World War II* (1994).
Hartmann, Susan M. *The Home Front and Beyond: American Women in the 1940s* (1982).
Honey, Maureen. *Creating Rosie the Riveter: Class, Gender and Propaganda During World War II* (1984).

Jeffries, John W. *Wartime America: The World War II Home Front* (1996).
Johnson, Marilynn S. *The Second Gold Rush: Oakland and the East Bay in World War II* (1993).
Kennedy, David M. *Freedom from Fear: The American People in Depression and War, 1929–1945* (1999).
Lawson, Steven. *Black Ballots: Voting Rights in the South, 1944–1969* (1975).
Lichtenstein, Nelson. *Labor's War at Home: The CIO in World War II* (1982).
Lipsitz, George. *Rainbow at Midnight: Labor and Culture in the 1940s* (1994).
May, Elaine Tyler. *Pushing the Limits: American Women, 1940–1961* (1994).
Mazon, Mauricio. *The Zoot-Suit Riots: The Psychology of Symbolic Annihilation* (1984).
Milkman, Ruth. *Gender at Work: The Dynamics of Job Segregation by Sex During World War II* (1987).
Nash, Gerald D. *The American West Transformed: The Impact of the Second World War* (1985).
Reed, Merl E. *Seedtime for the Modern Civil Rights Movement: The President's Committee on Fair Employment Practice, 1941–1946* (1991).
Ruiz, Vicki L. *Cannery Women, Cannery Lives: Mexican Women, Unionization, and the California Food Processing Industry, 1930–1950* (1987).
Shogan, Robert, and Tom Craig. *The Detroit Race Riot* (1964).
Tuttle, William M., Jr. *"Daddy's Gone to War": The Second World War in the Lives of America's Children* (1993).
Wynn, Neil A. *The Afro-American and the Second World War* (1976, 1993).

See also Chapters 2 and 7.

CHAPTER
7

Challenges and Changes
in Wartime American Culture

🌍

World War II was a time of sacrifice at home and abroad, yet it was also a time
when movies, musicals, and other forms of popular entertainment provided
audiences with timeless stories, welcome amusements, and needed distractions.
One story was Rogers and Hammerstein's musical Oklahoma! which broke all
box office records after it opened on Broadway in March 1943. As a story of love
and rivalry, the musical celebrated the resiliency of the American spirit. More
sentimental, but revealing of Americans' yearning for peace and safety, was the
hit song "White Christmas," sung by Bing Crosby in the 1942 movie Holiday
Inn. Music and stories helped people on the home front imagine a just past and
envision a fairer world for the future.

   Popular culture connected those at home to the men and women serving overseas. Celebrated films, including Sergeant York, winner of the Oscar in 1942,
and Casablanca, which won in 1943, explored the meanings of war. Among the
finest of the documentaries produced during the war were those of Frank Capra
in the series Why We Fight. Top male stars, and lesser ones like Ronald Reagan,
joined up, saw action, or, in the case of Reagan, helped make the propaganda
films that attempted to teach soldiers lessons about war, patriotism, and much
more. Screen stars came to life as soldiers were entertained by "pin-up girls" Betty
Grable and Rita Hayworth, whose pictures could be found in the possession of
many soldiers. Organizing entertainment for the troops was the U.S.O., or United
Service Organizations. Across the country, women followed the lead of Betty Grable
and volunteered their time serving coffee, talking with soldiers, or dancing the
jitterbug and the Lindy Hop.

   Newspapers, magazines, the radio, and film newsreels reported daily about
the carnage of war even as the reports attempted to boost the nation's morale. They
focused on gas and food rationing, and encouraged people to plant victory gardens.
On the radio, people listened to Edward R. Murrow as he described the Battle of
Britain in the summer of 1940. Readers learned from Ernie Pyle's newspaper columns about the military campaigns in North Africa, Europe, and the Pacific, and
his death there in 1944 brought another tragedy into American homes. More light-
hearted but just as revealing were the cartoon characters produced by Bill Mauldin.

Over one-third of Americans regularly read comic books, and special editions were sent to soldiers at home and abroad. Books, magazines, and newspapers were also sent overseas to GIs. Some, like the Stars and Stripes *newspapers that carried Mauldin's cartoons, were created specifically for military audiences. Magazine advertisements focused on the war as much as did the feature stories, reminding all Americans that they were involved in a total war. Advertisements revealed that even the fashions of the day reflected the equation of sacrifice at home with sacrifice in battle, as the fashion pages showed women opting for subdued grays instead of bright colors.*

Best-selling books, like William L. Shirer's Berlin Diary *about Hitler and Nazism, introduced readers to worlds outside their own communities as events of the day brought those worlds closer. Richard Wright's* Black Boy *and Lillian Smith's* Strange Fruit *conveyed new insights about race in America. Novels like* My Friend Flicka *by Mary O'Hara also sold in unprecedented numbers during the war. So successful was bookselling that publishers faced with paper shortages at the height of the war began to market softcover (or paperback) books. GIs also had access to cheap paperback books published under the direction of the Council on Books in Wartime. Soldiers looking for erotic or pacifist literature would not find it here, however, as the military librarians censored out such works, considering them ill suited to their audience. Movies were also widely distributed to soldiers serving in Europe and the Pacific. As parts of these areas were liberated, Hollywood's reach grew broader, especially in Europe, and the globalization of American mass media accelerated.*

The war opened up for many women and men the possibility of autonomous personal lives free of traditional family and community restrictions. For some people, the draw of military life or a job at a factory was about spending extended periods of time with the same sex; for others, it was the chance to socialize with a different sex. The war brought on changes in gay culture as people moved beyond their private networks into urban, commercial places like bars and clubs. Expressions of anxieties over sex and sexuality took many forms during the war years, but in general they aimed for two results: to keep men clean and women pure. Warnings against the corruptions of vice and venereal disease were equaled by prescriptive pronouncements about how women must not lose their "femininity" even as they took a factory job, joined minor league ball clubs, or volunteered for the WAC (Women's Army Corps). The ultimate challenge was to make sure that women and men understood the need for united families at the end of the war. The G.I. Bill provided free education to returning veterans, while FDIC (Federal Deposit Insurance Corporation) mortgages allowed them to buy the new suburban prefabricated tract houses that were constructed using methods perfected by the Kaiser shipyards during the war. Women took on the roles of mothers and housewives, having been displaced from their wartime jobs. The baby boom, suburbanization, and a conservative postwar ideology reshaped the American landscape after 1945.

War forced extraordinary demands on ordinary Americans in the 1940s. The documents and essays that follow provide evidence of the role cultural constructions played in helping people express and deal with those difficulties. Artists of all sorts—from comedians in a U.S.O. show to photographers capturing images on streetcorners—tried to depict the war's meanings: its tragedies, its moments of resolve, the grandeur of victory.

As you read through the documents, think especially about how ideas about womanhood and manhood—about gender—influenced people's reactions to war and the transformations brought on by war. In what ways were existing concepts of gender altered during the war? In what ways were they not altered? How did gender concepts influence people's reactions to the war? How did they influence people's reactions to the transformations brought on by the war?

D O C U M E N T S

Document 1 is excerpted from an address given by Oveta Culp Hobby, the director of the Women's Army Auxiliary Corps [later the Women's Army Corps, or WAC], to the mothers of WAAC volunteers. Document 2 is a newspaper article that provides an example of the concern with "victory girls" and the wartime issue of prostitution and venereal disease. Document 3 is an excerpt from another newspaper article on the role and reception of the women and men who entertained the troops overseas. Document 4 is a 1947 *Newsweek* article titled "Homosexuals in Uniform" that reveals not only the findings of the army but also the magazine's editorial voice about male sexuality. Document 5 consists of two graphs showing changes in marriage, divorce, and birth rates from prewar to postwar. The next two documents deal with how men and women were thinking about the relationship of wartime service to postwar families. Document 6 is from an article by movie star Ann Sothern directing women to think about how to prepare themselves for the return of their husbands from war. Document 7 is an excerpt from the last chapter of popular newspaper columnist Ernie Pyle's 1944 *Here Is Your War.* Document 8, an excerpt from Henry R. Luce's influential essay "The American Century," is also about the postwar world, but it was written before the United States entered the war. Document 9 shows one of the popular entertainers, Betty Grable, whose pin-up poster could be found wherever there were American soldiers. She was known as the woman with the million-dollar legs. Finally, Document 10, Alfred Eisenstadt's famous photograph of VJ Day in New York City, catches the American spirit at the end of the war, on August 14, 1945.

1. Oveta Culp Hobby, Director of the Women's Army Auxiliary Corps, Talks to American Mothers, 1943

I have seen and talked with a great many WAAC mothers all over the United States in the eleven months I have been Director of the Women's Army Auxiliary Corps. But never until this moment have I seen so many of you all at once. It is a very warming experience. I like it.

. . . There is a very great sense of responsibility in directing the lives of thousands of America's women through this most critical period in our nation's history, and I am deeply sensible of all that this sacrifice means to you. . . . I think nothing could have brought me more personal satisfaction than the evidence you have given, through organizing the WAAC Mother's Association, that you have taken us to your hearts.

A daughter is a precious possession, and you have given daughters to your country. You have given them gladly. This new association of WAAC mothers is

---

From "Address by Oveta Culp Hobby, Director, W.A.A.C., Pittsburgh, April 14, 1943," RG165 (Dir. WAC, 080), Entry 54, Box 15, National Archives.

full proof of that. You gave them because you knew that in total war such as this, women as well as men must be part of our necessary military establishment. And so you have given your dearest possession to your country's need. . . .

It is a new conception to think of daughters in the military service. It must require something of an adjustment from most mothers before the idea is readily accepted. With sons it is different. Throughout the history of this and every nation, mothers have watched their sons go off to war. Not that sending a son is easier than sending a daughter. But there has been a spiritual preparation in the hearts of women for this necessary sacrifice, passed on from generation to generation of mothers.

Until this war required the all-out service of the entire nation—women as well as men, civilians as well as soldiers—the military life was restricted to men. Even as recently as the World War of 1917, women did not serve in our Army's uniform.

I think that even if there had not been the vital need for manpower which made a women's corps inevitable, women would still have wanted to serve their country in uniform today. I sensed that before the Corps was ever brought into being by Congressional action and the President's executive order eleven months ago tomorrow. I caught it immediately in the great flood of applications we received from women all over the country and the serious, purposeful letters that accompanied them. They seemed to say, "This is our war, too, and we want to share it with the men who fight."

I have been proud, many times to find that simple eagerness to serve on the part of America's women. We wondered sometimes, in the early days of the Corps, whether women would find it easy to adapt themselves to the military life. It is not an easy life, and its basis is discipline. There is no turning over for another five minutes sleep in the Army. There is no time to practice those pleasant feminine ways of procrastination when the bugle is calling and a sergeant's whistle shrills through the barracks. We wondered a little whether the women would like that. The officers out at Fort Des Moines, which was the first WAAC Training Center, wondered, too.

I think that some of those good, hard-boiled officers and noncoms were a little astonished at what happened the first morning reveille sounded for American women in uniform. Because the WAACs came pouring out of the barracks in jig time. You see, most of them had been up long before reveille just to make sure they'd be on time.

So that was the way American women took to the military life. They liked it, and they've gone on liking it. I'm sure there was a good bit of pride behind the eagerness with which they took to the drilling and the discipline. They wanted to show those officers and noncoms that they could be just as good soldiers as any man. . . .

. . . I wonder if you have considered the new values which the military experience they are living through now is bringing them. I am not referring now to what they will learn as part of their military education, and yet I want to stress that they are acquiring a great deal of knowledge which they could have learned in no other way.

But it is the corollary effects of their experience that I am talking of now. And particularly, of the sense of responsibility which a great many thousands of American women are developing through their service in the WAAC.

In the first place, they are learning discipline. By that I do not mean simply obedience to orders, though that is part of it. They are learning the self-discipline which comes of consideration for others. In the Army a woman, as well as a man, lives in a large community of other individuals. . . .

In sixty-seven posts, camps and stations in these United States, WAACs are feeling these things today. They are abroad, too, and their service in North Africa has released men from headquarters to take their rifles up into the hills of Tunisia where American and British troops are pinching out the last of Rommel's resistance. Wherever they serve, these women are performing a man's job with the Army. They are contributing their full share to victory.

2. Robert P. Lane, Director of New York City's Welfare Council, Cites Home Front Concerns About "Victory Girls" and Venereal Disease, 1945

Commercialized prostitution keeps spreading venereal disease behind the smoke-screen set up by the current furor over so-called "Victory Girls," Robert P. Lane charged yesterday.

He said the police alone have not been able to curb the organized vice rings, and advocated medical examinations for men taken in vice raids, to keep down the disease rate.

Police Commissioner Valentine refused to comment.

Mr. Lane, executive director of the Welfare Council of New York City, announced an unmistakable rise in New York's venereal rate. He said:

> The root source of most venereal disease in New York City still lies in commercialized prostitution, and not, I am convinced, in a sudden, war-born lowering of moral standards among teen-age girls.
>
> More searching inquiry, compilation and analysis of the facts as to how service men and others pick up venereal disease will, I am confident, substantiate this statement. The furor over "Victory Girls" has become a convenient smokescreen to hide the operations of commercialized vice rings.

Organized prostitution in large cities such as New York, Mr. Lane maintained, continues to thrive because only women offenders are arrested, never the panderers, madams, call-house operators, landlords and other parasites who share the profits.

"Police action alone cannot achieve results," he continued. "It must be supported by public opinion." He contended that failure to seize men who frequent houses of prostitution is a major factor in spreading disease.

"I suggest that law make it mandatory for men picked up in raids to be under medical observation for the minimum disease incubation period."

He decried the "revolving door" process of fighting diseased prostitutes—arrest, trial, medical treatment, a short jail sentence or a fine, out on the streets again.

"Here is where social agencies should play a vital role," he argued, "in the re-habilitation of socially diseased persons, in re-directing their energies into more constructive channels, in providing vocational training, a new sense of security, a new set of goals to live for."

He said that without these adjuncts, rapid venereal disease treatment is merely "illusory in its social implications."

From "Commercial Vice Is Held Uncurbed," *The New York Times,* January 19, 1945, p. 34. Copyright © 1945 by *The New York Times.*

3. John Desmond, *New York Times* Writer, Praises Entertainers at the War Front, 1944

The stage is a rough board affair, supported by freshly hewn logs. On it a girl, dressed in a simple cotton dress like those you see on the boardwalk at Jones Beach on a summer afternoon, is singing. Behind her two other entertainers are sitting on camp stools and to the right an accordionist pumps his arms. His instrument pours out a volume of sound that somehow manages to approximate the tune of "Shoo-Shoo Baby."

The scene is in New Guinea. It is hot—115 degrees in back of the stage, 130 plus under the arc lights that are powered by a mobile Army generator standing nearby. . . .

. . . The singer's last note is cut short by a roar that breaks across the jungle stillness. A thousand pairs of hands are clapping. Men are shouting and whistling. Out of the din an occasional shout comes clear, "How about some more, baby?" or "Let's have 'Take It Easy,'" or "Give us 'Don't Sweetheart Me.'" The girl looks at the musician and nods. Then the roar suddenly ceases and the strains of another song float over the vast and almost unseen audience of United States servicemen.

The singer and the performers with her on New Guinea make up an overseas company of the Camp Shows branch of the United Service Organizations. At the present time, eighty such companies are out of the country, giving shows in bomb-damaged opera houses in Italy, in rickety Nissen huts in North Africa, in storage barns in Alaska and the Aleutians, in jungles, deserts, mountain hideouts—in fact, wherever American boys are stationed. . . .

The headquarters of this worldwide vaudeville circuit covers half-dozen floors in a building at 8 West Fortieth Street, New York City. Its funds come from the National War Fund and its audience is provided by the armed services. Camp Shows' job—with the help of the Hollywood Victory Committee, which makes available the services of motion-picture stars—is primarily one of finding talent and molding it into variety-type shows that won't be laughed off the boards.

The talent falls into two classifications. First there are the paid USO Camp Show performers, hired from theaters, vaudeville companies, night clubs, and shows, as permanent troupers. They form the backbone of the entertainment for our soldiers and sailors. In the second-class are Broadway, Hollywood, and radio volunteers who offer their services for a minimum of six weeks. Hollywood stars, unused as many of them are to personal appearances before large audiences, were at first reluctant to give camp performances because, as Gary Cooper put it, "What can I give them?" But Cooper and many others have been fitted into the variety-show pattern and they have made a tremendous hit.

Once the talent is gathered and a script is prepared, the Army takes over. It does this with exemplary military terseness. Special Services orders up entertainment much in the same fashion as it orders tanks or planes or other essentials of war. A typical requisition will read like this: "Immediately, five people, mixed, including personality. Musician essential. Tropical climate. Six weeks." . . .

From John Desmond, "The Troupers Go to the Troops," *The New York Times Magazine,* April 2, 1944, pp. 16–17, 46. Copyright © 1944 by *The New York Times.*

Perhaps the hardest part of an overseas tour is the first week. The company elegantly housed in its Hollywood hotel will leave in the early morning for an unannounced destination. The same evening they will put in at Hawaii, snatch a few hours sleep, and push off before dawn the next day. The bomber is relatively comfortable. In its electrically controlled cabin the players are unaware of the changing temperature outside. Then the plane circles in for a landing. As it drops, the occupants pick out a landing field, and as the ground comes closer, they can identify a landing strip and, finally, the hangars and troops' quarters. The plane taxis to a stop and the opening doors let in a swift rush of hot tropical air. The field is on the northern top of Australia. . . .

After a couple of days in Australia, with trips by jeep or truck over rutted roads to nearby camps, the company will move northward into the islands. The closer to the front, the greater the hardships. . . .

Enemy action frequently brings a show to a halt in the middle of its most dramatic scene. This happens in Italy more often than elsewhere, because in that theater the players are frequently close behind the front lines. George Raft was giving a performance south of Naples early this year when enemy planes came in overhead, and the audience and performers sat in the darkness until the alarm passed and the show could resume. . . .

. . . Overseas these players find that the soldiers like to laugh. Even the oldest jokes will virtually "roll 'em in the aisles." . . .

. . . Bob Hope, in his whirlwind circuit of the European and Mediterranean theaters late last year, would cheer up a couple of thousand weary men back from battle with gags like this: "I led such a sheltered life I didn't go out with girls till I was almost four," or "Fellas, the folks at home are having a terrible time about eggs. They can't get any powdered eggs at all. They've got to use the old-fashioned kind you break open."

It is the kind of broad humor, with some GI variations, that the boys heard for years in America. It reminds them of home. They like almost anything that smacks of home. One of Gary Cooper's best performances was a recitation of Lou Gehrig's speech in "Pride of the Yankees," and George Raft won many an audience reenacting scenes from some of his better-known films. . . .

Letters from all theaters flood into the USO-Camp Shows from soldiers and sailors in the fighting zones and from their parents at home attesting the gratitude of the servicemen for the "live shows." There is not an actor who has returned who has not had mail and telephone calls from parents in all parts of the United States to tell how much their sons liked the performances. If the trouper happened to have spoken personally to the soldier in a hospital or at mess, the boy's parents are sure to have heard about it and they call and write, grateful for any scrap of information about a son's whereabouts, his looks, his food. Such letters are a source of deep pleasure to the performers, but their greatest thrill comes from the spontaneous response of men in the fighting zones. Take this one:

Ella Logan, along with two other performers, was giving a show before several hundred men, half of them Negro, in a huge Nissen hut in North Africa. The program had lasted for about two hours and Miss Logan had been on the stage for more than one hour singing dozens of popular songs. After an encore she shouted to the audience, "Fellas, am I keeping you from anything?" And a young kid in the back of the room called back, "Yeh, sufferin'."

4. *Newsweek* Looks Back at Homosexuals in Uniform During Wartime, 1947

Although Army regulations strictly forbade the drafting of homosexuals, scores of these inverts managed to slip through induction centers during the second world war. Between 3,000 and 4,000 were discharged for this abnormality; others were released as neuropsychiatric cases. Last week, with most of the records on homosexuals tabulated, Army medical officers, for the first time, summed up their strange story.

To screen out this undesirable soldier-material, psychiatrists in induction-station interviews tried to detect them (1) by their effeminate looks or behavior and (2) by repeating certain words from the homosexual vocabulary and watching for signs of recognition. In some instances, the urinary hormone-secretion test showed a higher degree of estrogens (female hormones) than androgens (male hormones), just the opposite of a normal man. But this test was too uncertain and too expensive to try on every inductee.

Frequently, a latent homosexual, who had no knowledge of his predilection, was inducted into the service, only to develop alarming symptoms in camp and on the battlefield. Many of these men refused to admit homosexuality, even to themselves, and went to elaborate lengths to prove their masculinity. One of these ruses was regular and conspicuous absence without leave, always with female companions. Often the soldier's primary trouble was not discovered until he was hauled before Army psychiatrists on an AWOL charge.

From case histories in Army files, these facts about homosexuals were gleaned:

• They topped the average soldier in intelligence, education, and rating. At least 10 per cent were college graduates, more than 50 per cent had finished high school. Only a handful were illiterate.

• Including all ages, there were more whites than Negroes in this group. They came mostly from the cities rather than the country.

• Although the majority had no family history of nervous or mental disease, many were from homes broken by divorce or separation. In many instances the man had been brought up by his mother as a girl, or had been an only son in a large family of girls. About half assumed a "feminine" role, the other half "masculine." Most were either unmarried or had made a failure of marriage.

• As a whole, these men were law-abiding and hard-working. In spite of nervous, unstable, and often hysterical temperaments, they performed admirably as office workers. Many tried to be good soldiers.

Once this abnormality was detected, the man was usually evacuated by the unit doctors to a general hospital where he received psychiatric treatment while a military board decided whether or not he was reclaimable. A good number begged to be cured, but doctors usually doubted their sincerity and recommended discharge. At least half of the confirmed homosexuals, one psychiatrist estimated, were well-adjusted to their condition, and neither needed nor would respond to treatment. The majority, therefore, were released.

The Blue Discharge. Early in the war, the homosexuals were sent up for court-martial, but in 1943–1944, the Army decided to separate most of them quietly with a "blue" discharge (neither honorable nor dishonorable) unless some other breach of military law had been committed. Last week, however, the Army announced a stiff new policy, effective July 1.

Instead of leaving service with the vague and protective "blue" discharge, the homosexuals who had not been guilty of a definite offense would receive an "un-desirable" discharge. A few of this group with outstanding combat records might receive an honorable discharge. Those found guilty of homosexual violence or of impairing the morals of minors, would receive a "yellow" or dishonorable discharge.

5. Wartime and Postwar Conditions Affect Marriage, Divorce, and Birth Rates, 1930–1950

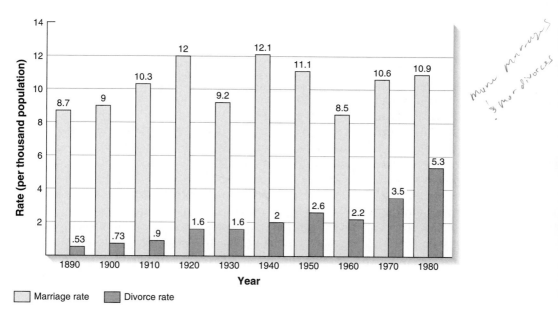

Sources: Marriage and Divorce, 1887–1906, Bulletin 96, Bureau of the Census, Department of Commerce and Labor, 1908. *Historical Statistics of the United States, Colonial Times to 1970,* Part 1, Bicentennial Edition, Bureau of the Census, U.S. Department of Commerce, 1975. *Statistical Abstract of the United States,* Bureau of the Census, U.S. Department of Commerce, 1983.

NOTE: The marriage and divorce rates are the annual number of marriages and divorces per 1,000 population.

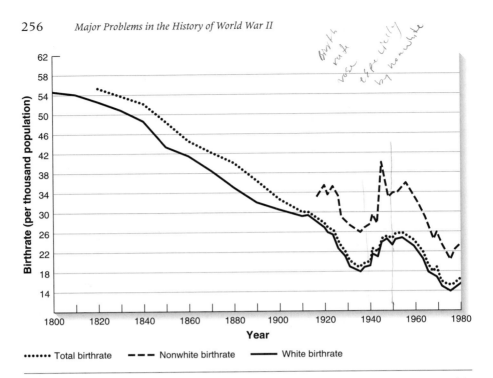

Sources: Historical Statistics of the United States, Colonial Times to 1970, Part 1, Bicentennial Edition, Bureau of the Census, U.S. Department of Commerce, 1975. *Perspectives on Working Women: A Databook,* Bulletin 2080, Bureau of Labor Statistics, U.S. Department of Labor. *Final Natality Statistics, 1978,* Monthly Vital Statistics Report, National Center for Health Statistics. *Statistical Abstract of the United States,* Bureau of the Census, U.S. Department of Commerce, 1981.

NOTE: Figures for nonwhites were not computed until World War I.

6. Movie Star Ann Sothern Asks, "What Kind of Woman Will Your Man Come Home To?" 1944

Nothing will ever be the same again. When you tell your man-in-uniform good-by and he picks up his kit and sets off for those far places, he carries with him a mental picture of you wearing your perkiest hat and your bravest smile . . . a picture of the girl he fell in love with and perhaps married, a picture he'll be seeing in his mind's eye for all the months and months to come.

Right then is the moment for *you* to begin to think, "What kind of woman will he come back to?" Because when he returns, he will have changed; you will have changed; the whole world in which we live will be different. His job and yours may be different ones. Your entire relation to work and life, even to one another, may have altered. . . .

Now I am more and more vividly conscious that not only I but every intelligent modern girl who wants more than anything else to preserve the delicate relationship of marriage must begin now to recognize the inevitability of change—right

From Ann Sothern, "What Kind of Woman Will Your Man Come Home To?" *Photoplay,* vol. 25, no. 6 (November 1944): 44–45, 85–86. Reprinted by permission of Argus Publishing Co. Ltd.

now—and to respond to it. I don't mean that any of us can plan or prepare ourselves for *definite* personal or general post-war changes. I mean merely that there
will *be* changes and there will be problems and we must keep abreast, as nearly as
we can, with what is going on around us as well as in our intimate lives.

I've thought about these things since Bob went into training and I think that
the smart girl will want to devise for herself a pattern of living which will assure
her that her man will come back, if not to the identical woman he left, to the sort of
woman who will be fitted to go hand in hand with him into whatever strange new
world will be emerging. She can't foresee what it will be like any more than he can.
So the best thing she can do is to live as fully and as usefully . . . and with as much
awareness . . . as she can in the world she sees now.

She must keep herself out of mental ruts. . . .

Millions of boys—and men who are too old to be called "boys"—are learning
to be serious about things they scarcely thought of before the war. They're beginning to realize what it is to die, to recognize the flat, dull fact of the possibility of
ceasing to be. They're becoming aware of dangers that are greater than personal
dangers; they're learning the nature of the people they will have to fight. They're
learning the meaning of righteous hate.

But I don't know a single man who has gone into the service who hasn't benefited by it—from the one who was too fat or the one who stood all wrong, on through
the ones who had never been on time in their lives, who had never known hardship, the ones who had never had to learn to live on equal terms with other people.

We have to *keep up* with them. We can't afford to sit in the middle of our tight
little circles and stay in our tidy little molds while they are expanding and learning
and growing so fast. . . .

One of the best ways I know for a woman to keep up with her soldier is to read
and read and read—everything she can get her hands on which has anything to
do with what he is doing, with what we are fighting for and with what will come
afterward. Begin with the morning paper and go through every book and magazine
you can find which has bearing on anything that interests him.

Your plans for your life together afterward are important. . . .

There may be even more serious things to consider than the kind of home you
will have. One woman I know, whose husband was in the last war, tells me that when
he came home it took him two or three years to "find himself."

But she was his haven. He clung to her because, in some strange way, he felt
safe with her. He began to see more clearly when he was with her. She realized that
she would have to be a sort of mental balance wheel for him for a time. That she succeeded is proved by the happy and successful life they've had together since.

Whatever happens to her man, the woman who loves him must be ready to
help him solve it and defeat it.

And always she has to come back to the realization that she will be different,
too. It's her job—not his—to see that the changes in both of them do not affect the
fundamental bonds between them. . . .

He wants to come back to those Four Freedoms for which he is fighting. But
he wants to come back to some comfort and ease of mind, too. And what else do
you think he is dreaming of while he is fighting in those far-off places? I know—
now—that a lot of men are dreaming of coming back not only to those girls who

waved good-by to them. They are dreaming of coming back to the mothers of their children! There is warmth and beauty and music, too—and *fun*. The fun he is missing by not being with you. . . .

Your morale is important, you know—to *him*, as well as to yourself. Sometimes if you feel like brooding or slumping mentally, an energetic burst of almost any sort of activity will clear the atmosphere. I don't mean necessarily rushing off to walk five miles or play hard tennis—although that will help. But do something with your hands. Some women like to trim a hat or recover a chair or make a pie. I don't happen to like those things. But I sew or knit like mad. I make pinafores for my friends or I knit for Bob. I've knitted him lots of army sox and I've already made him three post-war sweaters.

But most of all I've listened and listened to what Bob has told me and written me about what men in the service are thinking and what they will want and expect of the women they come back to. And the least we can do as women is try to live up to some of those expectations.

7. Newspaper Columnist Ernie Pyle Depicts the Realities of War for Americans at Home, 1943

The Tunisian campaign was ended. Our air forces moved on farther into Tunisia, to the very edge of the chasm of sea that separated them only so little from Sicily and Sardinia and then from Europe itself. We and the British leaped upon the demolished ports we had captured, cleared out enough wreckage for a foothold for ships, and as the ports grew and grew in usefulness they swarmed with thousands of men, and ships, and trucks. Our combat troops moved back—out of range of enemy strafers—to be cheered and acclaimed momentarily by the cities in the rear, to take a few days of wild and hell-roaring rest, and then to go into an invasion practice that was in every respect, except the one of actually getting shot, as rigorous as a real invasion.

Surely before autumn we of Tunisia would be deep into something new. Most of us realized and admitted to ourselves that horrible days lay ahead. The holocaust that at times seemed so big to us in Tunisia would pale in our memories beside the things we would see and do before another year ran out. . . .

It is hard for you at home to realize what an immense, complicated, sprawling institution a theater of war actually is. As it appears to you in the newspapers, war is a clear-cut matter of landing so many men overseas, moving them from the port to the battlefield, advancing them against the enemy with guns firing, and they win or lose.

To look at war that way is like seeing a trailer of a movie, and saying you've seen the whole picture. I actually don't know what percentage of our troops in Africa were in the battle lines, but I believe it safe to say that only comparatively few ever saw the enemy, ever shot at him, or were shot at by him. All the rest of those hundreds of thousands of men were churning the highways for two thousand

---

From Ernie Pyle, *Here is Your War* (New York: Henry Holt, 1943), pp. 295–299, 304.

miles behind the lines with their endless supply trucks, they were unloading the ships, cooking the meals, pounding the typewriters, fixing the roads, making the maps, repairing the engines, decoding the messages, training the reserves, pondering the plans.

To get all that colossal writhing chaos shaped into something that intermeshed and moved forward with efficiency was a task closely akin to weaving a cloth out of a tubful of spaghetti. . . .

What I have seen in North Africa has altered my own feelings in one respect. There were days when I sat in my tent alone and gloomed with the desperate belief that it was actually possible for us to lose this war. I don't feel that way any more. Despite our strikes and bickering and confusion back home, America is producing and no one can deny that. Even here at the far end of just one line the trickle has grown into an impressive stream. We are producing at home and we are hardening overseas. Apparently it takes a country like America about two years to become wholly at war. We had to go through that transition period of letting loose of life as it was, and then live the new war life so long that it finally became the normal life to us. It was a form of growth, and we couldn't press it. Only time can produce that change. . . . [W]e have about changed our character and become a war nation. I can't yet see when we shall win, or over what route geographically, or by which of the many means of warfare. But no longer do I have any doubts at all that we shall win.

The men over here have changed too. . . .

For a year, everywhere I went, soldiers inevitably asked me two questions: "When do you think we'll get to go home?" and "When will the war be over?" The home-going desire was once so dominant that I believe our soldiers over here would have voted—if the question had been put—to go home immediately, even if it meant peace on terms of something less than unconditional surrender by the enemy.

That isn't true now. Sure, they all still want to go home. So do I. But there is something deeper than that, which didn't exist six months ago. I can't quite put it into words—it isn't any theatrical proclamation that the enemy must be destroyed in the name of freedom; it's just a vague but growing individual acceptance of the bitter fact that we must win the war or else, and that it can't be won by running excursion boats back and forth across the Atlantic carrying homesick vacationers.

A year is a long time to be away from home, especially if a person has never been away before, as was true of the bulk of our troops. At first homesickness can almost kill a man. But time takes care of that. It isn't normal to moon in the past forever. Home gradually grows less vivid; the separation from it less agonizing. There finally comes a day—not suddenly but gradually, as a sunset-touched cloud changes its color—when a man is living almost wholly wherever he is. His life has caught up with his body, and his days become full war days, instead of American days simply transplanted to Africa.

That's the stage our soldiers are in now. . . .

Our men, still thinking of home, are impatient with the strange peoples and customs of the countries they now inhabit. They say that if they ever get home they never want to see another foreign country. But I know how it will be. The day will come when they'll look back and brag about how they learned a little Arabic, and how swell the girls were in England, and how pretty the hills of Germany were. Every day their scope is broadening despite themselves, and once they all get back with their global yarns and their foreign-tinged views, I cannot conceive of our nation ever being isolationist again. The men don't feel very international right now, but the influences are at work and the time will come. . . .

On the day of final peace, the last stroke of what we call the "Big Picture" will be drawn. I haven't written anything about the "Big Picture," because I don't know anything about it. I only know what we see from our worm's-eye view, and our segment of the picture consists only of tired and dirty soldiers who are alive and don't want to die; of long darkened convoys in the middle of the night; of shocked silent men wandering back down the hill from battle; of chow lines and Atabrine tablets and foxholes and burning tanks and Arabs holding up eggs and the rustle of high-flown shells; of jeeps and petrol dumps and smelly bedding rolls and C rations and cactus patches and blown bridges and dead mules and hospital tents and shirt collars greasy-black from months of wearing; and of laughter too, and anger and wine and lovely flowers and constant cussing. All these it is composed of; and of graves and graves and graves.

That is our war, and we will carry it with us as we go on from one battleground to another until it is all over, leaving some of us behind on every beach, in every field. We are just beginning with the ones who lie back of us here in Tunisia. I don't know whether it was their good fortune or their misfortune to get out of it so early in the game. I guess it doesn't make any difference, once a man has gone. Medals and speeches and victories are nothing to them any more. They died and others lived and nobody knows why it is so. They died and thereby the rest of us can go on and on. When we leave here for the next shore, there is nothing we can do for the ones beneath the wooden crosses, except perhaps to pause and murmur, "Thanks, pal."

8. Editor and Publisher Henry Luce Proclaims the "American Century," 1941

In the field of national policy, the fundamental trouble with America has been, and is, that whereas their nation became in the 20th Century the most powerful and the most vital nation in the world, nevertheless Americans were unable to accommodate themselves spiritually and practically to that fact. Hence they have failed to play their part as a world power—a failure which has had disastrous consequences for themselves and for all mankind. And the cure is this: to accept wholeheartedly our duty and our opportunity as the most powerful and vital nation in the world and in consequence to exert upon the world the full impact of our influence, for such purposes as we see fit and by such means as we see fit. . . .

America cannot be responsible for the good behavior of the entire world. But America is responsible, to herself as well as to history, for the world-environment in which she lives. Nothing can so vitally affect America's environment as America's own influence upon it, and therefore if America's environment is unfavorable

From Henry Luce, "The American Century," *Life*, February 17, 1941, pp. 61–65. Copyright © 1941 *Time*, Inc., reprinted with permission.

to the growth of American life, then America has nobody to blame so deeply as she must blame herself. . . .

Consider the 20th Century. It is not only in the sense that we happen to live in it but ours also because it is America's first century as a dominant power in the world. So far, this century of ours has been a profound and tragic disappointment. No other century has been so big with promise for human progress and happiness. And in no one century have so many men and women and children suffered such pain and anguish and bitter death.

It is a baffling and difficult and paradoxical century. No doubt all centuries were paradoxical to those who had to cope with them. But, like everything else, our paradoxes today are bigger and better than ever. Yes, better as well as bigger—inherently better. We have poverty and starvation—but only in the midst of plenty. We have the biggest wars in the midst of the most widespread, the deepest and the most articulate hatred of war in all history. We have tyrannies and dictatorships—but only when democratic idealism, once regarded as the dubious eccentricity of a colonial nation, is the faith of a huge majority of the people of the world. . . .

. . . [A]ny true conception of our world of the 20th Century must surely include a vivid awareness of at least these four propositions.

First: our world of 2,000,000,000 human beings is for the first time in history one world, fundamentally indivisible. Second: modern man hates war and feels intuitively that, in its present scale and frequency, it may even be fatal to his species. Third: our world, again for the first time in human history, is capable of producing all the material needs of the entire human family. Fourth: the world of the 20th Century, if it is to come to life in any nobility of health and vigor, must be to a significant degree an American Century.

As to the first and second: in postulating the indivisibility of the contemporary world, one does not necessarily imagine that anything like a world state—a parliament of men—must be brought about in this century. Nor need we assume that war can be abolished. All that it is necessary to feel—and to feel deeply—is that terrific forces of magnetic attraction and repulsion will operate as between every large group of human beings on this planet. Large sections of the human family may be effectively organized into opposition to each other. Tyrannies may require a large amount of living space. But Freedom requires and will require far greater living space than Tyranny. Peace cannot endure unless it prevails over a very large part of the world. Justice will come near to losing all meaning in the minds of men unless Justice can have approximately the same fundamental meanings in many lands and among many peoples.

As to the third point—the promise of adequate production for all mankind, the "more abundant life"—be it noted that this is characteristically an American promise. It is a promise easily made, here and elsewhere, by demagogues and proponents of all manner of slick schemes and "planned economics." What we must insist on is that the abundant life is predicated on Freedom—on the Freedom which has created its possibility—on a vision of Freedom under Law. Without Freedom, there will be no abundant life. With Freedom, there can be.

And finally there is the belief—shared let us remember by most men living—that the 20th Century must be to a significant degree an American Century. This knowledge calls us to action now. . . .

Once we cease to distract ourselves with lifeless arguments about isolationism, we shall be amazed to discover that there is already an immense American internationalism. American jazz, Hollywood movies, American slang, American machines and patented products, are in fact the only things that every community in the world, from Zanzibar to Hamburg, recognizes in common. Blindly, unintentionally, accidentally and really in spite of ourselves, we are already a world power in all the trivial ways—in very human ways. But there is a great deal more than that. America is already the intellectual, scientific and artistic capital of the world. Americans— Midwestern Americans—are today the least provincial people in the world. They have traveled the most and they know more about the world than the people of any other country. America's worldwide experience in commerce is also far greater than most of us realize.

Most important of all, we have that indefinable, unmistakable sign of leadership: prestige. And unlike the prestige of Rome or Genghis Khan or 19th Century England, American prestige throughout the world is faith in the good intentions as well as in the ultimate intelligence and ultimate strength of the whole American people. We have lost some of that prestige in the last few years. But most of it is still there. . . .

As America enters dynamically upon the world scene, we need most of all to seek and to bring forth a vision of America as a world power which is authentically American and which can inspire us to live and work and fight with vigor and enthusiasm. And as we come now to the great test, it may yet turn out that in all our trials and tribulations of spirit during the first part of this century we as a people have been painfully apprehending the meaning of our time and now in this moment of testing there may come clear at last the vision which will guide us to the authentic creation of the 20th Century—our Century. . . .

First, the economic. It is for America and for America alone to determine whether a system of free economic enterprise—an economic order compatible with freedom and progress—shall or shall not prevail in this century. We know perfectly well that there is not the slightest chance of anything faintly resembling a free economic system prevailing in this country if it prevails nowhere else. What then does America have to decide? Some few decisions are quite simple. For example: we have to decide whether or not we shall have for ourselves and our friends freedom of the seas—the right to go with our ships and our ocean-going airplanes where we wish, when we wish and as we wish. The vision of America as the principal guarantor of the freedom of the seas, the vision of America as the dynamic leader of world trade, has within it the possibilities of such enormous human progress as to stagger the imagination. Let us not be staggered by it. Let us rise to its tremendous possibilities. Our thinking of world trade today is on ridiculously small terms. For example, we think of Asia as being worth only a few hundred millions a year to us. Actually, in the decades to come Asia will be worth to us exactly zero—or else it will be worth to us four, five, ten billions of dollars a year. And the latter are the terms we must think in, or else confess a pitiful impotence.

Closely akin to the purely economic area and yet quite different from it, there is the picture of an America which will send out through the world its technical and artistic skills. Engineers, scientists, doctors, movie men, makers of entertainment, developers of airlines, builders of roads, teachers, educators. Throughout the world, these skills, this training, this leadership is needed and will be eagerly welcomed, if only we have the imagination to see it and the sincerity and good will to create the world of the 20th Century.

But now there is a third thing which our vision must immediately be concerned with. We must undertake now to be the Good Samaritan of the entire world. It is the manifest duty of this country to undertake to feed all the people of the world who as a result of this worldwide collapse of civilization are hungry and destitute—all of them, that is, whom we can from time to time reach consistently with a very tough attitude toward all hostile governments. For every dollar we spend on armaments, we should spend at least a dime in a gigantic effort to feed the world—and all the world should know that we have dedicated ourselves to this task. Every farmer in America should be encouraged to produce all the crops he can, and all that we cannot eat—and perhaps some of us could eat less—should forthwith be dispatched to the four quarters of the globe as a free gift, administered by a humanitarian army of Americans, to every man, woman and child on this earth who is really hungry.

But all this is not enough: All this will fail and none of it will happen unless our vision of America as a world power includes a passionate devotion to great American ideals. We have some things in this country which are infinitely precious and especially American—a love of freedom, a feeling for the equality of opportunity, a tradition of self-reliance and independence and also of co-operation. In addition to ideals and notions which are especially American, we are the inheritors of all the great principles of Western civilization—above all Justice, the love of Truth, the ideal of Charity. The other day Herbert Hoover said that America was fast becoming the sanctuary of the ideals of civilization. For the moment it may be enough to be the sanctuary of these ideals. But not for long. It now becomes our time to be the powerhouse from which the ideals spread throughout the world and do their mysterious work of lifting the life of mankind from the level of the beasts to what the Psalmist called a little lower than the angels.

America as the dynamic center of ever-widening spheres of enterprise, America as the training center of the skillful servants of mankind, America as the Good Samaritan, really believing again that it is more blessed to give than to receive, and America as the powerhouse of the ideals of Freedom and Justice—out of these elements surely can be fashioned a vision of the 20th Century to which we can and will devote ourselves in joy and gladness and vigor and enthusiasm.

Other nations can survive simply because they have endured so long—sometimes with more and sometimes with less significance. But this nation, conceived in adventure and dedicated to the progress of man—this nation cannot truly endure unless there courses strongly through its veins from Maine to California the blood of purposes and enterprise and high resolve.

Throughout the 17th Century and the 18th Century and the 19th Century, this continent teemed with manifold projects and magnificent purposes. Above them all and weaving them all together into the most exciting flag of all the world and of all history was the triumphal purpose of freedom.

It is in this spirit that all of us are called, each to his own measure of capacity, and each in the widest horizon of his vision, to create the first great American Century.

9. Betty Grable Becomes a Favorite "Pin-up Girl" Among Soldiers, 1943

Betty Grable, the "pin-up girl" with the "million-dollar legs," actively participated in the war effort, appearing across the country at war bond rallies and volunteering at the Hollywood Canteen.

An officer uses a Grable pin-up to instruct American troops in
map reading.

10. Photographer Alfred Eisenstadt Captures the American Spirit of Victory, August 14, 1945

As thousands jam the streets of New York City, a sailor kisses a nurse to celebrate VJ Day on August 14, 1945.

From *Life*, August 27, 1945, Volume 19, number 9, page 27. Alfred Eisenstadt/Timepix.

⊕ E S S A Y S

Most historians agree that World War II brought dramatic changes to American society and culture. The war itself involved real bodies of men and women. How people thought about those bodies, how they used them to represent positive and negative ideals, is one area of research for historians. Both of the following essays focus on the use and representation of women's bodies. In the first essay, Robert Westbrook of the University of Rochester, an influential intellectual and cultural historian, looks at the phenomenon of pin-ups. Westbrook argues that pin-ups of women like Betty Grable were less about lust and sex than they were icons through which men expressed their political obligations. In the second essay, historian Leisa D. Meyer, who teaches at the College of William and Mary, examines the constructions of gender and sexual identities, specifically focusing on the creation of the "female soldier." Both essays deal with the idea that part of the visual and written rhetoric of the war era concentrated on the issue of men's protection of women.

The "Pin-up Girls" Taught Americans Less About Sex and More About Political Obligations

ROBERT B. WESTBROOK

..., I would like to explain my interest in pin-ups, for the source of that interest is not what one might expect. I started thinking about pin-ups in the context of a study on the way in which political obligation was conceived in America during World War II. This study is an effort to see whether the conclusion of a number of political philosophers that liberal theory lacks a coherent conception of political obligation (a conclusion I find persuasive) is reflected empirically in the political culture of a liberal polity like that of the United States. My aim is to identify the philosophy of obligation at work in American practices and institutions and to highlight its distinctive features by means of a case study of a moment when Americans had reason to be more explicit than usual about such matters.

My working hypothesis (consistent with the expectations derived from political theory) is that, with some exceptions, Americans during World War II were not called upon to conceive of their obligation to participate in the war effort as a *political* obligation to work, fight, or die for their country. By and large, the representatives of the state and other American propagandists relied on two different moral arguments, neither of which constituted a claim of political obligation. First, they appealed to putatively universal moral values—such as those enumerated in the Atlantic Charter or Franklin Roosevelt's "Four Freedoms" speech—values such as "freedom," "equality," and "democracy" transcending obligations to the United States as a particular political community. Second, and more interestingly, they implored Americans as individuals and as families to join the war effort in order to protect the state that protected them, an appeal, philosophers have argued,

From Robert B. Westbrook, " 'I Want a Girl, Just Like the Girl That Married Harry James': American Women and the Problem of Political Obligation in World War II," *American Quarterly* 42, no. 4 (December 1990): 588–592, 595–596, 598–603, 605–607, 611. © The American Studies Association. Reprinted with permission of the Johns Hopkins University Press.

characteristic of liberal states and one that, at bottom, is an appeal to go to war to defend *private* interests and discharge *private* obligations. Over the course of the war, this latter sort of prescription became increasingly prominent, and the more elusive evidence of the felt obligations of Americans suggests that it was this sort of appeal that was most compelling for them and coincided most often with their own notions of "what we are fighting for."

One important body of evidence supporting this hypothesis is what might be termed the cultural construction of women as objects of obligation. This process is one I want to analyze here, examining principally the fabrication by communication elites of women as prescribed icons of male obligation. I also will suggest the ways in which women functioned as such for soldiers and the manner in which women themselves participated in their mobilization as a private interest for which men would fight. My focus will be on the pin-up, one of the most prominent documents in the material culture of World War II and, in particular, on the image of the most popular of the movie stars who found their way onto the walls of barracks from the Aleutians to North Africa: Betty Grable (hence my title).

Liberal Obligations

Before I turn to pin-ups, more should be said about the theoretical concerns that lie behind this effort to offer something other than the obvious reading of these documents—an attempt to see them as part of the wartime discourse on obligation without gainsaying their place in the story of the exploitation of women and their bodies in American mass culture. Wartime pin-ups can tell us much about liberal political theory, as well as much about sexual politics. Or, to be more precise, they can tell us something about the ways in which the American state attempted to draw on the moral obligations prescribed by prevailing gender roles to solve the problem of obligation posed by liberal ideology.

Arguing from a variety of perspectives, a number of philosophers have offered a powerful critique of the efforts of the giants of the liberal philosophical tradition from Thomas Hobbes to John Rawls to provide an adequate basis for political obligation and have concluded, as Carole Pateman puts it, that "political obligation in the liberal democratic state constitutes an insoluble problem; insoluble because political obligation cannot be given expression within the context of liberal democratic institutions." This critique of the liberal theory of political obligation has advanced on at least two fronts. On the one hand, philosophers such as John Simmons have used the tools of analytic philosophy to demonstrate that the traditional foundations of the liberal theory of political obligation—the notion of "tacit consent" and the claim that citizens are obligated to a liberal state because of the benefits they receive from it—cannot provide an adequate account of or justification for political obligation. On the other hand, communitarian critics of liberalism such as Michael Walzer have slighted these difficulties in favor of raising doubts about whether liberal theorists can be said to have ever advanced an account of *public* obligation, that is, obligation to a political community. It is this latter critique that is most pertinent to discussing the construction of women as icons of obligation.

In an essay entitled "The Obligation to Die for the State," Walzer addresses the problem of obligation in the context of war and asks whether the obligation citizens have to the state can be made the motive for risking their lives. The answer to this question, he suggests, depends in critical respects on the nature of the state, and, in the case of the liberal state, the answer is no. The reason, he argues, is that the end of the liberal state—as conceived in the social contract tradition of Hobbes, Locke, and their successors—is the security of the lives of the individuals who form it. Consequently, "a man who dies for the state defeats his only purpose in forming the state: death is the contradiction of politics. A man who risks his life for the state accepts the insecurity which it was the only end of his political obedience to avoid: war is the failure of politics. Hence there can be no political obligation either to die or to fight."

When a war begins, political authorities in a liberal society invite their sub-jects, as Hobbes put it, to "protect their protection"—an admission on their part of a failure to hold up their end of the bargain on which the state rests. Peculiar in any case as a call to men and women to risk their lives for their instrument, the invita-tion is doubly peculiar as one to defend an instrument that has failed its function. As Walzer says, when individuals "protect their protection they are doing nothing more than defending themselves, and so they cannot protect their protection after their protection ceases to protect them. At that point, it ceases to be their pro-tection. The state has no value over and above the value of the lives of the concrete individuals whose safety it provides. No man has a common life to defend, but only an individual life."

Walzer goes on to link more closely this problem that liberalism has with the "ultimate obligation" to its individualism and largely negative conception of liberty—which make for a conception of the citizen as an individual whom the state protects from interference by other individuals or by the state itself. This lib-eral view suggests "an indefinite number of distinct and singular relations between the individual citizens and the authorities as a body—a pattern that might best be symbolized by a series of vertical lines. There are no horizontal connections among citizens as citizens." The state is conceived "as an instrument which serves individual men (or families) but not or not necessarily as an instrument wielded by these men themselves" as constituents of a political community. Walzer concludes that any theory like liberalism which "begins with the absolute independence of freely willing individuals and goes on to treat politics and the state as instrumental to the achievement of individual purposes would seem by its very nature incapable of describing ultimate obligation."

It is very important to add, as Walzer does, that this difficulty in liberal theory does not mean that the citizens of a liberal state will not go to war and fight and die on behalf of ethical, if not political, obligations. As he says:

> Moved by love, sympathy, or friendship, men in liberal society can and obviously do incur ultimate obligations. They may even find themselves in situations where they are or think they are obliged to defend the state which defends in turn the property and enjoyment of their friends and families. But if they then actually risk their lives or die, they do so because they have incurred private obligations which have nothing to do with politics. The state may shape the environment within which these obligations are freely incurred, and it may provide the occasions and the means for their fulfillment. But this is only to say that, when states make war and men fight, the reasons of the two often are and ought to be profoundly different.

This argument leads one to expect that liberal states, bereft of a compelling argument for political obligation, will attempt to exploit private obligations in order to convince its citizens to serve its defense. Indeed, it was precisely these sorts of private obligations—to families, to children, to parents, to buddies, and generally, to an "American Way of Life" defined as a rich (and richly commodified) private experience—that formed a crucial element in the campaign to mobilize Americans for World War II. Yet few private obligations were more apparent in pronouncements about "why we fight" than those binding men and women.

Pin-Ups as Moral Arguments

Three years before American entry into the war, a team of copywriters drew up a recruiting advertisement to show what wartime enlistment propaganda might look like. . . . Though the most apparent feature of this ad is its racism—its call to white Americans to prevent "yellow feet" from ever reaching American soil—it is also a document that anticipates the privatization of obligation in World War II propaganda. Men are urged here to enlist in order to discharge a private (the "'other fellow' won't stop them") obligation to the women they, as individuals, protect ("*your* sister, *your* wife, *your* sweetheart"). This sort of appeal distinguishes this ad from other instances of the prominent genre of Allied "rape propaganda" of which it is a part. Often in such propaganda women are portrayed simply as the booty of war . . . , and the appeal is to men to protect their property in women's bodies from enemy male competitors. In the "*Your* Sister" ad, however, a more complex bond of obligation is said to tie American men to the women of their society. The copy suggests that the rights American men claim to "their" women's bodies are linked to a set of corresponding obligations; the threat of the "yellow hand of lust" is here less that of the expropriation of the bounty of their own lust than the rupturing of a moral relationship between themselves and the women in their lives. It also indicates that this relationship extends to their sisters and to other women to whom they have no proprietary sexual claim. When American soldiers said, as they often did, that it was American women that they were "fighting for," they sometimes, to be sure, were identifying women as the spoils of war, but more often "for" meant "for whom" or "on behalf of." They were articulating the moral obligations of the "protector" to the "protected," a relationship ethically problematic in its own right but nonetheless different from that of a man to a woman viewed simply as sexual property.

A similar argument is implicit in one of the ubiquitous visual components of the cultural landscape of the war: the pin-up. Unlike the "naughty postcard" that American troops brought back from France in World War I, the pin-up circulated above ground in World War II, and the Hollywood pin-up did so with official sanction. Despite the concerns of religious groups and some officials about the immorality of pin-ups, the United States government and the film industry cooperated closely during the war in the production and distribution of millions of photographs of Hollywood's leading ladies and rising starlets, and these pictures decorated the walls of barracks, the bulkheads of ships, and the fuselages of planes on all fronts. I suspect that many historians whose fathers fought in the war might find evidence in family archives of the avidity with which soldiers collected pin-ups. . . .

Obviously, pin-ups functioned as surrogate objects of sexual desire for soldiers far from home, and I do not mean to discount this. Soldiers viewed them as such, and some complained that the pin-ups in semi-official publications like *Yank* were too tame. "I know you want to keep it clean," wrote one private to *Yank,* "but after all the boys are interested in sex, and *Esquire* and a few other magazines give us sex and still get by the mail, so why can't *Yank*?" They reacted bitterly to charges that pin-ups were immoral and to the threat of censorship. "Maybe if some of those 'panty waists' had to be stuck out some place where there are no white women and few native women for a year and a half, as we were," wrote some GIs in Alaska, "they would appreciate even a picture of our gals back home."

American military officials linked the aggressiveness of the effective soldier with healthy, heterosexual desire and worried about sustaining such desire and thwarting homosexuality. Thus, it is plausible, as John D'Emilio and Estelle Freedman have said, that pin-ups were intended by the government to "encourage heterosexual fantasy in the sex-segregated military." Concerned also about epidemics of venereal disease, the government sought to provide activities in which sexual desire could be sublimated and even endorsed a measure of "autoeroticism," provided it did not become "habit-forming."

However, pin-ups were more than masturbatory aides. They also functioned as icons of the private interests and obligations for which soldiers were fighting. Several pieces of evidence suggest this point. First of all, many pin-ups were, as the complaints of some soldiers indicate, relatively demure. As Paul Fussell has said, they were hardly "triggers of lust," which is, in part, attributable to censorship; the War Department and Hollywood were only willing to go so far. Yet to attribute the limited erotic charge of pin-ups to censorship alone fails to explain why some of the most popular pin-ups were not those that flirted with the limits imposed by the censors. Above all, it fails to account for the appeal of far-and-away the most sought-after pin-up—that of Betty Grable [see Document 9]—for which, at one point, there were twenty thousand requests per week and which, by war's end, had been put in the hands of five million servicemen. This pin-up was modest compared with others like that of runner-up Rita Hayworth . . . , suggesting that Grable and many of the other most popular pin-up models were viewed not only as objects of sexual fantasy but also as representative women, standing in for wives and sweethearts on the homefront. . . .

Betty Grable's appeal, in particular, was less as an erotic "sex goddess" than as a symbol of the kind of woman for whom American men—especially American working-class men—were fighting. She was the sort of girl a man could prize. Her image, carefully cultivated by the star-making machinery of Twentieth Century Fox, was "straight-arrow, chintz-table-cloth." Darryl Zanuck, the head of the studio, correctly guessed that Grable would appeal to soldiers, and he featured her in a series of Technicolor musicals that highlighted her "pastel charms." In her movies, Grable repeatedly portrayed a young woman tempted by "flash" but, in the end, claimed for gentility. In *Pin-Up Girl* (1944), for example, she played Laurie Jones, a local pin-up girl popular with the soldiers at the USO Club in Missoula, Missouri, who is possessed of a vivid imagination and a weakness for the white lie. After moving to Washington to take up a job as a government stenographer, Laurie attempts to win the heart of Guadalcanal hero Tommy Dooley by pretending that she is glamorous showgirl "Laura Lorraine" only to discover that what Tommy really wants and needs is a girl like the real Laurie Jones: "sincere, honest, with both feet on the ground." In the film's finale, she reveals that Laurie Jones and Laura Lorraine are one and the same woman and accepts herself as she is: a level-headed small-town girl who happens to know her way around an elaborate production number.

This reading of Grable's appeal is not to deny a sexual dimension to her popularity. It is rather to situate her sexuality within a configuration of attributes that established her as a principal icon of obligation. Grable's sexiness was, as condescending middlebrow critics often sneered, "of the common sort"—and this was a key to her success. . . . If we place Grable's image within the context of the discourse of obligation as well as that of soft-core pornography, we can explain how it flourished despite bucking what André Bazin perceived as a drift of the gaze of American men during the war from the leg to the breast. By these lights, Grable's standing as the premier pin-up girl is inexplicable given that her legs were said to be her most striking attribute. Of course, Bazin might have been wrong, and Grable's popularity, compared to Rita Hayworth and Jane Russell, merely might indicate that "leg-men" still outnumbered "breast-men" during the war. Yet this conclusion, I think, is too simple. Even Grable's legs were celebrated less for their exceptional beauty than for their approximation to the "average." As *Life* reported, Grable's legs—"her private trademark"—were celebrated not as extraordinary but as "the Great American Average Legs: straight, perfectly rounded and shaped, but withal judged by the same standards as millions of others."

Finally, one must not forget that the war in the Pacific was a race war, and Grable's obvious "whiteness" gave her an advantage over competitors such as Hayworth (née Margarita Cansino) in the eyes of white soldiers waging a brutal struggle against a racial enemy in a setting in which, as they often complained, white women—especially women as white as Grable—were in short supply. . . . As *Time* reported, soldiers preferred Grable to other pin-ups "in direct ratio to their remoteness from civilization." Here again, in a nation still firmly in the grip of white supremacy, Betty Grable provided the superior image of American womanhood.

Packaged as the serviceman's favorite, Grable quickly caught on as such. No one received more fan mail from soldiers, and by the end of the war she was the most popular star in Hollywood, earning the largest salary of any woman in America. . . . "In her time," as Jane Gaines has said, Grable was "model girlfriend, wife, and finally mother." Indeed, her popularity *increased* after she married bandleader Harry James in 1943 and had a child later that year. She fared as well, if not better, as "pin-up mamma" as she had as pin-up girl.

Perhaps the most striking evidence of the way pin-ups functioned as wartime discourse about obligation is the way soldiers plastered the image of Grable and others to the machines of war, where they competed with and upstaged the insignias of the state. . . . As John Costello observes, "by 1945 there was hardly a tank or a plane in the U.S. military that was not adorned with its own painted icon of femininity as a good-luck talisman that also showed the enemy what it was that red-blooded Americans 'were fighting for.'" This practice was not just a matter of naming planes after girls (or of comparing girls to planes) but of removing the obfuscating veil of arguments for a soldier's obligation to die for the liberal state in order to reveal (nakedly) the private obligations upon which such states ultimately relied.

In suggesting that there was more to pin-ups than sexual exploitation and that pin-ups advanced a tacit moral argument, I do not mean to endorse the substance of that argument, for it is a troubling one. As Judith Hicks Stiehm has observed in an acute discussion of the disquieting features of the asymmetrical relationship between "protectors" and "protected," at the heart of this argument is the assignment of women to the role of the protected simply by virtue of their gender. Moreover, this argument has some disturbing effects on male protectors.

Men, who have a monopoly on the use of violent power, find their identity bound up with the effectiveness of the protection they provide to their dependents. Hence, they may tend to "overprotect" them, and, even more disturbing, "there is a tendency for the protector to become a predator" who turns on his dependents, especially when things go badly.

> When there is no real work or duty required of a protector the role is satisfying, it makes one proud. As role demands increase, and/or as the chances of fulfilling the role decrease, the practice of the role becomes less and less attractive. The protected become a nuisance, a burden, and finally a shame, for an unprotected protectee is the clearest possible evidence of a protector's failure. . . . As one gains ascendancy one gains dependents, as one gains dependents their requirements for protection increase. . . . Thus the most wholly dependent protectees may be just the ones most likely to trigger a nihilistic impulse in their protector.

The dynamic that Stiehm describes may help explain the misogynistic, often violently misogynistic, character of much of the literature produced by soldiers, which such critics as Susan Gubar have analyzed. Though pin-ups are not the best documents through which to explore this dynamic, there is a hint of it in the use of a Grable pin-up to instruct troops in map reading. . . . This device was said to be an aid to concentration, but it is difficult not to view it also as a "targeting" of Grable's anatomy, in which case Grable's image proved eminently adaptable to an expression of the darker side of the pressing obligations connecting men and women during the war [see Document 9].

Reciprocity

Though male soldiers were the principal collectors of pin-ups, the pin-up girl also addressed herself to American women, suggesting that, if men were obliged to fight for their pin-up girls, women were in turn obliged to fashion themselves into pin-up girls worth fighting for. Pin-ups, that is, argued for a reciprocity of obligation. Amidst a call to women to do their part by taking up (for the duration) the jobs that men had left behind, there was a simultaneous appeal to them to discharge an obligation to be the sort of women their men would be proud to protect. . . .

Here too Betty Grable was an important figure. She was admired by women as well as men. Her rise to box-office champion during the war was due as much to the women who flocked to her movies as to the soldiers who pinned her up overseas. "Girls can see me in a picture," she said, "and feel I could be one of them." During the war, she was offered to women—especially working-class women—as a model of female virtue on the homefront. . . . Young working-class women avidly followed Grable's career in the fan magazines where her domestic life, as they portrayed it, was held up as an example to readers. As Gaines says, "even though Grable was making a six-figure yearly salary, in the fan magazines she was still the little family budget-keeper, living within her million-dollar means and outfitting the ranch house with bargains from the Sears catalogue." Above all, it was Grable's self-effacing modesty that recommended her to women. . . .

It is important, of course, to try to figure out the extent to which the obligation of American women to be pin-ups men would die for was felt as well as prescribed, but it is much more difficult to find evidence on this score. Here I can only say that what evidence I have been able to gather thus far suggests that it was an obligation that many women took to heart. American soldiers marched into battle with pin-ups of not only Betty Grable but also of their own wives and girlfriends. Grable both explicitly and by example urged women who thought they looked good in a bathing suit to send a snapshot to servicemen, and many heeded her advice. . . .

Living Theory

Occasionally, citizens recognize that political theory is something more than the labor of those specialists called political theorists and come to realize that, in their everyday experience as citizens they are *living* theory. One of those occasions on which they become aware of this is when their nation goes to war. Reflecting then on the problems of political obligation, they ask themselves why they are obliged not only to obey the laws of their state but why they (or their loved ones) are obliged to risk their lives to defend that state. The representatives of the state supply them with answers to these questions that best serve their purposes, and citizens often accept these answers, which accord with their own sense of where their obligations lie, a sense developed within the confines of a particular political culture.

Because of the thinness of public life in a liberal political culture like that of the United States, modern American statesmen and their allies have found it difficult to call upon their fellow citizens *as citizens* to defend their nation in time of war. Though given to justify wars on behalf of principles transcending the values of any particular political community, they also have relied heavily on appeals to private (which is not to say selfish) obligations in order to legitimate the sacrifices of war, including the moral commitments believed to exist between men and women. These arguments are sometimes explicit; often they are not. As living theory, they can be found in some unexpected places, even in pin-ups.

Given the centrality of the mutual obligations, both prescribed and felt, between men and women to American mobilization in World War II, it is not surprising that pin-ups were sanctioned by the state. Nor is it surprising that the photograph that has come to signify the end of American participation in the war is one portraying the consummation of the bargain between protector and protected [see Document 10]. Here in Times Square in August 1945, *Life* photographer Alfred Eisenstadt captured a protector exacting his reward from a woman he grabbed on the street, a representative of the protected who happened to be close at hand. Apparently this sailor shared the conviction of fellow soldiers in New Guinea who, earlier in the war, had remarked that "we are not only fighting for the Four Freedoms, we are fighting also for the priceless privilege of making love to American women." Having helped win that fight, the sailor and other soldiers returned home to reap the rewards they believed were their due. If I am right about the character of American discourse concerning obligation during World War II, it is fitting to mark the end of the "Good War" with a representative kiss, manifesting in its mix of joy and violence the ambiguities of the moral contract binding protective men and protected women in a liberal state.

Creating GI Jane

LEISA D. MEYER

Several years after World War II ended, a journalist summed up the difficulties the Women's Army Corps encountered in recruiting women by observing:

> Of the problems that the WAC has, the greatest one is the problem of morals . . . of convincing mothers, fathers, brothers, Congressmen, servicemen and junior officers that women really can be military without being camp followers or without being converted into rough, tough gals who can cuss out the chow as well as any dogface. . . .

The sexual stereotypes of servicewomen as "camp followers" or "mannish women," prostitutes or lesbians, had a long history both in the construction of notions of femaleness in general and in the relationship of "woman" and "soldier" in particular. Historically, women had been most visibly associated with the military as prostitutes and crossdressers. The challenge before women and men who wanted to promote "women" as "soldiers" during World War II was how to create a new category which proclaimed female soldiers as both sexually respectable and feminine. The response of Oveta Culp Hobby, the Women's Army Corps director, to this challenge was to characterize female soldiers as chaste and asexual; such a presentation would not threaten conventional sexual norms. Clashing public perceptions of servicewomen and internal struggles within the U.S. Army over the proper portrayal and treatment of military women were the crucibles in which this new category was created. Such struggles profoundly shaped the daily lives of women in the Women's Army Auxiliary Corps (WAAC) and the Women's Army Corps (WAC) and framed the notorious lesbian witchhunts of the mid- to late-forties. . . .

The entrance of some women into the army paralleled the movement of other women into nontraditional jobs in the civilian labor force as the need for full utilization of all resources during World War II brought large numbers of white, married women into the labor force for the first time and created opportunities for many women and people of color in jobs historically denied them. Women's service in the armed forces was especially threatening, however, because of the military's function as the ultimate test of "masculinity."

The definition of the military as a masculine institution and the definition of a soldier as a "man with a gun who engages in combat" both excluded women. . . .

From Leisa D. Meyer, "Creating G.I. Jane: The Regulation of Sexuality and Sexual Behavior in the Women's Army Corps During World War II," originally published in *Feminist Studies* 18, no. 3 (Fall 1992): 581–601, by permission of the publisher, *Feminist Studies,* Inc.

Thus, the establishment of the WAAC in May 1942, marking women's formal entrance into this preeminently masculine domain, generated heated public debate. It heightened the fears already generated by the entry of massive numbers of women in the civilian labor force and by the less restrictive sexual mores of a wartime environment. . . .

In a culture increasingly anxious about women's sexuality in general, and homosexuality in particular, the formation of the WAAC, a women-only environment within an otherwise wholly male institution, sparked a storm of public speculation as to the potential breakdown of heterosexual norms and sexual morality which might result. Not surprisingly, these concerns focused on the potentially "masculinizing" effect the army might have on women and especially on the disruptive influence the WAAC would have on sexual standards. Public fears were articulated in numerous editorials and stories in newspapers and journals, as well as in thousands of letters to the War Department and the newly formed WAAC Headquarters in Washington, D.C. . . . Among other allegations, the public expressed fear that, in forming the WAAC, the military was trying to create an organized cadre of prostitutes to service male GI's. . . .

. . . Many civilians as well as some elements of the mainstream media characterized Waacs as sexual actors who engaged in the same type of promiscuity, drunkenness, and sexual adventure condoned in male GI's. Although explicit references to female homosexuality in the WAAC were seldom made in the mainstream press, reports of rumors submitted to WAAC Headquarters by recruiting officers in the field demonstrated that public concern with lesbianism was also pervasive. . . . Thus, "masculinization" implied both women's potential power over men and their sexual independence from them, a threat to gender and sexual norms. . . .

The army's response to this negative publicity was orchestrated by Col. Hobby. She organized this response around the need to assure an anxious public that servicewomen had not lost their "femininity." Hobby's definition of "femininity" was rooted in the Victorian linkage between sexual respectability and female passionlessness. As a result she characterized the woman soldier as chaste, asexual, and essentially middle-class. . . . She characterized the WAAC/WAC as acting *in loco parentis,* as a guardian of young women's welfare and morals. And to demonstrate that the WAAC/WAC attracted "better-quality" women, Hobby emphasized the greater educational requirements mandated for women compared with their male counterparts, illustrated by the high ratio of women with college degrees. . . .

. . . In responding to fears that the military would make women "mannish" or would provide a haven for women who were "naturally" that way, for instance, some army propaganda highlighted the femininity of WAAC/WAC recruits and stressed their sexual attractiveness to men. These articles assured an anxious public that "soldiering hasn't transformed these Wacs into Amazons—far from it. They have retained their femininity." Presenting women in civilian life in the period as sexually attractive to men did not necessarily imply that they were sexually available. . . .

The framework created by Hobby and disseminated in military propaganda efforts was occasionally undercut by the conflicting responses to the question of whether Waacs/Wacs should be treated and utilized as "soldiers" or as "women." On several occasions the male army hierarchy, much to Hobby's dismay, attempted to treat the regulation and control of women's sexuality and sexual behavior in the same manner as that of male soldiers. The army's approach to the issue of sexual regulation and control for men stressed health and combat readiness among troops, not morality. In fact, the army expected and encouraged heterosexual activity among male soldiers and controlled male sexuality with regulations prohibiting sodomy and addressing the prevention and treatment of venereal disease, as well as more informal mechanisms upholding prohibitions on interracial relationships. The male military hierarchy's desire for uniformity collided with the female WAAC director's firm belief in different moral standards for women and her insistence that this difference be reflected in army regulations. This struggle was clearly represented in the army's battle to fight the spread of venereal disease within its ranks.

Hobby believed the army's venereal disease program for men, premised on the assumption of heterosexual activity, would seriously damage the reputation of the corps if applied to women and would undermine her efforts to present Waacs as sexless, not sexual. Her strategy of moral suasion clashed with the U.S. surgeon general's efforts to institute a system of chemical prophylaxis in the women's corps. The surgeon general's plan for control of venereal disease in the WAAC included a full course of instruction in sex education and the distribution of condoms in slot machines placed in latrines so that even "modest" servicewomen might have access to them. This program was completely rejected by Hobby. She argued that even proposing such measures placed civilian and military acceptance of the WAAC in jeopardy. She pointed to public fears of women's military service and accusations of immorality already present as evidence that the course proposed by the surgeon general would result in catastrophic damage to the reputation of the WAAC and seriously hamper her efforts to recruit women to the corps.

Her concern was not with venereal disease per se, but rather with creating an aura of respectability around the WAAC. Her victory in this struggle resulted in the development of a social hygiene pamphlet and course which stressed the "high standards" of moral conduct (i.e., chastity) necessary for members of the corps and the potential damage one woman could do through her misbehavior or immoral conduct. The pamphlet, distributed to all WAAC officers, discussed venereal disease only in reference to the "frightful effects" of the disease on women and children, the difficulties in detection and treatment, and the ineffectiveness of all prophylactic methods for women. Hobby supported combining this policy with the maintenance of strict enlistment standards. She believed that if the corps accepted only "high types of women," no control measures would be necessary.

. . . Although her goals were to build and repair the reputation of the WAAC, as well as to protect individual women from potential sexual exploitation, her methods—withholding information and highlighting the dangers of heterosexual activity for women—served to institutionalize differential expectations and consequences for the behavior of female and male GI's. Waacs, for example, could be discharged for "illicit sexual activity," but such behavior was expected and often encouraged in male soldiers. Thus, Hobby's policies firmly reinforced the sexual double standard.

Hobby's fears of the adverse public reaction that might result from the distribution of prophylactics information and equipment to Waacs were confirmed by the slander campaign against the WAAC/WAC which started in mid-1943 and continued through early 1944. This "whispering campaign" began with the publication of a nationally syndicated article which reported that in a secret agreement between the War Department and the WAAC, contraceptives would be issued to all women in the army. This piece provoked a storm of public outcry and marked the resurgence of accusations of widespread sexual immorality in the women's corps.

Subsequent army investigations showed that most rumors about the WAAC/WAC originated with male servicemen and officers. Telling "slanderous" stories about the WAAC/WAC was one expression of the resentment men felt at women's entrance into a previously male-only preserve. These attitudes also indicated the confusion present on the command level and among rank-and-file enlisted personnel as to the purpose and function of a women's corps. Was the mission of the women's corps a military one or was the WAAC created to help "improve male morale"? Was a servicewoman's primary function as a soldier, supporting her comrades in arms, or as a woman boosting sagging male spirits and providing feminine companionship for the lonely? A number of servicemen answered these questions by writing home advising girlfriends and family members against joining the women's corps, both because of the "bad reputation" of its members and the belief of some GI's that the WAAC was created solely to "serve" male soldiers sexually. . . .

. . . Although "morale boosting" did not necessarily imply prostitution or sexual service, the two were often linked in the public consciousness. For example, one army investigator reported that in Kansas City, Kansas, it was believed that "Waacs were issued condoms and enrolled solely for the soldier's entertainment, serving as 'morale builders' for the men and nothing more." Hobby worked to eliminate all references to Waacs/Wacs being used for "morale purposes," believing that these bolstered public concerns with heterosexual immorality in the corps.

In addition, the occasional use of WAAC/WAC units to control male sexuality seemed to confirm suspicions that the role the army envisioned for women was sexual. For example, African American WAAC/WAC units were in general stationed only at posts where there were Black male soldiers present. In part this was a product of the army's policy of segregating its troops by race. However, white officers, particularly at southern posts, also explicitly referred to the "beneficial" presence of African American WAAC/WAC units as a way to insure that Black male troops would not form liaisons with white women in the surrounding communities. Thus, in this instance, African American WAAC/WAC units were used by the army as a means of upholding and supporting prohibitions on interracial relationships. . . .

The army's negotiation between anxieties about assertive female sexuality, whether heterosexual or homosexual, and the realities of servicewomen's sexual vulnerability to abuse by male GI's and officers can be seen by examining the army's efforts to control the sexuality of servicewomen in the Southwest Pacific Area. Upon arrival in Port Moresby, New Guinea, in May 1944, Wacs found their lives unexpectedly restricted. The theater headquarters directed that in view of the great number of white male troops in the area, "some of whom allegedly had not seen a nurse or other white woman in 18 months," Wacs should be locked within their barbed wire compound at all times except when escorted by armed guards to work or to approved group recreation. No leaves, passes, or one-couple dates were allowed at any time. Many Wacs found these restrictions unbearable and patronizing and complained that they were being treated as criminals and children. The mounting complaints from women at WAC Headquarters and rumors of plummeting morale moved Hobby to protest to the War Department and ask for a discontinuation of what many Wacs referred to as the "concentration camp system." The War Department responded that it was in no position to protest command policies, especially because the theater authorities insisted that the system was required "to prevent rape of Wacs by Negro troops in New Guinea." Societal stereotypes of African American men, in particular, as rapists, and of male sexuality, in general, as dangerous for women, were used to defend the extremely restrictive policies of the military toward Wacs in the Southwest Pacific Area. In this situation the army stepped in as the surrogate male protector defending white military women's honor and virtue by creating a repressive environment designed to insure a maximum of "protection" and supervision.

One consequence of the controls placed on women's heterosexual activities in the Southwest Pacific Area was a series of rumors in late 1944 claiming widespread homosexuality among Wacs in New Guinea. The concerns originated in letters of complaint from several Wacs stationed there who asserted that restrictive theater policies created an ideal habitat for some women to express and explore their "abnormal sexual tendencies." The War Department and Hobby sent a WAC officer to the theater to investigate the rumors. The report issued by Lt. Col. Mary Agnes Brown, the WAC staff director, noted that although homosexuality was certainly not widespread, several incidences of such behavior had occurred. Lieutenant Colonel Brown felt that the situation was accentuated by the rigid camp security system to which Wacs were subjected. She suggested increasing Wacs' opportunities for recreation "with a view of maintaining the normal relationships between men and women that exist at home and avoid the creation of abnormal conditions which otherwise are bound to arise." When faced with a choice of protecting women from men or "protecting" them from lesbian relationships which might occur in a sex-segregated and restricted compound, Lieutenant Colonel Brown's recommendation was to protect servicewomen from the possibility of homosexuality. . . .

Army regulations providing for the undesirable discharge of homosexuals were rarely used against lesbians in the WAC, and WAC officers were warned to consider this action only in the most extreme of situations. Hobby felt that such proceedings would only result in more intensive public scrutiny and disapproval of the women's corps. Instead, it was suggested that WAC officers use more informal methods of control. These included shifting personnel and room assignments, transferring individuals to different posts, and as was exemplified in New Guinea, insuring that corps members were provided with "opportunities for wholesome and natural companionship with men." Another recommended method for dealing with homosexuality was to encourage a woman with "homosexual tendencies" to substitute "hero worship" of a WAC officer for active participation in homosexual relations. . . . In addition, on several posts informal WAC policy prohibited women from dancing in couples in public and cautioned against the adoption of "mannish" hairstyles. . . .

Within these parameters, lesbians within the WAC developed their own culture and methods of identifying one another, although the risks of discovery and exposure remained. . . .

Despite the opportunities for creating and sustaining a lesbian identity or relationship within the WAAC/WAC, the process was also fraught with danger and uncertainty. Army policies provided a space in which female homosexuals could exist, recognize one another, and develop their own culture. Yet this existence was an extremely precarious one, framed by army regulations which also provided for the undesirable discharge of homosexuals, female and male. These regulations could be invoked at any time and were widely used in purges of lesbians from the military in the immediate postwar years, purges that were in part the result of the army's decreasing need for women's labor. . . .

The tensions between agency and victimization illustrated here are characteristic of women's participation within the U.S. Army during World War II. Hobby's attempts to portray Wacs as sexless and protected in response to accusations of heterosexual promiscuity were undercut by the need also to present Wacs as feminine and sexually attractive to men to ease fears that the military would attract or produce "mannish women" and lesbians. In addition, the army's occasional utilization of WAC units to control male sexuality seemed to confirm the belief that women's role within the military was sexual. Within this confusing and fluctuating environment, and in negotiation with army regulations and public opinion, Wacs tried to define their own sexuality and make their own sexual choices. Their actions sometimes challenged and other times reinforced entrenched gender and sexual ideologies and were crucial to the development of a role for women within the military. The process of creating a category of "female soldier" was defined by these interactions between Wacs, the army hierarchy (which was often divided along gender lines), and public opinion. The reformulation and reconstruction of gender and sexual norms involved in this process did not end with the war but is still going on today. Women's service continues to be circumscribed by debates over the contradictory concepts of "woman" and "soldier," and servicewomen continue to grapple with the sexual images of dyke and whore framing their participation.

FURTHER READING

Baker, Joyce. *Images of Women in Film: The War Years, 1941–1945* (1980).
Beidler, Philip D. *The Good War's Greatest Hits: World War II and American Remembering* (1998).
Berube, Alan. *Coming Out Under Fire: The History of Gay Men and Women in World War Two* (1990).
Bird, William L., and Harry Rubinstein. *Design for Victory: World War II Posters on the American Home Front* (1998).
Blum, John Morton. *V Was for Victory: Politics and American Culture During World War II* (1976).
Brandt, Allan M. *No Magic Bullet: A Social History of Venereal Disease in the United States Since 1880* (1985).
Cohen, Stan. *V for Victory: America's Home Front During World War II* (1991).
D'Emilio, John, and Estelle B. Freedman. *Intimate Matters: A History of Sexuality in America* (1988).
Dick, Bernard. *The Star-Spangled Screen: The American World War II Film* (1985).
Erenberg, Lewis A., and Susan E. Hirsch, eds. *The War in American Culture* (1996).
Fox, Frank. *Madison Avenue Goes to War: The Strange Military Career of American Advertising, 1941–1945* (1975).
Fussell, Paul. *Wartime* (1989).
Goodman, Jack. *While You Were Gone* (1946).

Harris, Mark J., Franklin D. Mitchell, and Steven J. Schecter, eds. *The Home Fro During World War II* (1984).

Honey, Maureen. *Creating Rosie the Riveter: Class, Gender and Propaganda Du World War II* (1984).

Koppes, Clayton R., and Gregory D. Black. *Hollywood Goes to War: How Politics, and Propaganda Shaped World War II Movies* (1987).

Lingemann, Richard R. *Don't You Know There's a War Going On? The American H Front* (1970).

Meyer, Leisa D. *Creating GI Jane: Sexuality and Power in the Women's Army Corps During World War II* (1996).

Nichols, David, ed. *Ernie's War: The Best of Ernie Pyle's World War II Dispatches* (1986).

Perrett, Geoffrey. *Days of Sadness, Years of Triumph: The American People, 1939–1945* (1973).

Polan, Dana. *Power and Paranoia: History, Narrative, and the American Cinema, 1940–1950* (1986).

Polenberg, Richard. *War and American Society: The United States, 1941–1945* (1972).

Roeder, George H., Jr. *The Censored War: American Visual Experience During World War II* (1993).

Rupp, Leila. *Mobilizing Women for War: German and American Propaganda, 1939–1945* (1978).

Short, K. R. M., ed. *Film and Radio Propaganda in World War II* (1983).

Terkel, Studs. *"The Good War": An Oral History of World War II* (1984).

Westbrook, Robert B. "'I Want a Girl, Just Like the Girl That Married Harry James': American Women and the Problem of Political Obligation in World War II," *American Quarterly* 42, no. 4 (December 1990): 588–612.

See also Chapters 2 and 6.

CHAPTER 8

The Impact of Science
and Intelligence

World War II witnessed revolutionary developments in the fields of science and technology. The most dramatic of these was, of course, the atomic bomb (see Chapter 11), but this destructive weapon was simply the proverbial tip of the iceberg. Throughout the war, the major belligerents produced an astounding array of scientific inventions (radar, sonar, rockets, and jet engines, to name but a few) that dramatically transformed the nature of warfare—and the postwar world. In the process, scientists themselves became key components of their nations' war machines.

Some of the most important, but for many years the least known, scientific and technological inventions and innovations occurred in the field of intelligence. Throughout recorded history, spies had been the primary source of intelligence about the enemy, and during World War II individual spies continued to play a critical role. Indeed, American spying activities were organized during the war within a special organization, the Office of Strategic Services (OSS), which became the predecessor for the postwar Central Intelligence Agency (CIA). In World War II, however, some of the most important intelligence about the enemy came not from individual spies but from revolutionary developments in the field of cryptography—the art of ciphering and deciphering messages in code.

Cryptography is probably as old as spying itself. In World War II, however, the belligerents for the first time sent many of their secret messages via radio signals. These signals could, of course, be intercepted from the airwaves, but they were written on special encoding machines in codes so complex as to be considered unbreakable. They were not. Even before Pearl Harbor, U.S. intelligence officials had broken the Japanese diplomatic code (MAGIC) and had been able to read messages between Tokyo and the Japanese embassy in Washington. By the spring of 1942 they had also broken a key Japanese naval code, which enabled them to anticipate and defeat a major Japanese offensive in the decisive Battle of Midway. These two codebreaking successes were made public soon after the war ended. Not until 1974, however, did U.S. and British officials begin to reveal the true extent and importance of their wartime codebreaking operations.

The most important of these activities focused on British possession of the German encryption machine (ENIGMA). This enabled the British to "read" the highest-level German military intelligence (ULTRA). But decrypting the numerous German codes sent on this machine, which were extremely complex and which changed daily, required the establishment of a special deciphering unit at Bletchley Park in England, staffed by some of the most brilliant British mathematicians.

Revelation of this ULTRA Secret in 1974, combined with the opening of Anglo-American wartime intelligence records, led to the creation of a new subfield in World War II history—Signals Intelligence, or "SIGINT." Although findings in this field did not always verify the early and often overstated claims regarding the importance of SIGINT, they did lead to numerous major reassessments in World War II military and diplomatic history—and to numerous new questions. Given the extraordinary information provided by the ENIGMA machine, for example, why did it take the Allies so long to defeat the Axis? Of related interest, just how important were ULTRA and other SIGINT to the Allied war effort? On a broader level, just what was the impact of the entire scientific/technological revolution in warfare, of which SIGINT was a part, on the outcome of World War II and the shape of the postwar world?

D O C U M E N T S

Pearl Harbor was one of the worst intelligence failures in U.S. history, and after the war many wondered how such a disaster could have occurred in light of MAGIC. Document 1 contains the conclusions of the 1946 majority and minority congressional reports regarding responsibility for this failure, with the majority focusing on the commanders at Pearl Harbor and the minority on their superiors in Washington. In Document 2, British wartime Bletchley Park cryptologist and historian Peter Calvocoressi explains how ENIGMA worked. Document 3 is a sample of an intercepted Japanese Army message in its different forms. Document 4 contains the alphabet and a few key words from one of the most successful American wartime codes—one the Axis was never able to break—the Navajo language that special Navajo "code talkers" used.

Codes and codebreaking were by no means the only forms of intelligence employed by the United States during World War II. As previously mentioned, the OSS used traditional spies in intelligence activities. It also made extensive use of scholars to analyze and interpret the intelligence it received. In Document 5, Allen Dulles, OSS chief in Switzerland during the war and later head of the CIA, describes some of his wartime activities. In Document 6, William Langer, a Harvard historian and wartime head of the Research and Analysis Branch of the OSS (R and A), describes the contributions of scholars to the intelligence war.

Spying was not limited to obtaining intelligence about the enemy. Recent scholarship has revealed an extensive Soviet spying effort within the United States, some of which was known to U.S. authorities during the war. In Document 7, Secretary of War Henry L. Stimson expresses to President Roosevelt concerns about the possible connection between union organizing and Soviet spying within the atomic bomb project.

Signals Intelligence was but a small part of the enormous use of science and technology that occurred during the war. In the July 1945 report excerpted in Document 8, Dr. Vannevar Bush, head of the wartime Office of Scientific Research and Development (OSRD), responds to a presidential request for recommendations regarding postwar continuation of government support for different types of scientific research.

1. A Congressional Committee Assesses Blame for the Pearl Harbor Disaster, 1946

Majority Report

. . .

2. The ultimate responsibility for the attack and its results rests upon Japan, an attack that was well planned and skillfully executed. Contributing to the effectiveness of the attack was a powerful striking force, much more powerful than it had been thought the Japanese were able to employ in a single tactical venture at such distance and under such circumstances. . . .

4. The committee has found no evidence to support the charges, made before and during the hearings, that the President, the Secretary of State, the Secretary of War, or the Secretary of Navy tricked, provoked, incited, cajoled, or coerced Japan into attacking this Nation in order that a declaration of war might be more easily obtained from the Congress. On the contrary, all evidence conclusively points to the fact that they discharged their responsibilities with distinction, ability, and foresight and in keeping with the highest traditions of our fundamental foreign policy.

5. The President, the Secretary of State, and high Government officials made every possible effort, without sacrificing our national honor and endangering our security, to avert war with Japan.

6. The disaster of Pearl Harbor was the failure, with attendant increase in personnel and material losses, of the Army and the Navy to institute measures designed to detect an approaching hostile force, to effect a state of readiness commensurate with the realization that war was at hand, and to employ every facility at their command in repelling the Japanese.

7. Virtually everyone was surprised that Japan struck the Fleet at Pearl Harbor at the time that she did. Yet officers, both in Washington and Hawaii, were fully conscious of the danger from air attack; they realized this form of attack on Pearl Harbor by Japan was at least a possibility; and they were adequately informed of the imminence of war.

8. Specifically, the Hawaiian commands failed—

(*a*) To discharge their responsibilities in the light of the warnings received from Washington, other information possessed by them, and the principle of command by mutual cooperation.

(*b*) To integrate and coordinate their facilities for defense and to alert properly the Army and Navy establishments in Hawaii, particularly in the light of the warnings and intelligence available to them during the period November 27 to December 7, 1941.

(*c*) To effect liaison on a basis designed to acquaint each of them with the operations of the other, which was necessary to their joint security, and to exchange fully all significant intelligence.

(*d*) To maintain a more effective reconnaissance within the limits of their equipment.

From *Report of the Joint Committee on the Investigation of the Pearl Harbor Attack,* 2nd sess., July 20 (legislative date July 5), 1946, S. Cong. Res. 27, 79th Cong., 251–252, 493, 504–505.

(e) To effect a state of readiness throughout the Army and Navy establishments designed to meet all possible attacks.

(f) To employ the facilities, matériel, and personnel at their command, which were adequate at least to have greatly minimized the effects of the attack, in repelling the Japanese raiders.

(g) To appreciate the significance of intelligence and other information available to them.

9. The errors made by the Hawaiian commands were errors of judgment and not derelictions of duty.

10. The War Plans Division of the War Department failed to discharge its direct responsibility to advise the commanding general he had not properly alerted the Hawaiian Department when the latter, pursuant to instructions, had reported action taken in a message that was not satisfactorily responsive to the original directive. . . .

12. Notwithstanding the fact that there were officers on twenty-four hour watch, the Committee believes that under all of the evidence the War and Navy Departments were not sufficiently alerted on December 6 and 7, 1941, in view of the imminence of war. . . .

Minority Report

We, the undersigned, find it impossible to concur with the findings and conclusions of the Committee's report because they are illogical, and unsupported by the preponderance of the evidence before the Committee. The conclusions of the diplomatic aspects are based upon incomplete evidence.

We, therefore, find it necessary to file a report setting forth the conclusions which we believe are properly sustained by evidence before the Committee.

HOMER FERGUSON.
OWEN BREWSTER.

. . .

8. Judging by the military and naval history of Japan, high authorities in Washington and the Commanders in Hawaii had good grounds for expecting that in starting war the Japanese Government would make a surprise attack on the United States.

9. Neither the diplomatic negotiations nor the intercepts and other information respecting Japanese designs and operations in the hands of the United States authorities warranted those authorities in excluding from defense measures or from orders to the Hawaiian commanders the probability of an attack on Hawaii. On the contrary, there is evidence to the effect that such an attack was, in terms of strategy, necessary from the Japanese point of view and in fact highly probable, and that President Roosevelt was taking the probability into account—before December 7. . . .

11. The decision of the President, in view of the Constitution, to await the Japanese attack rather than ask for a declaration of war by Congress increased the responsibility of high authorities in Washington to use the utmost care in putting the commanders at Pearl Harbor on a full alert for defensive actions before the Japanese attack on December 7, 1941. . . .

13. The messages sent to General Short and Admiral Kimmel [Hawaiian Commanders] by high authorities in Washington during November were couched in such conflicting and imprecise language that they failed to convey to the commanders definite information on the state of diplomatic relations with Japan and on Japanese war designs and positive orders respecting the particular actions to be taken—orders that were beyond all reasonable doubts as to the need for an all-out alert. In this regard the said high authorities failed to discharge their full duty.

14. High authorities in Washington failed in giving proper weight to the evidence before them respecting Japanese designs and operations which indicated that an attack on Pearl Harbor was highly probable and they failed also to emphasize this probability in messages to the Hawaiian commanders.

15. The failure of Washington authorities to act promptly and consistently in translating intercepts, evaluating information, and sending appropriate instructions to the Hawaiian commanders was in considerable measure due to delays, mismanagement, noncooperation, unpreparedness, confusion, and negligence on the part of officers in Washington.

2. Bletchley Park Cryptologist Peter Calvocoressi Explains How ENIGMA Worked During the War

Essentially Enigma was a transposition machine. That is to say, it turned every letter in a message into some other letter. The message stayed the same length but instead of being in German it became gobbledegook: it was garbled. That the Enigma machine did this was obvious. The problem was to find out how it performed its tricks. Only if its hidden workings were known, could a decypherer or cryptographer even begin to turn the gobbledegook back into German.

Even when he had got as far as to understand how Enigma worked the cryptographer was still no more than half way to decyphering any particular message. This was because the machine had a number of manually adjustable parts and the cryptographer needed to know not only how the machine was constructed and how it worked but also how these various movable parts were set by the operator at the moment when he began transmitting each particular message. These parts were adjusted every so often—in peace time once a month, later once every 24 hours, and from September 1942 some of them every 8 hours. In addition some parts moved automatically minute by minute when the machine was in use. And, the final complication, each separate message contained its own, individual key and this key was randomly selected. . . .

At first glance the Enigma machine looked like a typewriter but a peculiarly complicated one. It had a keyboard like the standard three-row keyboard of an ordinary typewriter but without numerals, punctuation marks or other extras. . . .

Behind the keyboard the alphabet was repeated in another three rows and in the same order, but this time the letters were not on keys but in small round glass holes which were set in a flat rectangular plate and could light up one at a time.

From Peter Calvocoressi, *Top Secret Ultra* (New York: Pantheon, 1980), 23–29. © 1980 by Peter Calvocoressi. Used by permission of Pantheon Books, a division of Random House, Inc.

When the operator struck a key one of these letters lit up. But it was never the same letter. By striking P the operator might, for example, cause L to appear; and next time he struck P he would get neither P nor L but something entirely different.

This operator called out the letters as they appeared in lights and a second operator sitting alongside him noted them down. This sequence was then transmitted by wireless in the usual Morse code and was picked up by whoever was supposed to be listening for it. It could also be picked up by an eavesdropper. The Germans experimented with a version of the machine which, by transmitting automatically as the message was encyphered, did away with the need for the second operator, but they never brought this version into use.

The legitimate recipient took the gobbledegook which had been transmitted to him and tapped it out on his machine. Provided he got the drill right the message turned itself back into German. The drill consisted in putting the parts of his machine in the same order as those of the sender's machine. This was no problem since he had a handbook or manual which told him what he had to do each day. In addition, the message which he had just received contained within itself the special key to that message.

The eavesdropper on the other hand had to work all this out for himself. Even assuming he had an Enigma machine in full working order it was no good to him unless he could discover how to arrange its parts—the gadgets which it had in addition to its keyboard. These were the mechanisms which caused L to appear when the operator struck P.

These parts or gadgets consisted of a set of wheels or drums and a set of plugs. Their purpose was not simply to turn P into L but to do so in so complex a manner that it was virtually impossible for an eavesdropper to find out what had gone on inside the machine in each case. And, furthermore, to ensure that if P became L this time it would become something else next time. It is quite easy to construct a machine that will always turn P into L but it is then comparatively easy to find out that L always means P: a simple substitution of this kind is inadequate for specially secret traffic.

The eavesdropper's basic task was to set his machine in exactly the same way as the legitimate recipient of the message had set his, since the eavesdropper would then be able to read the message with no more difficulty than the legitimate recipient. The more complex the machine and its internal workings, the more difficult and more time-consuming was it for the eavesdropper to solve this problem.

The Enigma machine fitted compactly into a wooden box which measured about $7 \times 11 \times 13$ inches.

As the operator sat at his machine he had in front of him, first, the rows of keys, then the spaces for the letters to appear illuminated, and beyond these again and in the far left-hand corner of the machine three slots to take three wheels or drums. Each wheel was about three inches in diameter. The wheels were much more than half embedded in the machine and end-on to the operator. They were covered by a lid and when this lid was closed the operator could see only the tops of them. He could easily lift them out and replace them.

Although there were three slots for three wheels, there were by 1939 five wheels. The operator had to use three of his set of five. He had to select the correct three and then place them in a prescribed order. This was crucial because the wheels, although outwardly identical, were different inside.

The German navy introduced a four-wheel machine at the beginning of March 1943. At this point the naval operator had six wheels for four slots but the new wheel had distinct limitations: it had to go to the left of the other three and it did not rotate, so that the number of permutations, though much increased by this innovation, was not nearly as large as it would have been if the four wheels had been as freely interchangeable as the three and if all four had rotated. In July of the same year a seventh wheel and fifth slot were added to the naval kit. The greater flexibility and inventiveness of the navy, which was still in evidence at the end of the war, may be ascribed to the fact that it used far fewer machines than either the army or the Luftwaffe. They could therefore be more easily replaced. Most of them moreover were static either in naval HQs ashore or in fleet units. In this context a ship, even when at sea, provides a static home for its machinery in a way which is impossible for an army division or an air squadron, for which moving means considerably more upheaval.

Finally, there were besides the wheels the plugs (in German *Stecker*). These were in pairs. They looked like the plugs on a telephone switchboard. . . . There was one plughole for every letter of the alphabet. Each pair of plugs coupled a pair of letters. Putting them in and taking them out to change the couplings was the work of a moment. The number of pairings varied from 5 to 10. In theory there could be 13 pairings of 26 letters but there never were, and for some mathematical reason which I do not understand the maximum number of permutations is obtained when 10 pairings are used. . . .

The Enigma machine ran on an electric battery. When the operator of an ordinary typewriter strikes P on his keyboard he mechanically and immediately produces P on the paper in his machine. When an Enigma operator struck his P the effect, though all but instantaneous, was neither mechanical nor immediate. The operator's touch did not move a key and there was of course no paper in his machine. What he did by his touch was to release an electric pulse and this pulse went on a tortuous journey round the machine before returning to illumine not P but L. The electric current passed through the plug system; then through each of the three removable wheels from right to left, entering each in turn and leaving each of them by any one of 26 different points of entry and exit; and then—after bouncing off a fixed wheel or reflector to the left of these removable three wheels—back from left to right by a different and equally multifarious route, back through the plug system again by a different route, and so to the light for L. The variety and unpredictability of each of these journeyings every time a key was struck were the inventor's pride and the cryptographer's headache.

Each journey from key to light—such was the complexity of Enigma's entrails—might take any one of an astronomical number of routes. The outcome, as shown in the row of lights, was not so multifarious. P could turn into one only of 25 different letters, i.e. 26 minus one. But that was not the point. The point was not what happened at the end of the journey but how it happened. What the cryptographer needed to know was the route, for without being able to establish and repeat the route he could not discover the journey's end.

Enigma, in the form in service when the war began, multiplied its permutations in various ways. First, there was the wheel-order. When there were just three different wheels to place in three slots the number of possible wheel-orders was six. Call the wheels A, B and C: the possible wheel-orders are ABC, ACB, BAC, BCA, CAB, CBA. But when the Germans added a fourth and a fifth wheel for the three slots, the number of possible three-wheel-orders rose from six to sixty.

But that was only the beginning. Not only were the wheels not identical; they were not stationary. They rotated. Each had a rotatable rim with 26 different contact points on either side. So each, independently of its fellows, could be set in any one of 26 different positions. And furthermore, every time the operator touched a key the right-hand wheel moved itself on by one notch. When it had done this 26 times the middle wheel began to behave likewise: and ultimately the left-hand wheel too. These shifts vastly raised the number of permutations—the number of different states in which the machine might be at a given moment.

Finally, the extra changes introduced by the plug couplings raised the total to an astronomical figure which, when laid out in full, had 88 digits.

All this sounds horribly complicated and so in one sense it was. But not in another. Although the Enigma machine was a highly complex piece of electrical machinery it was easy to operate. . . . [T]he essential difference between the legitimate recipient of an Enigma message and an enemy cryptographer was that, although both possessed and understood the machine, only the former had the handbook which told how the machine's parts were to be arranged each day.

3. Americans Decode and Translate a Japanese Encrypted Message, 1944

A Japanese Army Message Enciphered for Transmission

57[a]   491[b]   48[c]   12022240[d]

1887 1773 3972[e]

DD 6635 = 4761[f]

2345[g]	6966[h]	2804	6249	4481	2424	8376	6135	7994	9570
1115	0312	2284	6870	6683	5207	1397	3689	7290	1861
8944	1980	3848	8428	9292	7802	1864	7499	3588	8585
1199	6952	9759	3102	1750	0646	7871	5765	6085	9415
1489	8410	4835	5340	9436	3943	0900	6249		

[a]Circuit number
[b]Originating message center number (Army Operations Department, IGHQ)
[c]Group count (forty-eight four-digit groups of numbers in the message)
[d]File date and time (December 2/10:40 P.M. (Tokyo time)
[e]Disguised address (Second Area Army, Chief of Staff)
[f]Disguised points of origin and destination (DD = *den'dai* or telegraph address) (Tokyo = Davao)
[g]Discriminant code (3155 when converted from substitution table)
[h]Key indicator (2999 when converted from substitution table)

Source: History of the SSA, Vol. 3: *The Japanese Army Problem: Cryptanalysis, 1942–45,* 21–22, Record Group 457, U.S. National Archives and Records Administration, Washington, D.C.

From Edward J. Drea, *MacArthur's Ultra: Codebreaking and the War Against Japan, 1942–1945* (Lawrence: University Press of Kansas, 1992), 4, 6–7. Used by permission of the publisher.

The Japanese Army Message Transmitted in Morse Code

(RONSE/RONSE)[a]

7190/6720[b]	12022343[c]	(A)[d]	US00298367[e]

MA[f]	57[g]	MVN[h]	MW[i]	NZ/ZZMO[j]

NWWR   NRRS   SVRZ[k]

DD 6635 = 4767[l]

[m]ZSMA	TVTT	ZWOM	TZMV	MMWN	ZMZN	WSRT	TNSA	RVVM	VARO
NNNA	OSNZ	ZZWM	TWRO	TAWS	AZOR	NSVR	STWV	RZVO	NWTN
WVMM	NVWO	SWMW	WMZW	RWPZ	NWTM	RMVV	SAWW	WAWA	
NNVV	TVAZ	VRAV	SZON	ZRAO	OTMT	RWRN	ARTA	TOWA	VMNA
NMWV	WMNO	MWSA	ASMO	VSMT	SVMS	OOVO	TZMV	VE[n]	

[a]Circuit call between Tokyo and Manila
[b]Kilocycles to 7190 kilocycles from 6720.
[c]Day, month, and hour of interception (Tokyo time)
[d]Classification of quality of intercept
[e]Intercept station number and teletype transmission number
[f]Routing instruction indicating relay
[g]Circuit number
[h]Originating message center number
[i]Group count
[j]File date and time
[k]Enciphered address
[l]Geographic code indicating point of origin and destination
[m]Text of message including discriminant and key cipher groups
[n]Procedure signal indicating end of message

Source: History of the SSA, Vol. 3: *The Japanese Army Problem: Cryptanalysis, 1942–45,* 23, Record Group 457, U.S. National Archives and Records Administration, Washington, D.C.

Transliteration into Roman Letters

DAI ICHI. DAI JU YON SHIDAN WO DAI SAN HOMEN GUN NOO HENSO YORI WO NOZOKU DAI NI GUN SENTO JORETSU HENNYU SHI DAI NIJU KU SHIDAN WO KANTOGUN HENSO YORI WO NOZUKU DAI HACHI HOMEN GUN SENTO JORETSU HENNYU SHI.

Translation

Paragraph 1. The 14th Division is deleted from the Third Area Army Order of Battle and enrolled in the Second Area Army Order of Battle. Paragraph 2. The 29th Division is removed from the Kwantung Army Order of Battle and enrolled in the Eighth Area Army Order of Battle.

4. The Navajo Language Becomes an Unbreakable American Code, 1945

ALPHABET	NAVAJO WORD	LITERAL TRANSLATION
A	WOL-LA-CHEE	ANT
A	BE-LA-SANA	APPLE
A	TSE-NILL	AXE
B	NA-HASH-CHID	BADGER
B	SHUSH	BEAR
B	TOISH-JEH	BARREL
C	MOASI	CAT
C	TLA-GIN	COAL
C	BA-GOSHI	COW
D	BE	DEER
D	CHINDI	DEVIL
D	LHA-CHA-EH	DOG
E	AH-JAH	EAR
E	DZEH	ELK
E	AH-NAH	EYE
F	CHUO	FIR
F	TSA-E-DONIN-EE	FLY
F	MA-E	FOX
G	AH-TAD	GIRL
G	KLIZZIE	GOAT
G	JEHA	GUM
H	TSE-GAH	HAIR
H	CHA	HAT
H	LIN	HORSE
I	TKIN	ICE
I	YEH-HES	ITCH
I	A-CHI	INTESTINE
J	TKELE-CHO-G	JACKASS
J	AH-YA-TSINNE	JAW
J	YIL-DOI	JERK
K	JAD-HO-LONI	KETTLE
K	BA-AH-NE-DI-TININ	KEY
K	KLIZZIE-YAZZIE	KID
L	DIBEH-YAZZIE	LAMB
L	AH-JAD	LEG
L	NASH-DOIE-TSO	LION
M	TSIN-TLITI	MATCH
M	BE-TAS-TNI	MIRROR
M	NA-AS-TSO-SI	MOUSE
N	TSAH	NEEDLE
N	A-CHIN	NOSE
O	A-KHA	OIL
O	TLO-CHIN	ONION
O	NE-AHS-JAH	OWL
P	CLA-GI-AIH	PANT
P	BI-SO-DIH	PIG
P	NE-ZHONI	PRETTY
Q	CA-YEILTH	QUIVER
R	GAH	RABBIT
R	DAH-NES-TSA	RAM
R	AH-LOSZ	RICE

From U.S. Naval Historical Center; http://www.history.navy.mil/faqs/faq61-4.htm.

ALPHABET	NAVAJO WORD	LITERAL TRANSLATION
S	DIBEH	SHEEP
S	KLESH	SNAKE
T	D-AH	TEA
T	A-WOH	TOOTH
T	THAN-ZIE	TURKEY
U	SHI-DA	UNCLE
U	NO-DA-IH	UTE
V	A-KEH-DI-GLINI	VICTOR
W	GLOE-IH	WEASEL
X	AL-NA-AS-DZOH	CROSS
Y	TSAH-AS-ZIH	YUCCA
Z	BESH-DO-TLIZ	ZINC

NAMES OF COUNTRIES	NAVAJO WORD	LITERAL TRANSLATION
AMERICA	NE-HE-MAH	OUR MOTHER
BRITAIN	TOH-TA	BETWEN WATERS
GERMANY	BESH-BE-CHA-HE	IRON HAT
JAPAN	BEH-NA-ALI-TSOSIE	SLANT EYE

NAMES OF AIRPLANES	NAVAJO WORD	LITERAL TRANSLATION
PLANES	WO-TAH-DE-NE-IH	AIR FORCE
DIVE BOMBER	GINI	CHICKEN HAWK
TORPEDO PLANE	TAS-CHIZZIE	SWALLOW
OBS. PLANE	NE-AS-JAH	OWL
FIGHTER PLANE	DA-HE-TIH-HI	HUMMING BIRD
BOMBER PLANE	JAY-SHO	BUZZARD
PATROL PLANE	GA-GIH	CROW
TRANSPORT	ATSAH	EAGLE

NAMES OF SHIPS	NAVAJO WORD	LITERAL TRANSLATION
SHIPS	TOH-DINEH-IH	SEA FORCE
BATTLESHIP	LO-TSO	WHALE
AIRCRAFT	TSIDI-MOFFA-YE-HI	BIRD CARRIER
SUBMARINE	BESH-LO	IRON FISH
MINE SWEEPER	CHA	BEAVER
DESTROYER	CA-LO	SHARK
TRANSPORT	DINEH-NAY-YE-HI	MAN CARRIER
CRUISER	LO-TSO-YAZZIE	SMALL WHALE
MOSQUITO BOAT	TSE-E	MOSQUITO

VOCABULARY WORD	NAVAJO WORD	LITERAL TRANSLATION
ALLIES	NIH-HI-CHO	ALLIES
BOMB	A-YE-SHI	EGGS
COAST GUARD	TA-BAS-DSISSI	SHORE RUNNER
COMMUNICATION	HA-NEH-AL-ENJI	MAKING TALK
DETONATOR	AH-DEEL-TAHI (OR)	BLOWN UP
EXPLOSIVE	AH-DEL-TAHI (E)	EXPLOSIVE
HOSPITAL	A-ZEY-AL-IH	PLACE OF MEDICINE
PYROTECHNIC	COH-NA-CHANH	FANCY FIRE
SABOTAGE	A-TKEL-YAH	HINDERED
SUBMERGE	TKAL-CLA-YI-YAH	WENT UNDER WATER

5. Office of Strategic Services Official Allen Dulles Explains His Wartime Intelligence Activities, 1941–1945

The Craft of Intelligence

It was only in World War II, and particularly after the Pearl Harbor attack, that we began to develop, side by side with our military intelligence organizations, an agency for secret intelligence collection and operations. . . . The origin of this agency was a summons by President Franklin D. Roosevelt to William J. Donovan in 1941 to come down to Washington and work on this problem.

Colonel (later Major General) Donovan was eminently qualified for the job. A distinguished lawyer, a veteran of World War I who had won the Medal of Honor, he had divided his busy life in peacetime between the law, government service and politics. He knew the world, having traveled widely. He understood people. He had a flair for the unusual and for the dangerous, tempered with judgment. In short, he had the qualities to be desired in an intelligence officer.

The Japanese sneak attack on Pearl Harbor and our entry into the war naturally stimulated the rapid growth of the OSS and its intelligence operations.

It had begun, overtly, as a research and analysis organization, manned by a hand-picked group of some of the best historians and other scholars available in this country. By June, 1942, the COI (Coordinator of Information), as Donovan's organization had been called at first, was renamed the Office of Strategic Services (OSS) and told "to collect and analyze strategic information and to plan and operate special services."

By this time the OSS was already deep in the task of "special services," a cover designation for secret intelligence and secret operations of all kinds and character, particularly the support of various anti-Nazi underground groups behind the enemy lines and covert preparations for the invasion of North Africa.

During 1943, elements of the OSS were at work on a world-wide basis, except for Latin America, where the FBI was operating, and parts of the Far Eastern Command, which General MacArthur had already pre-empted.

Its guerrilla and resistance branch, modeled on the now well-publicized British Special Operations Executive (SOE) and working closely with the latter in the European Theater, had already begun to drop teams of men and women into France, Italy and Yugoslavia and in the China-Burma-India Theater of war. The key idea behind these operations was to support, train and supply already existing resistance movements or, where there were none, to organize willing partisans into effective guerrillas. The Jedburghs, as they were called, who dropped into France, and Detachment 101, the unit in Burma, were among the most famous of these groups. Later the OSS developed special units for the creation and dissemination of black propaganda, for counterespionage, and for certain sabotage and resistance tasks that required unusual talents, such as underwater demolitions or technical functions in support of regular intelligence tasks. In conjunction with all these undertakings, it had to develop its own training schools.

From *The Craft of Intelligence* by Allen W. Dulles (New York: Harper & Row, 1963; reprint, Boulder, Colo.: Westview Press, 1985), 41–43. Reprinted by permission of HarperCollins Publishers, Inc.

Toward the end of the war, as our armies swept over Germany, it created special units for the apprehension of war criminals and the recovery of looted art treasures as well as for tracking down the movements of funds which, it was thought, the Nazi leaders would take into hiding in order to make a comeback at a later date. There was little that it did not attempt to do at some time or place between 1942 and the war's end. . . .

The Secret Surrender

Unknown to the outside world, since the end of February, 1945, emissaries and messages had been passing secretly between the OSS mission in Switzerland, of which I was in charge, and German generals in Italy. For two crucial months the commanders of contending armies locked in battle had maintained secret communications through my office in Bern seeking the means to end the fighting on the front in Italy, hoping that a Nazi surrender there would bring in its wake a general surrender in Europe. We had given the code name "Sunrise" to this operation to facilitate speed and secrecy in the handling of our messages. We did not know until later that Winston Churchill, who was closely following the proceedings, had already named the operation "Crossword."

What prevented our early success was the stubborn and insane policy of one man, Adolf Hitler. Despite the hopeless position of his armies, he would not countenance any surrender anywhere. His generals had good reason to fear that they would pay with their lives for any unauthorized attempt to stop the fighting. This meant there could be no parliamentarians crossing enemy lines with white flags, no public parleys, no formalized negotiations. Instead, a secret intelligence organization took over the unusual function of establishing the first contact and actively pursuing the negotiations with the enemy until the surrender was ready to be signed. We became, in agreement with Field Marshal Alexander, the channel through which communications between the Allied and the German High Commands were maintained. . . .

Against Germany it was obvious from the start that our work would have to be of another sort. There were certain high-level resistance groups in Germany but no partisan activities of the kind we supported in France and Italy. Our best intelligence source on Germany materialized in the summer of 1943, in the person of a diplomat, one who had the kind of access which is the intelligence officer's dream. George Wood (our code name for him) was not only our best source on Germany but undoubtedly one of the best secret agents any intelligence service has ever had. He was an official in the German Foreign Office in Berlin and his job there was to screen and distribute for action the cable traffic between the Foreign Office and German diplomatic posts all over the world. Since the messages to and from German military and air attachés in Tokyo were also generally sent through Foreign Office channels, he saw these, too, and they became of great value as the war in the Far East was still to be fought out. He was frequently sent by the Foreign Office as a courier to Switzerland as well as to other posts, and it was on one of his courier trips to Switzerland that he succeeded in making contact with us, having convinced himself that in this way he could contribute to the fall of the Nazis, whom he hated.

From *The Secret Surrender* by Allen W. Dulles (New York: Harper & Row, 1966), 3, 22–25. Reprinted by permission of HarperCollins Publishers, Inc.

While at his post in Berlin, he would scour the files of official cables and copy or photograph (microfilm) for us everything he thought of importance. He would then bring the copies out in his locked diplomatic bag along with the material he was delivering to the German Legation in Bern or mail them to us by secret channels. It is impossible here to describe fully his coverage. He turned in to us some of the best technical and tactical information on the V-weapons, on the effects of Allied bombings, on German planning, on the gradually weakening fabric of the whole Nazi regime. General Donovan thought highly enough of this material to pass much of it on directly to President Roosevelt. . . .

Of direct practical value of the very highest kind among Wood's contributions was a copy of a cable in which the German Ambassador in Turkey, von Papen, proudly reported to Berlin (in November, 1943) the acquisition of top-secret documents from the British Embassy in Ankara through "an important German agent." This was, of course, the famous Cicero, the valet of the British Ambassador who had managed to procure the keys to the Ambassador's private safe and to photograph its contents. I immediately passed word of this to my British colleagues, and a couple of British security inspectors immediately went over to the British Embassy in Ankara and changed the safes and their combinations, thus putting Cicero out of business. Neither the Germans nor Cicero ever knew what was behind the security visit, which was, of course, made to appear routine and normal. Thus our rifling of the German Foreign Office safes in Berlin through an agent reporting to the Americans in Switzerland, put an end to the rifling of the British Ambassador's safe by a German agent in Turkey.

6. Historian and OSS Official William Langer Describes the Contribution of Scholars to the Intelligence War, 1943–1946

As the war progressed, the Joint Chiefs of Staff assigned more and, indeed, even more difficult operational assignments to the OSS. These fascinated [OSS Chief William J.] Donovan and gave full scope to his imagination. More and more of his attention was focused on these tasks, many of which required him to be abroad. Compared to plans for sabotage of enemy installations, aid and supplies to resistance groups, the penetration of enemy positions, etc., the work of the R and A [Research and Analysis] lacked drama and excitement. Hence, the books that have been written on the OSS have little to say of it and devote themselves to the narrative of adventure and heroism. But Donovan never lost his interest in R and A and its work. On the contrary, he rated it highly and interfered little, though he never failed to have visiting notables shown around, if only to see men and women busy at desks or typewriters.

The work of the R and A was so varied and so conditioned by the requirements of the war that it is extremely difficult to give a coherent account of it. At first we were ignored, if not opposed, by other agencies, and most of our reports were

From William Langer, *In and Out of the Ivory Tower* (New York: Neale Watson Academic Publications, 1977), 187–188, 190–192.

unsolicited. Our Projects Committee decided which problems were important or apt to become so, and directed and criticized the product. . . .

In the planning of the invasion of North Africa, all sorts of abstruse information was required and the contributions of our African section, headed by Sherman Kent, who for many years was to play a key role in foreign intelligence work and actually wrote a book on the subject, were gratefully received. The landing in Sicily and the Italian campaign were to tax our Italian section, and here, if I am not mistaken, we first began to make careful target studies for Air Force bombardment. . . .

. . . Almost anyone would admit that the outcome of the war hinged largely on the success or failure of the Russian forces, which in turn depended largely on the availability not only of tanks, airplanes, and trucks, but also of munitions. How were we to form an independent judgment on Russian capabilities and needs? Very few of our economists, even among the ablest, had any knowledge of the organization and workings of either the Soviet or the Nazi economy. The economics of the New Deal, which had brought many of them to Washington, were too fascinating and immediately important to study the functioning of the dictatorships.

Our economics section, headed by my distinguished colleague and life-long friend Edward S. Mason, was extraordinarily able, imaginative, and dynamic, staffed by a number of brilliant young scholars, who were for many later years to play important roles in Washington. They had no difficulty in recognizing the problems and mapping out approaches to their solution. There was only one serious obstacle—ignorance of the Russian language and hence inability to read many of the crucial materials.

According to Geroid T. Robinson, professor of Russian history at Columbia and author of a well-known study, *Rural Russia under the Old Regime* (based on two years of archival work in Russia in the 1930s), ignorance of the language vitiated the value of the reports on Russian affairs produced by the economics section. The latter replied that such work could not be abandoned to the Russian section because it knew no economics. Actually, I think Robinson and some of his staff knew more of Russian economics than the economics section knew of the Russian language; but fortunately, it never became necessary to rule apodictically on this important issue. Both Mason and Robinson were outstanding men, whose prime interest was in getting the work well done. It was soon arranged that on Russian problems appropriate members of each section should work together. This was the natural and successful solution. The R and A studies on Russian needs and productive capabilities were among the most effective of our products. Towards the end of the conflict, various sections working together produced an extended analysis of Soviet capabilities and intentions that may justly be called the first national intelligence estimate. In the budding "cold war," it was highly regarded by General Embick and the Joint Chiefs of Staff and may well be described as the very acme of intelligence analysis.

Before leaving the economics section, more than mere mention must be made of its contributions on the German side, where the economists had a better command of the language and where, too, close collaboration with the German section was gradually established. Using captured Nazi materiel, the economists discovered the key to the serial numbers of captured truck tires, engines, and other Nazi industrial products. Presently they could tell with astonishing accuracy which factory was producing what amount of what product, where the bottlenecks were (as with ball bearings), and which plants it was urgently necessary to destroy by bombardment.

Similarly, by the careful analysis of the local Nazi press (collected in Stockholm), it became possible to determine, through the officer obituaries, where different Nazi units were and sometimes what their losses were in recent engagements. I submit that these items were military intelligence of the highest order, attained by altogether new and ingenious methods. No other nation during the war was, or so far as I know, has since been able to bring such concentrated intellectual power to bear on wartime problems as did Donovan's R and A.

During the concluding year of the war, the German section had the crucial role of studying for the occupation and military governments of territories conquered from the enemy. This section was peculiarly fitted for this assignment because it had on its staff a number of German refugees with considerable firsthand knowledge about conditions and procedures. I think here of the late Hajo Holborn, professor of history at Yale, the late Franz Neumann, of the New School for Social Research, and Herbert Marcuse, whose later revolutionary role was then indiscernible. These senior scholars were supported by younger men, almost all of whom were eventually to fill chairs at our major universities. To mention Franklin L. Ford, Carl E. Schorske, Robert L. Wolff, H. Stuart Hughes, and Paul Sweet is only to cite those whom I knew best. Holborn was later to write an excellent book on occupation policies and military government, and all that need be said here is that by dint of hard and sustained work the R and A was able to make a major contribution in a difficult and troublesome field.

7. Secretary of War Henry L. Stimson Raises Concerns to President Roosevelt about Communist Union Organizing in the Atomic Bomb Project, 1943

September 9, 1943.

MEMORANDUM FOR THE PRESIDENT:

Subject: FAECT Organizational Activities
in the Radiation Laboratory.

1. There has been a marked increase recently in union organizing activity in the Radiation Laboratory at the University of California in Berkeley which is engaged upon one of the most important phases of the work on uranium fission. This organizational activity is being carried on by the Federation of Architects, Engineers, Chemists, and Technicians (CIO) Local No. 25. In the furtherance of their organizational activity this union is assembling lists of the scientific and technical personnel of the laboratory, and necessarily acquiring considerable information with respect to the work being carried on there.

2. The paid organizer of Local No. 25 . . . and the local FAECT International Vice-President . . . are definitely Communists. They are close associates of and receive the constant counsel of . . . a member of the National Committee of the Communist Party, U.S.A., and the head of the Communist Party in Alameda County, California . . . [who] induced . . . a member of the staff of the Radiation Laboratory to furnish

From Franklin D. Roosevelt Papers, Map Room File, Franklin D. Roosevelt Library, Hyde Park, N.Y.

him secret information concerning the work with the announced intention of transmitting it to the U.S.S.R. and it is believed he has done so.

3. Lists of the persons employed upon this Project are classified as secret because information as to the nature and extent of the work could be deduced therefrom. The security of the work has already been compromised by the activities of the union. Continued union activities will be extremely dangerous not only to security but to the speedy completion of the work and it is unquestionable that the union organization will be used to further espionage activity of agents of a foreign power.

4. It is urgently recommended that at the earliest opportunity you have a personal conference with . . . the head of the CIO and request him in the strongest terms to take such steps as are necessary to ensure that the FAECT immediately cease, for the duration of the war, all union activity whatsoever with respect to the Radiation Laboratory, University of California, at Berkeley. This should include disbanding the laboratory organization of Local No. 25. There is no objection, however, to employees of the laboratory retaining membership in the union, provided it is in a wholly inactive status during the war.

> Respectfully yours,
> Henry L. Stimson
> Secretary of War.

[handwritten] Unless this can be at once stopped, I think the situation very alarming.

> HLS

8. Office of Scientific Research and Development Director Dr. Vannevar Bush Reports to the President on the Importance of Science During and After the War, 1945

Scientific Progress Is Essential

Progress in the war against disease depends upon a flow of new scientific knowledge. New products, new industries, and more jobs require continuous additions to knowledge of the laws of nature, and the application of that knowledge to practical purposes. Similarly, our defense against aggression demands new knowledge so that we can develop new and improved weapons. This essential, new knowledge can be obtained only through basic scientific research.

Science can be effective in the national welfare only as a member of a team, whether the conditions be peace or war. But without scientific progress no amount of achievement in other directions can insure our health, prosperity, and security as a nation in the modern world.

For the War Against Disease. We have taken great strides in the war against disease. The death rate for all diseases in the Army, including overseas forces, has been reduced from 14.1 per thousand in the last war to 0.6 per thousand in this war.

From Vannevar Bush, *Science: The Endless Frontier; A Report to the President* (Washington, D.C.: U.S. Government Printing Office, 1945), 1–4.

In the last 40 years life expectancy has increased from 49 to 65 years, largely as a consequence of the reduction in the death rates of infants and children. But we are far from the goal. . . .

The responsibility for basic research in medicine and the underlying sciences, so essential to progress in the war against disease, falls primarily upon the medical schools and universities. Yet we find that the traditional sources of support for medical research in the medical schools and universities, largely endowment income, foundation grants, and private donations, are diminishing and there is no immediate prospect of a change in this trend. Meanwhile, the cost of medical research has been rising. If we are able to maintain the progress in medicine which has marked the last 25 years, the Government should extend financial support to basic medical research in the medical schools and in universities.

For Our National Security.   The bitter and dangerous battle against the U-boat was a battle of scientific techniques—and our margin of success was dangerously small. The new eyes which radar has supplied can sometimes be blinded by new scientific developments. V-2 was countered only by capture of the launching sites.

We cannot again rely on our allies to hold off the enemy while we struggle to catch up. There must be more—and more adequate—military research in peacetime. It is essential that the civilian scientists continue in peacetime some portion of those contributions to national security which they have made so effectively during the war. This can best be done through a civilian-controlled organization with close liaison with the Army and Navy, but with funds direct from Congress, and the clear power to initiate military research which will supplement and strengthen that carried on directly under the control of the Army and Navy.

And for the Public Welfare.   One of our hopes is that after the war there will be full employment. To reach that goal the full creative and productive energies of the American people must be released. To create more jobs we must make new and better and cheaper products. We want plenty of new, vigorous enterprises. But new products and processes are not born full-grown. They are founded on new principles and new conceptions which in turn result from basic scientific research. Basic scientific research is scientific capital. Moreover, we cannot any longer depend upon Europe as a major source of this scientific capital. Clearly, more and better scientific research is one essential to the achievement of our goal of full employment.

How do we increase this scientific capital? First, we must have plenty of men and women trained in science, for upon them depends both the creation of new knowledge and its application to practical purposes. Second, we must strengthen the centers of basic research which are principally the colleges, universities, and research institutes. These institutions provide the environment which is most conducive to the creation of new scientific knowledge and least under pressure for immediate, tangible results. With some notable exceptions, most research in industry and in Government involves application of existing scientific knowledge to practical problems. It is only the colleges, universities, and a few research institutes that devote most of their research efforts to expanding the frontiers of knowledge.

Expenditures for scientific research by industry and Government increased from $140,000,000 in 1930 to $309,000,000 in 1940. Those for the colleges and universities increased from $20,000,000 to $31,000,000, while those for the research institutes declined from $5,200,000 to $4,500,000 during the same period. If the colleges, universities, and research institutes are to meet the rapidly increasing demands of industry and Government for new scientific knowledge, their basic research should be strengthened by use of public funds. . . .

The most important ways in which the Government can promote industrial research are to increase the flow of new scientific knowledge through support of basic research, and to aid in the development of scientific talent. In addition, the Government should provide suitable incentives to industry to conduct research. . . .

A Program for Action

The Government should accept new responsibilities for promoting the flow of new scientific knowledge and the development of scientific talent in our youth. These responsibilities are the proper concern of the Government, for they vitally affect our health, our jobs, and our national security. It is in keeping also with basic United States policy that the Government should foster the opening of new frontiers and this is the modern way to do it. For many years the Government has wisely supported research in the agricultural colleges and the benefits have been great. The time has come when such support should be extended to other fields.

The effective discharge of these new responsibilities will require the full attention of some over-all agency devoted to that purpose. There is not now in the permanent Governmental structure receiving its funds from Congress an agency adapted to supplementing the support of basic research in the colleges, universities, and research institutes, both in medicine and the natural sciences, adapted to supporting research on new weapons for both Services, or adapted to administering a program of science scholarships and fellowships.

Therefore I recommend that a new agency for these purposes be established. Such an agency should be composed of persons of broad interest and experience, having an understanding of the peculiarities of scientific research and scientific education. It should have stability of funds so that long-range programs may be undertaken. It should recognize that freedom of inquiry must be preserved and should leave internal control of policy, personnel, and the method and scope of research to the institutions in which it is carried on. It should be fully responsible to the President and through him to the Congress for its program.

Early action on these recommendations is imperative if this nation is to meet the challenge of science in the crucial years ahead. On the wisdom with which we bring science to bear in the war against disease, in the creation of new industries, and in the strengthening of our Armed Forces depends in large measure our future as a nation.

ESSAYS

The congressional conclusions reproduced in Document 1 did not satisfy all Americans regarding how and why the United States could have been so surprised at Pearl Harbor, given the information provided by MAGIC. Some turned to a conspiracy theory and argued that President Roosevelt knew about the attack in advance but allowed it to take place. In the first essay, the late Roberta Wohlstetter denigrates such an interpretation by explaining how and why U.S. intelligence failed to predict the attack. In the process she emphasizes the limits of signals intelligence, both in this particular episode and in general. Despite such limits and failures, signals intelligence played an important role in Allied victory. In the second essay, Williamson Murray of the Institute for Defense Analysis attempts to clarify that role in regard to ULTRA. In the third essay, written before revelation of the ULTRA Secret, the late Stanford University historian Gordon Wright explores the broader issue of the role of science and technology in the war.

Pearl Harbor and the Limits of Signals Intelligence

ROBERTA WOHLSTETTER

Surprise

If our intelligence system and all our other channels of information failed to produce an accurate image of Japanese intentions and capabilities, it was not for want of the relevant materials. Never before have we had so complete an intelligence picture of the enemy. And perhaps never again will we have such a magnificent collection of sources at our disposal.

Retrospect

To review these sources briefly, an American cryptanalyst, Col. William F. Friedman, had broken the top-priority Japanese diplomatic code, which enabled us to listen to a large proportion of the privileged communications between Tokyo and the major Japanese embassies throughout the world. Not only did we know in advance how the Japanese ambassadors in Washington were advised, and how much they were instructed to say, but we also were listening to top-secret messages on the Tokyo-Berlin and Tokyo-Rome circuits, which gave us information vital for conduct of the war in the Atlantic and Europe. In the Far East this source provided minute details on movements connected with the Japanese program of expansion into Southeast Asia.

Besides the strictly diplomatic codes, our cryptanalysts also had some success in reading codes used by Japanese agents in major American and foreign ports. . . .

Our naval leaders also had at their disposal the results of radio traffic analysis. While before the war our naval radio experts could not read the content of any Japanese naval or military coded messages, they were able to deduce from a study of intercepted ship call signs the composition and location of the Japanese Fleet units. . . .

Extremely competent on-the-spot economic and political analysis was furnished by Ambassador Grew and his staff in Tokyo. Ambassador Grew was himself a most sensitive and accurate observer, as evidenced by his dispatches to the State Department. His observations were supported and supplemented with military detail by frequent reports from American naval attachés and observers in key Far Eastern ports. . .

During this period the data and interpretations of British intelligence were also available to American officers in Washington and the Far East, though the British and Americans tended to distrust each other's privileged information.

In addition to secret sources, there were some excellent public ones. Foreign correspondents for *The New York Times, The Herald Tribune,* and *The Washington Post* were stationed in Tokyo and Shanghai and in Canberra, Australia. Their reporting as well as their predictions on the Japanese political scene were on a very high level. Frequently their access to news was more rapid and their judgment of its significance as reliable as that of our Intelligence officers. . . .

The Japanese press was another important public source. During 1941 it proclaimed with increasing shrillness the Japanese government's determination to pursue its program of expansion into Southeast Asia and the desire of the military to clear the Far East of British and American colonial exploitation. This particular source was rife with explicit signals of aggressive intent. . . .

All of the public and private sources of information mentioned were available to America's political and military leaders in 1941. It is only fair to remark, however, that no single person or agency ever had at any given moment all the signals existing in this vast information network. The signals lay scattered in a number of different agencies; some were decoded, some were not; some traveled through rapid channels of communication, some were blocked by technical or procedural delays; some never reached a center of decision. But it is legitimate to review again the general sort of picture that emerged during the first week of December from the signals readily at hand. Anyone close to President Roosevelt was likely to have before him the following significant fragments.

There was first of all a picture of gathering troop and ship movements down the China coast and into Indochina. . . . [But] American radio analysts disagreed about the locations of the Japanese carriers. One group held that all the carriers were near Japan because they had not been able to identify a carrier call sign since the middle of November. Another group believed that they had located one carrier division in the Marshalls. The probability seemed to be that the carriers, wherever they were, had gone into radio silence; and past experience led the analysts to believe that they were therefore in waters near the Japanese homeland, where they could communicate with each other on wavelengths that we could not intercept. However, our inability to locate the carriers exactly, combined with the two changes in call signs, was itself a danger signal.

Our best secret source, MAGIC, was confirming the aggressive intention of the new military cabinet in Tokyo, which had replaced the last moderate cabinet on October 17. In particular, MAGIC provided details of some of the preparations for the move into Southeast Asia. Running counter to this were increased troop shipments to the Manchurian border in October. (The intelligence picture is never clear-cut.) But withdrawals had begun toward the end of that month. MAGIC also carried explicit instructions to the Japanese ambassadors in Washington to pursue diplomatic negotiations with the United States with increasing energy, but at the same time it announced a deadline for the favorable conclusion of the negotiations, first for November 25, later postponed until November 29. In case of diplomatic failure by that date, the Japanese ambassadors were told, Japanese patience would be exhausted, Japan was determined to pursue her Greater East Asia policy, and on November 29 "things" would automatically begin to happen.

On November 26 Secretary Hull rejected Japan's latest bid for American approval of her policies in China and Indochina. MAGIC had repeatedly characterized this Japanese overture as the "last," and it now revealed the ambassadors' reaction of consternation and despair over the American refusal and also their country's characterization of the American Ten Point Note as an "ultimatum."

On the basis of this collection of signals, Army and Navy Intelligence experts in Washington tentatively placed D-day *for the Japanese Southeastern campaign* during the week end of November 30, and when this failed to materialize, during the week end of December 7. They also compiled an accurate list of probable British and Dutch targets and included the Philippines and Guam as possible American targets. . . .

Perspective

On the basis of this rapid recapitulation of the highlights in the signal picture, it is apparent that our decisionmakers had at hand an impressive amount of information on the enemy. They did not have the complete list of targets, since none of the last-minute estimates included Pearl Harbor. They did not know the exact hour and date for opening the attack. They did not have an accurate knowledge of Japanese capabilities or of Japanese ability to accept very high risks. The crucial question then, we repeat, is, If we could enumerate accurately the British and Dutch targets and give credence to a Japanese attack against them either on November 30 or December 7, why were we not expecting a specific danger to *ourselves?* And by the word "expecting," we mean expecting in the sense of taking specific alert actions to meet the contingencies of attack by land, sea, or air.

There are several answers to this question that have become apparent in the course of this study. First of all, it is much easier *after* the event to sort the relevant from the irrelevant signals. After the event, of course, a signal is always crystal clear; we can now see what disaster it was signaling, since the disaster has occurred. But before the event it is obscure and pregnant with conflicting meanings. It comes to the observer embedded in an atmosphere of "noise," i.e., in the company of all sorts of information that is useless and irrelevant for predicting the particular disaster. For example, in Washington, Pearl Harbor signals were competing with a vast number of signals from the European theater. These European signals announced danger more frequently and more specifically than any coming from the Far East. The Far Eastern signals were also arriving at a center of decision where they had to compete with the prevailing belief that an unprotected offensive force acts as a deterrent rather than a target. In Honolulu they were competing *not* with signals from the European theater, but rather with a large number of signals announcing Japanese intentions and preparations to attack Soviet Russia rather than to move southward; here they were also competing with expectations of local sabotage prepared by previous alert situations.

In short, we failed to anticipate Pearl Harbor not for want of the relevant materials, but because of a plethora of irrelevant ones. Much of the appearance of wanton neglect that emerged in various investigations of the disaster resulted from the unconscious suppression of vast congeries of signs pointing in every direction except Pearl Harbor. It was difficult later to recall these signs since they had led nowhere. . . .

There is a difference, then, between having a signal available somewhere in the heap of irrelevancies, and perceiving it as a warning; and there is also a difference between perceiving it as a warning, and acting or getting action on it. These distinctions, simple as they are, illuminate the obscurity shrouding this moment in history. . . .

. . . [A]t the time there was a good deal of evidence available to support all the wrong interpretations of last-minute signals, and the interpretations appeared wrong only *after* the event. . . .

It is important to emphasize here that most of the men that we have cited in our examples, such as Captain Wilkinson and Admirals Turner and Kimmel—these men and their colleagues who were involved in the Pearl Harbor disaster—were as efficient and loyal a group of men as one could find. Some of them were exceptionally able and dedicated. The fact of surprise at Pearl Harbor has never been persuasively explained by accusing the participants, individually or in groups, of conspiracy or negligence or stupidity. What these examples illustrate is rather the very human tendency to pay attention to the signals that support current expectations about enemy behavior. If no one is listening for signals of an attack against a highly improbable target, then it is very difficult for the signals to be heard.

For every signal that came into the information net in 1941 there were usually several plausible alternative explanations, and it is not surprising that our observers and analysts were inclined to select the explanations that fitted the popular hypotheses. They sometimes set down new contradictory evidence side by side with existing hypotheses, and they also sometimes held two contradictory beliefs at the same time. We have seen this happen in G-2 estimates for the fall of 1941. Apparently human beings have a stubborn attachment to old beliefs and an equally stubborn resistance to new material that will upset them.

Besides the tendency to select whatever was in accord with one's expectations, there were many other blocks to perception that prevented our analysts from making the correct interpretation. We have just mentioned the masses of conflicting evidence that supported alternative and equally reasonable hypotheses. This is the phenomenon of noise in which a signal is embedded. Even at its normal level, noise presents problems in distraction; but in addition to the natural clatter of useless information and competing signals, in 1941 a number of factors combined to raise the usual noise level. First of all, it had been raised, especially in Honolulu, by the background of previous alert situations and false alarms. Earlier alerts, as we have seen, had centered attention on local sabotage and on signals supporting the hypothesis of a probable Japanese attack on Russia. Second, in both Honolulu and Washington, individual reactions to danger had been numbed, or at least dulled, by the continuous international tension.

A third factor that served to increase the natural noise level was the positive effort made by the enemy to keep the relevant signals quiet. The Japanese security system was an important and successful block to perception. It was able to keep the strictest cloak of secrecy around the Pearl Harbor attack and to limit knowledge only to those closely associated with the details of military and naval planning. In the Japanese Cabinet only the Navy Minister and the Army Minister (who was also Prime Minister) knew of the plan before the task force left its final port of departure.

In addition to keeping certain signals quiet, the enemy tried to create noise, and sent false signals into our information system by carrying on elaborate "spoofs." False radio traffic made us believe that certain ships were maneuvering near the mainland of Japan. The Japanese also sent to individual commanders false war plans for Chinese targets, which were changed only at the last moment to bring them into line with the Southeastern movement.

A fifth barrier to accurate perception was the fact that the relevant signals were subject to change, often very sudden change. This was true even of the so-called static intelligence, which included data on capabilities and the composition of military forces. In the case of our 1941 estimates of the infeasibility of torpedo attacks in the shallow waters of Pearl Harbor, or the underestimation of the range and performance of the Japanese Zero, the changes happened too quickly to appear in an intelligence estimate.

Sixth, our own security system sometimes prevented the communication of signals. It confronted our officers with the problem of trying to keep information from the enemy without keeping it from each other, and, as in the case of MAGIC, they were not always successful. As we have seen, only a very few key individuals saw these secret messages, and they saw them only briefly. They had no opportunity or time to make a critical review of the material, and each one assumed that others who had seen it would arrive at identical interpretations. Exactly who those "others" were was not quite clear to any recipient. Admiral Stark, for example, thought Admiral Kimmel was reading all of MAGIC. Those who were not on the list of recipients, but who had learned somehow of the existence of the decodes, were sure that they contained military as well as diplomatic information and believed that the contents were much fuller and more precise than they actually were. The effect of carefully limiting the reading and discussion of MAGIC, which was certainly necessary to safeguard the secret of our knowledge of the code, was thus to reduce this group of signals to the point where they were scarcely heard.

To these barriers of noise and security we must add the fact that the necessarily precarious character of intelligence information and predictions was reflected in the wording of instructions to take action. The warning messages were somewhat vague and ambiguous. . . .

Last but not least we must also mention the blocks to perception and communication inherent in any large bureaucratic organization, and those that stemmed from intraservice and interservice rivalries. The most glaring example of rivalry in the Pearl Harbor case was that between Naval War Plans and Naval Intelligence. A general prejudice against intellectuals and specialists, not confined to the military but unfortunately widely held in America, also made it difficult for intelligence experts to be heard. . . .

In view of all these limitations to perception and communication, is the fact of surprise at Pearl Harbor, then, really so surprising? Even with these limitations explicitly recognized, there remains the step between perception and action. Let us assume that the first hurdle has been crossed: An available signal has been perceived as an indication of imminent danger. Then how do we resolve the next questions: What specific danger is the signal trying to communicate, and what specific action or preparation should follow? . . .

Prospect

The history of Pearl Harbor has an interest exceeding by far any tale of an isolated catastrophe that might have been the result of negligence or stupidity or treachery, however lurid. For we have found the roots of this surprise in circumstances that affected honest, dedicated, and intelligent men. The possibility of such surprise at any time lies in the conditions of human perception and stems from uncertainties so basic that they are not likely to be eliminated, though they might be reduced. . . .

It is only human to want some unique and univocal signal, to want a guarantee from intelligence, an unambiguous substitute for a formal declaration of war. This is surely the unconscious motivation of all the rewriting of Pearl Harbor history, which sees in such wavering and uncertain sources of information as the [Japanese] winds code and all of the various and much-argued MAGIC texts a clear statement of Japanese intent. But we have seen how drastically such an interpretation over-simplifies the task of the analyst and decisionmaker. If the study of Pearl Harbor has anything to offer for the future, it is this: We have to accept the fact of uncertainty and learn to live with it. No magic, in code or otherwise, will provide certainty. Our plans must work without it.

Signals Intelligence As Critical to Allied Victory

WILLIAMSON MURRAY

Only now, nearly forty years after the end of the Second World War, has the essential role and contribution of intelligence to the winning of that conflict become clear. Central to the new evaluation of that importance has been the discovery of the fact that throughout the war the intelligence services of the Western powers (particularly the British) were able to intercept, break, and read a significant portion of the top secret message traffic of the German military. The dissemination of that crypto-graphic intelligence to Allied commanders under the code name Ultra played a substantial and critical role in fighting the Germans and achieving an Allied victory.

The breaking of the German high-level codes began with the efforts of the Polish secret service in the interwar period. By creating a copy of the basic German enciphering machine, the Poles were able to read German signal traffic through the 1930s with varying degrees of success. However, shortly before the Munich Conference in September 1938, the Germans introduced additional rotors into their enciphering machine—the so-called enigma machine—and in approximately mid-September, darkness closed over the German message traffic. The Poles continued their work nevertheless, and after the British guarantee in March 1939 to Poland, they passed along to Great Britain what they had thus far achieved. (Earlier, there had also been considerable cooperation between the Poles and the French.) Building on what they had learned from their continental allies, the British finally managed to break into

From Williamson Murray, "Ultra: Some Thoughts on Its Impact on the Second World War," *Air University Review* 35, no. 5 (July–August, 1984): 53–63.

some of the German codes in April 1940, just before the great German Offensive against France and the Low Countries.

This first success would soon be followed by others that would give Allied intelligence and commanders valuable insights into German intentions and capabilities. Nevertheless, these cryptographic successes covered only a small proportion of the specific codes that the Germans used. The German navy at the end of 1943, for example, used up to forty different ciphers, all requiring different settings on the enigma machines. Given the priorities in the Battle of the Atlantic, the transmissions from U-boat to shore and from the commander of submarines to his boats received the highest priorities from British code breakers at Bletchley Park (the location of the major Allied code-breaking effort in Europe). Even with the exceptional resources available at that location and at that time, it would take the experts several days and in some cases up to a week to find the solution for a particular day's settings to the enigma machine.

The task of getting invaluable intelligence information out to the field where it could be of direct help to Allied commanders was, of course, immensely difficult, especially given the fear that should the Germans find out that their codes were being compromised on a daily basis, the entire source of Ultra would dry up. In 1940 during the Battle of Britain, this need for concealment was not a great difficulty; but as the war spread throughout Europe and the Mediterranean, it became an increasing problem. Basically, the British and their American allies evolved a carefully segregated intelligence system that kept the flow of Ultra information down to a limited number of senior commanders. This entire Ultra dissemination process lay outside of normal intelligence channels. . . .

If Ultra information was misused at times, it is clear that such instances were the exception rather than the rule. However, it is difficult to access Ultra's full impact on the war. At times (particularly early in the war), no matter how much Ultra tipped the British off to German intentions, the overwhelming superiority of the Wehrmacht made any successful use of the information virtually impossible. . . .

In war, so many factors besides good intelligence impinge on the conduct of operations that it is difficult to single out any single battle or period in which Ultra was of decisive importance by itself. Yet there is one instance where one can say that the intelligence achieved through the breaking of the German codes by itself played a decisive role in mitigating enemy capabilities. By the first half of 1941, as more and more submarines were coming on line, the German U-boat force was beginning to have a shattering impact on the trade routes on which the survival of Great Britain depended. The curve of sinkings of British, Allied, and neutral shipping was climbing upward ominously. . . .

Through the spring of 1941, the British had had virtually no luck in solving the German navy's codes. In mid-May 1941, however, the British captured not only a German weather trawler with considerable material detailing the settings for the naval codes but also a German submarine, the U-110, with its cipher machine and *all* accompanying material. With these two captures, the British held the settings for the next two months for the German navy's enigma machines. Thus, the British were able to break into the U-boat traffic by the end of May. Also, because German U-boats were controlled closely from shore and a massive amount of signaling went back and forth to coordinate the movement of the wolf packs, the British gained invaluable information, ranging from the number of U-boats available to tactical dispositions and patrol lines. Moreover, once they had a full two months' experience inside the German U-boat traffic, British cryptologists were able to continue breaking the submarine message traffic for the next five months. The impact that this intelligence had on the Battle of the Atlantic was almost immediate. . . .

The dramatic decline in sinkings (compared with those that had occurred during the first five months of the year) has no explanation other than that Ultra information enabled the British to gain a decisive edge over their undersea opponent. There was no introduction of new technology, no significant increase in the number of escorts available, and no extension of air coverage. Ultra alone made the difference.

Unfortunately for the Anglo-American powers, within two months of U.S. entrance into the war, the Germans introduced an entirely new cipher, Triton, which closed off the flow of Ultra decrypts for the remainder of 1942. Thus, at the very time that the vulnerable eastern and southern coasts of the United States opened up to German submarine operations, Ultra information on German intentions and operations ceased. Direction-finding intelligence was available, of course, but it remained of limited assistance.

When the Germans turned their full attention back to the Atlantic in early 1943, enormous convoy battles occurred with increasing frequency. German Admiral Karl Dönitz had available to him in the North Atlantic nearly one hundred submarines. In opposition, the Allies possessed far greater numbers of escort vessels, including escort carriers whose aircraft made U-boat shadowing of convoys almost impossible. Moreover, long-range aircraft from Newfoundland, Iceland, and Northern Ireland were reaching farther and farther into the Atlantic.

At the beginning of 1943, the Allied naval commanders enjoyed one further great advantage. Bletchley Park had succeeded once again in breaking the German naval ciphers. That intelligence proved somewhat less useful than the Ultra intelligence in 1941 that had allowed the British to steer convoys around U-boat threats. The Allies were able to carry out similar evasive operations at times, but the large numbers of German submarines at sea at any given time made such maneuvers increasingly difficult and oftentimes impossible. Initially during the great three-month battle from March to May 1943, the Allies were badly battered. In May, however, the Allies smashed the U-boat threat so decisively that Dönitz was forced to end the battle. Ultra intelligence played a major role in the turnaround. However, because of additions to Allied escort strength and increases in long-range aircraft patrols, one must hesitate in identifying the Ultra contribution as decisive by itself. Yet, the leading German expert on the Battle of the Atlantic does note:

> I am sure that without the work of many unknown experts at Bletchley Park . . . the turning point of the Battle of the Atlantic would not have come as it did in May 1943, but months, perhaps many months, later. In that case the Allied invasion of Normandy would not have been possible in June 1944, and there would have ensued a chain of developments very different from the one which we have experienced.

Meanwhile, Ultra affected the air war on both the tactical and on the strategic levels. British decoding capabilities were not sufficient during the Battle of Britain to provide major help to Fighter Command to defeat the German air threat. Similarly, for the first three years of Bomber Command's war over the continent, Ultra could provide little useful intelligence. On the other hand, throughout 1942 and 1943, Ultra information provided valuable insights into what the Germans and Italians were doing in the Mediterranean and supplied Allied naval and air commanders with detailed, specific knowledge of the movement of Axis convoys from the Italian mainland to the North African shores. By March 1943, Anglo–American air forces operating in the Mediterranean had virtually shut down seaborne convoys to the Tunisian bridgehead. . . .

In the battles with German fighters for control of the air over Sicily, Ultra proved equally beneficial to Allied air commanders. It enabled them to take advantage of German fuel and ammunition shortages and to spot Axis dispositions on the airfields of Sicily and southern Italy. However, in regard to U.S. strategic bombing, Ultra may well have exerted a counterproductive influence in 1943. Intercepts from the Luftwaffe's message traffic indicated quite correctly how seriously Allied attacks in the air were affecting German air units, but these intercepts may have persuaded General Ira Eaker, Commander, Eighth Air Force in 1943, and his subordinate commanders to go to the well once too often. The second great attack on Schweinfurt in October 1943, as well as the other great raids of that month, proved to be disastrous for the Eighth Air Force crews who flew the missions. (Sixty bombers were lost in the Schweinfurt run.)

Moreover, U.S.A.A.F. theories about the vulnerability of the German economy to precision bombing proved somewhat unrealistic. While bomber attacks did inflict heavy damage on the German aircraft industry, the industry was in no sense destroyed. Likewise, the attacks on ball-bearing plants failed to have a decisive impact. True, damage to Schweinfurt caused the Germans some difficulties, but the batterings that Eighth's bombers took in the August and October attacks were such that despite intelligence information that the Germans would be back in business quickly, the Eighth could not repeat the mission again.

In 1944, however, the nature of Eighth's capabilities and target selection changed. Most important, the Eighth Air Force received the long-range fighter support to make deep penetration raids possible. The initial emphasis in the strategic bombing attacks in late winter and early spring of 1944 was in hitting the German aircraft industry and then in preparing the way for the invasion of the European continent. In May 1944, however, General Carl Spaatz persuaded Eisenhower that he possessed sufficient bomber strength to support both the invasion and a major new offensive aimed at taking out Germany's oil industry. . . .

Throughout the summer, Albert Speer's [German Minister of Armaments and Munitions] engineers and construction gangs scrambled to put Germany's oil plants back together. As fast as they succeeded, however, Allied bombers returned to undo their reconstruction efforts. Throughout the remainder of the year, Allied eyes, particularly of American bomber commanders, remained fixed on Germany's oil industry. The punishing, sustained bombing attacks prevented the Germans from ever making a lasting recovery in their production of synthetic fuel.

Clearly, Ultra played a major role in keeping the focus of the bombing effort on those fuel plants. Speer had warned Hitler after the first attack in May 1944:

> The enemy has struck us at one of our weakest points. If they persist at it this time, we will no longer have any fuel production worth mentioning. Our one hope is that the other side has an air force general staff as scatterbrained as ours!

Speer's hopes were not realized, largely because Ultra intelligence relayed to Allied air commanders both the size and successes of German reconstruction efforts, as well as the enormous damage and dislocations to Germany's military forces that the bombing of the plants was causing. The intelligence officer who handled Ultra messages at Eighth Air Force headquarters reported after the war that the intercepts and decrypts of enigma transmissions had indicated that shortages were general and not local. This fact, he indicated, convinced "all concerned that the air offensive had uncovered a weak spot in the German economy and led to [the] exploitation of this weakness to the fullest extent."

On the level of tactical intelligence during the preparation and execution of Overlord, Ultra also was able to provide immensely useful information. Intercepts revealed a clear picture of German efforts and successes in attempting to repair damage that the Allied air campaign was causing to the railroad system of northern France. A mid-May staff appreciation by Field Marshal Gerd von Rundstedt (Commander in Chief, Panzer Group West) warned that the Allies were aiming at the systematic destruction of the railway system and that the attacks had already hampered supply and troop movements. Ultra intelligence made clear to Allied "tactical" air commanders how effective the attacks on the bridge network throughout the invasion area were and the difficulties that German motorized and mechanized units were having in picking their way past broken bridges at night.

Ultra intercepts also gave Western intelligence a glimpse of the location and strength of German fighter units, as well as the effectiveness of attacks carried out by Allied tactical air on German air bases. Furthermore, these intercepts indicated when the Germans had completed repairs on damaged fields or whether they had decided to abandon operations permanently at particular locations. Armed with this information, the Allies pursued an intensive, well-orchestrated campaign that destroyed the Germans' base structure near the English Channel and invasion beaches. These attacks forced the Germans to abandon efforts to prepare bases close to the Channel and to select airfields far to the southeast, thereby disrupting German plans to reinforce *Luftflotte* 3 [German Air Force Unit, "Air Fleet 3"] in response to the cross-channel invasion. . . .

It is worth examining the reasons why the British were able to break some of the most important German codes with such great regularity and with such an important impact on the course of the war. The Germans seem to have realized midway through the war that the Allies were receiving highly accurate intelligence about their intentions and moves. Nevertheless, like postwar German historians, the German military looked everywhere but at their own signals. Enthralled with the technological expertise that had gone into the construction of the enigma machine, the Germans excluded the possibility that the British could decrypt their signals. . . .

The Germans made a bad situation worse by failing to take even the most basic security measures to protect their ciphers. Indeed, a significant portion of Bletchley Park's success was due to silly, procedural mistakes that the Germans made in governing their message traffic. . . .

The German navy proved no less susceptible to critical mistakes. Dönitz's close control of the U-boat war in the Atlantic rested on an enormous volume of radio traffic. The volume itself was of inestimable help to the cryptanalysts at Bletchley

Park. Although the Germans introduced a fourth rotor into the enigma machine in March 1943, thereby threatening once again to impose a blackout on their North Atlantic operations, the new machines employed only a small fraction of their technical possibilities. Unfortunately for the U-boats also, there was considerable overlapping between old and new machines. As a result of these and other technical errors, the British were back into the North Atlantic U-boat radio transmissions within ten days of the changeover. Furthermore, at about the same time, Bletchley Park decrypted a signal to U-boat headquarters indicating that the Germans were breaking the Allied merchant code. . . .

Obviously, there are important lessons that we in the West can learn from these German errors. To begin with, Patrick Beesly, who worked closely with the naval Ultra throughout the war, notes that "while each nation accepted the fact that its own cryptanalysts could read at least some of their enemy's ciphers, they were curiously blind to the fact that they themselves were being subjected to exactly the same form of eavesdropping." Above all, the Germans seem to have been overly impressed with their presumed superiority in technology. Thus, not only did they make elemental mistakes in their communications discipline, but they arrogantly refused to believe that their enemies might have technological and intelligence capabilities comparable to their own.

In recent years, there has been considerable interest in German operational and tactical competence on the field of battle. There is an important subheading to that competence: while the historians and military analysts tell us that the Germans were extraordinarily good in the operational and tactical spheres, we should also recognize that the Germans were sloppy and careless in the fields of intelligence, communications, and logistics, consistently (and ironically) holding their opponents in contempt in those fields. Thus, we would be wise to examine the German example closely in all aspects of World War II. We can learn from the Germans' high level of competence in the tactical and operational fields; equally, we have much to learn from their failures in other areas. Above all, the German defeat in World War II suggests that to underestimate the capabilities and intelligence of one's opponents can have only very dangerous and damaging consequences for one's own forces.

Science Revolutionizes Warfare

GORDON WRIGHT

I. Scientists, Soldiers, and Statesmen

As the Second World War ended in Europe, the British physicist Sir Henry Tizard noted in his diary: "I wonder if the part that scientists have played will ever be faithfully and fully recorded. Probably not." Tizard had some reason to be morose; historians of warfare have traditionally tended to concentrate on soldiers and strategies rather than on the technical advances that may have contributed to victory. But with

From Gordon Wright, *The Ordeal of Total War: 1939–1945* (New York: Harper & Row, 1968), 79–80, 82–103, 105–106. Copyright © 1968 by Gordon Wright. Reprinted with permission of HarperCollins Publishers, Inc.

the coming of technological war, the scientist's role became far more vital than ever before. When victory or defeat might hinge on the application of new theoretical discoveries, soldiers and statesmen could no longer afford to treat scientists as minor bureaucrats of a highly specialized type. In the forcing-ground of total war, a new and more intimate partnership was likely to grow up. And the product of this partnership, despite Tizard's gloomy forecast, was to be too important for either historians or informed citizens to ignore. That great phrasemaker Winston Churchill was to dramatize the scientists' contribution by labeling it "the wizard war."

In a sense, of course, the application of technology to warfare was centuries old. Until recent times, however, this effort had rarely transcended the rather elementary level of weapons development. Pure science, as contrasted to applied science, had seemed to have little direct relevance to war. The beginnings of change could be seen in the 1914 conflict, when chemists made a particular contribution in developing improved explosives, poison gases, and synthetics, and when aeronautics experts succeeded in building the first combat air force. That war left behind it a residue of military respect for the scientist's contribution; in all major nations, the armed forces maintained scientific research staffs during the interwar years. In general, however, these staffs were small and their prestige limited. Their function was seen as useful but essentially menial—rather like that of the blacksmith in cavalry days, except for the fact that weapons development required somewhat greater expertise than shoeing mules. . . .

II. Radar and Its Refinements

If any scientific device were to give its name to the Second World War, that device would probably be radar. In the air and on the sea, its importance for both defense and offense was to be crucial. Unlike the atomic bomb, it came into use at the beginning rather than the end of the war, and wartime improvements were to render it steadily more effective. . . .

Radar alone, however, would not have sufficed to win the Battle of Britain. The R.A.F. also needed an effective ground-control system to direct fighter planes on the basis of the early warnings that radar would provide; and such a system could not be hastily improvised. Tizard had been the first to foresee this need, and with his remarkable skill at interpreting scientific conceptions to military men, he had persuaded the air force to attack the problem of ground control even before the radar screen became operative—indeed, even before anyone could be sure that it would ever be operative. Beginning in 1937, the air force undertook exercises based on the presumption that radar would work; and by 1940, it had solved most of the initial difficulties. Thanks to these timely preparations, British fighters were employed so effectively in 1940 that German intelligence decided it must have seriously underestimated the R.A.F.'s strength. Gadgetry and foresight were thus combined with courage and daring to save Britain from defeat, and to alter the course of the entire war. . . .

By . . . [late 1942] the Atlantic powers had shifted their attention from the defensive to the offensive use of radar. Their bomber force had met unforeseen difficulties in the skies over Germany; planes often failed to find their targets, and even more often failed to hit those targets. They needed navigational aids to carry their aircraft through murky weather or darkness; bombing devices to permit them to strike accurately; techniques to frustrate the Germans' radar defenses. By 1942, all of these needs had been at least partially met by British scientists. A navigational system called "Gee" utilizing three radio pulse transmitters went into use early in 1942, but within six months the Germans had learned to jam it successfully. A blind-bombing device code-named "Oboe" was soon added; radar transmitting stations dispatched the attacking bomber along a beam, and kept track of its location by means of a device that measured its ground speed. On arrival over the unseen target, the ground station notified the crew by a special signal, so that in effect the bombs were dropped by a technician back on English soil. With the introduction of "Oboe," the age of visual bombing virtually came to an end.

Although "Oboe" was used until the end of the war, it was susceptible to German jamming, and it could be used for only limited numbers of aircraft. For mass raids, a new blind-bombing device was shortly added to the British arsenal: the so-called H2S system, an airborne radar set whose downward-looking transmitter allowed the air crews to "see" through clouds and darkness below them. The key component in H2S was the cavity magnetron, a small and simple device invented in 1940 by two physicists at Birmingham University. The magnetron, it has been said, "probably had a more decisive effect on the war than any other single new weapon." It produced a powerful high-frequency beam which made possible microwave radar, a vastly improved type which replaced the old longer-wave radar in fighter planes and ships as well as in bombers. H2S enabled Bomber Command to find certain types of targets at night with remarkable accuracy. Used for the first time over Hamburg in January 1943, it produced devastating results. It was soon utilized in the antisubmarine campaign as well. Heretofore, British bombers on Atlantic patrol had carried old-style radar to locate U-boats, but its effectiveness was lost as the German navy found ways to detect approaching planes. The new microwave radar, first used in search planes in March 1943, led to a slaughter of U-boats during the next three months. German scientists eventually devised countermeasures, but by that time the Battle of the Atlantic had been won by the Allies.

Once the main battlefield in the air war had shifted to the skies over Germany, the British had to seek ways to frustrate the Germans' radar defenses. Their most successful device, remarkably simple in conception, bore the code name "Window." It involved dropping tin foil or aluminum strips over a target city; each strip caused a blip on the German radar screens, exactly as though it had been an aircraft. For many months, however, the British hesitated to use this technique for fear the Germans might retaliate in kind over Britain. When "Window" was eventually employed for the first time over Hamburg in July 1943, British bomber losses were cut to one-tenth of those normally expected in such a raid. The device worked effectively for almost a year before the Germans developed adequate countermeasures. And while the Germans had worked out their equivalent of "Window" even earlier than the British, they could never utilize it, for they could no longer spare bombers and gasoline for raids on Britain.

III. Slide-Rule Warfare

Traditionally, scientists had been used in war to provide ideas for new weapons or to suggest improvements in old ones. The war of 1939 added a new function: the use of scientists in connection with actual military operations, with a view to greater effectiveness or economy of effort. For this function the British in 1940 coined the term "operational research." The term is not easy to define, but the physicist C. P. Snow sums it up as simply "thinking scientifically about operations."

Operational research began as a kind of accidental by-product of radar development. Scientists not only devised the new equipment; they then proceeded to join with air force personnel to test it out in team fashion. The essential contribution of the scientists impressed itself on the Air Ministry and the R.A.F., who became aware that hit-or-miss methods were no longer good enough in a technological war. During the early war years, operational research sections were quietly introduced into many different branches of the air force; and from 1941 onward, the other armed services and the civil defense authorities began to imitate the practice. Statistical techniques combined with the scrupulous habits of observation of the trained scientist provided a check on the effectiveness of current operations, and proved invaluable in working out better ways to do things.

As early as 1940, for example, the army called on operational research to study the complexities of applying radar to anti-aircraft fire. A team that carefully analyzed anti-aircraft operations during the Battle of Britain quickly spotted serious deficiencies, and proposed a regrouping of batteries and an altered firing pattern that yielded far better results. Highly detailed studies were made of bomb damage in British cities, both to improve civil defense measures and to help plan the eventual bomber attacks on Germany. When those attacks got under way, scientists tackled the problem of the traffic pattern involved in sending a thousand bombers over a target city. For the army, laboratory tests were run on the effects of various weapons in different sets of circumstances; and eventually, operational research teams accompanied the troops during actual military operations, studying battles in some cases from the initial assault to the end of the action. For the navy, the scientists studied the proper depth at which to detonate depth bombs; the best color to camouflage aircraft assigned to Atlantic patrol; and the optimum size of convoys as they passed through the danger zone. Indeed, operational research may have rivaled microwave radar for top honors as the most important single factor in winning the Battle of the Atlantic.

Of the other warring powers, only the United States developed the practice of slide-rule warfare to a degree that paralleled the British effort. The Germans' lesser interest in operational research techniques may seem surprising in light of their traditional excellence in science and their taste for the systematic. It may be that the neoromantic flavor of Nazi doctrine had something to do with it; for operational research tended to reduce war to a rational process, coldly analytical rather than subjectively heroic. Perhaps there is some truth in the epigrammatic remark of a British historian: "One reason why Hitler failed is that he was out-of-date."

IV. Weapons Technology

A much more traditional aspect of the application of science to warfare is the realm of weapons technology: the refinement of old weapons, the development of new ones. Here engineers and technicians played a considerably greater role than pure scientists, and their collaboration was more readily accepted by the soldiers. Military hardware was easier to comprehend than theoretical talk about bouncing radio waves off aircraft or calculating probabilities by the use of statistical method. . . .

Perhaps the most widely used new weapon of the war was the simple short-range powder rocket, fired in many cases from multibarreled launching devices. Although powder rockets had been used in warfare during the Middle Ages and again for a time during the early nineteenth century, they had long since been displaced by modern artillery. The war of 1939 reintroduced them on a large scale; rocket guns were installed on aircraft and naval vessels, or were hauled to the front on trucks. During the early weeks of the German attack on Russia, the Nebelwerfer and Wurfgerät rocket launchers were among the most effective weapons the Nazis possessed; but the Soviet armies quickly retaliated in kind with such devices as the "Stalin organ," which could fire forty-eight rockets at once. The Americans in Tunisia first introduced the small antitank rocket gun called the bazooka, and similar weapons came into prompt use everywhere. . . .

Rivaling the rocket in importance, but developed much later in the war, was the proximity fuse. This ingenious device, produced in quantity in the United States on the basis of research carried out in Britain, and invented independently by the Germans as well, greatly increased the effectiveness of anti-aircraft defense. Shells from ground batteries and fighter planes no longer had to score direct hits on the target; the proximity fuse exploded the shell when it came near enough the enemy craft to be activated by the noise.

One vital wartime race—the development of jet engines for aircraft—ended in a virtual dead heat between the Germans and the Anglo-Americans. . . .

V. The Medical Sciences

Improved devices for killing are natural by-products of warfare. Improved techniques of healing follow along at some distance in the rear; yet they too are likely to be stimulated by wartime needs. In earlier wars, the problem was simply to maintain armies at the peak of fighting fitness through control of epidemic diseases and better methods of battlefield surgery. The Second World War broadened the concerns of doctors and medical researchers to include the civilian populations as well, for home-front fitness and morale were almost as important as the physical state of the fighting forces. The strain of a long war, the unprecedented ratio of civilian casualties, and the need to ensure adequate nutrition in a time of consumer shortages confronted medical science with a greatly expanded list of problems. On the other hand, these same factors also provided medical scientists with unprecedented opportunities for experimentation and statistical analysis of disease. Even though most long-range research had to be suspended in favor of meeting immediate needs, medicine nevertheless profited by the fact that some governments devoted so large a share of their available resources to the advance of the healing arts.

Great Britain and the United States set the pace in this realm. . . . In most branches of medicine, notable progress occurred under the stimulus of war; in a few cases, the progress was spectacular. For its short-run effect during the war years, improved malaria control was probably most notable; for the longer future, the development of the sulfa drugs and of penicillin undoubtedly ranks first in importance. . . . Penicillin marked a kind of revolution in chemotherapy—the arrival of the antibiotic age. . . .

. . . Apparently the Germans made no attempt to develop penicillin, though they did a little experimenting with the sulfonamides. They also made some progress in the control of typhus, which was a serious threat on the eastern front. But until the last year of the war Germany suffered neither serious epidemics nor grave food shortages that might have stimulated crash programs of medical research. In the occupied countries and the concentration camps, on the other hand, such diseases as typhus were common toward the end, and German doctors were evidently unable to check their ravages. The British are said to have found sixty thousand typhus cases in the Bergen-Belsen camp alone when they liberated it in 1945. Malnutrition was also severe in many of the occupied countries, notably in eastern Europe and the Balkans. Infant mortality and the incidence of tuberculosis rose sharply there during the later war years, though the lasting damage from malnutrition was less grave than might have been expected. That permanent damage could result from wartime strain and shortages has been amply demonstrated, however, by follow-up studies of men who spent the war years in prisoner-of-war camps. Twenty years after the end of hostilities, specialists reported that ex-prisoners showed an abnormally high incidence of nervous and psychiatric disorders, of premature aging, and of susceptibility to such diseases as tuberculosis and hepatitis.

One notorious footnote to the story of wartime medical research in Germany was the use of concentration camp inmates as human guinea pigs. These unwilling victims were subjected to a wide variety of experiments designed to determine the effects of high altitude, low pressure, freezing, and exposure, and to test various types of vaccines and drugs. "Euthanasia" techniques were also tried out on prisoners, as a prelude to organizing programs of either mass sterilization or direct elimination of "racial inferiors" and "undesirables." The distorted motives behind many of these experiments would suffice to condemn them by any civilized standard. What made the procedure even more reprehensible was that it evidently failed to push back the frontiers of medical knowledge in any useful way. After the war, a number of SS doctors were convicted of war crimes for these concentration camp activities.

VI. The Coming of the Missile Age

For a generation before 1939, a handful of unorthodox scientists and a few widely-scattered lay enthusiasts had been fascinated by the idea of long-range self-propelled rockets. Few of these theorists and tinkerers had a new weapon in mind; their real interest was in rapid transportation or space travel. The earliest pioneer of the missile age was a self-educated Russian physics teacher named K. E. Tsiolkovsky who, beginning in 1903, preached the possibility of travel in space and worked out many of the theoretical problems of rocket construction. During the 1920's, Hermann Oberth in Germany and R. H. Goddard in the United States retraced Tsiolkovsky's theoretical steps, and Goddard moved from theory to practice by firing the world's first liquid-fueled rocket in 1926. Societies of rocket fanciers were organized in several countries, and their members were hard at work trying to build a workable rocket motor. . . .

By . . . [1943], British intelligence had begun to piece together bits of information about the German flying bomb and rocket programs. During the prewar years,

British officials had shown no interest in rocket research; the Air Ministry had been satisfied that heavy bombers would be sufficient if war came. This lack of interest doubtless contributed to the failure of British intelligence, in the period 1939–1942, to follow up some scattered items of evidence about the Peenemünde enterprise. In 1942–1943, however, air photographs revealed what appeared to be launching sites for missiles across the Channel, together with torpedo-shaped objects at Peenemünde and elsewhere that might be the missiles themselves. In August 1943 the R.A.F. carried out a massive raid on Peenemünde, which partially wrecked the facility and killed several hundred technicians and workers. Most of the key technicians survived, however, and were transferred to safer underground quarters in the Harz Mountains of central Germany. There, and at a new testing ground in occupied Poland, work on the rocket continued at top speed. The raid on Peenemünde had left the *Luftwaffe*'s flying-bomb station unscathed, and its work proceeded without interruption. . . .

British and American intelligence, meanwhile, remained uncertain about the nature of the new German weapon and the imminence of the threat it posed. As insurance, they did their best to obliterate the launching sites along the Channel; but until the eve of the Normandy landings, General Eisenhower and his staff feared that a sudden rain of rockets or flying bombs might disrupt the cross-Channel operation. The British government grew nervous, too; for several weeks it discussed the possible evacuation of a million Londoners and the transfer of the government itself to a less threatened city. But D-day came and went without interference by any kind of miracle weapon, comforting those who had always insisted that the whole thing was a German hoax, designed to mislead the Western Allies.

Then, just a week after the Normandy landings, the first German missile struck near London. It was not a rocket, but the *Luftwaffe*'s pilotless plane, promptly labeled "V-1" by Goebbels' propaganda machine, and "buzz bomb" by the British. During the next three months, 9300 V-1's were fired toward England, and about two-thirds of them reached the English coast. Their effect, however, was much less grave than the Germans had hoped. Their slow speed and their telltale buzz enabled the British to improvise defensive measures, and before long a large proportion were being shot down by British fighters and anti-aircraft batteries using the new proximity fuse. It was clear that V-1, though a dangerous nuisance, was not the kind of weapon that could win a war.

Meanwhile, Dornberger and his staff were pushing desperately to perfect what Goebbels was to call "V-2"—the larger, longer-range supersonic rocket. Almost three hundred of these had been built by the summer of 1944, but the German scientists were aware of certain defects in them, and wanted time to make some final improvements. Dornberger's superiors, despite his protests, ordered their immediate use. Employing a cleverly devised movable launching device that could easily escape the vigilance of British bombers, the Germans on September 8 fired the first long-range military rocket ever used in warfare. It fell without warning in London, only hours after a high British official, encouraged by the slacking-off of the V-1 attack, had announced that the Battle of London was at last over.

The new blitz continued intermittently for almost seven months until the Allied advance into the Netherlands at last drove the Germans back out of firing range. During that period about 4300 V-2 rockets were fired: 1500 of them toward England,

2100 toward the port of Antwerp which had been captured almost intact by the Allied forces. Their effect was far more devastating than had been that of the flying bomb. Furthermore, the British had found no way to counter this new weapon: rapid and soundless, it could not be overtaken or shot down by any existing aircraft or system of ground fire. If perfected a year or two earlier, Hitler might have had the "miracle weapon" of which he dreamed—the weapon that might have determined the outcome of the war. But if the German rocket scientists had failed to play the decisive role in the Second World War, they had possibly helped to reshape the character of all future wars.

VII. The Atomic Breakthrough

. . . Much of the scientific knowledge on which the atomic weapon was based had been building up during the first four decades of the twentieth century. . . .

The work of [Enrico] Fermi and [Niels] Bohr inspired a whole series of new experiments in Europe and the United States. One scientist, the Berlin chemist Otto Hahn, in 1938 achieved a surprising result: by bombarding uranium with neutrons, he produced radioactive isotopes not of uranium itself or of a neighboring element (as had been the case in the past) but of quite different elements possessing roughly half the atomic weight of uranium. It appeared that the nucleus in this case must have split into two approximately equal fragments, and that if such fission had really occurred, a great quantity of energy must have been released in the process. Tests run in Copenhagen by the refugee German physicist Otto Frisch soon confirmed this hypothesis. The news created a sensation in scientific circles everywhere. For, if the theory was sound, the fission of a uranium nucleus caused some free neutrons to be thrown out; these in turn might impinge on other nuclei, causing fissions in them as well; and thus a self-sustaining chain reaction might be set off, releasing enormous energy for constructive or destructive purposes. The next problems were to find out what kind of fissionable material would be most susceptible to use, and how much of the material would be required to permit the chain reaction to proceed. These problems were under intensive study when the war broke out; but theory was then still well ahead of experimental verification. . . .

Although investing vast resources in such a project seemed a dubious venture, Britain's situation in the late summer of 1941 was sufficiently grave to convince Churchill and his scientific adviser Lord Cherwell that it must be tried. . . . Under the cover name "Directorate of Tube Alloys," an all-out effort to produce a nuclear weapon was mounted late in 1941. . . .

Within a year, however, the British found themselves outpaced by the Americans. Atomic research had been proceeding in the United States also, though at a more leisurely pace. As the prospect of American entry into the war became imminent, the Americans suggested that the two nations pool their talent and their facilities in a joint project. The British government, perhaps because it then enjoyed a clear lead in atomic development, failed to respond to this approach. After Pearl Harbor, the Americans threw their vast resources into the enterprise and quickly forged ahead. Too late, the British in 1942 attempted to revive the partnership plan; it was the Americans who now evaded, on the ground that establishing joint machinery would delay progress. By the time a partnership agreement was finally worked out in August 1943, the American lead was so great as to ensure that if the bomb were to be built in time for use during the war, it would come from an American rather than a British plant.

Britain's most difficult problem involved production techniques: how could a sufficient supply of U-235 be turned out by Britain's overworked and partially outmoded industrial plant? Scientists and engineers were not even agreed on the proper method to use for the separation of U-235 from uranium; three different industrial processes had been proposed, each one expensive and difficult. While the British wrestled with the problem, the opulent Americans pushed ahead on all fronts. They built plants to separate U-235 by all three methods, plus still another plant to produce a second fissionable element—plutonium—which American scientists thought to be potentially superior to U-235. By 1945, enough of both materials was on hand to permit bombs of both types to be built. The first plutonium bomb was successfully tested in the New Mexico desert in July 1945; the first U-235 bomb fell three weeks later on Hiroshima. A new age in warfare had begun.

One of the most powerful drives behind the British decision to push wartime atomic research had been the fear that Germany might win the race for nuclear weapons. It was in Berlin, after all, that nuclear fission had first been achieved; and German science and industry seemed particularly well equipped to carry through such an enormous enterprise. When Lord Cherwell in 1941 advised Churchill to invest Britian's scarce resources in the development of an atomic bomb, he observed ominously: "It would be unforgivable if we let the Germans develop a process ahead of us by means of which they could defeat us or reverse the verdict after they had been defeated." Not until Germany was invaded in 1945 could the Western Allies be sure that their fears had been exaggerated. By that time the Germans, despite their initial advantages, had fallen far behind. Worse still, they were not aware that they had fallen behind; the progress of atomic development in the West largely escaped the German intelligence services. When the news of the Hiroshima bomb was announced in August 1945, several of Germany's top nuclear physicists who had been captured by the Western armies refused at first to believe the report, and insisted that it must be a propaganda trick. . . .

No atomic bomb was ever dropped in the European theater of war. Would it have been used against the Germans if completed in time? There is no adequate evidence to permit a sure answer, though the readiness of both British and American governments to pulverize German cities with "conventional" bombs suggests that they would not have hesitated to try the new weapon on fellow white men. The effects of certain "conventional" bombing raids were, after all, just as devastating as those by the first atomic bombs; indeed, the destruction of Dresden in February 1945 cost more lives than the nuclear attack on Hiroshima. Any doubters would probably have been reminded that the Nazis, if they had won the nuclear race, would not have let moral scruples deter them from using it on London, Moscow, or Washington.

More striking, perhaps, is the fact that the American and British officials in charge of developing atomic weapons were too preoccupied with their task to think very much about the long-term implications of this revolution in warfare. Despite the warnings contained in the Peierls-Frisch memorandum of 1940 [a report by refugee scientists Rudolf Peierls and Otto Frisch on the probable effectiveness and dangers of, as well as how to make, a nuclear bomb], there was evidently little concern about the possible genetic effects of radioactive fission; and when a few scientists (notably Niels Bohr) developed strong qualms of conscience about their brainchild, their concern found little echo among the statesmen and soldiers who shared the secret. Bohr, who escaped from Denmark in 1943 and came to England, sensed that the new weapon might fundamentally change the world. Along with some fellow scientists, he warned both British and American leaders that the Russians could almost certainly develop their own bomb within a few years after the war. On Bohr's urging, Sir John Anderson suggested to Churchill in the summer of 1944 that the Foreign Office begin at once a study of the postwar international control of atomic energy, and that it seek Soviet collaboration in this enterprise. Anderson was sharply rebuffed by the Prime Minister; thereafter until the war ended Bohr pursued his desperate but futile effort to get a hearing in the Allied capitals.

"Under pressure of war," declared Sir John Anderson in a broadcast to the British people just after Japan's final surrender, "development has been compressed within the space of a few years which might normally have occupied a century or more. . . ." Perhaps Sir John underestimated the speed of "normal" scientific advance in our day, even in time of peace. One can scarcely doubt, however, that the coming of the atomic age was materially hastened by the circumstances of the Second World War. Perhaps it was that war's principal contribution to the future, ensuring that there would never be another conflict on the lines of the war of 1939–1945. Henceforth, the world would know only lesser wars—or greater ones.

FURTHER READING

Andrew, Christopher. *Codebreaking and Signals Intelligence* (1986).
Andrew, Christopher, and David Dilks. *The Missing Dimension: Governments and Intelligence Communities in the Twentieth Century* (1984).
Beesly, Patrick. *Very Special Intelligence* (1977).
Bennett, Ralph. *Ultra and Mediterranean Strategy* (1989).
———. *Ultra in the West: The Normandy Campaign of 1944–45* (1979).
Boyd, Carl. *Hitler's Japanese Confidant: General Oshima Hiroshi and Magic Intelligence 1941–1945* (1993).
Brodie, Bernard, and Fawn M. Brodie. *From Crossbow to H-Bomb—The Evolution of Weapons and the Tactics of Warfare* (1973).
Brown, Anthony Cave. *Bodyguard of Lies* (1975).
Calvocoressi, Peter. *Top Secret Ultra* (1980).
Casey, William. *The Secret War Against Hitler* (1988).
Cockridge, E. H. *Inside SOE* (1965).
Crowther, J. G., and R. Whiddington. *Science at War* (1948).
Drea, Edward J. *MacArthur's Ultra* (1992).
Dulles, Allen. *The Secret Surrender* (1966).
Eggleston, Wildrid. *Scientists at War* (1950).
Foot, Michael. *SOE in France* (1966).
Garlinski, Jozef. *The Enigma War* (1980).
Guerlac, Henry. *Radar in World War II*, 2 vols. (1987).
Hartcap, Guy. *The Effect of Science on the Second World War* (2000).
Hinsley, F. H. et al. *British Intelligence in the Second World War,* 5 vols. (1979–1993).
Hinsley, F. H., and Alan Stripp, eds. *Codebreakers* (1993).
Jones, Reginald V. *The Wizard War: British Scientific Intelligence, 1939–1945* (1978).
Kahn, David. *The Codebreakers* (1967).

————. *Seizing the Enigma: The Race to Break the German U-Boat Codes* (1991).

Langhorne, Richard, ed. *Diplomacy and Intelligence During the Second World War* (1985).

Lewin, Ronald. *The American Magic: Codes, Ciphers and the Defeat of Japan* (1982).

————. *Ultra Goes to War* (1978).

Masterman, J. C. *The Double-Cross System in the War of 1939 to 1945* (1972).

Meigs, Montgomery C. *Slide Rules and Submarines: American Scientists and Subsurface Warfare in World War II* (1990).

Murray, Williamson. "Ultra: Some Thoughts on Its Impact on the Second World War," *Air University Review* 35 (July–August 1989) 53–83.

Parrish, Thomas. *The Ultra Americans: The U.S. Role in Ultra* (1991).

Persico, Joseph E. *Piercing the Reich* (1979).

Prange, Gordon. *At Dawn We Slept: The Untold Story of Pearl Harbor* (1981).

Prange, Gordon, et al. *Pearl Harbor: The Verdict of History* (1986).

Richards, Pamela Spence. *Scientific Information in Wartime: The Allied-German Rivalry 1939–1945* (1994).

Smith, R. Harris. *OSS* (1972).

Van Creveld, Martin. *Technology and War* (1991).

Welchman, Gordon. *The Hut Six Story: Breaking the Enigma Codes* (1982).

Winterbotham, Frederick W. *The Ultra Secret* (1974).

Wohlstetter, Roberta. *Pearl Harbor: Warning and Decision* (1962).

Wright, Gordon. *The Ordeal of Total War* (1968).

See also Chapters 1 and 11.

C H A P T E R
9

The United States and
the Holocaust

Much of World War II was a vicious race war waged without mercy on civilians as well as combatants. In Asia, Japanese soldiers butchered hundreds of thousands if not millions of Chinese civilians, most notably but far from exclusively in the notorious "rape of Nanking." In the Pacific, Japanese and American armed forces often fought without quarter in what historian John W. Dower has aptly labeled a "war without mercy" (see his essay in Chapter 5). It was in Nazi-ruled Europe, however, that the most widespread and notorious race war took place.

Racism was central to Nazi ideology. In the Nazi racial hierarchy, most of the peoples of Europe were considered biologically inferior to the "Aryan" Germans. Such beliefs justified not merely the conquest of these peoples, but also the expropriation of their property and often their death. This was particularly true in Eastern Europe, where one of Hitler's key aims was to obtain Lebensraum, or "living space" for Germany's burgeoning population. To provide that "living space," the Nazis intended to force out, enslave, and/or murder millions of Slavs living in the area. War provided the opportunity to do so. As a result, more than 25 million Soviet citizens perished during the war, the majority of them civilians. The percentage of the prewar Polish population to be murdered by the Germans was even higher.

In a separate racial category were the Jews of Europe, whom the Nazis demonized as the source of all evil in the world. Throughout the 1930s, one of Hitler's key goals was to isolate, expropriate, and force out of Germany the Jews living there. The process began with the Nuremberg racial laws, which defined and deprived German Jews of their rights and culminated in the November 1938 Kristallnacht, or "Night of Broken Glass," during which Jewish people, businesses, and houses of worship were savagely attacked in a government-sponsored assault. Thousands of Jews did leave Germany under the impact of these measures, but Nazi conquests from 1938 through 1942 brought millions more into the German empire. Nazi policy consequently shifted from expulsion of the Jews to outright murder as the way to make their empire "Jew Free," a policy begun in the years 1939–1941 and then codified in early 1942 as the notorious "Final Solution" to what the Nazis had labeled "the Jewish Problem." Death camps such as Auschwitz and Treblinka were established in German-occupied Poland for the systematic extermination of the Jews of Europe, as well as other "undesirables" such as homosexuals and gypsies. Extermination also took place at many of the concentration camps that the Nazis had already established.

The response of the United States to this atrocity has been the subject of much discussion and debate. The U.S. government did little if anything to help the Jewish refugees being forced out of Germany during the 1930s, or the millions of Jews being systematically murdered during the war years. President Franklin D. Roosevelt was exceptionally popular within the American Jewish community and spoke out against Nazi actions on numerous occasions. He also pressed in 1938 for an international conference to deal with the refugees and in 1944 established the War Refugee Board. But he proved unwilling to challenge existing U.S. laws that sharply limited the number of immigrants allowed into the country. Nor were Congress or the American people willing to modify those laws, and State Department officials proved unwilling to interpret them flexibly. During the war itself, the United States and its allies condemned Nazi war crimes and promised postwar justice. But no effort was made to bomb the extermination camps or in other ways actively halt the extermination process. Indeed, many government officials sought to suppress information about what we now call the Holocaust.

This American behavior has led to much controversy and raises numerous questions. What, if anything, was done to aid the Jews of Europe? What could have been done that was not done, and why? Why were the American people unwilling to modify their harsh immigration laws during the 1930s? Why was President Roosevelt unwilling to challenge these laws and call for their modification? Why did the State Department interpret these laws so rigidly and seek to suppress information about the "Final Solution"? Why were the extermination camps not bombed during the war? Were there other measures that could have been tried but were not? If so, why?

DOCUMENTS

U.S. immigration policy before and during World War II was based on the 1924 National Origins Act, which established immigration quotas particularly limiting to the peoples of Eastern and Southern Europe. Document 1 reproduces key sections of that act. Anti-Semitism was by no means limited to Germany; Document 2 provides a sample of the anti-Semitic writings of the famous American automaker Henry Ford. Document 3 consists of public opinion polls regarding Jews, refugees, and immigration taken before and during the war. Document 4 relates the tragic story of the *St. Louis,* a refugee ship denied the right to unload its passengers in 1939 and forced to return to Europe.

Document 5 is taken from one of the first eyewitness accounts of the Nazi extermination of the Jews. Written by Jan Karski of the Polish Underground and published in late 1944, it describes his 1942 visit, in disguise and in the company of a Nazi militiaman, to a camp in eastern Poland that served as a transit point on the way to the Belzec death camp. State Department officials had been informed of Nazi extermination plans in 1942 and had sought to suppress the information, as shown in Document 6. Document 7 is taken from Treasury Secretary Henry Morgenthau's January 1944 condemnation of State Department behavior in a letter to Roosevelt. Document 8 consists of the recollections of Clinton C. Gardner, who as a U.S. soldier participated in the liberation of a Nazi concentration camp in 1945.

1. The National Origins Act Restricts Immigration, 1924

Section 11

(a) The annual quota of any nationality shall be 2 per centum of the number of foreign-born individuals of such nationality resident in continental United States as determined by the United States census of 1890, but the minimum quota of any nationality shall be 100.

(b) The annual quota of any nationality for the fiscal year beginning July 1, 1927, and for each fiscal year thereafter, shall be a number which bears the same ratio to 150,000 as the number of inhabitants in continental United States in 1920 having that national origin (ascertained as hereinafter provided in this section) bears to the number of inhabitants in continental United States in 1920, but the minimum quota of any nationality shall be 100.

2. Henry Ford's *Dearborn Independent* Reveals American Anti-Semitism, 1921–1922

The international Jewish banker who has no country but plays them all against one another, and the International Jewish proletariat that roams from land to land in search of a peculiar type of economic opportunity, are not figments of the imagination except to the non-Jew who prefers a lazy laxity of mind.

Of these classes of Jews, one or both are at the heart of the problems that disturb the world today. The immigration problem is Jewish. The money question is Jewish. The tie-up of world politics is Jewish. The terms of the Peace Treaty are Jewish. The diplomacy of the world is Jewish. The moral question in movies and theaters is Jewish. The mystery of the illicit liquor business is Jewish.

These facts are unfortunate as well as unpleasant for the Jew, and it is squarely up to him to deal with the facts, and not waste time in trying to destroy those who define the facts. . . .

To say that the immigration problem is Jewish does not mean that Jews must be prohibited entry to any country; it means that they must become rooted to a country in loyal citizenship, as no doubt some are, and as no doubt most are not. To say that the money question is Jewish does not mean that Jews must get out of finance; it means that they must rid finance of the Jewish idea which has always been to use money to get a strangle-hold on men and business concerns, instead of using finance to help general business. . . .

It is not the true Jewishness of the Jew, nor yet the nationalism of the Jew that is on trial, but his anti-national internationalism. A true Mosaic Jew—not a Talmud Jew—would be a good citizen. A nationalist Jew would at least be logical. But an

(Document 1) From Public Law 139, Chapter 190, *United States Statutes at Large* 43 (1925): 153.

(Document 2) From Henry Ford's *Jewish Influences in American Life* and *Aspects of Jewish Power in the United States,* vols. 3 and 4 of *The International Jew: the World's Foremost Problem,* reprints of third and fourth selections from articles appearing in the *Dearborn Independent* (Dearborn, Mich.: Dearborn Publishing Co., Nov. 1921 and May 1922), vol. 3, pp. 243–244; vol. 4, pp. 41–44, 47–48, 50–51, 53.

international Jew has proved an abomination, because his internationalism is focused on his own racial nationalism which in turn is founded on his ingrained belief that the rest of humanity is inferior to him and by right his prey. Jewish leaders may indulge in all the platitudes they possess, the fact which they cannot deny is that the Jew has for centuries regarded the "goyim" as beneath him and legitimately his spoil.

The internationalism of the Jew is confessed everywhere by him. Listen to a German banker: imagine the slow, oily voice in which he said:

"We are international bankers. Germany lost the war?—what of it?—that is an affair of the army. We are international bankers."

And that was the attitude of every international Jewish banker during the war. . . .

The Jewish Question is not in the number of Jews who here reside, not in the American's jealousy of the Jew's success, certainly not in any objection to the Jew's entirely unobjectionable Mosaic religion; it is in something else, and that something else is the fact of Jewish influence on the life of the country where Jews dwell; in the United States it is *the Jewish influence on American life.* . . .

The essence of the Jewish Idea *in its influence on the labor world* is the same as in all other departments—the destruction of real values in favor of fictitious values. The Jewish philosophy of money is not to "make money," but to "get money." The distinction between these two is fundamental. That explains Jews being "financiers" instead of "captains of industry." It is the difference between "getting" and "making."

The creative, constructive type of mind has an affection for the thing it is doing. The non-Jewish worker formerly chose the work he liked best. He did not change employment easily, because there was a bond between him and the kind of work he had chosen. Nothing else was so attractive to him. He would rather draw a little less money and do what he liked to do, than a little more and do what irked him. The "maker" is always thus influenced by his liking.

Not so the "getter." It doesn't matter what he does, so long as the income is satisfactory. He has no illusions, sentiments or affections on the side of work. It is the "geld" that counts. He has no attachment for the things he makes, for he doesn't make any; he deals in the things which other men make and regards them solely on the side of their money-drawing value. "The joy of creative labor" is nothing to him, not even an intelligible saying. . . .

The idea of "get" is a vicious, anti-social and destructive idea *when held alone;* but when held in company with "make" and as second in importance, it is legitimate and constructive. As soon as a man or a class is inoculated with the strictly Jewish Idea of "getting"—("getting mine"; "getting while the getting is good"; "honestly if you can, dishonestly if you must—but *get* it"—all of which are notes of this treasonable philosophy), the very cement of society loses its adhesiveness and begins to crumble. . . .

Jewish influence on the thought of the workingmen of the United States, as well as on the thought of business and professional men, has been bad, thoroughly bad. This is not manifested in a division between "capital" and "labor," for there are no such separate elements; there is only the executive and operating departments of American business. The real division is between the Jewish idea of "get" and the Anglo-Saxon idea of "make," and at the present time the Jewish idea has been successful enough to have caused an upset.

All over the United States, in many branches of trade, Communist colleges are maintained, officered and taught by Jews. These so-called colleges exist in Chicago, Detroit, Cleveland, Rochester, Pittsburgh, New York, Philadelphia and other cities, the whole intent being to put all American labor on a "get" basis, which must prove the economic damnation of the country. And that, apparently, is the end sought, as in Russia.

Until Jews can show that the infiltration of foreign Jews and the Jewish Idea into the American labor movement has made for the betterment in character and estate, in citizenship and economic statesmanship, of the American workingman, the charge of being an alien, destructive and treasonable influence will have to stand. . . .

Colleges are being constantly invaded by the Jewish Idea. . . . Young men in the first exhilarating months of intellectual freedom are being seized with promissory doctrines, the source and consequences of which they do not see. There is a natural rebelliousness of youth, which promises progress; there is a natural venturesomeness to play free with ancient faiths; both of which are ebullitions of the spirit and significant of dawning mental virility. It is during the periods when these adolescent expansions are in process that the youth is captured by influences which deliberately lie in wait for him in the colleges. True, in after years a large proportion come to their senses sufficiently to be able "to sit on the fence and see themselves go by," and they come back to sanity. They find that "free love" doctrines make exhilarating club topics, but that the Family—the old-fashioned loyalty of one man and one woman to each other and their children—is the basis, not only of society, but of all personal character and progress. They find that Revolution, while a delightful subject for fiery debates and an excellent stimulant to the feeling of supermanlikeness, is nevertheless not the process of progress.

And, too, they come at length to see that the Stars and Stripes and the Free Republic are better far than the Red Star and Soviet sordidness. . . .

The only absolute antidote to the Jewish influence is to call college students back to a pride of race. We often speak of the Fathers as if they were the few who happened to affix their signatures to a great document which marked a new era of liberty. The Fathers were the men of the Anglo-Saxon Celtic race. The men who came across Europe with civilization in their blood and in their destiny; the men who crossed the Atlantic and set up civilization on a bleak and rock-bound coast; the men who drove west to California and north to Alaska; the men who peopled Australia and seized the gates of the world at Suez, Gibraltar and Panama; the men who opened the tropics and subdued the arctics—Anglo-Saxon men, who have given form to every government and a livelihood to every people and an ideal to every century. They got neither their God nor their religion from Judah, nor yet their speech nor their creative genius—they are the Ruling People, Chosen throughout the centuries to Master the world, by Building it ever better and better and not by breaking it down.

Into the camp of this race, among the sons of the rulers, comes a people that has no civilization to point to, no aspiring religion, no universal speech, no great achievement in any realm but the realm of "get," cast out of every land that gave them hospitality, and these people endeavor to tell the sons of the Saxons what is needed to make the world what it ought to be. . . .

Judah has begun the struggle. Judah has made the invasion. Let it come. Let no man fear it. But let every man insist that the fight be fair. Let college students and leaders of thought know that the objective is the regnancy of the ideas and the race that have built all the civilization we see and that promise all the civilization of the future; let them also know that the attacking force is Jewish.

3. Public Opinion Polls Reveal American Attitudes About Jews in Europe, Refugees, and Immigration, 1938–1945

Refugees

(US July '38) What is your attitude toward allowing German, Austrian and other political refugees to come into the United States?

We should encourage them to come even if we have to raise our
immigration quotas 4.9%
We should allow them to come but not raise immigration quotas 18.2
With conditions as they are, we should try to keep them out 67.4
Don't know. 9.5

Colonization

(US Nov 22 '38) Should we allow a larger number of Jewish exiles from Germany to come to the United State to live?

Yes   23%   No   77%

Jewish Questions

(US Nov '38) Do you believe that in this country there is very little hostility toward the Jewish people or that there is a growing hostility toward them?

	Little hostility	*Growing hostility*	*Don't know*
National total.	52.5%	32.5%	15.0%
BY EXTREMES IN SIZE OF COMMUNITY			
Cities over 1,000,000	44.1%	46.7%	9.2%
Towns under 2,500	55.9	22.0	22.1
BY RELIGION			
Jewish	50.3%	41.7%	8.0%
Catholic.	51.3	35.3	13.4
Protestant.	53.0	31.0	16.0
None	50.0	30.0	20.0

From Hadley Cantril, *Public Opinion, 1935–1946* (Princeton, N.J.: Princeton University Press, 1951), 382–385, 1150.

(US Apr '39) What do you feel is the reason for hostility toward Jewish people here or abroad?

	National total	*Jewish people*
Reasons favorable to Jews		
People are jealous and envious of Jews' accomplishments	5.5%	17.2%
Jews too clever and successful, have too much ability to make money	4.7	2.5
People who are against Jews are mean, narrow-minded, ignorant, crazy	1.5	10.8
Other favorable to Jews	1.1	5.1
	12.8%	35.6%
Reasons unfavorable to Jews		
Jews control and monopolize enterprise, hoard money, have too much power.	13.0%	8.9%
Unfair and dishonest in business; they cheat and swindle	6.4	1.3
Too grasping, covetous, avaricious, cheap	5.6	—
Their own fault; their manners, characteristics, and attitudes cause people to resent them	4.9	3.2
They're clannish, nonmixers, not good citizens, interested only in race	4.4	1.3
Aggressive, energetic; too aggressive	2.6	2.5
Overbearing; forward; noisy.	1.9	—
Lazy; parasitic; won't do manual labor or pioneer	1.1	—
Other unfavorable	2.4	1.9
	42.3%	19.1%
External and neutral reasons		
Religious and racial prejudice	3.7%	3.2%
Germans; Hitler; dictatorship.	2.6	5.1
Biblical prophecy being fulfilled; will of God—persecuted race	2.1	.6
Financial status of Germany; needs Jewish money to carry on.	2.0	8.3
Propaganda; agitation.	2.0	11.5
Political move; Jews made scapegoat to divert attention from defects of Nazism	1.1	7.6
Subjugation of minorities; fear of overthrow; desire for sole control	.6	1.9
Other; general reasons	2.0	6.4
	16.1	44.6
Don't know	43.3	22.9
	114.5%*	122.2%*

BY OPINIONS ON IMMIGRATION

	Let immi-grants in	*Keep immi-grants out*
Reasons unfavorable to the Jews	26.0%	46.1%
Reasons favorable.	21.8	12.4
Reasons neutral or external	29.0	15.2
Don't know	38.1	41.0
	114.9%*	114.7%*

BY OPINIONS ON ANTI-SEMITISM

	Anti-Semitism not growing	*Anti-Semitism growing*
Reasons unfavorable to the Jews	33.9%	67.7%
Reasons favorable.	17.8	11.0
Reasons neutral or external	19.8	16.3
Don't know	42.5	25.4
	114.0%*	120.4%*

*Percentages add to more than 100 because some respondents gave more than one answer.

(US July '39) Which of the following statements most nearly represents your general opinion on the Jewish question?

In the United States the Jews have the same standing as any other peoples and they should be treated in all ways exactly as any other Americans	38.9%
Jews are in some ways distinct from other Americans, but they make respected and useful citizens so long as they don't try to mingle socially where they are not wanted	10.8
Jews have some different business methods and, therefore, some measures should be taken to prevent Jews from getting too much power in the business world.	31.8
We should make it a policy to deport Jews from this country to some new homeland as fast as it can be done without inhumanity.	10.1
Don't know	6.5
Refused to answer.	3.0
	101.1%*

*Percentages add to more than 100 because some respondents gave more than one answer.

(US July 15 '42) Do you think the Jews have too much power and influence in this country?

Yes   44%   No   41%   No opinion and no answer   15%

(US Jan '43, Dec '44, Nov '45) Do you think that Jewish people in the United States have too much influence in the business world, not enough influence, or about the amount of influence they should have?

	Too much	Not enough	About right	Don't know	Qualified answers
Jan '43	49.7%	2.0%	33.4%	13.3%	1.6%
Dec '44	57	2	29	11	1
Nov '45	58	1	30	11	*

   *Less than 0.5%.

(US Jan 7 '43) It is said that two million Jews have been killed in Europe since the war began. Do you think this is true or just a rumor?

True   47%   Rumor   29%   No opinion   24%

(Germany Oct 26 '45) Which of these statements do you consider as generally true—(1) the treatment the Jews received under Hitler was just what they deserved. (2) Hitler went too far in his treatment of the Jews, but something had to be done to keep them within bounds. (3) The anti-Jewish measures were absolutely unjustified.

Statement 1	—
Statement 2	19%
Statement 3	77
No opinion	3
Other	1

4. *The New York Times* Reports on the *St. Louis* Tragedy, 1939

The saddest ship afloat today, the Hamburg-America liner *St. Louis,* with 900 Jewish refugees aboard, is steaming back toward Germany after a tragic week of frustration at Havana and off the coast of Florida. She is steaming back despite an offer made to Havana yesterday to give a guarantee through the Chase National Bank of $500 apiece for every one of her passengers, men, women, and children, who might land there. President Laredo Bru still has an opportunity to practice those humanitarian sentiments so eloquently expressed in his belated offer of asylum after the refugee ship had been driven from Havana Harbor. His cash terms have been met. But the *St. Louis* still keeps her course for Hamburg.

No plague ship ever received a sorrier welcome. Yet those aboard her had sailed with high hopes. About fifty of them, according to our Berlin dispatch, had consular

---

From "Topics of the Times: Refugee Ship," *The New York Times,* June 8, 1939.

visas. The others all had landing permits for which they had paid; they were unaware that these permits had been declared void in a decree dated May 5. Only a
score of the hundreds were admitted. At Havana the *St. Louis*'s decks became a
stage for human misery. Relatives and friends clamored to get aboard but were held
back. Weeping refugees clamoring to get ashore were halted at guarded gangways.
For days the *St. Louis* lingered within the shadow of Morro Castle, but there was no
relaxation of the new regulations. Every appeal was rejected. One man reached
land. He was pulled from the water with slashed wrists and rushed to a hospital. A
second suicide attempt led the captain to warn the authorities that a wave of self-
destruction might follow. The forlorn refugees themselves organized a patrol committee. Yet out of Havana Harbor the *St. Louis* had to go, trailing pitiful cries of "Auf
Wiedersehen." Off our shores she was attended by a helpful Coast Guard vessel
alert to pick up any passengers who plunged overboard and thrust them back on the
St. Louis again. The refugees could even see the shimmering towers of Miami rising
from the sea, but for them they were only the battlements of another forbidden city.

It is useless now to discuss what might have been done. The case is disposed of.
Germany, with all the hospitality of its concentration camps, will welcome these unfortunates home. Perhaps Cuba, as her spokesmen say, has already taken too many
German refugees. Yet all these 900 asked was a temporary haven. Before they sailed
virtually all of them had registered under the quota provisions of various nations,
including our own. Time would have made them eligible to enter. But there seems to
be no help for them now. The *St. Louis* will soon be home with her cargo of despair.

Her next trip is already scheduled. It will be a gay cruise for carefree tourists.

5. Jan Karski of the Polish Underground Gives an Eyewitness Account of the "Final Solution," 1942–1944

As we approached to within a few hundred yards of the camp, the shouts, cries, and
shots cut off further conversation. I noticed an unpleasant stench that seemed to
have come from decomposing bodies mixed with horse manure. This may have
been an illusion. [My guide] was, in any case, completely impervious to it. He even
began to hum some sort of folk tune to himself. We passed through a small grove of
decrepit-looking trees and emerged directly in front of the loud, sobbing, reeking
camp of death.

It was on a large, flat plain and occupied about a square mile. It was surrounded
on all sides by a formidable barbed-wire fence, nearly two yards in height and in
good repair. Inside the fence, at intervals of about fifteen yards, guards were standing, holding rifles with bayonets ready for use. Around the outside of the fence,
militiamen circulated on constant patrol. The camp itself contained a few small
sheds or barracks. The rest of the area was completely covered by a dense, pulsat-
ing, throbbing, noisy human mass—starved, stinking, gesticulating, insane human
beings in constant agitated motion. Through them, forcing paths if necessary with
their rifle butts, walked the German police and the militiamen. They walked in

From Jan Karski, "Polish Death Camp," *Collier's*, October 14, 1944, pp. 18–19, 60–61.

silence, their faces bored and indifferent. They looked like shepherds bringing in a flock to the market. They had the tired, vaguely disgusted appearance of men doing a routine, tedious job. . . .

The Jewish mass vibrated, trembled, and moved to and fro as if united in a single, insane rhythmic trance. They waved their hands, shouted, quarreled, cursed, and spat at one another. Hunger, thirst, fear, and exhaustion had driven them all insane. I had been told that they were usually left in the camp for three or four days without food or a drop of water. . . .

The chaos, the squalor, the hideousness of it all were simply indescribable. There was a suffocating stench of sweat, filth, decay, damp straw, and excrement. To get to my post we had to squeeze our way through this mob. It was a ghastly ordeal. I had to push foot by foot through the crowd and step over the limbs of those who were lying prone. It was like forcing my way through a mass of death and decomposition made even more horrible by its agonized pulsations. My companion had the skill of long practice, evading the bodies on the ground and winding his way through the mass with the ease of a contortionist. Distracted and clumsy, I would brush against people or step on a figure that reacted like an animal; quickly, often with a moan or a yelp. Each time this occurred I would be seized by a fit of nausea and come to a stop. But my guide kept urging and hustling me along.

In this way we crossed the entire camp and finally stopped about twenty yards from the gate which opened on the passage leading to the train. It was a comparatively uncrowded spot. I felt immeasurably relieved at having finished my stumbling, sweating journey. . . .

I remained there perhaps half an hour, watching this spectacle of human misery. At each moment I felt the impulse to run and flee. I had to force myself to remain indifferent, to practice stratagems to convince myself that I was not one of the condemned. Finally, I noticed a change in the motion of the guards. They walked less and they all seemed to be glancing in the same direction—at the passage to the track which was quite close to me.

I turned toward it myself. Two German policemen came to the gate with a tall, bulky SS man. He barked out an order and they began to open the gate. It was very heavy. He shouted at them impatiently. They worked at it frantically and finally shoved it open. They dashed down the passage as though they were afraid the SS man might come after them, and took up their positions where the passage ended. The whole system had been worked out with crude effectiveness. The outlet of the passage was blocked off by two cars of the freight train, so that any attempt on the part of one of the Jews to break out of the mob would have been completely impossible.

The SS man turned to the crowd, planted himself with his feet wide apart and his hands on his hips, and loosed a roar that must have actually hurt his ribs. It could be heard far above the hellish babble that came from the crowd:

"*Ruhe, ruhe!* Quiet, quiet! All Jews will board this train to be taken to a place where work awaits them. Keep order. Do not push. Anyone who attempts to resist or create a panic will be shot."

He stopped speaking and looked challengingly at the helpless mob that hardly seemed to know what was happening. Suddenly, accompanying the movement with a loud, hearty laugh, he yanked out his gun and fired three random shots into the crowd. A single, stricken groan answered him. He replaced the gun in his holster, smiled, and set himself for another roar:

"*Alle Juden, 'raus—'raus!*"

For a moment the crowd was silent. Those nearest the SS man recoiled from the shots and tried to dodge, panic-stricken, toward the rear. But this was resisted by the mob as a volley of shots from the rear sent the whole mass surging forward madly, screaming in pain and fear. The shots continued without letup from the rear and now from the sides, too, narrowing the mob down and driving it in a savage scramble onto the passageway. In utter panic they rushed down the passageway, trampling it so furiously that it threatened to fall apart.

Then new shots were heard. The two policemen at the entrance to the train were now firing into the oncoming throng corralled in the passageway, in order to slow them down and prevent them from demolishing the flimsy structure. The SS man added his roar to the bedlam.

"*Ordnung, ordnung!*" He bellowed like a madman.

"Order, order!" The two policemen echoed him hoarsely, firing straight into the faces of the Jews running to the trains. Impelled and controlled by this ring of fire, they filled the two cars quickly.

And now came the most horrible episode of all. The military rule stipulates that a freight car may carry eight horses or forty soldiers. Without any baggage at all, a maximum of a hundred passengers pressing against one another could be crowded into a car. The Germans had simply issued orders that 120 to 130 Jews had to enter each car. Those orders were now being carried out. Alternately swinging and firing their rifles, the policemen were forcing still more people into the two cars which were already overfull. The shots continued to ring out in the rear, and the driven mob surged forward, exerting an irresistible pressure against those nearest the train. These unfortunates, crazed by what they had been through, scourged by the policemen, and shoved forward by the milling mob, then began to climb on the heads and shoulders of those in the trains.

These latter were helpless since they had the weight of the entire advancing throng against them. They howled with anguish at those who, clutching at their hair and clothes for support; trampling on necks, faces, and shoulders; breaking bones; and shouting with insensate fury, attempted to clamber over them. More than another score of men, women, and children crushed into the cars in this fashion. Then the policemen slammed the doors across the arms and legs that still protruded, and pushed the iron bars in place.

The two cars were now crammed to bursting with tightly packed human flesh. All this while the entire camp reverberated with a tremendous volume of sound in which groans and screams mingled with shots, curses, and bellowed commands.

Nor was this all. I know that many people will not believe me, but I saw it, and it is not exaggerated. I have no other proofs, no photographs. All I can say is that I saw it, and it is the truth.

The floors of the car had been covered with a thick, white powder. It was quicklime. Quicklime is simply unslaked lime or calcium oxide that has been dehydrated. Anyone who has seen cement being mixed knows what occurs when water is poured on lime. The mixture bubbles and steams as the powder combines with the water, generating a searing heat.

The lime served a double purpose in the Nazi economy of brutality: The moist flesh coming in contact with the lime is quickly dehydrated and burned. The occupants of the cars would be literally burned to death before long, the flesh eaten from their bones. Thus the Jews would "die in agony," fulfilling the promise Himmler had issued "in accord with the will of the Fuehrer," in Warsaw in 1942. Secondly, the lime would prevent the decomposing bodies from spreading disease. It was efficient and inexpensive—a perfectly chosen agent for its purpose.

It took three hours to fill up the entire train. It was twilight when the forty-six cars were packed. From one end to the other the train, with its quivering cargo of flesh, seemed to throb, vibrate, rock, and jump as if bewitched. There would be a strangely uniform momentary lull and then the train would begin to moan and sob, wail and howl. Inside the camp a few score dead bodies and a few in the final throes of death remained. German policemen walked around at leisure with smoking guns, pumping bullets into anything that moaned or moved. Soon none were left alive. In the now quiet camp the only sounds were the inhuman screams that echoed from the moving train. Then these, too, ceased. All that was now left was the stench of excrement and rotting straw and a queer, sickening, acidulous odor which, I thought, may have come from the quantities of blood that had stained the ground.

The Last Incredible Journey

As I listened to the dwindling outcries from the train I thought of the destination toward which it was speeding. My informants had minutely described the entire journey. The train would travel about eight miles and finally come to a halt in an empty, barren field. Then nothing at all would happen. The train would stand stock-still, patiently waiting while death penetrated into every corner of its interior. This would take from two to four days.

When quicklime, asphyxiation, and injuries had silenced every outcry, a group of men would appear. They would be young, strong Jews, assigned to the task of cleaning out these cars until their own turn to ride in them should arrive. Under a strong guard they would unseal the cars and expel the heaps of decomposing bodies. The mounds of flesh that they piled up would then be burned and the remnants buried in a single huge hole. The cleaning, burning, and burial would consume one or two full days.

The entire process of disposal would take, then, from three to six days. During this period the camp would have recruited new victims. The train would return and the whole cycle would be repeated. . . .

. . . I walked to the store as quickly as I could, running when there was no one about to see me. I reached the grocery store so breathless that the owner became alarmed. I reassured him while I threw off my uniform, boots, stockings, and underwear. I ran into the kitchen and locked the door. In a little while my bewildered and worried host called out to me:

"Hey, what are you doing in there?"

"Don't worry. I'll be right out."

When I came out, he promptly entered the kitchen and called back in despair: "What the devil have you been doing? The whole kitchen is flooded!"

"I washed myself," I replied, "that is all. I was very dirty."

Then I collapsed. I was completely, violently, rackingly sick. Even today, when I remember those scenes, I become nauseated.

6. The State Department Receives and Suppresses News of the "Final Solution," 1942

August 8, 1942

MEMORANDUM

Subject: Conversation with Mr. Gerhart
M. RIEGNER, Secretary of World
Jewish Congress

This morning Mr. Gerhart M. RIEGNER, Secretary of the World Jewish Congress in Geneva, called in great agitation. He stated that he had just received a report from a German business man of considerable prominence, who is said to have excellent political and military connections in Germany and from whom reliable and important political information has been obtained on two previous occasions, to the effect that there has been and is being considered in Hitler's headquarters a plan to exterminate all Jews from Germany and German controlled areas in Europe after they have been concentrated in the east (presumably Poland). The number involved is said to be between three-and-a-half and four millions and the object is to permanently settle the Jewish question in Europe. The mass execution if decided upon would allegedly take place this fall.

Riegner stated that according to his informant the use of prussic acid was mentioned as a means of accomplishing the executions. When I mentioned that this report seemed fantastic to me, Riegner said that it had struck him in the same way but that from the fact that mass deportation had been taking place since July 16 as confirmed by reports received by him from Paris, Holland, Berlin, Vienna, and Prague it was always conceivable that such a diabolical plan was actually being considered by Hitler as a corollary.

According to Riegner, 14,000 Jews have already been deported from occupied France and 10,000 more are to be handed over from occupied France in the course of the next few days. Similarly from German sources 56,000 Jews have already been deported from the Protectorate together with unspecified numbers from Germany and other occupied countries.

From State Department Files, Record Group 59, National Archives, Washington, D.C.; reproduced in *America and the Holocaust,* vol. 1, ed. David S. Wyman (New York: Garland, 1990), 187, 191–194.

Riegner said this report was so serious and alarming that he felt it his duty to make the following requests: (1) that the American and other Allied Governments be informed with regard thereto at once; (2) that they be asked to try by every means to obtain confirmation or denial; (3) that Dr. Stephen Wise, the president of his organization, be informed of the report.

I told Riegner that the information would be passed on to the Legation at once but that I was not in a position to inform him as to what action, if any, the Legation might take. He hoped that he might be informed in due course that the information had been transmitted to Washington.

For what it is worth, my personal opinion is that Riegner is a serious and balanced individual and that he would never have come to the Consulate with the above report if he had not had confidence in his informant's reliability and if he did not seriously consider that the report might well contain an element of truth. Again it is my opinion that the report should be passed on to the Department for what it is worth.

There is attached a draft of a telegram prepared by Riegner giving in his own words a telegraphic summary of his statements to me.

Howard Elting, Jr.
American Vice Consul
[Geneva, Switzerland]

Copy

DR. STEPHEN WISE PRESIDENT AMERICAN JEWISH CONGRESS

330 WEST 42ND STREET ROOM 809

NEW YORK

RECEIVED ALARMING REPORT STATING THAT IN FUEHRERS HEADQUARTERS A PLAN HAS BEEN DISCUSSED AND BEING UNDER CONSIDERATION ACCORDING WHICH TOTAL OF JEWS IN COUNTRIES OCCUPIED CONTROLLED BY GERMANY NUMBERING THREEANDHALF TO FOUR MILLIONS SHOULD AFTER DEPORTATION AND CONCENTRATED IN EAST BE AT ONE BLOW EXTERMINATED IN ORDER RESOLVE ONCE FOR ALL JEWISH QUESTION IN EUROPE STOP   ACTION IS REPORTED TO BE PLANNED FOR AUTUMN WAYS OF EXECUTION STILL DISCUSSED STOP   IT HAS BEEN SPOKEN OF PRUSSIC ACID STOP   IN TRANSMITTING INFORMATION WITH ALL NECESSARY RESERVATION AS EXACTITUDE CANNOT BE CONTROLLED BY US BEG TO STATE THAT INFORMER IS REPORTED HAVE CLOSE CONNECTIONS WITH HIGHEST GERMAN AUTHORITIES AND HIS REPORTS TO BE GENERALLY RELIABLE

WORLD JEWISH CONGRESS
GERARD RIEGNER

ADDRESS OFFICIAL COMMUNICATIONS TO
THE SECRETARY OF STATE
WASHINGTON, D. C.

DEPARTMENT OF STATE
WASHINGTON

Do not send 🖋

In reply refer to
Eu:862.4016/2233

My dear Dr. Wise:

The following message, in paraphrase, has been received from the American Legation at Bern. It was sent at the request of Mr. Gerhardt M. Riegner, Secretary of the World Jewish Congress at Geneva.

In Hitler's headquarters a plan is being considered to wipe out at one blow from 3,500,000 to 4,000,000 Jews this autumn, following their expulsion from countries controlled or occupied by Germany and their concentration in the East, according to a report from a person whose previous reports have been generally reliable and who is alleged to have intimate connections among the highest German officials. Prussic acid has been contemplated but the manner of extermination has not yet been determined. The correctness of the report cannot be confirmed and the information is therefore sent with reservation.

The Legation at Bern has no information which would confirm this rumor and believes it is one of the many unreliable war rumors circulating in Europe today.

Sincerely yours,

For the Secretary of State:

Paul T. Culbertson

Paul T. Culbertson,
Assistant Chief, Division of
European Affairs.

Dr. Stephen S. Wise,
President, American Jewish Congress,
330 West 42nd Street,
New York, New York.

FOR DEFENSE
BUY
UNITED
STATES
SAVINGS
BONDS
AND STAMPS

DEPARTMENT OF STATE
_____

DIVISION OF EUROPEAN AFFAIRS

<u>MEMORANDUM</u>   August 13, 1942.

With reference to Bern's telegram no. 3697 [862.4016/2233] August 11, 3 p.m. transmitting information from Mr. Gerhardt M. Riegner, Secretary of the World Jewish Congress, Geneva, regarding the alleged plan of the Nazis to exterminate three and a half to four million Jews, it does not appear advisable in view of the Legation's comments, the fantastic nature of the allegation, and the impossibility of our being of any assistance if such action were taken, to transmit the information to Dr. Stephen Wise as suggested.

[Elbridge Durbrow]

7. Secretary of the Treasury Henry Morgenthau, Jr., Denounces State Department Behavior to Roosevelt, 1944

PERSONAL REPORT TO THE PRESIDENT

One of the greatest crimes in history, the slaughter of the Jewish people in Europe, is continuing unabated.

This Government has for a long time maintained that its policy is to work out programs to save those Jews and other persecuted minorities of Europe who could be saved.

You are probably not as familiar as I with the utter failure of certain officials in our State Department, who are charged with actually carrying out this policy, to take any effective action to prevent the extermination of the Jews in German-controlled Europe.

The public record, let alone the facts which have not yet been made public, reveals the gross procrastination of these officials. It is well known that since the time when it became clear that Hitler was determined to carry out a policy of exterminating the Jews in Europe, the State Department officials have failed to take any positive steps reasonably calculated to save any of these people. Although they have used devices such as setting up intergovernmental organizations to survey the whole refugee problem, and calling conferences such as the Bermuda Conference to explore the whole refugee problem, making it appear that positive action could be expected, in fact nothing has been accomplished.

The best summary of the whole situation is contained in one sentence of a report submitted on December 20, 1943, by the Committee on Foreign Relations of the Senate, recommending the passage of a Resolution (S.R. 203), favoring the appointment of a commission to formulate plans to save the Jews of Europe from extinction by Nazi Germany. . . .

> "We have talked; we have sympathized; we have expressed our horror; the time to act is long past due."

Whether one views this failure as being deliberate on the part of those officials handling the matter, or merely due to their incompetence, is not too important from my point of view. However, there is a growing number of responsible people and organizations today who have ceased to view our failure as the product of simple incompetence on the part of those officials in the State Department charged with handling this problem. They see plain Anti-Semitism motivating the actions of

---

From Henry Morgenthau, Jr., diaries, Franklin D. Roosevelt Library, Hyde Park, N.Y.; reproduced in *America and the Holocaust,* vol. 8, ed. David S. Wyman (New York: Garland, 1990), 498–506.

these State Department officials and, rightly or wrongly, it will require little more in the way of proof for this suspicion to explode into a nasty scandal. . . .

The facts I have detailed in this report, Mr. President, came to the Treasury's attention as a part of our routine investigation of the licensing of the financial phases of the proposal of the World Jewish Congress for the evacuation of Jews from France and Rumania. The facts may thus be said to have come to light through accident. How many others of the same character are buried in State Department files is a matter I would have no way of knowing. Judging from the almost complete failure of the State Department to achieve any results, the strong suspicion must be that they are not few.

This much is certain, however. The matter of rescuing the Jews from extermination is a trust too great to remain in the hands of men who are indifferent, callous, and perhaps even hostile. The task is filled with difficulties. Only a fervent will to accomplish, backed by persistent and untiring effort can succeed where time is so precious.

[Henry Morgenthau, Jr.
Jan. 16, 1944.]

8. U.S. Soldier Clinton C. Gardner Remembers the Liberation of the Buchenwald Concentration Camp, 1945

Clinton Gardner's report of the liberation of Buchenwald appears here as it did originally in The Dartmouth *on 15, 17, and 19 April 1946—except that a few misprints have been corrected. It reflects the time in which it was written, as well as the events of April 1945.*

. . .

As you go north from Weimar the road climbs a long well-forested hill. The trees whose arched limbs frame the way are beech, which is how the forest got its name: Buchenwald. It is an annoying, rutted road that you follow for a few kilometers, but at the top of the hill, where this road continues straight, there on your left is a broad, new concrete highway. When you take this left, as some three hundred thousand Europeans have done before you, you will find that you are on a one way road and there are no more turns.

A few more kilometers and the road bursts out into a huge clearing on the hill's north side. The view is breath-taking: thirty miles of patchwork scenery, brilliant green farmland and velvety purple forests. But to enjoy this view is uncommon. The hill is a bad place for weather; in winter it is one of the coldest, most bitter places in Germany.

Let your eyes drop from the view and focus on the clearing. On each side of the road are bombed-out factory buildings, junk heaps of brick and steel. To the left, a quarter of a mile away are twenty four-story brick barracks, the SS soldiers' garrison. Four thousand elite, black-uniformed Nazis lived here. Just to the right of the barracks begins another built-up area: neat rows of one-story wooden buildings

From *The Dartmouth,* April 15, 17, and 19, 1946, as reprinted with misprints corrected by David Scrase and Wolfgang Mieder, eds., *The Holocaust: Personal Accounts* (Burlington: Center for Holocaust Studies at the University of Vermont, 2001), 238–242.

and a few rows of two-story brick. These make up a compact block, five rows wide, eleven buildings to a row. The square thus formed is about three hundred yards on a side. In it, surrounded by an electrified, fifteen foot barbed wire fence, existed at one time forty-eight thousand human beings. That is the concentration camp—*Konzentrationslager Buchenwald. . . .*

There were twenty thousand prisoners left when we liberated the camp. A few days before another twenty thousand had been evacuated eastward. More than a thousand of these were found dead on the train at Dachau. No women stayed at Buchenwald; when families arrived the women were sent north to Bergen-Belsen. But children stayed behind. There were eight hundred children under fourteen kept behind the wire. Every nation in Europe was represented. Our first census showed: 4,000 Russians, 3,000 French, 3,000 Poles, 2,000 Germans, and 2,000 Czechs; many hundreds of Belgians, Dutch, Austrians, Yugoslavs, Spaniards and Italians; some Greeks, Norwegians, ex-Swedes, ex-Swiss, and ex-Americans.

The first thing we went to see inside the camp was the crematory. It was not far from the entrance gate and easy to find because it was stone and stood out from the flimsy wooden barracks. Its smokestack was tall, a sort of monument visible from all over the camp. There were lots of our soldiers waiting to see the crematory yard. You could easily smell what they were waiting to see. Dead bodies in the sun have a smell that is peculiarly indescribable. The sight of them, however, was far more powerful. It crystallized many a thought you had had on man's inhumanity to man. Now these men were only dust, but to the Nazis they had been dust long before their death. The four hundred bodies there were waiting to be burned, waiting to join the *fifty-one thousand* that had gone before them there.

They lay there because in the last few weeks there had been no coal. In fact two thousand others had collected in those few weeks and the SS had had to throw them into a huge natural pit up on the very top of the Buchenwald hill. . . .

Buchenwald is generally considered by the American public to have been the worst or at least one of the worst Nazi concentration camps. This is not true. Of the ten biggest, Buchenwald was the "best."

The probable reason for its reputation is that it received more publicity. First Army headquarters was at Weimar and with it, of course, was the press. It was very convenient for the reporters to hop into a jeep and go the few kilometers to Buchenwald for the horror story of the year.

Had they gone to Nordhausen, fifty miles north, they would have seen a camp whose name was whispered in awe at Buchenwald. At this camp, where V-2s were made, there were about ten-thousand prisoners, with a monthly death rate of one thousand—usually due to a combination of starvation and overwork.

Even more deadly than Nordhausen were the annihilation camps (*Vernichtungslager*). The best known of these are Auschwitz at Kraków and Majdanek at Lublin, Poland. Buchenwald was a health resort compared to these. It had its factories and stone quarries to run. Deaths were not its mission. Indeed they were not particularly sought after. If they occurred, it had to be charged up to operating expenses. After all, only fifty-one thousand died there. At Majdanek well over a million were gassed, shot and burned.

In that light, knowing that the prisoners preferred Buchenwald to the others (many of which they had passed through), it is perhaps even more significant to see what a "good" concentration camp was like.

A sharp distinction should be made at this point between what were called the Big and the Little Camps at Buchenwald. The Big Camp provided workers for the factories that made such things as artillery caissons, truck parts, and optical instruments. But men in the Little Camp had no work to do. They just had to exist, just had to wait.

Before 1943 the Little Camp had been a quarantine area. Newly arrived prisoners spent their first six weeks there. They slept on triple-decker plain wood shelves sixteen men to twelve feet of shelf space, two feet of headroom between shelves. Rations were soup twice a day, bread occasionally, but less of both than in the Big Camp where they were nominally the same. Most men lost forty per cent of their weight in those first six weeks. Often they didn't last. One night in 1941 seventy men went mad and had to be killed by the camp doctors.

When the Little Camp hospital got overcrowded the doctors took the same measures. Shortly after we liberated the camp we captured two Poles who, when they realized that we had found out about it, admitted to having helped in this hospital clearance. They had disposed of a thousand patients. One held the man while the other gave him an injection of carbolic acid in the base of the brain.

At the end of their six weeks initiation period a prisoner was supposed to graduate to the Big Camp. If he was a Jew, he seldom did. And after perhaps a year in the Big Camp, if a man got sick or feeble, he was sent back to the Little Camp. After all, if he was sick he was of no more use. By the winter of 1944–45 starvation was causing one hundred deaths a day in the Little Camp.

✸ E S S A Y S

U.S. response to the Holocaust became a controversial issue only in the late 1960s, when key documents were declassified and the Americans began a public discussion about this important event (see Peter Novick's essay in Chapter 12). The result was a series of popular and scholarly works sharply critical of U.S. inaction in general and of the Roosevelt administration in particular. The first essay is taken from one of these works, written by Henry Feingold of the City University of New York. In recent years this condemnation has itself come under attack from scholars who defend the behavior of the Roosevelt administration in light of the limits under which it had to operate and what it was able to accomplish. The second essay, by Franklin and Eleanor Roosevelt Institute president William J. Vanden Heuvel, summarizes this defense.

The American Failure to Rescue European Jews

HENRY L. FEINGOLD

Rescue in Retrospect

On those occasions during the Holocaust years when mass rescue appeared possible, it required of the nations a passionate commitment to save lives. Such a commitment did not exist in the Roosevelt Administration, although there were many individuals who wanted to do more.

From Henry L. Feingold, *The Politics of Rescue: The Roosevelt Administration and the Holocaust, 1938–1945* (New Brunswick: NJ: Rutgers University Press, 1970), 295–307.

Between 1938 and 1941 refugee-rescue advocates, most of whom were supporters of the New Deal, undoubtedly believed that the humanitarian concern which characterized Roosevelt's handling of domestic problems could be projected to the refuge crisis. That assumption was buttressed by the statements of concern which accompanied each White House announcement that visa procedures had been liberalized. Those who might have questioned the authenticity of the Administration's concern would have been hard pressed to explain other steps taken by Roosevelt in this early period. The President had, after all, taken the initiative in calling an international refugee conference to meet at Evian. The establishment of the IGC [Intergovernmental Committee on Political Refugees] which resulted from that conference was primarily an Administration-supported endeavor as were the Rublee-Schacht negotiations, which were designed to bring order into the refugee chaos. Moreover, a special procedure to rescue the cultural and scientific elite of Europe had been established and the Administration was busily occupied in searching for areas where the refugees might find new homes. What more could be asked?

Promise and Reality.   What refugee-rescue advocates could foresee only with some difficulty at the time was that all these steps would remain largely gestures which the Roosevelt Administration would not and sometimes could not follow up. There developed a gulf between the professed good intentions of the Administration and the implementation of policy. The hope of bringing refugees to the United States was severely circumscribed by the seemingly immutable immigration law. The invitation to the nations to meet at Evian was so qualified that from the outset there seemed little hope of solving the problem of where to put the growing number of refugees. Once at the Conference the American delegation was in the embarrassing position of lacking the bargaining power to convince others to undertake a serious effort to provide for refugees or the will to do so itself. The Intergovernmental Committee for Political Refugees which grew out of the Conference became a monument to the Administration's impotence on the rescue front. The IGC remained throughout those years to clutter and confuse the effort. The attempt by [Assistant Secretary of State] Breckinridge Long to resurrect this ineffective agency after the Bermuda Conference was little more than an effort to thwart more energetic rescue activity.

The Administration's search for resettlement havens shows a similar tendency to degenerate into mere humanitarian gestures. While the President dreamed of a United States of Africa and proposed visionary schemes of nation-building, a visible manifestation of the Administration's concern, a proposal to make Alaska and the Virgin Islands available to a limited number of refugees, was ultimately rejected. When the political risk of circumventing the immigration laws was finally taken in July 1944 by the establishment of a temporary haven in Oswego, New York, it was too late to make a difference.

The struggle over the administration of the visa procedure and the special visa lists throws some light on the conflicting tendencies within the Administration. The visa system became literally an adjunct to Berlin's murderous plan for the Jews. The quotas were underissued until 1939 and after June 1940 a skillful playing on the security fear resulted in ever more drastic reduction of refugee immigrants. In the critical year of 1941 only 47 percent of the German-Austrian quota was filled. A similar pattern is discernible in the procedure by which prominent refugees could receive special visitors' visas. Here again, the good intentions of the Administration were thwarted by the State Department and the consuls.

The calling of the Bermuda Conference in mid-1943 marks the fullest development of what might be called a politics of gestures. Held in inaccessible Bermuda, officials in London, where the initiative to hold such a conference developed, and Washington saw in the idea of holding another refugee conference the possibility of muting the growing agitation for a more active effort. The State Department confined the delegates to dealing with a group it called "political refugees," a euphemism for Jews, who bore the brunt of the Nazi liquidation program. The Conference was thereby confined to discussing ways and means of "rescuing" a handful of refugees who had found a precarious safety in Spain and other neutral havens and who were, in fact, already rescued, while those who faced death in the camps were ignored.

Reasons for the Gap in Implementing Rescue Policy.   The gulf which often exists between decision makers and administrators was especially wide in the case of rescue because the coterie of middle echelon career officers headed by Breckinridge Long and located primarily in the Special Problems Division of the State Department consistently opposed the professed humanitarian intentions of the Administration. The mobilization of a countervailing influence within the Administration which might have come from the Department of Interior, the Justice Department, and the Treasury Department, as well as numerous Jewish officials, did not materialize until the final months of 1943 when Henry Morgenthau, Jr., took up the cause. Before that time, Breckinridge Long, by his own account, usually had his way. He was able to capitalize on the weakness of White House leadership, so that the making and the administration of what amounted to the rescue program fell naturally in the purview of the State Department. An effective coalition of restrictionists and conservative legislators and Long's control of the flow of information to the White House abetted anti-rescue activities. After 1940, Breckinridge Long, by use of what I have called the security gambit, a playing on the fear that spies had infiltrated the refugee stream, was able to curtail the humanitarian activity of the Roosevelt Administration.

To place the responsibility for the failure of the Administration's rescue activity on Breckinridge Long alone would be to oversimplify. Roosevelt did intrude intermittently into the arena of rescue activity. We have seen that he was especially enthusiastic about the search for resettlement havens and he had some firm ideas about the form such ventures should take. Occasionally he mediated squabbles between rescue advocates and opponents within the Administration. But usually his suggestions, especially in the resettlement area, had an "above the battle" quality, being nowhere bound to the reality of the circumstances. Much of the inconsistency between the rhetoric of the Administration and the actual implementation of policy can be traced to the chief executive's uncertain mandate. Bound by a restrictive immigration law and perhaps an oversensitivity to the "Jew Deal" label which had been applied to his Administration on the one hand, and yet anxious to help the Nazi victims on the other, Roosevelt sought a balance between the opponents and advocates of a more active rescue policy. Such a middle road was never found, and to this day it is difficult for researchers to determine Roosevelt's personal role.

They must turn to the State Department for answers, and repeat the journey made by American Jewish leaders during the Holocaust.

The Role of American Jewry.   . . . On the surface, few groups appeared better equipped to exert pressure on the Roosevelt Administration than American Jewry. Yet between 1938 and 1943 Jews were not notably successful in influencing the establishment on rescue ground rules and that failure proved catastrophic. In one sense the rescue battle was lost in the first round. Why they did not have more influence on the making and administration of rescue policy is only partly answered by what was happening within the American Jewish community during those terrible years.

The role that fell to American Jewry was difficult, perhaps impossible, to fill. It was called upon not only to attempt to change restrictive immigration policies which a majority of American Jews had supported in 1938, but also to challenge the State Department's administrative fiat further limiting the number which might come to these shores. They had to counteract a hysterical fear of Nazi espionage which was abetted by Congress, the State Department, the White House, and the communications media. No "hyphenate" group had ever been faced with the prospect of total annihilation of its European brethren and, while there was great urgency to use its influence, it proved to be extremely difficult to impress the urgency for action on the Administration. The rescue case concerned the disposition and treatment of a foreign minority, took place largely during the war years and, most important, required Roosevelt to tangle with powerful restrictionists in Congress and his own Administration. The kind of influence required was not available to Jewish leaders.

When catastrophe threatened, the deep fissures between its "uptown" and "downtown" elements had barely been bridged. Jews were anxious to continue their rapid movement into the mainstream of American life and did not readily accept the mantle of leadership which for centuries had been worn by European Jewry. Much of their formidable organizational resources were dissipated in internal bickering until it seemed as if Jews were more anxious to tear each other apart than to rescue their coreligionists. . . . The Jews had achieved higher positions in the New Deal than in any prior Administration, but even with such resources they could not fully mobilize.

It is, of course, easy to know by hindsight what might have been done by American Jews. Disunity and powerlessness were characteristic of Jewish communities everywhere and the United States was no exception. The political behavior of American Jewry, moreover, exacerbated the situation. American Jews . . . supported Roosevelt because they thought his program evidenced concern for the "forgotten man." Such concern was a traditional part of the Jewish belief. When the New Deal moved further to the left after the election of 1936, the Jewish "love affair" with Roosevelt, in sharp contrast with other hyphenate groups, grew more ardent. The delivery of a voting bloc, the most potent weapon in any political arsenal, was not available to Jewish leaders. They could not gain leverage by threatening a withdrawal of votes and were therefore dependent on less certain rewards for political loyalty. If American Jews detected any failing in the rescue program it was not reflected in their voting. . . .

The growth of Zionist sentiment among American Jews as the crisis deepened was an additional factor interfering with the focusing of Jewish pressure on the

White House. The new power relationship naturally gave those organizations with Zionist inclinations reason to hope that Jewry might be unified under their auspices. But other organizations stubbornly protected their organizational integrity. The crisis posed a special dilemma for the Zionists, for while it convinced many Jews of the need for a Jewish national homeland it also gave the old territorialists a new lease on life. Roosevelt was only one of many world leaders who were taken with visionary resettlement schemes. For Zionists a national homeland in Palestine was so clearly the answer that to divert money and energy to resettlement elsewhere was akin to heresy. . . .

Unfortunately, the strife between Zionists and other groups did not remain merely academic. It not only interfered with the mobilization of American Jewry but spilled over into the largely Zionist-administered operation which maintained listening posts around the periphery of occupied Europe. The bickering between agents over credit for the handful that were brought out, which could be heard in Lisbon, Ankara and Stockholm, possesses an irony all its own. While the Nazi overlords endlessly projected a picture of a well-coordinated international Jewish conspiracy, the rescuers were in continuous conflict over questions of which Jews should be saved and who should get the credit.

Perspective on the Roosevelt Administration as Holocaust Witness.   To view the Administration's failure to do everything that might have been done to save Jewish lives in perspective, an appreciation of the domestic and international problems involved in mass rescue is necessary. The rescue of European Jewry, especially after the failure to act during the refugee phase (1939 to October 1941), was so severely circumscribed by Nazi determination that it would have required an inordinate passion to save lives and a huge reservoir of good will toward Jews to achieve it. Such passion to save Jewish lives did not exist in the potential receiving nations. In the case of the United States, one can readily see today that a projection of human concern inwards to its own domestic problems such as alleviating the misery of its own Negro minority had barely been begun by the New Deal. What hope of better treatment could be held for a foreign minority? But this was not the only reason that the energy and organization of the Administration's rescue effort, even at its apogee in January 1944, never remotely approached the effort Berlin was willing to make to see the Final Solution through to its bitter end.

There were factors on the domestic political scene that further circumscribed action on the Administration's part. We have noted the continued strength of the restrictionists who remained alert during the refugee phase to the slightest infringement of the quota system. The anti-Jewish thrust of the anti-refugee sentiment did not escape the notice of Jewish leadership, who had become sensitized to the mood in the nation in the thirties. Supported by the Depression-created tensions and the example and financial support of the Reich, Jews found it difficult to dismiss the rantings of Father Charles E. Coughlin and other spokesmen of anti-Semitism. In Congress, for example, the negative response to the Wagner-Rogers Bill to save German-Jewish refugee children as contrasted to the favorable response to the evacuation of non-Jewish British children was too apparent to escape notice. The growth of domestic anti-Semitism projected against what was happening in Europe brought out the latent insecurities of American Jewry and sharpened internal divisions. The bitter disputes over the boycott of German goods and other "emotional" forms of agitation as well as the continued apprehension about dual loyalties in some sections of American Jewry become more understandable in the light of this insecurity.

A hidden casualty to the renewed vigor of domestic anti-Semitism may have been Roosevelt's willingness to strengthen his Administration's strong link to American Jewry. Roosevelt's appointments of Jews to high positions were a far cry from extending a helping hand to a foreign minority whose coreligionists in America were not winning medals for popularity. Such a commitment entailed a political risk which Roosevelt was not willing to take, and the Administration's response was to go through the motions of rescue without taking the political risk of implementing them. Undoubtedly this partly explains the paradox of the State Department's use of the innocuous label "political refugees," and maintaining it long after it had become apparent that the Reich meant to liquidate Jews and was converting all "enemies," including Roosevelt, to the Jewish faith. By concealing the anti-Jewish character of the Nazi depredations behind a neutral or interdenominational cover, Roosevelt may have sought to lessen the predictable outcry about favoritism towards Jews at home. For example, he expressed disappointment at the specific mention of Jews when Rublee revealed the provisions of the statement of agreement to him in February 1939. Again in October 1939 Roosevelt told Ickes about his hope to admit ten thousand refugees to Alaska on the same nationality ratio by which the quota system admitted immigrants to the mainland. That would limit entrance to one thousand Jews, a figure which Roosevelt hoped "would avoid the undoubted criticism" which would surely result "if there were an undue proportion of Jews." In May 1944 Roosevelt was still worrying about such "undue proportions" when he instructed Robert Murphy, who was to make the selection for the camp in Oswego, to make certain that he gets "reasonable proportions" of all categories of persecuted minorities. Beyond traumatizing American Jewry, the startling growth of anti-Semitism in the thirties may have alerted Roosevelt, whose sensitivity to the ethnic strain in American politics was well known, to the perils of further strengthening his ties to American Jewry.

Aside from such domestic political considerations, there were other roadblocks in the way of rescue. In the refugee and later the rescue phase, certain legal technicalities plagued the rescue effort. Admittedly there is a certain unreality in talking of legal technicalities while mass murder is being committed, but the witnesses and the perpetrators of the Holocaust were affected by such considerations. Before being deprived of their national citizenship the Jews were an "internal problem," and after they had been stripped of their national rights and citizenship they were not legally the responsibility of the nations who might have acted as rescue agents. As much as France, Britain, and the United States were directly involved in Germany's extrusion policy by having to become receiving nations, they had no power to force her to cease and desist. When there was a clear legal responsibility or an opportunity to utilize international law, the nations often did act. Thus when the Nazis threatened American Jewish property in Germany with confiscation before December 1941, the State Department did make strong representations. When Hungarian Jews in France were forced to wear the yellow star and later concentrated to be deported, Hungary did intercede in Berlin. Italian Jews were not forced to wear the yellow star. As cobelligerents Hungary and Italy maintained their sovereignty and therefore control of the fate of their Jews. A neutral like Turkey was able to protect its Jewish nationals in France and Spain's willingness to extend citizenship to Sephardic Jews saved some lives. Often Latin-American legal papers could make the difference between life and death, for paradoxically, even in the midst of their bloody operation, Nazis observed certain legal niceties. When there was no clear-cut legal responsibility, it proved difficult to elicit from the nations a voluntary response on humanitarian or moral grounds. Nation states like the United States are man-made institutions, not man himself. They have no souls and no natural sense of morality, especially when it concerns a foreign minority which is clearly not their legal responsibility. It is difficult to separate the charge that the Roosevelt Administration did not do enough to rescue Jews during the Holocaust years from the assumption that modern nation-states can make human responses in situations like the Holocaust. One wonders if the history of the twentieth, or any other century, warrants such an assumption, especially when the nation-state feels its security threatened.

In those rare cases where governments are able to make human responses to catastrophes they do so at the behest of an aroused public opinion. The shipping of relief supplies to Biafra is a case in point. In the case of the Jews the Roosevelt Administration had no popular mandate for a more active rescue role. Public opinion was, in fact, opposed to the admission of refugees, because most Americans were not aware of what was happening. A Roper poll taken in December 1944 showed that the great majority of Americans, while willing to believe that Hitler had killed some Jews, could not believe that the Nazis, utilizing modern production techniques, had put millions to death. The very idea beggared the imagination. Perhaps there is such a thing as a saturation point as far as atrocity stories are concerned. In the American mind the Final Solution took its place beside the Bataan Death March and the Malmedy massacre as just another atrocity in a particularly cruel war. Not only were the victims unable to believe the unbelievable, but those who would save them found it extremely difficult to break through the "curtain of silence." The State Department's suppression of the details compounded the problem of credibility.

The Administration's reluctance to publicly acknowledge that a mass murder operation was taking place went far in keeping American public opinion ignorant and therefore unaroused while it helped convince men like Goebbels that the Allies approved or were at least indifferent to the fate of the Jews. Psychological warfare techniques such as threats of retribution and bombing did have some effect in Hungary. A statement by Washington that the massive raid on Hamburg in July 1943 was made in retribution for a Treblinka or better yet a bombing of the rail lines and crematoria would have gone far to pierce the "curtain of silence," not only in the United States but among the people of occupied Europe. Specific mention of the crime against Jews was omitted from war-crimes statements and not until March 1944 could Roosevelt be prevailed upon to make some correction in the Moscow War Crimes Declaration. That statement promised vengeance for crimes against Cretan peasants but neglected to mention the Final Solution. From that point of view the failure of John J. McCloy, then Assistant Secretary of War, to favorably consider a joint request by the World Jewish Congress and the WRB to bomb the crematoria because it would be of "doubtful efficacy" was especially tragic. It might have gone far to alert world opinion to the mass murder operation as well as disrupting the delicate strands which made it possible. Washington maintained its silence for fear, in McCloy's words, that it might "provoke even more vindictive action by the

Germans." Berlin, it was felt, was fully capable of escalating the terror. But for European Jewry, at least, it is difficult to imagine a terror greater than that of Auschwitz.

An effective rescue effort required not only inordinate energy and will but also coordination with other nations and agencies. It required the collective effort of the Vatican, the Committee of the International Red Cross (CIRC), other neutrals, the Allied governments, the governments in exile and the people of the occupied areas. While a determined effort by the Roosevelt Administration would have set a good precedent it did not mean that other nations and agencies would have automatically fallen in line. Latin America, for example, showed little propensity to follow Washington's advice regarding resettlement havens. The Taylor mission to the Vatican did not result in a change of Vatican policy and the CIRC was not fully activated until mid-1944. All maintained their own measure of commitment which they could claim fully matched that of the United States. The mere existence of separate national rescue efforts presented a problem of coordination. The IGC, which was established after the Evian Conference, might have furnished such coordination but, as we have seen, it became instead the first casualty of the lack of will. The early rescue effort was literally strangled by red tape, a reflection of the general lack of will to save lives. The State Department and Whitehall played a game which might be called "you've got the moral onus now" throughout the crisis.

The Holocaust was part of the larger insanity of World War II, and few world leaders possessed the foresight to comprehend that Auschwitz was a separate tragedy, a lethal combination of the most primitive atavism with the most advanced technology, a combination which summed up the agony of the twentieth century. Instead, there was a certain annoyance at the priority demanded by the Jews when the entire civilized world hovered on the brink of totalitarian domination. It was difficult for France to muster enthusiasm for a mass resettlement for refugees, which was suggested by Roosevelt at the meeting of the officers of the IGC in Washington in October 1939, when the existence of the French nation itself hung in the balance. Nor was Britain, while fighting for its life, anxious to accept more refugees. The priorities were for national survival and victory, and the rescue of Jews would be considered only if it could be accommodated to these priorities.

In the three years before America's entry into the war it faced no threat to its continued national existence as did France and Britain. But it acted as though it did and ordered its priorities accordingly. By June 1941 a nonbelligerent United States had more rigid screening procedures for refugees than Britain, which had been at war for almost two years. The security psychosis which was generously abetted by the State Department was the Administration's version of the national survival argument and had much the same effect on rescue activity. Once the war began the mania about spies having been infiltrated among the largely Jewish refugees could be muted in favor of the argument that the fastest road to rescue was to defeat Hitler. Nothing must be done to divert energy and resources from that goal. As it turned out, almost anything that could be done for rescue would cause such a diversion. Ships to transport refugees, which came back empty, could not be diverted because they were in short supply. Relief supplies could not be sent to camps because, according to Breckinridge Long, it would relieve the Reich from responsibility of feeding people under its control. Camps could not be bombed because aircraft could not be diverted to tasks of "doubtful efficacy." If one argued, as many rescue advocates did, that by the time victory came all Jews in Europe would be dead, one revealed a greater concern for Jewish survival than for the survival of the United States. Breckinridge Long's diary is full of charges that the rescue advocates, in pressing for a more humanitarian visa procedure or relief shipments to the camps, were really acting as Berlin's agents and subverting the nation's war effort. Counteracting such arguments proved to be a nigh impossible task.

These, then, were some of the reasons why the Roosevelt Administration responded only half-heartedly to the challenge of saving Jewish lives. But even if the problems that prevented rescue had been solved—if Breckinridge Long had been converted to the rescue cause; if the divisions within American Jewry had been magically healed; if the immigration laws had been circumvented earlier; if Alaska had been made available for resettlement; if Whitehall had abandoned its inhumanely political attitude towards Jewish immigration into Palestine; if the Pope had spoken out; if the CIRC had been more courageous; in short if there had been a will to save lives, we still have no assurance that mass rescue could have been realized, although many thousands more might have been saved. Something like such a miracle occurred in Hungary in 1944. Yet within full view of the world and when the Nazi authorities could no longer doubt that they had lost the war, the cattle cars rolled to Auschwitz as if they had a momentum of their own. Over half of Hungary's Jewry went up in smoke.

Appalling as it may sound, the saving of lives was a far more formidable task than the practice of genocide. Even a passionate will to save lives could prove insufficient, given Nazi determination to liquidate the Jews of Europe. Something more was required, something to soften the hearts of those in Berlin who were in physical control of the slaughter. Such a miracle was never in the power of the Washington policy makers. It belongs to a higher kingdom whose strange indifference has become an overriding concern of the theologians.

The Successes of American Rescue and The Limits of The Possible

WILLIAM J. VANDEN HEUVEL

It was Winston Churchill's judgment that the Holocaust "was probably the greatest and most terrible crime ever committed in the whole history of the world." The Holocaust, of course, was part of a colossal struggle in which fifty-three million people were killed, where nations were decimated, where democracy's survival was in the balance. In his campaign to exterminate the Jews of Europe, Hitler and his Nazi followers murdered six million men, women, and children for no other reason than that they were Jewish. This crime is of such profound proportions that it can never be fully understood; it must continue to be analyzed from every aspect as to how and why it happened, and its memory must unite all of us.

Nine million non-Jewish civilians were also murdered by the Nazis, as were three million Soviet prisoners of war, yet the Holocaust remains a uniquely horrible

From William J. Vanden Heuvel, "America and the Holocaust," *American Heritage* 50 (July/August 1999): 38–41, 43, 46, 48, 50–52. Reprinted by permission of *American Heritage,* Inc., 1999.

crime, and there can be no greater indictment than to allege complicity in it. Such an accusation was made against America in general and its leader, Franklin D. Roosevelt, in particular by a recent PBS documentary entitled "America and the Holocaust: Deceit and Indifference." The show drew on a substantial and growing body of scholarship that has caused many young American Jews to criticize and even condemn their grandparents and parents for being so absorbed in the effort to become assimilated in American society that they chose silence rather than voice outrage at the Nazi crimes and gave their overwhelming support to a President who was indifferent to the fate of Europe's Jews. Why did not the United States let the *St. Louis,* a German ship carrying Jewish refugees to Cuba in 1939, land at an American port when Cuba refused them admission? Also, perhaps the most frequently asked question of the last decade, why did the Allies not bomb Auschwitz and the railways that fed it? The people who pose these questions believe they know the answers. As one eminent spokesman for this viewpoint has written, "The Nazis were the murderers but we"—here he includes the American government, its President, and its people, Christians and Jews alike—"were the all too passive accomplices."

How much truth is there in these painful assertions? As we ask ourselves what more might have been done to save the innocent, we must frame our response in the context of the realities of World War II and the events and values of the years that preceded it.

Five weeks after Adolf Hitler became chancellor of Germany, in 1933, Franklin Roosevelt became President of the United States. Roosevelt's loathing for the whole Nazi regime was known the moment he took office; alone among the leaders of the world, he stood in opposition to Hitler from the very beginning. . . .

The America that elected Franklin Delano Roosevelt its President in 1932 was a deeply troubled country. Twenty-five percent of its work force was unemployed—this at a time when practically every member of that work force was the principal support of a family. The economy was paralyzed, while disillusion after the sacrifices of the First World War fomented profound isolationist sentiments.

The nation's immigration laws had been established by legislation in 1921 and 1924 under Presidents Harding and Coolidge and by a Congress that had rejected the League of Nations. A formula assigned a specific quota to countries based on the population origins of Americans living in the United States in 1890. The law was aimed at Eastern Europe, particularly Russia and Poland, which were seen as seedbeds of bolshevism. Italians were targeted, and Asians practically excluded. The total number of immigrants who could be admitted annually was set at 153,744; the two countries of origin given the highest quotas were Great Britain (65,721) and Germany (25,957). The deepening Depression encouraged an unusual coalition of liberal and conservative forces, labor unions and business leaders, to oppose any enlargement of the immigration quotas. Because of the relatively large German quota, Jewish refugees from Germany had an easier time than anticommunist refugees from the Soviet Union, not to mention Chinese victims of Japan's aggression, or Armenians. The Spanish who wanted to escape a civil war that between 1936 and 1939 killed half a million people faced an annual quota of 252.

The President and Mrs. Roosevelt were leaders in the effort to help those fleeing Nazi persecution. Eleanor Roosevelt was a founder, in 1933, of the International

Rescue Committee, which brought intellectuals, labor leaders, and political figures to sanctuary in the United States. President Roosevelt made a public point of inviting many of them to the White House. In 1936, in response to the Nazi confiscation of personal assets as a precondition to Jewish emigration, Roosevelt greatly modified President Hoover's strict interpretation of the refugee laws, thereby allowing a greater number of visas to be issued. As a result the United States accepted twice as many Jewish refugees as did all other countries put together. As the historian Gerhard L. Weinberg has shown, Roosevelt acted in the face of strong and politically damaging criticism for what was generally considered a pro-Jewish attitude.

When, in March 1938, the Anschluss put Austria's 185,000 Jews in jeopardy, Roosevelt called for an international conference "to facilitate the emigration from Germany and Austria of political refugees." There was no political advantage to FDR in this; no other major leader in any country matched his concern and involvement. The conference, which met in Evian, France, tried to open new doors in the Western Hemisphere. At first things went well; the Dominican Republic, for example, offered to give sanctuary to 100,000 refugees. Then came a devastating blow: The Polish and Romanian governments announced that they expected the same right as the Germans to expel their Jewish populations. There were fewer than 475,000 Jews left in Germany and Austria at this point—a number manageable in an emigration plan that the twenty-nine participating nations could prepare—but with the possibility of 3.5 million more from Eastern Europe, the concern now was that any offer of help would only encourage authoritarian governments to brutalize any unwanted portion of their populations, expecting their criminal acts against their own citizens to force the democracies to give them haven. National attitudes then were not very different from today's; no country allows any and every refugee to enter without limitations. Quotas are thought even now to deter unscrupulous and impoverished regimes from forcing their unwanted people on other countries. . . .

America's reaction to *Kristallnacht* was stronger than that of any of the other democracies. Roosevelt recalled his ambassador from Germany and at his next press conference said, "I myself can scarcely believe that such things could occur in a twentieth-century civilization." He extended the visitors' visas of twenty-thousand Germans and Austrians in the United States so they would not have to return. Americans in opinion polls showed anger and disgust with the Nazis and sympathy for the Jews; nevertheless, Roosevelt remained the target of the hard-core anti-Semites in America. He fought them shrewdly and effectively, managing to isolate them from mainstream America and essentially equating their anti-Semitism with treason destructive to both the national interest and national defense. Recognizing the inertia at the State Department, he entrusted Sumner Welles, the Undersecretary of State and a man wholly sympathetic to Jewish needs, to be his instrument of action.

Immigration procedures were complicated and sometimes harshly administered. The laws and quotas were jealously guarded by Congress, supported by a strong, broad cross section of Americans who were against all immigrants, not just Jews. Of course, there were racists and anti-Semites in the Congress and in the country, as there are today, only now they dare not speak their true attitudes. The State Department, deeply protective of its administrative authority in the granting of visas, was frequently more concerned with congressional attitudes and criticisms than with reflecting American decency and generosity in helping people in despair and panic. Roosevelt undoubtedly made a mistake in appointing as Assistant Secretary of State Breckenridge Long, who many allege was an anti-Semite. His presence at State was an assurance to Congress that the immigration laws would be strictly enforced. On the other hand there were countless Foreign Service officers who did everything possible to help persecuted, innocent people, just as they would today. There was an attitude that many sanctuaries besides the United States existed in the world, so the department, controlled by a career elite, conservative and in large part anti–New Deal and anti-FDR, was quite prepared to make congressional attitudes rather than those of the White House the guide for their administration of immigration procedures. Yet, between 1933 and 1941, 35 percent of all immigrants to America under quota guidelines were Jewish. After *Kristallnacht,* Jewish immigrants were more than half of all immigrants admitted to the United States.

Of course there were other countries of refuge; public opinion in democracies everywhere indicated that people had been repelled by the Nazi persecution. . . .

For his part, Roosevelt, knowing that he did not have the power to change the quota system of his own country, was constantly seeking havens for the refugees in other countries. His critics severely underestimate limitations on presidential power; clearly, the President could not unilaterally command an increase in quotas. . . .

By the time the war made further emigration impossible, 72 percent of all German Jews had left the country—and 83 percent of all those under twenty-one. . . .

Given the reality of the Holocaust, all of us in every country—and certainly in America—can only wish that we had done more, that our immigration barriers had been lower, that our Congress had had a broader world view, that every public servant had shared the beliefs of Franklin and Eleanor Roosevelt. If anyone had foreseen the Holocaust, perhaps, possibly, maybe . . . but no one did. Nevertheless, the United States, a nation remote from Europe in a way our children can hardly understand, took in double the number of Jewish refugees accepted by the rest of the world.

Among the anguishing events we read about is the fate of the ship *St. Louis* of the Hamburg-America Line, which left Germany and arrived in Cuba with 936 passengers, all but 6 of them Jewish refugees, on May 27, 1939. This was three months before the outbreak of the war and three years before the establishment of the death camps. Other ships had made the same journey, and their passengers had disembarked successfully, but on May 5 the Cuban government had issued a decree curtailing the power of the corrupt director general of immigration to issue landing certificates. New regulations requiring five-hundred-dollar bonds from each approved immigrant had been transmitted to the shipping line, but only 22 passengers of the *St. Louis* had fulfilled the requirements before leaving Hamburg on May 13. Those 22 were allowed to land; intense negotiations with the Cuban government regarding the other passengers—negotiations in which American Jewish agencies participated—broke down despite pressure from our government. It was not an unreported event. Tremendous international attention focused on the *St. Louis,* later made famous as the "Voyage of the Damned." Secretary of State Cordell Hull, Secretary of the Treasury Henry Morgenthau, Jr., and others, including Eleanor Roosevelt, worked to evade the immigration laws. . . . In the end, despite the legal inability of the United States to accept the passengers as immigrants, our diplomats were significantly helpful in resettling them. Not one was returned to Nazi Germany. They all went to democratic countries—288 in the United Kingdom, the rest in France, the Netherlands, Belgium, and Denmark. And who, in that spring of 1939, was prescient enough to foretell that in little more than a year all but one of those countries would be held by Nazi troops?

What were FDR's own attitudes toward Hitler and the Jews? Did he reflect the social anti-Semitism that was endemic in the America of that era? Contemporary Jews certainly didn't think so. Roosevelt opened the offices of government as never before to Jews. Henry Morgenthau, Jr., Samuel Rosenman, Felix Frankfurter, Benjamin Cohen, David Niles, Anna Rosenberg, Sidney Hillman, and David Dubinsky were among his closest advisers in politics and government. Rabbi Stephen Wise, the pre-eminent spokesman for American Zionism, said, "No one was more genuinely free from religious prejudice and racial bigotry."

. . .

[After the outbreak of war, t]he Jews of Central Europe, the Jews from the occupied nations of Western Europe, the Jews of the Soviet Union—the principal victims of the Holocaust—were not refugees; they were prisoners in a vast prison from which there was no escape and no possible rescue. . . . Once Hitler's armies marched, the Jews of Nazi-occupied Europe no longer had the possibility of being refugees.

The doors had been closed not by the United States or its allies but by Hitler. On January 30, 1942, Hitler, speaking to the Reichstag, said, "This war can end in two ways—either the extermination of the Aryan peoples or the disappearance of Jewry from Europe." Since the mid-1920s Hitler had never voluntarily spoken to a Jew. He was the most determined ideologue of racial superiority and racial conflict who ever led a country. Nothing diminished his mission—not the defeat of his armies, not the destruction of his country. As Germany lay in ruins, as its dictator prepared to end his life in his bunker in Berlin, his Nazi acolytes continued his campaign, diverting even urgently needed reinforcements for his retreating armies in order to complete the Final Solution.

The prisoners of Hitler could be saved only by the total, unconditional surrender of Nazi Germany, and that was a task that required four years and the unprecedented mobilization of all the resources, human and material, of Great Britain, the Soviet Union, and the United States.

Some critics of American policy during these years maintain that the news of the annihilation of Europe's Jews was deliberately kept secret so that our people would not know about it and that if Americans had been aware of the Final Solution, they would have insisted on doing more than was done. The facts are otherwise. President Roosevelt, Winston Churchill, General Eisenhower, General Marshall, the intelligence services of the Allied nations, every Jewish leader, the Jewish communities in America, in Britain, in Palestine, and yes, anyone who had a radio or newspaper in 1942 knew that Jews in colossal numbers were being murdered. They may have received the news with disbelief; there was, after all, no precedent for it in human history. But the general information of the genocide was broadly available to anyone who would read or listen. . . .

American Jewry was no passive observer of these events. Despite issues that bitterly divided them, primarily relating to Palestine, the Jewish community in America spoke the same words in pleading to do whatever was possible for Europe's Jews. Jewish leaders lobbied Congress. Mass rallies were held across the country with overflow crowds throughout those years, praying, pleading for action to stop the genocide. The unremitting massacre continued because no one, no nation, no alliance of nations could do anything to close down the death camps—save, as Roosevelt said over and over again, by winning the war.

Had FDR followed the national will, Japan would have been our military priority, but understanding the Nazi threat to civilization, he ordered Germany to be the focus of our efforts. Had Roosevelt listened to General Marshall and his other military advisers, he would not have sent the few tanks we had in 1942 to help General Montgomery win at El Alamein, thereby probably saving Palestine from the same fate as Poland. Roosevelt gave frequent audience to Jewish leaders; he sent messages to rallies of Jews across the country; he listened to every plea and proposal for rescue that came to him. But he knew that the diversion of resources from the purpose of defeating the Nazi armies might palliate the anguish felt by so many, would rescue no one, and in all likelihood would kill the would-be rescuers. As Richard Lichtheim, a representative of the World Jewish Congress in Switzerland and a hero in informing the world of the genocide, said in December 1942, "You cannot divert a tiger from devouring his prey by adopting resolutions or sending cables. You have to take your gun and shoot him."

The historian Gerhard Weinberg answers those who question America's policy by suggesting that they consider how many more Jews would have survived had the war ended even a week or ten days earlier—and how many more would have died had it lasted an additional week or ten days. Given that the slaughter of the Jews went on into the final moments of the Third Reich, that every day until the surrender there were thousands of deaths by murder, starvation, and disease, the number of Jews saved by winning the war as quickly as possible was vastly greater than the total number who could have been saved by any rescue efforts proposed by anyone between 1941 and 1945.

Serious proposals for rescue and response were not disregarded. . . .

The proposal to bomb Auschwitz in 1944 has become the symbol for those who argue American indifference and complicity in the Holocaust. Some would have us believe that many American Jewish groups petitioned our government to bomb Auschwitz; in fact, there was considerable Jewish opposition in both the United States and Palestine. The focal center of the Holocaust Museum's exhibit on bombing Auschwitz is a letter from Leon Kubowitzki, head of the Rescue Department of the World Jewish Congress, in which he forwarded, without endorsement, a request from the Czech State Council (in exile in London) to the War Department, in August 1944, to bomb the camp. Much is made of the Assistant Secretary John McCloy's response to Kubowitzki explaining the War Department's decision not to undertake such a mission. What is not on display and rarely mentioned is a letter dated July 1, 1944, from the same Leon Kubowitzki to the executive director of the War Refugee Board, arguing *against* bombing Auschwitz because "the first victims would be the Jews" and because the Allied air assault would serve as "a welcome pretext for the Germans to assert that their Jewish victims have been massacred not by their killers, but by Allied bombing."

Mainstream Jewish opinion was against the whole idea. The very thought of the Allied forces' deliberately killing Jews—to open the gates of Auschwitz so the survivors could run where?—was as abhorrent then as it is now. The Rescue Committee of the Jewish Agency in Jerusalem voted, at a meeting with the future Israeli prime minister David Ben-Gurion presiding, against even making the bombing request. Although only President Roosevelt or General Eisenhower could have ordered the bombing of Auschwitz, there is no record of any kind that indicates that either one ever heard of the proposal—even though Jewish leaders of all persuasions had clear access to both men.

A seemingly more reasonable proposal to bomb the railways to Auschwitz was made to Anthony Eden, the foreign minister of Great Britain, on July 6, 1944. Eden, with Churchill's immediate support, asked the RAF to examine the feasibility of doing so. The secretary of state for air, Sir Archibald Sinclair, replied several days later: "I entirely agree that it is our duty to consider every possible plan [to stop the murder of the Jews] but I am advised that interrupting the railways is out of our power. It is only by an enormous concentration of bomber forces that we have been able to interrupt communications in Normandy; the distance of Silesia from our bases entirely rules out doing anything of the kind." John McCloy had replied to a similar suggestion weeks earlier: "The War Department is of the opinion that the suggested air operation is impracticable for the reason that it could be executed only with the diversion of considerable air support essential to the success of our forces now engaged in decisive operations." Even the severest critics of America's response to the Nazi murder of the Jews acknowledge that successful interruption of railways required close observation of the severed lines and frequent rebombing, since repairs would take only a few days. Even bridges, which were costly to hit, were often back in operation in three or four days. Postwar studies of railway bombing totally vindicated the conclusion of the military authorities. Professor Istvan Deak of Columbia University asks in a recent article: "And if the rail lines had been bombed? The inmates of the cattle cars and those at the departure points would have been allowed to die of thirst, or of the heat, or of the cold, while the lines were being repaired."

It is often noted that American bombers were carrying out raids in the summer of 1944 on industrial targets only a few miles away from Auschwitz, suggesting how easy it would have been to bomb the gas chambers. They do not mention that preparation for the D-day invasion left only 12 percent of the U.S. Army Air Force available for the destruction of German fuel supplies, the primary mission as defined by Gen. Carl Spaatz. They point to the huge blowups of reconnaissance photographs at the Holocaust Museum that show not only the Farben synthetic-fuel plant, the target of the raids, but the outlines of Auschwitz and columns of prisoners. Yet the aerial photographs of Auschwitz on display were not developed until 1978, and their details were readable then only because advanced technology, developed by the CIA more than twenty years after the end of World War II, made it possible. *All* such strategic raids on military-industrial bases proceeded only after months of preparatory intelligence work, entailing the creation of a target folder with specific information about the size, hardness, structure placement, and defenses of the target and detailed aerial photography. These were costly, dangerous raids against heavily protected, frequently remote targets; the losses in men and planes were tragically heavy. The Allied air forces simply lacked the intelligence base necessary to plan and execute a bombing raid against the Auschwitz extermination camp. It would have been a nonmilitary mission. Only Roosevelt or Eisenhower could have ordered it, and as we have seen, no one proposed it to them.

Yet many insist that anti-Semitism alone spared Auschwitz the wrath of the Army Air Force. With this in mind, it is worth considering the plight of northern Holland, where during the last seven months of the war more than eighty thousand citizens starved to death because the German occupiers wanted to punish the Dutch for insurrection and strikes following the failed assault on Arnhem. The Allies knew what was happening. Allied armies were everywhere around this occupied segment of the Netherlands; air rescue, or at least the capacity for organizing food drops, was minutes away. Still, eighty thousand men, women, and children died while the forces that could have saved them remained intent on their objective of a military engagement with the Germans that would lead to victory in the shortest possible time. Perhaps these military decisions were wrong, but they were not made because of any bias against the Dutch—or, regarding Auschwitz, because of anti-Semitism.

And what of those who managed to escape the Nazis once the war had started? President Roosevelt created the War Refugee Board in January 1944, immediately upon Henry Morgenthau's presenting the case for doing so. There were thousands of refugees stranded on the outer peripheries of Nazi Europe. With the invasion of Italy in 1943, thousands more had sought safety in camps in the south. Tito's success in Yugoslavia had enabled many to escape from Croat fascism and Serb hatred. But those were refugees who were already saved. They were not escapees from the death camps. Under pressure from Roosevelt and Churchill, Spain kept open its frontiers, stating as its policy that "all refugees without exception would be allowed to enter and remain." Probably more than forty thousand, many of them Jewish, found safe sanctuary in Spain. Makeshift transit camps there and in Portugal, Italy, and North Africa housed them in abysmal conditions. Those who fought for these people to come to America were right to do so; then, as now, refugees are generally powerless and voiceless. Governments have to be reminded constantly of their humanitarian responsibilities. But perhaps the Allied nations can be forgiven, in the midst of a war for survival, for not doing more for refugees whose lives had already been saved. Perhaps not. In remembering what we did not do, maybe we can measure our response to today's tragedies and ask whether we—now the richest, most powerful nation in history—have responded adequately to the "ethnic cleansing" of Bosnia, to the genocide in Rwanda, to the Killing Fields of Cambodia. We might question the adequacy of our response to the catalogue of horrors visible to all of us in Sierra Leone, where thousands of children as young as seven years old are forced to become soldiers, human shields, sex slaves, and instruments of torture and killing, having already witnessed the slaughter of their parents and the hacking off of the hands and feet of countless innocent civilians.

Roosevelt's intervention with the government of Hungary, which by then understood that Nazi defeat was inevitable; the actions of the War Refugee Board, such as retaining the heroic Raoul Wallenberg; the bombing of the Budapest area—all played a role in the rescue of half the Jewish community in Hungary. President Roosevelt was deeply and personally involved in this effort. . . .

On April 12, 1945, General Eisenhower visited Ohrdruf Nord, the first concentration camp liberated by the American Army. "The things I saw beggar description," he wrote General Marshall. According to his biographer Stephen Ambrose, "Eisenhower had heard ominous rumors about the camps, of course, but never in his worst nightmares had he dreamed they could be so bad." He sent immediately for a delegation of congressional leaders and newspaper editors; he wanted to make sure Americans would never forget this. Five months later he dismissed his close friend and brilliant army commander Gen. George Patton for using former Nazi officials in his occupation structure and publicly likening "the Nazi thing" to differences between the Republicans and Democrats. (Patton had visited the Ohrdruf camp with Eisenhower and become physically ill from what he saw.)

Eisenhower got his first glimpse into the worst horrors at the heart of the Third Reich on the day death claimed the American who had done more than any other to bring them to an end. How ironic that Franklin Roosevelt—the man Hitler hated most, the leader constantly attacked by the isolationist press and derided by the anti-Semites, vilified by Goebbels as a "mentally ill cripple" and as "that Jew Rosenfeld"—should be faulted for being indifferent to the genocide. For all of us the shadow of doubt that enough was not done will always remain, even if there was little more that could have been done. But to say that "we are all guilty" allows the truly guilty to avoid that responsibility. It was Hitler who imagined the Holocaust and the Nazis who carried it out. We were not their accomplices. We destroyed them.

FURTHER READING

Abzug, Robert. *Inside the Vicious Heart: Americans and the Liberation of Nazi Concentration Camps* (1985).

Baldwin, Neil. *Henry Ford and the Jews: The Mass Production of Hate* (2001).

Bauer, Yehuda. *American Jewry and the Holocaust* (1981).

———. *Jewish Reactions to the Holocaust* (1989).

———. *Jews for Sale?* (1994).

Bourke-White, Margaret. *Dear Fatherland, Rest Quietly* (1946).

Breitman, Richard. *Official Secrets: What the Nazis Planned, What the British and Americans Knew* (1998).

Breitman, Richard, and Alan M. Kraut. *American Refugee Policy and European Jewry, 1933–1945* (1987).

Browning, Christopher. *The Path to Genocide* (1992).

Cole, Tim. *Selling the Holocaust: From Auschwitz to Schindler, How History Is Bought, Packaged and Sold* (1999).

Dinnerstein, Leonard. *America and the Survivors of the Holocaust: The Evolution of a U.S. Displaced Persons Policy, 1945–1950* (1982).

———. *Anti-Semitism in America* (1994).

Feingold, Henry. *Bearing Witness* (1995).

———. *The Politics of Rescue* (1970).

Flanzbaum, Hilene, ed. *The Americanization of the Holocaust* (1999).

Friedman, Saul. *No Haven for the Oppressed* (1973).

Gilbert, Martin. *Auschwitz and the Allies* (1981).

Hilberg, Raul. *The Destruction of the European Jews* (1961, 2002).

———. *Perpetrators, Victims and Bystanders* (1992).

Laqueur, Walter. *The Terrible Secret: Suppression of the Truth about Hitler's "Final Solution"* (1980).

Lipstadt, Deborah. *Beyond Belief: The American Press and the Coming of the Holocaust, 1933–1945* (1986).

Lookstein, Haskel. *Are We Our Brothers' Keepers? The Public Response of American Jews to the Holocaust, 1938–1944* (1985).

Marrus, Michael. *The Holocaust in History* (1987).

Medoff, Rafael. *The Deafening Silence: American Jewish Leaders and the Holocaust* (1986).

Morse, Arthur. *While Six Million Died* (1968).

Nawyn, William E. *American Protestantism's Response to Germany's Jews and Refugees* (1982).

Neufeld, Michael J., and Michael Berenbaum, eds. *The Bombing of Auschwitz* (2000).

Newton, Verne W., ed. *FDR and the Holocaust* (1996).

Novick, Peter. *The Holocaust in American Life* (1999).

Penkower, Monty. *The Jews Were Expendable* (1983).

Rubinstein, William. *The Myth of Rescue* (1997).

Scrase, David, and Wolfgang Mieder, eds. *The Holocaust: Personal Accounts* (2001).

Urofsky, Melvin I. *A Voice That Spoke for Justice: The Life and Times of Stephen S. Wise* (1982).

Wood, E. Thomas, and Stanislaw M. Jankowski. *Karski: How One Man Tried to Stop the Holocaust* (1994).

Wyman, David S. *The Abandonment of the Jews* (1984).

———. *Paper Walls* (1968).

CHAPTER
10

Franklin D. Roos~~~~
and Allied Diplomacy
for War and Peace

Wars are fought to achieve political as well as military goals. Indeed, the military
goals are themselves merely means to the political ends desired by belligerents. The
Axis powers in World War II, for example, sought military conquest to establish
extensive empires run in accord with their ideologies. Similarly, the Allies sought
not merely to militarily defeat the Axis powers to prevent this, but also to establish
a postwar world to their liking. But what would such a world look like? Each ally
had a different idea—a problem that made difficult not only postwar planning, but
even maintaining the coalition during the war. Chapter 3 of this volume explored the
serious Allied strategic differences and their resolution between 1941 and 1943. This
chapter explores the equally serious Allied political differences and their attempted
resolution from 1941 to 1945, with special emphasis on Franklin D. Roosevelt's
controversial policies.

As discussed in Chapter 3, the Allies agreed that Germany had to be defeated
before Japan but could not agree as to how this should be accomplished. Similarly,
they agreed that their great political objective was to create a world in which Axis
aggression and another world war could not occur, but they disagreed sharply as to
how this should be accomplished. Although they had agreed by the end of 1941 to a
series of broad principles enunciated in a document known as the Atlantic Charter,
in reality they disagreed sharply in their interpretation of the charter's provisions
and the postwar world they wished to create.

Great Britain favored a return to the international system that had existed
before the rise of the fascist powers, one based on a recreated balance of power in
Europe and the continued existence of the British and other European colonial
empires in Africa and Asia. For the Soviet Union and the United States, however,
this system had led to fascism and the war in the first place. Consequently they
pressed for alternative, and highly conflicting, postwar systems.

For Josef Stalin, the prewar system had also isolated the U.S.S.R. because of its
communist ideology and had sanctioned a huge loss of territory, first imposed on the

359

by Germany in 1918 and then ratified at Versailles (1919) and immediately after. By the terms of the Treaty of Versailles, the former Russian Empire was torn of some of its most valuable lands on its western borders, lands that went to Rumania and the recreated nations of Poland, Finland, and the three Baltic states of Estonia, Latvia, and Lithuania. Stalin regained most of this territory between 1939 and 1941 as a result of his 1939 pact with Hitler and the Soviet Union's subsequent takeover of the three Baltic states, eastern Poland, and portions of Rumania, as well as its war with Finland. Despite Hitler's quick conquest of this territory in 1941, Stalin demanded throughout the war that it be considered part of the postwar Soviet Union. He also pressed for the permanent weakening of Germany and the imposition of governments throughout Eastern Europe "friendly" to the Soviet Union. Britain opposed such moves because they would in effect make the Soviet Union the hegemonic power in Europe, thereby replacing the present German threat with a future Soviet threat.

The United States opposed both British and Soviet plans. Either one, Americans believed, would simply recreate the system that had led to World War II in the first place and violate the cherished principle of national self-determination—be it in Eastern Europe or in the Asian and African colonies of Britain and other European powers. But what could and should the United States offer as an alternative postwar vision, and how could it get its allies to agree?

Roosevelt desired an end to European colonialism, and national self-determination for Asians and Africans as well as Europeans. He also insisted that the Axis powers would have to be disarmed as well as defeated and kept under strict control in the postwar era. Officially he favored the creation of a new League of Nations to accomplish these objectives and maintain world peace. Given the failure of the original league, however, he insisted that the task would really belong to the three major allies and China, who, he argued, should act as "the Four Policemen" in the postwar world to prevent not only German or Japanese aggression, but any aggression that could trigger another world war. All of that would require the Allies to remain unified, despite their disputes with each other. It would also require acceptance by the American public of a major role for the United States in the postwar world. To prevent any damaging splits between Americans or between the Allies while the war was in progress, Roosevelt favored postponement of all controversial postwar issues, especially territorial issues. In their place he proposed merely a reassertion of the broad principles on which they could agree within the Atlantic Charter and insistence on the total defeat and unconditional surrender of the Axis powers. Churchill and Stalin concurred but consistently pressed for the detailed political discussions that Roosevelt opposed.

In late 1943, Roosevelt finally agreed to preliminary postwar discussions. These continued throughout 1944 and resulted in a series of important agreements about a postwar League of Nations at the Dumbarton Oaks Conference, the postwar economic order at the Bretton Woods Conference, and potential spheres of influence in the Balkans at a Churchill-Stalin summit in Moscow during October 1944. Then in February of 1945 the Big Three met in the Russian Crimean resort of Yalta to ratify these accords and try to reach agreement on remaining issues as well as plan final military operations against their Axis enemies.

The Yalta Accords broke down very soon after they were signed and led to bitter accusations among the Big Three. Then, on April 12, Roosevelt died of a massive stroke. What he would have done in this diplomatic crisis had he lived has remained one of the great "if" questions of World War II history.

Roosevelt's consistent efforts to compromise Allied differences and postpone post-war discussions raise a series of questions. Why did he pursue these policies? Were they wise, or would alternative policies have been better? Was he foolish to think he could cooperate with Stalin in the postwar era? Was he foolish to believe that China under Chiang Kai-shek could serve as one of the Four Policemen? Were the accords he signed at Yalta the best he could have achieved, or did they constitute a naïve and cowardly sellout of American principles, as critics have charged?

DOCUMENTS

In August of 1941, before the United States officially entered the war, Churchill and Roosevelt met off the coast of Newfoundland and issued the Atlantic Charter, a statement of broad, idealistic war aims. Document 1 reproduces those aims as enunciated in the charter. Document 2 consists of excerpts from the British and Soviet versions of the December 1941 meetings in Moscow, during which Josef Stalin made clear to British foreign secretary Anthony Eden Soviet territorial demands that conflicted with the charter, despite formal Soviet adherence to it. The January 1, 1942, Declaration of the United Nations, the official public announcement of the Grand Alliance, is reproduced as Document 3. Document 4 is an excerpt from the January 24, 1943, press conference at the Casablanca Conference, during which Roosevelt enunciated unconditional surrender as Allied policy instead of dealing with these territorial issues.

Document 5 reproduces the first formal Allied agreement on postwar policies, the Declaration on General Security, which was reached at the tripartite Foreign Ministers' Conference in October 1943. Document 6 consists of Roosevelt's more detailed postwar views, as expressed during his May 1942 conversations with Soviet foreign minister Vyacheslav Molotov and his November 1943 conversations with Churchill and Stalin at the Tehran Conference (see Chapter 5 for Roosevelt's views on decolonization during these meetings). Document 7 presents the August 1944 Dumbarton Oaks agreements on a postwar international organization that would lead to the formation of the United Nations. Document 8 presents Churchill's version of his October 1944 "deal" with Stalin regarding spheres of influence in the Balkans. Document 9 contains excerpts from the highly controversial Yalta protocols. Document 10 offers excerpts from two of Roosevelt's final messages to his Allied colleagues before his April 12 death.

1. The Atlantic Charter States Allied War Aims, 1941

Joint declaration of the President of the United States of America and the Prime Minister, Mr. Churchill, representing His Majesty's Government in the United Kingdom, being met together, deem it right to make known certain common principles in the national policies of their respective countries on which they base their hopes for a better future for the world.

First, their countries seek no aggrandizement, territorial or other;

Second, they desire to see no territorial changes that do not accord with the freely expressed wishes of the peoples concerned;

From State Department *Bulletin* 5 (Washington, D.C.: U.S. Government Printing Office, 1942): 125–126.

Third, they respect the right of all peoples to choose the form of government under which they will live; and they wish to see sovereign rights and self-government restored to those who have been forcibly deprived of them;

Fourth, they will endeavor, with due respect for their existing obligations, to further the enjoyment by all States, great or small, victor or vanquished, of access, on equal terms, to the trade and to the raw materials of the world which are needed for their economic prosperity;

Fifth, they desire to bring about the fullest collaboration between all nations in the economic field with the object of securing, for all, improved labor standards, economic advancement, and social security;

Sixth, after the final destruction of the Nazi tyranny, they hope to see established a peace which will afford to all nations the means of dwelling in safety within their own boundaries, and which will afford assurance that all the men in all the lands may live out their lives in freedom from fear and want;

Seventh, such a peace should enable all men to traverse the high seas and oceans without hindrance;

Eighth, they believe that all of the nations of the world, for realistic as well as spiritual reasons, must come to the abandonment of the use of force. Since no future peace can be maintained if land, sea, or air armaments continue to be employed by nations which threaten, or may threaten, aggression outside of their frontiers, they believe, pending the establishment of a wider and permanent system of general security, that the disarmament of such nations is essential. They will likewise aid and encourage all other practicable measures which will lighten for peace-loving peoples the crushing burden of armaments.

Franklin D Roosevelt
Winston S Churchill

2. Josef Stalin Demands Territorial Settlements, 1941

**British Foreign Secretary Anthony Eden's Summary
of His Conversations with Stalin**

At my first conversation with M. Stalin, M. Stalin set out in some detail what he considered should be the postwar territorial frontiers in Europe; and in particular his ideas regarding the treatment of Germany. He proposed the restoration of Austria as an independent state, the detachment of the Rhineland from Prussia as an independent state or protectorate, and possibly the constitution of an independent state of Bavaria. He also proposed that East Prussia should be transferred to Poland and the Sudetenland returned to Czechoslovakia. He suggested that Yugoslavia should be restored and even receive certain additional territories from Italy, that Albania should be reconstituted as an independent state, and that Turkey should

From U.S. Department of State, *Foreign Relations of the United States, 1942*, vol. 3 (Washington, D.C.: U.S. Government Printing Office, 1961), 499–500; and Oleg Rzheshevsky, *War and Diplomacy: The Making of the Grand Alliance; Documents from Stalin's Archives edited with a Commentary* (n.p.: Harwood Academic Publishers/Overseas Publishers Association, 1996), 28–33.

receive the Dodecanese, with possibly readjustments in favour of Greece as regards islands in the Aegean important to Greece. Turkey might also receive certain districts in Bulgaria, and possibly also in Northern Syria.

In general the occupied countries, including Czechoslovakia and Greece, should be restored to their prewar frontiers, and Mr. Stalin was prepared to support any special arrangements for securing bases, et cetera, for the United Kingdom in Western European countries, e.g., France, Belgium, the Netherlands, Norway and Denmark. As regards the special interests of the Soviet Union, Stalin desired the restoration of the position in 1941, prior to the German attack, in respect of the Baltic States, Finland and Bessarabia. The "Curzon Line" should form the basis for the future Soviet-Polish frontier, and Rumania should give special facilities for bases, et cetera, to the Soviet Union, receiving compensation from territory now occupied by Hungary.

In the course of this first conversation, Stalin generally agreed with the principle of restitution in kind by Germany to the occupied countries, more particularly in regard to machine tools, et cetera, and ruled out money reparations as undesirable. He showed interest in a postwar military alliance between the "democratic countries," and stated that the Soviet Union had no objection to certain countries of Europe entering into a federal relationship, if they so desired.

In the second conversation, M. Stalin pressed for the immediate recognition by His Majesty's Government of the future frontiers of the USSR, more particularly in regard to the inclusion within the USSR of the Baltic States and the restoration of the 1941 Finnish-Soviet frontier. He made the conclusion of any Anglo-Soviet agreement dependent on agreement on this point. I, for my part, explained to M. Stalin that in view of our prior undertakings to the United States Government it was quite impossible for His Majesty's Government to commit themselves at this stage to any postwar frontiers in Europe, although I undertook to consult His Majesty's Government in the United Kingdom, the United States Government, and His Majesty's Governments in the Dominions on my return. . . .

The Soviet Minutes

The Second Meeting. 17 December, 12.00 p.m.

Present: Comrades Stalin, Molotov and Maisky on the Soviet Side; Eden, Cripps and Cadogan on the British Side (Comrade Maisky Interprets)

Upon opening the meeting Eden began with the question of whether Comrade Stalin had seen the results of the morning's work on the texts of the agreements? . . .

Comrade Stalin said that the results were certainly interesting, but that he was much more interested in the question of the USSR's future frontiers. Had Eden not received a reply to this question from the British Government?

Eden answered that he had not and had not even tried to. The Prime Minister was on a voyage at present, on the ocean, and he could not communicate with him on the question raised by Comrade Stalin. *[Rzheshevsky: Eden reported earlier that Churchill had left for the USA to meet Roosevelt in connection with the development of events in the Pacific.]* In London, there was nobody who might give the decisive answer to this question with due authority and in the name of the British

Government. Eden could only repeat now what he had said yesterday, namely, that on his return to London he would place the question of the USSR western frontiers before the Government and consult with the United States on the same question.

Further communications on this matter would have to be conducted through normal diplomatic channels.

Comrade Stalin objected that the question of Soviet frontiers (irrespective of the general question of the frontiers in Central and Western Europe) was of exceptional importance to us. The Soviet Government was especially interested in it because, in particular, it was precisely the question of the Baltic States and Finland that had been the stumbling-block in the negotiations in 1939 on the pact of mutual assistance under Chamberlain's Government. . . .

Comrade Stalin then asked if special permission was required from the British Government to settle the question of the Baltic States? This question was axiomatic. The USSR is waging a fierce struggle against Hitlerite Germany. It is making heavy sacrifices, losing hundreds of thousand of people in the common fight together with Great Britain, its ally. It is bearing the brunt of the war on its shoulders. Is a decision of the British Government still needed to recognise the Soviet western frontier? Is not this question axiomatic? . . .

Eden again repeated the motivation of refusal stated above with slight variations.

Comrade Stalin then asked, where might such a formulation of the question lead Britain? Perhaps tomorrow Britain will declare that she does not recognise the Ukraine as part of the USSR.

Eden replied that there was an obvious misunderstanding here. Britain did not recognise only the changes of frontiers that have taken place during the war. The Ukraine had been part of the USSR before the war. Therefore the Premier's declaration as mentioned above could not in any way refer to the Ukraine.

Comrade Stalin replied that the position taken by Eden did not differ essentially from the position Chamberlain's Government had taken in its time on the question of the Baltic States. Comrade Stalin was greatly surprised at this circumstance and, if it was really the case, it would apparently be very difficult to come to terms and conclude the treaties.

Eden expressed regret at this and again returned to his argument, this time emphasizing the need for preliminary consultations with America on the question of the USSR's western frontier. In conclusion he pointed out the difference that, in his view, exists between the state of affairs in 1939 and 1941. At that time the British Government recognised the Baltic countries as independent States. Today it does not recognise their independent existence and, therefore, the actual situation has radically changed.

Comrade Stalin noted that a highly ridiculous situation had come about. . . .

Eden repeated his former argument and added only that the Atlantic Charter did not admit a change of a State's status without the consent of its population. And in this particular case this provision in the Atlantic Charter might possibly be considered as applicable.

Comrade Stalin responded that if Eden did not change his position, the signature of the treaties would have to be postponed.

Comrade Stalin replied that the whole war between the USSR and Germany started because of the USSR's western frontier including, in particular, the Baltic

States. He would like to know whether Britain, our ally, was ready to back us up in the restoration of these frontiers. . . .

Comrade Stalin replied that . . . he absolutely could not understand the position taken by the British Government. Presumably, one ally must support another ally. Should someone come to him and say that it was necessary to separate the Irish Free State from the British Empire, he would send him packing. If Britain wished to have air [and] naval bases in Belgium and Holland he would certainly render her all manner of assistance. That is the way an ally should behave. If Britain did not find it possible to take such a stand, then it would be better to postpone the signature of the treaties and hold to the pact of mutual assistance concluded between the two countries in July. . . .

Comrade Stalin replied that he certainly did not want to ask Eden for the impossible. He well understood the limits of his authority, and he did not address him, but the British Government through him. An involuntary impression was created that the Atlantic Charter was directed not against the people who were striving for global supremacy but against the USSR.

Eden started to dispute this inference resolutely, arguing that the question of Soviet frontiers was in no sense out of keeping with the Atlantic Charter. In view of the points he had already made, however, Eden simply did not have the power to recognise the Soviet western frontier immediately. This only requires time, a measure of postponement.

Comrade Stalin remarked that when Britain was giving her promises to America we were not yet allies. . . .

Comrade Molotov expressed surprise at Eden's persistent defence of his position. We are talking about common military goals, common struggle, but in one of the most important military goals, our western frontier, we cannot derive support from Great Britain. Is this really normal?

3. The Allies Announce Formation of the Grand Alliance: The Declaration by the United Nations, 1942

January 1, 1942

A Joint Declaration by the United States of America, the United Kingdom of Great Britain and Northern Ireland, the Union of Soviet Socialist Republics, China, Australia, Belgium, Canada, Costa Rica, Cuba, Czechoslovakia, Dominican Republic, El Salvador, Greece, Guatemala, Haiti, Honduras, India, Luxembourg, Netherlands, New Zealand, Nicaragua, Norway, Panama, Poland, South Africa, Yugoslavia

The Governments signatory hereto,

Having subscribed to a common program of purposes and principles embodied in the Joint Declaration of the President of the United States of America and the Prime Minister of Great Britain dated August 14, 1941, known as the Atlantic Charter,

From U.S. Department of State, *Foreign Relations of the United States: The Conferences at Washington, 1941–1942, and Casablanca, 1943* (Washington, D.C.: U.S. Government Printing Office, 1968), 375.

Being convinced that complete victory over their enemies is essential to defend life, liberty, independence and religious freedom, and to preserve human rights and justice in their own lands as well as in other lands, and that they are now engaged in a common struggle against savage and brutal forces seeking to subjugate the world,

Declare:

(1) Each Government pledges itself to employ its full resources, military or economic, against those members of the Tripartite Pact and its adherents with which such government is at war.

(2) Each Government pledges itself to cooperate with the Governments signatory hereto and not to make a separate armistice or peace with the enemies.

The foregoing declaration may be adhered to by other nations which are, or which may be, rendering material assistance and contributions in the struggle for victory over Hitlerism.

4. Roosevelt Enunciates the Unconditional Surrender Policy, 1943

CASABLANCA, January 24, 1943

. . . I think we have all had it in our hearts and heads before, but I don't think that it has ever been put down on paper by the Prime Minister and myself, and that is the determination that peace can come to the world only by the total elimination of German and Japanese war power.

Some of you Britishers know the old story—we had a General called U. S. Grant. His name was Ulysses Simpson Grant, but in my, and the Prime Minister's, early days he was called "Unconditional Surrender" Grant. The elimination of German, Japanese and Italian war power means the unconditional surrender by Germany, Italy, and Japan. That means a reasonable assurance of future world peace. It does not mean the destruction of the population of Germany, Italy, or Japan, but it does mean the destruction of the philosophies in those countries which are based on conquest and the subjugation of other people.

5. The Allies Agree on Postwar Policies: The Moscow Declaration on General Security, 1943

THE GOVERNMENTS of the United States of America, the United Kingdom, the Soviet Union and China:

united in their determination, in accordance with the Declaration by the United Nations of January 1, 1942, and subsequent declarations, to continue hostilities against those Axis powers with which they respectively are at war until such powers have laid down their arms on the basis of unconditional surrender;

From U.S. Department of State, *Foreign Relations of the United States: The Conferences at Washington, 1941–1942, and Casablanca, 1943* (Washington, D.C.: U.S. Government Printing Office, 1968), 726–727.

From U.S. Department of State, *Foreign Relations of the United States, 1943*, vol. 1 (Washington, D.C.: U.S. Government Printing Office, 1963), 755–756.

conscious of their responsibility to secure the liberation of themselves and the peoples allied with them from the menace of aggression; recognizing the necessity of ensuring a rapid and orderly transition from war to peace and of establishing and maintaining international peace and security with the least diversion of the world's human and economic resources for armaments; jointly declare:

1. That their united action, pledged for the prosecution of the war against their respective enemies, will be continued for the organization and maintenance of peace and security.

2. That those of them at war with a common enemy will act together in all matters relating to the surrender and disarmament of that enemy.

3. That they will take all measures deemed by them to be necessary to provide against any violation of the terms imposed upon the enemy.

4. That they recognize the necessity of establishing at the earliest practicable date a general international organization, based on the principle of the sovereign equality of all peace-loving states, and open to membership by all such states, large and small, for the maintenance of international peace and security.

5. That for the purpose of maintaining international peace and security pending the re-establishment of law and order and the inauguration of a system of general security, they will consult with one another and as occasion requires with other members of the United Nations with a view to joint action on behalf of the community of nations.

6. That after the termination of hostilities they will not employ their military forces within the territories of other states except for the purposes envisaged in this declaration and after joint consultation.

7. That they will confer and co-operate with one another and with other members of the United Nations to bring about a practicable general agreement with respect to the regulation of armaments in the post-war period.

6. Roosevelt Informs His Allies of His Postwar Plans, 1942 and 1943

May 29, 1942

While serving cocktails, the President discussed at length certain basic considerations on post-war organization. Mr. Churchill (he said) had expressed some idea of reestablishing a post-war international organization which was in effect a revived League of Nations. The President had given Mr. Churchill his own opinion that such an organization would be impractical, because too many nations would be involved. The President conceived it the duty of the four major United Nations (Britain, U. S., U. S. S. R., and China, provided the last achieves a unified central government, opposite which there was still a question-mark) to act as the policemen of the world. The first step was general disarmament. But the four major nations would maintain

From U.S. Department of State, *Foreign Relations of the United States, 1942*, vol. 3 (Washington, D.C.: U.S. Government Printing Office, 1961), 568–569; and U.S. Department of State, *Foreign Relations of the United States: The Conferences at Cairo and Tehran, 1943* (Washington, D.C.: U.S. Government Printing Office, 1961), 509–511, 530–532.

sufficient armed forces to impose peace, together with inspection privileges which would guard against the sort of clandestine rearmament in which Germany had notoriously engaged during the pre-war years. If any nation menaced the peace, it could be blockaded and then if still recalcitrant, bombed. The President added that which concerned him was the establishment of a peace which would last 25 years, at least the lifetime of the present generation. He and Mr. Stalin were over 60, Mr. Molotov 53; his aim was thus peace in our time. He thought that all other nations save the Big Four should be disarmed (Germany, Japan, France, Spain, Belgium, Netherlands, Scandinavia, Turkey, Rumania, Hungary, Poland, Czechoslovakia, etc.).

Mr. Molotov remarked that this might be a bitter blow to the prestige of Poland and Turkey. "The Turks," he added, "are an extremely pretentious people." He also inquired about the reestablishment of France as a great power. The President replied that might perhaps be possible within 10 or 20 years. He added that other nations might eventually be accepted progressively at various times among the guarantors of peace whenever the original guarantors were satisfied of their reliability. This might be peace by dictation, but his hope was that it might be so administered that the peoples of the previous aggressor nations might eventually come to see that they have infinitely more to gain from permanent peace than from periodically recurrent wars. . . .

November 28, 1943

MARSHAL STALIN then raised the question of the future of France. He described in considerable length the reasons why, in his opinion, France deserved no considerate treatment from the Allies and, above all, had no right to retain her former empire. He said that the entire French ruling class was rotten to the core and had delivered over France to the Germans and that, in fact, France was now actively helping our enemies. He therefore felt that it would be not only unjust but dangerous to leave in French hands any important strategic points after the war.

THE PRESIDENT replied that he in part agreed with Marshal Stalin. That was why this afternoon he had said to Marshal Stalin that it was necessary to eliminate in the future government of France anybody over forty years old and particularly anybody who had formed part of the French Government. He mentioned specifically the question of New Caledonia and Dakar, the first of which he said represented a threat to Australia and New Zealand and, therefore, should be placed under the trusteeship of the United Nations. In regard to Dakar, THE PRESIDENT said he was speaking for twenty-one American nations when he said that Dakar in unsure hands was a direct threat to the Americas.

MR. CHURCHILL at this point intervened to say that Great Britain did not desire and did not expect to acquire any additional territory out of this war, but since the 4 great victorious nations—the United States, the Soviet Union, Great Britain and China—will be responsible for the future peace of the world, it was obviously necessary that certain strategic points throughout the world should be under the [*their?*] control. . . .

The conversation then turned to the question of the treatment to be accorded Nazi Germany.

THE PRESIDENT said that, in his opinion, it was very important not to leave in the German mind the concept of the Reich and that the very word should be stricken from the language.

MARSHAL STALIN replied that it was not enough to eliminate the word, but the very Reich itself must be rendered impotent ever again to plunge the world into war. He said that unless the victorious Allies retained in their hands the strategic positions necessary to prevent any recrudescence of German militarism, they would have failed in their duty.

In the detailed discussion between the President, Marshal Stalin and Churchill that followed Marshal Stalin took the lead, constantly emphasizing that the measures for the control of Germany and her disarmament were insufficient to prevent the rebirth of German militarism and appeared to favor even stronger measures. He, however, did not specify what he actually had in mind except that he appeared to favor the dismemberment of Germany.

MARSHAL STALIN particularly mentioned that Poland should extend to the Oder and stated definitely that the Russians would help the Poles to obtain a frontier on the Oder.

THE PRESIDENT then said he would be interested in the question of assuring the approaches to the Baltic Sea and had in mind some form of trusteeship with perhaps an international state in the vicinity of the Kiel Canal to insure free navigation in both directions through the approaches. Due to some error of the Soviet translator Marshal Stalin apparently thought that the President was referring to the question of the Baltic States. On the basis of this understanding, he replied categorically that the Baltic States had by an expression of the will of the people voted to join the Soviet Union and that this question was not therefore one for discussion. Following the clearing up of the misapprehension, he, however, expressed himself favorably in regard to the question of insuring free navigation to and from the Baltic Sea.

THE PRESIDENT, returning to the question of certain outlying possessions, said he was interested in the possibility of a sovereignty fashioned in a collective body such as the United Nations; a concept which had never been developed in past history. . . .

November 29, 1943

THE PRESIDENT then said the question of a post war organization to preserve peace had not been fully explained and dealt with and he would like to discuss with the Marshal the prospect of some organization based on the United Nations.

THE PRESIDENT then outlined the following general plan:

(1) There would be a large organization composed of some 35 members of the United Nations which would meet periodically at different places, discuss and make recommendations to a smaller body.

MARSHAL STALIN inquired whether this organization was to be world wide or European, to which the President replied, world-wide.

THE PRESIDENT continued that there would be set up an executive committee composed of the Soviet Union, the United States, United Kingdom and China, together with two additional European states, one South American, one Near East, one

Far Eastern country, and one British Dominion. He mentioned that Mr. Churchill did not like this proposal for the reason that the British Empire only had two votes. This Executive Committee would deal with all non-military questions such as agriculture, food, health, and economic questions, as well as the setting up of an International Committee. This Committee would likewise meet in various places.

MARSHAL STALIN inquired whether this body would have the right to make decisions binding on the nations of the world.

THE PRESIDENT replied, yes and no. It could make recommendations for settling disputes with the hope that the nations concerned would be guided thereby, but that, for example, he did not believe the Congress of the United States would accept as binding a decision of such a body. THE PRESIDENT then turned to the third organization which he termed "The Four Policemen," namely, the Soviet Union, United States, Great Britain, and China. This organization would have the power to deal immediately with any threat to the peace and any sudden emergency which requires this action. He went on to say that in 1935, when Italy attacked Ethiopia, the only machinery in existence was the League of Nations. He personally had begged France to close the Suez Canal, but they instead referred it to the League which disputed the question and in the end did nothing. The result was that the Italian Armies went through the Suez Canal and destroyed Ethiopia. THE PRESIDENT pointed out that had the machinery of the Four Policemen, which he had in mind, been in existence, it would have been possible to close the Suez Canal. THE PRESIDENT then summarized briefly the idea that he had in mind. . . .

. . . THE PRESIDENT added that he saw two methods of dealing with possible threats to the peace. In one case if the threat arose from a revolution or developments in a small country, it might be possible to apply the quarantine method, closing the frontiers of the countries in question and imposing embargoes. In the second case, if the threat was more serious, the four powers, acting as policemen, would send an ultimatum to the nation in question and if refused, [it] would result in the immediate bombardment and possible invasion of that country.

7. The Allies Agree to a Postwar International Organization: The Dumbarton Oaks Agreement, 1944

Proposals for the Establishment of a General International Organization

There should be established an international organization under the title of The United Nations, the Charter of which should contain provisions necessary to give effect to the proposals which follow.

CHAPTER I.—PURPOSES

The purposes of the Organization should be:

1. To maintain international peace and security; and to that end to take effective collective measures for the prevention and removal of threats to the peace and the

From U.S. Department of State, *Foreign Relations of the United States, 1944,* vol. 1 (Washington, D.C.: U.S. Government Printing Office, 1966), 890–891.

suppression of acts of aggression or other breaches of the peace, and to bring about by peaceful means adjustment or settlement of international disputes which may lead to a breach of the peace;

2. To develop friendly relations among nations and to take other appropriate measures to strengthen universal peace;

3. To achieve international cooperation in the solution of international economic, social and other humanitarian problems; and

4. To afford a center for harmonizing the actions of nations in the achievement of these common ends.

CHAPTER II.—PRINCIPLES

In pursuit of the purpose mentioned in Chapter I the Organization and its members should act in accordance with the following principles:

1. The Organization is based on the principle of the sovereign equality of all peace-loving states.

2. All members of the Organization undertake, in order to ensure to all of them the rights and benefits resulting from membership in the Organization, to fulfill the obligations assumed by them in accordance with the Charter.

3. All members of the Organization shall settle their disputes by peaceful means in such a manner that international peace and security are not endangered.

4. All members of the Organization shall refrain in their international relations from the threat or use of force in any manner inconsistent with the purposes of the Organization.

5. All members of the Organization shall give every assistance to the Organization in any action undertaken by it in accordance with the provisions of the Charter.

6. All members of the Organization shall refrain from giving assistance to any state against which preventive or enforcement action is being undertaken by the Organization.

The Organization should ensure that states not members of the Organization act in accordance with these principles so far as may be necessary for the maintenance of international peace and security.

CHAPTER III.—MEMBERSHIP

1. Membership of the Organization should be open to all peaceloving states.

CHAPTER IV.—PRINCIPAL ORGANS

1. The Organization should have as its principal organs:

   a. A General Assembly;
   b. A Security Council;
   c. An international court of justice; and
   d. A Secretariat.

2. The Organization should have such subsidiary agencies as may be found necessary.

8. Churchill and Stalin Divide Eastern Europe, 1944

The moment was apt for business, so I [Churchill] said, "Let us settle about our affairs in the Balkans. Your armies are in Rumania and Bulgaria. We have interests, missions, and agents there. Don't let us get at cross-purposes in small ways. So far as Britain and Russia are concerned, how would it do for you to have ninety per cent predominance in Rumania, for us to have ninety per cent of the say in Greece, and go fifty-fifty about Yugoslavia?" While this was being translated I wrote out on a half-sheet of paper:

Rumania	
Russia	90%
The others	10%
Greece	
Great Britain (in accord with U.S.A.)	90%
Russia	10%
Yugoslavia	50–50%
Hungary	50–50%
Bulgaria	
Russia	75%
The others	25%

I pushed this across to Stalin, who had by then heard the translation. There was a slight pause. Then he took his blue pencil and made a large tick upon it, and passed it back to us. It was all settled in no more time than it takes to set down.

Of course, we had long and anxiously considered our point, and were only dealing with immediate war-time arrangements. All larger questions were reserved on both sides for what we then hoped would be a peace table when the war was won.

After this there was a long silence. The pencilled paper lay in the centre of the table. At length I said, "Might it not be thought rather cynical if it seemed we had disposed of these issues, so fateful to millions of people, in such an offhand manner? Let us burn the paper." "No, you keep it," said Stalin.

9. The Allies Reach Postwar Agreements at the Yalta Conference, 1945

The Yalta Protocol of Proceedings, 1945

I. World Organization

It was decided:

1. that a United Nations Conference on the proposed world organization should be summoned for Wednesday, 25th April, 1945, and should be held in the United States of America.

(Document 8) Excerpt from Winston S. Churchill, *The Second World War,* vol. 6, *Triumph and Tragedy* (Boston: Houghton Mifflin, 1953), 227–228. Copyright 1953 by Houghton Mifflin Company; copyright © renewed 1981 by The Honourable Lady Sarah Audley and The Honourable Lady Soames. Reprinted by permission of Houghton Mifflin Company. All rights reserved.

(Document 9) From U.S. Department of State, *Foreign Relations of the United States: The Conferences at Malta and Yalta, 1945* (Washington, D.C.: U.S. Government Printing Office, 1955), 975–982, 984.

2. the Nations to be invited to this Conference should be:
   a. the United Nations as they existed on the 8th February, 1945; and
   b. such of the Associated Nations as have declared war on the common enemy by 1st March, 1945. (For this purpose by the term "Associated Nations" was meant the eight Associated Nations and Turkey). When the Conference on World Organization is held, the delegates of the United Kingdom and United States of America will support a proposal to admit to original membership two Soviet Socialist Republics, i.e. the Ukraine and White Russia.
3. that the United States Government on behalf of the Three Powers should consult the Government of China and the French Provisional Government in regard to decisions taken at the present Conference concerning the proposed World Organization.
4. that the text of the invitation to be issued to all the nations which would take part in the United Nations Conference should be as follows:

Invitation

The Government of the United States of America, on behalf of itself and of the Governments of the United Kingdom, the Union of Soviet Socialist Republics, and the Republic of China and the Provisional Government of the French Republic, invite the Government of ————— to send representatives to a Conference of the United Nations to be held on 25th April, 1945, or soon thereafter, at San Francisco in the United States of America to prepare a Charter for a General International Organization for the maintenance of international peace and security.

The above named governments suggest that the Conference consider as affording a basis for such a Charter the Proposals for the Establishment of a General International Organization, which were made public last October as a result of the Dumbarton Oaks Conference, and which have now been supplemented by the following provisions for Section C of Chapter VI:

C. Voting
1. Each member of the Security Council should have one vote.
2. Decisions of the Security Council on procedural matters should be made by an affirmative vote of seven members.
3. Decisions of the Security Council on all other matters should be made by an affirmative vote of seven members including the concurring votes of the permanent members; provided that, in decisions under Chapter VIII, Section A, and under the second sentence of paragraph 1 of Chapter VIII, Section C, a party to a dispute should abstain from voting.

Further information as to arrangements will be transmitted subsequently.

In the event that the Government of ————— desires in advance of the Conference to present views or comments concerning the proposals, the Government of the United States of America will be pleased to transmit such views and comments to the other participating Governments.

Territorial Trusteeship. It was agreed that the five Nations which will have permanent seats on the Security Council should consult each other prior to the United Nations Conference on the question of territorial trusteeship.

The acceptance of this recommendation is subject to its being made clear that territorial trusteeship will only apply to (a) existing mandates of the League of Nations; (b) territories detached from the enemy as a result of the present war; (c) any other territory which might voluntarily be placed under trusteeship; and (d) no discussion of actual territories is contemplated at the forthcoming United Nations Conference or in the preliminary consultations, and it will be a matter for subsequent agreement which territories within the above categories will be placed under trusteeship.

II. Declaration on Liberated Europe

The following declaration has been approved:

> The Premier of the Union of Soviet Socialist Republics, the Prime Minister of the United Kingdom and the President of the United States of America have consulted with each other in the common interests of the peoples of their countries and those of liberated Europe. They jointly declare their mutual agreement to concert during the temporary period of instability in liberated Europe the policies of their three governments in assisting the peoples of the former Axis satellite states of Europe to solve by democratic means their pressing political and economic problems.
>
> The establishment of order in Europe and the rebuilding of national economic life must be achieved by processes which will enable the liberated peoples to destroy the last vestiges of Nazism and Fascism and to create democratic institutions of their own choice. This is a principle of the Atlantic Charter—the right of all peoples to choose the form of government under which they will live—the restoration of sovereign rights and self-government to those peoples who have been forcibly deprived of them by the aggressor nations.
>
> To foster the conditions in which the liberated peoples may exercise these rights, the three governments will jointly assist the people in any European liberated state or former Axis satellite state in Europe where in their judgment conditions require (a) to establish conditions of internal peace; (b) to carry out emergency measures for the relief of distressed peoples; (c) to form interim governmental authorities broadly representative of all democratic elements in the population and pledged to the earliest possible establishment through free elections of governments responsible to the will of the people; and (d) to facilitate where necessary the holding of such elections.
>
> The three governments will consult the other United Nations and provisional authorities or other governments in Europe when matters of direct interest to them are under consideration.
>
> When, in the opinion of the three governments, conditions in any European liberated state or any former Axis satellite state in Europe make such action necessary, they will immediately consult together on the measures necessary to discharge the joint responsibilities set forth in this declaration.
>
> By this declaration we reaffirm our faith in the principles of the Atlantic Charter, our pledges in the Declaration by the United Nations, and our determination to build in cooperation with other peace-loving nations world order under law, dedicated to peace, security, freedom and general well-being of all mankind.
>
> In issuing this declaration, the Three Powers express the hope that the Provisional Government of the French Republic may be associated with them in the procedure suggested.

III. Dismemberment of Germany

It was agreed that Article 12 (a) of the Surrender Terms for Germany should be amended as follows:

> The United Kingdom, the United States of America and the Union of Soviet Socialist Republics shall possess supreme authority with respect to Germany. In the exercise of such

authority they will take such steps, including the complete disarmament demilitarization and dismemberment of Germany as they deem requisite for future peace and security. . . .

IV. Zone of Occupation for the French and Control Council for Germany

It was agreed that a zone in Germany, to be occupied by the French Forces, should be allocated to France. This zone would be formed out of the British and American zones and its extent would be settled by the British and Americans in consultation with the French Provisional Government.

It was also agreed that the French Provisional Government should be invited to become a member of the Allied Control Council of Germany.

V. Reparation

The heads of the three governments agreed as follows:

1. Germany must pay in kind for the losses caused by her to the Allied nations in the course of the war. Reparations are to be received in the first instance by those countries which have borne the main burden of the war, have suffered the heaviest losses and have organized victory over the enemy.
2. Reparation in kind to be exacted from Germany in three following forms:
   a. Removals within 2 years from the surrender of Germany or the cessation of organized resistance from the national wealth of Germany located on the territory of Germany herself as well as outside her territory (equipment, machine-tools, ships, rolling stock, German investments abroad, shares of industrial, transport and other enterprises in Germany etc.), these removals to be carried out chiefly for purpose of destroying the war potential of Germany.
   b. Annual deliveries of goods from current production for a period to be fixed.
   c. Use of German labor.
3. For the working out on the above principles of a detailed plan for exaction of reparation from Germany, an Allied Reparation Commission will be set up in Moscow. It will consist of three representatives—one from the Union of Soviet Socialist Republics, one from the United Kingdom and one from the United States of America.
4. With regard to the fixing of the total sum of the reparation as well as the distribution of it among the countries which suffered from the German aggression the Soviet and American delegations agreed as follows:

The Moscow Reparation Commission should take in its initial studies as a basis for discussion the suggestion of the Soviet Government that the total sum of the reparation in accordance with the points (a) and (b) of the paragraph 2 should be 20 billion dollars and that 50% of it should go to the Union of Soviet Socialist Republics.

The British delegation was of the opinion that pending consideration of the reparation question by the Moscow Reparation Commission no figures of reparation should be mentioned.

The above Soviet-American proposal has been passed to the Moscow Reparation Commission as one of the proposals to be considered by the Commission.

VI. Major War Criminals

The Conference agreed that the question of the major war criminals should be the subject of enquiry by the three Foreign Secretaries for report in due course after the close of the Conference.

VII. Poland

The following Declaration on Poland was agreed by the Conference:

> A new situation has been created in Poland as a result of her complete liberation by the Red Army. This calls for the establishment of a Polish Provisional Government which can be more broadly based than was possible before the recent liberation of [the] Western part of Poland. The Provisional Government which is now functioning in Poland should therefore be reorganized on a broader democratic basis with the inclusion of democratic leaders from Poland itself and from Poles abroad. This new Government should then be called the Polish Provisional Government of National Unity.
>
> M. Molotov, Mr. Harriman and Sir A. Clark Kerr are authorized as a commission to consult in the first instance in Moscow with members of the present Provisional Government and with other Polish democratic leaders from within Poland and from abroad, with a view to the reorganization of the present Government along the above lines. This Polish Provisional Government of National Unity shall be pledged to the holding of free and unfettered elections as soon as possible on the basis of universal suffrage and secret ballot. In these elections all democratic and anti-Nazi parties shall have the right to take part and to put forward candidates.
>
> When a Polish Provisional Government of National Unity has been properly formed in conformity with the above, the Government of the U.S.S.R., which now maintains diplomatic relations with the present Provisional Government of Poland, and the Government of the United Kingdom and the Government of the United States of America will establish diplomatic relations with the new Polish Provisional Government of National Unity, and will exchange Ambassadors by whose reports the respective Governments will be kept informed about the situation in Poland.
>
> The three Heads of Government consider that the Eastern frontier of Poland should follow the Curzon Line with digressions from it in some regions of five to eight kilometers in favor of Poland. They recognize that Poland must receive substantial accession of territory in the North and West. They feel that the opinion of the new Polish Provisional Government of National Unity should be sought in due course on the extent of these accessions and that the final delimitation of the Western frontier of Poland should therefore await the Peace Conference.

[Following this declaration, but omitted here for reasons of space, are brief statements on Yugoslavia, the Italo-Yugoslav frontier and Italo-Austrian frontier, Yugoslav-Bulgarian relations, Southeastern Europe, Iran, meetings of the three foreign secretaries, and the Montreux Convention and the Straits.]

The Yalta Agreement on Soviet Entry into the War Against Japan, 1945

The leaders of the three Great Powers—the Soviet Union, the United States of America and Great Britain—have agreed that in two or three months after Germany has surrendered and the war in Europe has terminated the Soviet Union shall enter into the war against Japan on the side of the Allies on condition that:

1. The *status quo* in Outer-Mongolia (The Mongolian People's Republic) shall be preserved;
2. The former rights of Russia violated by the treacherous attack of Japan in 1904 shall be restored, viz:
   a. the southern part of Sakhalin as well as all the islands adjacent to it shall be returned to the Soviet Union,
   b. the commercial port of Dairen shall be internationalized, the preeminent interests of the Soviet Union in this port being safeguarded and the lease of Port Arthur as a naval base of the USSR restored,
   c. the Chinese-Eastern Railroad and the South-Manchurian Railroad which provides an outlet to Dairen shall be jointly operated by the establishment of a joint Soviet-Chinese Company; it being understood that the preeminent interests of the Soviet Union shall be safeguarded and that China shall retain full sovereignty in Manchuria;
3. The Kurile islands shall be handed over to the Soviet Union.

It is understood, that the agreement concerning Outer-Mongolia and the ports and railroads referred to above will require concurrence of Generalissimo Chiang Kai-shek. The President will take measures in order to obtain this concurrence on advice from Marshal Stalin.

The Heads of the three Great Powers have agreed that these claims of the Soviet Union shall be unquestionably fulfilled after Japan has been defeated.

For its part the Soviet Union expresses its readiness to conclude with the National Government of China a Pact of friendship and alliance between the USSR and China in order to render assistance to China with its armed forces for the purpose of liberating China from the Japanese yoke.

10. Roosevelt Sends Letters to Stalin and Churchill, 1945

Roosevelt's Anger with Stalin, [April 4] 1945

I have received with astonishment your message of April 3 containing an allegation that arrangements which were made between Field Marshals [Harold] Alexander and [Albert] Kesselring at Berne [Switzerland] "permitted the Anglo-American troops to advance to the East and the Anglo-Americans promised in return to ease for the Germans the peace terms."

In my previous messages to you in regard to the attempts made in Berne to arrange a conference to discuss a surrender of the German army in Italy I have told you that: (1) No negotiations were held in Berne, (2) The meeting had no political implications whatever, (3) In any surrender of the enemy army in Italy there would be no violation of our agreed principle of unconditional surrender, (4) Soviet officers would be welcomed at any meeting that might be arranged to discuss surrender.

For the advantage of our common war effort against Germany, which today gives excellent promise of an early success in a disintegration of the German

From U.S. Department of State, *Foreign Relations of the United States, 1945* (Washington, D.C.: U.S. Government Printing Office, 1967–1968), vol. 3, 745–746; vol. 5, 210.

armies, I must continue to assume that you have the same high confidence in my truthfulness and reliability that I have always had in yours.

I have also a full appreciation of the effect your gallant army has had in making possible a crossing of the Rhine by the forces under General [Dwight D.] Eisenhower and the effect that your forces will have hereafter on the eventual collapse of the German resistance to our combined attacks.

I have complete confidence in General Eisenhower and know that he certainly would inform me before entering into any agreement with the Germans. He is instructed to demand and will demand unconditional surrender of enemy troops that may be defeated on his front. Our advances on the Western Front are due to military action. Their speed has been attributable mainly to the terrific impact of our air power resulting in destruction of German communications, and to the fact that Eisenhower was able to cripple the bulk of the German forces on the Western Front while they were still west of the Rhine.

I am certain that there were no negotiations in Berne at any time and I feel that your information to that effect must have come from German sources which have made persistent efforts to create dissension between us in order to escape in some measure responsibility for their war crimes. If that was [General Karl] Wolff's purpose in Berne, your message proves that he has had some success.

With a confidence in your belief in my personal reliability and in my determination to bring about, together with you, an unconditional surrender of the Nazis, it is astonishing that a belief seems to have reached the Soviet Government that I have entered into an agreement with the enemy without first obtaining your full agreement.

Finally I would say this, it would be one of the great tragedies of history if at the very moment of the victory, now within our grasp, such distrust, such lack of faith should prejudice the entire undertaking after the colossal losses of life, material and treasure involved.

Frankly I cannot avoid a feeling of bitter resentment toward your informers, whoever they are, for such vile misrepresentations of my actions or those of my trusted subordinates.

Roosevelt's Last Letter to Churchill, [April 11] 1945

I would minimize the general Soviet problem as much as possible because these problems, in one form or another, seem to arise every day and most of them straighten out as in the case of the Berne meeting.

We must be firm, however, and our course thus far is correct.

☘ *E S S A Y S*

For more than five decades scholars have debated the wisdom of Franklin Roosevelt's wartime diplomacy. To many historians, especially but far from exclusively those writing in the first years of the Soviet-American Cold War that followed World War II, Roosevelt was exceptionally naïve and foolish to believe he could collaborate with Stalin. He was equally foolish to attack the colonial empires of the Western European nations that he would need as strong postwar allies against the Soviet Union. Other historians have defended FDR, emphasizing the domestic and international constraints under which he had to operate, his prescience regarding the Third World, and his overall realism. The following two essays are representative of these two schools of thought. In the first, independent scholar Frederick W. Marks III attacks Roosevelt for ignorance, parochialism, and numerous diplomatic blunders during the war. In the second, Robert Dallek of the University of Southern California strongly defends FDR against such criticisms.

The Ignorance and Naïveté of Roosevelt's Wartime Diplomacy

FREDERICK W. MARKS III

. . . There were weaknesses at nearly every point along the line of Roosevelt's thought. If he felt that Russia could be made amenable, he also assumed that Britain would remain America's chief commercial rival and that postwar France would be unable to raise a finger. Especially did he bank on the idea that China would survive the war as a strong and viable nation. According to much of the advice he received at the time, there were no real communists in China and Chiang's domestic feuding came down to a simple matter of personalities. By knocking heads together, by pressing Chiang for social democratic reform and insisting on coalition government, China would coalesce and find herself. Needless to say, on each of these counts Churchill knew Roosevelt to be mistaken, but there was no way the English leader could prevail upon his opposite number. When the truth finally began to dawn in Washington, pundits were to speak of a "Cold War." But again, London knew differently. America's Cold War was nothing but a continuation of Britain's age-old struggle to contain the power of the czars. International life had changed but little. . . .

. . . In addition to promising Stalin a second military front in Europe, Roosevelt acquiesced in a Soviet protectorate over Mongolia, against Chiang's wishes, as well as Soviet acquisition of the Kurile Islands and the southern half of Sakhalin Island. He violated another solemn engagement to Chiang Kai-shek at the same conference when he bestowed his official blessing upon the internationalization of Dairen and the cession of Port Arthur to the Soviet Union as a naval base on long-term lease. Dairen and Port Arthur were among China's most vital ports. Finally, he agreed unilaterally, again in violation of the spirit of his understanding with Chiang, to a half-interest for Russia in the operation of Manchurian railways, with Soviet interests throughout the area to be recognized as "preeminent." Other questions follow along a similar line. During the Big Three Conference at Yalta in February 1945, Roosevelt obtained a modicum of Soviet cooperation regarding the structure of the United Nations. In return, he threw American support to the communist-sponsored Lublin government of Poland, broadened to include various noncommunist elements, but communist nevertheless. Was this a wise bargain? Did the president have to reject, out of hand, Churchill's pleas for practical safeguards to ensure the outcome of "free elections" as promised for eastern Europe? And did he have to side with Stalin

From Frederick W. Marks III, *Wind Over Sand: The Diplomacy of Franklin Roosevelt* (Athens: University of Georgia Press, 1988), 169–173, 175–176, 179–181, 193–196, 201–203, 216, 276–277, 281, 284–285, 287–288. Reprinted by permission of Frederick W. Marks III.

against Churchill on miscellaneous questions regarding reparations, industry, and labor in postwar Germany?

Few will deny that there were many tactics Roosevelt might have used to contain communist expansion in eastern Europe and the Far East, although how successful they would have been will continue to be a matter for speculation. Some have argued that Russia's postwar gains were inevitable and even morally justifiable given her enormous sacrifice in human life, estimated at twenty million (approximately ten times the figure for all the rest of the Allied forces). To be sure, there is an element of truth in this argument. Few things in history are inevitable, and Stalin did carry weight at the conference table. The specter of a separate peace between Russia and Germany could never be laid. Moreover, Stalin proved masterful in the use of veiled threats. No Western leader was ever permitted to forget that Moscow had engaged 270 German divisions as compared with only 90 for Washington and London combined. Roosevelt needed Stalin's cooperation and he needed it badly since his goal was to win the war at minimum cost to his country while securing the unconditional surrender of Germany and Japan. Nevertheless, had he operated on a different set of assumptions, his strategy and prospects would also have been different. The crux of the issue is simple: *he never grasped the need* for an alternative approach. He believed that the Soviet Union would exhaust itself against Germany and, in association with a cooperative West, evolve gradually toward capitalism and democracy. The Russian empire was too cumbersome, he felt, to absorb additional territory, and he was convinced that by charming Stalin he could lead him gently along the path to postwar unity. "I think I can personally handle Stalin better than either your Foreign Office or my State Department," he confided to Churchill. "Stalin hates the guts of all your top people. He thinks he likes me better, and I hope he will continue to do so."

Had FDR glimpsed the true contours of power in a world aborning, he might have given more support to Mao Tse-tung or backed Chiang with less reserve. It was his to decide which would be more important in negotiating with Stalin, the United Nations charter or the composition of eastern European government. He might have accepted de Gaulle's advice that Polish interests dictated an Anglo-American demand for access to Baltic ports in return for Soviet access to terminals in the North Sea. Furthermore, had he assumed, as Eden and the Red Chinese did, that Russia had a natural interest in entering the war against Japan, he might have yielded far less in exchange. Never was he the absolute prisoner of events.

On the one hand, Stalin derived powerful leverage from his option to grant or withhold aid against Japan. Atomic warfare, still in the experimental stage, offered little assurance of instantaneous surrender, particularly given the depth of Japanese commitment, and Roosevelt's military advisers were as one in stressing the importance of Moscow's aid. On the other hand, it is clear that Roosevelt gave away much of his hand in a game whose rules he did not comprehend. He did not have to *volunteer* to hand over such prizes as Dairen and the Kurile Islands. . . .

Possibilities abound. FDR might have baited his line with the promise of a credit or loan for Soviet postwar rehabilitation, as recommended by Harriman and Morgenthau. He might have been more stringent on conditions for the continuation of Lend-Lease. He did not have to announce his intention of withdrawing from Europe at the end of the war, particularly when a contrary policy had the support of public opinion, as well as of powerful political leaders and top military advisers. . . . There was no reason why Roosevelt had to rule out American spy activity in Russia, just as it fell within his province to file a much stronger protest on the Soviet takeover of Romania. In addition, his armies might have rolled on into Berlin and Prague as Churchill advised. . . . To lengthen the list of alternatives, Roosevelt might have sided with Churchill on the value of Germany and France as potential makeweights against Soviet power. He might have bargained on questions affecting the partition of Germany, the sum of reparations to be exacted, or the question of a fair trial for prisoners of war.

Above all, he might have given the Polish government in exile more of an opportunity to survive. When Russian armies were about to enter Warsaw and pro-Western underground forces rose to attack retreating Nazi units, Stalin ordered his troops to halt on the Vistula River. There they stayed until German gunners had all but annihilated the prospective leadership of a democratic Poland. Churchill proposed an airlift to relieve the embattled patriots, but Stalin refused to permit American or British planes to land at nearby airfields. When Churchill insisted that Roosevelt go ahead with or without Soviet permission, the president could not be budged. He declined even to write Stalin a note of protest. As it happened, a detailed American plan for the United Nations was under consideration at Dumbarton Oaks, and what FDR wanted was Soviet support on voting procedure along with assembly membership and location of the organization in New York City. This, rather than Poland, was the apple of his eye. . . .

. . . [I]f the Polish people were ever represented in the counsels of the Big Three, they found their voice in Winston Churchill rather than in Franklin Roosevelt. Ultimately, the difference between London and Washington came down to a question of diplomatic judgment. Churchill concluded that while it might be futile to contest the Polish boundary issue, one must nevertheless fight for a pro-Western government in Warsaw. Roosevelt, on the other hand, demonstrated scant concern about the future of Poland because he never shared Churchill's suspicion of the Soviet Union. Churchill insisted on a total scrapping of the Lublin puppet government; FDR was content with a broadening. The former urged strong representations against Lublin while the latter sent weak ones accompanied by a slur against the London Poles. Where Churchill wanted to insist on Western observers, Roosevelt again demurred. When Mikolajczyk asked that Western troops be sent to Poland to prevent Russian reprisals, Roosevelt not only declined to send troops but proposed a political cease-fire, which could only help Russia. Churchill nudged him to intervene personally, but he preferred to let the ambassadors handle it. Exasperated, the prime minister opened fire: "Poland has lost her frontier. Is she now to lose her freedom? . . . We are in the presence of a great failure." Roosevelt, who diagnosed the problem as one of semantics, could not even be brought to the point of prodding Stalin.

Perhaps it is suggestive that Roosevelt never appointed an ambassador to the London Poles once Biddle resigned in the aftermath of Teheran. Before this, he sided with Stalin on the hotly contested question of responsibility for the Katyn Forest Massacre, telling him that the London Poles must learn to act "with more common sense." After Teheran, from 1 December 1943 until August 1945, the United States continued in the same posture, with Roosevelt counseling Mikolajczyk to trust Stalin and pressing him to replace anti-Soviet cabinet members with neutrals or communist sympathizers. Secretly, he sent two pro-Soviet American Poles to Moscow against the advice of Hull and Stettinius, and in the months after Teheran he rejected two requests by Mikolajczyk and four by Ambassador Jan Ciechanowski for a personal meeting. When he did see the Polish prime minister in June of 1944, he promised he would help him establish his claim to Lvov, Tarnopol, and the oil fields of eastern Galicia. In truth, Poland might well have done without such help as it consisted in Roosevelt's telling Stalin that Polish demands were not to be regarded as demands but merely as suggestions for Soviet consideration. Mikolajczyk promptly resigned.

Without question, Stalin held a strong hand. His armies were on the ground. Nevertheless, nothing about the shape of postwar Polish politics had been fore-ordained. There was more than empty pride in Mikolajczyk's charge that "we were sacrificed by our allies." Nowhere was it written that twenty thousand pro-Western Polish patriots had to die in the Warsaw Uprising. Roosevelt did not have to boost Soviet hopes at Teheran by conceding that Polish affairs were "of special concern" to Stalin. Nor did he have to remain silent when Churchill depicted Poles as the type of people who would never be satisfied. He need not have repeated to Stalin at Yalta what he had already told him, that his only interest in Poland was to appear "in some way involved with the question of freedom of elections." And he did not have to characterize Poles as a "quarrelsome people not only at home but also abroad." By stressing that his principal interest lay in six million Polish-American voters and alleging that in some years there had not really been any Polish government, he was sinking saber teeth into the future of eastern Europe. It is strange to read the minutes of the plenary meetings at Yalta and to discover that Stalin, of all people, was the only one to volunteer anything complimentary on the subject of Poland or its people.

FDR made Stalin's work relatively easy. In the face of American willingness to grant unconditional Lend-Lease, Stalin responded with condescension: he was "willing to accept" it. When Admiral William H. Standley, Roosevelt's ambassador to Moscow, spoke out against unconditional aid, the president dismissed him with a curt reminder that his mission had but one purpose: "full and friendly cooperation" with the Soviet Union. Again and again, Roosevelt described himself as "deeply appreciative" and "thrilled" at Soviet cooperation, and eventually the United States would succeed in shipping some four hundred thousand trucks, two million tons of petroleum products, four million tons of food, two thousand locomotives, and ten thousand flatcars, along with vast quantities of clothing. All to the Soviet Union. . . .

By the end of the year, Stalin had extended his power beyond anything dreamed of by the czars and given Americans a succession of lessons in the art of statecraft. To Hopkins, he termed it a mistake to believe that just because a state was small, it was necessarily innocent. To Davies, who hoped that a top-level meeting between Soviet and American leaders would resolve all outstanding problems, Stalin replied that he was not so sure. Litvinov instructed Ambassador Bullitt in like manner: there was no such thing as "really friendly" relations between nations. When FDR took the liberty of calling Stalin "Uncle Joe," the reaction proved unexpectedly frigid. Always, it seemed, one man spoke as teacher while the other listened as pupil. On one occasion, when Roosevelt suggested that India needed reform from the bottom up, Stalin remarked that in a land with so many tiers of culture and no interchange between the castes, this would invite revolutionary chaos. The Soviet chairman also favored restoration of the monarchy in Yugoslavia. On another occasion, when

Roosevelt called Hitler mad, Stalin again corrected him, pointing out that whatever one might think of Hitler's methods or his level of cultural and political sophistication, there was no ground for judging him mentally unbalanced. Only a very able man could have succeeded in unifying the German people. Finally, as if to make the picture complete, FDR advocated a peace imposed by "four policemen" only to be reminded by the Soviet leader of the feelings of smaller nations. Realistically, Stalin predicted that China, one of the prospective four, would not be powerful enough in the aftermath of the war to assume such responsibility.

Of Roosevelt's relationship with Chiang Kai-shek there is only one thing to be said. It was nearly the reverse of what has been observed in the case of Stalin. FDR made practically no effort to assuage Chiang's fears or to cater to him personally. In the epic battle for China, he extended remarkably little material or moral aid, and such sacrifices as were made by the United States tended to undermine Chiang politically. Intentionally or not, great blows were leveled against the prestige of Nationalist China as Roosevelt broke one promise after another. . . .

. . . He [FDR] shipped less than 10 percent of the aid pledged. He went back on his commitment to assist Chiang's Burma campaign with an amphibious invasion. At various times, supplies earmarked for Chungking were diverted without consultation. Scores of bombers and transports, once the entire U.S. Tenth Air Force in India, were rerouted to bypass China after the United States had given its word. Roosevelt pledged a loan of a billion dollars which was never delivered. And more than once, he promised increased tonnage to be flown from India over the Himalayan Hump. In almost every instance, such tonnage failed to eventuate.

Only the whipcord of public insult can compare with this array of broken promises as a factor in Chiang's ultimate defeat on the mainland, at least insofar as Roosevelt's role is concerned. . . . It would have cost Roosevelt little to have greeted the Chinese leader when his plane landed in Cairo. Barred from the Atlantic Conference of 1941, China took no part in major Allied planning groups such as the Joint Chiefs of Staff and the Munitions Board, to name two of the more prestigious ones. . . .

Chiang felt humiliated when Roosevelt failed to inform him of developments as they broke during the Casablanca Conference of late January 1943. He was likewise prevented from sending an official representative to the Teheran and Yalta conferences, where the fate of a vital portion of his realm would be settled. . . . For Chiang to be given only a week's notice before the ill-fated Doolittle raid, then to have Washington go ahead with it over his strenuous objection, constituted a stunning indignity. . . .

Even if Chiang had managed to survive such treatment, he would still have had to withstand the kind of diplomatic punishment meted out to him and his country behind his back, something already mentioned but worth repeating. After solemnly promising at Cairo that China would recover all of Manchuria, including the ports of Dairen and Port Arthur, which together held the key to surrounding industrial areas, Roosevelt went on at Teheran to say that he thought Dairen should be converted to an open port subject to Soviet "preeminent interests." When Stalin replied that Chiang might object, Roosevelt would not hear of it. So, too, in the case of Port Arthur, which went to the Soviet navy on a ninety-nine-year lease. . . .

. . . FDR seems to have been convinced that he had only two choices in China: either he must compel Chiang to embrace thoroughgoing democratic reform, albeit in the crucible of civil and foreign war, or he must write him off. Ultimately, of course, he did neither. His peculiar blend of action and inaction undermined Chiang even as it fell short of providing the basis for a positive relationship with Mao. . . .

Many have assumed that there was a friendly, if not affectionate, relationship between Downing Street and the White House. Historians have also taken note of the surface camaraderie that existed to the degree that both sides stood to benefit. Nor can one forget FDR's playful cable to Churchill about "how much fun" it was to be in the same decade with him. At the same time, beneath all the gaiety and merriment lay a hard substratum of distrust. . . .

It is interesting to note certain differences of character which separated the protagonists. Of the four mottoes that ring out from Churchill's history of World War II ("In War: Resolution. In Defeat: Defiance. In Victory: Magnanimity. In Peace: Goodwill."), it is the third that most clearly distinguishes one man from the other. As painter, philosopher, savant, and wit, there were few individuals or groups to which Churchill's understanding and sympathy did not extend in one form or another. . . .

Roosevelt, too, preached magnanimity and understanding, but he did not always practice it. It was not out of character for him to speak of castration for the Germans, sterilization for Puerto Ricans, and a frying pan for Burma's people to "stew in their own juice." Perhaps the wartime issue that sets off British and American leadership most graphically in this respect relates to the question of trial for German prisoners of war. In Stalin's mind, summary execution was a convenient means of eliminating opposition. Having tested it to dispose of Polish officers as well as balky Soviet generals, he anticipated it would again prove serviceable in dealing with Germans. This pleased FDR. . . .

. . . [W]hen Stalin spoke at Teheran on behalf of automatic execution of fifty thousand German officers, he knew he could count on American support. Churchill, unwilling to be cowed, adopted the role of challenger as he was to do at Moscow and later at Yalta, and Roosevelt's contribution was equally predictable. He encouraged Stalin. He and his son Elliot proposed banquet toasts seconding the marshal until Churchill stalked indignantly out of the hall. . . .

Having come this far in our analysis, we are free to go a step further and address the knotty question of what Winston Churchill really thought of his distant cousin, Franklin Roosevelt. In Churchill's widely read war memoirs, America's chief executive appears noble, far-seeing, and valiant; he is a man of knowledge and experience who possessed "commanding gifts." Each of the six volumes, moreover, contains at least one special term of endearment. It may also be recalled that Churchill was selected by Parliament to deliver a fitting eulogy on the death of FDR and that on this particular occasion the president was lauded for his upright and generous disposition: he was a man of "clear vision and vigour upon perplexing and complicated matters," in fact "the greatest American friend we have ever known" and "the greatest champion of freedom who has ever brought help and comfort from the New World to the Old."

Such encomiums must, of course, be evaluated within the context of their immediate background as well as against a body of countervailing evidence. Even if it were not apparent that Churchill leaned heavily upon his American connection, there are other grounds for questioning the genuineness of his regard for Roosevelt. Nearly all his praise is contained in the memoirs, which, according to Halifax, were askew in certain places and designed to make a record. Maurice Ashley, after four years as Churchill's research assistant, commented on his employer's "extraordinary gift for irony." . . .

Eden stated flatly that Churchill "had to play the courtier" and that if he had ever aired his real opinion he would have described the president as a charming country gentleman without any businesslike method for dealing with serious situations. In de Gaulle's judgment, Churchill "bitterly resented" the "tone of supremacy" which FDR adopted toward him, while the prime minister's physician relates that his patient was most reticent when it came to criticizing Roosevelt. Nowhere is it recorded that Churchill ever uttered a word of praise in private. On the contrary, Lord Coleraine, who saw him shortly after the news of Roosevelt's death, remembered that he seemed "remarkably unmoved." . . .

A number of individuals, including Australian Prime Minister Robert Menzies, marveled at the way Roosevelt, after singling Hitler out as a threat to world freedom, acted with imagination and persistence to convert strict neutrality into benevolent neutrality and thence into all aid short of war. On balance, however, the respect that Roosevelt might have earned as president of the United States simply did not materialize. Nothing is more misleading than the eulogies that poured from foreign chancelleries in 1945, when few failed to see the benefit, if not the necessity, of cultivating the party of Roosevelt. Within two years, veteran diplomat George Kennan would be moved to declare that world opinion toward the United States was "at worst hostile and at best resentful." Thoughtful Americans might well have wondered at the time, reading Kennan's dour appraisal, how their nation's standing could have fallen off so precipitately. But the more one sees of FDR, in particular his image in the eyes of the world, the more one is inclined to take Kennan at his word. America's reputation did not fall suddenly, however. It had been in semi-eclipse for more than a decade. . . .

Had Hoover, Stimson, and Roosevelt leaned less upon the reed of world opinion, had they been more familiar with the general course of world history as it bore upon their growing dilemma, one can only wonder if the outcome might not have been somewhat different. In a manner of speaking, nearly all of the problems affecting America's standing and reputation during this period can be traced to one pervasive quality—that of parochialism—which brings us full circle. Greater sensitivity to foreign attitudes would have implied more of a readiness to arm. It would have counseled less deference to a fickle and often uninformed public opinion. Above all, it would have dictated a broader spirit of understanding, hence of tolerance and compromise. Like all mortals, Roosevelt was a man thrown up by time and place. But it is clear that his options were dictated as much by personal preference as they were by force of circumstance. What is unfortunate about the foundation upon which he based much of his thinking is that it shut so many doors to peace. The ideas upon which he rested his case from 1933 to 1945 proved to be a veritable bed of sand. The rain fell, the floods came, the winds blew and beat against that house, and it fell.

In the last analysis, statesmanship depends upon the ability to reduce events to an intelligible pattern, to devise long-range strategy, and to settle on appropriate tactics. Just as victory at chess hinges on a series of adjustments adhering to an overall game plan, so too in foreign policy. The diplomatic gambit may vary in accord with challenge and response, but it must be drawn and redrawn from a single harmonious point of view, either the president's or that of a trusted adviser. Because Roosevelt played diplomatic chess by seeking fresh counsel with every new move, ambivalence became the dominant feature of his policy. The observer is confronted with a continual balancing of dissimilar points of view, one against the other, and all of them against public opinion. By having at his side a Morgenthau and a Hull, he virtually ensured cross purposes. His delegation to the Brussels Conference consisted of Moffat and Hornbeck, who stood on opposite sides of the spectrum, with Norman Davis in the middle. Each of the three spoke for a distinct current of opinion, while Davis received two different sets of instructions. Likewise, when Hull played croquet, he often flanked himself with Moffat and Hornbeck, with Dunn situated somewhere in between. From this essentially fragmented center of policy making there came the "two stools" approach to difficult decisions. . . .

When all factors are weighed, it is perhaps the parochial aspect of America, as much as anything else, which frustrated its chance for a more fruitful international exchange. There was no compelling reason why Washington had to select envoys incapable of conducting an official conversation in the tongue of the country to which they were accredited, particularly such nations as Mexico, Italy, Czechoslovakia, Russia, Germany, China, and Japan. . . . Roosevelt need not have chosen men to serve as secretary of state and chief of the Division of Western Europe who spoke no language but their own. . . .

We are speaking of a president who upheld the democratic norm and championed the rights of smaller nations yet suggested that the world be governed by Four Policemen and organized according to three regional Monroe Doctrines. Before proposing a system of Four Policemen, he had spoken in terms of three and before that of two (the United States and Britain). Hull may have promised to obliterate spheres of influence, but such thinking did not originate in the mind of FDR. When the British argued the case for world organization at Argentia, and then again a year later, the president demurred, causing Welles to protest that the less powerful nations might at least be given a forum for complaint. It was Churchill, not his American counterpart, who pressed for "a wider and more permanent system of general security." London, not Washington, looked first and most penetratingly at the question of postwar organization. Only after Willkie published *One World* and Churchill's ideas had begun to gain currency in America and England did Roosevelt attempt to propel himself from the rear of the movement to its van. Senator Fulbright told him that unless he moved quickly Republicans would gain a monopoly on plans for world organization. Thus it was that on returning from Teheran, where he had just advocated a four-power condominium, he spoke over the radio of "the rights of every nation, large or small": "The doctrine that the strong shall dominate the weak is the doctrine of our enemies—and we reject it."

He has been called a hero of world order and acclaimed as herald of the destruction of the system of plural state sovereignty. But whatever sacrifices he may have made to obtain Soviet cooperation on behalf of a new league, whatever arrangements he may have made to locate it in New York, he hardly deserves to be placed on a level with the Prophet of Princeton. In the twelve years from 1933 to 1945, the United States did not divest itself of a single imperial possession, notwithstanding its plan for release of the Philippines. It did not abrogate one colonial leasehold. On the contrary, control over foreign peoples grew, alike in terms of population and acreage. The idea of a renascent American imperialism, sometimes referred to as "the American peril" overseas, remained very much alive, as we have had occasion to observe. It was mainly the imperialism of other countries that Roosevelt found despicable, which may help to explain Churchill's remark that "idealism at others' expense and without regard to the consequences of ruin and slaughter which fall upon millions of humble homes cannot be considered as its highest or noblest form." . . .

The man who presided over American fortunes for more than a decade was not without magic. There was an electricity in his voice, an intuitive brilliance about his style, that made him the salesman par excellence of domestic legislation. One cannot but admire the skill with which he launched Destroyers for Bases and coaxed Lend-Lease through a skittish Congress. Few presidents have been as eloquent in the cause of democracy or breathed as much optimism into a people that needed dearly to be encouraged.

Nonetheless, it is possible to mistake form for substance, magnetism for the man. This holds especially true in the realm of foreign policy where FDR accumulated the largest overseas credibility gap of any president on record. Scores of promises made to leaders of other nations were retracted or broken. Most were to Britain, but they included a great many to China and France. The French, revolted as always by the slightest whiff of cant or humbug, could speak in certain quarters of Roosevelt and "the Missouri winds" while German officials could liken the Western democracies to "shifting sand." In point of fact, there is something close to the heart of New Deal diplomacy which has about it the quality of *both* wind *and* sand.

The Astuteness and Appropriateness of Roosevelt's Wartime Diplomacy

ROBERT DALLEK

In the years since 1945, Roosevelt has come under sharp attack for his handling of foreign affairs. To be sure, historians generally agree that he was an architect of victory in World War II, but they find little to compliment beyond that: his response to the London Economic Conference of 1933, his neutrality and peace plans of the thirties, his pre–Pearl Harbor dealings with Japan, and his wartime approach to China, France, and Russia have evoked complaints of superficiality and naïveté; his cautious reactions to the Italian conquest of Ethiopia, the demise of the Spanish Republic, Japanese expansion in China, Nazi victories from 1938 to 1941, the destruction of Europe's Jews, and apparent wartime opportunities for cementing ties with Russia, transforming China, ending colonialism, and establishing a truly effective world body have saddled him with a reputation for excessive timidity about world affairs; his indirection and guarded dealings with the public before Pearl Harbor and his secret wartime agreements have provoked charges of arbitrary leadership destructive to American democracy.

These complaints certainly have some merit. Roosevelt made his share of errors in response to foreign affairs. His acceptance of Britain's lead in dealing with the Spanish Civil War, his sanction of wiretaps and mail openings, his wartime internment of the Japanese, and his cautious response to appeals for help to Jewish victims of Nazi persecution were unnecessary and destructive compromises of legal and moral principles. Beyond these matters, however, I believe that too much has been made of Roosevelt's shortcomings and too little of the constraints under which he had to work in foreign affairs. . . .

Historians generally give Roosevelt high marks for his direction of wartime strategy. As this and other recent studies conclude, Roosevelt was the principal architect of the basic strategic decisions that contributed so heavily to the early defeat of Germany and Japan. Commentators immediately after 1945, however, thought otherwise. Generalizing from the actualities in the last stages of the war, they described Roosevelt's thinking on wartime strategy as almost entirely a reflection of decisions reached by the Joint Chiefs. Undoubtedly for reasons of wartime unity, Roosevelt encouraged this idea, saying that he never overruled his Staff and that they had no basic differences or even minor disagreements. But the record of the years 1938–43 shows otherwise. Until the first Quebec Conference in August 1943, military historian William Emerson has written, "it is no exaggeration to say that . . . the basic decisions that molded strategy were made by the Commander-in-Chief himself, against the advice of his own chiefs and in concert with Churchill and the British chiefs." Indeed, "whenever the military advice of his chiefs clearly diverged from his own notions," Emerson also says, "Roosevelt did not hesitate to ignore or override them." In 1940, for example, when an air force planner presented detailed figures showing aid to Britain was undermining American air rearmament, "the President cut him off with a breezy 'Don't let me see that again!'" Roosevelt was rarely so blunt. With few exceptions, he masked differences with his Chiefs by having the British carry the burden of the argument. As in so many other things, this allowed him to have his way without acrimonious exchanges which could undermine his ability to lead.

In his handling of major foreign policy questions as well, Roosevelt was usually his own decision-maker. Distrustful of the State Department, which he saw as conservative and rigid, he divided responsibility for foreign affairs among a variety of agencies and men. "You should go through the experience of trying to get any changes in the thinking, policy and action of the career diplomats and then you'd know what a real problem was," he once told Marriner Eccles of the Federal Reserve Board. By pitting Welles against Hull, political envoys against career diplomats, Treasury against State, Stimson against Morgenthau, and a host of other official and personal representatives against each other for influence over foreign policy, he became a court of last resort on major issues and kept control in his own hands. In 1943, for example, when George Kennan, then in charge of the American mission in Portugal, objected to Washington's method of gaining military facilities in the Azores as likely to antagonize the Portuguese government and possibly push Spain into the war on Germany's side, the State Department called him back to Washington. After a meeting with Stimson, Knox, Stettinius, and the Joint Chiefs in which he made no headway, Kennan gained access to the President, who endorsed his solution to the problem. But what about the people in the Pentagon, who seemed intent on a different course? Kennan inquired. "Oh, don't worry," said the President with a debonair wave of his cigarette holder, "about all those *people* over there."

Outwardly, Roosevelt's diplomatic appointments also suggest an *ad hoc,* disorganized approach to foreign affairs. Career diplomats, wealthy supporters of his campaign, academics, military men, journalists, and old friends made up the varied list of heads of mission abroad. But, as with major decisions on foreign policy, there was more method and purpose behind Roosevelt's selection of diplomats than meets the eye. William E. Dodd, the Jeffersonian Democrat in Berlin, signaled the President's antipathy for Nazi views and plans. Openly sympathetic to the Soviets, Bullitt and Davies had been sent to Moscow to improve relations between Russia and the United States. Nelson T. Johnson in China and Joseph C. Grew in Japan, both holdovers from the previous administration, reflected Roosevelt's desire for a continuation of the Hoover-Stimson Far Eastern policy. Joseph Kennedy, who went to London in 1938, seemed likely to keep his distance from the British government and provide critical estimates of the appeasement policy. His failure to do so disappointed and annoyed FDR. John G. Winant, a former Republican Governor of New Hampshire who succeeded Kennedy in London in 1941, reflected the President's commitment to Britain's triumph over Berlin. Standley and Harriman, both skeptics in differing degrees about Soviet intentions, had been sent to Moscow partly to provide a contrary perspective to the wartime euphoria about Russia. All these men were instruments of presidential purpose, expressions of Roosevelt's designs in foreign affairs.

No part of Roosevelt's foreign policy has been less clearly understood than his wartime diplomacy. The portrait of him as utterly naïve or unrealistic about the Russians, for example, has been much overdrawn. Recognizing that postwar stability would require a Soviet-American accord, and that Soviet power would then extend into East-Central Europe and parts of East Asia, Roosevelt openly accepted these emerging realities in his dealings with Stalin. The suggestion that Roosevelt could have restrained this Soviet expansion through greater realism or a tougher approach to Stalin is unpersuasive. As an aftermath of World War II, George Kennan has written, no one could deny Stalin "a wide military and political *glacis* on his Western frontier . . . except at the cost of another war, which was unthinkable." Since the West could not defeat Hitler without Stalin's aid, which "placed him automatically in command of half of Europe," and since public questions about postwar Soviet intentions would have shattered wartime unity at home and with the Russians, Roosevelt endorsed the new dimensions of Soviet power, in the hope that it would encourage future friendship with the West. As his conversation with Niels Bohr in 1944 indicated, Roosevelt also left open the question of whether he would share control of atomic power with the Russians.

At the same time, however, he acted to limit the expansion of Russian power in 1945 by refusing to share the secret of the atomic bomb, agreeing to station American troops in southern Germany, endorsing Churchill's arrangements for the Balkans, working for the acquisition of American air and naval bases in the Pacific and the Atlantic, and encouraging the illusion of China as a Great Power with an eye to using her as a political counterweight to the U.S.S.R. Mindful that any emphasis on this kind of *Realpolitik* might weaken American public resolve to play an enduring role in world affairs, Roosevelt made these actions the hidden side of his diplomacy. Yet however much he kept these actions in the background, they were a significant part of his wartime Soviet policy. Hence, in the closing days of his life, when he spoke of becoming "'tougher' [with Russia] than has heretofore appeared advantageous to the war effort," he was not suddenly departing from his conciliatory policy but rather giving emphasis to what had been there all along. Moreover, had he lived, Roosevelt would probably have moved more quickly than Truman to confront the Russians. His greater prestige and reputation as an advocate of Soviet-American friendship would have made it easier for him than for Truman to muster public support for a hard line.

Did Roosevelt's equivocal wartime approach to Russia poison postwar Soviet-American relations? Many forces played a part in bringing on the Cold War, James MacGregor Burns contends, "but perhaps the most determining single factor was the gap between promise and reality that widened steadily during 1942 and 1943." Roosevelt's failure to give full rein to the policy of common goals and sacrifices by delaying a second front in France until 1944, Burns believes, aroused Soviet anger and cynicism and contributed "far more than any other factor" to the "postwar disillusionment and disunity" we call the Cold War. But could Roosevelt have arranged an earlier cross-Channel attack? British opposition and want of military means, particularly landing craft, made a pre-1944 assault difficult to undertake and unlikely to succeed. Such a campaign would not only have cost more American lives, it would also have played havoc with the President's entire war strategy, undermining the nation's ability to break German and Japanese power as quickly and as inexpensively as it did.

More to the point, would an earlier, less successful or unsuccessful European attack have quieted Soviet suspicions of the West? Failure would certainly have brought forth a new round of Soviet complaints, and even a successful cross-Channel attack in 1942 or 1943 would have been no hedge against the Cold War. The Soviets, according to Adam B. Ulam, were not easily dissuaded from "their suspicions about the intentions of the Western Powers. Not the most intensive credits, not even the turning over to the Russians of sample atomic bombs could have appeased them or basically affected their policies. Suspicion was built into the Soviet system."

Roosevelt's thinking about China has also been imperfectly understood. Because he so often countered wartime pressures over China with glib remarks about his family ties to the China trade or exaggerated statements of China's power, Roosevelt has been described as sentimental and shallow or unrealistic about Chinese affairs. In fact, he had a good general grasp of Chinese realities, a clear conception of how he hoped to use China during and after the war, and a healthy appreciation of his limited powers to influence events there. From the beginning of American involvement in the war to the fall of 1944, when the China theater was at the bottom of the priority list, Roosevelt felt compelled to meet Chiang Kai-shek's wishes for an air campaign in China at the expense of a ground buildup and an attack in Burma. Eager to keep China going until they could make a strong effort to reopen the Burma Road and turn China into an effective base against Japan and trying to assure against serious political repercussions in the United States, Roosevelt refused to do anything that might risk a China collapse. During 1944, when it became clear that Chiang's strategy promised little Chinese help against Japan and might even lose China as a base of attack, Roosevelt pressed Chiang to give Stilwell command of all forces in China. By the fall, however, with Chiang unwilling to follow the American lead and promises of Russian help against Japan reducing the importance of effective military action by Chiang, Roosevelt gave up on expecting any significant military contribution from the Chinese.

Instead, he focused on China's postwar role. Believing that China was a valuable asset in persuading American opinion to assume a major part in world affairs and that China could be a useful balance wheel in any political test of will with the Soviets in the United Nations or in possible areas of joint occupation such as Japan and Korea, Roosevelt encouraged Great Power status for China. Since a Nationalist collapse or a civil war in China would jeopardize this plan, Roosevelt also urged the creation of a coalition regime. He appreciated that this was not easy to arrange. It was certainly clear to him that Chiang strongly opposed the idea, but he hoped that the choice between a likely collapse in a civil war against Soviet-backed Communist forces and Soviet-American support for a coalition government led by the Nationalists would persuade Chiang to pick the latter. In this, however, Roosevelt, like almost all other American political and military leaders dealing with China, mistakenly assumed that a coalition was a realizable aim. In fact, neither the United States nor the Soviet Union had the wherewithal to compel this result.

Roosevelt has been strongly criticized for uncritically backing Chiang's corrupt and doomed regime. "What should have been our aim in China," Barbara Tuchman has written, "was not to mediate or settle China's internal problem, which was utterly beyond our scope, but to preserve viable and as far as possible amicable relations with the government of China whatever it turned out to be." But Roosevelt operated under political constraints he could not easily bend or ignore. Pressure in the United States for a continued Nationalist, or at least non-Communist, government in China commanded Roosevelt's respect. As demonstrated by his concern in the fall of 1944 to prepare a defense of the administration's China policy in case of a collapse, he believed that Chiang's demise would have political consequences that could play havoc with his ability to organize the peace. Moreover, as a democratic leader concerned with checking the expansion of Soviet influence and power, he could not have welcomed the prospect of a Chinese Communist regime, however shallow, as the Soviets alleged, its Communist ties may have been. Unlike many others at the time, Roosevelt was not certain that China's Communists were simply "agrarian democrats" or "margarine" Communists. Were the Chinese Communists "real Communists" and were the Russians "bossing them?" Roosevelt asked journalist Edgar Snow in March 1945. In sum, appreciating better than either his Joint Chiefs or Stalin how little staying power Chiang might show in a civil war and determined to avoid the domestic and international problems that would flow from a Nationalist collapse, Roosevelt supported a coalition government under Chiang's control.

On other major postwar questions as well, Roosevelt was more perceptive than commonly believed. His desire for a new world league with peace-keeping powers rested less on a faith in the effectiveness of Wilsonian collective security than on the belief that it was a necessary vehicle for permanently involving the United States in world affairs. Though convinced that postwar affairs would operate under a system of Great Power control, with each of the Powers holding special responsibility in their geographical spheres, Roosevelt felt compelled to obscure this idea through a United Nations organization which would satisfy widespread demand in the United States for new idealistic or universalist arrangements for assuring the peace.

His commitment to a trusteeship system for former colonies and mandates is another good example of how he used an idealistic idea to mask a concern with power. Believing that American internationalists would object to the acquisition of postwar air and naval bases for keeping the peace, Roosevelt disguised this plan by proposing that dependent territories come under the control of three or four countries designated by the United Nations. The "trustees" were to assume civil and military responsibilities for the dependent peoples until they were ready for self-rule. In this way, the United States would both secure strategic bases and assure self-determination for emerging nations around the globe.

This idea strongly influenced Roosevelt's wartime policy toward France. He opposed de Gaulle's plans for taking control in France and resurrecting the French Empire as dangerous to postwar stability in Europe and around the world. De Gaulle's assumption of power seemed likely to provoke civil strife in France, feed revolutionary movements in French African and Asian colonies longing to be free, and inhibit American or Great Power control over areas that were strategic for keeping postwar peace. Roosevelt preferred a malleable French Government ready to accept the reality of reduced French power and ultimate independence for former colonies temporarily under United Nations civil and military control.

Roosevelt's broad conception of what it would take to assure the postwar peace was fundamentally sound: a greatly expanded American role abroad, a Soviet-American accord or "peaceful coexistence," a place for a Great Power China, and an end to colonial empires have all become fixtures on the postwar world scene. But these developments emerged neither in the way nor to the extent Roosevelt had wished. His plans for a United States with substantial, but nevertheless limited, commitments abroad, an accommodation with the U.S.S.R., a stable, cooperative China, a passive France, and a smooth transition for dependent peoples from colonial to independent rule could not withstand the historical and contemporary forces ranged against them. Roosevelt was mindful of the fact that uncontrollable conditions—Soviet suspicion of the West and internal divisions in China, for example—might play havoc with his postwar plans. His decision to hold back the secret of the atomic bomb from Stalin and his preparation to meet a political storm over Chiang's collapse testify to these concerns. But his vision of what the world would need to revive and remain at peace after the war moved him to seek these ends neverthe-less. That he fell short of his aims had less to do with his naïveté or idealism than with the fact that even a thoroughgoing commitment to *Realpolitik* or an exclusive reliance on power would not have significantly altered developments in Europe and Asia after the war. Russian expansion, Chinese strife, and colonial revolutions were beyond Roosevelt's power to prevent.

By contrast with these developments, external events played a central part in helping Roosevelt bring the country through the war in a mood to take a major role in overseas affairs. Much of Roosevelt's public diplomacy during the war was directed toward this goal: the portraits of an effective postwar peace-keeping body, of a friendly Soviet Union, and of a peaceful China had as much to do with creating an internationalist consensus at home as with establishing a fully effective peace system abroad. Principally influenced by Pearl Harbor, which destroyed isolationist contentions about American invulnerability to attack, and by the country's emergence as the world's foremost Power, the nation ended the war ready to shoulder substantial responsibilities in foreign affairs.

One may assume that postwar developments would not have surprised or greatly disappointed FDR. As he once told someone impatient for presidential action, Abraham Lincoln "was a sad man because he couldn't get it all at once. And nobody can. . . . You cannot, just by shouting from the housetops, get what you want all the time." No doubt American willingness to play a large part in postwar international affairs would have impressed him as a major advance, while postwar world tensions would surely have stimulated him to new efforts for world peace. And no doubt, as so often during his presidency, a mixture of realism and idealism, of practical short-term goals tied to visions of long-term gains would have become the hallmark of his renewed struggle to make the world a better place in which to live.

FURTHER READING

Bennett, Edward M. *Franklin D. Roosevelt and the Search for Victory* (1990).
Buhite, Russell. *Decisions at Yalta* (1986).
Campbell, Thomas M. *Masquerade Peace: America's UN Policy, 1944–1945* (1973).
Clemens, Diane Shaver. *Yalta* (1970).
Dallek, Robert. *Franklin D. Roosevelt and American Foreign Policy, 1932–1945* (1979).
Edmonds, Robin. *The Big Three* (1991).
Eubank, Keith. *Summit at Teheran* (1985).
Feis, Herbert. *Churchill, Roosevelt, Stalin* (1957).
Gardner, Lloyd C. *Spheres of Influence* (1993).
Gilbert, Martin. *Winston S. Churchill,* vol. 7, *Road to Victory* (1986).
Hilderbrand, Robert C. *Dumbarton Oaks* (1990).
Hoopes, Townsend, and Douglas Brinkley. *FDR and the Creation of the UN* (1997).
Kimball, Warren F. *Churchill & Roosevelt: The Complete Correspondence,* 3 vols. (1984).
———. *Forged in War: Roosevelt, Churchill and the Second World War* (1997).
———. *The Juggler: Franklin Roosevelt as Wartime Statesman* (1991).
Kolko, Gabriel. *The Politics of War* (1968).
Louis, William Roger. *Imperialism at Bay: The United States and the Decolonization of the British Empire, 1941–1945* (1978).
Marks, Frederick W., III. *Wind Over Sand: The Diplomacy of Franklin Roosevelt* (1988).
Mastny, Vojtech. *Russia's Road to the Cold War* (1979).
Miner, Steven M. *Between Churchill and Stalin* (1988).
Neumann, William L. *After Victory* (1967).
Nisbet, Robert. *Roosevelt and Stalin* (1988).
O'Connor, Raymond G. *Diplomacy for Victory: FDR and Unconditional Surrender* (1967).
Reynolds, David, et al. *Allies at War* (1994).
Sainsbury, Keith. *Churchill and Roosevelt at War* (1994).
———. *The Turning Point: Roosevelt, Stalin, Churchill, and Chiang Kai-shek, 1943— The Moscow, Cairo, and Teheran Conferences* (1985).
Sbrega, John. *Anglo-American Relations and Colonialism in East Asia* (1983).
Schild, Georg. *Bretton Woods and Dumbarton Oaks* (1995).
Smith, Gaddis. *American Diplomacy During the Second World War* (1985).
Snell, John. *Illusion and Necessity: The Diplomacy of Global War* (1963).
Stoler, Mark A. "A Half Century of Conflict: Interpretations of U.S. World War II Diplomacy," *Diplomatic History* 18 (1994): 375–403.
Thorne, Christopher. *Allies of a Kind: The United States, Britain, and the War Against Japan, 1941–1945* (1978).
———. *The Issue of War* (1985).
Van Minnen, Cornelius, and John F. Sears, eds. *FDR and His Contemporaries* (1992).
Woods, Randall. *A Changing of the Guard: Anglo-American Relations, 1941–1946* (1990).

See also Chapters 1 and 3.

CHAPTER
11

The Atomic Bomb and
the End of World War II

With German surrender on May 7–8, 1945, the United States began to focus all its military attention on the Pacific War. By this time Japan was under naval blockade and air bombardment, and its military position was hopeless. Nevertheless its forces continued to fight furiously, using suicide tactics and inflicting massive casualties on U.S. forces during the early 1945 battles for the islands of Iwo Jima and Okinawa (see Chapter 5).

During July and August of 1945, the military and diplomatic situation in the Far East changed dramatically. Throughout World War II, scientists had been working on a top-secret project, code-named Manhattan in the United States and Tube Alloys in Britain, to create a nuclear weapon (see Chapter 8). On July 16, the United States successfully tested the world's first such weapon at Alamagordo, New Mexico. Three weeks later, on August 6, it destroyed the entire city of Hiroshima with a single atomic bomb. Two days later, on August 8, the Soviet Union declared war on Japan and attacked the Japanese Army in Manchuria. Then on August 9 the United States used another atomic bomb to destroy the city of Nagasaki. On August 14 Japan agreed to surrender on condition that it be allowed to retain its emperor. Formal surrender took place in Tokyo Bay on September 2, 1945, officially ending the bloodiest war in history.

The atomic bomb clearly played a major role in ending World War II. But it resulted in the deaths of nearly 200,000 Japanese civilians at Hiroshima and Nagasaki, and it also played a major role in starting the Soviet-American Cold War that followed World War II. Consequently, the policies surrounding the development and use of this awesome new weapon aroused intense postwar controversies. Critics argue that its use against civilians was barbaric as well as unnecessary to obtain Japanese surrender, and that keeping it a secret during the war poisoned postwar Soviet-American relations and led to both the Cold War and the nuclear arms race. Others counter that civilians had been legitimate targets throughout World War II, that dropping the bomb was necessary to obtain Japanese surrender without a much bloodier invasion of the home islands, that its use therefore saved thousands if not hundreds of thousands of lives, and that different policies could not have avoided the Cold War or the nuclear arms race.

The documents and essays that follow are designed to introduce you to different aspects of, and viewpoints regarding, this highly controversial issue. In reading them, you should ask yourself numerous questions. Why did the United States decide to ini- tiate an atomic bomb project in 1939? Why did it agree to work with Great Britain on this project, but to keep it a secret from the Soviet Union? Why did the United States decide to drop atomic bombs on Hiroshima and Nagasaki? What other policies were available, and why were they rejected? What role did this decision and the pre- ceding secretiveness play in the origins of the Cold War and the nuclear arms race?

DOCUMENTS

In 1939 President Roosevelt initiated the U.S. atomic bomb project as a result of a letter sent to him by Albert Einstein, which is reproduced as Document 1. By 1942–1943 Roosevelt and Churchill had decided to pool their research and resources in this project, and to exclude the Soviet Union. Noted Danish physicist Niels Bohr challenged this policy, as recounted in a letter from Supreme Court Justice Felix Frankfurter to Roosevelt in Document 2. But, as shown in the memorandum repro- duced in Document 3, Churchill and Roosevelt forcefully rejected Bohr's proposal to share atomic secrets with the Soviet Union.

By the time of Roosevelt's death in April 1945, the Manhattan Project was on the verge of producing a usable weapon. So secret had the project been, however, that Harry Truman, former senator and vice president and now the new president, did not even know of its existence. In Document 4, Truman recalls how he learned about the project.

To examine the numerous wartime and postwar issues that now needed to be addressed, Truman appointed a special Interim Committee. By this time, other scien- tists were echoing and amplifying the concerns and recommendations Bohr had voiced in 1944. These were summarized in the so-called Franck Petition to Secretary of War Henry L. Stimson, which is excerpted in Document 5. A scientific panel appointed by the Interim Committee disagreed with most of the Franck Petition recommendations. The panel's recommendations on the use of the weapon against Japan are reproduced in Document 6. It should be noted that everyone involved in the decision agreed that the new weapon should be used; the question was *how*—via a demonstration or by actual use against a Japanese target and, if the latter, what kind of target and with or without warning.

Document 7 presents the objections of Ralph Bard, undersecretary of the navy and a member of the Interim Committee, who opposed unannounced use of the bomb and resigned over the issue. Secretary of War Henry L. Stimson, who had played a major role in the creation of U.S. policies regarding the bomb, had second thoughts about continued secrecy after the Japanese surrender. Document 8 consists of excerpts from the report Truman received at the Potsdam Conference of the July 16 Alamagordo test, after which he "casually mentioned" to Stalin on July 24 "that we had a new weapon of unusually destructive force." Truman noted in his memoirs that Stalin "showed no special interest. All he said was that he was glad to hear it and hoped we would make 'good use of it against the Japanese.'" Actually, Stalin knew exactly what Truman was talking about and immediately ordered acceleration of the Soviet atomic bomb project. The postwar Soviet-American nuclear arms race thus began even before the bombing of Hiroshima and the end of World War II.

Document 9 is a photograph of Hiroshima soon after the B-29 bomber *Enola Gay* dropped the atomic bomb on it. Most Americans strongly supported the bombing, as is illustrated by the public opinion polls in Document 10. That support was far from unanimous, however. In Document 11, taken from his last memorandum to Truman prior to his retirement, Stimson calls for a change in that policy.

1. Albert Einstein Informs President Roosevelt of the Potential for an Atomic Bomb, 1939

August 2nd, 1939

F.D. Roosevelt,
President of the United States,
White House
Washington, D.C.

Sir:

Some recent work by E. Fermi and L. Szilard, which has been communicated to me in manuscript, leads me to expect that the element uranium may be turned into a new and important source of energy in the immediate future. Certain aspects of the situation which has arisen seem to call for watchfulness and, if necessary, quick action on the part of the Administration. I believe therefore that it is my duty to bring to your attention the following facts and recommendations:

In the course of the last four months it has been made probable—through the work of Joliot in France as well as Fermi and Szilard in America—that it may become possible to set up a nuclear chain reaction in a large mass of uranium, by which vast amounts of power and large quantities of new radium-like elements would be generated. Now it appears almost certain that this could be achieved in the immediate future.

This new phenomenon would also lead to the construction of bombs, and it is conceivable—though much less certain—that extremely powerful bombs of a new type may thus be constructed. A single bomb of this type, carried by boat and exploded in a port, might very well destroy the whole port together with some of the surrounding territory. However, such bombs might very well prove to be too heavy for transportation by air.

The United States has only very poor ores of uranium in moderate quantities. There is some good ore in Canada and the former Czechoslovakia, while the most important source of uranium is Belgian Congo.

In view of this situation you may think it desirable to have some permanent contact maintained between the Administration and the group of physicists working on chain reactions in America. One possible way of achieving this might be for you to entrust with this task a person who has your confidence and who could perhaps serve in an inofficial capacity. His task might comprise the following:

a) to approach Government Departments, keep them informed of the further development, and put forward recommendations for Government action, giving

From Franklin D. Roosevelt Papers, President's Secretary's File, Roosevelt Library, Hyde Park, N.Y.; reproduced in Michael B. Stoff, Jonathan F. Fanton, and R. Hal Williams, *The Manhattan Project: A Documentary Introduction to the Atomic Age* (New York: McGraw Hill, 1991), 18–19.

particular attention to the problem of securing a supply of uranium ore for the United States;

b) to speed up the experimental work, which is at present being carried on within the limits of the budgets of University laboratories, by providing funds, if such funds be required, through his contacts with private persons who are willing to make contributions for this cause, and perhaps also by obtaining the co-operation of industrial laboratories which have the necessary equipment.

I understand that Germany has actually stopped the sale of uranium from the Czechoslovakian mines which she has taken over. That she should have taken such early action might perhaps be understood on the ground that the son of the German Under-Secretary of State, von Weizäcker, is attached to the Kaiser-Wilhelm-Institut in Berlin where some of the American work on uranium is now being repeated.

Yours very truly,
(Albert Einstein)

2. Supreme Court Justice Felix Frankfurter Shares with FDR Physicist Niels Bohr's Suggestion that the Soviets Be Informed of the Atomic Bomb Project, 1944

September 8, 1944

Dear Frank: ✳ Makes a strong point

Here is a letter from my Danish friend [Niels Bohr—letter not reproduced here].

From many long talks with him I gather that there are three solid reasons for believing that knowledge of the pursuit of our project can hardly be kept from Russia: (1) they have very eminent scientists, particularly Peter Kapitza, entirely familiar through past experience with these problems; (2) some leakage, even if not of results and methods, must inevitably have trickled to Russia; (3) Germans have been similarly busy, and knowledge of their endeavors will soon be open to the Russians. Therefore, to open the subject with Russia, without of course making essential disclosures before effective safeguards and sanctions have been secured and assured, would not be giving them anything they do not already—or soon will—substantially have.

In a word, the argument is that appropriate candor would risk very little. Withholding, on the other hand, might have grave consequences. There may be answers to these considerations. I venture to believe, having thought a good deal about it, that in any event these questions are very serious.

My very best wishes for successful days in the tasks immediately ahead.

Affectionately yours,

[Felix Frankfurter,
Supreme Court Justice]

From Franklin D. Roosevelt Papers, President's Secretary's File, Roosevelt Library, Hyde Park, N.Y.; reproduced in Michael B. Stoff, Jonathan F. Fanton, and R. Hal Williams, *The Manhattan Project: A Documentary Introduction to the Atomic Age* (New York: McGraw-Hill, 1991), 64–65.

3. Churchill and Roosevelt Reject Informing the Soviets, 1944

Aide-Mémoire of Conversation Between the President and the Prime Minister at Hyde Park, September 18, 1944

1. The suggestion that the world should be informed regarding TUBE ALLOYS, with a view to an international agreement regarding its control and use, is not accepted. The matter should continue to be regarded as of the utmost secrecy; but when a "bomb" is finally available, it might perhaps, after mature consideration, be used against the Japanese, who should be warned that this bombardment will be repeated until they surrender.

2. Full collaboration between the United States and the British Government in developing TUBE ALLOYS for military and commercial purposes should continue after the defeat of Japan unless and until terminated by joint agreement.

3. Enquiries should be made regarding the activities of Professor Bohr and steps taken to ensure that he is responsible for no leakage of information, particularly to the Russians.

F[ranklin] D R[oosevelt]   W[inston] S C[hurchill]

4. President Harry S Truman Recalls How He Learned About the Atomic Bomb Project, 1945

The ceremony at which I had taken the oath of office [on April 12, 1945] had lasted hardly more than a minute, but a delay followed while the inevitable official photographs were taken. Then, after most of those present had gripped my hand—often without a word, so great were their pent-up emotions—and after Mrs. Truman and Margaret had left, everyone else withdrew except the members of the Cabinet. . . .

That first meeting of the Cabinet was short, and when it adjourned, the members rose and silently made their way from the room—except for Secretary [of War Henry] Stimson.

He asked to speak to me about a most urgent matter. Stimson told me that he wanted me to know about an immense project that was under way—a project looking to the development of a new explosive of almost unbelievable destructive power. That was all he felt free to say at the time, and his statement left me puzzled. It was the first bit of information that had come to me about the atomic bomb, but he gave me no details. It was not until the next day that I was told enough to give me some understanding of the almost incredible developments that were under way and the awful power that might soon be placed in our hands.

That so vast an enterprise had been successfully kept secret even from the members of Congress was a miracle. I had known, and probably others had, that

(Document 3) From U.S. Department of State, *Foreign Relations of the United States: The Conference at Quebec, 1944* (Washington, D.C.: U.S. Government Printing Office, 1972), 492–493.

(Document 4) From Harry S Truman, *Memoirs,* vol. 1, *Year of Decisions* (Garden City, N.Y.: Doubleday & Co., 1955), 9–11.

something that was unusually important was brewing in our war plants. Many months before, as part of the work of the Committee to Investigate the National Defense Program, of which I was chairman, I had had investigators going into war plants all over the country. I had even sent investigators into Tennessee and the state of Washington with instructions to find out what certain enormous constructions were and what their purpose was.

At that time, when these investigators were sent out, Secretary Stimson had phoned me to say that he wanted to have a private talk with me. I told him that I would come to his office at once, but he said he would rather come to see me.

As soon as he arrived, I learned that the subject he had in mind was connected with the immense installations I had sent the committee representatives to investigate in Tennessee and the state of Washington.

"Senator," the Secretary told me as he sat beside my desk, "I can't tell you what it is, but it is the greatest project in the history of the world. It is most top secret. Many of the people who are actually engaged in the work have no idea what it is, and we who do would appreciate your not going into those plants."

I had long known Henry L. Stimson to be a great American patriot and statesman.

"I'll take you at your word," I told him. "I'll order the investigations into those plants called off."

I did so at once, and I was not to learn anything whatever as to what that secret was until the Secretary spoke to me after that first Cabinet meeting. The next day Jimmy Byrnes, who until shortly before had been Director of War Mobilization for President Roosevelt, came to see me, and even he told me few details, though with great solemnity he said that we were perfecting an explosive great enough to destroy the whole world. It was later, when Vannevar Bush, head of the Office of Scientific Research and Development, came to the White House, that I was given a scientist's version of the atomic bomb.

5. The Franck Committee Warns of a Nuclear Arms Race and Calls for a Noncombat Demonstration of the Bomb, 1945

If no efficient international agreement is achieved, the race for nuclear armaments will be on in earnest not later than the morning after our first demonstration of the existence of nuclear weapons. After this, it might take other nations three or four years to overcome our present head start, and eight or ten years to draw even with us if we continue to do intensive work in this field. . . .

The consequences of nuclear warfare, and the type of measures which would have to be taken to protect a country from total destruction by nuclear bombing, must be as abhorrent to other nations as to the United States. England, France, and the smaller nations of the European continent, with their congeries of people and

J. Franck, D. J. Hughes, J. J. Nickson, E. Rabinowitch, G. T. Seaborg, J. C. Stearns, and L. Szilard, "Political and Social Problems," June 11, 1945, Manhattan Engineer District Records, National Archives, Washington, D.C., reprinted in *Bulletin of the Atomic Scientists* 1 (May 1946), and in Michael B. Stoff, Jonathan F. Fanton, and R. Hal Williams, *The Manhattan Project* (New York: McGraw Hill, 1991), 140–147.

industries, would be in a particularly desperate situation in the face of such a threat. Russia and China are the only great nations at present which could survive a nuclear attack. However, even though these countries may value human life less than the peoples of Western Europe and America, and even though Russia, in particular, has an immense space over which its vital industries could be dispersed and a government which can order this dispersion the day it is convinced that such a measure is necessary—there is no doubt that Russia will shudder at the possibility of a sudden disintegration of Moscow and Leningrad and of its new industrial cities in the Urals and Siberia. Therefore, only lack of mutual *trust,* and not lack of *desire* for agreement, can stand in the path of an efficient agreement for the prevention of nuclear warfare. The achievement of such an agreement will thus essentially depend on the integrity of intentions and readiness to sacrifice the necessary fraction of one's own sovereignty, by all the parties to the agreement.

From this point of view, the way in which the nuclear weapons now being secretly developed in this country are first revealed to the world appears to be of great, perhaps fateful importance.

One possible way—which may particularly appeal to those who consider nuclear bombs primarily as a secret weapon developed to help win the present war—is to use them without warning on an appropriately selected object in Japan. It is doubtful whether the first available bombs, of comparatively low efficiency and small size, will be sufficient to break the will or ability of Japan to resist, especially given the fact that the major cities like Tokyo, Nagoya, Osaka and Kobe already will largely have been reduced to ashes by the slower process of ordinary aerial bombing. Although important tactical results undoubtedly can be achieved by a sudden introduction of nuclear weapons, we nevertheless think that the question of the use of the very first available atomic bombs in the Japanese war should be weighed very carefully, not only by military authorities, but by the highest political leadership of this country. If we consider international agreement on total prevention of nuclear warfare as the paramount objective, and believe that it can be achieved, this kind of introduction of atomic weapons to the world may easily destroy all our chances of success. Russia, and even allied countries which bear less mistrust of our ways and intentions, as well as neutral countries may be deeply shocked. It may be very difficult to persuade the world that a nation which was capable of secretly preparing and suddenly releasing a weapon as indiscriminate as the rocket bomb and a million times more destructive, is to be trusted in its proclaimed desire of having such weapons abolished by international agreement. We have large accumulations of poison gas, but do not use them, and recent polls have shown that public opinion in this country would disapprove of such a use even if it would accelerate the winning of the Far Eastern war. It is true that some irrational element in mass psychology makes gas poisoning more revolting than blasting by explosives, even though gas warfare is in no way more "inhuman" than the war of bombs and bullets. Nevertheless, it is not at all certain that American public opinion, if it could be enlightened as to the effect of atomic explosives, would approve of our own country being the first to introduce such an indiscriminate method of wholesale destruction of civilian life.

Thus, from the "optimistic" point of view—looking forward to an international agreement on the prevention of nuclear warfare—the military advantages and the saving of American lives achieved by the sudden use of atomic bombs against Japan may be outweighed by the ensuing loss of confidence and by a wave of horror and repulsion sweeping over the rest of the world and perhaps even dividing public opinion at home.

From this point of view, a demonstration of the new weapon might best be made, before the eyes of representatives of all the United Nations, on the desert or a barren island. The best possible atmosphere for the achievement of an international agreement could be achieved if America could say to the world, "You see what sort of a weapon we had but did not use. We are ready to renounce its use in the future if other nations join us in this renunciation and agree to the establishment of an efficient international control."

After such a demonstration the weapon might perhaps be used against Japan if the sanction of the United Nations (and of public opinion at home) were obtained, perhaps after a preliminary ultimatum to Japan to surrender or at least to evacuate certain regions as an alternative to their total destruction. This may sound fantastic, but in nuclear weapons we have something entirely new in order of magnitude of destructive power, and if we want to capitalize fully on the advantage their possession gives us, we must use new and imaginative methods.

It must be stressed that if one takes the pessimistic point of view and discounts the possibility of an effective international control over nuclear weapons at the present time, then the advisability of an early use of nuclear bombs against Japan becomes even more doubtful—quite independently of any humanitarian considerations. If an international agreement is not concluded immediately after the first demonstration, this will mean a flying start toward an unlimited armaments race. . . .

One may point out that scientists themselves have initiated the development of this "secret weapon" and it is therefore strange that they should be reluctant to try it out on the enemy as soon as it is available. The answer to this question was given above—the compelling reason for creating this weapon with such speed was our fear that Germany had the technical skill necessary to develop such a weapon, and that the German government had no moral restraints regarding its use. . . .

The development of nuclear power not only constitutes an important addition to the technological and military power of the United States, but also creates grave political and economic problems for the future of this country.

Nuclear bombs cannot possibly remain a "secret weapon" at the exclusive disposal of this country for more than a few years. The scientific facts on which their construction is based are well known to scientists of other countries. Unless an effective international control of nuclear explosives is instituted, a race for nuclear armaments is certain to ensue following the first revelation of our possession of nuclear weapons to the world. Within ten years other countries may have nuclear bombs, each of which, weighing less than a ton, could destroy an urban area of more than ten square miles. In the war to which such an armaments race is likely to lead, the United States, with its agglomeration of population and industry in comparatively few metropolitan districts, will be at a disadvantage compared to nations whose population and industry are scattered over large areas.

We believe that these considerations make the use of nuclear bombs for an early unannounced attack against Japan inadvisable. If the United States were to be the first to release this new means of indiscriminate destruction upon mankind, she would sacrifice public support throughout the world, precipitate the race for armaments, and prejudice the possibility of reaching an international agreement on the future control of such weapons.

Much more favorable conditions for the eventual achievement of such an agreement could be created if nuclear bombs were first revealed to the world by a demonstration in an appropriately selected uninhabited area. . . .

To sum up, we urge that the use of nuclear bombs in this war be considered as a problem of long-range national policy rather than of military expediency, and that this policy be directed primarily to the achievement of an agreement permitting an effective international control of the means of nuclear warfare.

The vital importance of such a control for our country is obvious from the fact that the only effective alternative method of protecting this country appears to be a dispersal of our major cities and essential industries.

> J. FRANCK, CHAIRMAN
> D. J. HUGHES
> J. J. NICKSON
> E. RABINOWITCH
> G. T. SEABORG
> J. C. STEARNS
> L. SZILARD

6. The Scientific Panel of the Interim Committee Recommends Combat Use of the Bomb Against Japan, 1945

You have asked us to comment on the initial use of the new weapon. This use, in our opinion, should be such as to promote a satisfactory adjustment of our international relations. At the same time, we recognize our obligation to our nation to use the weapons to help save American lives in the Japanese war.

(1) To accomplish these ends we recommend that before the weapons are used not only Britain, but also Russia, France, and China be advised that we have made considerable progress in our work on atomic weapons, that these may be ready to use during the present war, and that we would welcome suggestions as to how we can cooperate in making this development contribute to improved international relations.

(2) The opinions of our scientific colleagues on the initial use of these weapons are not unanimous: they range from the proposal of a purely technical demonstration to that of the military application best designed to induce surrender. Those who advocate a purely technical demonstration would wish to outlaw the use of atomic weapons, and have feared that if we use the weapons now our position in future

---

From A. H. Compton, E. O. Lawrence, J. R. Oppenheimer, and E. Fermi, "Recommendations on the Immediate Use of Nuclear Weapons," June 16, 1945, Manhattan Engineer District Records, National Archives, Washington, D.C.; reproduced in Michael B. Stoff, Jonathan F. Fanton, and R. Hal Williams, *The Manhattan Project* (New York: McGraw Hill, 1991), 149–150.

negotiations will be prejudiced. Others emphasize the opportunity of saving American lives by immediate military use, and believe that such use will improve the international prospects, in that they are more concerned with the prevention of war than with the elimination of this specific weapon. We find ourselves closer to these latter views; we can propose no technical demonstration likely to bring an end to the war; we see no acceptable alternative to direct military use.

(3) With regard to these general aspects of the use of atomic energy, it is clear that we, as scientific men, have no proprietary rights. It is true that we are among the few citizens who have had occasion to give thoughtful consideration to these problems during the past few years. We have, however, no claim to special competence in solving the political, social, and military problems which are presented by the advent of atomic power.

7. Undersecretary of the Navy Ralph Bard Objects to the Unannounced Use of the Bomb, 1945

MEMORANDUM ON THE USE OF S-1 BOMB

Ever since I have been in touch with this program I have had a feeling that before the bomb is actually used against Japan that Japan should have some preliminary warning for say two or three days in advance of use. The position of the United States as a great humanitarian nation and the fair play attitude of our people generally is responsible in the main for this feeling.

During recent weeks I have also had the feeling very definitely that the Japanese government may be searching for some opportunity which they could use as a medium of surrender. Following the three-power conference emissaries from this country could contact representatives from Japan somewhere on the China Coast and make representations with regard to Russia's position and at the same time give them some information regarding the proposed use of atomic power, together with whatever assurances the President might care to make with regard to the Emperor of Japan and the treatment of the Japanese nation following unconditional surrender. It seems quite possible to me that this presents the opportunity which the Japanese are looking for.

I don't see that we have anything in particular to lose in following such a program. The stakes are so tremendous that it is my opinion very real consideration should be given to some plan of this kind. I do not believe under present circumstances existing that there is anyone in this country whose evaluation of the chances of the success of such a program is worth a great deal. The only way to find out is to try it out.

RALPH A. BARD

27 June 1945

From the Manhattan Engineer District Records, National Archives, Washington, D.C.; reproduced in Michael B. Stoff, Jonathan F. Fanton, and R. Hal Williams, *The Manhattan Project* (New York: McGraw Hill, 1991), 162, and in Martin Sherwin, *A World Destroyed* (New York: Knopf, 1975), 307–308.

8. Manhattan Project Commanding General Leslie Groves Reports the Results of the Alamagordo Test, 1945

WASHINGTON, 18 JULY 1945.

MEMORANDUM FOR THE SECRETARY OF WAR

SUBJECT: THE TEST.

1. This is not a concise, formal military report but an attempt to recite what I would have told you if you had been here on my return from New Mexico.

2. At 0530, 16 July 1945, in a remote section of the Alamogordo Air Base, New Mexico, the first full scale test was made of the implosion type atomic fission bomb. For the first time in history there was a nuclear explosion. And what an explosion! . . . The bomb was not dropped from an airplane but was exploded on a platform on top of a 100-foot high steel tower.

3. The test was successful beyond the most optimistic expectations of anyone. Based on the data which it has been possible to work up to date, I estimate the energy generated to be in excess of the equivalent of 15,000 to 20,000 tons of TNT; and this is a conservative estimate. Data based on measurements which we have not yet been able to reconcile would make the energy release several times the conservative figure. There were tremendous blast effects. For a brief period there was a lighting effect within a radius of 20 miles equal to several suns in midday; a huge ball of fire was formed which lasted for several seconds. This ball mushroomed and rose to a height of over ten thousand feet before it dimmed. The light from the explosion was seen clearly at Albuquerque, Santa Fe, Silver City, El Paso and other points generally to about 180 miles away. The sound was heard to the same distance in a few instances but generally to about 100 miles. Only a few windows were broken although one was some 125 miles away. A massive cloud was formed which surged and billowed upward with tremendous power, reaching the substratosphere at an elevation of 41,000 feet, 36,000 feet above the ground, in about five minutes, breaking without interruption through a temperature inversion at 17,000 feet which most of the scientists thought would stop it. Two supplementary explosions occurred in the cloud shortly after the main explosion. The cloud contained several thousand tons of dust picked up from the ground and a considerable amount of iron in the gaseous form. Our present thought is that this iron ignited when it mixed with the oxygen in the air to cause these supplementary explosions. Huge concentrations of highly radioactive materials resulted from the fission and were contained in this cloud.

4. A crater from which all vegetation had vanished, with a diameter of 1200 feet and a slight slope toward the center, was formed. In the center was a shallow bowl 130 feet in diameter and 6 feet in depth. The material within the crater was deeply pulverized dirt. The material within the outer circle is greenish and can be distinctly seen from as much as 5 miles away. The steel from the tower was evaporated. 1500 feet away there was a four-inch iron pipe 16 feet high set in concrete and strongly guyed. It disappeared completely.

From the Manhattan Engineer District Records, National Archives, Washington, D.C.; reproduced in Michael B. Stoff, Jonathan F. Fanton, and R. Hal Williams, *The Manhattan Project* (New York: McGraw Hill, 1991), 188–191, and in Martin Sherwin, *A World Destroyed* (New York: Knopf, 1975), 308–314.

9. A Photographer Captures Hiroshima Two Months After the Atomic Bomb of August 6, 1945

This photograph was taken from the rooftop of the Hiroshima Chamber of Commerce building and shows the physical effects of an atomic weapon.

10. Public Opinion Polls Show Strong Support for the Atomic Bomb, August, September, and December 1945

(US Aug 8 '45) Do you approve or disapprove of using the new atomic bomb on Japanese cities? Asked of a cross-section of people who had heard of the bomb. 96% of a national sample is represented.

	Approve	*Disapprove*	*No opinion*
United States	85%	10%	5%

(Document 9) From Hiroshima Panorama Project; http://titan.iwu.edu/~rwilson/hiroshima/rama3.htm.

(Document 10) From Hadley Cantril, *Public Opinion, 1935–1946* (Princeton, N.J.: Princeton University Press, 1951), 20, 21, 23.

(US Sept '45) Do you think the United States should try to keep the secret of how to make atomic bombs as long as we can, or do you think we should let some other countries also know how to make them?

	Share	Keep	Miscellaneous or Don't know
United States	12%	85%	3%

(US Dec '45) Which of these comes closest to describing how you feel about our use of the atomic bomb?

We should not have used any atomic bombs at all 4.5%
We should have dropped one first on some unpopulated region, to show
   the Japanese its power, and dropped the second one on a city only
   if they hadn't surrendered after the first one 13.8
We should have used the two bombs on cities, just as we did 53.5
We should have quickly used many more of them before Japan had a
   chance to surrender 22.7
Don't know. 5.5

11. Secretary of War Henry L. Stimson Has Second Thoughts on Atomic Secrecy, 1945

11 September 1945

MEMORANDUM FOR THE PRESIDENT:

In many quarters it [America's development of the atomic bomb] has been interpreted as a substantial offset to the growth of Russian influence on the continent. We can be certain that the Soviet government has sensed this tendency and the temptation will be strong for the Soviet political and military leaders to acquire this weapon in the shortest possible time. Britain in effect already has the status of a partner with us in the development of this weapon. Accordingly, unless the Soviets are voluntarily invited into the partnership upon a basis of cooperation and trust, we are going to maintain the Anglo-Saxon bloc over against the Soviet in the possession of this weapon. Such a condition will almost certainly stimulate feverish activity on the part of the Soviet toward the development of this bomb in what will in effect be a secret armament race of a rather desperate character. There is evidence to indicate that such activity may have already commenced. . . .

    Whether Russia gets control of the necessary secrets of production in a minimum of say four years or a maximum of twenty years is not nearly as important to the world and civilization as to make sure that when they do get it they are willing and cooperative partners among the peace loving nations of the world. It is true that if we approach them now, as I would propose, we may be gambling on their

From Henry L. Stimson Papers, Yale University Library, New Haven, Conn.; reproduced in Henry L. Stimson and McGeorge Bundy, *On Active Service in Peace and War* (New York: Harper & Brothers, 1947), 642–646.

good faith and risk their getting into production of bombs a little sooner than they would otherwise.

To put the matter concisely, I consider the problem of our satisfactory relations with Russia as not merely connected with but as virtually dominated by the problem of the atomic bomb. Except for the problem of the control of that bomb, those relations, while vitally important, might not be immediately pressing. The establishment of relations of mutual confidence between her and us could afford to await the slow progress of time. But with the discovery of the bomb, they became immediately emergent. Those relations may be perhaps irretrievably embittered by the way in which we approach the solution of the bomb with Russia. For if we fail to approach them now and merely continue to negotiate with them, having this weapon rather ostentatiously on our hip, their suspicions and their distrust of our purposes and motives will increase. . . .

The chief lesson I have learned in a long life is that the only way you can make a man trustworthy is to trust him; and the surest way to make him untrustworthy is to distrust him and show your distrust.

If the atomic bomb were merely another though more devastating military weapon to be assimilated into our pattern of international relations, it would be one thing. We could then follow the old custom of secrecy and nationalistic military superiority relying on international caution to prescribe the future use of the weapon as we did with gas. But I think the bomb instead constitutes merely a first step in a new control by man over the forces of nature too revolutionary and dangerous to fit into the old concepts. I think it really caps the climax of the race between man's growing technical power for destructiveness and his psychological power of self-control and group control—his moral power. If so, our method of approach to the Russians is a question of the most vital importance in the evolution of human progress. . . .

My idea of an approach to the Soviets would be a direct proposal after discussion with the British that we would be prepared in effect to enter an arrangement with the Russians, the general purpose of which would be to control and limit the use of the atomic bomb as an instrument of war and so far as possible to direct and encourage the development of atomic power for peaceful and humanitarian purposes. Such an approach might more specifically lead to the proposal that we would stop work on the further improvement in, or manufacture of, the bomb as a military weapon, provided the Russians and the British would agree to do likewise. It might also provide that we would be willing to impound what bombs we now have in the United States provided the Russians and the British would agree with us that in no event will they or we use a bomb as an instrument of war unless all three Governments agree to that use. We might also consider including in the arrangement a covenant with the U.K. and the Soviets providing for the exchange of benefits of future developments whereby atomic energy may be applied on a mutually satisfactory basis for commercial or humanitarian purposes. . . .

I emphasize perhaps beyond all other considerations the importance of taking this action with Russia as a proposal of the United States—backed by Great Britain—but peculiarly the proposal of the United States. Action of any international group of nations, including many small nations who have not demonstrated their potential power or responsibility in this war would not, in my opinion, be taken seriously by the Soviets.

Scholars disagree very sharply over the questions of why the United States dropped atomic bombs on Japan and whether this action was justified. For nearly four decades Gar Alperovitz has been one of the leading revisionist critics, arguing that the bombs were dropped primarily to intimidate the Soviet Union, that their use was not necessary to avoid a costly invasion of the home islands and obtain Japanese surrender, and that claims to the contrary by Truman and his associates constitute a deception and enduring myth. The first essay is taken from Alperovitz's most recent and comprehensive work on the subject.

Numerous historians have challenged such conclusions. They strongly defend Truman's decision as motivated by a desire to end the war as quickly as possible and with minimum U.S. casualties, and they conclude that the atomic bombs were both necessary and effective in this regard. In the second essay, Robert P. Newman of the University of Pittsburgh explains why and directly counters Alperovitz's conclusions. Whereas Alperovitz labels Newman's conclusions a myth, Newman labels Alperovitz's work part of an ahistorical "cult."

During the 1970s, historians Barton Bernstein of Stanford University and Martin Sherwin of Tufts University took a middle ground by arguing that Truman and his advisers inherited policies from Roosevelt, that they were primarily motivated by a desire to end the war as quickly as possible and with minimal U.S. casualties, but that impressing the Soviets with the new weapon constituted a "diplomatic bonus." In the third essay, Bernstein summarizes this argument and then examines what in hindsight appear to be alternatives to using the bomb. In the process he analyzes why these alternatives were not seriously considered at the time, tries to assess whether they could have worked, and emphasizes the different contexts of 1945 and the present.

Dropping the Atomic Bomb Was Neither Necessary Nor Justifiable

GAR ALPEROVITZ

Quite simply, it is not true that the atomic bomb was used because it was the only way to save the "hundreds of thousands" or "millions" of lives as was subsequently claimed. The readily available options were to modify the surrender terms and/or await the shock of the Russian attack. Three months remained before a November Kyushu landing could take place even in theory; there were six to seven months before the spring invasion of Honshu could begin under the existing planning assumptions.

If we accept the conclusion of either the U.S. Strategic Bombing Survey (which did not even assume a modification of the unconditional surrender formula or the impact of a Russian declaration of war) or the War Department study which judged the war would almost certainly have ended when the Red Army attacked—then in retrospect, minimally, the bombings were, as Hanson Baldwin put it, a "mistake."

From Gar Alperovitz, *The Decision to Use the Atomic Bomb and the Architecture of an American Myth* (New York: Random House, 1995), 629–636, 645, 665–668. Used by permission of Alfred A. Knopf, a division of Random House, Inc.

However, the evidence—especially from the MAGIC intercepts, the records of the Joint Chiefs of Staff, the 1945 intelligence studies, numerous statements by military leaders close to the decision process, and the Leahy, Stimson, Forrestal, McCloy, and Brown diaries—allows us to go beyond this. It is impossible to peer into the hearts and minds of men fifty years after the fact. Nevertheless, although matters of nuance and degree can be endlessly debated, it is quite clear that alternatives to using the bomb existed—and that the president and his advisers were aware of them. . . .

Modern evidence . . . suggests not only that the president and [Secretary of State James] Byrnes knew Japan was on the verge of surrender, but that once the new weapon had been successfully tested, rushing to end the war before an expected mid-August Red Army attack was indisputably a major concern. . . .

It is sometimes held that no real "decision" to use the atomic bomb ever took place, that the "momentum" of war (or of bureaucracy, etc.) produced the bombings—and that, besides, there is no surviving contemporaneous evidence that anyone directly challenged the decision. . . .

The truth is that at least three very clear and explicit decisions (and probably more) were made which set the terms of reference for the bomb's subsequent seemingly "inevitable" use. Indeed, once they were made, they so tightly framed the remaining issues as to make it all but impossible thereafter to oppose the bombings.

The first decision involved rejection of the recommendation that to offer any meaningful possibility of surrender a statement to Japan would have to allow enough time for the development of a serious response. As we have seen, a conscious choice not to allow a meaningful interval was made early on—and explicitly reaffirmed at Potsdam.

The second and more fundamental choice was the decision not to offer Japan assurances for the Emperor. Once this decision had been made—and the Japanese were allowed to believe the Emperor might be removed and possibly hanged as a war criminal—it was obvious to all concerned that the fighting would continue. . . .

The decision to delete assurances for the Emperor from the Potsdam Proclamation was one relegated to political authority. Once the president had made his choice on this matter—and since it was known that therefore the fighting would now unquestionably continue—the basic military options were narrowed to two: The only choice now was to use the bomb or go forward with an invasion.

In this situation the silence and seeming momentum of events is not difficult to comprehend. For any official—military or civilian—to oppose the bombing in these circumstances would have been absurd. It would have been equivalent to arguing for a bloody invasion. It would also have been to challenge the president after he had made his decision quite clear.

The third fundamental choice has now also been fully documented. It was the decision not to test the impact of the Russian declaration of war—indeed, to weaken the military challenge posed to Japan by attempting to put off an event which all understood would have extraordinary impact. This decision, too, was made at the political level. . . .

All of this also obviously bears on the issue of the number of lives which may possibly have been saved by the atomic bomb. As we have seen, over the last decade scholars working in very different fields—Barton Bernstein, Rufus E. Miles, Jr., and John Ray Skates—all separately have demonstrated that even if the first landing and subsequent invasion had gone forward, at the time it was officially estimated that the number of lives which might have been lost (and therefore possibly saved by the atomic bomb) was of the order of magnitude of 20,000 to 26,000 for Kyushu, and a maximum of 46,000 in the unlikely event of a full invasion in 1946.

However, even these numbers confuse the central issues (as do other nonofficial estimates). The fact is if the war could have been ended by clarifying the terms and/or the Russian shock, there would have been no lives lost in an invasion. Fighting was reduced as both sides regrouped, and the most that may be said is that the atomic bombs may have saved the lives which might have been lost in the time it would have taken to arrange the final surrender terms. . . .

In the decades since World War II, writers who have defended the bombings have repeatedly pointed to the hard-line Japanese army faction which was opposed to surrender and which was clearly preparing to defend against a possible invasion. Some have even offered dramatic, detailed descriptions of battles which in theory might possibly have been fought. The intricacies of various arguments are taken up in the Afterword, but the essential points to note here are rather straightforward:

In the first place it is an obvious non sequitur to argue from the fact that preparations were going forward that what was "planned" was also what, in fact, was likely to happen. The U.S. military, after all, was also engaged in preparations and plans for an invasion. It is quite clear that the Japanese both wished to be prepared for an invasion and wanted to make sure U.S. officials believed they would fight to the death if invaded.

Much more important, no knowledgeable historian would dispute the idea that so long as the Emperor's position was in doubt—as it was throughout this entire period—the Japanese would likely have resisted to the end. The army faction held all the cards so long as the Emperor was threatened. And so long as the Russians were neutral they could also argue it was not totally insane to continue the war.

Nor is it surprising that after the war some Japanese leaders honestly recalled that they had planned to fight on. That is, in fact, what they had expected to do, given that U.S. policy continued to threaten the Emperor. This was what the fundamental debate was all about inside the U.S. government—and precisely why American military leaders urged the president to offer Japan assurances for the Emperor.

Put another way, eliminating the political-psychological props holding up the army faction and securing the shock of a Red Army attack were the central thrust of top intelligence and other advice throughout the summer. That even without such changes so many U.S. military leaders felt the war could have been ended before a November landing only underscores the narrow focus of some arguments which point to opposition to surrender within Japan yet ignore or downplay the options available to U.S. leaders at the time.

Nor, contrary to some theories, did political considerations compel the president's choices. . . .

Perhaps it is here, most poignantly, that we confront our own reluctance to ask the difficult questions—for even if one were to accept the most inflated estimates of lives saved by the atomic bomb, the fact remains that it was an act of violent destruction aimed deliberately at large concentrations of noncombatants.

We do not like to speak of such things. "The knowledge of horrible events periodically intrudes into public awareness," professor of psychiatry Judith Herman observes, but it "is rarely retained for long. Denial, repression, and dissociation operate on a social as well as an individual level." . . .

There are, of course, historians who still disagree with the judgment that the war would have ended in any event before an invasion. Also, some general scholars have not as yet caught up with the modern expert research findings. However, it is difficult to believe that Japan would have fought on once the Russians actually attacked and once assurances for the Emperor were actually given. And it is very difficult—given what we now know—to believe that in the end assurances would not have been given if the alternative was an invasion. Truman and Byrnes, as Stimson noted, were hardly "obdurate" about the point. . . .

. . . [T]he modern evidence does not support the view that diplomatic considerations were merely a "bonus" in the minds of top U.S. officials. Although it is impossible to reach a full and final answer to the question of emphasis, what we now know even more strongly suggests—but does not as yet definitively prove—that diplomatic factors were of far greater significance. The most important points concern Byrnes' attitude and his influence on the president—especially when compared with virtually all the other top advisers (and Churchill). Some matters are no longer in doubt:

First, in general Byrnes clearly saw the weapon as important to his diplomacy vis-à-vis the Soviet Union.

Second, of particular significance are features of the context established during the two weeks in Germany. It is no longer seriously disputed that Byrnes and the president took a hard-line position on a variety of issues during the Potsdam discussion because of—in anticipation of—the atomic bomb. This fact itself set the terms of reference for the next stage of decision-making. . . .

Third, it was in this specific context—and at this specific time—that Byrnes arranged for the elimination of language offering assurances for the Emperor.

Fourth, it is beyond question that once the atomic bomb was successfully tested, Byrnes saw it as a way to end the war before the Red Army entered Manchuria—and urgently attempted both to get a surrender and to stall the Russians. . . .

My own view has shifted slightly in recent years. By the early 1960s it was clear that the Potsdam conference had been postponed in order to have the weapon tested before negotiating with Stalin. It was also obvious from the Stimson diaries that as early as May 16 Truman himself believed that the United States would "hold more cards in our hands later than now"—and that by June 6 the president had "postponed [the Big Three meeting] . . . on purpose to give us more time." Stimson had first brought information to the president about the atomic bomb because of its bearing on the crisis over Poland. And at the end of May, according to Szilard, Byrnes saw the bomb as a way to make Russia more manageable in Europe. . . .

In the early 1980s I was impressed by the research Robert Messer had done on Byrnes' concerns—especially his demonstration that having been sent by Roosevelt to sell the Yalta agreement to the Senate and to the American public, Byrnes had a strong interest in achieving a satisfactory settlement in Eastern Europe. Moreover, Byrnes' personal political stature now rested almost entirely on his performance as secretary of state—and in general it is evident that the bomb appeared critical in this regard as well.

Although it still seems clear that considerations related to Europe established key aspects of the diplomatic context as Potsdam and the Alamogordo test approached, there was considerable uncertainty until the force of the test was actually experienced. Byrnes seems genuinely to have wanted Russia to enter the war prior to mid-July. Almost surely the combination of news of the Emperor's intervention (July 13) with the news of the successful test immediately thereafter (July 16) crystallized the final decisions: Now the bomb might end the war not only before an invasion but also before the Red Army moved into Manchuria.

In this regard, Truman's strong interest in the Manchurian question—perhaps partly because of its importance to many Republicans—probably also played a role. In any event, both European and Asian issues appear to have weighed heavily on the minds of American leaders in the final weeks before Hiroshima. However, we simply do not have enough information to make a final judgment as to emphasis— and we will probably never know what passed between Truman and Byrnes in their unrecorded private discussions.

Dropping the Bomb Was Necessary and Justifiable

ROBERT P. NEWMAN

I take the meaning of "cult" from *Merriam-Webster's Ninth New Collegiate:* "a great devotion to a person, idea, or thing: esp: such a devotion regarded as literary or intellectual fad." The intellectual idea to which Hiroshima cultists are devoted is that since Japan was about to surrender when the bombs were dropped, the slaughter of innocents at Hiroshima and Nagasaki was not motivated by military reasons. It was instead motivated primarily by the desire to intimidate the Russians (so-called atomic diplomacy), by racism (we did not drop the bomb on Germany), by the desire of Robert Oppenheimer and company to experiment with a new toy, by the fear of Secretary of War Henry Stimson and others that Congress would investigate if their $2 billion dollar expenditure was found not useful, or by the sheer unthinking momentum of a bureaucratic juggernaut (Manhattan Project).

This cult has a shrine, a holy day, a distinctive rhetoric of victimization (it can also be called a Japanese-as-victim cult), various items of scripture (John Hersey's *Hiroshima,* The Franck Report, P.M.S. Blackett's 1949, *Fear, War, and the Bomb*), and, in Japan, support from a powerful constituency (Marxist). As with other cults, it is ahistorical. Its devotees elevate fugitive and unrepresentative events to cosmic status. And most of all, *they believe.*

The Hiroshima cult is the mirror image of the nuclear cult—those evangelists of the 1950s and 1960s who saw the energy of the atom as the means to make the desert bloom, to air condition whole cities for pennies (the electricity would be too cheap to meter), to power an airplane across the oceans on a thimbleful of fuel, and to do other wonderful things. Daniel Ford dealt with these matters in his 1982 book, *The Cult of the Atom. This* cult has demonstrated its bankruptcy.

But the Hiroshima cult is not bankrupt. It gained ascendancy in 1994 in the Smithsonian's Air and Space Museum, and its faithful still flock to the shrine in Japan. This

Reprinted with permission from Robert P. Newman, *Truman and the Hiroshima Cult* (East Lansing: Michigan State University Press, 1995), xi–xii, 17–18, 21, 28–29, 31, 57, 71, 76–77, 94, 96–99, 101–103, 108–109, 130, 136–139, 185, 196–197.

book is about how things got that way, and it is judgmental. My focus, however, is not on the cultists as such; rather it is on the arguments they use to proselytize. . . .

. . . [E]ven ULTRA,* accurate as it was in revealing Japanese reinforcement on Kyushu, missed a few troops. At the end of fighting, the Japanese had 900,000 soldiers defending Kyushu, with more to come, opposing the 766,700 Americans readying for the invasion.

General Marshall was following the ULTRA decrypts; they jarred him out of his complacent 31,000 thirty-day estimate as given the president on 18 June. Truman claims in a letter dated 12 January 1953 that he had asked Marshall at Potsdam "what it will cost in lives to land on the Tokyo plain and other places in Japan. It was his opinion that such an invasion would cost at a minimum one quarter of a million casualties, and might cost as much as a million, on the American side, with an equal number of the enemy."

Many historians write this estimate off as self-serving, nothing more than wishful reconstruction of a failing memory. Perhaps. But the laughably unrealistic underestimates *put on paper* by casualty-shy military people certainly do not command the high ground of credibility. Marshall may have given such an estimate orally. Truman may have accurately remembered. Those who are so certain that landing on Kyushu would have been a walk (meaning only 31,000 casualties at D plus 30) must engage the ULTRA intelligence, as well as the confident beliefs of the Imperial Japanese Army commanders that they could not only have severely damaged the first wave attack, but beaten it back so convincingly that the United States would have sued for peace. . . .

Even with Hiroshima and Nagasaki, with the Soviet entry, and with an impressive (though outnumbered) American invasion fleet shaping up, surrender barely came off in mid-August. Despite the final submission of War Minister Anami, Army Chief of Staff Umezu, and Navy Chief of Staff Toyoda, who had been the three Supreme Council holdouts, army hotheads got out of control. Dissident forces seized the Imperial Compound the night before the emperor's broadcast, turned the place inside out trying to find the recording of his surrender rescript, assassinated Lt. Gen. Mori Takeshi (commander of the Imperial Guard at the palace), attempted to assassinate Premier Suzuki Kantaro and burned down his house when they found he had escaped, and tried to take over the radio station that was to broadcast the emperor's surrender the next day.

The sticking point in Japanese surrender in August 1945 was *not* the terms of surrender; it was the still unknown ability of the emperor to make a surrender *of any kind* hold.

John Dower has the ultimate answer to those who tell us now that peace was there to be had in 1944 and early 1945 if we had only modified the unconditional surrender rhetoric, and signaled acceptance of the emperor: "The suggestion that there may have been serious lost opportunities for a peace settlement in 1944 or early 1945 remains almost unbelievable, and the small murmurs about peace which Iriye [Newman: in his rose-tinted book *Power and Culture*] seizes upon seem as candles set against an inferno of hate."

---

*See Chapter 8.

The inferno of hate was stilled only by the inferno of the atom.

The preponderance of evidence shows that *at the time of decision* the Truman administration believed, with good reason, that invasion plans threatened an unacceptable loss of life, to Japanese as much as to Americans. Hiroshima cultists deny this and go beyond it to claim that whatever Truman thought, postwar investigation showed Kyushu defenses to have been weak, and OLYMPIC [Planned Invasion of Kyushu] if it had gone forward would not have been traumatic. . . .

Harry Truman ordered the bombing of Hiroshima and Nagasaki primarily to end the war as soon as possible and save lives. This conclusion is compelled by the evidence, and yet there are challenges to this motivation. The most powerful challenge is based on the belief that atomic bombs were dropped on Japan, and nowhere else, because of American racism. . . .

There are two intractable facts that destroy this argument: (1) Hiroshima cultists cannot challenge the timetable that made the first bomb available only after Germany had surrendered, leaving Japan as the sole Axis power yet to be overwhelmed. What evidence anywhere implies that the United States would not have used atomic weapons on Germany had it been still a belligerent, when the bombs were developed precisely out of fear Germany would get them first, and when the Allies obliterated Dresden and several other towns as thoroughly as the atom destroyed Hiroshima and Nagasaki? (2) The directive issued to Col. Paul Tibbets in September 1944 instructed him to train *two* bomber groups to make simultaneous drops on Germany and Japan. This also is unanswerable.

Japan's sense of victimization is so deeply rooted that the racism argument cannot be successfully countered in that country. There is no justification for its acceptance elsewhere.

Then there is the atomic diplomacy argument, the main stock in trade of some American Hiroshima cultists: Truman dropped the bomb to intimidate the Soviet Union. This possesses a kernel of truth. Anticommunism and anti-Sovietism had burgeoned in 1920s America, receded during the war, and began growing in 1944 as the Russians occupied Eastern Europe. President Truman, James Byrnes, Ambassador Averell Harriman, and a few others worried about the extension of Soviet power, and welcomed the clout that possession of nuclear weapons gave the United States. But uneasiness about the Soviets in the summer of 1945 was not a full-blown cold war. Checkmating Soviet moves did not dominate the Truman White House until much later. . . .

Atomic diplomacy and other cultist variants purport to show a White House fixated on Russia, or strongly racist, or dominated by bureaucrats. One cannot quarrel with the claim that many bureaucratic and personal motives of the makers of the bomb were brought to bear upon the president; these analyses do not, however, remove the pressure point of *decision,* which lay with the president. He ordered the dropping of the first bombs "as available" as surely as he ordered cancellation of the third. And the White House was fixated on securing Japan's surrender, on terms that would obviate recrudescence of militarism, as quickly and with as few casualties as possible.

Almost as important in the theology of Hiroshima cultists as the atomic diplomacy and racism doctrines is the claim that the unconditional surrender policy kept Japan from capitulating. Had this policy been repudiated, we are told, the bombs would not have been necessary. . . .

Careful inspection of the attitudes of leaders of the Japanese peace party yields different conclusions. They saw in the Potsdam terms an acceptable alternative to the destruction Japan would otherwise sustain.

Foreign Minister Togo Shigenori was foremost among them. He felt that the phrase "Following are our terms" clearly indicated that there *were* terms, that surrender was not without conditions. . . .

. . . [O]n the big strategic question: Did substantially carrying out Roosevelt's unconditional surrender doctrine in the Pacific War teach Japan a lesson, eradicate militarism, promote "peace in our time"? The answer is "perhaps." But had Truman officially abandoned the doctrine, the war party, not the peace party, would have benefitted. Anami, Umezu and Toyoda would have been better able to resist pressure from the emperor: "Look, now the Americans are backing down. If we just hold out long enough to severely punish their invasion forces we can get an armistice with no occupation, no war crimes trials, no American-conducted disarmament." As Brian Villa emphasizes in his discussion of the final tense moments, "There was present the eternal dilemma of truce making, the endless truism, 'If the enemy is weak, concessions are unnecessary, if he appears strong, concessions look like a confession of weakness.' "

Thus, what Hiroshima cultists insist was a viable alternative for Truman to end the war early without using the bomb—retaining the emperor—was really no alternative at all. It would not have converted the Japanese military to surrender, but would instead have stiffened their resolve to fight the decisive battle of the homeland. Had the United States been willing to grant *all* of Anami's demands, the determination of the military to fight it out would have been even more intensified. Even if the emperor could have overpowered the military before Hiroshima and secured a cease fire on the basis of softening of the unconditional surrender demand, it would not have been wise. A Japanese conviction that they had not really been defeated would have taken firm hold. . . .

In the interrogations of Japanese leaders conducted by the United States Strategic Bombing Survey, and by MacArthur's G-2, I have been unable to find any Japanese leaders who claim that the destruction of Hiroshima and Nagasaki could have been avoided, and Japan brought to surrender, by a nonlethal demonstration of the bomb. Instead, there is abundant testimony that the Japanese military even minimized the significance of the damage at Hiroshima. Fortunately the civilian elite, the peace party, knew that something disastrous had occurred; and the emperor used it to face down Anami.

Hiroshima cultists never come to grips with the very cogent reasons why the Interim Committee and its scientific advisers rejected the idea of a demonstration. . . . The pressure point of the argument is whether a nonlethal demonstration could have produced the triumph of the peace party and the acquiescence of the militarists. On this matter, the pro-demonstration argument is bankrupt. Its supporters do not even attempt to analyze the proposal from the Japanese viewpoint as of the summer of 1945; they assume a strictly Western point of view. . . .

But what about a warning?

Many scientists and philosophers felt a warning was called for; the very sober General Marshall felt the same way; even the Far Eastern Department of the British Foreign Office took that point of view. Stimson and his advisers, and hence Truman, believed otherwise.

The only analyst to consider the "no warning" position in depth is Lawrence Freedman of the Royal Institute of International Affairs in London. In a 1978 article, "The Strategy of Hiroshima," he concludes: "As more thought was given to the most effective use of the bomb, the strategy evolved from a simple one based on maximizing the impact of the bomb's destructive power to one aimed at maximizing its shock value. To achieve this it became necessary to distinguish the use of this new weapon from conventional strategic bombing." . . .

Robert Oppenheimer sensed the true potentialities of the new bomb. It was not just an extension of LeMay's conventional bombing campaign; it was something new under the sun. Lawrence Freedman observes, "It was on the basis of this spectacular quality that those considering the use of the bomb began to move away from the previous, implicit, strategy of cumulative pressure to one of maximum shock." Maximum shock demanded maximum surprise; a specific warning would have eliminated this factor.

It was precisely the shock of the bombs and the assumption that more were coming that brought about Japan's surrender *at that time*. The emperor, by mid-June, agreed with the peace party that the time to give up had arrived. He could not, however, despite his godlike stature, simply impose his will on a military machine determined to fight a decisive battle of the homeland, and capable of governing by assassination if thwarted. Kido, Suzuki, Togo could have been assassinated and the emperor taken into protective custody in order to keep fighting.

The shock of the atom gave the emperor the leverage he needed to compel compliance with his decision. . . .

Anami and others made convincing arguments that the United States could not have more bombs. Nagasaki, when it came so soon after, was equally a shock. These shocks were fundamental to ending the stalemate in the cabinet and the Supreme Council for the Direction of the War, *and* needed to convince Anami, Toyoda, and Umezu not to join Hatanaka, Ida, and the other insurgents who assassinated the commander of the Palace Guard and attempted to reverse the emperor's decision. . . .

The point at issue here is not what *defeated* Japan; naval, army, and air forces can all claim much credit. Nor is it *when* Japan realized it was defeated; this happened at various times, some admitting defeat after the loss of Saipan, others after MacArthur retook the Philippines, or after Iwo Jima or Okinawa. What is at issue is the trigger that motivated the emperor to surrender and emasculated military opposition. No revisionist historian even begins to come to grips with the best evidence here. . . .

Henry Stimson and the Interim Committee did not perceive the true fulcrum of Japanese decision making in this crisis; the effect of bombs on the Japanese *people* was largely irrelevant. The people were kept in the dark about how destructive the atom had been. But the leaders knew, and they were shaken. Robert Butow captures the essence of the event:

> The revulsion with which these *samurai*-inspired men viewed defeat and surrender often made them blind to all other considerations. Their thinking processes were befuddled by the emphasis they placed upon the ability of the spirit to triumph miraculously over the power of material force. These men, who had once been the wardens of the prison in which they had confined the whole nation, had now joined the ranks of the inmates. The real significance of the explosions over Hiroshima and Nagasaki and the Soviet dash into Manchuria was that these events produced a shock great enough to crack the walls

of the prison. Even this shock did not result in an escape but it did force everyone, the guards and guarded alike, to face the full and glaring light of day—to acknowledge a fact which could no longer be denied. It was not that the military men had suddenly become reasonable . . . it was rather that they, like the machinery of government with which they had been tinkering, had momentarily been caught off balance.

In the furious controversy over surrender that shook the Japanese government in the first days of August 1945, the atomic bombing of Hiroshima and Nagasaki was the decisive event. . . .

. . . Evidence that the emperor made his firm decision to recommend peace after the Hiroshima bombing and before the Nagasaki bombing has been available for decades. The sticking point during this interim was not the will of the emperor; it was the refusal of Anami and the military to give up their hopes for a decisive battle of the homeland, at which they would finally convince the United States to back off and negotiate.

No account of the deliberations in the Supreme Council for the Direction of the War, or in the Japanese cabinet, on 9 August warrants the belief that absent Nagasaki, the emperor would have been able to prevail when he finally declared himself. *Japan's Longest Day* is quite clear; the Hiroshima bomb, the Soviet entry into the war, and the Nagasaki bomb were *together* insufficient to move the military. Only the Emperor's opinion, stated twice, ended the war. How can one believe any lesser trauma could have been effective? . . .

Everything we know about the death throes of the Japanese empire indicates that even with the modification of the unconditional surrender doctrine to allow continuation of the emperor, even with the devastation caused by conventional bombing and two atomic bombs, even with the feared entry of the Soviet Union, surrender hung by a thread. Twice the emperor had to direct his ministers to accept the Potsdam terms. When they finally gave in, obedience by the fanatical junior officers was not assured. . . .

Hiroshima was no Dresden. The Japanese, even more than the Germans, threatened to fight to the last death and take tens of thousands of Allied soldiers with them. Churchill was right on this matter, and the quotation Walzer uses from Churchill to show the latter's insensitivity instead goes precisely to the heart of the reason for using the atomic bombs: "To avert a vast, indefinite butchery . . . at the cost of a few explosions seemed, after all our toils and perils, a miracle of deliverance."

Averting a vast indefinite butchery even at the cost of several hundred thousand noncombatant casualties was worth it. The doctrine of noncombatant immunity needs contemporary rethinking. In previous times when soldiers were volunteers, in the business of soldiering for money, a distinction between them and ordinary folk had some moral force. In times when soldiers are mostly conscripts, when noncombatants are often as implicated in the war-fighting policies and economies of the state as those in uniform, it is not self-evident why the lives of conscripts should be valued less than their fellow-citizens. In the case at issue here, Japanese citizens were not abject (and hence innocent) victims of a militaristic regime. . . .

How *do* justice and revenge differ? Is it not true that the people and factories of Hiroshima and Nagasaki, as well as the rest of Japan, armed Tojo's butchers and sent them forth on their campaigns of pillage, rape, and murder? . . .

. . . [H]ad Hiroshima not become a shrine to the peaceminded, the anguish of Japan's victims might be more on our consciences.

And it is not just their anguish; it is their sheer numbers. Only after several years of study did I realize that, for some reason, I could find no one who had put together comprehensive figures showing the extent of Japanese-caused *deaths*. Statistics of the numbers who died at Hitler's hands are in every account of his crimes. The same for victims of Stalin. Deaths during World War II's battles in the European-African theaters are readily available. Why is there no similar compilation for deaths caused by the Japanese? Perhaps that would be more difficult to compile than Hitler's statistics. Japan did conquer more different and far-flung territories and put Allied captives in 424 prison camps scattered over one-quarter of the globe.

Nevertheless, it is possible to put together an estimate of how many people perished at Japanese hands. John Dower gives death figures for nine countries in his book; a United Nations (UN) document covers four other countries. Problem cases are China, where estimates of deaths from 1931 to 1945 range from two to thirty million; the Burma-Siam railway, where Murakami Hyoe gives a low estimate of 32,000, the Associated Press lists 116,000; and the Dutch East Indies, where the UN lists three million for Java, one million for the other islands; but the probable error must be high. I use the lowest figure in all cases except China, where ten million is a consensus figure, and the Burma-Siam railway, where I use the figure of the Allied War Graves Registration Unit:

Deaths Attributable to the Japanese Empire, 1931–1945

China	10,000,000
Java (Dutch Indies)	3,000,000
Outer Islands	1,000,000
Philippines	120,000
India	180,000
Bengal famine	1,500,000
Korea	70,000
Burma-Siam railway	82,500
Indonesia, Europeans	30,000
Malaya	100,000
Vietnam	1,000,000
Australia	30,000
New Zealand	10,000
United States	100,000
Total	17,222,500

The summary cannot do justice to the details. From the viewpoint of seeking justice, Pearl Harbor is no big deal; a mere 2,400 casualties. This pales before seventeen million. At least ten million of these occurred between 7 December 1941 and 30 August 1945. During these forty-five months, 200,000 to 300,000 persons died each month at Japanese hands. The last months were in many ways the worst; starvation and disease aggravated the usual beatings, beheadings, and battle deaths. It is plausible to hold that upwards of 250,000 people, mostly Asian but some

Westerners, *would have died each month the Japanese Empire struggled in its death throes beyond July 1945. . . .*

Overshadowing every other consideration, continuation of the Pacific War, had Truman not used atomic bombs in August, would have produced unmitigated evil. The extent of the evil would have depended on the duration of the war. Hiroshima cultists' fanaticism blinds them to everything except the casualties from the atom. The prospect, however, was for far greater casualties, from (1) continued Japanese mistreatment of prisoners and slave laborers; (2) intensified disruption of food supplies and transportation throughout the empire; (3) continued land and sea battles with losses like that of the *Indianapolis;* and (4) continued conventional bombing by Gen. Curtis LeMay's B-29s. These things together would have produced *monthly death rates* well in excess of the Hiroshima-Nagasaki total. . . .

Possession of nuclear weapons did reinforce American messianism and truculence. Gar Alperovitz and Kai Bird may be right in believing that without nuclear weapons, the United States might not have rearmed Germany nor intervened in the Korean War. But this is irrelevant to the Hiroshima question. Truman did not let this genie out of the bottle. The United States would have had nuclear weapons as soon as it did no matter who was president. And in all probability, any president would have made ending the war quickly with minimum loss of life his top priority, would have known from intercepts that the Japanese peace party was impotent and the dominant generals were determined to fight a final battle of the homeland, and would have brought the new weapon into play exactly as Truman did. One would hope, however, that with the war over, a different president might not have succumbed so quickly to the chimera of national security, or have gone off as eagerly in search of places to intervene against Communism.

One argument against use of the bomb against Japan does score. Karel van Wolferen is assuredly right that if the bombs had not been dropped, the Japanese cult of victimhood could not have grown as fast.

Were There Viable Alternatives to Dropping the Atomic Bomb?

BARTON J. BERNSTEIN

Few events in modern American history have attracted as much attention, and provoked as much dispute, as the use of the atomic bomb. The analysis of the use of that weapon has had a curious, and often polemical, history. One school ("orthodox") stresses that the atomic bombing was necessary, that the bomb saved many American lives (possibly a quarter million or more), and that not using it would have been unconscionable. Another school ("revisionist") argues that the atomic bombing was unnecessary, that American leaders knew that Japan was near defeat and hence near surrender, and that the bomb was used for an ulterior purpose. In

From Barton J. Bernstein, "Understanding the Atomic Bomb and the Japanese Surrender: Missed Opportunities, Little-Known Near Disasters, and Modern Memory," *Diplomatic History* 19, no. 2 (Spring 1995): 229–230, 235–238, 240–244, 247–260, 262, 269.

this framework, the motive of intimidating the Soviet Union is usually cited as primary, though sometimes analysts define it as secondary but essential, and occasionally historians also stress bureaucratic interests as playing a controlling role in the decision to drop the A-bomb on Japan. By implication, and often by assertion, the revisionists are quite sure that the war against Japan could have been ended without the bomb, that ulterior motives blocked other approaches, and that the use of the bomb was clearly immoral.

Between these two schools, a third has emerged, employing parts of the revisionist and orthodox analyses to conclude in a new synthesis: that the A-bomb was conceived as a legitimate weapon to be used against the enemy; that this assumption under President Franklin D. Roosevelt went largely unexamined and unchallenged; that Truman comfortably inherited this assumption, and that it also fit his inclinations and desires; and that the combat use of the bomb on Japan even came to seem both necessary and desirable. For President Harry S. Truman, the bomb could help end the war on American terms, possibly avoid the dreaded invasions, punish the Japanese for Pearl Harbor and their mistreatment of POWs, fulfill bureaucratic needs, conform to the desires of the American people, and *also* intimidate the Soviets, perhaps making them tractable in Eastern Europe.

According to this formulation, the atomic bomb might well have been used against Japan on the same days, in the same ways, even if the Bolshevik Revolution had never occurred and the Soviet Union had not existed. But the prospect of intimidating the Soviet Union added another reason, a kind of bonus, or what some would call over-determination. In turn, the prospects of this bonus may have blocked some policymakers from reconsidering in July or early August the use of the atomic bomb; but there is no reason to conclude that such a reconsideration—had it occurred—would have produced a different policy. In short, the combat use of the A-bomb was, unfortunately, virtually inevitable. Truman's commitment to its use was, basically, the implementation of the assumption that he had inherited.

For President Truman and his top advisers in 1945, the use of the atomic bomb was never a question. For them, the important question was how militarily to produce Japan's surrender, and sometimes what kind of surrender was likely. All had come by mid-June 1945, if not somewhat earlier, to endorse the military strategy of invading Kyushu in early November 1945. On 18 June 1945, urged by his united military advisers, Truman had approved full planning for this invasion. . . .

In 1945, American leaders were not seeking to avoid the use of the A-bomb. Its use did not create ethical or political problems for them. Thus, they easily rejected or never considered most of the so-called alternatives to the bomb: 1) a non-combat demonstration as a dramatic warning; 2) modification of the unconditional-surrender demand and an explicit guarantee of the imperial system; 3) pursuit of Japan's peace feelers; 4) a delay of the A-bomb until well after Soviet entry into the war; and 5) reliance (without the A-bomb) on heavy conventional bombing and a naval blockade. American leaders felt no incentive to pursue these strategies as *alternatives to dropping the bomb on Japan*.

Even by framing a post-Hiroshima analysis in terms of *alternatives* to the use of the A-bomb, there is some risk of distorting history by seeming—though not intending—to imply that American leaders before Hiroshima considered these various approaches, with the single exception of a non-combat demonstration, as alternatives to the bomb. They did not. In examining these so-called alternatives, post-Hiroshima analysts can conclude that these strategies, with various probabilities, *might* have served as alternatives to the bomb by producing a surrender before November 1945. But that is the view from a *post-*, not *pre-*, Hiroshima perspective. In the pre-Hiroshima months, when and if these strategies were considered, and delaying use of the bomb went unconsidered, they were not examined (with the exception of the non-combat demonstration) in terms of avoiding the use of the bomb but sometimes assessed within the context of *avoiding the invasion.* Even the siege strategy of bombing and blockade, though often linked to the November invasion, raised for policymakers the hope that it might compel a Japanese surrender before the November invasion. Put bluntly, for American leaders, avoiding the dread invasion, even if "only" twenty-five thousand Americans might die in the attack, was a major concern. Avoiding the use of the bomb was never a real concern for policymakers.

After the fact, however, avoiding the use of that weapon is properly an analytical theme for historians who seek to understand, explain, and assess the use of the A-bomb in August 1945. In conducting that historical study, they must be careful not to conflate their morality, that the bomb was a terrible weapon to be avoided, with the beliefs of American leaders before Hiroshima. Such a conflation, though tempting to some analysts, gravely misunderstands Truman and his associates in the pre-Hiroshima world. Such a conflation greatly distorts the past and makes understanding the use of the bomb very difficult, because it leads analysts to search for some hidden ulterior motive that compelled policymakers to overcome their scruples to use the bomb. Policymakers did not have such scruples—and there is no need to look for overwhelming hidden motives. Their primary motives were not hidden.

Only had American leaders viewed the bomb as profoundly immoral, or (like the Franck Committee) had they feared the postwar consequences of the bomb's combat use, might they have sought ways not to use it. They did not regard it as profoundly immoral, they were largely inured to the mass killing of the enemy, and they also looked forward to the A-bomb's international-political benefits—intimidating the Soviets. American leaders also knew that they might risk a great outcry at home if they did not use the bomb. How could they have justified spending $2 billion on the Manhattan Project, and even diverting scarce wartime resources to that project, and then not using the A-bomb against a hated enemy—especially if the war continued past 1 November 1945 and thousands of Americans died in the invasion? Such lurking domestic-political reasons easily blended into very powerful patriotic motives and easily found additional support in personal and bureaucratic reasons for those American leaders such as Stimson and Marshall, as well as the new president, all of whom bore particular responsibility for the A-bomb project.

Despite these general explanations, there is still need to look closely at *each* of these so-called alternatives and ask two questions: Why were they not pursued *instead* of the bomb? And what might have happened if *one or more* had instead been pursued? Answers to the first question are strictly historical; but answers to the second (what might have happened if?), though greatly influenced by evidence, must necessarily remain somewhat speculative. They rest, in part, on projections of trends, actors' behavior, and events into a future that did not occur.

Alternative I: Non-combat Demonstration. This alternative was really only raised on two sets of occasions—at the 31 May 1945 Interim Committee lunch and then in the Franck Committee Report of 11 June, leading to its rejection by the Scientific Advisory Panel on 16 June and by the Interim Committee on 21 June. Each time, this proposal was speedily disposed of because, variously, the bomb might not work, a dud might embolden the Japanese, or Allied POWs might be moved into the demonstration area and be killed by the bomb. Because each of these risks was deeply troubling, and because there was *no strong desire* (and usually no desire) to avoid the combat use of the bomb, the alternative of a non-combat demonstration was easily rejected. . . .

In retrospect, given what we now know of the strong opposition among the "militarists" in the Japanese government even after two atomic bombings and Soviet entry, it is difficult to believe that a non-combat demonstration, even if preceded by a warning, would have produced a surrender before 1 November 1945 and the likely invasion of Kyushu. At best, the probabilities seem slight—maybe 5 or 10 percent. And the likelihood is even skimpier of a warning, without such a demonstration, being successful.

Alternative II: Modification of Unconditional Surrender and Guarantee of the Emperor. Some American leaders, most notably Undersecretary of State Joseph Grew and Secretary of War Stimson, pleaded for this strategy—not as an alternative to the A-bomb, but rather as a way, they hoped, of avoiding the invasion. Grew did not even know of the bomb, and Stimson hoped that a guarantee of the emperor, *together* with the A-bomb and heavy conventional bombing, as well as the blockade, might produce a surrender before 1 November. Grew and Stimson lost on the guarantee because Truman and James F. Byrnes, the new secretary of state, feared a political backlash in America, where Hirohito was likened to Hitler and judged a war criminal, and because Truman and Byrnes feared that such modified surrender terms might also embolden the Japanese to fight on for better terms.

Some analysts have argued that maintenance of the imperial system was the *only* issue blocking a Japanese surrender in late July or early August (before the A-bomb), and that American leaders knew this or should have known it. Such an interpretation of the Japanese position is ill-founded. The Japanese government was badly split both on how and whether to end the war, and even the Japanese "peace" forces were unsure, unsteady, and uncertain. . . .

Given the power of the militarists and their desire, it is *quite unlikely*—but not impossible—that an American guarantee of the imperial system would have produced a Japanese surrender before 1 November on terms acceptable to the United States. Certainly, given American plans for the political reconstruction of Japan and the destruction of Japanese militarism, postwar occupation was essential—even at the price of a prolonged war. Very probably, American concessions on all *four* conditions (the emperor, postwar occupation, self-disarmament, and war trials) could have produced a speedy surrender. But that would not have been the victory that American leaders, as well as much of the public, desired. War is fought for political purposes, and World War II, as historians have come to understand, certainly had its politics, influenced by a desire to shape the postwar world.

Alternative III: Pursuit of Japanese Peace Feelers. During the summer, Japanese middle-level diplomats and military attachés in Switzerland and elsewhere in Europe approached intermediaries and American officials to try to move toward a surrender. . . .

... These peace feelers were, unfortunately, usually directed by Japanese officials through non-American intermediaries, and there was no evidence that these Japanese were acting on authority from their government. In fact, they were not. At best, they had loose approval from some peace forces within the sharply divided Japanese government, but the "Magic" intercepts (America's decoding of top-secret Japanese messages) revealed that the government in Tokyo could not agree on specific terms and that the militarists in the government wanted far more than a guarantee of the emperor. . . .

Had the A-bomb not been dropped and had the informal discussions ("back channels") in Switzerland continued for a few more months, while America pummeled Japan from the air and tightened its naval strangulation, perhaps a surrender with a guarantee of the emperor could have been secured before November. But that would have required Japan's powerful militarists to give up their hope for one more battle and sharply cut back their demands for a peace settlement. There is little evidence, only slim hope, that the militarists would have shown such tractability and so redefined honor and necessity unless other events, very painful events, intervened to help, or propel, them to accede to what Emperor Hirohito on 10 August justified as a surrender "to save the nation from destruction."

Alternative IV: Awaiting Soviet Entry into the War. No top American leader (Truman, Marshall, Byrnes, Stimson, Leahy, Forrestal, King, or Arnold) generally saw Soviet entry into the war as likely to be decisive *without* the A-bomb, before the scheduled invasion. Some analysts have cited—incorrectly, I think—two sources in order to reach a contrary conclusion: that Soviet entry was foreseen as likely to be decisive *without* the bomb. . . .

In retrospect, we can conclude that Soviet entry on 15 August (without the A-bomb) might well (maybe 20–30 percent probability) have produced a surrender before 1 November. But let me stress that this is a conclusion based on what we now know, not on what American leaders believed at the time. Had they closely, empathetically, and imaginatively read the intercepted and decoded Sato-Togo cables, perhaps American leaders might have anticipated the profound psychological *shock* that Soviet entry into the war produced among Japanese leaders, many of whom were hoping until that fateful day of 8 August 1945 that the Soviets might be entreated to remain outside the Pacific war. To distinguish psychological shock from military significance required subtlety and perhaps the willingness to speculate about the uneasiness and vulnerability of the enemy. No American leader—including Stimson, who had argued for a guarantee of the emperor—had the inclination, and perhaps the capacity, in the last weeks of July and the early days of August to engage in such analysis.

In retrospect, we can conclude that American leaders' unwillingness to delay the bomb's use and await Soviet entry, and then, if necessary, to delay the A-bombing for a longer period, may well have been a "missed opportunity." But such a possibility was not adequately understood in late July or early August. And delaying the A-bomb would have seemed a very risky, and unnecessary, gamble—far too risky for men not seeking to avoid its use. . . .

Alternative V: Bombing and Blockade—The Strategy of Siege Without the Atomic Bomb. Probably the most likely way of achieving a Japanese surrender before November 1945 (without the A-bomb) was by continuing the siege strategy of the heavy bombing of Japanese cities—the terror-bombing and the destruction of military and industrial installations—and the strangling naval blockade, including mining operations. . . .

[But these] did not *promise* that the November 1945 invasion would be unnecessary, or that bombing alone would make the decisive difference. For all understood that this bombing would occur *within* the context of the ongoing blockade, and that such linked devastation, while adding to the substance of Japan's defeat, did not automatically translate into Japan's surrender. Better than many later analysts, the Joint Chiefs well understood the gap between the conditions for defeat and the production of an actual surrender, because the chiefs knew that enemy leaders did not automatically surrender when defeat was both inevitable and possibly near.

If heavy bombing could contribute to surrender before the planned Kyushu invasion, however, and Arnold and the other Joint Chiefs hoped in mid-July that it would, they were neither assuming nor suggesting that they thought that the A-bomb was unnecessary. For Arnold, as for the other military chiefs before and even shortly after Hiroshima, heavy bombing was not a substitute—but a supplement—to the A-bomb. And the A-bomb was, in turn, for them, a supplement to heavy bombing. In their pre-Hiroshima thinking, conventional heavy bombing may even have seemed a more powerful contributor to ultimate victory than the A-bomb. . . .

Amid the strangling naval blockade, and without the A-bomb, perhaps the heavy bombing of Japanese cities in August, September, and October 1945 would have forced Japan to surrender before November. . . .

But the question remains, to be asked even after nearly a half-century, whether Japan's military leaders would have been willing to surrender, or whether they would have insisted on fighting at Kyushu and perhaps at Honshu, too? The movement from recognizing defeat to offering surrender can be jagged, and the process can be filled with self-deception, the quest for glory, and the faith in hope. Surrender, for many leaders, can be the most devastating failure—an event to be resisted at great cost to self and others. . . .

Had American leaders been willing to risk prolonging the war, there is no question that a naval blockade, as King later wrote, "would *in the course of time,* have starved the Japanese into submission through lack of oil, rice, medicine, and other materials." . . .

The siege strategy (without the A-bomb) might have produced the desired Japanese surrender by 1 November. The probabilities are not very high (maybe 25–30 percent) because the crucial problems, in this counterfactual history, are whether Japan's peace forces would have pushed ardently for surrender, whether the emperor would have intervened if his government had been divided, whether the militarists would have yielded to his sense of necessity, whether the government would have accepted defeat and moved to surrender, and whether Japanese military leaders in the field would have abided by the Tokyo government's order. That whole process would have involved many contingencies and have required the Japanese government to deal directly with the United States.

Single and Multiple Alternatives. There is good reason to have serious doubts that any *single* "alternative"—trying a non-combat demonstration, guaranteeing the emperor, pursuing peace feelers, awaiting Soviet entry, or continuing heavy conventional bombing and the blockade—would *alone* have produced surrender before November without the use of the A-bomb. But it does seem very likely, though certainly not definite, that a synergistic combination of guaranteeing the emperor, awaiting Soviet entry, and continuing the siege strategy would have ended the war in time to avoid the November invasion. And quite possibly, in the absence of a guarantee of the emperor, the impact of Soviet entry amid the strangling blockade and the heavy bombing of cities could have accomplished that goal without dropping the atomic bomb.

There was, then, more probably than not, a missed opportunity to end the war without the A-bomb and without the November invasion. And it is virtually definite, had the Kyushu invasion occurred with these other strategies, and without the A-bomb, that Japan would have surrendered well before the March 1946 invasion. Such conclusions, though emerging from the uneasy realm of counterfactual history, do place in question the contention that the atomic bomb was necessary. These conclusions challenge that concept of "necessity" and require that its meanings be carefully spelled out, that the implied costs be carefully expressed and analyzed, and that scholars and laypeople, in discussing these issues, carefully distinguish between what now seems known, what was known or believed before Hiroshima, and whether the pre-Hiroshima processes of decision making and analysis were adequate, on ethical and international-political grounds, to the important actions being taken.

To dwell upon the process of decision making alone would be unduly mechanistic, but it is certainly important to recognize that the A-bomb decision, contrary to some contentions, was not "carefully considered" and that the movement toward the November invasion, despite Truman's desires, was not fully and critically examined in his presence. He never sought "carefully" to consider the use of the A-bomb, nor did he feel any need to hold a meeting with advisers on whether it should be used, because he and they all assumed that it would be used. The process that he followed implemented that assumption. The question of the invasion was far more troubling to him. Had Japan not surrendered by the summer or early autumn, probably Truman would have returned to another session with his military advisers to discuss the necessity for the November invasion. At such a meeting, perhaps they would have served him better than they did in mid-June, at the special White House session, where they smoothed over earlier differences and thus presented the siege strategy with the Kyushu invasion of November as the only reasonable approach. . . .

World War II was a terribly bloody war. It killed many millions and maimed many more. It helped transform morality. It ushered in the atomic age. It dramatized the dark side of human capacity and prompted some to redefine "human nature." In America, the war—with its barbarism—was a helpful midwife in the shift in liberal sensibility from the optimistic rationality of John Dewey to the emphasis on the pessimistic irrationality of Reinhold Niebuhr. For some, the names of Buchenwald, Dachau, and Auschwitz would be joined, perhaps uneasily, to Dresden, Hamburg, and Tokyo, and occasionally also to Hiroshima and Nagasaki. They were not moral equivalents, because intentional genocide and intentional mass killing of some noncombatants were not morally identical, but all were powerful testimonials to the fact of massive deaths organized by nation-states, implemented by modern warriors, and endorsed by their civilian populations.

Had events turned out differently, Kyushu might be linked with Hiroshima and Nagasaki in modern memory as sites of mass nuclear death. For, had the war continued into the November invasion, some American leaders planned to use atomic weapons as tactical devices, directed against enemy soldiers, in that attack. General Marshall, earlier appalled by the prospect of killing non-combatants with nuclear weapons, was a strong supporter of this tactical-nuclear strategy. . . .

Ultimately, to understand, to rue, and even to deplore the use of the A-bomb are separable, and not necessarily linked, judgments. To fail to understand the reasons for the bombings of Hiroshima and Nagasaki is regrettable. To judge those actions by a set of ethical standards usually abandoned in World War II and sometimes revived in later years is appropriate. But to ascribe those moral standards to the leaders and citizens of the United States, or the other major powers, during World War II is to distort the history of that terrible war and to misinterpret the important decisions made in it.

FURTHER READING

Allen, Thomas B., and Norman Polmar. *Code-Name Downfall: The Secret Plan to Invade Japan and Why Truman Dropped the Bomb* (1995).
Alperovitz, Gar. *Atomic Diplomacy* (1965, 1985).
———. *The Decision to Use the Atomic Bomb* (1995).
Bernstein, Barton J. "The Atomic Bombings Reconsidered," *Foreign Affairs* 74 (1995): 135–142.
———. "Roosevelt, Truman and the Atomic Bomb, 1945: A Reinterpretation," *Political Science Quarterly* 90 (1975): 23–69.
———. "Understanding the Atomic Bomb and Japanese Surrender," *Diplomatic History* 19 (Spring 1995): 227–273.
———, ed. *The Atomic Bomb* (1975).
Boyer, Paul. *By the Bomb's Early Light* (1986).
Butow, Robert. *Japan's Decision to Surrender* (1954).
Feis, Herbert. *The Atomic Bomb and the End of World War II* (1966).
Frank, Richard B. *Downfall: The End of the Imperial Japanese Empire* (1999).
Fussell, Paul. *Thank God for the Atomic Bomb and Other Essays* (1988).
Hersey, John. *Hiroshima* (1946, 1985).
Hershberg, James. *James B. Conant and the Birth of the Nuclear Age* (1994).
Hogan, Michael J., ed. *Hiroshima in History and Memory* (1996).
Holloway, David. *Stalin and the Bomb* (1994).
Linenthal, Edward T., and Tom Englehart. *History Wars* (1996).
Maddox, Robert J. *Weapons for Victory* (1995).
Newman, Robert P. *Truman and the Hiroshima Cult* (1995).
Rhodes, Richard. *The Making of the Atomic Bomb* (1986).
Sherwin, Martin. *A World Destroyed* (1975, 1987, 2000).
Sigal, Leon. *Fighting to a Finish: The Politics of War Termination in the United States and Japan* (1988).
Skates, John R. *The Invasion of Japan: Alternative to the Bomb* (1994).
Takaki, Ronald. *Hiroshima* (1995).
Walker, J. Samuel. "The Decision to Drop the Bomb: A Historiographical Update," *Diplomatic History* 14 (1993): 97–114.
———. *Prompt and Utter Destruction* (1997).

See also Chapters 4, 5, and 12.

History and Memory:
The Legacy of World War II

World War II has had, and continues to have, an enormous impact on virtually all facets of American life. It has shaped the thoughts and actions of Americans since 1945 in much the same way the Civil War shaped American thoughts and actions for decades after 1865. This concluding chapter explores some of the areas and ways in which it has done so.

At least as important as the war itself in the shaping of American thoughts and values are the memories of the war that Americans came to hold in the years after 1945. As many of the authors in this chapter note, those memories differed substantially from what had actually occurred during the war, and with the belief system that had existed at that time. Indeed, issues that appear historically important about the war today differ substantially from issues considered important while the war was in progress. As with other major events in history, World War II has been consistently reinterpreted in light of changing postwar concerns. But contemporary Americans often disagree with each other on these reinterpretations. This has resulted in numerous conflicts over the war's meaning and "lessons." Changing and conflicting memories of the war have thus resulted in changing and conflicting meanings, making memory itself an important subject for historical study.

Below you will find excerpts from six recent historical works that explore in different ways questions of memory and meaning regarding World War II. Questions emerging from these essays are both numerous and extremely relevant to your lives today. How, for example, do your values differ from the values of the World War II era? How have these differences affected memories of World War II and the appropriate historical "lessons" of that conflict? How have historical events since 1945 affected such values, memories, and lessons? Are any of these lessons valid, or are they all distortions of the past? What, in other words, can history "teach" us, if anything? How exactly does the present affect memories of the past, and what is the proper relationship between the two? How does all of this relate to conflicting interpretations of World War II events and issues? In more general terms, what is the nature of historical inquiry and historical memory, what is the importance of each in your lives today, and what insights do these essays provide in helping you to answer these questions?

In the first essay, Michael C. C. Adams of Northern Kentucky University explores some of the distortions and mythmaking that have occurred as World War II became the "good war" in American memory. In the next two essays, David Kennedy of Stanford University and Alan Brinkley of Columbia University assess some of the consequences of the war as perceived today—Kennedy in a comprehensive sweep taken from the epilogue to his Pulitzer prize–winning history of the years 1929–1945, and Brinkley in terms of war-induced changes to the broad American liberal ideology. The final three essays examine specific wartime subjects that became matters of intense postwar concern and controversy: the wartime internment of Japanese Americans, the atomic bombing of Hiroshima and Nagasaki, and the U.S. response to the Nazi destruction of European Jewry. Each of these subjects has been explored in previous chapters (see Chapters 2, 9, and 11). The focus in these three essays is not on the events themselves, but on postwar controversy over their meaning and memory. In the fourth essay, Roger Daniels of the University of Cincinnati explores how and why Americans moved from wartime demands for internment of Japanese Americans to formal apologies and financial compensation by 1988 for what all admitted had been a grievous violation of American law and values. He also deals with similar threats to civil liberties that have arisen since World War II and the possibility of a future repetition of the events of 1942—a subject of obvious concern today in the aftermath of the events of September 11, 2001. In the fifth essay, Richard Kohn of the University of North Carolina examines the public uproar that arose in 1994–1995 over the Smithsonian Institution's plans to commemorate the fiftieth anniversary of the bombing of Hiroshima, focusing on conflicting memories and meanings that Americans had come to hold of that event as well as on the controversy itself and the numerous issues that were involved. In the sixth essay, Peter Novick of the University of Chicago interprets the emergence of intense interest and controversy over the Holocaust and U.S. wartime responses to that event as a product of postwar issues and concerns. In the process he questions what "lessons," if any, can be drawn from this or any historical event.

Postwar Mythmaking About World War II

MICHAEL C. C. ADAMS

All societies to some degree reinvent their pasts. This is not intended, not a pattern of deliberate lying; but too much has happened for it all to be retained in popular memory. Therefore, to make our understanding of history manageable, we try to retrieve from the huge clutter of the past only those events that seem to be particularly useful, interesting, or exciting. Usable historical events appear to offer helpful insights into how people of the past confronted problems or situations similar to our own.

Examples of functional and engaging past happenings are dramatic disasters, such as the sinking of the *Titanic,* which serve as warnings, or great triumphs, such as World War II. We tend to dwell on the victories because they make us feel good about ourselves. We see them as events that showcase our national strength, collective courage, idealism, and other desirable traits.

Sometimes we conjure up the past in such a way that it appears better than it really was. We forget ugly things we did and magnify the good things. This is wishful

Excerpt from Michael C. C. Adams, *The Best War Ever: America and World War II,* 1–2, 4–17, 19. © 1993 by copyright holder. Reprinted with permission of the Johns Hopkins University Press.

thinking, the desire to retell our past not as it was but as we would like it to have been. If the past is remolded too drastically, it ceases to be real history. It becomes what we call myth, or folklore, instead. One task of the historian is to try to keep our knowledge of the past as complete and accurate as possible so that our popular version does not depart too far from reality. If history becomes too mythologized, it may lose its value as a tool for understanding our course as a society. Adolf Hitler presented a deeply distorted view of Germany's history and role in the twentieth century. When this was accepted by his people, they embarked on a course leading to national disaster.

The influence of historians is, however, limited. Because they must be comprehensive in their treatment of the past and cannot simply choose to highlight the exciting and dramatic, their work often strikes people as boring and tedious. It cannot compete with modern vehicles of folklore history: film and television. In addition, historians, too, are victims of the immenseness of the past: they can never read, digest, and describe all there is to know about an event or character (there are one million documents in the Lyndon Baines Johnson Library alone). They must be highly selective in what they choose to present to us, so their picture is incomplete, a distortion to some degree. And as they are creatures of their time and place, members of the society as well as professional observers of it, their retelling of history will be molded partly by the same biases and constraints that shape the popular view. Then, through repetition, people come to believe that this partial portrait is the whole landscape of history, and what is forgotten will be thought never to have existed.

Such a process happened with World War II, which has been converted over time from a complex, problematic event, full of nuance and debatable meaning, to a simple, shining legend of the Good War. For many, including a majority of survivors from the era, the war years have become America's golden age, a peak in the life of society when everything worked out and the good guys definitely got a happy ending. It was a great war. For Americans it was the best war ever.

This was the film age, and the script could have been written in Hollywood. The original villains were the Nazis and the Fascists, many of whom obligingly dressed in black. They bullied the weak-willed democratic politicians who tried to buy them off, which gave us the word *appeasement* as a catchall term of contempt for anyone who suggests a diplomatic solution to potential international aggression. The bad guys then took the first rounds, driving opponent after opponent out of the fighting. The Americans gave material aid to their cousins, the British, who finally fought pluckily with their backs to the wall, until the United States was brought into the fighting by the treacherous Japanese, who crippled the Pacific fleet at Pearl Harbor.

For a while, it looked grim all over, but then the Allies fought back, their victories culminating in the unconditional surrender of all enemy nations, who were then made over in our image. America emerged from the war strong, united, prosperous, and the unrivaled and admired leader of the free world.

In the search for a usable past, Americans increasingly return to this best war ever. Its image, as a time of glorious success, sparkles in the imagination. . . .

The era has become a benchmark of excellence, not only in things military but in all areas of life. We think that products were made better and lasted longer. Kids were supposedly better behaved and learned more. Listening to some contemporary critics of education, one is led to believe that college students of the thirties and forties walked daily with Plato and Thomas Jefferson. And families loved each other more;

in a recent biography of President George Bush, Joe Hyams asserted that "Bush's generation seems to have had more respect for their marriage vows than young people today." Bush was a naval pilot, and Hyams would also have us believe that all the airmen on his carrier were happy warriors who, despite having flown over fifty missions, "were always vying with one another to see who could get in the most."

In creating a usable past, we seek formulas to apply in solving today's problems. Americans believe that World War II proved one rule above all others. It goes like this. By 1938 at the latest it was clear that Hitler was a bully bent on world domination. Britain and France should have stood up to him at the Munich conference (September 1938), when he demanded parts of Czechoslovakia as the price for peace. By their failure, World War II was made bloodier than it might have been. Conclusion: it is usually better to fight than to talk.

The political commentator Andy Rooney said that perhaps Hitler's worst crime was to convince Americans that international opponents are invariably bullies who must be met with military force. Admiral Gene LaRocque, like Rooney a veteran and a dissenter from the mainstream, said that "World War Two has warped our view of how we look at things today. We see things in terms of that war, which in a sense was a good war. But the twisted memory of it encourages the men of my generation to be willing, almost eager, to use military force anywhere in the world."

Undoubtedly, the memory of Munich was partly responsible for the decision to use force rather than continued sanctions in the Persian Gulf crisis of 1990–91. President Bush took along a history of World War II as his reading material on Air Force One. He compared Saddam Hussein to Hitler, the Iraqi occupation of Kuwait to a German SS operation, and the UN alliance to a new world order, a phrase popular with both sides in World War II. Newspapers and readers' columns were full of warnings about appeasement. . . .

In 1990–91 we came close to believing that we could wish upon a war: if we applied the magic formula of an allied war effort against an aggressive dictator, we could again have national unanimity of purpose, renewed world prestige, and a return of the leaping prosperity that was a hallmark of American life during the best war ever. Some people wanted to turn the clock back badly enough to believe the *World's* claim that a very old Hitler (he would have been 111 years of age in 1990) had been captured by U.S. forces on his way to Iraq. . . .

The idea that World War II was the best war America had is not entirely off the mark; like any enduring myth, it rests on a solid core of credible argument. America cemented its final rise to world power with relatively light losses: about 300,000 Americans died; a further 1 million were wounded, of whom 500,000 were seriously disabled. Tragic as these figures are, they are dwarfed by those for other belligerents. The Japanese lost 2.3 million, Germany about 5.6 million, China perhaps as many as 10 million, and the Soviet Union a staggering 20 million. Put another way, the death rate in the American Civil War of 1861–65 was 182 per ten thousand population. For World War II, the proportion of Americans killed was 30 per ten thousand.

Of the major belligerents, the United States was alone in enjoying a higher standard of living as a result of the war. Following the lean Depression years, the gross national product for 1940 was $97 billion. By 1944 it had reached $190 billion. The average gross weekly wage rose from $25.20 in 1940 to $43.39 in 1945, an increase of 72 percent. The United States was unique among the principal combatants in being neither invaded nor bombed, and most people, in or out of uniform, never saw a fighting front. As a result, the war was for many a prosperous, exciting, even safe change from the "ruined and colorless landscape of the Depression," as Russell Baker, a writer who grew up in the 1930s, termed the decade. . . . World War II for a time gave Americans a sense of belonging, of community, as they were caught up in the war fever.

Most of us still agree that nazism was an evil so monstrous that the war in Europe had to be fought. "Unlike Vietnam—the war that dominated our children's lives," said 1940s veteran Roger Hilsman, "World War II was a 'good' war. Hitler was a maniacal monster, and young as we were, we saw this and understood its implications." Hilsman was correct about the need to fight. Yet he was writing with the benefit of hindsight. This is problematic, and it gives us a window through which to begin exploring what is wrong with the myth.

At the time, many Americans didn't fully understand the threat of Hitler; they wanted to beat the Japanese first because they hated them more (a 1942 poll showed 66 percent of Americans wanting the Pacific war to have priority). The Pacific campaigns were fought with a mutual ferocity that culminated in the Japanese kamikaze attacks and the Allied incendiary and atomic bombings of Japan's major cities. Many Americans of the war generation like to divorce the atom bombings from the conflict, seeing them as the curtain raiser on the nuclear age rather than the last act of our best war. But they were in fact the final destructive episode in a fight that, as historian John Ellis said, was won and lost by brute force.

Here is the point. To make World War II into the best war ever, we must leave out the area bombings and other questionable aspects while exaggerating the good things. The war myth is distorted not so much in what it says as in what it doesn't say. Combat in World War II was rarely glamorous. It was so bad that the breakdown rate for men consistently in action for twenty-eight days ran as high as 90 percent. Soldiers of all nations performed deeds of courage, but they also shot prisoners, machine-gunned defenseless enemies in the water or in parachutes, and raped women, including their own military personnel. And they had nightmares afterward about what they had seen and done. About 25 percent of the men still in the hospital from the war are psychiatric cases.

Posttraumatic stress disorder no more originated with Vietnam than did napalm. This terrible weapon, a jellied gasoline that burns its victims, was invented by American scientists during World War II and used in all major combat zones, along with phosphorous, another flesh-searing load for bombs and shells. On all battlefronts where there were perceived ethnic differences, the war was fought without many rules. Russians and Germans butchered each other indiscriminately. The Japanese abused Allied prisoners and were in turn often seen as subhuman "gooks."

Contrary to the popular myth that dumps all negatives on Vietnam, the worst war we had, there was significant discrimination in the armed forces during World War II. Many soldiers didn't know what the war was about, and some resented their war-long terms of service, feeling they were doing everybody's fighting. The majority of returning soldiers got no parades. James Jones, a veteran, noted that wounded men repatriated to the United States were treated as though diseased, and people rushed to wash their hands after greeting them. Civilians feared that the GIs would think the country owed them a living, while veterans felt that "when you come back they treat you just like scum." Said this anonymous soldier: "If you ever get the boys all together they will probably kill all the civilians." . . .

After the initial post–Pearl Harbor bursts of unity and willing sacrifice, Americans showed the average amount of selfishness and cupidity. Politics became politics again. The administration collected gossip about General Douglas MacArthur's sex life to use if he ran for president on the Republican ticket. And innuendos about homosexuality helped to force Sumner Welles out of the State Department when it was decided he was too pro-Soviet. Labor-management disputes continued. Merchant seamen, taking badly needed supplies to the troops on Guadalcanal, turned back when they were refused extra pay. An elderly gentleman on a bus in Viola, Kentucky, home of a munitions plant, hit a female passenger with his umbrella when she said she hoped the war wouldn't end until she had worked long enough to buy a refrigerator.

The war massively altered the face of American society. Small farmers and storeowners went under, while big businesses became great corporations. Fed by the emergency, the federal bureaucracy mushroomed from 1 million to 3.8 million. Most people paid income tax for the first time. Millions of Americans moved, usually to the cities, which experienced considerable racial tension and some violence as ethnic groups were thrown together. The stress of social change also showed up in a record number of hospital admissions for patients suffering from psychoses. Family dislocation came to be a concern: with fathers in the armed forces and mothers working, kids seemed to go wild, and people worried about juvenile delinquency. In a 1946 opinion poll, a majority of adults said adolescent behavior had degenerated during the war; only 9 percent thought it had improved. And people may now think that marriages were more sacred back then, but marital strain led to a record high 600,000 divorces in 1946.

Americans may have been better educated then, too, but a 1942 poll showed that 59 percent of them couldn't locate China, a major ally, on the map. In the same year, Philip Wylie, a disillusioned federal official, published *Generation of Vipers,* a book cataloguing America's ills. The list is startlingly modern. Young people, he said, could no longer think because education failed to challenge them—and nobody flunked. They listened to radio and watched movies instead of reading books. Teachers who were intellectually demanding got fired. Consumerism and uncritical boosterism were pervasive, making discussion of social issues like pollution, urban congestion, drug addiction, and materialism impossible. Many of Wylie's strictures were ignored at the time and have been forgotten since.

The selective process by which only positive aspects of the war received mainstream attention began during the conflict itself—one of the most censored events in modern history. Every nation rigorously edited the news. No Japanese or American newspaper, for example, carried a single report of atrocities by their own military, though there were in fact many. The beating and even killing of African-American soldiers by other U.S. service personnel also went undisclosed. Canadian correspondent Charles Lynch spoke for the whole international press corps when he said of the reporters: "We were cheerleaders." Perhaps, he thought, this was necessary for national survival in a total war. But "it wasn't good journalism. It wasn't journalism at all."

The U.S. military censored all reports from the front, and those who broke the rules were sent home. In America, the Office of Censorship vetted public and private communications, while the Office of Facts and Figures, and later the Office of War Information, published propaganda in support of the war effort. The result was a cleaned-up, cosmetically-enhanced version of reality. The war, said writer Fletcher Pratt, was reported like a polite social function. . . . When Walter Cronkite filed a report that the Eighth Air Force had blindly bombed Germany through solid cloud cover, challenging the myth that all American bombing was pinpoint accurate and hit only military targets, his copy was held up. A combat photographer who recorded the murder of SS soldiers by their American guards was told the film couldn't be screened because of technical difficulties. And when Eric Sevareid tried to broadcast descriptions of faceless, limbless boys in military hospitals, the censors told him to write about new miracle drugs and medical instruments instead.

But the news wasn't manipulated only by the censors. John Steinbeck, a tough-minded writer who exposed human misery during the Depression, admitted that as a war reporter he deliberately slanted his stories to omit anything that might shock civilians. He didn't report on the rotten conditions suffered by the infantry or on homosexual activity in the military.

Censorship in the interests of military security, even protection of civilian morale, has its purpose. But the image-making went beyond this. Generals, even whole branches of the service like the paratroops and the Marine Corps, employed platoons of public relations officers and advertising agencies to make sure they looked good. General Douglas MacArthur was a notorious publicity hound. During the first months of 1942, when the Japanese were smashing his defenses in the Philippines, he still found time to publish 140 press releases. Manufacturing an enemy body count is usually associated with Vietnam, but for one two-year period in the Pacific war, MacArthur reported 200,000 Japanese killed for 122 Allied losses. After he was driven from the Philippines, the general became famous for the line, "I shall return." But this sound bite was manufactured from his speeches by staffers. When he did return, the dramatic scenes of him wading ashore were filmed several times on different beaches to get the right effect.

Similarly, when Eisenhower and his generals went ashore in Normandy after the D-Day landings, fifty cameramen were on hand and were told which profiles to shoot. Eisenhower saw reporters as part of the army and expected them to report the news as loyal soldiers and subordinates, not as independent observers. "Public opinion wins wars," he said. "I have always considered as quasi-staff officers, correspondents accredited to my headquarters." . . .

The public lapped up the images. This was a media generation; it had come of age with talking pictures and radio. By 1940 radio was a billion-dollar industry, and twenty-eight million families owned sets. Commercials, with their snappy pace and upbeat messages, already dominated format and programming. The public's concentration span and ability to tolerate any but optimistic messages were being eroded. To meet this challenge the print media responded with glossy magazines and the *Reader's Digest,* whose circulation jumped in the 1930s from a quarter of a million to seven million. The *Digest,* like the commercials, offered short, easily digested concepts, laced with a philosophy of optimism. Gloomy endings, skepticism, and complexity were out. The media age also spawned comic books, whose superheroes further simplified the issues and made them black or white. By 1942, twelve million comic books a month were sold, one-third to people over eighteen. They were the favorite reading of the private soldier.

Towering above all other popular entertainments were the movies. They had allowed audiences a fantasy release from the Depression, and now they glamorized the war for them. Movie attendance, around sixty million per week in the 1930s, rose to an all-time peak of ninety million during the war. Hollywood made more than 300 feature films, over 40 percent of them musicals—like Irving Berlin's *This Is the Army* and Danny Kaye in *Up in Arms*. Movies like these offered a winning combination of escapism and toe-tapping patriotism. Hollywood, more than any other agency, made this into the best war ever. Daffy Duck got drafted, Donald Duck told filmgoers how saving would beat the Axis, and Bugs Bunny sold war bonds.

The censors hardly needed to tell the film producers that war movies should showcase American heroism and patriotism and that the enemy must be cruel, devious, and unprincipled. The infantry platoon became America's melting pot, where an Irish boy from Brooklyn, a Texas sharecropper, a fresh-faced midwesterner, a Chicago Italian, and even an intellectual all found their Americanism. When an American was killed, it was quick and painless (except for blacks or Hispanics, who might die in a more ghastly way). Wounds were clean and healed well. Grisly endings or lingering deaths were usually saved for the enemy. . . .

Ernie Pyle, arguably one of America's top war reporters, admitted that at the front he lost focus on the war: amid the muck and death, the bits and pieces didn't add up to a grand, proud whole. He had to read the magazines from America to get the "true" picture, to recapture the glamor and excitement. "Only in the magazine from America could I catch the *real* spirit of the war"(italics added). For much of his time as a war reporter, Pyle tried to impose the cheerful, sanitized media version of war upon reality. In his reports from North Africa and Sicily, all the infantry were gung ho, especially the wounded, who "were anxious to return to their outfits" at the front. (Actually, American wounded were rarely returned to their original units but were funneled into other formations as needed, where they were treated as rookies, which was deeply demoralizing to these veteran soldiers.) . . .

Yet try as he might, Pyle could not avoid the actuality of misery and death in war, which eventually became sickeningly real for him. Tired and demoralized, he tried to go home. But he was too popular. Reassigned to the Pacific war, his reports became more bitter, more honest. He no longer got on well with the troops, whom he thought were being brutalized by the slaughter of the Japanese. Finally, an unhappy and disillusioned man, he was killed by a sniper.

Pyle had the integrity to ultimately confront the full nature of war, but most Americans didn't have to. Like Walter Mitty, the protagonist of James Thurber's 1941 story about a hen-pecked husband who makes life tolerable by fantasizing that he is a hero, they could still dream large dreams about the glamour of war without ever having to challenge their assumptions.

The imposition of the media construct upon reality continued after the war. . . .

The star most associated with World War II is John Wayne. Through many film roles he has come to epitomize the Hollywood version of the American fighting man, even though he was never a combat soldier. *Sands of Iwo Jima,* made in 1949, was perhaps the best of the genre. The movie had the integrity to suggest that Wayne's character, Sergeant Stryker, was not a perfect man. His devotion to the military cost him his marriage, and he could not communicate with his son. But the film continued the erosion of reality about the nature of combat. Stryker was a man's man who molded boys into marines: in battle, they became seasoned veterans and mature adults who knew what they were fighting for and had an infinite strength denied to their devious yellow enemy.

There were dissonant voices. The film *A Walk in the Sun* (1946) tried to show the confusion and random butchery of combat. *Let There Be Light* (1946) was a documentary dealing with psychologically damaged veterans. But these films did not have wide audiences. Veterans like Norman Mailer in *The Naked and the Dead* (1948) and James Jones in *The Thin Red Line* (1962) wrote starkly of the war, its brutality, confusion, insensitivity, the political ambitions of generals, and the sexual undertones inherent in the killing process. But their novels were not read by the mainstream, and the authors tended to be written off as the intellectual fringe, if not actually psychotics and sex perverts. Many would not read their works because they contained "bad language," even though it is an unfortunate truth of military life that the most important noun, adjective, and verb is *fuck*.

By 1962 at the latest, when Hollywood produced *The Longest Day,* its epic tribute to the D-Day landings, the movie replica had completely displaced the original. Films copied earlier films to get the "authentic" period look. For example, the film *December 7th,* made in 1943, used studio sets to recreate aspects of the attack on Pearl Harbor. But when *Winds of War* was made in 1983, the earlier film was assumed to be actual combat footage, and so the substitute reality was studiously copied. People went to the cinema to see what the war had been like, and the stars became synonymous with the generals they played. George C. Scott *was* George Patton. A real-life hero such as Audie Murphy, America's most decorated soldier in World War II, when he couldn't make the transition to the screen as a film hero, was remembered largely as a failed movie actor. The war had become a part of American folklore, captured forever in a manageable format and with a message acceptable to the public. As an advertisement for a John Wayne reproduction army pistol put it, "from *Sands of Iwo Jima* to *The Green Berets* to *The Longest Day,* he captured our essence. Our Strength. Our values."

No group believed more fervently that this was the best war ever than the young men who enthusiastically left for Vietnam believing they were following in the footsteps of their WWII film fathers. A blue-collar veteran from Boston said he went to "kill a Commie for Jesus Christ and John Wayne." Ron Kovic, a soldier who became partially paralyzed in Vietnam, said in his memoir *Born on the Fourth of July* that *Sands of Iwo Jima* so moved him as a youth that he cried each time he heard the music from it. Wayne "became one of my heroes." Some Vietnam veterans realized that in Vietnam they had discovered the reality of war and that, on a day-to-day basis, it was not much different from what their fathers' generation had endured in the Pacific during World War II. They understood that the movies had misled them about what war would be like. Others continued to think of the films as the way war really was in the 1940s and blamed themselves for having fought a "bad war" in Vietnam. They forgot that media coverage of Vietnam was more candid and that therefore our view of the war was inevitably more realistic, less cosmetic. . . .

Two recent public figures most closely represent the aura of the Good War era: George Bush, a WWII combat veteran, and Ronald Reagan, a film actor who came to embody America's good feelings about the golden years of the 1940s. Reagan's immense popularity as president rested partly on his remarkable talent to create a partial reality based on wishful thinking. This engagement with image-making began early in Reagan's radio career, when he made up the play-by-play for baseball games neither he nor the audience could see. His exciting illusions proved more popular than the real games. Though he saw no combat in World War II, and indeed was only out of the country once before he became president, Reagan later seemed to believe that he was a veteran who had been present at the U.S. opening of a Nazi concentration camp and that he did top secret work on the atom bomb project (all he actually did was work in Hollywood on the voice-over for a film made to help pilots locate their bombing targets in Japan). He told anecdotes about combat situations in the war that he believed were real, yet all of these scenarios were from films he had either worked on or had seen.

He is the ultimate symbol of the movie version becoming the reality. Thus, Reagan related the story of the bomber pilot on a doomed plane who refused to parachute because a young wounded gunner couldn't evacuate the ship. The pilot went down cradling the youngster's head in his lap until the very end. The story is obviously from a film, because, since all the men on the plane died, we cannot know what they did at the very end; the only witnesses are those who have seen the movie. Yet Reagan refused to accept that the story was a fiction. Because he had seen WWII films in which black and white soldiers fought side by side, Reagan insisted that the WWII armed forces were racially integrated. In fact, they were rigidly segregated; it was only in 1948, three years after the war ended, that President Truman ordered racial mixing in military units to begin.

Even Reagan's Star Wars project, the strategic defense initiative aimed at putting weapons in space to knock out incoming hostile missiles, was inspired partly by a film he acted in during World War II; *Murder in the Air*, made in 1940, used an "inertia projector," a primitive Star Wars device, to strike enemy planes from the skies. Not unexpectedly, SDI as projected is not considered feasible by most experts because it is not rooted in reality.

Reagan's deep belief in the legitimacy of the movie version of American history made him a living symbol for many Americans of their best war ever and the magic formula for success that they thought was the special possession of the 1940s generation. He was the final embodiment of the movie star as war hero. "He's a real, live hero whose impact transcends his overwhelming success at the polling booths," said one young supporter, commenting on Reagan's success in the 1984 election. . . .

The situation of the belly gunner on a B-17 Flying Fortress provides a small but illuminating example of how the mythmaking process has damaged our ability to seriously comprehend the WWII experience. To protect the vulnerable underside of the aircraft against attack by enemy fighter planes, a gunner was stationed in a bubblelike plexiglass revolving ball turret protruding from the bottom of the ship. He was literally suspended in space, along with his machine guns, sealed off from the rest of the crew.

In his cramped turret, the gunner could not even wear his parachute. Worse still, should the electrical system of the plane malfunction or be shot out by enemy fire, he would not be able to open the turret doors. If, at the same time, the hydraulic system failed and the landing wheels could not be lowered or were shot away, the ship would have to make a belly flop or pancake landing, coming down on the turret and smashing the gunner to pulp. He would know exactly what was going to happen to him until the moment of impact, one of the most grotesque deaths one can imagine. The nature of these terrible deaths was kept from the home front audience of the war, which was most likely to see the belly gunner in an ad for Talon slide fasteners, useful to both the housewife and the flyer. Here, he was depicted as a hell-bent-for-leather hero, raining lead from his machine guns. This commercial was captioned, "Giving 'Em Hell from a 'Goldfish Bowl,' " as though fighting your war from a fish tank was a magnificent experience.

In 1945, veteran and poet Randall Jarrell tried to tell America what it was like to hang suspended six miles above the earth with only the protection of a plexiglass bubble. In his poem "The Death of the Ball Turret Gunner," the gunner is hit by flak, flying shrapnel from an anti-aircraft shell burst. The impact turns his body into mush: "they washed me out of the turret with a hose." One of my undergraduate students, imbued with the myth that every WWII soldier got a flag, a parade, and if necessary, a decent burial, wrote an essay on this poem in 1990. He wrote, "This man's death was not overlooked. I feel this man probably was praised on his burial for his services." The student transformed the awful, lonely, anonymous fate of the gunner into a hero's death, even though there wasn't a body for the honorable burial the student envisioned.

Steven Spielberg provided the final touch in one of his *Amazing Stories,* "The Mission," aired on television in the 1985–86 season. In harshly realistic detail, Spielberg recreated the nightmare scenario: the turret jammed and the landing gear shot away. The gunner will die, and we grieve with him on the flight home. But wait. One crewman is a doodler; on a sketchpad he draws the Fortress, then crayons in new wheels with candy-striped legs. Miraculously, these wheels appear on the plane, and it lands safely. Surely, this was the best war ever.

The World the War Made

DAVID M. KENNEDY

America was officially at peace [on September 2, 1945], and so was Japan. Elsewhere in Asia peace remained elusive. The war in that region had been more than a struggle between the United States and Japan, or even between China and Japan. The conflict also marked the penultimate chapter in the history of Western colonialism in Asia that had lasted since the fifteenth century. "It almost seems that the Japs were a necessary evil in order to break down the old colonial system," Franklin Roosevelt had told a journalist in 1942. From that perspective, it might be said that Japan had won the war

---

From David M. Kennedy, *Freedom From Fear: The American People in Depression and War, 1929–1945,* 853–858. Copyright © 1999 by David M. Kennedy. Used by permission of Oxford University Press.

after all, finishing the work begun with Admiral Togo's victory over the Russians at Tsushima Strait in 1905, a victory that Nagumo had so vividly memorialized when his aircraft carriers descended on Pearl Harbor flying Togo's old battle flag. If a major Japanese war aim had been to evict the Westerners and build "Asia for the Asians," that aim had been accomplished as early as 1942 and was never effectively reversed. The Philippines proceeded on schedule toward independence on July 4, 1946. India wrested its nationhood from Britain in 1947; Ceylon (Sri Lanka) and Burma (Myanmar), in 1948. In other countries, where the old colonial powers tried to reassert their authority, the final chapter of the struggle to rid Asia of Western dominance took longer to write and was often written in blood, but written it was. Rebellion against the reimposition of Dutch rule went on for four years in the East Indies after 1945, until Indonesia established its independence at last in 1949. Malaya slipped the British harness only in 1957. Japan's former colony of Korea remained divided for the remainder of the century, sucking the United States into a second Asian war within half a decade of the ceremony on the *Missouri*'s deck. The French waged a futile struggle to recolonize Indochina until they gave up in 1954, leaving a messy legacy that eventually precipitated America's third twentieth-century Asian war in Vietnam.

As for China, whose friendship had been the great goal of American diplomacy before 1941, a friendship deemed so valuable as to set the United States on the collision course with Japan that led to Pearl Harbor, there the results were peculiarly ironic, and not a little bitter. Mao Tse-tung finally defeated Chiang Kai-shek in 1949. The new Communist regime openly declared its hostility to the United States and committed itself to force-marching China into the modern era. Everywhere in Asia it was clear by century's end that World War II had set the stage for the definite finale of a five-century saga of Western imperial hegemony.

In Europe the end of World War II almost instantly introduced a new era of conflict with a martial name of its own, the Cold War. Of the traditional great European powers, France was humbled, Britain exhausted, Germany demolished and divided. Hitler had brewed a catastrophe so vast that for his own people it seemed to sunder the web of time itself. Germans would call the moment of their surrender on May 8, 1945, *Stunde null*—zero hour, when history's clock must be made to start anew. Stalin closed his fist over eastern Europe and dared the Western powers to break his grip. Counting on the resurgence of traditional American isolationism, he anticipated having a free hand with which to harvest the fruits of victory in the vast domain he had conquered at the price of more than twenty million Soviet dead.

The Americans surprised him, and perhaps themselves, by taking up Stalin's challenge, inaugurating the four and a half decades of Soviet-American confrontation known as the Cold War, the unwanted war baby conceived in the fragile marriage of convenience that was the Grand Alliance. Who could have predicted that the nation that had repudiated the League of Nations in 1920 would emerge as the foremost champion of the United Nations a generation later? That the Congress that had passed five neutrality statutes in the 1930s would vote overwhelmingly to make the United States a charter member of the North Atlantic Treaty Organization in 1949? That the country that had so reluctantly armed itself in 1941 would become a virtual garrison state in the postwar decades? Or that the people who had refused asylum to Europe's Jews in their hour of greatest peril would welcome some seven hundred thousand refugees in the decade and a half after 1945?

World War II led directly to the Cold War and ended a century and a half of American isolationism. Yet future historians may well conclude that the Cold War that came to an end in 1989 was neither the most surprising nor the most important or durable of the war's legacies for American diplomacy. In the long sweep of time, America's half-century-long ideological, political, and military face-off with the Soviet Union may appear far less consequential than America's leadership in inaugurating an era of global economic interdependence. In this dimension, too, there was much that was surprising. Who could have foretold that the nation that had flintily refused to cancel the Europeans' war debts in the 1920s would establish the World Bank in 1945 and commit $17 billion to the Marshall Plan in 1948? That the country that had embraced the Fordney-McCumber and Smoot-Hawley tariffs would take the lead in establishing the General Agreement on Tariffs and Trade, and later the World Trade Organization? That the government that had torpedoed the London Economic Conference in 1933 would create the International Monetary Fund in 1944? That isolationist America would step forward to midwife the European Union, another war baby whose maturation muted centuries of old-world rivalries and symbolized the international regime that by century's end came to be called "globalization"? And who could deny that globalization—the explosion in world trade, investment, and cultural mingling—was the signature and lasting international achievement of the postwar era, one likely to overshadow the Cold War in its long-term historical consequences?

Americans could not see that future clearly in 1945, but they could look back over the war they had just waged. They might have reflected with some discomfort on how slowly they had awakened to the menace of Hitlerism in the isolationist 1930s; on how callously they had barred the door to those seeking to flee from Hitler's Europe; on how heedlessly they had provoked Japan into a probably avoidable war in a region where few American interests were at stake; on how they had largely fought with America's money and machines and with Russia's men, had fought in Europe only late in the day, against a foe mortally weakened by three years of brutal warfare in the east, had fought in the Pacific with a bestiality they did not care to admit; on how they had profaned their constitution by interning tens of thousands of citizens largely because of their race; on how they had denied most black Americans a chance to fight for their country; on how they had sullied their nation's moral standards with terror bombing in the closing months of the war; on how their leaders' stubborn insistence on unconditional surrender had led to the incineration of hundreds of thousands of already defeated Japanese, first by fire raids, then by nuclear blast; on how poorly Franklin Roosevelt had prepared for the postwar era, how foolishly he had banked on goodwill and personal charm to compose the conflicting interests of nations, how little he had taken his countrymen into his confidence, even misled them, about the nature of the peace that was to come; on how they had abandoned the reforming agenda of the New Deal years to chase in wartime after the sirens of consumerism; on how they alone among warring peoples had prospered, emerging unscathed at home while 405,399 American soldiers, sailors, marines, and airmen had died. Those men were dignified in death by their service, but they represented proportionately fewer military casualties than in any other major belligerent country. Beyond the war's dead and wounded and their families, few Americans had been touched by the staggering sacrifices and unspeakable anguish that the war had visited upon millions of other people around the globe.

That would have been a reasonably accurate account of America's role in World War II, but it did not describe the war that Americans remembered. In the mysterious zone where history mixes with memory to breed national myths, Americans after 1945 enshrined another war altogether. It was the "good war," maybe the last good war, maybe, given the advent of nuclear weapons, the last war that would ever be fought by huge armies and fully mobilized industrial economies in a protracted contest of attrition. The future of warfare, if there was one, lay not on the traditional battlefield but in cities held hostage by weapons of mass destruction that the war had spurred American science to create.

Americans remembered World War II as a just war waged by a peaceful people aroused to anger only after intolerable provocation, a war stoically endured by those at home and fought in far-away places by brave and wholesome young men with dedicated women standing behind them on the production lines, a war whose justice and necessity were clinched by the public revelations of Nazi genocide in 1945, a war fought for democracy and freedom and, let the world beware, fought with unstinting industrial might and unequaled technological prowess—an effort equivalent, one journalist wrote at war's end, to "building two Panama Canals every month, with a fat surplus to boot."

The dimensions of the surpluses that rested in America's hands at war's end were staggering. "The United States," said Winston Churchill in 1945, "stand at this moment at the summit of the world." Americans commanded fully half of the entire planet's manufacturing capacity and generated more than half of the world's electricity. America owned two-thirds of the world's gold stocks and half of all its monetary reserves. The United States produced two times more petroleum than the rest of the world combined; it had the world's largest merchant fleet, a near monopoly on the emerging growth industries of aerospace and electronics, and, for a season at least, an absolute monopoly on the disquieting new technology of atomic power.

The war had shaken the American people loose and shaken them up, freed them from a decade of economic and social paralysis and flung them around their country into new regions and new ways of life. It was a war that so richly delivered on all the promises of the wartime advertisers and politicians that it nearly banished the memory of the Depression. At the end of the Depression decade, nearly half of all white families and almost 90 percent of black families had still lived in poverty. One in seven workers remained unemployed. By war's end unemployment was negligible. In the ensuing quarter century the American economy would create some twenty million new jobs, more than half of them filled by women. Within less than a generation of the war's end, the middle class, defined as families with annual incomes between three and ten thousand dollars, more than doubled. By 1960 the middle class included almost two-thirds of all Americans, most of whom owned their own homes, unprecedented achievements for any modern society. The birth dearth of the Depression years gave way to the baby boom, as young couples confident about their futures filled the Republic's empty cradles with some fifty million bawling babies in the decade and a half after the war. The social and economic upheavals of wartime laid the groundwork for the civil rights movement as well as for an eventual revolution in women's status.

Small wonder that Americans chose to think of it as the good war. It was a war that had brought them as far as imagination could reach, and beyond, from the ordeal of the Great Depression and had opened apparently infinite vistas to the future. The huge expenditures for weaponry clinched the Keynesian doctrine that government spending could underwrite prosperity and inaugurated a quarter century of the most robust economic growth in the nation's history—an era of the very grandest expectations.

The young Americans who went off to war in the twilight years of the New Deal came home to a different country. By 1950, for the first time in history, a majority of Americans were women, thanks to battle deaths, improvements in maternal health care, and the paucity of immigrants in the preceding generation. Because of the birth slump in the prewar decade, the statistically typical thirty-year-old American woman in 1950 was four years older than her statistically abstracted male counterpart on the eve of the Depression. She had been born in the aftermath of the Great War, spent her childhood in the prosperous twenties, and became a teenager in the year Franklin Roosevelt became president. The Depression had blighted her youth, but as she entered adulthood the country was mobilizing for war and she had found a good job, not in a defense plant but in a clerical position that she had left at war's end and intended one day to take up again. She had married a veteran, a young man who had gone to war believing it was just and necessary and came back still believing so. The GI Bill had sent him to college, and he was on his way up. On his income of almost $3,445 a year they were flush beyond their parents' dreams, or their own Depression-era dreams either, for that matter. They bought a freshly built suburban tract home with room enough for their three children. Their parents talked about the days of outhouses and kerosene lanterns, but their place was plumbed and wired and fitted out with every kind of modern appliance: telephone, radio, refrigerator, washing machine, and the newest gadget of all, television.

They had cast their first presidential ballot for Franklin Roosevelt, in 1944, and their second for his scrappy little successor, Harry Truman, in 1948, though they were uneasy that Truman's party was promising at last to secure full civil rights for Negroes. The Russians had just exploded their own atomic bomb, and the Communists had recently taken power in China. Somehow the good war had not settled things to the degree that Roosevelt had promised. They had inherited a new world, and a brave one too. Like all worlds, it held its share of peril as well as promise.

The War Transformed American Liberalism

ALAN BRINKLEY

Few would disagree that World War II changed the world as profoundly as any event of this century, perhaps any century. What is less readily apparent, perhaps, is how profoundly the war changed America—its society, its politics, and . . . its image of itself. Except for the combatants themselves, Americans experienced the war at a remove of several thousand miles. They endured no bombing, no invasion, no massive dislocations, no serious material privations. Veterans returning home in 1945 and 1946 found a country that looked very much like the one they had left— something that clearly could not be said of veterans returning home to Britain, France, Germany, Russia, or Japan.

But World War II did transform America in profound, if not immediately visible, ways. Not the least important of those transformations was in the nature of American liberalism, a force that would play a central role in shaping the nation's postwar political and cultural life. Liberalism in America rests on several consistent and enduring philosophical assumptions: the high value liberals believe society should attribute to individual rights and freedoms and the importance of avoiding rigid and immutable norms and institutions. But in the half century since the New Deal, liberalism in America has also meant a prescription for public policy and political action; and in the 1940s this "New Deal liberalism" was in a state of considerable uncertainty and was undergoing significant changes. Several broad developments of the war years helped lay the foundations for the new liberal order that followed the war.

Among those developments was a series of important shifts in the size, distribution, and character of the American population. Not all the demographic changes of the 1940s were a result of the war, nor were their effects on liberal assumptions entirely apparent until well after 1945. But they were a crucial part of the process that would transform American society and the way liberals viewed their mission in that society.

Perhaps the most conspicuous demographic change was the single biggest ethnic migration in American history: the massive movement of African Americans from the rural South to the urban North, a migration much larger than the "great migration" at the time of World War I. . . .

This second great migration carried the question of race out of the South and into the North, out of the countryside and into the city, out of the field and into the factory. African American men and women encountered prejudice and discrimination in the urban, industrial world much as they had in the agrarian world; but in the city they were far better positioned to organize and protest their condition, as some were beginning to do even before the fighting ended. World War II therefore began the process by which race would increase its claim on American consciousness and, ultimately, transform American liberalism.

Just as the war helped lay the groundwork for challenges to racial orthodoxies, so it contributed to later challenges to gender norms. Three million women entered the paid workforce for the first time during the war, benefiting—like black workers—from the labor shortage military conscription had created. . . .

No one living in the era of multiculturalism will be inclined to argue with the proposition that the changing composition of the American population over the past fifty years—and the changing relations among different groups within the population—is one of the most important events in the nation's recent history. Those changes have reshaped America's economy, its culture, its politics, and its intellectual life. They have forced the nation to confront its increasing diversity in more direct and painful ways than at any time since the Civil War. They have challenged

America's conception of itself as a nation and a society. And they have transformed American liberalism. In the 1930s, most liberals considered questions of racial, ethnic, or gender difference of distinctly secondary importance (or in the case of gender, virtually no importance at all). Liberal discourse centered much more on issues of class and the distribution of wealth and economic power. By 1945 that was beginning to change. One sign of that change was the remarkable reception among liberals of Gunnar Myrdal's *An American Dilemma,* published in 1944. Myrdal identified race as the one issue most likely to shape and perplex the American future. The great migration of the 1940s helped ensure that history would vindicate Myrdal's prediction and that American liberals would adjust their outlook and their goals in fundamental ways in the postwar years.

Perhaps the most common and important observation about the domestic impact of World War II is that it ended the Great Depression and launched an era of unprecedented prosperity. Between 1940 and 1945 the United States experienced the greatest expansion of industrial production in its history. After a decade of depression, a decade of growing doubts about capitalism, a decade of high unemployment and underproduction, suddenly, in a single stroke, the American economy restored itself and—equally important—seemed to redeem itself. Gross national product in the war years rose from $91 billion to $166 billion; 15 million new jobs were created, and the most enduring problem of the depression—massive unemployment—came to an end; industrial production doubled; personal incomes rose (depending on location) by as much as 200 percent. The revival of the economy is obviously important in its own right. But it also had implications for the future of American political economy, for how liberals in particular conceived of the role of the state in the postwar United States.

One of the mainstays of economic thought in the late 1930s was the belief that the United States had reached what many called "economic maturity": the belief that the nation was approaching, or perhaps had reached, the end of its capacity to grow, that America must now learn to live within limits. This assumption strengthened the belief among many reformers that in the future it would be necessary to regulate the economy much more closely and carefully for the benefit of society as a whole. America could not rely any more on a constantly expanding pie; it would have to worry about how the existing pie was to be divided.

The wartime economic experience—the booming expansion, the virtual elimination of unemployment, the creation of new industries, new "frontiers"—served as a rebuke to the "mature economy" idea and restored the concept of growth to the center of liberal hopes. The capitalist economy, liberals suddenly discovered, was not irretrievably stagnant. Economic expansion could achieve, in fact had achieved, dimensions beyond the wildest dreams of the 1930s. Social and economic advancement could proceed, therefore, without structural changes in capitalism, without continuing, intrusive state management of the economy. It could proceed by virtue of growth. . . .

But along with this celebration of economic growth came a new and urgent fear: that the growth might not continue once the war was over. What if the depression came back? What if there was a return to massive unemployment? What could be done to make sure that economic growth continued? That was the great liberal challenge of the war years—not to restructure the economy, not to control corporate behavior, not to search for new and more efficient forms of management, but to find a way to keep things going as they were.

And in response to that challenge, a growing number of liberal economists and policymakers became interested in a tool that had begun to attract their attention in the 1930s and that seemed to prove itself during the war: government spending. That was clearly how the economy had revived—in response to the massive increase in the federal budget in the war years, from $9 billion in 1939 to $100 billion in 1945. And that was how the revival could be sustained—by pumping more money into the economy in peacetime. What government needed to do, therefore, was to "plan" for postwar full employment. . . .

The wartime faith in economic growth led, in other words, to several developments of great importance to the future of American liberalism. It helped relegitimize capitalism among people who had, in the 1930s, developed serious doubts about its viability. It helped rob the "administrative" reform ideas of the late 1930s—the belief in ever greater regulation of private institutions—of their urgency. It helped elevate Keynesian ideas about indirect management of the economy to the center of reform hopes. And it made the idea of the welfare state—of Social Security and public works and other social welfare efforts—come to seem a part of the larger vision of sustaining economic growth by defining welfare as a way to distribute income and stimulate purchasing power. It helped channel American liberalism into a new, less confrontational direction—a direction that would produce fewer clashes with capitalist institutions; that tried to define the interests of capitalists and the interests of the larger public in identical terms; that emphasized problems of consumption over problems of production; that shaped the liberal agenda for more than a generation and helped shape the next great episode in liberal policy experiments: the Great Society of the 1960s.

World War II had other important and more purely ideological effects on American liberalism—some of them in apparent conflict with others, but all of them important in determining the permissible range of liberal aspirations for the postwar era. First, the war created, or at least greatly reinforced, a set of anxieties and fears that would become increasingly central to liberal thought in the late 1940s and 1950s. It inflamed two fears in particular: a fear of the state and a fear of the people. Both were a response, in large part, to the horror with which American liberals (and most other Americans as well) regarded the regimes the United States was fighting in World War II. Both would be sustained and strengthened by the similar horror with which most Americans came to view the regime the nation was beginning to mobilize against in peacetime even before the end of the war: the Soviet Union. . . .

The war, in other words, pushed a fear of totalitarianism (and hence a general wariness about excessive state power) to the center of American liberal thought. In particular, it forced a reassessment of the kinds of associational and corporatist arrangements that many had found so attractive in the aftermath of World War I. Those, after all, were the kinds of arrangements Germany and Italy had claimed to be creating. But it also created a less specific fear of state power that made other kinds of direct planning and management of the economy or society seem unappealing as well. . . . This fear of the state was one of many things that lent strength to the emerging Keynesian–welfare state liberal vision of political economy, with its much more limited role for government as a manager of economic behavior.

Along with this fear of the state emerged a related fear: a fear of "mass politics" or "mass man"; a fear, in short, of the people. Nazi Germany, fascist Italy, even the Soviet Union, many liberals came to believe, illustrated the dangers inherent in trusting the people to control their political life. The people, the "mass," could too easily be swayed by demagogues and tyrants. They were too susceptible to appeals to their passions, to the dark, intolerant impulses that in a healthy society remained largely repressed and subdued. Fascism and communism were not simply the products of the state or of elite politics, many liberals believed; they were the products of mass movements, of the unleashing of the dangerous and irrational impulses within every individual and every society.

This fear of the mass lay at the heart of much liberal cultural and intellectual criticism in the first fifteen years after World War II. It found expression in the writings of Hannah Arendt, Theodor Adorno, Richard Hofstadter, Lionel Trilling, Daniel Bell, Dwight Macdonald, and many others. Like the fear of the state, with which it was so closely associated, it reinforced a sense of caution and restraint in liberal thinking; a suspicion of ideology, a commitment to pragmatism, a wariness about moving too quickly to encourage or embrace spontaneous popular movements; a conviction that one of the purposes of politics was to defend the state against popular movements and their potentially dangerous effects.

There were, in short, powerful voices within American liberalism during and immediately after World War II arguing that the experience of the war had introduced a dark cloud of doubt and even despair to human society. A world that could produce so terrible a war; a world that could produce Hiroshima, Nagasaki, the Katyn Forest, Auschwitz; a world capable of profound evil and inconceivable destruction: such a world, many American liberals argued, must be forever regarded skeptically and suspiciously. Humankind must move cautiously into its uncertain future, wary of unleashing the dark impulses that had produced such horror.

Some liberal intellectuals went further. Americans, they argued, must resist the temptation to think of themselves, in their hour of triumph, as a chosen people. No people, no nation, could afford to ignore its own capacity for evil. Reinhold Niebuhr spoke for many liberals when he wrote of the dangers of the "deep layer of Messianic consciousness in the mind of America" and warned of liberal culture's "inability to comprehend the depth of evil to which individuals and communities may sink, particularly when they try to play the role of God in history." Americans, he said, would do well to remember that "no nation is sacred and unique. . . . Providence has not set Americans apart from lesser breeds. We too are part of history's seamless web."

But Niebuhr's statements were obviously written to refute a competing assumption. And as it suggests, there was in the 1940s another, very different ideological force at work in America, another form of national self-definition that affected liberal thought and behavior, at home and in the world, at least as much as the somber assessments of Niebuhr and others. Indeed even many liberal intellectuals attracted to Niebuhr's pessimistic ideas about human nature and mass politics were simultaneously drawn to this different and, on the surface at least, contradictory assessment of the nation's potential. For in many ways the most powerful ideological force at work in postwar American liberalism, and in the postwar United States generally, was the view of America as an anointed nation; America as a special moral force in the world; America as a society with a unique mission, born of its righteousness. This is an ideological tradition that is often described as the tradition of American innocence. But innocence is perhaps too gentle a word for what has often been an aggressive and intrusive vision, a vision that rests on the belief that America is somehow insulated from the sins and failures and travails that affect other nations, that America stands somehow outside of history, protected from it by its own strength and virtue.

World War II did not create those beliefs. They are as old as the nation itself. But the American experience in the conflict, and the radically enhanced international stature and responsibility of the United States in the aftermath of the war, strengthened such ideas and gave them a crusading quality that made them as active and powerful as they had been at any moment in the nation's history.

It is not difficult, perhaps, to understand how and why that happened. Fighting a war against Nazi Germany would encourage any nation to think of itself as a moral force in an immoral world, to believe in the righteousness of its cause, to consider itself the champion of freedom and justice in a battle against tyranny and darkness. But it was not just the contrast between America's democratic potential and the autocracies of Germany and Japan that influenced the liberal vision of the postwar world. There was also a strengthened sense that the United States had something worth sharing with *all* nations, that it had a commitment to freedom and justice that could serve as a model for the rest of the world. That was the message of, among others, Henry Luce in a small book he published in 1941, titled *The American Century.* In that book Luce—the crusading founder and publisher of *Time* and *Life* magazines—sketched a picture of the nation's destiny that probably only slightly exaggerated what would, by the late 1940s, be a widely shared and increasingly powerful view.

The American century, Luce said, must be a time when the American people would share with the rest of the world the special virtues of their own society. . . .

Luce's vision had obvious implications for America's international role: it must be active and forceful, to ensure that less worthy nations did not shape the future. But it had implications for American domestic life as well. If the American example was to inspire the world, Americans must make sure their own society was worthy of emulation.

Luce was a Republican, an often bitter opponent of Roosevelt and the New Deal, and a man mistrusted and even despised by many liberals, most of whom considered his idea of an American century excessively nationalistic, even imperialistic. Yet even many liberals who disliked Luce and whose visions of the postwar world were strongly anti-imperialist spoke at times in a similar language, imbued with much the same sense of American mission. Vice President Henry A. Wallace, for example, described America's wartime (and by implication postwar) mission to extend democracy, both at home and abroad, in almost floridly idealistic language in a 1942 statement: "No compromise with Satan is possible. . . . The people's revolution is on the march, and the devil and all his angels can not prevail against it.

They can not prevail, for on the side of the people [America and its allies] is the Lord." The belief that America had a powerful destiny in the postwar world, that it had special virtues worth sharing with other peoples, that it could (and should) serve as a model to the democratic strivings of all nations—this belief was penetrating deep into American culture and forming the liberal concept of the nation's postwar mission. It helped reconcile liberals (and other Americans) to the active, crusading international role that victory had thrust upon the nation. It enabled liberals (and other Americans) to rationalize the continued development of methods of mass destruction by harnessing that effort to a perceived moral imperative. It made possible widespread public support for the cold war. It helped create considerable support for much of the domestic political repression the cold war later produced and made it difficult for liberals to find an effective position from which to criticize that repression. But by increasing popular sensitivity to America's image in the world (and to the impact of its own social problems on that image), it also created support for some of the ambitious liberal reform efforts of the postwar years. Theodore White, one of the most eloquent and prolific chroniclers of the experiences of the World War II generation, suggested something of the ambiguous impact of this sense of world mission when he wrote very near the end of his life:

> For a proper historian of our times, there was only one overtowering beginning—the Year of Victory, 1945. All things flowed from that victory. . . . The intoxication of [it] . . . lasted for a generation. First, the sense of power which had convinced a peaceful nation that its armed force . . . could and should forever police and reorder the world. Second, the seductive belief that in any contest between good and evil, good always triumphs. We, our soldiers, had proved that Right makes Might. The imperative legacy of Virtue descended from the war.

The war left other ideological legacies for American liberalism as well. In the glow of the nation's victory, in the sense of old orders shattered and a new world being born, came an era of exuberant innovation, an era in which, for a time, nothing seemed more appealing than the new. The allure of the new was visible in the brave new world of architectural modernism, whose controversial legacy is so much a part of the postwar American landscape. It was visible in the explosive growth of the innovative and iconoclastic American art world, which made New York in the 1940s and 1950s something of what Paris had been in the nineteenth century. It was visible in the increased stature and boldness of the American scientific community, and in the almost religious faith in technological progress that came to characterize so much of American life.

Above all, perhaps, it was visible in the way it excited, and then frustrated, a generation of American liberals as they imagined new possibilities for progress and social justice. That is what Archibald MacLeish meant in 1943 when he spoke about the America of the imagination, the society that the war was encouraging Americans to create:

> We have, and we know we have, the abundant means to bring our boldest dreams to pass—to create for ourselves whatever world we have the courage to desire. . . . We have the tools and the skill and the intelligence to take our cities apart and put them together, to lead our roads and rivers where we please to lead them, to build our houses where we want our houses, to brighten the air, to clean the wind, to live as men in this Republic,

free men, should be living. We have the power and the courage and the resources of good-will and decency and common understanding . . . to create a nation such as men have never seen. . . . We stand at the moment of the building of great lives, for the war's end and our victory in the war will throw that moment and the means before us.

There was, of course, considerable naïveté, and even arrogance, in such visions. But there was also an appealing sense of hope and commitment—a belief in the possibility of sweeping away old problems and failures, of creating "great lives." Out of such visions came some of the postwar crusades of American liberals—the battle for racial justice, the effort to combat poverty, the expansion of individual rights. And although all of those battles had some ambiguous and even unhappy consequences, they all reflected a confidence in the character and commitment of American society—and the possibility of creating social justice within it—that few people would express so blithely today. Postwar liberalism has suffered many failures and travails in the half century since 1945. But surely its postwar faith in the capacity of America to rebuild—and perhaps even redeem—itself remains one of its most appealing legacies.

Americans Reevaluate
Japanese American Incarceration

ROGER DANIELS

The roundup, expulsion, and incarceration of more than a hundred thousand Japanese Americans in the months following the outbreak of the Pacific War between the United States and Japan is a major blot on the record of American democracy, an ironic counterpoint to a war that was fought to preserve and establish what Franklin D. Roosevelt called the *Four Freedoms*. The event attracted little attention during the war, and, in the decades immediately following it, was generally written off as an aberration, or, as one scholar put it, America's "worst wartime mistake," and the mistreatment and abuse suffered by the West Coast Japanese American civilian men, women and children, more than two-thirds of them native-born American citizens, was usually ignored by the nation's historians. Since the early 1970s, however, historians and others have placed this wartime atrocity squarely in the historical canon so that almost every textbook carries at least a brief and usually a condemnatory account. And, beginning in 1980, the federal government itself began a process which resulted in the passage of the Civil Liberties Act of 1988, entailing a payment of $20,000 tax-free to each of the more than sixty-thousand Japanese American survivors, and apologies from both Congress and the president for wartime wrongdoing. The investigative body which made the recommendations on which the government acted in the 1980s reported that the incarceration of Japanese Americans "was not justified by military necessity. . . . The broad historical causes . . . were race prejudice, war hysteria, and a

From Roger Daniels, "Incarcerating Japanese Americans: An Atrocity Revisited," *Peace & Change* 23, no. 2 (April 1998); 117–118, 120–122, 124–128. © Peace History Society and Consortium on Peace Research, Education, and Development.

failure of political leadership. Widespread ignorance of Japanese Americans contributed to a policy conceived in haste and executed in an atmosphere of fear and anger at Japan. A grave injustice was done to American citizens and resident aliens of Japanese ancestry who, without individual review or any probative evidence against them, were excluded, removed, and detained by the United States during World War II."

More recently, in a speech commemorating the fiftieth anniversary of the Pearl Harbor attack, President George H. W. Bush acknowledged that "the internment of Americans of Japanese ancestry was a great injustice" and vowed that "it will never be repeated." In this paper, I will briefly recapitulate the relevant events of 1941–42, attempt to explain the changes in the climates of opinion which caused Americans to reevaluate the significance of the wartime incarceration, and attempt to answer the haunting question—could such a thing happen again? . . .

. . . Not one single case of espionage or sabotage by an ethnic Japanese was ever detected in the United States after war came, but few American officials or political leaders chose to make this point, which is what the 1981 presidential commission report meant by "a failure of political leadership." Added to that, some important federal officials fanned the fires of prejudice. . . .

On February 19, 1942, Franklin Roosevelt signed an executive order (E.O.), numbered 9066, in the form that the Army had submitted it to him. The executive order, based on a war powers act passed in 1918 and amended in 1940 and 1941, was a sweeping grant of power. . . . We know that some in the military considered using it on the East Coast and against large numbers of German and Italian aliens, but that was never done. Although *individual* German and Italian aliens on the West Coast were forced to move, the order and almost all of the subsequent execution of it was directed against Japanese Americans living on the West Coast. As defined by the United States Army, it affected all persons of Japanese birth or ancestry living in California, the western halves of Oregon and Washington, and a small portion of Arizona. . . .

During and immediately after the war, the incarceration of most of the Japanese Americans was a popular move. Indeed, many politicians complained about "coddling Japs" and public opinion polls indicated not only support for what the government had done, but a willingness to support even more draconian actions, such as the postwar expatriation of all ethnic Japanese. This obviously did not happen, although a little-known postwar program did result in sending some forty-seven hundred Japanese persons to Japan, more than three thousand of them American citizens.

But even before the war was over, the improvement of the image of the Japanese Americans had begun, promoted largely by civilian liberals within the government. Agencies such as the Office of War Information and the War Relocation Administration issued reams of pro–Japanese American propaganda, stressing the wartime heroism of Japanese American troops in Italy and the quiet good-citizenship of the Nisei generally. In addition, even though the United States fought World War II with segregated armed forces, the notion was beginning to prevail that equal opportunity—or something approaching it—ought to have a place on the national agenda. Eight months before he issued E.O. 9066, Franklin Roosevelt had put out E.O. 8802 establishing a Fair Employment Practices Committee "to encourage full participation in the national defense program by all citizens regardless of race, creed, color, or national origin."

In July 1946, Roosevelt's successor, Harry S. Truman, who as a senator had silently acquiesced in the incarceration, held a special ceremony on the Ellipse behind the White House for members of the 442nd Regimental Combat Team composed of Japanese Americans and told them that they had "fought not only the enemy, but [also] prejudice—and you have won." Nineteen months later, he sent Congress a ten-point civil rights message whose last three points were of special concern to Japanese Americans. Point eight called for Hawaiian (and Alaskan) statehood, point nine for dropping racial bars in naturalization, and point ten for providing some compensation for economic losses Japanese Americans had sustained when they were forced to abandon their property.

The last point was quickly achieved. The president pointed out that "more than one hundred thousand Japanese-Americans were evacuated from their homes in the Pacific states solely because of their racial origin"—he made no mention of the fictitious "military necessity"—and urged Congress to pass legislation which was already before it. On July 2, 1948, Truman signed the Japanese-American Claims Act which appropriated $38 million to settle all property claims, a figure which almost all commentators now agree was not nearly enough.

The other objectives took longer. Full equality in naturalization came first. The first turn of the tide had occurred back in 1943 when Congress repealed the fifteen separate pieces of legislation which had enforced Chinese exclusion and granted Chinese persons naturalization rights. Separate pieces of legislation in 1946 had made similar grants to Filipinos and "natives of India," but other Asians remained "aliens ineligible to citizenship" until 1952. In that year, Congress enacted the McCarran-Walter Act over Truman's veto. The president's veto message praised those parts of the law which made naturalization color blind but found "this most desirable provision . . . embedded in a mass of legislation which would perpetuate injustice." The admission of Hawaii as the fiftieth state was delayed even longer, until near the end of Dwight D. Eisenhower's term in 1959. It was significant for Japanese and other Asian Americans because the heavy Asian American majority in the new state made Asian American legislators in Washington a certainty.

Although much has been written "explaining" the practical benefits Truman sought to gain from his general civil rights program, it is difficult to imagine what domestic political gains he can have hoped for by advocating legislation to benefit Japanese and other Asian Americans. The president himself gave two reasons which can be taken at face value. He said that he believed in it as a matter of justice and fairness *and* as he put it: "If we wish to inspire the peoples of the world whose freedom is in jeopardy, if we wish to restore hope to those who have already lost their civil liberties, if we wish to fulfill the promise that is ours, we must correct the remaining imperfections in our practice of democracy." Thus, both a desire to improve democracy at home and certain cold war imperatives explain the steps that the United States took in the postwar decades to improve the status of Japanese Americans.

To explain the passage of the Civil Liberties Act of 1988 other reasons must be considered, although a continuing struggle for ethnic equality is a constant. The combined effects of Lyndon Johnson's Great Society programs of the mid-1960s and of the eventual rejection of the misbegotten war in Vietnam contributed to a climate of opinion in which the acts of the 1940s could be reconsidered. In 1976, President Gerald R. Ford, hardly a radical, repealed F.D.R.'s Executive Order 9066 and, in a proclamation noting that the nation was celebrating its two-hundredth birthday, insisted that "an honest reckoning" must take account "of our national mistakes as well as our national achievements." The president continued: "We know now what we should have known then—not only was that evacuation wrong, but Japanese Americans were and are loyal Americans. On the battlefield and at home, Japanese Americans . . . have been and continue to be written into our history for the sacrifices and contributions they have made to the well-being and security of this, our common Nation."

Four years later, at the urging of Japanese American activists and ethnic organizations, and with the guidance of Japanese American legislators, Congress passed and President Jimmy Carter signed legislation creating the Presidential Commission on the Wartime Relocation and Internment of Civilians (CWRIC) whose mission was to "review the facts and circumstances surrounding" E.O. 9066 and its sequelae and to "recommend appropriate remedies." A detailed investigation confirmed what most scholars had been saying since 1959, and a series of hearings held in Washington and in Midwestern and Far Western centers of Japanese American population produced unexpected and unprecedented displays of anger and other emotions by survivors and their descendants nearly forty years after the event. In 1983 the CWRIC, as noted above, recommended a tax-free payment of $20,000 to each survivor and a formal apology. Five years later Congress enacted, and President Ronald W. Reagan signed, the Civil Liberties Act of 1988, but it was not until well into the Bush administration that payments were actually made. After nearly half a century, the legal and legislative ramifications of Executive Order 9066 seemed to have been played out.

What, however, of the future? Could it happen again, or was what happened to Japanese Americans, as George Bush believed, something that "will never be repeated"? Prediction is not the historian's primary task, but those of us who study the past have learned that although the precise circumstances which trigger any specific historical situation are unique, similar forces acting within a society can produce similar results. Racist and xenophobic forces still exist in American (and most other) societies. An extended external or internal crisis somehow associated with a minority group, whether political or ethnic, could produce similar results. Rather than trying to imagine what such future crises might be, I will note several separate occasions since the end of World War II in which the United States has seemed to be on the verge of effecting mass incarceration.

At the height of the cold war, Congress passed the Emergency Detention Act, which after a great deal of rhetoric about a monolithic worldwide communist conspiracy, authorized the president to declare, by executive order, an "Internal Security Emergency." In such a circumstance, the attorney general was then empowered to "apprehend and . . . detain . . . each person as to whom there is reason to believe that such person probably will engage in, or probably will conspire with others to engage in, acts of espionage or espionage." The statute also provided for the creation of a number of stand-by concentration camps. Although the law was clearly aimed at ideological rather than ethnic "enemies" of the republic, it was distinctly modeled on the procedure, upheld by the Supreme Court, under which the Japanese Americans had been incarcerated. The statute, although never utilized, remained on the books until 1969 when it was repealed.

Every recent American administration has at least considered some kind of massive incarceration of individuals. During the hostage crisis growing out of the seizure of the American embassy in Teheran, the Carter administration took preliminary steps against Iranians—mostly college students—living in the United States. When the Immigration and Naturalization Service's filing system proved so chaotic that it could not provide the White House with even approximate numbers, no less names and addresses, the administration instructed the nation's colleges and universities to provide them and most complied. Happily, no mass incarceration resulted, but it is clear that the White House was at least contemplating some punitive action. There was also sporadic mob violence against Iranians.

The Reagan administration caused the detention of large numbers of illegal Haitian immigrants—while welcoming illegal Cubans with open arms—although some of the worst aspects of their treatment were modified by federal judges unconstrained by a wartime crisis. Partly to avoid both federal courts and immigration lawyers, the Bush administration set up a camp for Haitian refugees inside the American military base at Guantanamo Bay, Cuba, a policy the Clinton administration continued and used for Cubans as well.

The Bush administration, just before and during the brief hostilities in the Persian Gulf in 1990–91, had some of its agents interrogate Arab American leaders, both citizen and alien. When spokespersons for Arab communities and some civil liberties organizations protested, the interrogations were stopped; the government made the lame excuse that the federal agents were only trying to protect those whom they had questioned. And there was sporadic violence against Arab American individuals and businesses.

These events, spread across nearly half a century, do not amount to very much when compared to what was done to Japanese Americans. But, similarly, no crisis comparable to World War II has occurred. All of these instances were violations of the spirit of the Constitution, and they did happen even in a society in which both racial prejudice and xenophobia have been reduced. What might have happened had they been accompanied by some great crisis or outrage—suppose, for example, that Iran had decided to execute the American hostages on television, say at the rate of one a day—is frightening to contemplate. But these "minor" events do demonstrate an ongoing American propensity to react against "foreigners" in the United States in time of crisis, especially when those foreigners have dark skins. Despite the amelioration of American race relations, there are still huge inequities between whites and non-whites, and potentially explosive emotions exist in both the oppressing and the oppressed populations. While optimists claim that American concentration camps are a thing of the past—and I certainly hope that they are—many Japanese Americans, the only group of citizens ever incarcerated *en masse* because of their genes, would argue that what has happened in the past can happen again. This student of Japanese American history can only agree with them.

Culture War Erupts Over the 1994–1995 Smithsonian Institution's *Enola Gay* Exhibition

RICHARD H. KOHN

The cancellation of the National Air and Space Museum's (NASM) original *Enola Gay* exhibition in January 1995 may constitute the worst tragedy to befall the public presentation of history in the United States in this generation. In displaying the *Enola Gay* without analysis of the event that gave the B-29 airplane its significance, the Smithsonian Institution forfeited an opportunity to educate a worldwide audience in the millions about one of this century's defining experiences. An exhibition that explored the dropping of the atomic bombs on Japan—an event historians view as significant in itself and symbolic of the end of World War II, the beginning of the Cold War, and the dawn of the nuclear age—might have been the most important museum presentation of the decade and perhaps of the era. The secretary and the Board of Regents of the Smithsonian abandoned this major exhibition for political reasons: Veterans' groups, political commentators, social critics, and politicians had charged that the exhibition script dishonored the Americans who fought the war by questioning the motives for using the bombs, by portraying the bomb as unnecessary to end the war, and by sympathizing too much with the Japanese killed by the bombs and, by implication, with the Japanese cause. Thus one of the premiere cultural institutions of the United States, its foremost museum system, surrendered its scholarly independence and a significant amount of its authority in American intellectual life to accommodate to a political perspective. . . .

The *Enola Gay* conflict began at least two decades ago. The controversy comprised at least five stories; they fused together in 1994 to set off the national explosion that resulted in cancellation of the exhibition. The first story traces planning for the exhibition in a museum whose staff was increasingly determined to apply professional, scholarly standards in a previously celebratory institution. The second concerns the uneasy relationship between the museum and many in the military aviation community. The third, of course, tells of the larger culture wars and the reaction of the museum to its critics. The fourth and fifth concern the appointment of a new secretary of the Smithsonian Institution just when political power in Congress shifted, for the first time in almost two generations, from Democrats to Republicans. Although what follows treats some of the stories at greater length than others, each was crucial to the character and timing of the outcome.

The first and most basic ingredient was the exhibition script itself, a product of the National Air and Space Museum and its history over the last twenty years. Since its opening in the mid-1970s, Air and Space had gained a worldwide reputation for breathtaking artifacts, huge and laudatory crowds of visitors (the highest numbers in the world, as many as 10 million in some years), but little intellectual or scholarly content. . . .

From Richard H. Kohn, "History and the Culture Wars: The Case of the Smithsonian Institution's *Enola Gay* Exhibition, "*Journal of American History* 82, no. 3 (December 1995): 1036–1044, 1047–1056, 1060–1063.

The appointment in 1987 of Martin Harwit, a respected astrophysicist from Cornell University with a longstanding interest in the history of science, seemed to promise a solution to many of the problems. The first academic and scholar to head the museum (his predecessors had been scientists, engineers, or aviators), Harwit was selected by Robert McCormick Adams, secretary of the Smithsonian from 1984 to 1994. Very much an academic, Adams eschewed such Washington power folkways as dark suits and the trappings of office. He managed the institution in a style that Smithsonian insiders characterized as "laissez-faire in a funny way . . . like academia," "collegial," and an effort "to stimulate more independence." But his management was also criticized, from within and without. Adams's priority was research. He aimed to put the institution on the cutting edge of scholarship, or at least to modernize exhibits and programs where the institution had fallen behind—in Adams's words, "deepening the intellectual structure of the place." Adams aimed to encourage critical scholarship in an institution whose reputation for scholarly leadership had waned as its reputation for uninspired establishmentarianism flourished. . . .

Martin Harwit, whom Adams chose over a distinguished retired four-star United States Air Force general with a graduate history degree, embraced Adams's agenda of scholarship and apparently shared his views of military affairs and air power. Harwit set out to encourage the curators to extend their historical research and writings, to hire bright young scholars, to help staff members finish graduate degrees, to increase the intellectual content of displays and exhibitions, and to foster scientific as well as historical study, but not to lessen either the appeal of the museum or its service to public, professional, industrial, and military constituencies. . . .

The *Enola Gay* exhibition would advance Harwit's agenda of promoting scholarship, exploring the social contexts and human implications of the aviation and space experiences, and avoiding uncritical celebration of technology. Restoration of the famous airplane began under his predecessor. From the outset the museum staff recognized how controversial the airplane would be, even if it were displayed with only an identifying label. For years, veterans had badgered the museum to restore the *Enola Gay* and display it or to loan or transfer it to a site or institution where it would receive the honor its historic flight deserved. During the 1980s, the NASM's Research Advisory Committee several times debated whether the aircraft should be restored and displayed. Members of the committee favored restoration and exhibition because of the plane's educational value in an exhibition. The only dissenter was the outspokenly antinuclear retired admiral and former commander of United States armed forces in the Pacific, Noel Gayler, who argued forcefully against any act that could be interpreted to celebrate such destruction or to memorialize the killing of so many innocent civilians. Thus well before the museum began mounting an exhibition, even before it began the expensive restoration of the aircraft, the Hiroshima atomic bomber had already come to symbolize both conflicting perspectives on American war making—emphasizing either innovative technological achievement or the mass death of enemy civilians—and, more widely, positive and negative judgments on the American past. The airplane had become, and within the museum was understood to have become, a flash point of profound, often emotional disagreement about how to observe, or even whether to observe, the event that had made this most famous of military aircraft significant. . . .

In keeping with the goals of scholarship and education and in spite of the conflict any exhibition was sure to provoke, the museum embedded in the exhibit a didactic objective that exacerbated the potential for controversy. According to the 1993 planning document, the exhibition's "primary goal" was "to encourage visitors to make a thoughtful and balanced re-examination of the atomic bombings in the light of the political and military factors leading to the decision to use the bomb, the human suffering experienced by the people of Hiroshima and Nagasaki and the long-term implications of the events of August 6 and 9, 1945." In other words, the chief purpose was not simply to present a historical investigation of what happened, why, and what it meant, but to revisit the American decision to use the bomb in 1945, to ask whether the bomb was needed or justified, and to suggest "an uncertain, potentially dangerous future for all of civilization." "The exhibition would conclude, as it began, by noting the debatable character of the atomic bombings," read an earlier document. Secretary Adams expressed worry about the contentious nature of the proposal. In response, the chairman of the Aeronautics Department, Tom Crouch, who would oversee production of the exhibit script, told Harwit: "Do you want to do an exhibition intended to make veterans feel good, or do you want an exhibition that will lead our visitors to think about the consequences of the atomic Bombing of Japan? Frankly, I don't think we can do both." From the beginning, then, the *Enola Gay* exhibit was designed to provoke its audience; and in the mind of the chief supervising curator, the museum faced an unbridgeable chasm between scholarship and commemoration. Harwit insisted that the museum could do both, impartially and responsibly, and he suggested that Crouch and Michael Neufeld, the lead curator, could withdraw if work on the exhibit would violate their professional ethics. Both agreed that it would not, and they continued.

The first script, finished in January 1994, titled the exhibition "The Crossroads: The End of World War II, the Atomic Bomb, and the Origins of the Cold War"; it combined patriotic commemoration with serious scholarship. The 303 pages of text, comprising narrative explanation and labels to connect and identify dozens of photographs, paintings, maps, charts, documents, videos, and artifacts, including the fuselage of the *Enola Gay*, was a sophisticated historical collage. The exhibition told the story with a clarity and completeness designed to appeal to varied audiences, while compromising none of the complexity. . . .

In presenting historical interpretations, the texts were cautious and balanced, choosing words precisely so as to treat controversial subjects with a tone of distance and detachment. . . .

What most bothered the critics, including some historians, and led to the public campaign of opposition by the Air Force Association, other veterans' groups, politicians, and commentators were not the carefully crafted statements of interpretation, virtually all of which were consensus scholarship. (A very few statements, mostly taken out of context, were used publicly to accuse the museum of an anti-American and pro-Japanese portrayal.) The problems with the script were the omission of material, the emphasis on other material, the order and placement of facts and analysis, and the tone and the mood. Taken as a whole and read with the emotional impact on viewers in mind, the exhibition *was* in fact unbalanced; it possessed a very clear and potent point of view. On a level of feeling that could be reached more powerfully through the senses of sight and sound than through the intellectuality of words, the exhibit appealed to viewers' emotions, and its message could be read to be tendentious and moralizing; the exhibition script could be read to condemn American behavior at the end of World War II.

On the first panel of text at the entry to the exhibition, in the second sentence mentioning the atomic bomb, visitors would learn that "To this day, controversy has raged about whether dropping this weapon on Japan was necessary to end the war quickly." Nearly every section of the exhibit that followed would contribute, directly or by juxtaposition, to doubts not only about the necessity and appropriateness of the bomb but about American motives, honor, decency, and moral integrity in wreaking such destruction on what the script portrayed as a defeated (but not surrendering) enemy. . . .

Read in this fashion with the probable reaction of visitors imagined, the entire exhibition cast a wholly negative interpretation on the development, use, and impact of the atomic bombs. It was thus possible, looking beyond the careful wording of each individual panel or label, to detect in the five sections of the exhibit an interpretation that was in today's parlance revisionist, countercultural, and condemnatory of the United States: the war was a racist conflict waged by Americans for vengeance, a war essentially won by mid-1945; the bombing was an unnecessary act, growing out of bureaucratic, diplomatic, and political as well as military impulses, that wreaked an atrocity upon a defeated Japanese population. The bombing made an uncertain contribution to ending the conflict but an unquestionable one to a more dangerous, depressing world that still troubles us today.

To be fair to the curators, few readers saw such extremes in the first draft or voiced strong objections, at least before the controversy over the script burst into public view. The exhibit followed recent innovations in the museological community: to explore the broad contexts of important events, particularly their human dimensions; to include complexity; to stimulate viewer interest and evoke controversy; to educate as well as to commemorate; and to combine the best recent scholarship with artifacts and other materials in multimedia, interactive "shows" that draw in audiences in powerful ways, intellectually and emotionally. The exhibit contained a balance of techniques and approaches. The first section, on 1945, provided context, and it was strongly interpretative. The second, on the decision to use the bomb, emphasized recent historical scholarship. The third—on the bomb, the airplanes, and the mission—memorialized American science, technology, industry, and fighting men. The fourth roused powerful emotions in viewers, while memorializing people the museum perceived as among the major stakeholders, the Japanese. The fifth, on Japan's surrender and the nuclear age, explored implications and meanings. If the story featured civilian death, a case could be made that the most enduring significance of strategic bombing and of the atomic bombs, perhaps even of World War II, was to spread destruction to civilian populations in ways and with results heretofore unknown in the history of war. . . .

The second story was the reaction of the Air Force Association and its public attack on the exhibition, undertaken either to force a revision or to stop it altogether. The association, formed immediately after World War II by Army Air Forces veterans to promote air power and the air force, had evolved over two generations into a large, powerful advocate for a strong national defense and a chief connecting link between the air force and its industrial suppliers. A private organization with an elected leadership and professional staff, it is separate from the United States Air Force, although the association's membership includes many active-duty and reserve serv-icemen and -women and many veterans, overwhelmingly of the air forces, of World War II and the Cold War. Some of the association's Washington staff had come to view Smithsonian in general and NASM in particular with suspicion; the exhibit script confirmed their worst fears. This was the fourth planning document for the *Enola Gay* exhibition that they had seen. They had detected hidden political mes-sages in all those documents. Especially offensive to people who viewed their or-ganization as representing tens of thousands of Army Air Forces veterans of World War II, living and dead, were the hints of doubt about the ethics and morality of the way the United States fought Japan and, by implication, about the honor of those who did the fighting. From the association's perspective, this "emotionally charged program," which "was fundamentally lacking in balance and context," was all the more suspect because the museum had been assuring veterans for years that the exhibition would honor their service. Association staff members believed their ob-jections were disregarded, although NASM officials believed they were consulting and listening (if not exactly responding) to a primary stakeholder and an important potential opponent. Having shared its plans, the museum leadership was therefore shocked when *Air Force Magazine* published, in April 1994, a virulent attack on the exhibit script, the curators, the director, and the museum, less than two months after the Exhibit Advisory Committee had seemingly approved the script.

The violence of the Air Force Association's public assault—the personal at-tacks on Smithsonian secretary Robert Adams and Air and Space director Martin Harwit, the accusation that the museum had been neglecting its primary task of preserving its priceless artifacts, the charges of political correctness—indicated something deeper at work. Just as that first script cannot be understood apart from the museum's history of the previous ten years, so the Air Force Association's public blast, which brought the controversy over the exhibit to the nation's atten-tion, cannot be understood apart from the unhappiness with the museum felt by some in the air force community. They believed that Smithsonian as a whole and Air and Space curators in particular were antimilitary, that displays downplayed military as opposed to commercial or general aviation, that the museum sometimes took a skeptical or disparaging attitude toward aviation, flight, air power, space exploration, even science and technology per se. . . .

A further problem lay in the lack of public monuments or national memorials to air power and the air force in Washington, in comparison with the army, navy, and marines. There may have been a subtle resentment that the most public reminder of aviation's contribution to American life and the nation's security was left by default to the Smithsonian. . . .

In other words, the willingness of the Air Force Association to initiate and lead a public campaign against the exhibit must be understood within two contexts beyond the content of the exhibit: resentment of the National Air and Space Museum and the churning culture war that surfaced during the 1980s and rose to crescendo in 1994.

That culture war is the third element that helps explain the calamity of the *Enola Gay* controversy. The Air Force Association's attack of April 1994 landed like a match on dry tinder. There exploded over the summer and fall of 1994, among veterans' groups and in the speeches of politicians, a rising chorus of criticism, almost all of it directed at the museum, and from the liberal press and columnists as well as conservatives. Much of the outcry was almost certainly spontaneous, but the Air Force Association and veterans' groups did much to plan and manage the public criticism. . . .

Historians and other scholars will need to locate the *Enola Gay* exhibit battle in the wider culture wars, but from the initial attack by *Air Force Magazine* to the postmortems after the exhibit was canceled, those involved in the battle connected the exhibition and the argument over it to the campaigns over political correctness, provocative art, multiculturalism, equal opportunity programs, gender and sexual orientation, the national history standards and revisionist history, and just about every other divisive social and cultural issue rending American society, save abortion and prayer in the schools. "What can't be altered," opined the *Wall Street Journal,* "is the clear impression given by the Smithsonian that the American museum whose business it is to tell the nation's story is now in the hands of academics unable to view American history as anything other than a woeful catalog of crimes and aggressions against the helpless peoples of the earth."

The museum responded in a number of ways. Harwit, in a letter to *Air Force Magazine* and in short essays, appealed to verifiable history and to recent scholarship, acknowledging the differing views of the function of the museum and the differing perspectives of the World War II and Cold War generations on the atomic bombings. During the spring and summer of 1994, museum officials also undertook to defuse the criticism by changing the exhibit. Harwit gave the script another careful reading to judge balance, and he found "much of the criticism . . . understandable." Having circulated the draft script with the intention of consulting widely, listening to responses, and altering the exhibit where appropriate, the museum changed the script, making use of criticism from Department of Defense historians and from a team inside the museum consisting chiefly of senior retired military aviators. The museum leadership also began to negotiate content with groups outside the museum with political agendas and no claim to scholarly knowledge, museum expertise, or a balanced perspective. Museums customarily consult, consider, react, and modify their products according to the best advice they can gather, but to negotiate a rendering of the past in exchange for acquiescence poses special dangers. . . .

Thus by the fall of 1994, the museum had not succeeded in satisfying the veterans and had alienated many historians; its actions had called into question the credibility of the exhibition's scholarship. Harwit had lost the trust of both groups. Mired in a senseless contest over the number of casualties expected in the planned invasion of Japan—a symbol of whether the bombing was necessary—the museum had become the target of a United States Senate resolution demanding history in proper context and exhibits reflecting positively on veterans of the Pacific war; the Smithsonian faced a troubling number of critics and politicians calling for Harwit's resignation or removal and the abandonment of the exhibition as planned. Not until too late did the museum leadership realize that the exhibit could be canceled from the outside.

The fourth and fifth elements came together after November 1994 with a speed and power that decided the outcome. First came the largely unexpected victory of the Republicans in the fall congressional elections. For those in the House of

Representatives who had made the culture war central to their critique of American society, canceling this exhibit seemed a necessary victory, and one essential to rolling back the cultural Left in American intellectual life. After the exhibit was canceled, newly installed House Speaker Newt Gingrich told the nation's state governors that the *"Enola Gay* fight was a fight, in effect, over the reassertion by most Americans that they're sick and tired of being told by some cultural elite that they ought to be ashamed of their country." As part of the larger battle over American values, the *Enola Gay* exhibit seemed to its critics more emotional, significant, and less ambiguous than the debate over the National History Standards, the National Endowment for the Humanities and the National Endowment for the Arts, the Public Broadcasting Corporation, and the suspected left bias of the press and other institutions. If an exhibition that appeared to be openly unpatriotic, planned by a national, publicly funded museum on the fiftieth anniversary of the winning of World War II, could not be shut down or altered, then fashions and institutions more insulated from the levers of power might be truly unreachable. No matter that forcing the cancellation might excite charges of political censorship or the suppression of free speech, open debate, or the search for truth, values the critics professed; stopping the *Enola Gay* exhibition or converting it into a patriotic celebration would have deterrent and collateral effects. The threat of large cuts in the Smithsonian budget and hearings into how the Smithsonian was managed and administered were just the weapons to wield.

The final element in the story was a new Smithsonian secretary, brought in to raise money, who was unable or unwilling even to contest the political pressure to cancel the exhibition. And that pressure was intense. By January 1995, eighty-one members of Congress had called for firing Harwit; twenty thousand subscribers to *Smithsonian* magazine had complained about the exhibit. Some 72 percent of the Smithsonian's operating budget and 77 percent of construction monies came from federal appropriations; the percentage of federal support had been rising as dollars from the private sector dwindled. In the middle of January 1995, the American Legion, using as an excuse Harwit's intention to change a casualty estimate for the invasion of Japan, suddenly demanded cancellation of the exhibition, called on Congress to help, demanded hearings into Smithsonian's management, and asked that the *Enola Gay* be transferred to another museum for display in a positive context. The secretary met with legion officials on January 18 and refused; thirteen days later he reversed himself and abandoned the exhibition.

History has had many functions in human society, the accurate reconstruction of the past being only one. "What happened, what we recall, what we recover, what we relate, are often sadly different," the scholar of the Middle East Bernard Lewis wrote twenty years ago. "The temptation is often overwhelmingly strong to tell it, not as it really was, but as we would wish it to have been." The conflict over the *Enola Gay* exhibition was in part generational, for to World War II veterans a critical presentation of this climactic event, on the Washington Mall during the fiftieth anniversary, seemed to discredit all that they had done in a cause that had defined their lives and connected them to American history. But Americans have frequently fought over how to commemorate anniversaries, design monuments, observe holidays, and mount displays and exhibitions. The United States government, like other national governments in the last two centuries, has used the memory of war to construct the identity and to build the cohesion of the modern nation-state. At the state and local levels, people have had different agendas. Throughout our history, the memorializations of battles and wars have been important cultural and political rituals that have had varied and changing meanings for individuals and groups—something all too easily forgotten as the fiftieth-anniversary commemorations of World War II come to a close. Because of its fame and mission, the *Enola Gay,* displayed alone or in an exhibit, in Washington fifty years after the event and in a heretofore celebratory museum, was sure to arouse passion.

But the causes of the controversy and the cancellation lay in the diverse circumstances that came together in 1994: an exhibit designed to provoke its viewers with powerful (perhaps tendentious) interpretations; a difficult relationship between a museum and an important constituency; long-developing and increasingly bitter contests over education, social relationships, historical interpretations, public culture, and other issues rending American society; mistakes of process and response by the Air and Space Museum; a new, aggressive, determined Republican majority in the Congress; and a new, peculiarly vulnerable Smithsonian leader who did not resist pressures generated by an enormous national outcry. Before we read wider implications for presenting history in American society into this experience, we had better know and reflect on the events and conditions that help explain the event. . . .

. . . An exhibit that provided the context of the entire war, that explained in even tones the decision to drop the bomb from the American government's viewpoint (including the disagreements among historians over American motives), that memorialized the artifacts and the fliers as the original script did, that recounted the effect of the bombs on the ground without attempting to arouse emotion or to use repetition in a way that might appear moralizing, and that explored the implications of the bomb for the future with the ambivalence most Americans have felt about the nuclear age seemed possible to many historians. What was *not* possible was "to honor the veterans" in an exhibition that was, in its first form, essentially antiwar and antinuclear, one that emphasized "the reality of atomic war and its consequences." This was the fundamental predicament, Martin Harwit explained, in a thoughtful essay aptly titled "The *Enola Gay:* A Nation's, and a Museum's, Dilemma."

The controversy could be read to indicate that the American people can tolerate honest history presented in full, that they can detect biased or partisan interpretation, and that they recognize the necessity of independent judgment and interpretation in public historical presentation. Americans know that if the complex, scholarly history of controversial events cannot be presented to the public, the United States will be behaving like its former enemies, the Soviet Union and Japan: one abused history for propaganda; the other is still unwilling to acknowledge its behavior during World War II in spite of the harm such silence does to Japanese foreign policy across Asia. As a student of Japanese literature about the bomb wrote recently, "Americans' ambivalence over Hiroshima and . . . Japan's ambivalence over its role in the war, involve a common reluctance to think too carefully or long about anything that threatens the national sense of legitimacy." Perhaps a Briton, the great spy novelist of the Cold War John Le Carré, recognized something deeper at work in American culture in the aftermath of the Cold War.

"The fight against communism diminished us," he wrote two years ago, lamenting the inaction on Bosnia. "It left in us a state of false and corrosive orthodoxy." "The strength of America is in her frankness, her nobility of mind, her willingness to declare herself, take risks and change. Not in her secrecy."

The tragedy of the cancellation is that a major opportunity to inform the American people and international visitors about warfare, air power, World War II, and a turning point in world history was lost. Certainly, the *Enola Gay* exhibition, even in its unbalanced versions, would have revealed the power and effectiveness of bombing and of nuclear weapons. Ironically, the effects for American foreign policy could have been salutary. Millions of people, including many of the world's leaders, would have seen how destructive nuclear bombs are and how difficult it is to control the passion unleashed in nations during wartime, perceptions that might help prevent nuclear proliferation and deter aggression. Viewers would have seen a reminder of what happens when an aggressor sets out on a war of con-quest, attacks American interests, and provokes the American people. Placed just a few blocks from the United States Holocaust Memorial Museum and from the exhibit on the World War II internment of the West Coast Japanese Americans at the Smithsonian's National Museum of American History, the atomic bombing exhibit would have attracted many visitors. Those who saw all three might have reflected on the folly of racism and concluded that some wars are worth fighting, World War II being one of them.

Why Did the Holocaust Become
a Major Postwar Issue?

PETER NOVICK

This book had its origin in curiosity and skepticism. The curiosity, which engaged me as an historian, had to do with why in 1990s America —fifty years after the fact and thousands of miles from its site—the Holocaust has come to loom so large in our culture. The skepticism, which engaged me as a Jew and as an American, had to do with whether the prominent role the Holocaust has come to play in both American Jewish and general American discourse is as desirable a development as most people seem to think it is. . . .

. . . Generally speaking, historical events are most talked about shortly after their occurrence, then they gradually move to the margin of consciousness. It was in the 1920s and 1930s, not the 1950s and 1960s, that novels, films, and collective consciousness were obsessed with the carnage of Passchendaele and the Somme. By the fifties and sixties—forty years and more after the events of the Great War— they had fallen down a memory hole where only historians scurry around in the dark. The most-viewed films and the best-selling books about the Vietnam War almost all appeared within five or ten years of the end of that conflict, as did the

Vietnam Veterans Memorial in Washington. With the Holocaust the rhythm has been very different: hardly talked about for the first twenty years or so after World War II; then, from the 1970s on, becoming ever more central in American public discourse—particularly, of course, among Jews, but also in the culture at large. What accounts for this unusual chronology?

. . . There is nothing surprising about the Holocaust's playing a central role in the consciousness of Germany, the country of the criminals and their descendants. The same might be said of Israel, a country whose population—or much of it—has a special relationship to the victims of the crime. To a somewhat lesser extent, this could be said of nations occupied by Germany during the war which were the scene of the deportation to death (or the actual murder) of their Jewish citizens. In all of these countries the parents or grandparents of the present generation directly confronted—resisted, assisted, in any case witnessed—the crime; in all cases, a fairly close connection. In the case of the United States none of these connections is present. The Holocaust took place thousands of miles from America's shores. Holocaust survivors or their descendants are a small fraction of 1 percent of the American population, and a small fraction of American Jewry as well. Only a handful of perpetrators managed to make it to the United States after the war. Americans, including many American Jews, were largely unaware of what we now call the Holocaust while it was going on; the nation was preoccupied with defeating the Axis. The United States was simply not connected to the Holocaust in the ways in which these other countries are. So, in addition to "why now?" we have to ask "why here?" . . .

. . . In the 1920s the French sociologist Maurice Halbwachs began to study what he was one of the first to call "collective memory." Instead of viewing collective memory as the past working its will on the present, Halbwachs explored the ways in which present concerns determine what of the past we remember and how we remember it. (There is a grim appropriateness in adopting Halbwachs's approach to the study of Holocaust memory. When, in occupied France, he protested the arrest of his Jewish father-in-law, Halbwachs was sent to Buchenwald, where he died.)

Collective memory, as Halbwachs used the phrase, is not just historical knowledge shared by a group. Indeed, collective memory is in crucial senses ahistorical, even anti-historical. To understand something historically is to be aware of its complexity, to have sufficient detachment to see it from multiple perspectives, to accept the ambiguities, including moral ambiguities, of protagonists' motives and behavior. Collective memory simplifies; sees events from a single, committed perspective; is impatient with ambiguities of any kind; reduces events to mythic archetypes. Historical consciousness, by its nature, focuses on the *historicity* of events—that they took place then and not now, that they grew out of circumstances different from those that now obtain. Memory, by contrast, has no sense of the passage of time; it denies the "pastness" of its objects and insists on their continuing presence. Typically a collective memory, at least a significant collective memory, is understood to express some eternal or essential truth about the group—usually tragic. A memory, once established, comes to define that eternal truth, and, along with it, an eternal identity, for the members of the group. . . .

Thinking about collective memory in this way helps us to separate ephemeral and relatively inconsequential memories from those that endure and shape consciousness. "Remember the Alamo," "Remember the *Maine*," and "Remember Pearl

Harbor" were briefly very resonant, but were pretty much abandoned when their work was done. There are "memory spasms" on the occasion of round-numbered anniversaries—the bicentennial of the American Revolution, the quincentenary of Columbus's first voyage—but the flurry of commemorations on such occasions doesn't signify that we're in the presence of important collective memory. . . .

If in looking at Holocaust memory in the United States we take Halbwachs's approach, relating memory to current concerns, we're led to look at just what those concerns have been, how they've been defined, and who has defined them. . . . [T]hose concerns have, in one period, made Holocaust memory seem inappropriate, useless, or even harmful; in another period, appropriate and desirable. . . . [T]he changing fortunes of Holocaust memory . . . relate to changing circumstances and, particularly among American Jews, changing decisions about collective self-understanding and self-representation.

One way of looking at these contrasting notions of the operation of collective memory is to say that Freud treats memory as imposed, while Halbwachs treats it as chosen. But that doesn't get it quite right unless we qualify the word "chosen." People often think of "choice" as implying *free* choice, but the sort of choices we're speaking of are shaped and constrained by circumstances. (The circumstances we'll be looking at include the cold war and the continuing conflict in the Middle East, changing attitudes toward the muting or the parading of ethnic differences, changes in attitudes toward victims, and strategies of communal survival.) Often people take the word "choice" to imply a thoughtful decision arrived at after consideration of all the pros and cons, a calculation of advantages and disadvantages. But while, as we'll see, there are some examples of that sort of choice in matters having to do with Holocaust memory, more often than not we'll find intuitive choices, or tacit choices, made without much thought for their consequences. And we always have to ask ourselves *whose* choices we're talking about. Concerning our collective memories, as in other aspects of collective consciousness, most of us are pretty conformist and take our cues from others. Finally, there is the institutionalization of memory, something that Halbwachs thought particularly important. An accumulation of previous choices, considered and unconsidered, has produced a set of institutions dedicated to Holocaust memory and a substantial cadre of Holocaust-memory professionals. Together, these provide self-perpetuating momentum to the centering of the Holocaust, independent of any further decision-making. . . .

. . . [T]hough it was Jewish initiative that put the Holocaust on the American agenda, we have to ask what characteristics of late-twentieth-century American society and culture made gentile Americans receptive to that initiative. Some of the influences that have shaped how, and how much, we talk about the Holocaust are well known and can be traced in the printed record; others are more obscure and can be reconstructed only from archival sources. And these influences have interacted in complicated ways. . . .

The meaning for American Jewry of its centering of the Holocaust is inseparable from the context in which that centering has taken place. One of the most important elements of that context has been the decline in America of an integrationist ethos (which focused on what Americans have in common and what unites us) and its replacement by a particularist ethos (which stresses what differentiates and divides us). The leaders of American Jewry, who once upon a time had sought to demonstrate that Jews were "just like everybody else, except more so," now had to establish, for both Jews and gentiles, what there was about Jews that made them different.

What *does* differentiate American Jews from other Americans? On what grounds can a distinctive Jewish identity in the United States be based? These days American Jews can't define their Jewishness on the basis of distinctively Jewish religious beliefs, since most don't have much in the way of distinctively Jewish religious beliefs. They can't define it by distinctively Jewish cultural traits, since most don't have any of these either. American Jews are sometimes said to be united by their Zionism, but if so, it is of a thin and abstract variety. . . . What American Jews *do* have in common is the knowledge that but for their parents' or (more often) grandparents' or great-grandparents' immigration, they would have shared the fate of European Jewry. Within an increasingly diverse and divided American Jewry, this became the historical foundation of that endlessly repeated but empirically dubious slogan "We are one."

. . . We choose to center certain memories because they seem to us to express what is central to our collective identity. Those memories, once brought to the fore, reinforce that form of identity. And so it has been with the Holocaust and American Jewry. The Holocaust, as virtually the only common denominator of American Jewish identity in the late twentieth century, has filled a need for a consensual symbol. And it was a symbol well designed to confront increasing communal anxiety about "Jewish continuity" in the face of declining religiosity, together with increasing assimilation and a sharp rise in intermarriage, all of which threatened demographic catastrophe. The Holocaust as central symbol of Jewishness has furthered in the late twentieth century what German Jews in the early nineteenth century had called *Trotzjudentum,* "Jewishness out of spite": a refusal to disappear, not for any positive reason, but, nowadays, so as not to grant Hitler a "posthumous victory." . . .

Another, parallel development in contemporary American culture has . . . been a change in the attitude toward victimhood from a status all but universally shunned and despised to one often eagerly embraced. On the individual level, the cultural icon of the strong, silent hero is replaced by the vulnerable and verbose antihero. Stoicism is replaced as a prime value by sensitivity. Instead of enduring in silence, one lets it all hang out. The voicing of pain and outrage is alleged to be "empowering" as well as therapeutic. . . .

. . . In practice, the assertion of the group's historical victimization—on the basis of race, ethnicity, gender, or sexual orientation—is always central to the group's assertion of its distinctive identity.

The growth of a "victim culture" wasn't the cause of American Jewry's focusing on the Holocaust in recent decades, but it has been an important background condition. . . . [I]n the 1940s and 1950s American Jews believed they had more reason than others to shun a victim identity, and this resulted in conscious decisions to downplay the Holocaust. By the 1980s and 1990s many Jews, for various reasons, wanted to establish that they too were members of a "victim community." Their contemporary situation offered little in the way of credentials. American Jews were by far the wealthiest, best-educated, most influential, in-every-way-most-successful group in American society—a group that, compared to most other identifiable minority groups, suffered no measurable discrimination and no disadvantages on account of that minority status. But insofar as Jewish identity could be anchored in the agony of European Jewry, certification as (vicarious) victims could be claimed, with all the moral privilege accompanying such certification.

The grounding of group identity and claims to group recognition in victimhood has produced not just a game of "show and tell." . . . In Jewish discourse on the Holocaust we have not just a competition for recognition but a competition for primacy. This takes many forms. Among the most widespread and pervasive is an angry insistence on the uniqueness of the Holocaust. Insistence on its uniqueness (or denial of its uniqueness) is an intellectually empty enterprise for reasons having nothing to do with the Holocaust itself and everything to do with "uniqueness." A moment's reflection makes clear that the notion of uniqueness is quite vacuous. Every historical event, including the Holocaust, in some ways resembles events to which it might be compared and differs from them in some ways. These resemblances and differences are a perfectly proper subject for discussion. But to single out those aspects of the Holocaust that were distinctive (there certainly were such), and to ignore those aspects that it shares with other atrocities, and on the basis of this gerrymandering to declare the Holocaust unique, is intellectual sleight of hand. The assertion that the Holocaust is unique—like the claim that it is singularly incomprehensible or unrepresentable—is, in practice, deeply offensive. What else can all of this possibly mean except "your catastrophe, unlike ours, is ordinary; unlike ours is comprehensible; unlike ours is representable." . . .

Apart from being our ticket of admission to this sordid game, American Jewish centering of the Holocaust has had other practical consequences. For many Jews, though this is much less true now than it was a few years ago, it has mandated an intransigent and self-righteous posture in the Israeli-Palestinian conflict. As the Middle Eastern dispute came to be viewed within a Holocaust paradigm, that tangled imbroglio was endowed with all the black-and-white moral simplicity of the Holocaust. And in this realm the Holocaust framework has promoted as well a belligerent stance toward any criticism of Israel. . . .

Turning the Holocaust into the emblematic Jewish experience has also, I think, and as I'll try to show, been closely connected to the inward and rightward turn of American Jewry in recent decades. If, as Cynthia Ozick has written, "all the world wants the Jews dead," and if the world was, as many have argued, indifferent to Jewish agony, why should Jews concern themselves with others? Once again, we're dealing with a complex phenomenon in which cause and effect are all mixed up. But I think the centering of the Holocaust in the minds of American Jews has contributed to the erosion of that larger social consciousness that was the hallmark of the American Jewry of my youth—post-Holocaust, but pre–Holocaust-fixation.

In a way, the guarding of the memory of the Holocaust is very much in the Jewish tradition; certainly, forgetting the Holocaust—hardly an option—would be contrary to tradition. As Yosef Yerushalmi has reminded us, the Hebrew Bible contains the verb "to remember," in its various declensions, 169 times (along with numerous injunctions not to forget). Yet what Jews are enjoined to remember is almost always God's handiwork; secular history, insofar as such a category is even admitted by the tradition, gets short shrift. Mourning and remembering the dead are, of course, traditional Jewish obligations. But Judaism has consistently disparaged excessive or overly prolonged mourning. Cremation is forbidden because it would dispose of the body too soon, but also forbidden is embalming, because it would preserve the body too long. Mourn, to be sure, is the message, but then move on: "choose life." . . .

. . . The principal "address" of American Jewry—the representation of Jewishness and the Jewish experience visited by more Americans than any other, and for most the only one they'll ever visit—is the Holocaust museum on the Mall in Washington. There surely isn't going to be a *second* Jewish institution on the Mall, presenting an alternative image of the Jew. And there surely isn't going to be *another* set of legislatively mandated curricula about Jews in American public schools, besides the proliferating Holocaust curricula zealously promoted by Jewish organizations—something to balance the existing curricula, in which, for enormous numbers of gentile children (Jewish ones too, for that matter), the equation Jew-equals-victim is being inscribed.

So I wind up asking a traditional question—a question often mocked but sometimes appropriate. I ask about our centering of the Holocaust in how we understand ourselves and how we invite others to understand us: "Is it good for the Jews?"

Then there's the balance sheet for our nation as a whole. There are many reasons why concern with the Holocaust among the 2 or 3 percent of the American population that is Jewish came to pervade American society. I will mention one important reason here, if only because it is often nervously avoided. We are not just "the people of the book," but the people of the Hollywood film and the television miniseries, of the magazine article and the newspaper column, of the comic book and the academic symposium. When a high level of concern with the Holocaust became widespread in American Jewry, it was, given the important role that Jews play in American media and opinion-making elites, not only natural, but virtually inevitable that it would spread throughout the culture at large.

Whatever its origin, the public rationale for Americans' "confronting" the Holocaust—and I don't doubt that it is sincerely argued and sincerely accepted—is that the Holocaust is the bearer of important lessons that we all ignore at our peril. Where once it was said that the life of Jews would be "a light unto the nations"—the bearer of universal lessons—now it is the "darkness unto the nations" of the death of Jews that is said to carry universal lessons. There is a good deal of confusion, and sometimes acrimonious dispute, over what these lessons are, but that has in no way diminished confidence that the lessons are urgent. Individuals from every point on the political compass can find the lessons they wish in the Holocaust; it has become a moral and ideological Rorschach test.

The right has invoked the Holocaust in support of anti-Communist interventions abroad: the agent of the Holocaust was not Nazi Germany but a generic totalitarianism, embodied after 1945 in the Soviet bloc, with which there could be no compromise. On a philosophical level, the Holocaust has been used by conservatives to demonstrate the sinfulness of man. It has provided confirmation of a tragic worldview, revealing the fatuousness of any transformative—or even seriously meliorative—politics. For other segments of the right, the Holocaust revealed the inevitable consequence of the breakdown of religion and family values in Germany. And, as is well known, the "abortion holocaust" figures prominently in American debate on that question.

For leftists, the claim that American elites abandoned European Jewry during the war has been used to demonstrate the moral bankruptcy of the establishment, including liberal icons like FDR. For liberals, the Holocaust became the locus of "lessons" that teach the evils of immigration restriction and homophobia, of nuclear weapons and the Vietnam War. Holocaust curricula, increasingly mandated in public schools, frequently link the Holocaust to much of the liberal agenda—a source of irritation to American right-wingers, including Jewish right-wingers like the late Lucy Dawidowicz.

For the political center—on some level for all Americans—the Holocaust has become a moral reference point. As, over the past generation, ethical and ideological divergence and disarray in the United States advanced to the point where Americans could agree on nothing else, all could join together in deploring the Holocaust— a low moral consensus, but perhaps better than none at all. (This banal consensus is indeed so broad that, in a backhanded way, it even includes that tiny band of malicious or deluded fruitcakes who deny that the Holocaust took place. "If it happened," they say in effect, "we would deplore it as much as anyone else. But it didn't, so the question doesn't arise.") And in the United States the Holocaust is explicitly used for the purpose of national self-congratulation: the "Americanization" of the Holocaust has involved using it to demonstrate the difference between the Old World and the New, and to celebrate, by showing its negation, the American way of life.

. . . If there are, in fact, lessons to be drawn from history, the Holocaust would seem an unlikely source, not because of its alleged uniqueness, but because of its extremity. Lessons for dealing with the sorts of issues that confront us in ordinary life, public or private, are not likely to be found in this most extraordinary of events. There are, in my view, more important lessons about how easily we become victimizers to be drawn from the behavior of normal Americans in normal times than from the behavior of the SS in wartime. In any case, the typical "confrontation" with the Holocaust for visitors to American Holocaust museums, and in burgeoning curricula, does not incline us toward thinking of ourselves as potential victimizers—rather the opposite. It is an article of faith in these encounters that one should "identify with the victims," thus acquiring the warm glow of virtue that such a vicarious identification brings. (Handing out "victim identity cards" to museum visitors is the most dramatic example of this, but not the only one.) And it is accepted as a matter of faith, beyond discussion, that the mere act of walking through a Holocaust museum, or viewing a Holocaust movie, is going to be morally therapeutic, that multiplying such encounters will make one a better person. . . .

Another ground on which I find the idea of lessons of the Holocaust questionable can be called pragmatic: what is the payoff? The principal lesson of the Holocaust, it is frequently said, is not that it provides a set of maxims, or a rule book for conduct, but rather that it sensitizes us to oppression and atrocity. In principle it might, and I don't doubt that sometimes it does. But making it the benchmark of oppression and atrocity works in precisely the opposite direction, trivializing crimes of lesser magnitude. It does this not just in principle, but in practice. American debate on the bloody Bosnian conflict of the 1990s focused on whether what was going on was "truly holocaustal or merely genocidal"; "truly genocidal or merely atrocious." A truly disgusting and not a merely distasteful mode of speaking and of decisionmaking, but one we are led to when the Holocaust becomes the touchstone of moral and political discourse.

The problem transcends the Bosnian tragedy, which is simply its most dramatic illustration. It is connected to the axiom of the uniqueness of the Holocaust and its corollary, that comparing anything to the Holocaust is illegitimate, indeed indecent. I have suggested that the very notion of uniqueness is vacuous, but rhetorically—for ideological or other purposes—the claim of uniqueness (or its denial) can be powerful. Whatever its success, the intention of talking in Germany of the uniqueness and incomparability of the Holocaust is to prevent Germans from evading confrontation with that which is most difficult, painful, and therefore probably most useful to confront. Let us remember the context in which many Germans—decent Germans—objected to the so-called relativization of the Holocaust in recent years. The context included the insistence of Chancellor Helmut Kohl's party that as a price for supporting a law against denying the Holocaust, the law had to include a provision making it illegal to deny the suffering of Germans expelled from the East after 1945. In this German context—and context, as always, is decisive—"relativization" meant equating crimes *against* Germans to crimes *by* Germans. Which, of course, many Germans wished to do. Those Germans who insisted on the uniqueness of the Holocaust, who condemned its relativization, did so to block what they correctly regarded as a move to evade confrontation with a painful national past, evade the implications of such a confrontation for the present and future.

The identical talk of uniqueness and incomparability surrounding the Holocaust in the United States performs the opposite function: it promotes *evasion* of moral and historical responsibility. The repeated assertion that whatever the United States has done to blacks, Native Americans, Vietnamese, or others pales in comparison to the Holocaust is true—and evasive. And whereas a serious and sustained encounter with the history of hundreds of years of enslavement and oppression of blacks might imply costly demands on Americans to redress the wrongs of the past, contemplating the Holocaust is virtually cost-free: a few cheap tears.

So, in the end, it seems to me that the pretense that the Holocaust is an American memory—that Americans, either diffusely, as part of Western civilization, or specifically, as complicit bystanders, share responsibility for the Holocaust—works to devalue the notion of historical responsibility. It leads to the shirking of those responsibilities that *do* belong to Americans as they confront their past, their present, and their future.

I have . . . expressed doubts about the usefulness of the Holocaust as a bearer of lessons. In large part these doubts are based on the Holocaust's extremity, which on the one hand makes its practical lessons of little applicability to everyday life; on the other hand makes anything to which it is compared look "not so bad." But there's another dimension to this. Along with most historians, I'm skeptical about the so-called lessons of history. I'm especially skeptical about the sort of pithy lessons that fit on a bumper sticker. If there is, to use a pretentious word, any wisdom to be acquired from contemplating an historical event, I would think it would derive from confronting it in all its complexity and its contradictions; the ways in which it resembles other events to which it might be compared as well as the ways it differs from them. It is not—least of all when it comes to the Holocaust—a matter of approaching the past in a neutral or value-free fashion, or of abstaining from moral judgment. And it's not a matter of taking a disengaged academic stance. It is medical researchers' commitment to conquering diseases that makes researchers want to understand them in their messy complexity, to acknowledge things about them that violate their preconceptions. Expressions of moral outrage don't help. Talk of evil humors in the blood leads you to try bleeding as a remedy (it doesn't work). Talk of demonic possession leads you to try exorcism (which doesn't work either). If there *are* lessons to be extracted from encountering the past, that encounter has to be with the past in all its messiness; they're not likely to come from an encounter with a past that's been shaped and shaded so that inspiring lessons will emerge.

In early writings about the Holocaust—particularly in Israel but also in the United States—Jewish resistance was inflated for inspirational purposes. In much cold war writing in America responsibility for the Holocaust was transferred from Nazi Germany to "totalitarianism," so that the appropriate anti-Soviet lessons could be learned. More recently, the possibilities for rescue available to the Allies and to gentiles in Hitler's Europe have been exaggerated so as to teach lessons about indifference.

And, of course, these shapings and shadings to accommodate lessons are of crucial importance when lessons move to the top of the agenda. In the Bosnian debate, they served both sides. Those who were for intervention argued—sometimes explicitly, always implicitly—that the history of the Holocaust proved that rescue efforts like bombing Auschwitz could have saved countless lives then, and similar measures would save countless lives now. Those against intervention repeatedly insisted that the Serbs' desire to live in a territory from which Bosnian Muslims had been "cleansed" was a rational, albeit deplorable, aspiration; not at all like Hitler's desire to eliminate Jews from a Europe under German domination.

If, despite my skepticism, there are lessons to be learned from the Holocaust, they're not likely to be derived from lesson-driven versions of it. And there are perhaps a few modest lessons to be learned. As George Steiner pointed out some years ago:

> We who come after know that whatever the news is, it may be so. Whatever the massacre, the torture . . . it may be so. We no longer have that complex psychological blindness whereby many decent human beings, when the first reports leaked through . . . about railroads taking 9,000 people a day to a camp, could say: "This cannot be. . . . This is beyond human reason." We have no more such excuse.

There was also a disposition, before the Holocaust, to think of the most barbarous deeds as being the work of the most barbarous folk—the least cultured, the least advanced. We've learned from the Holocaust that that's wrong. Perhaps there are other lessons, but nothing that will fit on a bumper sticker, and nothing to inspire. Awe and horror when confronting the Holocaust—for the first time or the thousandth time; then, now, and forever—are surely appropriate. Yet no matter how broadly we interpret the word "lesson," that's not a lesson—certainly not a useful one.

The desire to find and teach lessons of the Holocaust has various sources— different sources for different people, one supposes. Probably one of its principal sources is the hope of extracting from the Holocaust something that is, if not redemptive, at least useful. I doubt it can be done.

FURTHER READING

Adams, Michael C. C. *The Best War Ever* (1994).

Anderson, Benedict. *Imagined Communities: Reflections on the Origin and Spread of Nationalism* (1983).

Bodnar, John E. *Remaking America: Public Memory, Commemoration, and Patriotism in the Twentieth Century* (1992).

Butler, Thomas, ed. *Memory: History, Culture and the Mind* (1989).

Cole, Tim. *Selling the Holocaust: From Auschwitz to Schindler. How History is Bought and Sold* (1999).

Connerton, Paul. *How Societies Remember* (1989).

Daniels, Roger. "Incarcerating Japanese Americans: An Atrocity Revisited," *Peace & Change* 23 (April 1998): 117–130.

Erenberg, Lewis A., and Susan E. Hirsch, eds. *The War and American Culture* (1996).

Friedlander, Saul, ed. *Probing the Limits of Representation: Nazism and the "Final Solution"* (1992).

Gillis, John R., ed. *Commemorations: The Politics of National Identity* (1994).

Gross, David. *Lost Time: On Remembering and Forgetting in Late Modern Culture* (2000).

Halbwachs, Maurice. *On Collective Memory* (1992).

Hartman, Geoffrey H., ed. *Holocaust Remembrance: The Shapes of Memory* (1994).

Hobsbawm, Eric, and Terence Ranger, eds. *The Invention of Tradition* (1983).

Homans, Peter, ed. *Symbolic Loss: The Ambiguity of Mourning and Memory at Century's End.* (2000).

Hutton, Patrick. "Recent Scholarship on History and Memory." *The History Teacher.* 33/4 (August 2000): 533–548.

———. *History as an Art of Memory* (1993).

Kammen, Michael. *Mystic Chords of Memory: The Transformation of Tradition in American Culture* (1991).

Kennedy, David. *Freedom From Fear: The American People in Depression and War, 1929–1945* (1999).

Le Goff, Jacques. *History and Memory.* Trans. Steven Rendall and Elizabeth Claman (1992).

Linenthal, Edward T., et. al., eds. *History Wars* (1996).

Lipsitz, George. *Time Passages: Collective Memory and American Popular Culture* (1990).

Marling, Karal Ann, and John Wetenhall. *Iwo Jima: Monuments, Memories, and the American Hero* (1991).

Mayo, James. *War Memorials as Political Landscape* (1988).

Middleton, David, and Derek Edwards, eds. *Collective Remembering* (1990).

Nora, Pierre, ed. *Realms of Memory* (1996).

Novick, Peter. *The Holocaust in American Life* (1999).

Schama, Simon. *Landscape and Memory* (1996).

Stoler, Mark A. "The Second World War in U.S. History and Memory," *Diplomatic History* 25 (3) (Summer 2001): 383–392.

Thelen, David. "Memory and American History." *Journal of American History* 75 (March 1989): 117–129.

Thelen, David, et. al. "History and the Public: What Can We Handle? A Round Table About History after the *Enola Gay* Controversy," *Journal of American History* 82 (3) (December 1995): 1029–1144.

Wallace, Mike. *Mickey Mouse History and Other Essays on American History* (1996).

Young, James E. *The Texture of Memory: Holocaust Memorials and Meaning* (1993).

APPENDIX

General World War II Histories and Reference Works

An enormous literature exists on World War II. This volume covers only a small portion of that literature—the portion associated with American participation in the conflict. Readers interested in other aspects of the war are advised to consult the following general histories and reference works.

Boatner, Mark M., III. *Biographical Dictionary of World War II* (1996).

Calvocoressi, Peter, Guy Wint and John Pritchard. *Total War* (1995).

Churchill, Winston S. *History of the Second World War* (1948–54).

Dear, I. C. B., and M. R. D. Foot. *The Oxford Companion to World War II* (1995).

Ellis, John. *World War II: A Statistical Survey* (1993).

Enser, A. G. S. *A Subject Bibliography of the Second World War* (1977, 1990).

Funk, Arthur L., ed. *The Second World War: A Select Bibliography of Books in English* (1975, 1985).

Hess, Gary R. *The United States at War* (2000).

James, D. Clayton and Anne Sharp Wells. *Pearl Harbor to V-J Day* (1995).

Keegan, John. *The Second World War* (1990).

Kimball, Warren F., et. al. "The Future of World War II Studies: A Roundtable," *Diplomatic History* 25 (Summer 2001): 347–499.

Kitchen, Martin. *A World in Flames* (1990).

Leckie, Robert. *Delivered From Evil* (1987).

Lee, Loyd. *World War II* (1999).

———. *World War II in Europe, Africa, and the Americas, with General Sources: A Handbook of Literature and Research* (1997).

———. *World War II in Asia and the Pacific and the War's Aftermath, with General Themes: A Handbook of Literature and Research* (1998).

Leopard, Donald D. *World War II* (1992).

Liddell Hart, B. H. *History of the Second World War* (1970).

Lyons, Michael J. *World War II: A Short History* (1999).

Maddox, Robert J. *The United States and World War II* (1992).
Michel, Henri. *The Second World War,* 2 vols. (1975).
Milward, Alan S. *War, Economy and Society, 1939–1945* (1977).
Murray, Williamson, and Allan Millett. *A War to be Won* (2000).
Parker, R. A. C. *The Second World War* (1997).
Purdue, A. W. *The Second World War* (1999).
Royal Institute of International Affairs. *Chronology and Index of the Second World War 1938–1945* (1990).
Stokesbury, James L. *A Short History of World War II* (1980).
Weinberg, Gerhard. *A World at Arms: A Global History of World War II* (1994).
Willmott, H. P. *The Great Crusade* (1989).
Ziegler, Janet. *World War II; Books in English* (1971).